SOCIOLOGICAL FOOTPRINTS

INTRODUCTORY READINGS IN SOCIOLOGY

SECOND EDITION

LEONARD CARGAN
Wright State University

JEANNE H. BALLANTINE
Wright State University

Wadsworth Publishing Company
Belmont, California
A Division of Wadsworth, Inc.

Sociology Editor: Curt Peoples
Production Editor: Judith McKibben
Managing Designer: Lois Stanfield
Text Designer: Cheryl Carrington
Cover Designer: Lois Stanfield
Copy Editor: Pamela Evans
Signing Representative: Miriam Nathanson

*To the three professors whose advice
and encouragement made it all possible:
Edward Jandy, Leonard Moss, and Louis Ferman.*

L. C.

*To Mildred and Paul Klohr, who have
provided for me a model of what scholars
and professors should be.*

J. H. B.

ISBN 0-534-01078-4

Library of Congress Cataloging in Publication Data
Main entry under title:

Sociological footprints.

Includes bibliographical references.
   1. Sociology—Addresses, essays, lectures.
I. Cargan, Leonard.   II. Ballantine, Jeanne.
HM51.S66328 1982   301   81-14752
ISBN 0-534-01078-4   AACR2

Printed in the United States of America

   3 4 5 6 7 8 9 10—86 85 84 83

CONTENTS

CORRELATION CHART

	Science and Sociology	Socialization	Culture	Social Structure & Group Interaction	Stratification	Family	Education	Religion	Economics	Politics	Minority Relations	Deviance	Population & Ecology	Urban Affairs	Collective Behavior	Social Change
BABBIE 2ND ED. 1980	1, 2 3	5, 11	4	7, 8	9	12	13	13	14	14	10	6	16	17	18	19
BALDRIDGE 2ND ED. 1980	1, 2	4	3	6, 14	11	7	8	7	10	9	12	5	13	13	15	
BASSIS, ET AL. 1ST ED. 1980	1, 2	4	3	5, 6	9, 11	12	13	13	14	14	10	7	15	15	8	
BENKIN 1ST ED. 1981	Pro-logue	1	2	3, 5	7, 8	6	6	6				4, 9			10	11
BROOM, SELZNICK, DARROCH 7TH ED. 1981	1, 2	4	3	6, 7	11	12	13	14		16	8, 9 10	7	17	18	5	19
DE FLEUR, ET AL. 3RD ED. 1981	1, 2	6, 8	4	3, 5	9	15	17	16	18	18	10	7	13	12	14	11
DENISOFF & WAHRMAN 2ND ED. 1979	1, 2 3	6, 7	4, 14	5	9	8					10	11	12		15	16
DUBERMAN & HARTTEN 1ST ED. 1979		4, 5 11	1	2	13	6	7	8	9	10	12	15	16			3
EITZEN 1ST ED. 1978	1	5, 6	4	2, 6 13	9	14	16	15	17	10	11 12	7, 8				18
FEDERICO 2ND ED. 1979	1	3	2	4, 9	7	12	14	13	15	16	6	8	17	10	11	18
GREENBLAT 1ST ED. 1981	1, 2	5, 10	3	4, 7	8	11	13	12	14	14	9	6	15 16		17	18
HORTON & HUNT 5TH ED. 1980	1, 2	5	3, 4	6, 7 9	15 16	11	13	12	14	14	17	8	19	20	18	21
KENKEL 2ND ED. 1980	1, 2	4, 7	3	5, 6	8	9	11	10	12	12	16	17	14	15		13
LESLIE, LARSON, GORMAN 3RD ED. 1980	1, 2	7, 8	4, 6	3, 5 10 12	15	17	19	18	20	21	16	9	13	14	11	
LIGHT & KELLER 2ND ED. 1979	1, 2	5, 6	4	3, 7 8	10	13	14	15	12	12	11	9	16	17	18	19

CORRELATION CHART

	Science and Sociology	Socialization	Culture	Social Structure & Group Interaction	Stratification	Family	Education	Religion	Economics	Politics	Minority Relations	Deviance	Population & Ecology	Urban Affairs	Collective Behavior	Social Change
LLOYD, MACK, PEASE 6TH ED. 1979	1, 2	6, 7	5	3, 4 8, 9	11	17	18	19	15	16	12	22	13	14	19	20
MCGEE 2ND ED. 1980	1, 2 19	4, 7	3	5, 6	7	11	12	13	14	14	8	16	10	9	17	18
MCKEE 1ST ED. 1981	1	4	3	2, 5 6, 7	9, 10	13	14	15	16	17	11 12	18		8	19	20
POPENOE 4TH ED. 1980	1, 2	6, 7 8	5	3, 4 10	11	13	14	15	16	16	12	9	17	18	19	20
ROBERTSON 2ND ED. 1980	1, 2 17	5, 9	3	4, 6 7	10 11	14	15	16	18	19	12 13	8	20	21	22	23
ROSE 4TH ED. 1980	1, 2	3	4	5, 11 12	6	13		14		15	7	8, 9	16		10	17
SHEPARD 1ST ED. 1981	1, 2	5, 10	3	4, 6	8	11	12	14	13	13	9	7	15	16	17	
SMELSER 1ST ED. 1981	Appen. 1	2	8	3, 5 6	9, 10 11 12	13	14	15	16	17		4	18	7	19	20
SPENCER 2ND ED. 1979	1, 2	4, 5	3	6, 8	9	12	14	13	16	15	10	7	17	18	11	19
STEWART 2ND ED. 1981	1, 2	4	3	5	6, 8	11	12	13	15	14	7	9	17	18	10	19
STEWART & GLYNN 3RD ED. 1979	1	4	3	2	6	11	13	12	14	15	7	5	8	9	10	16
STORER 2ND ED. 1980	Appen. 1, 2	4, 5	3	7, 9 10	6	13		14	11	12		15 16	8		17	18
TURNER 2ND ED. 1981	1, 2 3	4, 8 15 16	5	6, 7 10 11	13	17	21	18	19	20	14	9	22	12	23	24
ZANDEN 4TH ED. 1979	1	3, 10	2	4, 5	8	12	15	13	14			9	6	16	17	7	11
ZEITLIN 1ST ED. 1981	1	2	3	4, 5	6, 7	9		10			8	12		13	11	14

SOURCES FOR CORRELATION CHART

Babbie, E. R. *Sociology: An Introduction.* 2nd ed. Belmont, Calif.: Wadsworth, 1980.

Baldridge, J. V. *Sociology: A Critical Approach to Power, Conflict, and Change.* 2nd ed. New York: John Wiley, 1980.

Bassis, M. S., Gelles, R. J., Levine, A. *Sociology: An Introduction.* New York: Random House, 1980.

Benkin, R. L. *Sociology: A Way of Seeing.* Belmont, Calif.: Wadsworth, 1981.

Broom, L., Selznick, P., Darroch, D. B. *Sociology.* 7th ed. New York: Harper & Row, 1981.

Defleur, M. L., D'Antonio, W. V., Defleur, L. B. *Sociology: Human Society.* 3rd ed. Glenview, Ill.: Scott, Foresman, 1981.

Denisoff, R. S., Wahrman, R. *An Introduction to Sociology.* 2nd ed. New York: Macmillan, 1979.

Duberman, L., Hartten, C. A. *Sociology: Focus on Society.* Glenview, Ill.: Scott, Foresman, 1979.

Eitzen, D. S. *In Conflict and Order: Understanding Society.* Boston, Mass.: Allyn & Bacon, 1978.

Federico, R. C. *Sociology.* 2nd ed. Reading, Mass.: Addison-Wesley, 1979.

Greenblatt, C. S. *An Introduction to Sociology.* New York: Alfred A. Knopf, 1981.

Horton, P. B., Hunt, C. L. *Sociology.* 5th ed. New York: McGraw-Hill, 1980.

Kenkel, W. F. *Society in Action: Introduction to Sociology.* 2nd ed. New York: Harper & Row, 1980.

Leslie, G. R., Larson, R. F., Gorman, B. L. *Introductory Sociology.* 3rd ed. New York: Oxford University Press, 1980.

Light, D. Jr., Keller, S. *Sociology.* 2nd ed. New York: Alfred A. Knopf, 1979.

Lloyd, J., Mack, R., Pease, J. *Sociology and Social Life.* 6th ed. New York: D. Van Nostrand Company, 1979.

McGee, R. *Sociology: An Introduction.* 2nd ed. New York: Holt, Rinehart & Winston, 1980.

McKee, J. B. *Sociology: The Study of Society.* New York: Holt, Rinehart & Winston, 1981.

Popenoe, D. *Sociology.* 4th ed. Englewood Cliffs, N.J.: Prentice-Hall, 1980.

Robertson, I. *Sociology.* 2nd ed. New York: Worth, 1980.

Rose, J. D. *Introduction to Sociology.* 4th ed. Chicago: Rand McNally, 1980.

Shepard, J. M. *Sociology.* St. Paul, Minnesota, 1981.

Smelser, N. T. *Sociology.* Englewood Cliffs, N.J.: Prentice-Hall, 1981.

Spencer, M. *Foundations of Modern Sociology.* 2nd ed. Englewood Cliffs, N.J.: Prentice-Hall, 1979.

Stewart, E. W. *Sociology: The Human Science.* 2nd ed. New York: McGraw-Hill, 1981.

Stewart, E. W., Glynn, J. A. *Introduction to Sociology.* 3rd ed. New York: McGraw-Hill, 1979.

Storer, N. *Focus on Society: An Introduction to Sociology.* 2nd ed. Reading, Mass.: Addison-Wesley, 1980.

Turner, J. H. *Sociology: Studying the Human System.* 2nd ed. Santa Monica, Calif.: Goodyear, 1981.

Vander Zanden, J. W. *Sociology.* 4th ed. New York: John Wiley, 1979.

Zeitlin, I. M. *The Social Condition of Humanity: An Introduction to Sociology.* New York: Oxford University Press, 1981.

PREFACE

The primary objective of this anthology is to provide a link between the theoretical sociology presented in textbooks and classroom presentations by presenting actual samples of classical and current sociological studies. For students to grasp the full meaning of sociological terms and topics, they must be able to translate the jargon of textbooks into real and useful concepts that are applicable to everyday life. To this end, *Sociological Footprints* presents viewpoints that demonstrate the broad range of sociological applications and the value of sociological research.

The selection of articles involved a number of important steps. As with the first edition, we constantly received feedback from more than a thousand students. We were pleased that most of the articles were approved overwhelmingly by the students. We then conducted an exhaustive search of the literature for more articles that are interesting and highly readable, that present concepts clearly, that represent both recent and classical sociology, and that feature authors of diverse background. Finally, we worked with manuscript reviewers' comments to make other aspects of the anthology relevant and useful.

The process, though complex, was valuable. *Sociological Footprints* includes readings from such interesting classics as Kingsley Davis's "Final Note on a Case of Extreme Isolation," C. Wright Mills's *The Sociological Imagination*, Horace Miner's "Body Ritual Among the Nacirema," and Paul Lazarsfeld's "The American Soldier." While presenting a wide spectrum of classical sociological issues, the anthology also covers such contemporary topics as the changing role of women ("The Changing Door Ceremony"), the rapid growth of the singles population ("Perceptions of Singlehood: 1900–1975"), school desegregation ("Sorting Out the Issues and Trends of School Desegregation"), and the need for political reform ("'The Political System Cannot Cope' with Today's Diversity"). The range of authors includes such experts as Jessie Bernard on marriage ("Marriage: His and Hers") and Raymond Hull on bureaucracy ("The Peter Principle"). Even the light side of sociology is accounted for in such articles as James Skipper's "Stripteasers: A Six-Year History of Public Reaction to a Study" and Richard Wynn's "The Wynn Principle." In sum, this anthology contains a balance of articles in each section that, according to students, instructors, and reviewers, is highly readable.

Our major concern, however, was to make this anthology as valuable a teaching aid as it is enjoyable—an intention reflected in the book's organization. First, each section has an introduction that covers the major themes of that topic area, noting how each article relates to those themes. Second, although anthologies do not usually define the concepts used in their articles, we include a glossary of important concepts at the end of the text. We urge that students preview the glossary for each article before they begin to read; this will give them a basic understanding of any special terminology used.

For the convenience of the instructor, the Instructor's Manual cross-lists chapters in major sociology texts with corresponding sections in this anthology. This list will facilitate the use of *Sociological Footprints* with almost all of the major introductory texts. This valuable aid also summarizes the theme, findings, and conclusions of each article; offers both multiple-choice and essay questions; suggests appropriate films by subject matter; and includes a section on games, simulations, and alternative classroom activities.

Both the anthology and the Instructor's Manual can be used in several ways to aid the instruction process: to expand students' comprehension of main topics, to illustrate lecture materials, and to provide a basis for class discussion. Those articles that deal with controversial issues can be used for debate or as the basis of small-group activities.

Several of the articles have been condensed, but the original material was in no way altered. In order to emphasize key points, we omitted digressions, repetitions, and detailed descriptions of quantitative data.

We wish to thank all those who made this second edition of *Sociological Footprints* possible: the reviewers—Carla B. Howery of the American Sociological Association and Kathryn Mueller of Baylor University, the many students who took the time to give us their opinions, the departmental secretaries and aides who helped to assemble and type the material—they were invaluable. To all we give a most heartfelt "thank you"!

L. C.

J. H. B.

TO THE STUDENT

The purpose of this anthology is to introduce you, the beginning student in sociology, to a wide range of sociological perspectives and their application to real-life situations. As you apply sociological perspectives to everyday events, you will begin to realize that sociology is more than jargon, more than dry statistics, more than endless terminology to be memorized. It is an exciting and useful field of study. Unfortunately, no textbook can fully describe the many applications of sociology. This anthology should help to fill the gap by supplying classical articles balanced with applications of current research.

From our experience in teaching introductory sociology, we know some of the problems that anthologies can present to the student: unexplained terms, articles difficult to relate to the text, and a different emphasis from that of the instructor's lectures. Therefore, to fully enjoy and benefit from *Sociological Footprints*, you should take the following steps.

1. Read and study the related textbook chapter and lecture materials. You must be familiar with the concepts and perspectives before you can clearly observe their daily application.
2. Read the introductions to the assigned sections in the anthology. They are designed to summarize the primary themes of the topic area and relate them to specific articles. In fact, the introductions will not only make the articles easier to understand—they will facilitate their application to other class materials and real-life situations.
3. Use the glossary before you read each article. Knowing the terms will make the articles more interesting and understandable.
4. Read each article through. Note the problem or issue being discussed, the evidence the author supplies in support of his or her contentions, and the conclusions drawn from this evidence.
5. Summarize the main ideas of each article in your own terms, relating them to other material in the course and to your own everyday experiences.

Step 5 is particularly important. Many of the articles address topics of current interest: women's liberation, the growing divorce rate, singlehood, the growth of fundamentalist religions, population control, environmental issues, and more. Because these are contemporary problems, you will see related materials in newspapers and magazines and on television. By applying what you have learned from the text, the lectures, and this anthology—your sociological knowledge, in short—to these other materials, you should develop a clearer understanding of current issues and how sociology has aided you in this understanding.

We feel quite strongly that sociology is a field of study highly relevant to your world: that it can give you a fuller comprehension of day-to-day living. Our aim has been to provide you with a readable, understandable, and enlightening anthology that will convey this relevance.

WHAT CAN YOU DO WITH A SOCIOLOGY DEGREE?*

*All positions are actual jobs held by sociology majors from The Ohio State University.

Reprinted by permission of the Department of Sociology, Ohio State University. Research and design compliments of the Visual Research Laboratory, Ohio State University, Department of Sociology, Timothy Jon Curry, Director, and Scott, Foresman and Company.

Part One

THE DISCIPLINE OF SOCIOLOGY

Although the term sociology *may be familiar, many students are unaware of the areas of study included in the field. Sociology ranges from the study of small groups—perhaps two people—to that of such large entities as corporations and societies. It is the study of interactions within, between, and among groups; and these group interactions encompass all areas of human behavior, as noted in the following article.*

. . . Leading thinkers in all ages have been concerned about society, human conduct, and the creation of a social order that would bring forth the best man is capable of. But, the study of these problems with the techniques and approaches of science (sociology) is only a little more than a century old.

It was only about 125 years ago that Auguste Comte published his *Cours de philosophie positive* which first included sociology as one of the scientific disciplines. No course in sociology was available in an American university until 1876 at Yale. . . . Before 1900 all the men who identified themselves as professional sociologists were trained originally in other fields such as history, politics, economics, law, and religion. Today, undergraduate students can obtain training in sociology in almost all American four-year liberal arts colleges and in many agricultural colleges and specialized schools; more than 70 schools offer a doctoral program in sociology and many additional schools offer Masters' degree programs.

Before World War I the opportunities for employment of men and women with professional training in sociology were largely limited to college teaching and research. Besides teaching and research, sociologists today are engaged in more than 25 different kinds of work in professional schools, in local, state, federal, and private agencies, and in business. They work in the fields of education, medicine, law, theology, corrections, agricultural extension, welfare, population study, community development, health, technological change, and the like. In short, sociologists are working on almost all the problems that concern man in relation to his fellow man and the consequences of this relationship for himself and others. . . . (Reprinted by permission of the Sociology Department, University of Kentucky.)

I

SCIENCE AND SOCIOLOGY
Is It Just Common Sense?

Sociologists are interested in discovering the realities of group interactions. To distinguish their conclusions from everyday, commonsense observations or intuitions, sociologists use scientific data-gathering techniques. Common sense is the feeling one has about a situation without systematic analysis; that is, appearances alone are accepted as the criteria for truth. In reality, what is commonsense truth for one person may not be for another. Good examples of such "truths" are found in advice columns such as Ann Landers and Dear Abby. In contrast, the scientific approach may be defined as a procedure for analyzing data according to an *objective, logical, systematic method* to produce *reliable* knowledge. By examining the five major terms in this definition we can clarify the difference between commonsense and scientific observations.

The first major term in the definition is *objective*. To be objective, you must be aware of how your opinions can and do influence a research operation. An essential part of the discipline of sociology is the rules of the scientific method; these rules reduce the influence of personal biases on our research experiences. Complete freedom from bias is difficult to achieve because we are products of our society and times and what we "see" is influenced by these conditions. This difficulty is the main theme of the first article in this section. Mills states that our perceptions are limited by our family, work, and other social experiences. In short, what we observe is bounded by these particular experiences, and therefore may lead to biased statements based on commonsense beliefs. However, the author believes that such limited perspective can be expanded by means of a "sociological imagination," which allows us to note relationships that exist between our personal experiences and general social issues.

The next two major terms in our definition are *logical* and *systematic*. *Logical* refers to the arrangement of facts and their interrelations according to accepted rules of reasoning. *Systematic* means that there is consistency in the internal order of the presentation of material. However, regardless of the logic and consistency of the research, the material is subject to the personal biases of the reader. The article on strippers reveals how nonscientists (journalists, moral crusaders, for example) misunderstand findings or become interested in the scientist's motives rather than in the findings.

The term *method* refers to the techniques used in the research effort. The third article in this section discusses one of the major methods used by sociologists and other scientists: the survey. Through the use of this methodological tool, commonsense and intuitive beliefs are tested for accuracy. Lazarsfeld indicates the importance of such testing when he cites as an example six rationally supported commonsense beliefs that were shown to be the opposite of the factual data supplied through scientific means.

The final term in our definition is *reliability*, which means that the knowledge produced can be depended on: the observations can be repeated with similar data for a predictably similar outcome. Sociological techniques can be used to make predictions about human behavior. However, unlike mechanical behavior, human behavior is subject to the whims and fads of people, and so, such behavior can only be predicted within a reliable *range*.

As the articles in this chapter argue, adherence to the rules of scientific method produces reliable knowledge that can be used to prove or disprove commonsense observation. This approach also can expand perspectives limited by the material boundaries of time and space, and help deal efficiently with society's needs. For example, in the first article Mills notes the need for a "sociological imagination" to overcome such boundaries of time as age bracket or historical period, to overcome such limitations of space as neighborhood or region of the country. The third article by Lazarsfeld reveals how the sociological method was utilized in dealing with some of society's needs in relation to World War II, and after the war when sociological techniques were used to design the basis for mustering out the soldiers.

Finally, the publication of the results of scientific investigation may lead to the recognition of other truths, resulting in developments beneficial to society. This would be true, for example, on reforms in education and prisons. As you read this chapter, keep these ideas in mind and apply them to your own commonsense beliefs.

1

THE PROMISE

C. Wright Mills

Nowadays men often feel that their private lives are a series of traps. They sense that within their everyday worlds, they cannot overcome their troubles, and in this feeling, they are often quite correct: What ordinary men are directly aware of and what they try to do are bounded by the private orbits in which they live; their visions and their powers are limited to the close-up scenes of job, family, neighborhood; in other milieux, they move vicariously and remain spectators. And the more aware they become, however vaguely, of ambitions and of threats which transcend their immediate locales, the more trapped they seem to feel.

From *The Sociological Imagination* by C. Wright Mills. Copyright © 1959 by Oxford University Press, Inc. Reprinted by permission.

Underlying this sense of being trapped are seemingly impersonal changes in the very structure of continent-wide societies. The facts of contemporary history are also facts about the success and the failure of individual men and women. When a society is industrialized, a peasant becomes a worker; a feudal lord is liquidated or becomes a businessman. When classes rise or fall, a man is employed or unemployed; when the rate of investment goes up or down, a man takes new heart or goes broke. When wars happen, an insurance salesman becomes a rocket launcher; a store clerk, a radar man; a wife lives alone; a child grows up without a father. Neither the life of an individual nor the history of a society can be understood without understanding both.

Yet men do not usually define the troubles they endure in terms of historical change and institutional contradiction. The well-being they enjoy, they do not usually impute to the big ups and downs of the societies in which they live. Seldom aware of the intricate connection between the patterns of their own lives and the course of world history, ordinary men do not usually know what this connection means for the kinds of men they are becoming and for the kinds of history-making in which they might take part. They do not possess the quality of mind essential to grasp the interplay of man and society, of biography and history, of self and world. They cannot cope with their personal troubles in such ways as to control the structural transformations that usually lie behind them.

Surely it is no wonder. In what period have so many men been so totally exposed at so fast a pace to such earthquakes of change? That Americans have not known such catastrophic changes as have the men and women of other societies is due to historical facts that are now quickly becoming "merely history." The history that now affects every man is world history. Within this scene and this period, in the course of a single generation, one sixth of mankind is transformed from all that is feudal and backward into all that is modern, advanced, and fearful. Political colonies are freed; new and less visible forms of imperialism installed. Revolutions occur; men feel the intimate grip of new kinds of authority. Totalitarian societies rise, and are smashed to bits—or succeed fabulously. After two centures of ascendancy, capitalism is shown up as only one way to make society into an industrial apparatus. After two centuries of hope, even formal democracy is restricted to a quite small portion of mankind. Everywhere in the underdeveloped world, ancient ways of life are broken up and vague expectations become urgent demands. Everywhere in the overdeveloped world, the means of authority and of violence become total in scope and bureaucratic in form. Humanity itself now lies before us, the super-nation at either pole concentrating its most co-ordinated and massive efforts upon the preparation of World War Three.

The very shaping of history now outpaces the ability of men to orient themselves in accordance with cherished values. And which values? Even when they do not panic, men often sense that older ways of feeling and thinking have collapsed and that newer beginnings are ambiguous to the point of moral stasis. Is it any wonder that ordinary men feel they cannot cope with the larger worlds with which they are so suddenly confronted? That they cannot understand the meaning of their epoch for their own lives? That—in defense of selfhood—they become morally insensible, trying to remain altogether private men? Is it any wonder that they come to be possessed by a sense of the trap?

It is not only information that they need—in this Age of Fact, information often dominates their attention and overwhelms their capacities to assimilate it. It is not only the skills of reason that they need—although their struggles to acquire these often exhaust their limited moral energy.

What they need, and what they feel they need, is a quality of mind that will help them to use information and to develop reason in order to achieve lucid summations of what is going on in the world and of what may be happening within themselves. It is this quality, I am going to contend, that journalists and scholars, artists and publics, scientists and editors are coming to expect of what may be called the sociological imagination.

I

The sociological imagination enables its possessor to understand the larger historical scene in terms of its meaning for the inner life and the external career of a variety of individuals. It enables him to take into account how individuals, in the welter of their daily experience, often become falsely conscious of their social positions. Within that welter, the framework of modern society is sought, and within that framework the psychologies of a variety of men and women are formulated. By such means the personal uneasiness of individuals is focused upon explicit troubles and the indifferences of publics is transformed into involvement with public issues.

The first fruit of this imagination—and the first lesson of the social science that embodies it—is the idea that the individual can understand his own experience and gauge his own fate only by locating himself within his period; that he can know his own chances in life only by becoming aware of those of all individuals in his circumstances. In many ways it is a terrible lesson; in many ways a magnificent one. We do not know the limits of man's capacities for supreme effort or willing degradation, for agony or glee, for pleasurable brutality or the sweetness of reason. But in our time we have come to know the limits of "human nature" are frighteningly broad. We have come to know that every individual lives, from one generation to the next, in some society; that he lives out a biography, and that he lives it out within some historical sequence. By the fact of his living he contributes, however minutely, to the shaping of this society and to the course of its history, even as he is made by society and by its historical push and shove.

The sociological imagination enables us to grasp history and biography and the relations between the two within society. That is its task and its promise. To recognize this task and this promise is the mark of the classic social analyst. It is characteristic of Herbert Spencer—turgid, polysyllabic, comprehensive; of E. A. Ross—graceful, muckraking, upright; of Auguste Comte and Emile Durkheim; of the intricate and subtle Karl Mannheim. It is the quality of all that is intellectually excellent in Karl Marx; it is the clue to Thorstein Veblen's brilliant and ironic insight, to Joseph Schumpeter's many-sided constructions of reality; it is the basis of the psychological sweep of W.E.H. Lecky no less than of the profundity and clarity of Max Weber. And

it is the signal of what is best in contemporary studies of man and society.

No social study that does not come back to the problems of biography, of history, and of their intersections within a society has completed its intellectual journey. Whatever the specific problems of the classic social analysts, however limited or however broad the features of social reality they have examined, those who have been imaginatively aware of the promise of their work have consistently asked three sorts of questions:

1. What is the structure of this particular society as a whole? What are its essential components, and how are they related to one another? How does it differ from other varieties of social order? Within it, what is the meaning of any particular feature for its continuance and for its change?

2. Where does this society stand in human history? What are the mechanics by which it is changing? What is its place within and its meaning for the development of humanity as a whole? How does any particular feature we are examining affect, and how is it affected by, the historical period in which it moves? And this period—what are its essential features? How does it differ from other periods? What are its characteristic ways of history-making?

3. What varieties of men and women now prevail in this society and in this period? And what varieties are coming to prevail? In what ways are they selected and formed, liberated and repressed, made sensitive and blunted? What kinds of "human nature" are revealed in the conduct and character we observe in this society in this period? And what is the meaning of "human nature" of each and every feature of the society we are examining?

Whether the point of interest is a great power state or a minor literary mood, a family, a prison, a creed—these are the kinds of questions the best social analysts have asked. They are the intellectual pivots of classic studies of man in society—and they are the questions inevitably raised by any mind possessing the sociological imagination. For that imagination is the capacity to shift from one perspective to another—from the political to the psychological; from examination of a single family to comparative assessment of the national budgets of the world; from the theological school to the military establishment; from considerations of an oil industry to studies of contemporary poetry. It is the capacity to range from the most impersonal and remote transformations to the most intimate features of the human self—and to see the relations between the two. Back of its use there is always the urge to know the social and historical meaning of the individual in the society and in the period in which he has his quality and his being.

That, in brief, is why it is by means of the sociological imagination that men now hope to grasp what is going on in the world, and to understand what is happening in themselves as minute points of the intersections of biography and history within society. In large part, contemporary man's self-conscous view of himself as at least an outsider, if not a permanent stranger, rests upon an absorbed realization of social relativity and of the transformative power of history. The sociological imagination is the most fruitful form of this self-consciousness. By its use men whose mentalities have swept only a series of limited orbits often come to feel as if suddenly awakened in a house with which they had only supposed themselves to be familiar. Correctly or incorrectly, they often come to feel that they can now provide themselves with adequate summations, cohesive assessments, comprehensive orientations. Older decisions that once appeared sound now seem to them products of a mind unaccountably dense. Their capacity for astonishment is made lively again. They acquire a new way of thinking,

they experience a transvaluation of values: in a word, by their reflection and by their sensibility, they realize the cultural meaning of the social sciences.

II

Perhaps the most fruitful distinction with which the sociological imagination works is between "the personal troubles of milieu" and "the public issues of social structure." This distinction is an essential tool of the sociological imagination and a feature of all classic work in social science.

Troubles occur within the character of the individual and within the range of his immediate relations with others; they have to do with his self and with those limited areas of social life of which he is directly and personally aware. Accordingly, the statement and the resolution of troubles properly lie within the individual as a biographical entity and within the scope of his immediate milieu—the social setting that is directly open to his personal experience and to some extent his willful activity. A trouble is a private matter: values cherished by an individual are felt by him to be threatened.

Issues have to do with matters that transcend these local environments of the individual and the range of his inner life. They have to do with the organization of many such milieux into the institutions of an historical society as a whole, with the ways in which various milieux overlap and interpenetrate to form the larger structure of social and historical life. An issue is a public matter: some value cherished by publics is felt to be threatened. Often there is a debate about what that value really is and about what it is that really threatens it. This debate is often without focus if only because it is the very nature of an issue, unlike even widespread trouble, that it cannot very well be defined in terms of the immediate and everyday environment of ordinary men. An issue, in fact, often involves a crisis in institutional arrangements, and often too it involves what Marxists call "contradictions" or "antagonisms."

In these terms, consider unemployment. When, in a city of 100,000, only one man is unemployed, that is his personal trouble, and for its relief we properly look to the character of the man, his skills, and his immediate opportunities. But when in a nation of 50 million employees, 15 million men are unemployed, that is an issue, and we may not hope to find its solution within the range of opportunities open to any one individual. The very structure of opportunities has collapsed. Both the correct statement of the problem and the range of possible solutions require us to consider the economic and political institutions of the society, and not merely the personal situation and character of a scatter of individuals.

Consider war. The personal problem of war, when it occurs, may be how to survive it or how to die in it with honor; how to make money out of it; how to climb into the higher safety of the military apparatus; or how to contribute to the war's termination. In short, according to one's values, to find a set of milieux and within it to survive the war or make one's death in it meaningful. But the structural issues of war have to do with its causes; with what types of men it throws up into command; with its effects upon economic and political, family and religious institutions, with the unorganized irresponsibility of a world of nation-states.

Consider marriage. Inside a marriage a man and a woman may experience personal troubles, but when the divorce rate during the first four years of marriage is 250 out of every 1,000 attempts, this is an indication of a structural issue having to do with the institutions of marriage and the family and other institutions that bear upon them.

Or consider the metropolis—the horrible, beautiful, ugly, magnificent sprawl of the great city. For many upper-class people, the personal solution to "the problem of the city" is to have an apartment with private garage under it in the heart of the city, and forty miles out, a house by Henry Hill, garden by Garrett Eckbo, on a hundred acres of private land. In these two controlled environments—with a small staff at each end and a private helicopter connection—most people could solve many of the problems of personal milieux caused by the facts of the city. But all this, however splendid, does not solve the public issues that the structural fact of the city poses. What should be done with this wonderful monstrosity? Break it all up into scattered units, combining residence and work? Refurbish it as it stands? Or, after evacuation, dynamite it and build new cities according to new plans in new places? What should those plans be? And who is to decide and to accomplish whatever choice is made? These are structural issues; to confront them and to solve them requires us to consider political and economic issues that affect innumerable milieux.

Insofar as an economy is so arranged that slumps occur, the problem of unemployment becomes incapable of personal solution. Insofar as war is inherent in the nation-state system and in the uneven industrialization of the world, the ordinary individual in his restricted milieu will be powerless—with or without psychiatric aid—to solve the troubles this system or lack of system imposes upon him. Insofar as the family as an institution turns women into darling little slaves and men into their chief providers and unweaned dependents, the problem of a satisfactory marriage remains incapable of purely private solution. Insofar as the overdeveloped megalopolis and the overdeveloped automobile are built-in features of the overdeveloped society, the issues of urban living will not be solved by personal ingenuity and private wealth.

What we experience in various and specific milieux, I have noted, is often caused by structural changes. Accordingly, to understand the changes of many personal milieux we are required to look beyond them. And the number and variety of such structural changes increase as the institutions within which we live become more embracing and more intricately connected with one another. To be aware of the idea of social structure and to use it with sensibility is to be capable of tracing such linkages among a great variety of milieux. To be able to do that is to possess the sociological imagination.

III

What are the major issues for publics and the key troubles of private individuals in our time? To formulate issues and troubles, we must ask what values are cherished yet threatened, and what values are cherished and supported, by the characterizing trends of our period. In the case both of threat and of support we must ask what salient contradictions of structure may be involved.

When people cherish some set of values and do not feel any threat to them, they experience *well-being*. When they cherish values but *do* feel them to be threatened, they experience a crisis—either as a personal trouble or as a public issue. And if all their values seem involved, they feel the total threat of panic.

But suppose people are neither aware of any cherished values nor experience any threat? That is the experience of *indifference*, which, if it seems to involve all their values, becomes apathy. Suppose, finally, they are unaware of any cherished values, but still are very much aware of a threat? That is the experience of *uneasiness*, of anxiety, which, if it is total enough, becomes a deadly unspecified malaise.

Ours is a time of uneasiness and indifference—not yet formulated in such ways as to permit the work of reason and the play of sensibility. Instead of troubles—defined in terms of values and threats—there is often the misery of vague uneasiness; instead of explicit issues there is often merely the beat feeling that all is somehow not right. Neither the values threatened nor whatever threatens them has been stated; in short, they have not been carried to the point of decision. Much

less have they been formulated as problems of social science.

In the 'thirties there was little doubt—except among certain deluded business circles—that there was an economic issue which was also a pack of personal troubles. In these arguments about "the crisis of captalism," the formulations of Marx and the many unacknowledged reformulations of his work probably set the leading terms of the issue, and some men came to understand their personal troubles in these terms. The values threatened were plain to see and cherished by all; the structural contradictions that threatened them also seemed plain. Both were widely and deeply experienced. It was a political age.

But the values threatened in the era after World War Two are often neither widely acknowledged as values nor widely felt to be threatened. Much private uneasiness goes unformulated; much public malaise and many decisions of enormous structural relevance never become public issues. For those who accept such inherited values as reason and freedom, it is the uneasiness itself that is the trouble; it is the indifference itself that is the issue. And it is this condition, of uneasiness and indifference, that is the signal feature of our period.

All this is so striking that it is often interpreted by observers as a shift in the very kinds of problems that need now to be formulated. We are frequently told that the problems of our decade, or even the crisis of our period, have shifted from the external realm of economics and now have to do with the quality of individual life—in fact with the question of whether there is soon going to be anything that can properly be called individual life. Not child labor but comic books, not poverty but mass leisure, are at the center of concern. Many great public issues as well as many private troubles are described in terms of "the psychiatric"—often, it seems, in a pathetic attempt to avoid the large issues and problems of modern society. Often this statement seems to rest upon a provincial narrowing of interest to the Western societies, or even to the United States—thus ignoring two-thirds of mankind; often, too, it arbitrarily divorces the individual life from the larger institutions within which that life is enacted, and which on occasion bear upon it more grievously than do the intimate environments of childhood.

Problems of leisure, for example, cannot even be stated without considering problems of work. Family troubles over comic books cannot be formulated as problems without considering the plight of the contemporary family in its new relations with the newer institutions of the social structure. Neither leisure nor its debilitating uses can be understood as problems without recognition of the extent to which malaise and indifference now form the social and personal climate of contemporary American society. In this climate, no problems of "the private life" can be stated and solved without recognition of the crisis of ambition that is part of the very career of men at work in the incorporated economy.

It is true, as psychoanalysts continually point out, that people do often have "the increasing sense of being moved by obscure forces within themselves which they are unable to define." But it is *not* true, as Ernest Jones asserted, that "man's chief enemy and danger is his own unruly nature and the dark forces pent up within him." On the contrary: "Man's chief danger" today lies in the unruly forces of contemporary society itself, with its alienating methods of production, its enveloping techniques of political domination, its international anarchy—in a word, its pervasive transformations of the very "nature" of man and the conditions and aims of his life.

It is now the social scientist's foremost political and intellectual task—for here the two coincide—to make clear the elements of contemporary uneasiness and indifference. It is the central demand made upon him by other cultural workmen—by physical scientists and artists, by the intellectual community in general. It is because of this task and these demands, I believe, that the social sciences are becoming the common denominator of our cultural period, and the sociological imagination our most needed quality of mind. . . .

2

STRIPTEASERS
A SIX-YEAR HISTORY OF PUBLIC REACTION
TO A STUDY

James K. Skipper, Jr.

Seven years ago in 1969 in San Francisco at the Annual Meeting of the American Sociological Convention, we presented a paper before a section on deviant behavior entitled: "Stripteasers: The Anatomy and Career Contingencies of a Deviant Occupation" (Skipper and McCaghy, 1969). We had hoped that it would be accepted by the academic community as making a contribution to our knowledge of deviant behavior and that it would be looked upon favorably enough to eventually become part of the published literature on the subject. In this regard, our expectations were more than met. The total study has been reported in a series of published papers. What we did not anticipate, however, was both the academic and non-academic interest, curiosity, and controversy which the study generated.

Too seldom do we find any extensive recorded reports of public reactions to behavioral science research, especially that which has no explicit policy implications. There is even less available literature on the effects which a given piece of research may have on the personal and professional life of the

researchers. Yet, these would seem to be legitimate topics for individuals interested in understanding the popular culture of the age in which we live. Therefore, the purpose of this paper is to present some of the public reactions to our study of the occupation of stripteasing, and comment briefly on how they affected us.

In order to better understand the meaning of our experiences, rather than present them in chronological order, I have classified them under five broad, non-inclusive, and somewhat overlapping generalizations. They are as follows: The Sensationalism Principle, The Erotic Principle, The Evergreen Principle, The Instant Expert and Expert-by-Association Principle, and The Conversation Piece Principle.

THE SENSATIONALISM PRINCIPLE

If a social, scientific study is novel and related to sex, it is likely that its scholarly value may be ignored or forgotten in comparison to aspects of the study which lend themselves to sensationalism.

At the time of the original presentation, I brought 60 copies of the paper to the speaker's table for possible distribution to interested individuals after the address. All

Reprinted with permission of the author. This is a condensed version of a longer paper entitled "Public Reactions to a Popular Study: The Case of Stripteasers."

copies were taken before the address was completed. The following morning I discovered the *San Francisco Chronicle* carried an article with my picture, "Why Girls Become Stripteasers" (Bess, 1969). For the next three days, excerpts from the Associated Press appeared in various forms in newspapers throughout the United States and a number of foreign countries. I have no idea of the total extent of the coverage. Back in Cleveland, my wife was besieged with phone calls about the paper. The story that was printed in *The Cleveland Plain Dealer* (1969) was derogatory and attempted to belittle the research and make it look ridiculous. This was to cause problems for us later.

The immediate media coverage focused on two passages in the paper, which evidently were easy to sensationalize and completely ignore the scientific value of the research. The first passage concerned the physical characteristics of the strippers:

In terms of body types, the strippers' measurements showed considerable variation. However, compared to the average American women between the ages of 20 and 30, and even Playboy Playmates of the Month, the strippers were taller, heavier, with large hips, and had extremely well-developed busts, several approaching astronomical proportions.

The second passage the press chose to highlight was the strippers' relationships with their fathers:

Although our data are not complete in all cases, there is a clear indication that at least 60 percent of the girls came from broken and unstable homes where they received little attention and affection. A characteristic feature was the absence of the father from the home, or, if he was present, his disintegrating influence on family relationships (Skipper and McCaghy, 1969).

The captions to the various stories illustrate beautifully the way in which these two passages were sensationalized. Examples are: "Study Finds Stripper Outpoints Wife" (*Cleveland Plain Dealer*, 1969), "Profs Discover Strippers Have Big Busts" (*New York Post*, 1969), "Strippers Lacked Tender Care From Fathers" (Barmann, 1971). Finally, a quotation from the publication *Screw* summarizes the treatment given to the paper by the press:

It took a study by top level social scientists to discover that strippers are built like proverbial brick shithouses (*Screw*, 1970).

We can conclude that the principle of sensationalism involves a selective process. Out of the many papers presented at an academic convention, only a few are selected to be featured in the press. The criterion is not their scientific value or how other scientists may evaluate them, but their human interest and attractiveness to a large, pluralistic audience. In our case, it was the novelty of the study and its sexual content. From the paper itself are extracted those passages which most lend themselves to sensationalism. These are used to prepare a general press release. This provides the fodder by which each individual publication can decide what portion or all of the general press release it cares to print and make up its own catchy title to lure and whet the reader's interest. There would seem to be little felt obligation to report objectively. A good example of this is the actual number of strippers we interviewed. We stated it was 35. The figures used in different newspapers were 35, 55, 70, 75, 119, and 130.

THE EROTIC PRINCIPLE

If a social scientific study is novel and related to sex, it is likely to become a subject of intense curiosity and humor by some individuals and a subject of intense ridicule and scorn by other individuals. One of the significant happenings at the American Sociological Association convention in 1969 was the development of the Women's Caucus under the leadership of Professor Alice Rossi. The stated purpose of the Caucus was to " . . . transform the role of women in the Association, on campuses and society in general" (*Los Angeles Times*, 1969). The day after we presented our paper, a handout sheet was distributed to members of the Association. It read as follows:

WOMEN AGAINST VICTIM SOCIOLOGY

"We believe," Professor Skipper said, "that in order to meet love and affection needs, these girls began to use and display their bodies as a means of gaining attention and recognition they did not receive at home."

Professor Skipper's paper demonstrates not the weakness of women but the perverse nature of male thinking. No one—not even Skipper—gets love and affection from being an object. How can one who cannot understand human feeling talk about another's human feeling—especially the feeling of women who are oppressed by male supremacy?

THE WOMEN PROBLEM IS MALE SUPREMACY

White males get their professional mobility by the blood of those whose suffering upholds their dominant status. They are easy-to-administer, simple-minded survey research (or, with Skipper's strippers, prostitutes, etc. "casual contacts"). They "explain" the dependent variable, characteristics of the victim, by other psychological characteristics of that same victim. With this vicious and inadequate methodology they self-righteously explain the "deviant" behavior of the victim as the victim's own psychological makeup. This leads to an irrelevant, non-structural analysis of society. Their inability to examine real causes stems from the researchers' own involvement and stake as oppressor. This kind of sociology is used to keep the oppressed in their place and to justify their oppression.

I do not know who was responsible for the handout, although one might suspect that it was someone close to the Women's Caucus. I do know, however, that the coining of the phrase "Skipper's Strippers" as the title for their remarks on our paper exacerbated the situation. That phrase has been picked up by students, colleagues, friends, and others to the extent that I sometimes dread meeting new people for fear they, too, will say, "Oh, so you are Skipper of 'Skipper's Strippers.'" As a sociologist employed by a medical school, it is not particularly advantageous to be identified in such a manner. In large part, due to the rhyming phrase, I am associated more with strippers than 15 years of research in the area of medical sociology.

A second source of negative reactions stemmed from the local academic community.

To put it bluntly, the study and its ensuing publicity embarrassed university officials and created an atmosphere of benign resentment among faculty. The university administration from the president on down received calls and letters from alumni, members of the community, and even members of the Board of Trustees questioning the value of the research, our motive in conducting it, and the morality of the university in sponsoring it. Fortunately, we were able to answer that no one had sponsored or funded the study besides ourselves.

We also received a number of scornful and/or crank letters, especially from religious fanatics chiding us for engaging in such a study and interacting with sinful people. One individual even sent several pages of scriptures entitled: "God's Word on the Sex Deviant and Offender."

In addition to the scorn and ridicule made of the study, there was also a great deal of curiosity about it and good natured humor connected with it. For example, there were 525 letters of inquiry and requests for reprints and/or information from individuals in the United States and 12 foreign countries.

There were many humorous aspects to the exotic interest and curiosity in the study, although they often did not seem funny to us at the time. Several days after the "Women Against Victim Sociology" handout had been distributed, a major midwestern radio station announced that we had received their "Losers of the Day" award. Columnists around the country had a field day poking fun at us. They called us dedicated sociologists who were "expanding science's front," "pioneer researchers who laid bare exciting facts," and "front row peeper professors." With tongue in cheek, one man wrote that it must have been exhaustive research discovering strippers are "big-busted broads." Another columnist stated that if he had known you could get paid for such work and make headlines to boot, he would have changed his occupation long ago. A Pulitzer prize-winning dramatist, Morrie Ryskind (1969) pointed out in his column that although we stated we investigated the background characteristics of strippers, we must also have been interested in their foregrounds.

THE EVERGREEN PRINCIPLE

If a social scientific study is novel and related to sex, its newsworthiness to the mass media is not likely to be tied to any time-space framework, medium, or form of usage.

Several days after returning to Cleveland, we were interviewed by a local television station on the campus of the university. After the interview was completed, I asked the reporter when it would appear on television. He replied: "I do not know. With this type of material it really does not matter—today, tomorrow, next week, next month, next year—it is Evergreen, man, Evergreen!"

In spite of this opinion, on a time basis under the category of *reporting* news, most of the coverage of the paper took place within three days of its presentation. In terms of space, it was covered throughout North America, parts of Latin America, Europe, and perhaps elsewhere. We do not know the extent of the initial coverage through mediums of radio and television. However, the vast majority of the people who contacted us learned of the study through newspaper accounts. The effect of the Evergreen Principle can first be seen in radio and television usage, which began slightly later than that of the newspapers. It did not take the form of straight reporting, but more as the final, 15 second, humorous, human interest story on the local six o'clock news.

Further television coverage lasted for five years. It took four separate forms. During the first year, we were invited to appear on "game shows," which we refused on the basis that they were likely to be exploitive and definitely nonacademic. Second, for three years we were asked to appear as guests on several talk shows, of which we were selective in our acceptance. Third, for three years from time to time there would be television coverage of a public presentation which we would make concerning strippers. Finally, for five years we were aware of the fact that the research was discussed on various "talk shows" especially, but not exclusively, when strippers were invited guests.

The Evergreen Principle is probably best exemplified by the use made of the papers by newspapers and magazines one to three years after its original presentation. It was utilized as cannon fodder by newspaper columnists who tended to poke fun and make light of it and use it for their own purposes. The feature writers on the other hand usually presented a much more thorough and objective analysis. They were also more sympathetic and awarded merit to the research. There was one exception. The West German publication *Der Spiegel* in describing the methodology of the study stated:

In theater dressing rooms, restaurants, and bars, and sometimes while drinking whiskey and playing cards, the researchers measured and interviewed all 35 strippers (1970, p. 218).

Evidently, something was lost in translation since we were not drinking whiskey or playing cards, and we certainly did not measure any of the girls ourselves.

In summary, perhaps the beauty of evergreen material to those in the mass media is that it does not have to be implemented immediately. It does not have to be scheduled. When there is nothing else about which to talk or write, it may be utilized, and it will be just as valuable as the day it was discovered.

THE INSTANT EXPERT AND EXPERT-BY-ASSOCIATION PRINCIPLE

If a social scientific study investigates an area which has not been explored before, the researchers are likely to be considered instantly experts in that area of study and also related areas.

Immediately after presentation of the

paper, people began to refer to us as experts on stripteasers and to some extent this attitude still exists today.

Of equal importance is the notion that because you are considered an expert in one area, by some means of association you are considered to be an expert in related or semi-related areas. The following are examples of this generalization. I suppose it was to be expected that I would receive letters, including some from strippers and former strippers, asking for advice on sexual problems, or that a medical journal would ask me to answer a reader's question about whether nude dancers are sexually aroused by their own performance (Skipper, 1975). However, I never expected to be asked to be a sex counselor for college students, nor did I think my experience qualified me to be an advisor to a campus lesbian group. These, then, are just a few examples of the events which occurred following the presentation of the paper. Yet, I believe they amply illustrate how, if one's research is in an area that has not previously been investigated, one can almost instantly become an expert in not only that area, but also a host of related areas.

THE CONVERSATION PIECE PRINCIPLE

If a social scientific study is novel and concerns sex, it is likely to have appeal to individuals in a variety of walks of life and may be used as a topic of conversation in a variety of social situations. Since September of 1969, I have met and talked with hundreds of sociologists at conventions, conferences, college campuses, cocktail parties, etc. Regardless of whether they approve or disapprove of the research, or how high they value its scientific usefulness, they are either eager to discuss it or at least tolerant enough to listen to discussion of it without public indications of boredom. This latter quality is one that I have not found to be particularly common among sociologists.

In almost every course that I have taught

in sociology since the paper was presented, some individual before, during, or after one of the sessions has asked me if I could take a few minutes to tell them about stripteasers. If I assign term papers in an undergraduate class, often someone will want to make stripteasers their topic. This is somewhat difficult to justify in courses in medical sociology.

Finally, over the last few years I have presented guest lectures and seminars in medical sociology to a number of different groups of behavioral scientists and various members of the health professions. Usually, but not always, after I have concluded my remarks and there have been a few questions asked and answered, some one will say: "Now could you tell us about stripteasers?"

To conclude, it is fascinating to realize that you have a wealth of information on a topic of conversation which can draw attention in almost any informal group and many formal ones. At the same time, it is a commentary on present day American culture that the topic is stripteasers.

CONCLUSION

The aftermath of the stripper study was a moving one for me. It affected my self-image, my personal life, and, to an extent, my career. This paper, then, is a very personal one and as such probably lacks objectivity and suffers from my own ego involvement. On this basis, I decided it was best at this time to focus on a description rather than an analytical analysis, a narrative rather than a strict sociological interpretation and not attempt to draw out implications for research.

From what started out to be what we considered a small contribution to sociological knowledge in the area of deviant behavior, there arose some major unanticipated consequences. I have suggested five generalizations which may make these consequences more understandable, if not more predictable (The Sensationalism Principle, The Erotic Principle, The Evergreen Principle, The Instant

Expert and Expert-by-Association Principle, and The Conversation Piece Principle). They convey a part of the popular culture of the age in which we live. I suggest that anyone who

engages in areas of research which have not been systematically explored before, are considered novel and involve sex, to a more or less degree are going to experience them.

REFERENCES

Barmann, George. 1971. "Strippers Lacked Tender Loving Care From Fathers," *Cleveland Plain Dealer*, September 25.

Bess, Donovan, 1969. "Why Girls Become Stripteasers," *San Francisco Chronicle*, September 3.

Cleveland Plain Dealer. 1969. "Study Finds Stripper Outpoints Wife," September 3.

Der Spiegel. 1970. "Striptease—A Real Science," September 2:18.

Los Angeles Times. 1969. "Woman Power Major Issue for Sociologists," September 3.

New York Post. 1969. "Profs Discover Strippers Have Big Busts," September 3.

Ryskind, Morrie. "Sneering at Sociologists." (Date and source unknown.)

Screw. 1970. "Anatomy of a Stripper," June 8:14.

Skipper, James K., Jr. and Charles McCaghy. 1969. "Stripteasers: The Anatomy and Career Contingencies of a Deviant Occupation." Paper presented to the annual meetings of the American Sociological Association, San Francisco.

———. 1970. "Stripteasers: The Anatomy and Career Contingencies of a Deviant Occupation." *Social Problems* 17:391–405.

3

THE AMERICAN SOLDIER—
AN EXPOSITORY REVIEW

Paul F. Lazarsfeld

THE NATURE OF ATTITUDE SURVEYS

. . . The limitations of survey methods are obvious. They do not use experimental techniques; they rely primarily on what people say, and rarely include objective observations; they deal with aggregates of individuals rather

than with integrated communities; they are restricted to contemporary problems—history can be studied only by the use of documents remaining from earlier periods.

In spite of these limitations survey methods provide one of the foundations upon which social science is being built. The finding of regularities is the beginning of any science, and surveys can make an important contribution in this respect. For it is necessary that we know what people usually do under many and different circumstances if we are to develop theories explaining their behavior. Furthermore, before we can devise an experiment we must know what problems are worthwhile; which should be investigated in greater detail. Here again surveys can be of service.

Finding regularities and determining criteria of significance are concerns the social sciences have in common with the natural sciences. But there are crucial differences between the two fields of inquiry. The world of social events is much less "visible" than the realm of nature. That bodies fall to the ground, that things are hot or cold, that iron becomes rusty, are all immediately obvious. It is much more difficult to realize that ideas of right and wrong vary in different cultures; that customs may serve a different function from the one which the people practicing them believe they are serving; that the same person may show marked contrasts in his behavior as a member of a family and as a member of an occupational group. The mere description of human behavior, of its variation from group to group and of its changes in different situations, is a vast and difficult undertaking. It is this task of describing, sifting and ferreting out inter-relationships which surveys perform for us. And yet this very function often leads to serious misunderstandings. For it is hard to find a form of human behavior that has not already been observed somewhere. Consequently, if a study reports a prevailing regularity, many readers respond to it by thinking "of course that is the way things are." Thus, from time to time, the argument is advanced that surveys only put into complicated form observations which are already obvious to everyone.

Understanding the origin of this point of view is of importance far beyond the limits of the present discussion. The reader may be helped in recognizing this attitude if he looks over a few statements which are typical of many survey findings and carefully observes his own reaction. A short list of these, with brief interpretive comments, will be given here in order to bring into sharper focus probable reactions of many readers.

1. Better educated men showed more psycho-neurotic symptoms than those with less education. (The mental instability of the intellectual as compared to the more impassive psychology of the man-in-the-street has often been commented on.)
2. Men from rural backgrounds were usually in better spirits during their Army life than soldiers from city backgrounds. (After all, they are more accustomed to hardships.)
3. Southern soldiers were better able to stand the climate in the hot South Sea Islands than Northern soldiers. (Of course, Southerners are more accustomed to hot weather.)
4. White privates were more eager to become non-coms than Negroes. (The lack of ambition among Negroes is almost proverbial.)
5. Southern Negroes preferred Southern to Northern white officers. (Isn't it well known that Southern whites have a more fatherly attitude toward their "darkies"?)
6. As long as the fighting continued, men were more eager to be returned to the States than they were after the German surrender. (You cannot blame people for not wanting to be killed.)

We have in these examples a sample list of the simplest type of interrelationships which provide the "bricks" from which our empirical social science is being built. But why, since they are so obvious, is so much money and energy given to establish such findings? Would it not be wiser to take them for granted and proceed directly to a more sophisticated type of analysis? This might be so except for one interesting point about the list. *Every one of these statements is the direct opposite of what actually was found.* Poorly educated soldiers were more neurotic than those with high education; Southerners showed no greater ability than Northerners to adjust to a tropical climate; Negroes were more eager for promotion than whites; and so on. . . .

If we had mentioned the actual results of the investigation first, the reader would have labeled these "obvious" also. Obviously something is wrong with the entire argument of "obviousness." It should really be turned on its head. Since every kind of human reaction is conceivable, it is of great importance to know which reactions actually occur most frequently and under what conditions; only then will a more advanced social science develop. . . .

Part Two

BECOMING A MEMBER OF SOCIETY

An infant quickly learns that certain actions bring responses from other people. In this way the transformation of the newborn child into a social being begins. We call this transformation the socialization process.

The family is the first agent in the process. It protects and cares for the helpless infant, providing the training needed for the child to survive and become a participating member of society. As the years pass, the child will come in contact with other agents of the socialization process, including peer groups, school and church.

The socialization process is lifelong. We must continuously learn to deal with the changes that occur throughout our lifetime, and all that we learn is part of the complex whole known as culture. Culture provides the knowledge and the materials necessary for survival in any society and for the ongoing existence of that society. Learning our culture may also have complications as we try to master such subtleties as "the silent language."

Only through our interaction with groups such as the family do we become social beings. However, this learning process is not always smooth; nor does society always function with perfect order. For example, families provide nurturance, but violence may contribute as well to our family experience. Group contact may provide needed social contact and belonging, but also may be frustrating. And chance places us in a rich or poor family, which in turn greatly influences our life opportunities. Group membership is our vehicle for carrying out the process of socialization and maintaining the social system, whatever that system might be.

Although specifics of each of these three elements—socialization, culture, and groups— will vary from society to society, each element will be found in every society.

Two results of the process of becoming a member of society must be mentioned because they influence how and what we learn. First, every society ranks its members according to its own values, which creates differing styles of living within the society. We call this creation of varying status levels *stratification*. Through socialization, children ingest the class values and beliefs held by their families, which in turn tends to perpetuate the status quo. The second influence is *ethnocentrism*: the belief that one's culture is superior to others. This influence is based on our familiarity with our own culture and on the comfort that this familiarity breeds. However, what begins as provincial lack of understanding can lead to the criticism of foreign cultures, the rejection of others, and the reluctance to accept change.

As you read this section, consider the processes that influence a baby and that turn the child into a productive member of groups within a particular culture. Also consider the different experiences that baby would undergo if reared in another social class or culture.

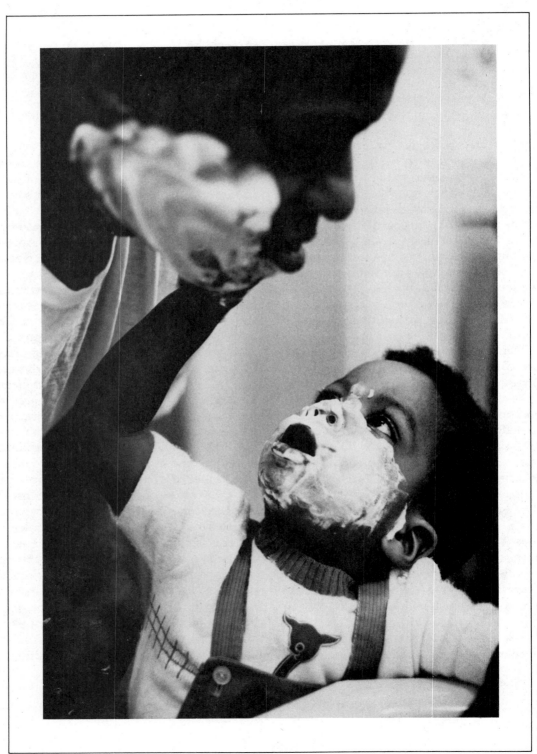

II

SOCIALIZATION
A Lifelong Learning Process

Through the process of socialization we learn to be social beings, members of our culture. Socialization shapes us into social beings from the day we are born, by teaching us the behaviors of our culture that make social existence possible. We are totally submerged into our cultures, first through our family—parents, siblings, and extended family members—then through the formal institutions of church and school, and later through political and economic institutions. The learning that takes place is important to our adjustment and even to our survival in society, for it is by these learned, patterned expectations that society is made possible.

We can see from the series of socialization agents mentioned that the process takes place through interaction with others—an interaction that seems vital to our social development. It might be asked, however, if such group contact is really necessary. Is not social development a natural outgrowth of physical maturity? To answer that question, some social scientists have focused their studies on cases of social isolation.

In rare instances, children do not experience early socialization in the family. For example, many orphanages provide only minimal care and human contact; children growing up in this environment have been found to show a higher percentage of physical and mental retardation. There are only a handful of cases of almost total isolation. In the first reading, Davis describes the case histories of Anna and Isabelle, and considers the impact of isolation on their development. He writes that severe retardation is likely to occur when consistent contact with other human beings is absent, and concludes that while socialization can take place after prolonged periods of isolation, some of the effects may be permanent.

Socialization begins at birth and lasts throughout life, for each time we face a new expe-options available to them than ever before, our sex roles are so deeply imbedded in us from our early years that they form a non-conscious ideology. This produces subtle sex-role behaviors that we hardly recognize, but that affect all of us from early childhood, through schooling and career choice, to marriage and childrearing.

The most obvious results of socialization are our language acquisition and behavior patterns. However, there is a less obvious form of socialization taking place simultaneously. The Halls call this "silent language," or nonverbal communication. Because of its subtleties and the vast range of possible nonverbal cues, it is a more difficult language to master than verbal speech. Body language involves physical cues—glances, movement, facial expressions—and the social distance or personal space we need. To complicate matters, each culture and subcul-rience or assume a new role we learn new ways of performing the role. Some roles are achieved: we work to earn them, just as you have learned the role of student and are being socialized into an occupational role. Other roles are ascribed: we are born into them and cannot change them—for instance, our age, sex, race and nationality.

The socialization process can be very rigid and difficult to change when it involves these ascribed roles. In the second article, Sandra and Daryl Bem address sex-role socialization. Even though our values and attitudes concerning woman's role are changing, and women have more

ture is socialized with different expectations. Close contact may be either erotic or annoying to a person of one culture, but an accepted conversational distance to one of another.

As you read the selections in this chapter, consider the three aspects of socialization we have mentioned. What are the effects of isolation, or lack of socialization through normal human contact, on humans? What are the effects of the socialization processes we take for granted, such as sex-role stereotyping? What are some of the subtleties of the socialization process that result in silent language?

4

FINAL NOTE ON A CASE OF EXTREME ISOLATION

Kingsley Davis

Early in 1940 there appeared . . . an account of a girl called Anna.[1] She had been deprived of normal contact and had received a minimum of human care for almost the whole of her first six years of life. At this time observations were not complete and the report had a tentative character. Now, however, the girl is dead, and with more information available,[2] it is possible to give a fuller and more definitive description of the case from a sociological point of view.

Anna's death, caused by hemorrhagic jaundice, occurred on August 6, 1942. Having been born on March 1 or 6,[3] 1932, she was approximately ten and a half years of age when she died. The previous report covered her development up to the age of almost eight years; the present one recapitulates the earlier period on the basis of new evidence and then covers the last two and a half years of her life.

Reprinted from *American Journal of Sociology*, Vol. III, No. 5, March 1947, pp. 432–437 by permission of the author. © 1947 by the University of Chicago Press.

EARLY HISTORY

The first few days and weeks by Anna's life were complicated by frequent changes of domicile. It will be recalled that she was an illegitimate child, the second such child born to her mother, and that her grandfather, a widowed farmer in whose house her mother lived, strongly disapproved of this new evidence of the mother's indiscretion. This fact led to the baby's being shifted about.

Two weeks after being born in a nurse's private home, Anna was brought to the family farm, but the grandfather's antagonism was so great that she was shortly taken to the house of one of her mother's friends. At this time a local minister became interested in her and took her to his house with an idea of possible adoption. He decided against adoption, however, when he discovered that she had vaginitis. The infant was then taken to a children's home in the nearest large city. This agency found that at the age of only three weeks she was already in a miserable condition, being "terribly galled and otherwise in very bad shape." It did not regard her as a likely subject for adoption but took her in for a while anyway, hoping to benefit her. After Anna had spent nearly eight weeks in this place, the agency notified her mother to come to get her. The mother responded by sending a man and his wife to the children's home with a view to their adopting Anna, but they made such a poor impression on the agency that permission was refused. Later the mother came herself and took the child out of the home and then gave her to this couple. It was in the home of this pair that a social worker found the girl a short time thereafter. The social worker went to the mother's home and pleaded with Anna's grandfather to allow the mother to bring the child home. In spite of threats, he refused. The child, by then more than four months old, was next taken to another children's home in a near-by town. A medical examination at this time revealed that she had impetigo, vaginitis, umbilical hernia, and a skin rash.

Anna remained in this second children's home for nearly three weeks, at the end of which time she was transferred to a private foster-home. Since, however, the grandfather would not, and the mother could not, pay for the child's care, she was finally taken back as a last resort to the grandfather's house (at the age of five and a half months). There she remained, kept on the second floor in an attic-like room because her mother hesitated to incur the grandfather's wrath by bringing her downstairs.

The mother, a sturdy woman weighing about 180 pounds, did a man's work on the farm. She engaged in heavy work such as milking cows and tending hogs and had little time for her children. Sometimes she went out at night, in which case Anna was left entirely without attention. Ordinarily, it seems, Anna received only enough care to keep her barely alive. She appears to have been seldom moved from one position to another. Her clothing and bedding were filthy. She apparently had no instruction, no friendly attention.

It is little wonder that, when finally found and removed from the room in the grand-father's house at the age of nearly six years, the child could not talk, walk, or do anything that showed intelligence. She was in an extremely emaciated and undernourished condition, with skeletonlike legs and a bloated abdomen. She had been fed on virtually nothing except cow's milk during the years under her mother's care.

Anna's condition when found, and her subsequent improvement, have been described in the previous report. It now remains to say what happened to her after that.

LATER HISTORY

In 1939, nearly two years after being discovered, Anna had progressed, as previously reported, to the point where she could walk, understand simple commands, feed herself, achieve some neatness, remember people, etc. But she still did not speak, and, though she was much more like a normal infant of something over one year of age in mentality, she was far from normal for her age.

On August 30, 1939, she was taken to a private home for retarded children, leaving the county home where she had been for more than a year and a half. In her new setting she made some further progress, but not a great deal. In a report of an examination made November 6 of the same year, the head of the institution pictured the child as follows:

Anna walks about aimlessly, makes periodic rhythmic motions of her hands, and, at intervals, makes guttural and sucking noises. She regards her hands as if she had seen them for the first time. It was impossible to hold her attention for more than a few seconds at a time—not because of distraction due to external stimuli but because of her inability to concentrate. She ignored the task in hand to gaze vacantly about the room. Speech is entirely lacking. Numerous unsuccessful attempts have been made with her in the hope of developing initial sounds. I do not believe that this failure is due to negativism or deafness but that she is not sufficiently developed to accept speech at this time. . . . The prognosis is not favorable. . . .

More than five months later, on April 25, 1940, a clinical psychologist, the late Professor Francis N. Maxfield, examined Anna and reported the following: large for her age; hearing "entirely normal"; vision apparently normal; able to climb stairs; speech in the "babbling stage" and "promise for developing intelligible speech later seems to be good." He said further that "on the Merrill-Palmer scale she made a mental score of 19 months. On the Vineland social maturity scale she made a score of 23 months."[4]

Professor Maxfield very sensibly pointed out that prognosis is difficult in such cases of isolation. "It is very difficult to take scores on tests standardized under average conditions of environment and experience," he wrote, "and interpret them in a case where environment and experience have been so unusual." With this warning he gave it as his opinion at that time that Anna would eventually "attain an adult mental level of six or seven years."[5]

The school for retarded children, on July 1, 1941, reported that Anna had reached 46 inches in height and weighed 60 pounds. She could bounce and catch a ball and was said to conform to group socialization, though as a follower rather than a leader. Toilet habits were firmly established. Food habits were normal, except that she still used a spoon as her sole implement. She could dress herself except for fastening her clothes. Most remarkable of all, she had finally begun to develop speech. She was characterized as being at about the two-year level in this regard. She could call attendants by name and bring in one when she was asked to. She had a few complete sentences to express her wants. The report concluded that there was nothing peculiar about her, except that she was feebleminded—"probably congenital in type."[6]

A final report from the school made on June 22, 1942, and evidently the last report before the girl's death, pictured only a slight advance over that given above. It said that Anna could follow directions, string beads, identify a few colors, build with blocks, and differentiate between attractive and unattractive pictures. She had a good sense of rhythm and loved a doll. She talked mainly in phrases but would repeat words and try to carry on a conversation. She was clean about clothing. She habitually washed her hands and brushed her teeth. She would try to help other children. She walked well and could run fairly well, though clumsily. Although easily excited, she had a pleasant disposition.

INTERPRETATION

Such was Anna's condition just before her death. It may seem as if she had not made much progress, but one must remember the condition in which she had been found. One must recall that she had no glimmering of speech, absolutely no ability to walk, no sense of gesture, not the least capacity to feed herself even when the food was put in front of her, and no comprehension of cleanliness. She was so apathetic that it was hard to tell whether or not she could hear. And all this at the age of nearly six years. Compared with this condition, her capacities at the time of her death seem striking indeed, though they do not amount to much more than a two-and-a-half-year mental level. One conclusion therefore seems safe, namely, that her isolation prevented a considerable amount of mental development that was undoubtedly part of her capacity. Just what her original capacity was, of course, is hard to say; but her development after her period of confinement (including the ability to walk and run, to play, dress, fit into a social situation, and, above all, to speak) shows that she had at least this capacity—capacity that never could have been realized in her original condition of isolation.

A further question is this: What would she have been like if she had received a normal upbringing from the moment of birth? A definitive answer would have been impossible in any case, but even an approximate answer is made difficult by her early death. If one assumes, as was tentatively surmised in the previous report, that it is "almost impossible for any child to learn to speak, think, and act

BECOMING A MEMBER OF SOCIETY

like a normal person after a long period of early isolation," it seems likely that Anna might have had a normal or near-normal capacity, genetically speaking. On the other hand, it was pointed out that Anna represented "a marginal case, [because] she was discovered before she had reached six years of age," an age "young enough to allow for some plasticity."[7] While admitting, then, that Anna's isolation *may* have been the major cause (and was certainly a minor cause) of her lack of rapid mental progress during the four and a half years following her rescue from neglect, it is necessary to entertain the hypothesis that she was congenitally deficient.

In connection with this hypothesis, one suggestive though by no means conclusive circumstance needs consideration, namely, the mentality of Anna's forebears. Information on this subject is easier to obtain, as one might guess, on the mother's than on the father's side. Anna's maternal grandmother, for example, is said to have been college educated and wished to have her children receive a good education, but her husband, Anna's stern grandfather, apparently a shrewd, hard-driving, calculating farmowner, was so penurious that her ambitions in this direction were thwarted. Under the circumstances her daughter (Anna's mother) managed, despite having to do hard work on the farm, to complete the eighth grade in a country school. Even so, however, the daughter was evidently not very smart. "A schoolmate of [Anna's mother] stated that she was retarded in school work; was very gullible at this age; and that her morals even at this time were discussed by other students." Two tests administered to her on March 4, 1938, when she was thirty-two years of age, showed that she was mentally deficient. On the Stanford Revision of the Binet-Simon Scale her performance was equivalent to that of a child of eight years, giving her an I. Q. of 50 and indicating mental deficiency of "middle-grade moron type."[8]

As to the identity of Anna's father, the most persistent theory holds that he was an old man about seventy-four years of age at the time of the girl's birth. If he was the one, there is no indication of mental or other biological deficiency, whatever one may think of his morals. However, someone else may actually have been the father.

To sum up: Anna's heredity is the kind that *might* have given rise to innate mental deficiency, though not necessarily.

COMPARISON WITH ANOTHER CASE

Perhaps more to the point than speculations about Anna's ancestry would be a case for comparison. If a child could be discovered who had been isolated about the same length of time as Anna but had achieved a much quicker recovery and a greater mental development, it would be a stronger indication that Anna was deficient to start with.

Such a case does exist. It is the case of a girl found at about the same time as Anna and under strikingly similar circumstances. A full description of the details of this case has not been published, but in addition to newspaper reports, an excellent preliminary account by a speech specialist, Dr. Marie K. Mason, who played an important role in the handling of the child, has appeared.[9] Also the late Dr. Francis N. Maxfield, clinical psychologist at Ohio State University, as was Dr. Mason, has written an as yet unpublished but penetrating analysis of the case.[10] Some of his observations have been included in Professor Zingg's book on feral man.[11] The following discussion is drawn mainly from these enlightening materials. The writer, through the kindness of Professors Mason and Maxfield, did have a chance to observe the girl in April, 1940, and to discuss the features of her case with them.

Born apparently one month later than Anna, the girl in question, who has been given the pseudonym Isabelle, was discovered in November, 1938, nine months after the discovery of Anna. At the time she was found she was approximately six and a half years of age. Like Anna, she was an illegitimate child and had been kept in seclusion for that reason. Her mother was a deaf-mute, having become so at the age of two, and it appears that she and Isabelle had spent most of their time together in a dark room shut off from the rest of the mother's family. As a result Isabelle had no chance to develop speech; when she communicated with her mother, it was by means of gestures. Lack of sunshine and inadequacy of diet had caused Isabelle to become rachitic. Her legs in particular were affected; they "were so bowed that as she stood erect the soles of her shoes came nearly flat together, and she got about with a skittering gait."[12] Her behavior toward strangers, especially men, was almost that of a wild animal, manifesting much fear and hostility. In lieu of speech she made only a strange croaking sound. In many ways she acted like an infant. "She was apparently utterly unaware of relationships of any kind. When presented with a ball for the first time, she held it in the palm of her hand, then reached out and stroked my face with it. Such behavior is comparable to that of a child of six months."[13] At first it was even hard to tell whether or not she could hear, so unused were her senses. Many of her actions resembled those of deaf children.

It is small wonder that, once it was established that she could hear, specialists working with her believed her to be feeble-minded. Even on nonverbal tests her performance was so low as to promise little for the future. Her first score on the Stanford-Binet was 19 months, practically at the zero point of the scale. On the Vineland social maturity scale her first score was 39, representing an age level of two and a half years.[14] "The general impression was that she was wholly uneducable and that any attempt to teach her to speak, after so long a period of silence, would meet with failure."[15]

In spite of this interpretation, the individuals in charge of Isabelle launched a systematic and skillful program of training. It seemed hopeless at first. The approach had to be through pantomime and dramatization, suitable to an infant. It required one week of intensive effort before she even made her first attempt at vocalization. Gradually she began to respond, however, and, after the first hurdles had at last been overcome, a curious thing happened. She went through the usual stages of learning characteristic of the years from one to six not only in proper succession but far more rapidly than normal. In a little over two months after her first vocalization she was putting sentences together. Nine months after that she could identify words and sentences on the printed page, could write well, could add to ten, and could retell a story after hearing it. Seven months beyond this point she had a vocabulary of 1,500–2,000 words and was asking complicated questions. Starting from an educational level of between one and three years (depending on what aspect one considers), she had reached a normal level by the time she was eight and a half years old. In short, she covered in two years the stages of learning that ordinarily require six.[16] Or, to put it another way, her I. Q. trebled in a year and a half.[17] The speed with which she reached the normal level of mental development seems analogous to the recovery of body weight in a growing child after an illness, the recovery being achieved by an extra fast rate of growth for a period after the illness until normal weight for the given age is again attained.

When the writer saw Isabelle a year and a half after her discovery, she gave him the impression of being a very bright, cheerful, energetic little girl. She spoke well, walked and ran without trouble, and sang with gusto and accuracy. Today she is over fourteen years old and has passed the sixth grade in a public school. Her teachers say that she participates in all school activities as normally as other children. Though older than her classmates, she has fortunately not physically matured too far beyond their level.[18]

Clearly the history of Isabelle's development is different from that of Anna's. In both cases there was an exceedingly low, or rather blank, intellectual level to begin with. In both cases it seemed that the girl might be congenitally feeble minded. In both a considerably higher level was reached later on. But the Ohio girl achieved a normal mentality with two years, whereas Anna was still marked inadequate at the end of four and a half years. This difference in achievement may suggest that Anna had less initial capacity. But an alternative hypothesis is possible.

One should remember that Anna never received the prolonged and expert attention that Isabelle received. The result of such attention, in the case of the Ohio girl, was to give her speech at an early stage, and her subsequent rapid development seems to have been a consequence of that. "Until Isabelle's speech and language development, she had all the characteristics of a feeble-minded child." Had Anna, who, from the standpoint of psychometric tests and early history, closely resembled this girl at the start, been given a mastery of speech at an earlier point by intensive training, her subsequent development might have been much more rapid.[19]

The hypothesis that Anna began with a sharply inferior mental capacity is therefore not established. Even if she were deficient to start with, we have no way of knowing how much so. Under ordinary conditions she might have been a dull normal or, like her mother, a moron. Even after the blight of her isolation, if she had lived to maturity, she might have finally reached virtually the full level of her capacity, whatever it may have been. That her isolation did have a profound effect upon her mentality, there can be no doubt. This is proved by the substantial degree of change

during the four and a half years following her rescue.

Consideration of Isabelle's case serves to show, as Anna's case does not clearly show, that isolation up to the age of six, with failure to acquire any form of speech and hence failure to grasp nearly the whole world of cultural meaning, does not preclude the subsequent acquisition of these. Indeed, there seems to be a process of accelerated recovery in which the child goes through the mental stages at a more rapid rate than would be the case in normal development. Just what would be the maximum age at which a person could remain isolated and still retain the capacity for full cultural acquisition is hard to say. Almost certainly it would not be as high as age fifteen; it might possibly be as low as age ten. Undoubtedly various individuals would differ considerably as to the exact age.

Anna's is not an ideal case for showing the effects of extreme isolation, partly because she was possibly deficient to begin with, partly because she did not receive the best training available, and partly because she did not live long enough. Nevertheless, her case is instructive when placed in the record with numerous other cases of extreme isolation. This and the previous article about her are meant to place her in the record. It is to be hoped that other cases will be described in the scientific literature as they are discovered (as unfortunately they will be), for only in these rare cases of extreme isolation is it possible "to observe *concretely separated* two factors in the development of human personality which are always otherwise only analytically separated, the biogenic and the sociogenic factors."[20]

NOTES

[1]Kingsley Davis, "Extreme Social Isolation of a Child," *American Journal of Sociology*, XLV (January, 1940), 554–65.
[2]Sincere appreciation is due to the officials in the Department of Welfare, Commonwealth of Pennsylvania, for their kind co-operation in making available the records concerning Anna and discussing the case frankly with the writer. Helen C. Hubbell, Florentine Hackbusch, and Eleanor Meckelnburg were particularly helpful, as was

Fanny L. Matchette. Without their aid neither of the reports on Anna could have been written.

[3] The records are not clear as to which day.

[4] Letter to one of the state officials in charge of the case.

[5] *Ibid.*

[6] Progress report of the school.

[7] Davis, *op. cit.*, p. 564.

[8] The facts set forth here as to Anna's ancestry are taken chiefly from a report of mental tests administered to Anna's mother by psychologists at a state hospital where she was taken for this purpose after the discovery of Anna's seclusion. This excellent report was not available to the writer when the previous paper on Anna was published.

[9] Marie K. Mason, "Learning to Speak after Six and One-Half Years of Silence," *Journal of Speech Disorders*, VII (1942), 295–304.

[10] Francis N. Maxfield, "What Happens When the Social Environment of a Child Approaches Zero." The writer is greatly indebted to Mrs. Maxfield and to Professor Horace B. English, a colleague of Professor Maxfield, for the privilege of seeing this manuscript and other materials collected on isolated and feral individuals.

[11] J.A.L. Singh and Robert M. Zingg, *Wolf-Children and Feral Man* (New York: Harper & Bros., 1941), pp. 248–51.

[12] Maxfield, unpublished manuscript cited above.

[13] Mason, *op. cit.*, p. 299.

[14] Maxfield, unpublished manuscript.

[15] Mason, *op. cit.*, p. 299.

[16] *Ibid.*, pp. 300–304.

[17] Maxfield, unpublished manuscript.

[18] Based on a personal letter from Dr. Mason to the writer, May 13, 1946.

[19] This point is suggested in a personal letter from Dr. Mason to the writer, October 22, 1946.

[20] Singh and Zingg, *op. cit.*, pp. xxi–xxii, in a foreword by the writer.

5

HOMOGENIZING THE AMERICAN WOMAN: THE POWER OF AN UNCONSCIOUS IDEOLOGY

Sandra L. Bem and Daryl J. Bem

"In the beginning God created the heaven and the earth. . . . And God said, Let us make man in our image, after our likeness; and let him have dominion over the fish of the sea, and over the fowl of the air, and over the cattle, and over all the earth. . . . And the rib, which the Lord God had taken from man, made he a woman and brought her unto the man. . . . And the Lord God said unto the woman, What is this that thou hast done? And the woman said, The serpent beguiled me, and I did eat. . . . Unto the woman God said, I will greatly multiply thy sorrow and thy conception; in sorrow thou shalt bring forth children; and thy desire shall be to thy husband, and he shall rule over thee." (Gen. 1, 2, 3)

There is a moral to that story. St. Paul spells it out even more clearly.

"For a man . . . is the image and glory of God; but the woman is the glory of the man. For the man is not of the woman, but the woman of the man. Neither was the man created for the woman, but the woman for the man." (1 Cor. 11)

"Let the woman learn in silence with all subjection. But I suffer not a woman to teach, nor to usurp authority over the man, but to be in silence. For Adam was first formed and then Eve. And Adam was not deceived, but the

Reprinted with permission of the authors. Originally titled "Training the Woman to Know Her Place." Citations should be made to the published version of this article: Bem, S. L. & Bem, D. J. Case study of a non-conscious ideology: training the woman to know her place. In D. J. Bem, *Beliefs, attitudes and human affairs*. Belmont, California: Brooks/Cole, 1970. Order of authorship determined by the flip of a coin.

woman, being deceived, was in the transgression. Notwithstanding, she shall be saved in childbearing, if they continue in faith and charity and holiness with sobriety." (1 Tim. 2)

Now one should not assume that only Christians have this kind of rich heritage of ideology about women. So consider now, the morning prayer of the Orthodox Jew:

"Blessed art Thou, O Lord our God, King of the Universe, that I was not born a gentile.

"Blessed art Thou, O Lord our God, King of the Universe, that I was not born a slave.

"Blessed art Thou, O Lord our God, King of the Universe, that I was not born a woman."

Or, consider the Koran, the sacred text of Islam:

"Men are superior to women on account of the qualities in which God has given them preeminence."

Because they think they sense a decline in feminine "faith, charity, and holiness with sobriety," many people today jump to the conclusion that the ideology expressed in these passages is a relic of the past. Not so, of course. It has simply been obscured by an equalitarian veneer, and the same ideology has now become unconscious. That is, we remain unaware of it because alternative beliefs and attitudes about woman, until very recently, have gone unimagined. We are very much like the fish who is unaware of the fact that his environment is wet. After all, what else could it be? Such is the nature of all unconscious ideologies in a society. Such, in particular, is the nature of America's ideology about women. What we should like to do in this paper is to discuss today's version of this same ideology.

When a baby boy is born, it is difficult to predict what he will be doing 25 years later. We can't say whether he will be an artist, a doctor, a lawyer, a college professor, or a bricklayer, because he will be permitted to develop and fulfill his own unique potential— particularly, of course, if he happens to be white and middle class. But if that same new-born child happens to be a girl, we can predict with almost complete confidence how she is likely to be spending her time some 25 years later. Why can we do that? Because her individuality doesn't have to be considered. Her individuality is irrelevant. Time studies have shown that she will spend the equivalent of a full working day, 7.1 hours, in preparing meals, cleaning house, laundering, mending, shopping and doing other household tasks. In other words, 43% of her waking time will be spent in activity that would command an hourly wage on the open market well below the federally set minimum for menial industrial work.

Of course, the point really is not how little she would earn if she did these things in someone else's home. She will be doing them in her own home for free. The point is that this use of time is virtually the same for home-makers with college degrees and for home-makers with less than a grade school education, for women married to professional men and for women married to blue-collar workers. Actually, that's understating it slightly. What the time study really showed was that college-educated women spend slightly *more* time cleaning their houses than their less-educated counterparts!

Of course, it is not simply the full-time

homemaker whose unique identity has been rendered largely irrelevant. Of the 31 million women who work outside the home in our society, 78% end up in dead-end jobs as clerical workers, service workers, factory workers, or sales clerks, compared to a comparable figure of 40% for men. Only 15% of all women workers in our society are classified by the Labor Department as professional or technical workers, and even this figure is misleading— for the single, poorly-paid occupation of non-college teacher absorbs half of these women, and the occupation of nurse absorbs an additional quarter. In other words, the two jobs of teacher and nurse absorb three-quarters of all women classified in our society as technical or professional. That means, then, that fewer than 5% of all professional women—fewer than 1% of all women working—fill those positions which to most Americans connote "professional": physician, lawyer, engineer, scientist, college professor, journalist, writer, and so forth.

Even an I. Q. in the genius range does not guarantee that a woman's unique potential will find expression. There was a famous study of over 1300 boys and girls whose I.Q.'s averaged 151 (Terman and Oden, 1959). When the study began in the early 1900s, these highly gifted youngsters were only ten years old, and their careers have been followed ever since. Where are they today? 86% of the men have now achieved prominence in professional and managerial occupations. In contrast, only a minority of the women were even employed. Of those who were, 37% were nurses, librarians, social workers, and non-college teachers. An additional 26% were secretaries, stenographers, bookkeepers, and office workers! Only 11% entered the higher professions of law, medicine, college teaching, engineering, science, economics, and the like. And even at age 44, well after all their children had gone to school, 61% of these highly gifted women remained full-time homemakers. Talent, education, ability, interests, motivations: all irrelevant. In our society, being female uniquely qualifies an individual for domestic work—either by itself or in conjunction with typing, teaching, nursing, or (most often) unskilled labor. It is this homogenization of America's women which is the major consequence of our society's sex-role ideology.

It is true, of course, that most women have several hours of leisure time every day. And it is here, we are often told, that each woman can express her unique identity. Thus, politically interested women can join the League of Women Voters. Women with humane interests can become part-time Gray Ladies. Women who love music can raise money for the symphony. Protestant women play canasta; Jewish women play Mah Jongg; brighter women of all denominations and faculty wives play bridge.

But politically interested *men* serve in legislatures. *Men* with humane interests become physicians or clinical psychologists. *Men* who love music play in the symphony. In other words, why should a woman's unique identity determine only the periphery of her life rather than its central core?

Why? Why nurse rather than physician, secretary rather than executive, stewardess rather than pilot? Why faculty wife rather than faculty? Why doctor's mother rather than doctor? There are three basic answers to this question: (1) discrimination, (2) sex-role conditioning, and (3) the presumed incompatibility of family and career.

DISCRIMINATION

In 1968, the median income of full-time women workers was approximately $4500. The comparable figure for men was $3000 higher. Moreover, the gap is widening. Ten years ago, women earned 64% of what men did; that percentage has now shrunk to 58%. Today, a female college graduate working full-time can expect to earn less per year than a male high school dropout.

There are two reasons for this pay differ-ential. First, in every category of occupation, women are employed in the lesser-skilled, lower-paid positions. Even in the clerical field, where 73% of the workers are women, females are relegated to the lowest status positions and hence earn only 65% of what male clerical workers earn. The second reason for this pay differential is discrimination in its purest form: unequal pay for equal work. According to a survey of 206 companies in 1970, female college graduates were offered jobs which paid $43 per month less than those offered to their male counterparts in the same college major.

New laws should begin to correct both of these situations. The Equal Pay Act of 1963 prohibits employers from discriminating on the basis of sex in the payment of wages for equal work. In a landmark ruling on May 18, 1970, the U. S. Supreme Court ordered that $250,000 in back pay be paid to women employed by a single New Jersey glass company. This decision followed a two-year court battle by the Labor Department after it found that the company was paying men selector-packers 21.5 cents more per hour than women doing the same work. In a similar case, the Eighth Circuit Court of Appeals ordered a major can company to pay more than $100,-000 in back wages to women doing equal work. According to the Labor Department, an estimated $17 million is owed to women in back pay. Since that estimate was made, a 1972 amendment extended the Act to cover executive, administrative and professional employees as well.

But to enjoy equal pay, women must also have access to equal jobs. Title VII of the 1964 Civil Rights Act prohibits discrimination in employment on the basis of race, color, religion, national origin—and sex. Although the sex provision was treated as a joke at the time (and was originally introduced by a Southern Congressman in an attempt to defeat the bill), the Equal Employment Opportunities Commission discovered in its first year of operation that 40% or more of the complaints warranting investigation charged discrimination on the basis of sex (Bird, 1969).

Title VII has served as one of the most effective instruments in helping to achieve sex equality in the world of work. According to a report by the E.E.O.C., nearly 6,000 charges of sex discrimination were filed with that agency in 1971 alone, a 62% increase over the previous year.

But the most significant legislative breakthrough in the area of sex equality was the passage of the Equal Rights Amendment by both houses of Congress in 1972. The ERA simply states that "Equality of rights under the law shall not be denied or abridged by the United States or by any state on account of sex." This amendment had been introduced into every session of Congress since 1923, and its passage now is clearly an indication of the changing role of the American women. All of the various ramifications are hard to predict, but it is clear that it will have profound consequences in private as well as public life.

Many Americans assume that the recent drive for equality between the sexes is primarily for the benefit of the middle-class woman who wants to seek self-fulfillment in a professional career. But in many ways, it is the woman in more modest circumstances, the woman who *must* work for economic reasons, who stands to benefit most from the removal of discriminatory barriers. It is *she* who is hardest hit by unequal pay; it is *she* who so desperately needs adequate day-care facilities; it is *her* job which is often dead-ended while her male colleagues in the factory get trained and promoted into the skilled craft jobs. And if both she and her husband work at unfulfilling jobs eight hours a day just to make an adequate income, it is still *she* who carries the additional burden of domestic chores when they return home.

We think it is important to emphasize these points at the outset, for we have chosen to focus our remarks in this particular paper on those fortunate men and women who can afford the luxury of pursuing self-fulfillment through the world of work and career. But every societal reform advocated by the new feminist movement, whether it be the Equal Rights Amendment, the establishment of child-care centers, or basic changes in America's sex-role ideology, will affect the lives of men and women in every economic circumstance. Nevertheless, it is still economic discrimination which hits hardest at the largest group of women, and it is here that the drive for equality can be most successfully launched with legislative and judicial tools.

SEX-ROLE CONDITIONING

But even if all discrimination were to end tomorrow, nothing very drastic would change. For job discrimination is only part of the problem. It does impede women who choose to become lawyers or managers or physicians. But it does not, by itself, help us to understand why so many women "choose" to be secretaries or nurses rather than executives or physicians; why only 3% of 9th grade girls as compared to 25% of the boys "choose" careers in science or engineering; or why 63% of America's married women "choose" not to work at all. It certainly doesn't explain those young women whose vision of the future includes only marriage, children, and living happily ever after; who may, at some point, "choose" to take a job, but who almost never "choose" to pursue a career. Discrimination frustrates choices already made. Something more pernicious perverts the motivation to choose.

That "something" is an unconscious ideology about the nature of the female sex, an ideology which constricts the emerging self-image of the female child and the nature of her aspirations from the very beginning; an ideology which leads even those Americans who agree that a black skin should not uniquely qualify *its* owner for a janitorial or domestic service to act as if the possession of a uterus uniquely qualifies *its* owner for precisely such service.

Consider, for example, the 1968 student rebellion at Columbia University. Students from the radical Left took over some administration buildings in the name of equalitarian ideals which they accused the university of flouting. Here were the most militant spokesmen one could hope to find in the cause of equalitarian ideals. But no sooner had they occupied the buildings than the male militants blandly turned to their sisters-in-arms and assigned them the task of preparing the food, while they—the menfolk—would presumably plan future strategy. The reply these males received was the reply that they deserved—we will leave that to your imagination—and the fact that domestic tasks behind the barricades were desegregated across the sex line that day is an everlasting tribute to the class consciousness of these ladies of the Left. And it was really on that day that the campus women's liberation movement got its start—when radical women finally realized they they were never going to get to make revolution, only coffee.

But these conscious co-eds are not typical, for the unconscious assumptions about a woman's "natural" talents (or lack of them) are at least as prevalent among women as they are among men. A psychologist named Phillip Goldberg (1968) demonstrated this by asking female college students to rate a number of professional articles from each of six fields. The articles were collated into two equal sets of booklets, and the names of the authors were changed so that the identical article was attributed to a male author (e.g., John T. McKay) in one booklet and to a female author (e.g., Joan T. McKay) in the other booklet. Each student was asked to read the articles in her booklet, and to rate them for value, competence, persuasiveness, writing style, and so forth.

As he had anticipated, Goldberg found that the identical article received significantly lower ratings when it was attributed to a female author than when it was attributed to a male author. He had predicted this result for articles from professional fields generally considered the province of men, like law or city planning, but to his surprise, these women also downgraded articles from the fields of dietetics and elementary school education when they were attributed to female authors. In other words, these students rated the male authors as better at everything, agreeing with Aristotle that "we should regard the female nature as afflicted with a natural defectiveness." Such is the nature of America's unconscious ideology about women.

When does this ideology begin to affect the life of a young girl? Research now tells us that from the day a newborn child is dressed in pink, she is given "special" treatment. Perhaps because they are thought to be more fragile, six-month-old infant girls are actually touched, spoken to, and hovered over more by their mothers while they are playing than are infant boys (Goldberg and Lewis, 1969). One study even showed that when mothers and babies are still in the hospital, mothers smile at, talk to, and touch their female infants more than their male infants at two days of age (Thoman, Leiderman, and Olson, 1972). Differential treatment can't begin much earlier than that.

As children begin to read, the storybook characters become the images and the models that little boys and girls aspire to become. What kind of role does the female play in the world of children's literature? The fact is that there aren't even very many females in that world. One survey (Fisher, 1970) found that five times as many males as females appear in the titles of children's books; the fantasy world of Doctor Seuss is almost entirely male; and even animals and machines are represented as male. When females do appear, they are noteworthy primarily for what they do *not* do. They do not drive cars, and they seldom even ride bicycles. In one story in which a girl does ride a bicycle, it's a two-seater. Guess where the girl is seated! Boys in these stories climb trees and fish and roll in the leaves and skate. Girls watch, fall down, and get dizzy. Girls are never doctors, and although they may be nurses or librarians or teachers, they are never principals. There seemed to be only one children's book about mothers who work, and it concludes that what mothers love "best of all" is "being your very own Mommy and coming home to you." And although this is no doubt true of many daddies as well, no book about working fathers has ever found it necessary to apologize for working in quite the same way.

As children grow older, more explicit sex-role training is introduced. Boys are encouraged to take more of an interest in mathematics and science. Boys, not girls, are usually given chemistry sets and microscopes for Christmas. Moreover, all children quickly learn that mommy is proud to be a moron when it comes to math and science, whereas daddy is a little ashamed if he doesn't know all about such things. When a young boy returns from school all excited about biology, he is almost certain to be encouraged to think of becoming a physician. A girl with similar enthusiasm is usually told that she might want to consider nurse's training later on, so she can have "an interesting job to fall back upon in case—God forbid—she ever needs to support herself." A very different kind of encouragement. And any girl who doggedly persists in her enthusiasm for science is likely to find her parents as horrified by the prospect of a permanent love affair with physics as they would be either by the prospect of an interracial marriage or, horror of horrors, no marriage at all. Indeed, our graduate women report that their families seem convinced that the menopause must come at age 23.

These socialization practices take their toll. When they apply for college, boys and girls are about equal on verbal aptitude tests, but boys score significantly higher on mathematical aptitude tests—about 60 points higher on the College Board Exams, for example

(Brown, 1965). Moreover, for those who are convinced that this is due to female hormones, it is relevant to know that girls improve their mathematical performance if the problems are simply reworded so that they deal with cooking and gardening, even though the abstract reasoning required for solutions remains exactly the same (Milton, 1959). That's not hormones! Clearly, what has been undermined is not a woman's mathematical ability, but rather her confidence in that ability.

But these effects in mathematics and science are only part of the story. The most conspicuous outcome of all is that the majority of America's women become full-time homemakers. And of those who do work, nearly 80% end up in dead-end jobs as clerical workers, service workers, factory workers or sales clerks. Again, it is this "homogenization" of America's women which is the major consequence of America's sex-role ideology.

The important point is not that the role of homemaker is necessarily inferior, but rather that our society is managing to consign a large segment of its population to the role of homemaker—either with or without a dead-end job—solely on the basis of sex just as inexorably as it has in the past consigned the individual with a black skin to the role of janitor or domestic. The important point is that in spite of their unique identities, the majority of American women end up in virtually the *same* role.

The socialization of the American male has closed off certain options for him, too. Men are discouraged from developing certain desirable traits such as tenderness and sensitivity, just as surely as women are discouraged from being assertive and, alas, "too bright." Young boys are encouraged to be incompetent at cooking and certainly child care, just as surely as young girls are urged to be incompetent at math and science. The elimination of sex-role stereotyping implies that each individual would be encouraged to "do his own thing." Men and women would no longer be stereotyped by society's definitions of masculine and feminine. If sensitivity, emotionality, and warmth are desirable *human* characteristics, then they are desirable for men as well as for women. If independence, assertiveness, and serious intellectual commitment are desirable *human* characteristics, then they are desirable for women as well as for men. Thus, we are not implying that men have all the goodies and that women can obtain self-fulfillment by acting like men. That is hardly the utopia implied by today's feminist movement. Rather, we envision a society which raises its children so flexibly and with sufficient respect for the integrity of individual uniqueness that some men might emerge with the motivation, the ability, and the opportunity to stay home and raise children without bearing the stigma of being peculiar. Indeed, if homemaking is as glamorous as women's magazines and television commercials would have us believe, then men, too, should have that option. And even if homemaking isn't all that glamorous, it would probably still be more fulfilling for some men than the jobs in which they now find themselves forced because of their role as breadwinner. Thus, it is true that a man's options are also limited by our society's sex-role ideology, but as the "predictability test" reveals, it is still the women in our society whose identity is rendered irrelevant by America's socialization practices.

Further Psychological Barriers

But what of the woman who arrives at age 21 still motivated to be challenged and fulfilled by a growing career? Is she free to choose a career if she cares to do so? Or is there something standing even in her way?

There is. Even the woman who has managed to finesse society's attempt to rob her of her career motivations is likely to find herself blocked by society's trump card: the feeling that one cannot have a career and be a successful woman simultaneously. A competent and motivated woman is thus caught in a double-bind which few men have ever faced. She must worry not only about failure, but also about success.

This conflict was strikingly revealed in a study which required college women to complete the following story: "After first-term finals, Anne finds herself at the top of her medical-school class" (Horner, 1969). The stories were then examined for concern about the negative consequences of success. The women in this study all had high intellectual ability and histories of academic success. They were the very women who could have successful careers. And yet, over two-thirds of their stories revealed a clear-cut inability to cope with the concept of a feminine, yet career-oriented, woman.

The most common "fear-of-success" stories showed fears of social rejection as a result of success. The woman in this group showed anxiety about becoming unpopular, unmarriageable, and lonely:

Anne starts proclaiming her surprise and joy. Her fellow classmates are so disgusted with her behavior that they jump on her in a body and beat her. She is maimed for life.

Anne is an acne-faced bookworm. . . . She studies twelve hours a day, and lives at home to save money. "Well, it certainly paid off. All the Friday and Saturday nights without dates, fun—I'll be the best woman doctor alive." And yet a twinge of sadness comes through—she wonders what she really has. . . .

Anne doesn't want to be number one in her class. . . . She feels she shouldn't rank so high because of social reasons. She drops to ninth and then marries the boy who graduates number one.

In the second "fear-of-success" category were stories in which the women seemed concerned about definitions of womanhood. These stories expressed guilt and despair over success and doubts about their femininity and normality:

Unfortunately Anne no longer feels so certain that she really wants to be a doctor. She is worried about herself and wonders if perhaps she is not normal. . . . Anne decides not to continue with her medical work but to take courses that have a deeper personal meaning to her.

Anne feels guilty. . . . She will finally have a nervous breakdown and quit medical school and marry a successful young doctor.

A third group of stories could not even face up to the conflict between having a career and being a woman. These stories simply denied the possibility that any woman could be so successful:

Anne is a code name for a nonexistent person created by a group of med students. They take turns writing for Anne. . . .

Anne is really happy she's on top, though Tom is higher than she—though that's as it should be. Anne doesn't mind Tom winning.

Anne is talking to her counselor. Counselor says she will make a fine nurse.

By way of contrast, here is a typical story written not about Anne, but about John:

John has worked very hard and his long hours of study have paid off. . . . He is thinking about his girl, Cheri, whom he will marry at the end of med school. He realizes he can give her all the things she desires after he becomes established. He will go on in med school and be successful in the long run.

Nevertheless, there were a few women in the study who welcomed the prospect of success:

Anne is quite a lady—not only is she top academically, but she is liked and admired by her fellow students— quite a trick in a man-dominated field. She is brilliant— but she is also a woman. She will continue to be at or near the top. And . . . always a lady.

Hopefully the day is approaching when as many "Anne" stories as "John" stories will have happy endings. But notice that even this story finds it necessary to affirm repeatedly that femininity is not necessarily destroyed by accomplishment. One would never encounter a comparable story written about John who, although brilliant and at the top of his class, is "still a man, still a man, still a man."

It seems unlikely that anyone in our society would view these "fear-of-success" stories as portraits of mental health. But even our concept of mental health has been distorted by America's sex-role stereotypes. Here we must indict our own profession of psy-chology. A recent survey of 79 clinically-trained psychologists, psychiatrists, and social workers, both male and female, revealed a double standard of mental health (Broverman, Broverman, Clarkson, Rosenkrantz, and Vogel, 1970). That is, even professional clinicians have two different concepts of mental health, one for men and one for women; and these concepts parallel the sex-role stereotypes prevalent in our society. Thus, according to these clinicians, a woman is to be regarded as healthier and more mature if she is: more submissive, less independent, less adventurous, more easily influenced, less aggressive, less competitive, more excitable in minor crises, more susceptible to hurt feelings, more emotional, more conceited about her appearance, less objective, and more antagonistic toward math and science! But this was the very same description which these clinicians used to characterize an unhealthy, immature man or an unhealthy, immature adult (sex unspecified)! The equation is clear: Mature woman equals immature adult.

Given this concept of a mature woman, is it any wonder that few women ever aspire toward challenging and fulfilling careers? In order to have a career, a woman will probably need to become relatively more dominant, independent, adventurous, aggressive, competitive, and objective, and relatively less excitable, emotional and conceited than our ideal of femininity requires. If she were a man (or an adult, sex unspecified), these would all be considered positive traits. But because she is a woman, these same traits will bring her disapproval. She must then either be strong enough to have her "femininity" questioned; or she must behave in the prescribed feminine manner and accept second-class status, as an adult and as a professional.

And, of course, should a woman faced with this conflict seek professional help, hoping to summon the strength she will need to pursue her career goals, the advice she is likely to receive will be of virtually no use.

For, as this study reveals, even professional counselors have been contaminated by the sex-role ideology.

It is frequently argued that a 21-year-old woman is perfectly free to choose a career if she cares to do so. No one is standing in her way. But this argument conveniently overlooks the fact that our society has spent 20 years carefully marking the woman's ballot for her, and so it has nothing to lose in that 21st year by pretending to let her cast it for the alternative of her choice. Society has controlled not her alternatives (although discrimination does do that), but more importantly, it has controlled her motivation to choose any but one of those alternatives. The so-called "freedom to choose" is illusory, and it cannot be invoked to justify a society which controls the woman's motivation to choose.

BIOLOGICAL CONSIDERATIONS

Up to this point, we have argued that the differing life patterns of men and women in our society can be chiefly accounted for by cultural conditioning. The most common counter argument to this view, of course, is the biological one. The biological argument suggests that there may really be inborn differences between men and women in, say, independence or mathematical ability. Or that there may be biological factors beyond the fact that women can become pregnant and nurse children which uniquely dictate that they, but not men, should stay home all day and shun serious outside commitment. What this argument suggests is that maybe female hormones really are responsible somehow. One difficulty with this argument, of course, is that female hormones would have to be different in the Soviet Union, where one third of the engineers and 75% of the physicians are women (Dodge, 1966). In America, by way of contrast, women constitute less than 1% of the engineers and only 7% of the physicians. Female physiology *is* different, and it may account for some of the psychological differ-

ences between the sexes, but America's sex-role ideology still seems primarily responsible for the fact that so few women emerge from childhood with the motivation to seek out any role beyond the one that our society dictates.

But even if there really were biological differences between the sexes along these lines, the biological argument would still be irrelevant. The reason can best be illustrated with an analogy.

Suppose that every black American boy were to be socialized to become a jazz musician on the assumption that he has a "natural" talent in that direction; or suppose that parents and counselors should subtly discourage him from other pursuits because it is considered "inappropriate" for black men to become physicians or physicists. Most Americans would disapprove. But suppose that it *could* be demonstrated that black Americans, *on the average*, did possess an inborn better sense of rhythm than white Americans. Would *that* justify ignoring the unique characteristics of a *particular* black youngster from the very beginning and specifically socializing him to become a musician? We don't think so. Similarly, as long as a woman's socialization does not nurture her uniqueness, but treats her only as a member of a group on the basis of some assumed *average* characteristic, she will not be prepared to realize her own potential in the way that the values of individuality and self-fulfillment imply that she should.

THE PRESUMED INCOMPATIBILITY OF FAMILY AND CAREER

If we were to ask the average American woman why she is not pursuing a full-time career, she would probably not say that discrimination had discouraged her; nor would she be likely to recognize the pervasive effects of her own sex-role conditioning. What she probably would say is that a career, no matter how desirable, is simply incompatible with the role of wife and mother.

As recently as the turn of the century, and

in less technological societies today, this incompatibility between career and family was, in fact, decisive. Women died in their forties and they were pregnant or nursing during most of their adult lives. Moreover, the work that a less technological society requires places a premium on mobility and physical strength, neither of which a pregnant woman has a great deal of. Thus, the historical division of labor between the sexes—the man away at work and the woman at home with the children—was a biological necessity. Today it is not.

Today, the work that our technological society requires is primarily mental in nature; women have virtually complete control over their reproductive lives; and most important of all, the average American women now lives to age 74 and has her last child before age 30. This means that by the time a woman is 35 or so, her children all have more important things to do with their daytime hours than to spend them entertaining some adult woman who has nothing fulfilling to do during the entire second half of her life span.

But social forms have a way of outliving the necessities which gave rise to them. And today's female adolescent continues to plan for a 19th century life style in a 20th century world. A Gallup poll has found that young women give no thought whatever to life after forty (Gallup and Hill, 1962). They plan to graduate from high school, perhaps go to college, and then get married. Period!

THE WOMAN AS WIFE

At some level, of course, this kind of planning is "realistic." Because most women do grow up to be wives and mothers, and because, for many women, this means that they will be leaving the labor force during the child-rearing years, a career is not really feasible. After all, a career involves long-term commitment and perhaps some sacrifice on the part of the family. Furthermore, as every "successful" woman knows, a wife's appropriate role is to encourage her husband in *his* career. The "good" wife puts her husband through school, endures the family's early financial difficulties without a whimper, and, if her husband's career should suddenly dictate a move to another city, she sees to it that the transition is accomplished as painlessly as possible. The good wife is selfless. And to be seriously concerned about one's own career is selfish—if one is female, that is. With these kinds of constraints imposed upon the work life of the married woman, perhaps it would be "unrealistic" for her to seriously aspire toward a career rather than a job.

There is some evidence of discontent among these "selfless" women, however. A 1962 Gallup poll (Gallup and Hill, 1962) revealed that only 10% of American women would want their daughters to live their lives the way they did. These mothers wanted their daughters to get more education and to marry later. And a 1970 study of women married to top Chicago-area business and professional men (Ringo, 1970) revealed that if these women could live their lives over again, they would pursue careers.

Accordingly, the traditional conception of the husband-wife relationship is now being challenged, not so much because of this widespread discontent among older, married women, but because it violates two of the most basic values of today's college generation. These values concern personal growth, on the one hand, and interpersonal relationships on the other. The first of these emphasizes the individuality and self-fulfillment; the second stresses openness, honesty, and equality in all human relationships.

Because they see the traditional male-female relationship as incompatible with these basic values, today's young people are experimenting with alternatives to the traditional marriage pattern. Although a few are testing out ideas like communal living, most seem to be searching for satisfactory modifications of the husband-wife relationship, either in or out of the context of marriage. An increasing number of young people claim to be seeking fully equalitarian relationships and they cite examples like the following:

"Both my wife and I earned college degrees in our respective disciplines. I turned down a superior job offer in Oregon and accepted a slightly less desirable position in New York where my wife would have more opportunities for part-time work in her specialty. Although I would have preferred to live in a suburb, we purchased a home near my wife's job so that she could have an office at home where she would be when the children returned from school. Because my wife earns a good salary, she can easily afford to pay a housekeeper to do her major household chores. My wife and I share all other tasks around the house equally. For example, she cooks the meals, but I do the laundry for her and help her with many of her other household tasks."

Without questioning the basic happiness of such a marriage or its appropriateness for many couples, we can legitimately ask if such a marriage is, in fact, an instance of interpersonal equality. Have all the hidden assumptions about the woman's "natural" role really been eliminated? Have our visionary students really exorcised the traditional ideology as they claim? There is a very simple test. If the marriage is truly equalitarian, then its description should retain the same flavor and tone even if the roles of the husband and wife were to be reversed:

EGALITARIAN SAME

"Both my husband and I earned college degrees in our respective disciplines. I turned down a superior job offer in Oregon and accepted a slightly less desirable position in New York where my husband would have more opportunities for part-time work in his specialty. Although I would have preferred to live in a suburb, we purchased a home near my husband's job so that he could have an office at home where he would be when the children returned from school. Because my husband earns a good salary, he can easily afford to pay a housekeeper to do his major household chores. My husband and I share all other tasks around the house equally. For example, he cooks the meals, but I do the laundry for him and help him with many of his other household tasks."

Somehow it sounds different, and yet only the pronouns have been changed to protect the powerful! Certainly no one would ever mistake the marriage *just* described as equalitarian or even very desirable, and thus it

becomes apparent that the ideology about the woman's "natural" place unconsciously permeates the entire fabric of such "pseudo-equalitarian" marriages. It is true the wife gains some measure of equality when she can have a career rather than have a job and when her career can influence the final place of residence. But why is it the unquestioned assumption that the husband's career solely determines the initial set of alternatives that are to be considered? Why is it the wife who automatically seeks the part-time position? Why is it *her* housekeeper rather than *their* housekeeper? Why *her* household tasks? And so forth throughout the entire relationship.

The important point is not that such marriages are bad or that their basic assumptions of inequality produce unhappy, frustrated women. Quite the contrary. It is the very happiness of the wives in such marriages that reveals society's smashing success in socializing its women. It is a measure of the distance our society must yet traverse toward the goal of full equality that such marriages are widely characterized as utopian and fully equalitarian. It is a mark of how well the woman has been kept in her place that the husband in such a marriage is almost always idolized by women, including his wife. Why? Because he "permits her" to squeeze a career into the interstices of their marriage as long as his own career is not unduly inconvenienced. Thus is the white man blessed for exercising his power benignly while his "natural" right to that power forever remains unquestioned. Such is the subtlety of America's ideology about women.

In fact, however, even these "benign" inequities are now being challenged. More and more young couples really are entering marriages of full equality, marriages in which both partners pursue careers or outside commitments which carry equal weight when all important decisions are to be made, marriages in which both husband and wife accept some compromise in the growth of their respective careers for their mutual partnership. Certainly such marriages have more tactical difficulties than more traditional ones: It is simply more difficult to coordinate two independent lives rather than one-and-a-half. The point is that it is not possible to predict ahead of time *on the basis of sex*, who will be doing the compromising at any given point of decision.

It should be clear that the man or woman who places career above all else ought not to enter an equalitarian marriage. The man would do better to marry a traditional wife, a wife who will make whatever sacrifices his career necessitates. The woman who places career above all else would do better—in our present society—to remain single. For an equalitarian marriage is not designed for extra efficiency, but for double fulfillment.

THE WOMAN AS MOTHER

In all marriages, whether traditional, pseudo-equalitarian or fully equalitarian, the real question surrounding a mother's career will probably continue to be the well-being of the children. All parents want to be certain that they are doing the very best for their children and that they are not depriving them in any important way, either materially or psychologically. What this has meant recently in most families that could afford it was that mother would devote herself to the children on a full-time basis. Women have been convinced—by their mothers and by the so-called experts—that there is something wrong with them if they even want to do otherwise.

For example, according to Dr. Spock (1963), any woman who finds full-time motherhood unfulfilling is showing "a residue of difficult relationships in her own childhood." If a vacation doesn't solve the problem, then she is probably having emotional problems which can be relieved "through regular counseling in a family social agency, or if severe, through psychiatric treatment. . . . Any mother of a pre-school child who is considering a job should discuss the issues with a social worker

before making her decision." The message is clear: If you don't feel that your two-year-old is a stimulating, full-time, companion, then you are probably neurotic.

In fact, research does not support the view that children suffer in any way when mother works. Although it came as a surprise to most researchers in the area, maternal employment in and of itself does not seem to have any negative effects on the children; and part-time work actually seems to benefit the children. Children of working mothers are no more likely than children of non-working mothers to be delinquent or nervous or withdrawn or anti-social; they are no more likely to show neurotic symptoms; they are no more likely to perform poorly in school; and they are no more likely to feel deprived of their mothers' love. Daughters of working mothers are more likely to want to work themselves, and, when asked to name one woman in the world that they most admire, daughters of working mothers are more likely to name their own mothers! (Nye and Hoffman, 1963). This is one finding that we wish every working woman in America could hear, because the other thing that is true of almost every working mother is that she *thinks* she is hurting her children and she feels guilty. In fact, research has shown that the worst mothers are those who would like to work, but who stay home out of a sense of duty (Yarrow, Scott, de Leeuw, and Heinig, 1962). The major conclusion from all the research is really this: What matters is the quality of a mother's relationship with her children, not the time of day it happens to be administered. This conclusion should come as no surprise; successful fathers have been demonstrating it for years. Some fathers are great, some fathers stink, and they're all at work at least eight hours a day.

Similarly, it is true that the quality of substitute care that children receive while their parents are at work also matters. Young children do need security, and research has shown that it is not good to have a constant turnover of parent-substitutes, a rapid succession of changing baby-sitters or housekeepers (Maccoby, 1958). Clearly, this is why the establishment of child care centers is vitally important at the moment. This is why virtually every woman's group in the country, no matter how conservative or how radical, is in agreement on this one issue: that child care centers ought to be available to those who need them.

Once again, it is relevant to emphasize that child care centers, like the other reforms advocated, are not merely for the benefit of middle-class women who wish to pursue professional careers. Of the 31 million women in the labor force, nearly 40% of them are working mothers. In 1960, mothers constituted more than one-third of the total woman labor force. In March, 1971, more than one out of three working mothers (4.3 million of them) had children under six years of age, and about half of these had children under three years of age. And most of these women in the labor force—like most men—work because they cannot afford to do otherwise. Moreover, they cannot currently deduct the full costs of child care as a business expense as the executive can often deduct an expensive car. At the moment, the majority of these working women must simply "make do" with whatever child care arrangements they can manage. Only 6% of their children under 6 years of age currently receive group care in child care centers. *This* is why child-care centers are a central issue of the new feminist movement. This is why they are not just an additional luxury for the middle-class family with a woman who wants to pursue a professional career.

But even the woman who is educationally and economically in a position to pursue a career must feel free to utilize these alternative arrangements for child care. For once again, America's sex-role ideology intrudes. Many people still assume that if a woman wants a full-time career, then children must be unimportant to her. But of course, no one makes this assumption about her husband. No one assumes that a father's interest in his career necessarily precludes a deep and abiding affection for his children or a vital interest in their development. Once again, America applies a double standard of judgment. Suppose that a father of small children suddenly lost his wife. No matter how much he loved his children, no one would expect him to sacrifice his career in order to stay home with them on a full-time basis—even if he had an independent source of income. No one would charge him with selfishness or lack of parental feeling if he sought professional care for his children during the day.

It is here that full equality between husband and wife assumes its ultimate importance. The fully equalitarian marriage abolishes this double standard and extends the same freedom to the mother. The equalitarian marriage provides the framework for both husband and wife to pursue careers which are challenging and fulfilling and, at the same time, to participate equally in the pleasures and responsibilities of childrearing. Indeed, it is the equalitarian marriage which has the potential for giving children the love and concern of two parents rather than one. And it is the equalitarian marriage which has the most potential for giving parents the challenge and fulfillment of two worlds—family and career—rather than one.

In addition to providing this potential for equalized child care, a truly equalitarian marriage embraces a more general division of labor which satisfies what we like to call "the roommate test." That is, the labor is divided just as it is when two men or two women room together in college or set up a bachelor apartment together. Errands and domestic chores are assigned by preference, agreement, flipping a coin, alternated, given to hired help, or—perhaps most often the case— left undone.

It is significant that today's young people, so many of whom live precisely this way prior to marriage, find this kind of arrangement within marriage so foreign to their thinking. Consider an analogy. Suppose that a white male college student decided to room or set up a bachelor apartment with a black male friend. Surely the typical white student would not blithely assume that his black roommate was to handle all the domestic chores. Nor would his conscience allow him to do so even in the unlikely event that his roommate would say: "No, that's okay. I like doing housework. I'd be happy to do it." We suspect that the typical white student would still not be comfortable if he took advantage of this offer because he and America have finally realized that he would be taking advantage of the fact that such a roommate had been socialized by our society to be "happy" with such obvious inequity. But change this hypothetical black roommate to a female marriage partner, and somehow the student's conscience goes to sleep. At most it is quickly tranquilized by the comforting thought that "she is happiest when she is ironing for her loved one." Such is the power of an unconscious ideology.

Of course, it may well be that she *is* happiest when she is ironing for her loved one.

Such, indeed, is the power of an unconscious ideology.

REFERENCES

Bird, C. *Born female: the high cost of keeping women down.* New York: Pocket Books, 1969.

Broverman, I. K., Broverman, D. M., Clarkson, F. E., Rosenkrantz, P. S., & Vogel, S. R. Sex-role stereotypes and clinical judgments of mental health. *Journal of Consulting and Clinical Psychology,* 1970, 34, 1–7.

Brown, R. *Social psychology.* New York: Free Press, 1965.

Dodge, N. D. *Women in the Soviet economy.* Baltimore: Johns Hopkins Press, 1966.

Fisher, E. The second sex, junior division. *The New York Times Book Review,* May, 1970.

Gallup, G., & Hill, E. The American woman. *The Saturday Evening Post,* Dec. 22, 1962, pp. 15–32.

Goldberg, P. Are women prejudiced against women? *Transaction,* April, 1968, 5, 28–30.

Goldberg, S., & Lewis, M. Play behavior in the year-old infant: early sex differences. *Child Development,* 1969, 40, 21–31.

Horner, M. S. Fail: bright women. *Psychology Today,* November, 1969.

Maccoby, E. E. Effects upon children of their mothers' outside employment. In *Work in the lives of married women.* New York: Columbia University Press, 1958.

Milton, G. A. Sex differences in problem solving as a function of role appropriateness of the problem content. *Psychological Reports,* 1959, 5, 705–708.

Nye, F. I., & Hoffman, L. W. *The employed mother in America.* Chicago: Rand McNally, 1963.

Ringo, M. The well-placed wife. Unpublished manuscript, John Paisios & Associates, 332 South Michigan Ave., Chicago, Illinois. 60604.

Spock, B. Should mothers work? *Ladies' Home Journal,* February, 1963.

Terman, L. M., & Oden, M. H. *Genetic studies of genius, V. The gifted group at mid-life: Thirty-five years' follow-up of the superior child.* Stanford, California: Stanford University Press, 1959.

Thoman, E. B., Leiderman, P. H., & Olson, J. P. Neonate-mother interaction during breast feeding. *Developmental Psychology,* 1972, 6, 110–118.

U. S. Department of Labor, Wage and Labor Standards Administration, Women's Bureau. Fact sheet on the earnings gap, February, 1970.

U. S. Department of Labor, Wage and Labor Standards Administration, Women's Bureau. *Handbook on women workers,* 1969. Bulletin 294.

Yarrow, M. R., Scott, P., de Leeuw, L., and Heinig, D. Child-rearing in families of working and non-working mothers. *Sociometry,* 1962, 25, 122–140.

6

THE SOUNDS OF SILENCE

Edward T. Hall
Mildred Reed Hall

Bob leaves his apartment at 8:15 A.M. and stops at the corner drugstore for breakfast. Before he can speak, the counterman says, "The usual?" Bob nods yes. While he savors his Danish, a fat man pushes onto the adjoining stool and overflows into his space. Bob scowls and the man pulls himself in as much as he can. Bob has sent two messages without speaking a syllable.

Henry has an appointment to meet Arthur at 11 o'clock; he arrives at 11:30. Their conversation is friendly, but Arthur retains a lingering hostility. Henry has unconsciously communicated that he doesn't think the appointment is very important or that Arthur is a person who needs to be treated with respect.

George is talking to Charley's wife at a party. Their conversation is entirely trivial, yet Charley glares at them suspiciously. Their physical proximity and the movements of their eyes reveal that they are powerfully attracted to each other.

José Ybarra and Sir Edmund Jones are at the same party and it is important for them to establish a cordial relationship for business reasons. Each is trying to be warm and friendly, yet they will part with mutual distrust and their business transaction will probably fall through. José, in Latin fashion, moved closer and closer to Sir Edmund as they spoke, and this movement was miscommunicated as pushiness to Sir Edmund, who kept backing away from this intimacy, and this was miscommunicated to José as coldness. The silent languages of Latin and English cultures are more difficult to learn than their spoken languages.

In each of these cases, we see the subtle power of nonverbal communication. The only language used throughout most of the history of humanity (in evolutionary terms, vocal communication is relatively recent), it is the first form of communication you learn. You use this preverbal language, consciously and unconsciously, every day to tell other people how you feel about yourself and them. This language includes your posture, gestures, facial expressions, costume, the way you walk, even your treatment of time and space and material things. All people communicate on several different levels at the same time but are usually aware of only the verbal dialog and don't realize that they respond to nonverbal messages. But when a person says one thing and really believes something else, the dis-

Excerpted from "The Sounds of Silence" by Edward T. Hall and Mildred Reed Hall. Originally appeared in *Playboy* Magazine. Copyright © 1981 by Edward T. Hall and Mildred Reed Hall. Reprinted with permission of the authors.

crepancy between the two can usually be sensed. Nonverbal-communication systems are much less subject to the conscious deception that often occurs in verbal systems. When we find ourselves thinking, "I don't know what it is about him, but he doesn't seem sincere," it's usually this lack of congruity between a person's words and his behavior that makes us anxious and uncomfortable.

Few of us realize how much we all depend on body movement in our conversation or are aware of the hidden rules that govern listening behavior. But we know instantly whether or not the person we're talking to is "tuned in" and we're very sensitive to any breach in listening etiquette. In white middle-class American culture, when someone wants to show he is listening to someone else, he looks either at the other person's face or, specifically, at his eyes, shifting his gaze from one eye to the other.

If you observe a person conversing, you'll notice that he indicates he's listening by nodding his head. He also makes little "Hmm" noises. If he agrees with what's being said, he may give a vigorous nod. To show pleasure or affirmation, he smiles; if he has some reservations, he looks skeptical by raising an eyebrow or pulling down the corners of his mouth. If a participant wants to terminate the conversation, he may start shifting his body position, stretching his legs, crossing or uncrossing them, bobbing his foot or diverting his gaze from the speaker. The more he fidgets, the more the speaker becomes aware that he has lost his audience. As a last measure, the listener may look at his watch to indicate the imminent end of the conversation.

Talking and listening are so intricately intertwined that a person cannot do one without the other. Even when one is alone and talking to oneself, there is part of the brain that speaks while another part listens. In all conversations, the listener is positively or negatively reinforcing the speaker all the time. He may even guide the conversation without knowing it, by laughing or frowning or dismissing the argument with a wave of his hand.

The language of the eyes—another age-old way of exchanging feelings—is both subtle and complex. Not only do men and women use their eyes differently but there are class, generation, regional, ethnic and national cultural differences. Americans often complain about the way foreigners stare at people or hold a glance too long. Most Americans look away from someone who is using his eyes in an unfamiliar way because it makes them self-conscious. If a man looks at another man's wife in a certain way, he's asking for trouble, as indicated earlier. But he might not be ill-mannered or seeking to challenge the husband. He might be a European in this country who hasn't learned our visual mores. Many American women visiting France or Italy are acutely embarrassed because, for the first time in their lives, men really look at them—their eyes, hair, nose, lips, breasts, hips, legs, thighs, knees, ankles, feet, clothes, hairdo, even their walk. These same women, once they have become used to being looked at, often return to the United States and are overcome with the feeling that "No one ever really looks at me anymore."

Analyzing the mass of data on the eyes, it is possible to sort out at least three ways in which the eyes are used to communicate: dominance versus submission, involvement versus detachment and positive versus negative attitude. In addition, there are three levels of consciousness and control, which can be categorized as follows: (1) conscious use of the eyes to communicate, such as the flirting blink and the intimate nose-wrinkling squint; (2) the very extensive category of unconscious but learned behavior governing where the eyes are directed and when (this unwritten set of rules dictates how and under what circumstances the sexes, as well as people of all status categories, look at each other); and (3) the response of the eye itself, which is completely outside both awareness and control—

changes in the cast (the sparkle) of the eye and the pupillary reflex.

The eye is unlike any other organ of the body, for it is an extension of the brain. The unconscious pupillary reflex and the cast of the eye have been known by people of Middle Eastern origin for years—although most are unaware of their knowledge. Depending on the context, Arabs and others look either directly at the eyes or deeply *into* the eyes of their interlocutor. We became aware of this in the Middle East several years ago while looking at jewelry. The merchant suddenly started to push a particular bracelet at a customer and said, "You buy this one." What interested us was that the bracelet was not the one that had been consciously selected by the purchaser. But the merchant, watching the pupils of the eyes, knew what the purchaser really wanted to buy. Whether he specifically knew *how* he knew is debatable.

A psychologist at the University of Chicago, Eckhard Hess, was the first to conduct systematic studies of the pupillary reflex. His wife remarked one evening, while watching him reading in bed, that he must be very interested in the text because his pupils were dilated. Following up on this, Hess slipped some pictures of nudes into a stack of photographs that he gave to his male assistant. Not looking at the photographs but watching his assistant's pupils, Hess was able to tell precisely when the assistant came to the nudes. In further experiments, Hess retouched the eyes in a photograph of a woman. In one print, he made the pupils small, in another, large; nothing else was changed. Subjects who were given the photographs found the woman with the dilated pupils much more attractive. Any man who has had the experience of seeing a woman look at him as her pupils widen with reflex speed knows that she's flashing him a message.

The eye-sparkle phenomenon frequently turns up in our interviews of couples in love. It's apparently one of the first reliable clues in the other person that love is genuine. To date,

there is no scientific data to explain eye sparkle; no investigation of the pupil, the cornea or even the white sclera of the eye shows how the sparkle originates. Yet we all know it when we see it.

One common situation for most people involves the use of the eyes in the street and in public. Although eye behavior follows a definite set of rules, the rules vary according to the place, the needs and feelings of the people, and their ethnic background. For urban whites, once they're within definite recognition distance (16–32 feet for people with average eyesight), there is mutual avoidance of eye contact—unless they want something specific: a pickup, a handout or information of some kind. In the West and in small towns generally, however, people are much more likely to look at and greet one another, even if they're strangers.

It's permissible to look at people if they're beyond recognition distance; but once inside this sacred zone, you can only steal a glance at strangers. You *must* greet friends, however; to fail to do so is insulting. Yet, to stare too fixedly even at them is considered rude and hostile. Of course, all of these rules are variable.

A great many blacks, for example, greet each other in public even if they don't know each other. To blacks, most eye behavior of whites has the effect of giving the impression that they aren't there, but this is due to white avoidance of eye contact with *anyone* in the street.

Another very basic difference between people of different ethnic backgrounds is their sense of territoriality and how they handle space. This is the silent communication, or miscommunication, that caused friction between Mr. Ybarra and Sir Edmund Jones in our earlier example. We know from research that everyone has around himself an invisible bubble of space that contracts and expands depending on several factors: his emotional state, the activity he's performing at the time and his cultural background. This bubble is a kind of mobile territory that he will defend against intrusion. If he is accustomed to close personal distance between himself and others, his bubble will be smaller than that of someone who's accustomed to greater personal distance. People of North European heritage—English, Scandinavian, Swiss and German—tend to avoid contact. Those whose heritage is Italian, French, Spanish, Russian, Latin American or Middle Eastern like close personal contact.

People are very sensitive to any intrusion into their spatial bubble. If someone stands too close to you, your first instinct is to back up. If that's not possible, you lean away and pull yourself in, tensing your muscles. If the intruder doesn't respond to these body signals, you may then try to protect yourself, using a briefcase, umbrella or raincoat. Women—especially when traveling alone—often plant their pocketbook in such a way that no one can get very close to them. As a last resort, you may move to another spot and position yourself behind a desk or a chair that provides screening. Everyone tries to adjust the space around himself in a way that's comfortable for him; most often, he does this unconsciously.

Emotions also have a direct effect on the size of a person's territory. When you're angry or under stress, your bubble expands and you require more space. New York psychiatrist Augustus Kinzel found a difference in what he calls Body-Buffer Zones between violent and nonviolent prison inmates. Dr. Kinzel conducted experiments in which each prisoner was placed in the center of a small room and then Dr. Kinzel slowly walked toward him. Nonviolent prisoners allowed him to come quite close, while prisoners with a history of violent behavior couldn't tolerate his proximity and reacted with some vehemence.

Apparently, people under stress experience other people as looming larger and closer than they actually are. Studies of schizophrenic patients have indicated that they sometimes have a distorted perception of space, and several psychiatrists have reported patients who experience their body boundaries as filling up an entire room. For these patients, anyone who comes into the room is actually inside their body, and such an intrusion may trigger a violent outburst.

Unfortunately, there is little detailed information about normal people who live in highly congested urban areas. We do know, of course, that the noise, pollution, dirt, crowding and confusion of our cities induce feelings of stress in most of us, and stress leads to a need for greater space. The man who's packed into a subway, jostled in the street, crowded into an elevator and forced to work all day in a bull pen or in a small office without auditory or visual privacy is going to be very stressed at the end of his day. He needs places that provide relief from constant overstimulation of his nervous system. Stress from overcrowding is cumulative and people can tolerate more crowding early in the day than later; note the increased bad temper during the evening rush hour as compared with the morning melee. Certainly one factor in people's desire to commute by car is the need for privacy and relief from crowding (except, often, from other cars); it may be the only time of the day when nobody can intrude.

In crowded public places, we tense our muscles and hold ourselves stiff, and thereby communicate to others our desire not to intrude on their space and, above all, not to touch them. We also avoid eye contact and the total effect is that of someone who has "tuned out." Walking along the street, our bubble expands slightly as we move in a stream of strangers, taking care not to bump into them. In the office, at meetings, in restaurants, our bubble keeps changing as it adjusts to the activity at hand.

Most white middle-class Americans use four main distances in their business and social relations: intimate, personal, social and public. Each of these distances has a near and a far phase and is accompanied by changes in the volume of the voice. Intimate distance varies from direct physical contact with another person to a distance of six to eighteen inches and is used for our most private activities—caressing another person or making love. At this distance, you are overwhelmed by sensory inputs from the other person—heat from the body, tactile stimulation from the skin, the fragrance of perfume, even the sound of breathing—all of which literally envelop you. Even at the far phase, you're still within easy touching distance. In general, the use of intimate distance in public between adults is frowned on. It's also much too close for strangers, except under conditions of extreme crowding.

In the second zone—personal distance—the close phase is one and a half to two and a half feet; it's at this distance that wives usually stand from their husbands in public. If another woman moves into this zone, the wife will most likely be disturbed. The far phase—two and a half to four feet—is the distance used to "keep someone at arm's length" and is the most common spacing used by people in conversation.

The third zone—social distance—is employed during business transactions or exchanges with a clerk or repairman. People who work together tend to use close social distance—four to seven feet. This is also the distance for conversation at social gatherings. To stand at this distance from someone who is seated has a dominating effect (for example, teacher to pupil, boss to secretary). The far phase of the third zone—seven to twelve feet—is where people stand when someone says, "Stand back so I can look at you." This distance lends a formal tone to business or social discourse. In an executive office, the desk serves to keep people at this distance.

The fourth zone—public distance—is used by teachers in classrooms or speakers at public gatherings. At its farthest phase—25 feet and beyond—it is used for important public figures. Violations of this distance can lead to serious complications. During his 1970 U. S. visit, the president of France, Georges Pom-pidou, was harassed by pickets in Chicago, who were permitted to get within touching distance. Since pickets in France are kept behind barricades a block or more away, the president was outraged by this insult to his person, and President Nixon was obliged to communicate his concern as well as offer his personal apologies.

It is interesting to note how American pitchmen and panhandlers exploit the unwritten, unspoken conventions of eye and distance. Both take advantage of the fact that once explicit eye contact is established, it is rude to look away, because to do so means to brusquely dismiss the other person and his needs. Once having caught the eye of his mark, the panhandler then locks on, not letting go until he moves through the public zone, the social zone, the personal zone, and finally, into the intimate sphere, where people are most vulnerable.

Touch also is an important part of the constant stream of communication that takes place between people. A light touch, a firm touch, a blow, a caress are all communications. In an effort to break down barriers among people, there's been a recent upsurge in group-encounter activities, in which strangers are encouraged to touch one another. In special situations such as these, the rules for not touching are broken with group approval and people gradually lose some of their inhibitions.

Although most people don't realize it, space is perceived and distances are set not by vision alone but with all the senses. Auditory space is perceived with the ears, thermal space with the skin, kinesthetic space with the muscles of the body and olfactory space with the nose. And, once again, it's one's culture that determines how his senses are programmed—which sensory information ranks highest and lowest. The important thing to remember is that culture is very persistent. In this country, we've noted the existence of culture patterns that determine distance between people in the third and fourth generations of some families, despite their prolonged contact with people of very different cultural heritages.

Whenever there is great cultural distance between two people, there are bound to be problems arising from differences in behavior and expectations. An example is the American couple who consulted a psychiatrist about their marital problems. The husband was from New England and had been brought up by reserved parents who taught him to control his emotions and to respect the need for privacy. His wife was from an Italian family and had been brought up in close contact with all the members of her large family, who were extremely warm, volatile and demonstrative.

When the husband came home after a hard day at the office, dragging his feet and longing for peace and quiet, his wife would rush to him and smother him. Clasping his hands, rubbing his brow, crooning over his weary head, she never left him alone. But when the wife was upset or anxious about her day, the husband's response was to withdraw completely and leave her alone. No comforting, no affectionate embrace, no attention—just solitude. The woman became convinced her husband didn't love her and, in desperation, she consulted a psychiatrist. Their problem wasn't basically psychological but cultural.

Why has man developed all these different ways of communicating messages without words? One reason is that people don't like to spell out certain kinds of messages. We prefer to find other ways of showing our feelings. This is especially true in relationships as sensitive as courtship. Men don't like to be rejected and most women don't want to turn a man down bluntly. Instead, we work out subtle ways of encouraging or discouraging each other that save face and avoid confrontations.

How a person handles space in dating others is an obvious and very sensitive indicator of how he or she feels about the other person. On a first date, if a woman sits or stands so close to a man that he is acutely conscious of her physical presence—inside the intimate-distance zone—the man usually construes it to mean that she is encouraging him. However, before the man starts moving in on the woman, he should be sure what message she's really sending; otherwise, he risks bruising his ego. What is close to someone of North European background may be neutral or distant to someone of Italian heritage. Also, women sometimes use space as a way of misleading a man and there are few things that put men off more than women who communicate contradictory messages—such as women who cuddle up and then act insulted when a man takes the next step.

How does a woman communicate interest in a man? In addition to such familiar gambits as smiling at him, she may glance shyly at him, blush and then look away. Or she may give him a real come-on look and move in very close when he approaches. She may touch his arm and ask for a light. As she leans forward to light her cigarette, she may brush him lightly, enveloping him in her perfume. She'll probably continue to smile at him and she may use what ethologists call preening gestures—touching the back of her hair, thrusting her breasts forward, tilting her hips as she stands or crossing her legs if she's seated, perhaps even exposing one thigh or putting a hand on her thigh and stroking it. She may also stroke her wrists as she converses or show the palm of her hand as a way of gaining his attention. Her skin may be unusually flushed or quite pale, her eyes brighter, the pupils larger.

If a man sees a woman whom he wants to attract, he tries to present himself by his posture and stance as someone who is self-assured. He moves briskly and confidently. When he catches the eye of the woman, he may hold her glance a little longer than normal. If he gets an encouraging smile, he'll move in close and engage her in small talk. As they converse, his glance shifts over her face and body. He, too, may make preening gestures—straightening his tie, smoothing his hair or shooting his cuffs.

How do people learn body language? The same way they learn spoken language—by observing and imitating people around them as they're growing up. Little girls imitate their mothers or an older female. Little boys imitate their fathers or a respected uncle or a character on television. In this way, they learn the gender signals appropriate for their sex. Regional, class and ethnic patterns of body behavior are also learned in childhood and persist throughout life.

Such patterns of masculine and feminine body behavior vary widely from one culture to another. In America, for example, women stand with their thighs together. Many walk with their pelvis tipped slightly forward and their upper arms close to their body. When they sit, they cross their legs at the knee or cross their ankles. American men hold their arms away from their body, often swinging them as they walk. They stand with their legs apart (an extreme example is the cowboy, with legs apart and thumbs tucked into his belt). When they sit, they put their feet on the floor with legs apart and, in some parts of the country, they cross their legs by putting one ankle on the other knee.

Leg behavior indicates sex, status and personality. It also indicates whether or not one is at ease or is showing respect or disrespect for the other person. Young Latin American males avoid crossing their legs. In their world of *machismo,* the preferred position for young males when with one another (if there is no older dominant male present to whom they must show respect) is to sit on the base of their spine with their leg muscles relaxed and their feet wide apart. Their respect position is like our military equivalent: spine straight, heels and ankles together—almost identical to that displayed by properly brought up young women in New England in the early part of this century.

American women who sit with their legs spread apart in the presence of males are *not* normally signaling a come-on—they are simply (and often unconsciously) sitting like men. Middle-class women in the presence of other women to whom they are very close may on occasion throw themselves down on a soft chair or sofa and let themselves go. This is a signal that nothing serious will be taken up. Males, on the other hand, lean back and prop their legs up on the nearest object.

The way we walk, similarly, indicates status, respect, mood and ethnic or cultural affiliation. The many variants of the female walk are too well known to go into here, except to say that a man would have to be blind not to be turned on by the way some women walk—a fact that made Mae West rich before scientists ever studied these matters. To white Americans, some French middle-class males walk in a way that is both humorous and suspect. There is a bounce and looseness to the French walk, as though the parts of the body were somehow unrelated. Jacques Tati, the French movie actor, walks this way: so does the great mime, Marcel Marceau.

Blacks and whites in America—with the exception of middle- and upper-middle-class professionals of both groups—move and walk very differently from each other. To the blacks, whites often seem incredibly stiff, almost mechanical in their movements. Black males, on the other hand, have a looseness and coordination that frequently makes whites a little uneasy; it's too different, too integrated, too alive, too male. Norman Mailer has said that squares walk from the shoulders, like bears, but blacks and hippies walk from the hips, like cats.

All over the world, people walk not only in their own characteristic way but have walks that communicate the nature of their involvement with whatever it is they're doing. The purposeful walk of North Europeans is an important component of proper behavior on the job. Any male who has been in the military knows how essential it is to walk properly (which makes for a continuing source of tension between blacks and whites in the Service). The quick shuffle of servants in the Far East in the old days was a show of respect. On the island of Truk, when we last visited, the inhabitants even had a name for the respectful walk that one used when in the presence of a chief or when walking past a chief's house. The term was *sufan*, which meant to be humble and respectful.

The notion that people communicate volumes by their gestures, facial expressions, posture and walk is not new; actors, dancers, writers and psychiatrists have long been aware of it. Only in recent years, however, have scientists begun to make systematic observations of body motions. Ray L. Birdwhistell of the University of Pennsylvania is one of the pioneers in body-motion research and coined the term *kinesics* to describe this field. He developed an elaborate notation system to record both facial and body movement, using an approach similar to that of the linguist, who studies the basic elements of speech. Birdwhistell and other kinesicists such as Albert Shellen, Adam Kendon and William Condon take movies of people interacting. They run the film over and over again, often at reduced speed for frame-by-frame analysis, so that they can observe even the slightest body movements not perceptible at normal interaction speeds. These movements are then recorded in notebooks for later analysis.

To appreciate the importance of nonverbal-communication systems, consider the unskilled inner-city black looking for a job. His handling of time and space alone is sufficiently different from the white middle-class pattern to create great misunderstandings on both sides. The black is told to appear for a job interview at a certain time. He arrives late. The white interviewer concludes from his tardy arrival that the black is irresponsible and not really interested in the job. What the interviewer doesn't know is that the black time system (often referred to by blacks as C.P.T.—colored people's time) isn't the same as that of whites. In the words of a black student who

had been told to make an appointment to see his professor: "Man, you *must* be putting me on. I never had an appointment in my life."

The black job applicant, having arrived late for his interview, may further antagonize the white interviewer by his posture and his eye behavior. Perhaps he slouches and avoids looking at the interviewer: to him, this is playing it cool. To the interviewer, however, he may well look shifty and sound uninterested. The interviewer has failed to notice the actual signs of interest and eagerness in the black's behavior, such as subtle shift in the quality of the voice—a gentle and tentative excitement—an almost imperceptible change in the cast of the eyes and a relaxing of the jaw muscles.

Moreover, correct reading of black-white behavior is continually complicated by the fact that both groups are comprised of individuals—some of whom try to accommodate and some of whom make it a point of pride *not* to accommodate. At present, this means that many Americans, when thrown into contact with one another, are in the precarious position of not knowing which pattern applies. Once identified and analyzed, nonverbal-communication systems can be taught, like a foreign language. Without this training, we respond to nonverbal communications in terms of our own culture; we read everyone's behavior as if it were our own, and thus we often misunderstand it.

Several years ago in New York City, there was a program for sending children from predominantly black and Puerto Rican low income neighborhoods to summer school in a white upper-class neighborhood on the East Side. One morning, a group of young black and Puerto Rican boys raced down the street, shouting and screaming and overturning garbage cans on their way to school. A doorman from an apartment building nearby chased them and cornered one of them inside a building. The boy drew a knife and attacked the doorman. This tragedy would not have occurred if the doorman had been familiar with the behavior of boys from low-income neighborhoods, where such antics are routine and socially acceptable and where pursuit would be expected to invite a violent response.

The language of behavior is extremely complex. Most of us are lucky to have under control one subcultural system—the one that reflects our sex, class, generation and geographic region within the United States. Because of its complexity, efforts to isolate bits of nonverbal communication and generalize from them are in vain; you don't become an instant expert on people's behavior by watching them at cocktail parties. Body language isn't something that's independent of the person, something that can be donned and doffed like a suit of clothes.

Our research and that of our colleagues have shown that, far from being a superficial form of communication that can be consciously manipulated, nonverbal-communication systems are interwoven into the fabric of the personality and, as sociologist Erving Goffman has demonstrated, into society itself. They are the warp and woof of daily interactions with others and they influence how one expresses oneself, how one experiences oneself as a man or a woman.

Nonverbal communications signal to members of your own group what kind of person you are, how you feel about others, how you'll fit into and work in a group, whether you're assured or anxious, the degree to which you feel comfortable with the standards of your own culture, as well as deeply significant feelings about the self, including the state of your own psyche. For most of us, it's difficult to accept the reality of another's behavioral system. And, of course, none of us will ever become fully knowledgeable of the importance of every non-verbal signal. But as long as each of us realizes the power of these signals, this society's diversity can be a source of great strength rather than a further—and subtly powerful—source of division.

III

CULTURE
Why We Do Things the Way We Do

Human behavior is both patterned and orderly, because within our society we are taught to follow similar rules of behavior (*norms*) and to cherish similar objects and behaviors (*values*). These similarities create the culture of a society: its total way of life. The importance of culture is indicated by the fact that most human behavior is learned.

Because we are taught mainly the norms, values, language, and beliefs of our own culture, we frequently find it difficult to see our culture objectively. What we do routinely we accept as right without question and, possibly, even without understanding. This *ethnocentrism*—the belief that one's own culture is superior to others—can make it difficult for us to accept the different ways of others and to change our own ways. Through *cultural relativity*—looking at other cultures in an objective manner—we attempt to understand the behaviors that exist within various cultures by considering the functions the behaviors serve. In the first article of this chapter, Miner examines the societal needs served by the unusual attitude of the Nacirema toward the human body.

Although the second article also deals with ethnocentrism, the main focus of Linton's tongue-in-cheek summary is *cultural diffusion*—the spread of cultural behaviors and materials from one society to another. In fact, many if not most of the items used in any given culture are neither invented nor discovered in that culture, but adopted from other societies.

The final article in this chapter emphasizes that culture is not stagnant: it is constantly changing. In discussing social change, William Ogburn, an early sociologist, noted that change may occur more rapidly in the material parts of culture than in its ideological parts. However, ideological change can and does occur: the ideas, the values, and the beliefs of a society do undergo transformation. Walum writes about the confusion and difficulties we encounter with a changing folkway.

As you read this chapter, ask yourself why the Nacirema have this seemingly pathological concern with the body, what the origins are of your everyday objects, what other norms are undergoing change, and what are the implications of that change.

7

BODY RITUAL AMONG THE NACIREMA

Horace Miner

The anthropologist has become so familiar with the diversity of ways in which different peoples behave in similar situations that he is not apt to be surprised by even the most exotic customs. In fact, if all of the logically possible combinations of behavior have not been found somewhere in the world, he is apt to suspect that they must be present in some yet undescribed tribe. This point has, in fact, been expressed with respect to clan organization by Murdock (1949:71). In this light, the magical beliefs and practices of the Nacirema present such unusual aspects that it seems desirable to describe them as an example of the extremes to which human behavior can go.

Professor Linton first brought the ritual of the Nacirema to the attention of anthropologists twenty years ago (1936:326), but the culture of this people is still very poorly understood. They are a North American group living in the territory between the Canadian Cree, the Yaqui and Tarahumare of Mexico, and the Carib and Arawak of the Antilles. Little is known of their origin, although tradition states that they came from the east. According to Nacirema mythology, their nation was originated by a culture hero, Notgnihsaw, who is otherwise known for two

great feats of strength—the throwing of a piece of wampum across the river Pa-To-Mac and the chopping down of a cherry tree in which the Spirit of Truth resided.

Nacirema culture is characterized by a highly developed market economy which has evolved in a rich natural habitat. While much of the people's time is devoted to economic pursuits, a large part of the fruits of these labors and a considerable portion of the day are spent in ritual activity. The focus of this activity is the human body, the appearance and health of which loom as a dominant concern in the ethos of the people. While such a concern is certainly not unusual, its ceremonial aspects and associated philosophy are unique.

The fundamental belief underlying the whole system appears to be that the human body is ugly and that its natural tendency is to debility and disease. Incarcerated in such a body, man's only hope is to avert these characteristics through the use of the powerful influences of ritual and ceremony. Every household has one or more shrines devoted to this purpose. The more powerful individuals in the society have several shrines in their houses and, in fact, the opulence of a house is often referred to in terms of the number of such ritual centers it possesses. Most houses are of wattle and daub construction, but the shrine rooms of the more wealthy are walled

Reproduced by permission of the American Anthropological Society from the *American Anthropologist*, 58, (3), 1956, pp. 503–507.

with stone. Poorer families imitate the rich by applying pottery plaques to their shrine walls.

While each family has at least one such shrine, the rituals associated with it are not family ceremonies but are private and secret. The rites are normally only discussed with children, and then only during the period when they are being initiated into these mysteries. I was able, however, to establish sufficient rapport with the natives to examine these shrines and to have the rituals described to me.

The focal point of the shrine is a box or chest which is built into the wall. In this chest are kept the many charms and magical potions without which no native believes he could live. These preparations are secured from a variety of specialized practitioners. The most powerful of these are the medicine men, whose assistance must be rewarded with substantial gifts. However, the medicine men do not provide the curative potions for their clients, but decide what the ingredients should be and then write them down in an ancient and secret language. This writing is understood only by the medicine men and by the herbalists who, for another gift, provide the required charm.

The charm is not disposed of after it has served its purpose, but is placed in the charm-box of the household shrine. As these magical materials are specific for certain ills, and the real or imagined maladies of the people are many, the charm-box is usually full to overflowing. The magical packets are so numerous that people forget what their purposes were and fear to use them again. While the natives are very vague on this point, we can only assume that the idea in retaining all the old magical materials is that their presence in the charm-box, before which the body rituals are conducted, will in some way protect the worshipper.

Beneath the charm-box is a small font. Each day every member of the family, in succession, enters the shrine room, bows his head before the charm-box, mingles different sorts of holy water in the font, and proceeds with a brief rite of ablution. The holy waters are secured from the Water Temple of the community, where the priests conduct elaborate ceremonies to make the liquid ritually pure.

In the hierarchy of magical practitioners, and below the medicine men in prestige, are specialists whose designation is best translated "holy-mouth-men." The Nacirema have an almost pathological horror of and fascination with the mouth, the condition of which is believed to have a supernatural influence on all social relationships. Were it not for the rituals of the mouth, they believe that their teeth would fall out, their gums bleed, their jaws shrink, their friends desert them, and their lovers reject them. They also believe that a strong relationship exists between oral and moral characteristics. For example, there is a ritual ablution of the mouth for children which is supposed to improve their moral fiber.

The daily body ritual performed by everyone includes a mouth-rite. Despite the fact that these people are so punctilious about care of the mouth, this rite involves a practice which strikes the uninitiated stranger as revolting. It was reported to me that the ritual consists of inserting a small bundle of hog hairs into the mouth, along with certain magical powders, and then moving the bundle in a highly formalized series of gestures.

In addition to the private mouth-rite, the people seek out a holy-mouth-man once or twice a year. These practitioners have an impressive set of paraphernalia, consisting of a variety of augers, awls, probes, and prods. The use of these objects in the exorcism of the evils of the mouth involves almost unbelievable ritual torture of the client. The holy-mouth-man opens the client's mouth and, using the above mentioned tools, enlarges any holes which decay may have created in the teeth. Magical materials are put into these holes. If there are no naturally occurring holes in the teeth, large sections of one or more teeth are gouged out so that the supernatural substance can be applied. In the client's view, the purpose of these ministrations is to arrest decay and to draw friends. The extremely sacred and traditional character of the rite is evident in the fact that the natives return to the holy-mouth-man year after year, despite the fact that their teeth continue to decay.

It is to be hoped that, when a thorough study of the Nacirema is made, there will be careful inquiry into the personality structure of these people. One has but to watch the gleam in the eye of a holy-mouth-man, as he jabs an awl into an exposed nerve, to suspect that a certain amount of sadism is involved. If this can be established, a very interesting pattern emerges, for most of the population shows definite masochistic tendencies. It was to these that Professor Linton referred in discussing a distinctive part of the daily body ritual which is performed only by men. The part of the rite involves scraping and lacerating the surface of the face with a sharp instrument. Special women's rites are performed only four times during each lunar month, but what they lack in frequency is made up in barbarity. As part of this ceremony, women bake their heads in small ovens for about an hour. The theoretically interesting point is that what seems to be a preponderantly masochistic people have developed sadistic specialists.

The medicine men have an imposing temple, or *latipso*, in every community of any size. The more elaborate ceremonies required to treat very sick patients can only be performed at this temple. These ceremonies involve not only the thaumaturge but a permanent group of vestal maidens who move sedately about the temple chambers in distinctive costume and headdress.

The *latipso* ceremonies are so harsh that it is phenomenal that a fair proportion of the really sick natives who enter the temple ever recover. Small children whose indoctrination is still incomplete have been known to resist attempts to take them to the temple because "that is where you go to die." Despite this fact, sick adults are not only willing but eager to undergo the protracted ritual purification, if they can afford to do so. No matter how ill the supplicant or how grave the emergency, the guardians of many temples will not admit a client if he cannot give a rich gift to the custodian. Even after one has gained admission and survived the ceremonies, the guardians will not permit the neophyte to leave until he makes still another gift.

The supplicant entering the temple is first stripped of all his or her clothes. In every-day life the Nacirema avoids exposure of his body and its natural functions. Bathing and excretory acts are performed only in the secrecy of the household shrine, where they are ritualized as part of the body-rites. Psychological shock results from the fact that body secrecy is suddenly lost upon entry into the *latipso*. A man, whose own wife has never seen him in an excretory act, suddenly finds himself naked and assisted by a vestal maiden while he performs his natural functions into a sacred vessel. This sort of ceremonial treatment is necessitated by the fact that the excreta are used by a diviner to ascertain the course and nature of the client's sickness. Female clients, on the other hand, find their naked bodies are subjected to the scrutiny, manipulation, and prodding of the medicine men.

Few supplicants in the temple are well enough to do anything but lie on their hard beds. The daily ceremonies, like the rites of the holy-mouth-men, involve discomfort and torture. With ritual precision, the vestals awaken their miserable charges each dawn and roll them about on their beds of pain while performing ablutions, in the formal movements of which the maidens are highly trained. At other times they insert magic wands in the supplicant's mouth or force him to eat substances which are supposed to be healing. From time to time the medicine men come to their clients and jab magically treated needles into their flesh. The fact that these temple ceremonies may not cure, and may even kill the neophyte, in no way decreases the people's faith in the medicine men.

There remains one other kind of practitioner, known as a "listener." This witch-doctor has the power to exorcise the devils that lodge in the heads of people who have been bewitched. The Nacirema believe that parents bewitch their own children. Mothers are particularly suspected of putting a curse on children while teaching them the secret body rituals. The counter-magic of the witch-doctor is unusual in its lack of ritual. The patient simply tells the "listener" all his troubles and fears, beginning with the earliest difficulties he can remember. The memory displayed by the Nacirema in these exorcism sessions is truly remarkable. It is not uncommon for the patient to bemoan the rejection he felt upon being weaned as a babe, and a few individuals even see their troubles going back to the traumatic effects of their own birth.

In conclusion, mention must be made of certain practices which have their base in native esthetics but which depend upon the pervasive aversion to the natural body and its functions. There are ritual fasts to make fat people thin and ceremonial feasts to make thin people fat. Still other rites are used to make women's breasts larger if they are small, and smaller if they are large. General dissatisfaction with breast shape is symbolized in the fact that the ideal form is virtually outside the range of human variation. A few women afflicted with almost inhuman hypermammary development are so idolized that they make a handsome living by simply going from village to village and permitting the natives to stare at them for a fee.

Reference has already been made to the fact that excretory functions are ritualized, routinized, and relegated to secrecy. Natural reproductive functions are similarly distorted. Intercourse is taboo as a topic and scheduled as an act. Efforts are made to avoid pregnancy by the use of magical materials or by limiting intercourse to certain phases of the moon. Conception is actually very infrequent. When pregnant, women dress so as to hide their condition. Parturition takes place in secret, without friends or relatives to assist, and the majority of women do not nurse their infants.

Our review of the ritual life of the Nacirema has certainly shown them to be a magic-ridden people. It is hard to understand how they have managed to exist so long under the burdens which they have imposed upon themselves. But even such exotic customs as these take on real meaning when they are viewed with the insight provided by Malinowski when he wrote (1948:70):

Looking from far and above, from our high places of safety in the developed civilization, it is easy to see all the crudity and irrelevance of magic. But without its power and guidance early man could not have mastered his practical difficulties as he has done, nor could man have advanced to the higher stages of civilization.

REFERENCES

Linton, Ralph. 1936. The Study of Man. New York, D. Appleton-Century Co.

Malinowski, Bronislaw. 1948. Magic, Science, and Religion. Glencoe, The Free Press.

Murdock, George P. 1949. Social Structure. New York, The Macmillan Co.

8

ONE HUNDRED PERCENT AMERICAN

Ralph Linton

There can be no question about the average American's Americanism or his desire to preserve this precious heritage at all costs. Nevertheless, some insidious foreign ideas have already wormed their way into his civilization without his realizing what was going on. Thus dawn finds the unsuspecting patriot garbed in pajamas, a garment of East Indian origin; and lying in a bed built on a pattern which originated in either Persia or Asia Minor. He is muffled to the ears in un-American materials; cotton, first domesticated in India; linen, domesticated in the Near East; wool from an animal native to Asia Minor; or silk, whose uses were first discovered by the Chinese. All these substances have been transformed into cloth by methods invented in Southwestern Asia. If the weather is cold enough he may even be sleeping under an eiderdown quilt invented in Scandinavia.

On awakening he glances at the clock, a medieval European invention, uses one potent Latin word in abbreviated form, rises in haste, and goes to the bathroom. Here, if he stops to think about it, he must feel himself in the presence of a great American institution; he will have heard stories of both the quality and frequency of foreign plumbing and will know that in no other country does the average man perform his ablutions in the midst of such splendor. But the insidious foreign influence pursues him even here. Glass was invented by the ancient Egyptians, the use of glazed tiles for floors and walls in the Near East, porcelain in China, and the art of enameling on metal by Mediterranean artisans of the Bronze Age. Even his bathtub and toilet are but slightly modified copies of Roman originals. The only purely American contribution to the ensemble is the steam radiator, against which our patriot very briefly and unintentionally places his posterior.

In this bathroom the American washes with soap invented by the ancient Gauls. Next he cleans his teeth, a subversive European practice which did not invade America until the latter part of the eighteenth century. He then shaves, a masochistic rite first developed by the heathen priests of ancient Egypt and Sumer. The process is made less of a penance by the fact that his razor is of steel, an iron-carbon alloy discovered in either India or Turkestan. Lastly, he dries himself on a Turkish towel.

Returning to the bedroom, the unconscious victim of un-American practices removes his clothes from a chair, invented in the Near East, and proceeds to dress. He puts on close-fitting tailored garments whose form derives

Reprinted by permission from *American Mercury*, Vol. 40, April 1937, pp. 427–430, P. O. Box 1306, Torrance, CA 90505.

from the skin clothing of the ancient nomads of the Asiatic steppes and fastens them with buttons whose prototypes appeared in Europe at the close of the Stone Age. This costume is appropriate enough for outdoor exercise in a cold climate, but is quite unsuited to American summers, steam-heated houses, and Pullmans. Nevertheless, foreign ideas and habits hold the unfortunate man in thrall even when common sense tells him that the authentically American costume of gee string and moccasins would be far more comfortable. He puts on his feet stiff coverings made from hide prepared by a process invented in ancient Egypt and cut to a pattern which can be traced back to ancient Greece, and makes sure they are properly polished, also a Greek idea. Lastly, he ties about his neck a strip of bright-colored cloth which is a vestigial survival of the shoulder shawls worn by seventeenth-century Croats. He gives himself a final appraisal in the mirror, an old Mediterranean invention, and goes downstairs to breakfast.

Here a whole new series of foreign things confronts him. His food and drink are placed before him in pottery vessels, the popular name of which—china—is sufficient evidence of their origin. His fork is a medieval Italian invention and his spoon a copy of a Roman original. He will usually begin the meal with coffee, an Abyssinian plant first discovered by the Arabs. The American is quite likely to need it to dispel the morning-after effects of over-indulgence in fermented drinks, invented in the Near East; or distilled ones, invented by the alchemists of medieval Europe. Whereas the Arabs took their coffee straight, he will probably sweeten it with sugar, discovered in India; and dilute it with cream, both the domestication of cattle and the technique of milking having originated in Asia Minor.

If our patriot is old-fashioned enough to adhere to the so-called American breakfast, his coffee will be accompanied by an orange, domesticated in the Mediterranean region, a cantaloupe domesticated in Persia, or grapes, domesticated in Asia Minor. He will follow this with a bowl of cereal made from grain domesticated in the Near East and prepared by methods also invented there. From this he will go on to waffles, a Scandinavian invention, with plenty of butter, originally a Near-Eastern cosmetic. As a side dish he may have the egg of a bird domesticated in Southeastern Asia or strips of the flesh of an animal domesticated in the same region, which have been salted and smoked by a process invented in Northern Europe.

Breakfast over, he places upon his head a molded piece of felt, invented by the nomads of Eastern Asia, and, if it looks like rain, puts on outer shoes of rubber, discovered by the ancient Mexicans, and takes an umbrella, invented in India. He then sprints for his train—the train, not the sprinting, being an English invention. At the station he pauses for a moment to buy a newspaper, paying for it with coins invented in ancient Lydia. Once on board he settles back to inhale the fumes of a cigarette invented in Mexico, or a cigar invented in Brazil. Meanwhile, he reads the news of the day, imprinted in characters invented by the ancient Semites by a process invented in Germany upon a material invented in China. As he scans the latest editorial pointing out the dire results to our institutions of accepting foreign ideas, he will not fail to thank a Hebrew God in an Indo-European language that he is a one hundred per cent (decimal system invented by the Greeks) American (from Americus Vespucci, Italian geographer).

9

THE CHANGING DOOR CEREMONY
NOTES ON THE OPERATION OF SEX ROLES
IN EVERYDAY LIFE

Laurel Richardson Walum

A young woman and a young man, total strangers to each other, simultaneously reach the closed classroom door. She steps slightly aside, stops, and waits. He positions himself, twists the handle, pulls open the door, and holds it while she enters. Once she is safely across the threshold, he enters behind her. An everyday, commonplace social ceremony has been performed. It is not accidental that their performance in this ceremonial ritual of "door-opening" has gone so smoothly, although they have never rehearsed it with each other. Nor is it by chance that such trivial, commonplace ceremonies between the sexes occur day after day.

Of the multitude of such ceremonial occasions between the sexes in middle-class society—occasions wherein the interplay of cultural values and self-image are displayed—the "Door Ceremony" is probably the most common. We are confronted constantly with doors: car doors, house doors, bathroom doors, revolving doors, electric eye doors. Ad infinitum are the physical structures which must somehow be penetrated if we are to complete our daily round of activities. And nearly as often as we confront the door, we are in a social situation in which a ceremonial ritual concerning it may occur. The pervasiveness of the occasion is difficult to deny. The relevance of the ceremony for the maintenance of cultural values and self esteem, its true *nontriviality*, was initially suggested to me by entries in student journals—the journals having been written for a Sociology of Women course. It was subsequently underscored by a series of norm violation experiments performed by undergraduates and by my own observation. I draw my illustration and develop my analysis from these data sources.

I am concerned with four major questions: (1) How does this ceremony function to bind the society together? (2) What cultural values are being enacted? (3) What consequences has the women's movement had on the ceremony? and finally, speculatively (4) What might the future hold?

Goffman has paid special attention to these ceremonial occasions. In our everyday associations we abide by rules of conduct, a kind of guide book which is followed "not because it is pleasant, cheap or effective, but

"The Changing Door Ceremony: Notes on the Operation of Sex Roles in Everyday Life," by Laurel Richardson Walum is reprinted from *Urban Life and Culture*, Vol. 2, No. 4 (January 1974), pp. 506–515, © Sage Publications, Beverly Hills, by permission of the publisher.

because it is suitable and just" (1967:48). These rules establish both our obligations—the way we are morally constrained to act—and our expectations—the way others are morally required to act towards us. Commitment to the rule becomes a commitment to a given self-image. Ceremonial rules guide

conduct in matters felt to have secondary importance—officially anyway—as a conventionalized means of communication by which the individual expresses his character or conveys his appreciation of other participants in the situation [Goffman 1967: 54].

These rules are incorporated in what we call "etiquette." To be properly mannered we convey an appropriate demeanor, expressed through our dress, deportment, bearing, and an appropriate deference, or appreciation and confirmation of an actor's relationship to a recipient.

The rules of conduct bind actors and recipients in appropriate interaction, encourage their interaction, and serve in a daily pedestrian way to hold together the social order. The very dailiness of the ceremonies, the lack of substantive investment, permits the constant reaffirmation of the kinds of persons we think we are and the kinds of rules we deem appropriate. The ceremony, then, affirms the nature of the social order, the morality of it, as well as the properness of the self who is engaged in the action. As Goffman succinctly states, "The gestures which we sometimes call empty are perhaps, in fact, the fullest things of all" (1967:91).

BINDING THE SOCIETY

The Door Ceremony exemplifies the etiquette developed to "bind" the sexes together. The daily drama of Betty Co-ed and Joe College at the Classroom Door, which began this analysis, is descriptive of the usual ritual. Joe College, under the ceremonial rules of conduct, is *obliged* to open the door for Betty Co-ed, and Betty Co-ed *expects* to be the recipient of his courtesy. In the ritual, both of them have confirmed their images of themselves as respectively, male and female. As one "Joe College" wrote in his course journal:

I have dated several girls including my fiancée who want to be treated like a lady. My courtesy like opening the car door makes them feel more feminine and they enjoy this. I enjoy also being a gentleman and making them feel this way. Personally, I prefer a girl who is feminine over a more rugged-looking and -acting girl.

And as a Betty Co-ed declared:

Tonight I had a date with a gentleman. When I opened the door to let myself in, he closed it and opened it again. To tell the truth it made me feel good. He said he enjoyed doing these little things for me because he derived a feeling of protectiveness. I was reassured. I didn't want him to think I was crude. It's nice to *feel* like a woman.

The activity as traditionally structured, then, affirms the generalized notion of "masculinity" and "femininity." But what are the components, the elements, of the personal self-image enacted in the door ceremony that lead the male to perceive himself as "masculine," and the female to see herself as "feminine"?

To be masculine, first and foremost, means to have authority, to be in charge, in control. And in our culture, in most encounters, the person with higher authority holds the door. The doctor ushers in his patient, the mother her children, the Dean his faculty, and the young and able facilitate the old and infirm. Note that the phrase, the "gatekeepers of knowledge," symbolically acknowledges the role of authority vested in those responsible for the door.

Secondly, and pervasively, to be "masculine" means to be "active"; to be "feminine" means to be "passive." This distinction pervades the entire ceremony. The male is the active party in the encounter; the female waits passively for the door to open and for the door to close. The passivity is closely linked to another prescribed feminine trait, namely "dependence." By waiting for the service to be performed, the woman communicates that she *needs* someone to help her through her daily round of activities. The male, in turn, communicates his independence by actively meeting the challenge of the door and overcoming it. Other male virtues of physical strength, mechanical ability, worldliness, self-confidence, and efficacy are called into play in the ceremony. If Joe College goes through his routine without mishap, he has engaged all these traits culturally associated with masculinity, and of course, he does *feel* masculine. And Betty Co-ed, by acting out her expectations, has drawn upon the perceptions of femininity recognized by the culture: frailty, weakness, ineptitude, and protectibility. She *feels* womanly.

AFFIRMATION OF CULTURAL VALUES

The door ceremony, then, reaffirms for both sexes their sense of gender-identity, of being a "masculine" or "feminine" person. It is not accidentally structured. In a very profound way the simple ceremony daily makes a reality of the moral perspective of their culture: the *ideology of patriarchy*. These virtues of "masculinity" are precisely those which are the dominant values of the culture: aggression, efficacy, authority, prowess, and independence. And these virtues are assigned to the dominant group, the males (see Millet, 1970: 23–58). Opening a door for a woman, presumably only a simple, common courtesy, is also a *political* act, an act which affirms a patriarchal ideology. The male who wrote the following recognized not the irony of his words.

Some women feel that if you open a door for them it is a sign of male chauvinism. In other words, you can't be nice to a female without showing your true colors.

His words, however, are perhaps less naive than this more commonly heard statement.

I'm all for Woman's Lib. I think women should get equal pay for equal work. But women should keep their femininity. I like being treated like a lady.

One might suggest that these people are missing the relevance of minor courtesies perpetuating the ideology of patriarchy. Analytically,

in terms of our understandings of the relationship between the cultural values and everyday ceremonies, women can't have it both ways.

EFFECTS OF THE WOMEN'S MOVEMENT

As more and more women and men "recognize" the meaning that common courtesies have for the perpetuation of the patriarchal ideology, increasing numbers of what Goffman refers to as deference confrontations occur. The world which has been taken for granted, the rules of conduct once abided by, are called into question. Ceremonial rituals, once performed with propriety, become imbued with substantive meaning and are perceived by some as insulting, assaulting, and degrading. As a consequence, the once routine, matter-of-fact door-opening ceremony becomes situationally problematic to increasing numbers of people. What are some of the responses to the altered consciousness? What stances do persons take to make sense out of their changed ceremonial world? I offer a kind of typology of such stances based on empirical observations and student reports. I do not claim that it is an exhaustive theoretical accounting, but, rather, only an analytical categorization of known patterns.

1. The Confused

Many persons confronted for the first time with a ceremonial profanation are uncertain what to do about it. They have practiced the standard behaviors and do not know how to respond when one of the actors is out of "character." A woman reports the following:

I approached a door ahead of a fellow and then with common courtesy, I held it open for him to go through. He bumped right into me even though he could see me. He looked awfully puzzled and it took him forever to get through.

The "confused" man could indeed see her but he could not perceive what was "happening" and was unable to make sense out of it. He acted along his normal path—destined for collision. Confusion is even more explicit in another reported episode.

I came to a door at the same time as this guy. He reached to open it for me but then I started to open it myself and he just let me do it. *It was like neither of us knew what to do.*

The Confused, embarrassed and awkward, literally don't know yet how to make sense out of the situation.

2.   The Tester

The Tester, unlike the Confused, *recognizes* that the routine rules of conduct in any given encounter are violable, and yet wants to maintain proper demeanor as well as proper deference. For example, a woman reports that "A man opening a door holds it open for me asking, 'Are you a liberated woman? If not, I'll hold this door open for you.' " Or, take the following overheard conversation.

Female: Well, aren't you going to open the door for me?
Male: I didn't know that girls still like for boys to do that.
Female: I'm not in Woman's Lib.

Often, the Tester has other motives in mind, such as wanting to act properly in order to "score." This excerpt from a male student's journal is illustrative.

It's almost like discovering a third sex to deal with liberated women. In the past I would make advances to my date almost as a matter of course. Now, I must "discover" if my date is sexually traditional or not before I decide on the conduct of our date. I can't just open doors and light cigarettes and expect to score. In fact, if I do treat those so-called "liberated" women like chattels, we never make it.

This male has found, then, that the whole course of his sexual life can hinge on the perception of appropriate deference.

3.   The Humanitarian

The Humanitarian, like the Tester, recognizes that the situation is changing but has drawn upon other cultural values to explain and guide behavior, particularly the values of "sensitivity" and of "considerateness" of all people. For example, one male states,

A male shouldn't *circle* the car to open the door for a woman. I believe each sex should treat the other with mutual courtesy. If a woman reaches the car first, there is nothing wrong with her opening it.

Or, as another male student writes,

I had a 15 second encounter with a pro-libber which has left a bad taste in my mouth all day. She had a large stack of papers and I pushed open and held the door for her. I would have done this for a woman or a man. Instead of thank you I got the coldest, bitterest, most glaring stare that went right through me. I resent being seen as a Pig when I was being courteous to her as a *person*.

There are women humanitarians, also, who open doors for men in similar straits. As one reports,

I entered the elevator ahead of a football player who lives in my building who had an armful of groceries. I quickly held the door back so he could get on. He was so embarrassed he couldn't even say thank-you.

4.   The Defender

The Defender recognizes there is change afoot in the land but wants no part of it. For example, one woman relates:

I opened a door to enter a building and a boy walked in ahead of me. It was just like he expected me to open the door for him. My first reaction was frowning and thinking some people have a lot of nerve. I believe in manners that did not enter the mind of the boy. I wondered if most boys now take it for granted that girls are woman's liberationists and will want to hold the door open for boys.

And a male student observes:

It happens many times in this University that the female *purposefully* beats the male to the door and opens it herself. To the male, this is a discourtesy and an example of bad manners. To him it appears that the female is a hard and calloused woman who has never been taught proper manners. They are trying to assert their person over their sex.

Another male student concluded a multiparagraph moral indictment of "lady dooropeners" with this clincher: "It's fine that women are liberating themselves, but I wouldn't want to marry one." The vehemence of Defenders occasionally creates poignant episodes, as evidenced by this journal entry.

"I don't care how uncomfortable you are. You are not going until you act like my wife should," my husband stormed. I conceded. I let him open the car door. I had to give in. I don't have a driving license.

5. The Rebel

The Rebel recognizes that the rules of conduct are changing and is anxious to speed the change on its way. Rebels are oftimes involved in badly demeanored profanations and report pleasure in their sacrilege. One woman states,

I had a date with this same fellow [previously referred to as a gentleman] and this time I *deliberately* opened the door. He looked distressed. So I rubbed it in and told him I was capable of opening the door myself. I never wanted to go out with him in the first place. Ha!

Another woman student reports:

So this Dude says to me, "Hey, let me help you with the door." And I say, "You ain't got nothin' to help me with."

Males appear also in the Rebel ranks. Says one,

I don't open doors for women. I'm glad not to. I don't want to serve them just because they're women. If they had their heads screwed on right they wouldn't trade doing laundry for me lighting their cigarettes.

WHAT THE FUTURE HOLDS

As is obvious from the illustrations, these five types are in frequent interaction with each other, making the ceremonial occasion increasingly complex and non-routine. Where do we go from here? Can we expect to get through those doors? Durkheim and Goffman argue that the social order is dependent on the routine daily acting-out of the morality of people who are simultaneously being bound together and providing living testimony of the cultural values. If altered consciousness continues and courtesies are rebuked, then ceremonial profanations will increase in frequency. The increase in violations of rules of conduct leads to increasing normlessness—anomie. The anomic period provides a time for the emergence of new *substantive* rules of conduct. A potential substantive change, then, might be forthcoming. If patriarchal values, which now govern the ceremonial conduct between the sexes, cannot be routinely enacted, these values cannot persist. Looking to changing values in other realms, and speaking optimistically, we might even be able to foresee ceremonial occasions dominated by a humanitarian perspective. If so, we might all get through our daily rounds with increased efficacy and joy.

REFERENCES

Goffman, E. (1967) "The Nature of Deference and Demeanor," pp. 47–96 in Interaction Ritual: Essays on Face-to-Face Behavior. Garden City, N.Y.: Doubleday Anchor.

Millett, K. (1970) Sexual Politics. Garden City, N.Y.: Doubleday.

IV

INTERACTION AND GROUP BEHAVIOR
Life Is with People

Life begins in a primary group, in the warm, intimate, face-to-face environment of the family. Here our early socialization takes place and we learn how to relate to others in group situations. However, the complexity of socialization in primary groups, particularly the family, makes for problems. Our socialization to families as warm, loving groups makes us ill-prepared for the normal, conflictual interactions which occur in all families; thus, family violence is a more common occurrence than most of us realize. In our first article, Dibble and Straus say violence is in fact as typical as love, and ranges from the corporal punishment of children to torture and murder. In their article they discuss some of the theories and myths of family violence.

Socialization is a lifelong process of learning the ways of society through association with a variety of groups. As we grow, so do our group contacts and experiences and our roles within those groups. Familial relations expand first to other primary groups such as play and peer groups, then to more formal groups such as the school. When we become adults, many of our interactions are with these secondary groups or organizations characterized by more formal relations.

These group relations reflect the changes in society itself. The transition to a larger, industrial, urbanized (*Gesellschaft*) society has meant for some a longing for the past—for a simple, traditional, close-knit society with predominantly primary relationships (*Gemeinschaft* society). It has also led to frustration with the impersonal, bureaucratic society, characterized mostly by secondary relationships. As defined by Max Weber, bureaucratic organizations include formal contractual relationships, rules and regulations, and hiring and firing based on merit or competence. However, the way in which bureaucracy really works is not always the same as Weber's "ideal type." Competence in one position does not necessarily mean competence in a higher position. The Peter Principle points out this irony: workers are promoted due to good work, until they reach their level of incompetence, and there they stop, filling up positions with incompetents. The Hull article considers the results of this tendency and suggests how we as individuals might avoid reaching our own level of incompetence.

With the growth of bureaucratic society has come an increasing division of labor and more jobs of limited prestige. As a means of gaining status, if not higher pay, euphemistic job titles have proliferated, illustrating the Wynn Principle.

As you read the selections in this chapter, consider the definition of primary and secondary groups, and reflect on examples of these groups in modern society. Since primary groups are our most intimate contact with others in an interaction situation, are familial conflict and violence inevitable? Are some of the problems of bureaucratic society inevitable outcomes of attempts to attain efficiency?

10

SOME SOCIAL STRUCTURE DETERMINANTS OF INCONSISTENCY BETWEEN ATTITUDES AND BEHAVIOR: THE CASE OF FAMILY VIOLENCE

Ursula Dibble
Murray A. Straus

Many investigators of family violence explain the presence or absence of domestic violence in terms of individual beliefs or personality dispositions (see, for example, Walker, 1977–1978). According to this approach, violent behavior should be a consequence of violent attitudes. Rather than concentrating on attitudes as determinants of family violence, or on violent behavior as a determinant of violent attitudes, this study is concerned with the degree to which attitudes and behavior are mutually consistent. In particular, the paper focuses on the social structural determinants of attitude-behavior consistency.

Social structure in this context refers to a system of patterned social interactions. For example, families are social structures which consist of various role relationships. Each role relationship involves mutual expectations and obligations between members, as, for example, those between husband and wife, or between mother and son. One of the characteristics of primary group interaction is that the role expectations and obligations of members of primary groups (such as the members

of a family) are diffuse rather than segmental, exposing us to conflicting demands and expectations (Goode, 1960). The likelihood that one member is unwilling or unable to live up to another member's expectations is, therefore, increased, enhancing the possibility of family conflict.

In short, from a theoretical perspective, this study tries to avoid the false dichotomy between individual dispositions and social structural variables as determinants of family violence. Instead, the theoretical focus is on the ways in which variations in patterns of family interaction are related to the extent to which behavior and attitude are consistent.

The empirical literature to date shows little association between attitude and behavior with respect to domestic violence. Ball-Rokeach (1973) reports a weak association between attitudes which favor violence and violent behavior. Straus (1977) found only a low positive relationship between approval of marital violence and violent behavior.[1] What accounts for this lack of consistency?

According to Ball-Rokeach, the reason for the lack of association between attitudes which favor violence and violent behavior is that violence and norms about violence are primarily interpersonal rather than intraper-

From *Journal of Marriage and the Family*, February 1980. Copyrighted 1980 by the National Council on Family Relations. Reprinted by permission.

sonal. One, therefore, should not expect a causal connection between attitudes and behavior when the attitudes and behavior of only one interacting party are taken into account. For example, in order to study the attitude-behavior consistency of wives with respect to domestic violence, it is necessary to take the attitudes and behavior of the husband into consideration.

In the family, as in any other social structure, there are forces which help to maintain the status quo as well as forces which produce change (Straus and Hotaling, 1979: Chapter 1). For some, the contingencies of everyday life work toward what "should be" in terms of the normative system of the traditional family. For many, however, the contingencies of everyday life work against the realization of what "should be." For example, we may prefer having a job to hitting other people. However, a person may end up without a job and find himself hitting his wife. What we actually end up doing is always influenced by a host of factors, such as what a spouse does, how much money we have, or what our friends think of us.

The specific questions considered in this paper include: What are some of the patterns of interaction inside the family which affect domestic violence? How are variations in the norms concerning the sex-linked division of labor in a marriage related to consistency of attitudes and behavior with respect to family violence? Are the patterns of interaction inside the family related to the family's position in the larger society (using total family income as an indicator of the family's economic position)? The theory which the paper is designed to explore underlies each of these questions. This theory asserts that the extent to which a person's attitudes and behavior with respect to domestic violence are consistent is related, not only to patterns of interaction within the family, but also to the extent to which larger social forces enable husbands and wives to live up to their mutual role obligations as socially defined or inhibit them from doing so.

SAMPLE AND METHOD

The findings are based on a national probability sample of 2,143 American adults living as members of conjugal units in January, 1976, of whom 1,146 had at least one child living at home. The full sample is used when the data refer to spousal violence, and the smaller N when the data concern parental violence.[2]

The survey contains information on the violent or nonviolent *behaviors* of both the respondent and of the respondent's spouse. As regards *attitudes* with respect to violence, it contains data only on respondents. It will, therefore, not be possible to examine how spouse's attitude affects the consistency of respondent's attitude and behavior. However, it will be possible to investigate whether spouse's behavior is related to respondent's attitude and behavior. Spouse's behavior may affect respondent's behavior independently of respondent's attitude. Or spouse's behavior may affect the attitude-behavior consistency of the respondent because it affects the relationship between respondent's attitude and respondent's behavior.

The survey contains two semantic differential items (Osgood et al., 1957). One asks about parents' attitudes towards slapping or spanking a 12-year-old. The other item refers to respondent's attitude towards couples slapping each other. For each of these, respondents indicate the degree to which they consider this kind of behavior "necessary," "normal," and "good" on scales with a range from 1 to 7. Each rating was dichotomized to read 1 versus 2–7; for example, "unnecessary" versus "necessary." The scales were dichotomized in this way so that people can be classified unambiguously into "nonviolent" versus "all other." A clearly nonviolent attitude should be related to nonviolent behavior and vice versa.

The dependent variables consist of two "minor violence counts," made up of answers to items K, L, and M of the Conflict Tactics Scales (Straus, 1979:87–88):

No matter how well a couple gets along, there are times when they disagree on major decisions, get annoyed about something the other person does, or just have spats or fights because they're in a bad mood or tired or for some other reason. They also use many different ways of trying to settle their differences. I . . . would like you to tell me . . . how often you: K. threw something at the other one; L. pushed, grabbed, or shoved the other one; M. slapped your (partner) . . . in the past year.

Those who reported any of the above behavior were classified as having engaged in minor violence. The others were not. In addition, a minor violence count for respondent's spouse was made up of answers to a parallel set of questions. In this case, the respondents acted as informants about their spouses' behavior (see footnote 7). Twelve percent of the respondents (N = 2,122) pushed, shoved, slapped, or threw something at their spouse during the 12 months preceding the interview.

A similar minor violence count was made up of answers to the three parallel items in the parent-child section of the Conflict Tactics Scales (Straus, 1979:77–78):

Parents and children use many different ways of trying to settle differences between them . . . would you like to tell me how often you: K. threw something at . . .; L. pushed, grabbed, or shoved . . .; M. slapped or spanked . . . the child during the last year.

Those who engaged in any of the above behaviors during the past year were classified as having engaged in minor violence. The others were not. Sixty-three percent of the parents (N = 1,146) pushed, shoved, or slapped their child during the 12 months preceding the interview.

Yule's Q will be used as a measure of the consistency between attitude and behavior for two reasons. First, the skewed distribution of one of the dependent variables (respondent's violence agaist spouse) precludes the use of parametric statistics. Second, Yule's Q is an appropriate measure of consistency because it does not make any assumptions about the direction of causality. Our theoretical approach, as stated earlier, and the limitations of cross-sectional data, led to the focus on the consistency between attitude and behavior, as distinguished from the question of whether attitude causes behavior or behavior causes attitude.

ATTITUDES AND BEHAVIOR

The findings show, first, that slapping a 12-year-old is normatively more acceptable than slapping one's spouse. Almost all parents (81.5 percent) expressed at least some approval of one or more of the three parental violence items (belief that slapping a 12-year-old is necessary, normal, or good), and 65 percent indicated approval along all three dimensions (N = 1,098). In contrast, only 27.6 percent of the respondents indicated that slapping a *spouse* was either necessary, normal, or good; and only five percent answered positively on all three dimensions (N = 2,048).

Second, our data show that such attitudes do have at least some relation to actual slapping, especially in relation to parental violence. Of the parents who believe that slapping a 12-year-old is necessary, normal, and good (N = 714), 72 percent actually used violence against their children during the survey year. But, of the respondents who believe that slapping one's *spouse* is necessary, normal, and good (N = 96), only 33 percent reported an actual act of violence against their spouses. Thus, among those with pro-violence attitudes, the consistency is greater in the parent-child relationship than in the husband-wife relationship.

However, among those with nonviolent attitudes, inconsistent behavior is also greater in the parent-child relationship than in the husband-wife relationship.[3] Of the respondents who believe that slapping one's spouse is not necessary, not normal, and bad (N = 1,479), only 8 percent engaged in minor violence against their spouses. In contrast, of the parents who think that slapping a 12-year-old is unnecessary, not normal, and bad (N =

199), over one-third, 37 percent, engaged in violence against their children.[4]

In analyzing these data further, we explored several alternatives: using a typology of attitudes, treating each of the three attitudes in question separately, and creating an index of violent attitudes.[5] It turns out, however, that the findings remain essentially unchanged, whether an index or the single attitude "normal versus not normal," is used. This is the case because there are very few respondents who believe that slapping a member of one's family is not normal, but who believe at the same time that it is necessary and/or good. Believing that slapping another member of one's family is "not normal" is, therefore, an adequate measure of the most antiviolent attitudes. Hence, for simplicity of presentation, we will report only those findings that deal with the "normal-not normal" attitude.

Control for Sex

Parental violence. The findings in the [upper] panel of Table 1 show that, among both mothers and fathers, a pro-violent attitude is related to parent's minor violence. The table also shows that mothers are more likely to slap their children than are fathers (see also Gelles, 1978). However, in relation to the objectives of this paper, the most interesting finding in Table 1 is the fact that there is an inconsistency between attitudes and behavior for a larger proportion of the mothers than the fathers. Among the 117 mothers who believe that slapping a 12-year-old is not normal, 42 percent did actually hit the child and were therefore inconsistent, as opposed to 32 percent of the 116 fathers who engaged in minor violence against their children despite their beliefs to the contrary.

Spousal violence. The findings in the [lower] panel of Table 1 show that, among both husbands and wives, a pro-violent attitude is related to minor violence against one's spouse. Those who believe that slapping one's spouse

TABLE 1.
PERCENTAGE OF RESPONDENTS WHO WERE VIOLENT BY SEX AND BELIEF IN THE NORMALITY OF VIOLENCE

A. Parent-Child Violence

Belief that Slapping a 12-Year-Old is Normal	Percentage of Parents with Minor Violence Against Their Child	
	Fathers	Mothers
Not Normal	32% (116)	42% (117)
Normal	65% (390)	74% (477)

B. Spousal Violence

Belief that Slapping a Spouse is Normal	Percentage of Respondents with Minor Violence Against Their Spouse	
	Husbands	Wives
Not Normal	8% (658)	8% (867)
Normal	24% (259)	22% (264)

is normal are more likely to have pushed, slapped, or thrown something at their spouse than those with an antiviolent attitude. In contrast to the data on fathers and mothers, there is no difference between husbands and wives in the rate of minor violence against their spouse, nor in the percentage who are inconsistent.

STRUCTURAL FACTORS AND PARENTAL VIOLENCE

Role Differentiation

Why do more mothers than fathers tend to be inconsistent in slapping their children when they don't believe in it? This greater inconsistency among mothers is probably due to the fact that full-time mothers tend to spend more time with their children than do fathers. They are more often "at risk" of behaving in a way which is inconsistent with their beliefs.

To test this explanation, we need a measure of the sex-linked division of labor in the family. Although there is no direct measure in the survey of sex-linked division of labor with the family as the unit of analysis, there are six items on segregated decision norms as seen by the husband, and the same six for the wife.[6] The total number of segregated decision norm items is therefore 12. The index has a range of 0–12.

The findings in Table 2 show that the attitude-behavior inconsistency among mothers increases with an increase in the number of segregated decision norms. For mothers who believe that child slapping is not normal, the greater the number of segregated decision norms in the family, the more likely they are to have a minor violence count against their children. For mothers in families with the highest number of segregated decision norms, Yule's Q is smallest (.35), confirming the relatively low consistency between attitude and behavior. In contrast, for fathers in families with the highest number of segregated deci-

sion norms, $Q = .52$, which shows a higher consistency between their attitudes and their behavior.

More detailed analysis produced further data which support the idea that the greater inconsistency of mothers is due to their being the ones responsible for the children most of the time. These mothers tend to be full-time housewives. It is among full-time housewives that number of segregated decision norms increases the inconsistency between attitude and behavior. In families with a low number of segregated decision norms (0–4), 37 percent of the full-time housewives slap their children when they don't believe in it (N = 27). In contrast, in families with a high number of segregated decision norms (8–12), 69 percent of the full-time housewives slap their children when they don't believe in it (N = 29). The number of segregated decision norms seems to have no such effect among mothers who have a full-time job, whether they believe in child slapping or not.

Partner's Violence

One might assume that wives who physically punish their children do the job for their hus-

TABLE 2.
PERCENTAGE OF FATHERS AND MOTHERS WHO WERE VIOLENT TO THEIR CHILDREN BY BELIEF REGARDING THE NORMALITY OF SLAPPING A 12-YEAR-OLD AND BY NUMBER OF SEGREGATED DECISION NORMS

Number of Segregated Decision Norms	Percentage Violent Among *Fathers* Who Believe Slapping Is:			Percentage Violent Among *Mothers* Who Believe Slapping Is:		
	Not Normal	Normal	Q	Not Normal	Normal	Q
0–4	34% (32)	63% (73)	.53	29% (35)	66% (124)	.66
5–7	30% (33)	72% (151)	.70	43% (40)	82% (195)	.71
8–12	36% (42)	64% (135)	.52	61% (36)	77% (133)	.35

BECOMING A MEMBER OF SOCIETY

bands so that the latter do not have to do it themselves. But this is not what the data show. On the contrary, as seen in Table 3, controlling for attitude, both fathers and mothers are much more likely to be violent to their children when their partners have used physical punishment against their children than when they have not.

Table 3 shows that attitude-behavior consistency is greatest among fathers whose wives physically punish their children, while among mothers whose husbands use physical punishment, attitude makes little difference. They are uniformly high on minor violence against their children. A Q of .25 confirms the relatively low consistency of the behavior of those mothers with nonviolent attitudes whose husbands have also physically punished their children. In contrast, among mothers whose husbands do not use physical punishment, the attitude-behavior consistency is increased (Q = .53).

In short, parent's behavior tends to be in agreement with spouse's behavior even if it is in disagreement with respondent's own attitude. The findings suggest that the partner's behavior serves as legitimation or has a reinforcing influence on the parent's own behavior with respect to child punishment.[7] Among mothers, their partners' behavior tends also

to legitimize the respondents' violent behavior towards their children when they appear to have internalized the opposite norm.

Other Social Relationships

What if a third party enters the picture in the form of a relative or friend with whom the respondent has talked about domestic problems? Table 4 shows that talking to relatives and friends about a domestic problem decreases the consistency between attitude and behavior among parents who do not believe in slapping a 12-year-old, but whose spouses have used physical punishment (as shown by the drop in the value of Q from .50 to .20). Also, consulting with relatives and friends increases the consistency between attitude and behavior among parents who believe in slapping a 12-year-old, but whose spouses do not do it (Q = .57). However, among parents whose own attitudes with respect to child punishment are in agreement with their spouses' behavior, consulting with relatives and friends makes little difference with regard to their violent behavior. For example, among parents with a pro-violent attitude whose partner physically punished their child, 88 percent of those who consulted with relatives and friends and 85 percent of

TABLE 3.
PERCENTAGE OF FATHERS AND MOTHERS WHO WERE VIOLENT TO THEIR
CHILDREN BY BELIEF REGARDING THE NORMALITY OF SLAPPING A 12-YEAR-OLD
AND BY ACTUAL PHYSICAL PUNISHMENT OF CHILD BY PARTNER

Partner Physically Punished Child	Percentage Violent Among *Fathers* Who Believe Slapping Is:			Percentage Violent Among *Mothers* Who Believe Slapping Is:		
	Not Normal	Normal	Q	Not Normal	Normal	Q
No	18% (77)	34% (143)	.40	26% (81)	53% (184)	.53
Yes	61% (36)	83% (234)	.52	81% (32)	88% (286)	.25

TABLE 4.

PERCENTAGE OF PARENTS WHO WERE VIOLENT TO THEIR CHILDREN BY ACTUAL PHYSICAL PUNISHMENT OF CHILD BY PARTNER, BY BELIEF REGARDING THE NORMALITY OF SLAPPING A 12-YEAR-OLD, AND BY DISCUSSION OF PROBLEMS WITH RELATIVES AND FRIENDS

Talked About Domestic Problems with Relatives, Friends	Percentage Violent Among Those Whose Partner Hit Child and Who Believe Slapping a 12-Year-Old Is:			Percentage Violent Among Those Whose Partner Did *Not* Hit Child and Who Believe Slapping a 12-Year-Old Is:		
	Not Normal	Normal	Q	Not Normal	Normal	Q
Yes	83% (23)	88% (260)	.20	26% (43)	56% (142)	.57
No	65% (43)	85% (244)	.50	20% (95)	38% (161)	.42

those who did not consult engaged in minor violence.

These findings show that, among those with a nonviolent spouse and a violent attitude or a violent spouse and a nonviolent attitude, consultation with relatives and friends is related to higher rates of violence. If there is a domestic problem and disagreement over the use of violence, consultation with relatives and friends may be a last ditch attempt for those who have a violent spouse and a nonviolent attitude (or vice versa) to resolve the problem. In this case, third parties may sanction the use of violence.

To recapitulate, the data show that the partner's behavior is *vis-a-vis* the child lends further sanctioning to the parent's own behavior. Do these findings also apply to spousal violence? It can be argued that the partner's behavior should make an even greater difference for respondent's own behavior than in the case of physical punishment of children.[8]

STRUCTURAL FACTORS AND MARITAL VIOLENCE

Partner's Violence

The findings in Table 5 are in line with the above reasoning. The data show that for both men and women who believe that slapping one's spouse is normal, violence by their partner increases attitude-behavior consistency.[9] A possible reason for the increase in consistency is that being hit by one's spouse is not just an act of provocation. It also seems to provide moral sanctioning or justification of one's own violent behavior. Spousal violence is most frequent in those families in which the respondent's own violent attitude is accompanied by the violent behavior of the respondent's spouse. This pattern continues despite a control for talking to third parties, such as relatives and friends, about a domestic problem. Whether they have consulted with relatives and friends or not, the majority of these respondents tend to have engaged in minor violence against their spouses.

These findings suggest that, with respect to domestic violence, involvement in a personal network of friends and relatives can support, not only acts which are normative, but also acts which are clearly deviant as far as the "standard" norms of the society are concerned. The following section will attempt to show why this should be the case.

Family Position in the Economic System

Data not reported here show that parents' violence against their children declines only

TABLE 5.
PERCENTAGE OF RESPONDENTS WHO WERE VIOLENT TO THEIR SPOUSES BY BELIEF REGARDING THE NORMALITY OF SLAPPING A SPOUSE AND BY MARITAL PARTNER'S VIOLENCE

Was Marital Partner Violent?	Percentage of *Husbands* Who Hit Spouse Among Husbands Who Believe Slapping a Spouse Is:			Percentage of *Wives* Who Hit Spouse Among Wives Who Believe Slapping a Spouse Is:		
	Not Normal	Normal	Q	Not Normal	Normal	Q
No	5% (607)	9% (196)	.31	4% (794)	6% (202)	.23
Yes	57% (42)	76% (58)	.40	52% (62)	74% (61)	.45

TABLE 6.
PERCENTAGE OF RESPONDENTS WHO WERE VIOLENT TO THEIR SPOUSES BY BELIEF REGARDING THE NORMALITY OF SLAPPING A SPOUSE, BY MARITAL PARTNER'S VIOLENCE AND BY TOTAL FAMILY INCOME

Total Family Income	Percentage Violent Among Those Whose Partner is Nonviolent and Who Believe Couple Slapping Is:			Percentage Violent Among Those Whose Partner is Violent and Who Believe Couple Slapping Is:		
	Not Normal	Normal	Q	Not Normal	Normal	Q
0-$11,999	5% (414)	10% (122)	.34	67% (39)	71% (63)	.11
$12,000 or more	4% (854)	7% (254)	.24	49% (59)	78% (49)	.56

in the highest income group ($20,000 or more). In contrast, violence against spouses decreases as income goes up. The lower the total family income, the greater the probability of violence (see O'Brien, 1971; Straus et al., 1979). The two-variable relationships are significant, even though they are not very strong. On the other hand, *belief* that for a husband or wife to slap the other is normal, is not related to income. These findings suggest that the family's position in the economic system affects the role relationships inside the family but not attitudes about violence.

The findings in Table 6 show that, when the marital partner has not engaged in vio-

lence, there is a low rate of spousal violence, irrespective of attitude or income. However, among those who have marital partners who have hit them, being in the lower income groups sharply decreases the consistency between attitudes and behavior (as shown by the decrease in Q from .56 to .11).

Other analyses of the data show that the above findings tend to hold for women rather than for men. That is, lower-income women who consider slapping "not normal" but whose husbands have hit them, are highly inconsistent. Very likely these are the women who hit in self-defense or just "hit back." But, among women in the higher income groups who have been hit by their husbands, being pro-violent increases the consistency between attitude and behavior.[10]

Among husbands who have been hit by their wives, those who have a pro-violent attitude are more likely to have been violent than those who do not. This is especially pronounced in the lower income groups though the Ns are too small to draw any definite conclusions. However, the data are in line with another finding. Among men, the lower the total family income, the greater the consistency of those respondents who believe that slapping one's spouse is normal. Of the husbands who have a total family income under $6,000, 52 percent of those who believe that slapping one's spouse is normal (N = 23) engaged in minor violence against their spouse as against 13 percent of those who have the nonviolent attitude (N = 64). In contrast, among the husbands with a total family income of $20,000 or more, only 11 percent of those who believe that slapping one's spouse is normal (N = 74) and 7 percent of those with the nonviolent attitude (N = 185) were actually violent.

We think that these findings reflect the fact that lower-income husbands are less able to fulfill the provider role and are, therefore, less able to live up to the expectations of other family members than are husbands with higher incomes (Rodman, 1968). In contrast to the higher social classes, in which husbands have more prestige, money, and power, lower-income men have no such resources to fall back on to control their wives. Physical violence can be used as a resource by lower-class men to control their wives when other resources are lacking (Allen and Straus, 1979; Steinmetz and Straus, 1974). In the higher income groups, men are able to control their wives in other than violent ways. "Money belongs to him who earns it, not her who spends it, since he who earns it may withhold it" (Hill and Becker, 1955:790). Violence is, therefore, used as a means to obtain a socially approved goal, namely the leadership role in

the family, when society withholds legitimate means to obtain that goal (Merton, 1938).

Another reason why marital violence is somewhat less frequent in higher-income families than in lower-income families may be because middle-class women have internalized a social-emotional, expressive, supportive role to a greater extent than have working-class woman. This is, in part, because of different socialization patterns and, in part, because they are compensated in other ways, namely through the prestige, power, and income of their husbands' positions (Goode, 1971). For these reasons, middle-class wives with nonviolent attitudes are less likely to retaliate when they are hit by their spouses than are their lower-class counterparts.

CONCLUSION

It is now possible to answer the questions posed at the beginning of this paper: to what extent are social structural variables, such as patterns of interaction inside the family and the family's position in the economic system, related to domestic violence and to the consistency or inconsistency between attitudes and behavior?

The findings show that attitudes and behavior are indeed related. However, they also show that *violent behavior by the spouse has a much greater impact on the respondent's violence than the respondent's own attitudes about violence.* This applies to both hitting one's child and hitting one's spouse. With respect to spousal violence, the consistency between attitude and behavior is greatest among those respondents who have pro-violence attitudes and a violent partner.

More generally, the findings suggest that consistency between attitude and behavior depends, not simply on a person's attitude, but also on social structural factors which reinforce or inhibit violent behavior. Whether one's behavior is consistent with one's beliefs about violence (*e.g.*, slapping a spouse when one believes this is permissible under certain circumstances, or not slapping a spouse when one believes this is never permissible), depends on being in roles and life circumstances which bring forth behavior that is consistent. Consistency can also occur by being in life circumstances which make it unnecessary to engage in the behavior believed to be wrong.

For example, low-income husbands are less in a position to live up to their role obligations as providers than are middle-class husbands. Their wives are, therefore, less likely to recognize the male as the head of the house than are their middle-class counterparts. When such recognition and other resources are lacking, husbands may, in turn, use force to control their wives. Thus, lack of resources increases the consistency between attitude and behavior among those husbands who have a pro-violent attitude.

In contrast, among high-income husbands, attitude about spousal violence shows little relation to behavior. They may approve of slapping a wife under certain circumstances, but they are uniformly low in actual slapping. We suggest that this is because high-income husbands have economic and prestige resources which let them control their wives without the need to use force.

Turning now to wives, the higher the total family income, the greater the consistency between their attitudes and behavior with respect to spousal violence even when they have been hit by their husbands. Middle-class wives less often have paid employment and are economically more dependent on their husbands than are wives from lower-income families. They are, therefore, more likely than their lower-class counterparts to practice what they have been taught to believe in, namely to refrain from hitting their husbands. The risks and costs involved in doing otherwise are great.

Lower-class wives are more likely to be hit than their middle-class counterparts. Furthermore, the data show that being hit by one's spouse has a greater impact on respondent's violent behavior than respondent's own attitude. These findings, plus the lack of access to resources, might account for the fact that lower-class wives who have been hit by their husbands tend to have a relatively high rate of spousal violence, irrespective of attitude.

In short, the results of this research show that the consistency between attitude and behavior cannot be taken for granted in the study of family violence. Patterns of interaction with spouse and kin are at least as important in the study of domestic violence as are respondents' attitudes. These patterns of interaction, in turn, are related to the extent to which the environment facilitates or inhibits the performance of various roles in the family, such as that of parent, provider, or spouse.

NOTES

[1] These findings are consistent with some of the studies reviewed by Liska (1974, 1975) which show an inconsistency between attitude and behavior. The classic study indicating a lack of association between attitude and behavior is that by LaPiere (1934). LaPiere discovered that there was little relationship between hotel-managers' verbally expressed attitudes concerning the accommodation of a Chinese couple and their actual behavior. For a review of the literature on the consistency between attitude and behavior, see Schuman and Johnson (1976).

[2] A description of the sampling procedures is given in Straus et al., 1979. Eligible families consisted of a couple who identified themselves as married or being a "couple" (man and woman living together as a conjugal unit). A random procedure was used so that approximately half of the respondents would be male and half female. Interviews were conducted with 960 men and 1,183 women.

[3] When we discuss those with a *violent* attitude, the percentages in the tables indicate the degree of consistency between the respondent's attitude and violent behavior. When we discuss those with a *nonviolent* attitude, the percentages in the tables indicate the degree of *inconsistency* between the respondent's attitude and violent behavior.

[4]The relationship between parental attitudes and parental behavior has a Q of .59, while the relationship between spousal attitudes and behavior has a Q of .56.

[5]The index in question assigns a code of 0 to all respondents who believe that slapping a member of one's family is unnecessary, not normal, and bad; and it assigns a code of 1 to everyone else.

[6]These involve normative expectations on who should have the final say on: "Buying a car; Having children; What house or apartment to take; What job your (husband/partner) should take; Whether you should go to work or quit work; How much money to spend on food per week" (answers: wife only or mostly; or husband only or mostly). In about half of the cases, husbands were interviewed. They also acted as informants concerning their wives' beliefs. In about half of the cases, wives were interviewed who also acted as informants about their husbands' beliefs.

[7]This implicit legitimation by the spouse seems to be important also in families with a high number of segregated decision norms. For example, in families with a high number of segregated decision norms (8–12) in which the spouse also uses physical punishment, 100 percent of the mothers who do not believe in slapping (N = 14), and 92 percent of the mothers who think slapping a 12-year-old is normal (N = 73) were violent.

[8]It will be remembered that the respondent was the wife in a random half of the sample, and the husband in the other half of the cases. The reader may wonder to what extent we can depend on the husband to accurately report the frequency of the wife's violence and vice versa. A detailed analysis of the accuracy of respondent's reports when respondent is used as an informant (Bulcroft and Straus, 1975) suggests that the latter depends on the type of information gathered. Fortunately, the data show that the incidence rates obtained for husband's violence using the husband as the respondent (12.8 per hundred) are almost identical to the incidence rates obtained when asking the wives about the husband's violence (12.9). Similarly, the incidence of violence per hundred wives is 11.2 when the data are based on interviewing husbands, and 11.5 when they are based on interviewing wives. Of course, this similarity could come about in a number of ways; for example, the spouses might be reporting only incidents in which both were violent. That this was not the case can be seen from the fact that violence was reported for only one of the two spouses in about half the couples among whom there was a violent incident during the survey year.

[9]There might appear to be an interaction effect in Table 5, but the relationships are additive. In this as in most other tables, we used hierarchical models as developed by Goodman (1970, 1971, 1972) and exposited by Davis (1973-1974) to test for interaction effects. The final hierarchical model for the data in Table 6 is additive. It consists of four two-variable relationships: Sex, Attitude; Attitude, Respondent's Minor Violence Count; Attitude, Partner's Minor Violence Count; Partner's Minor Violence Count, Respondent's Minor Violence Count. The final model has a *Chi*-Square Likelihood Ratio of 2.5556 with 7 D.F. The Probability of *Chi*-Square = 0.9226.

[10]Among wives whose husbands have hit them and who are in the 0-$11,999 income group, 67 percent of those with the nonviolent attitude (N = 24) and 62 percent of those with the pro-violent attitude (N = 29) were actually violent. In contrast, among women who have been hit by their spouses and who are in the $12,000 or more income group, 45 percent of the antiviolent (N = 33) as opposed to 86 percent of the pro-violent (N = 28) were actually violent to their spouse.

REFERENCES

Allen, Craig M., and Murray A. Straus
  1979 "Resources, power, and husband-wife violence." Chapter 12 in M. A. Straus and G. T. Hotaling (Eds.), The Social Causes of Husband-Wife Violence. Minneapolis: University of Minnesota Press.

Ball-Rokeach, Sandra J.
  1973 "Values and violence: A test of the subculture of violence thesis." American Sociological Review 38 (December): 736–749.

Bulcroft, Richard A., and Murray A. Straus
  1975 "Validity of husband, wife, and child reports of conjugal violence and power." Unpublished manuscript, University of New Hampshire (mimeo).

Davis, James A.
  1973– "The Goodman system for significance tests in
  1974 multivariate contingency tables." Pp. 189–231 in Herbert L. Costner (Ed.), Sociological Methodology. San Francisco: Jossey-Bass.

Gelles, Richard J.
  1978 "Violence towards children in the United States." American Journal of Orthopsychiatry 48 (4): 580–592.

Goode, William J.
  1960 "A theory of role strain." American Sociological Review 25 (August):483–496.
  1971 "Force and violence in the family." Journal of Marriage and the Family 33 (November): 624–636.

Goodman, Leo A.
  1970 "The multivariate analysis of qualitative data: Interaction among multiple classifications." Journal of the American Statistical Association 65 (March): 226–256.
  1971 "The analysis of multidimensional contingency tables: Stepwise procedures and direct estimation methods for building models for multiple classifications." Technometrics 13 (February): 33–61.
  1972 "A general model for the analysis of surveys." American Journal of Sociology 77 (May): 1035–1086.

Hill, Reuben, and Howard P. Becker (Eds.)
  1955 "Plans for strengthening family life." Pp. 773–806 in R. Hill (Ed.), Family, Marriage and Parenthood. Boston: D. C. Heath.

LaPiere, Richard T.
  1934 "Attitudes vs. actions." Social Forces 13 (December): 230–237.

Liska, A. E.
  1974 "Emergent issues in the attitude-behavior consistency controversy." American Sociological Review 39 (April): 261–272.
  1975 The Consistency Controversy: Readings on the Impact of Attitude on Behavior. New York: John Wiley and Sons.

Merton, Robert K.
  1938 "Social structure and anomie." American Sociological Review 3 (October): 672–682.

Osgood, Charles, George Suci, and Perry Tannenbaum

  1957 The Measurement of Meaning. Urbana, Illinois: University of Illinois Press.

Rodman, Hyman
  1968 "Family and social pathology in the ghetto." Science 161 (August): 756–762.

Schuman, Howard, and Michael P. Johnson
  1976 "Attitudes and behavior." Pp. 161–207 in Alex Inkeles (Ed.), Annual Review of Sociology 2. Palo Alto: Annual Review Inc.

Steinmetz, Suzanne K., and Murray A. Straus (Eds.)
  1974 Violence in the Family. New York: Harper and Row.

Straus, Murray A.
  1977 "Normative and behavioral aspects of violence between spouses: Preliminary data on a nationally representative USA sample." Paper presented at the Symposium on Violence in Canadian Society, Simon Fraser University (March).
  1979 "Measuring intrafamily conflict and violence: The Conflict Tactics (CT) Scales." Journal of Marriage and the Family 41 (February): 75–88.

Straus, Murray A., Richard J. Gelles, and Suzanne K. Steinmetz
  1979 Behind Closed Doors: Violence in the American Family. New York: Anchor/Doubleday.

Straus, Murray A., and Gerald T. Hotaling (Eds.)
  1979 The Social Causes of Husband-Wife Violence. Minneapolis: University of Minnesota Press.

Walker, Lenore E.
  1977– "Battered women and learned helplessness."
  1978 Victimology 2 (3–4): 525–534.

11

THE PETER PRINCIPLE

Raymond Hull

Bunglers are always with us and always have been. Winston Churchill tells us, in his history of World War II, that in August, 1940, he had to take charge personally of the Armed

Forces' Joint Planning Committee because, after almost twelve months of war, the Committee had not originated a single plan.

In the 1948 Presidential election, the advance public-opinion polls awarded an easy victory to Thomas E. Dewey. In the Fifties, there was the Edsel bungle. In 1965, Hous-

---

ton's domed baseball stadium opened and was so ill-suited to baseball that, on sunny days, fielders could not see fly balls against the blinding glare from the skylights.

We have come to expect incompetence as a necessary feature of civilization. We may be irked, but we are no longer amazed, when our bosses make idiotic decisions, when automobile makers take back thousands of new cars for repairs, when store clerks are insolent, when law reforms fail to check crime, when moon rockets can't get off the ground, when widely used medicines are found to be poisons, when universities must teach freshmen to read, or when a hundred-ton airliner is brought down by a duck.

We see these malpractices and mishaps as unconnected accidents, inevitable results of human fallibility.

But one man says, "These occurrences are not accidents; they are simply the fruits of a system which, as I have shown, *develops, perpetuates and rewards incompetence.*"

The Newton of incompetence theory is a burly, black-haired, slow-spoken Canadian philosopher and iconoclast, Dr. Lawrence J. Peter, who made his living as Assistant Professor of Education at the University of British Columbia until recently, when he moved down the coast to become a Professor of Education at the University of Southern California.

There is nothing incompetent about Dr. Peter. He is a successful author: his *Prescriptive Teaching* is a widely used text on the education of problem children. He built a house with his own hands, makes his own wine, is an expert cook, a skilled woodcarver, and an inventor. (He created a new tool rack for school woodwork shops and perfected an apparatus for marking fifty exam papers at once). Yet his chief claim to fame may be his founding of the science of hierarchiology.

"Hierarchiology," he says, "is the study of hierarchies. 'Hierarchy' originally meant 'church government by clergy graded into ranks.' The term now includes any organiza-

tion whose members or employees are arranged by rank or grade.

"Early in life, I faced the problem of occupational incompetence. As a young schoolteacher I was shocked, baffled, to see so many knot-heads as principals, inspectors and superintendents.

"I questioned older teachers. All I could find was that the knot-heads, earlier in their careers, had been capable, and that was why they had been promoted.

"Eventually I realized that the same phenomenon occurs in all trades and professions, because the same basic rule governs the climb through every hierarchy. A competent employee is eligible for promotion, but incompetence is a bar to promotion. So an employee's final position must be one for which he is incompetent!

"Suppose you own a drug-manufacturing firm, Perfect Pill Incorporated. Your foreman pill-roller dies of a perforated ulcer; you seek a replacement among the rank-and-file pill-rollers. Miss Cylinder, Mrs. Ellipse and Mr. Cube are variously incompetent and so don't qualify. You pick the best pill-roller, Mr. Sphere, and promote him to foreman.

"Suppose Sphere proves highly competent in this new job; later, when deputy-works-manager Legree moves up one step, Sphere will take his place.

"But if Sphere is incompetent as foreman, he won't be promoted again. He has reached what I call his *level of incompetence* and there he will stay till he retires."

An employee may, like Mr. Cube, reach his level of incompetence at the lowest rank: he is never promoted. It may take one promotion to place him at his level of incompetence; it may take a dozen. But, sooner or later, he does attain it.

Dr. Peter cites the case of the late General A. Jacks.[1] "His hearty manner, informal dress, scorn for petty regulations and disregard for personal safety made him the idol of his men. He led them from victory to victory.

"Had the war ended sooner, Jacks might

have retired, covered in glory. But he was promoted to the rank of field marshal. Now he had to deal, not with fighting men, but with politicians of his own country, and with two punctilious Allied field marshals.

"He quarreled with them all and took to spending whole days drunk, sulking in his trailer. The conduct of the war slipped out of his hands and into those of his subordinates.

"The final promotion had brought him from doing what he *could* do, to attempting what he could not do. He had reached his level of incompetence."

The Jacks case exemplified the Peter Principle, the basic theorem of hierarchiology. *In a hierarchy each employee tends to rise to his level of incompetence: every post tends to be occupied by an employee incompetent to execute its duties.*

How is it, then, that any work is done at all? Peter says, "Work is done by people who have not yet attained final placement at their level of incompetence."

And how is it that we occasionally see a competent person at the very top of a hierarchy? "Simply because there are not enough ranks for him to have reached his level of incompetence; in other words, *in that hierarchy* there is no task beyond his abilities.

"As a rule, such a prodigy of competence eventually sidesteps into another hierarchy—say from the Armed Forces into industry, from law to politics, from business to government—and there finds his level of incompetence. A well-known example is Macbeth, a successful general, but an incompetent king."

In an unpublished monograph, *The Pathology of Success: Morbidity and Mortality at the Level of Incompetence,* Peter expands his theory to take in matters of health.

"Certain physical conditions are associated with final placement: peptic ulcers, high blood pressure, nervous disorders, migraine headaches, alcoholism, insomnia, obesity and cardiovascular complaints. Obviously such symptoms indicate the patient's constitutional incompetence for his level of responsibility.

"Edgar Allan Poe, a highly competent writer, proved incompetent when raised to the rank of editor. He became 'nervous in a very unusual degree,' took to drink and then to drugs in a vain search for relief."

Such ailments, usually appearing two or more together, constitute the Final Placement Syndrome.

"Medication and surgery are often prescribed for F.P.S. patients, but they miss the root cause of the condition. Psychoanalysis fails for the same reason. The analyst is probing into the patient's subconscious for Oedipus complex, castration-complex, penis-envy or whatnot, when the trouble really lies outside, in the patient's hierarchal placement."

Is there no escape? Must every worker reach his level of incompetence, suffer the miseries of Final Placement Syndrome, and become a laughingstock for his behavioral or temperamental symptoms?

Peter describes two escape routes. The first is for a man who realizes that he has reached his level of incompetence, yet still wants to preserve health, self-respect, and sanity.

"Many an employee adjusts to final placement by the process of Substitution. Instead of executing his proper duties, he substitutes a set of irrelevant duties, and these self-imposed tasks he carries out to perfection.

"A. L. Tredwell, assistant principal of a secondary school, was intellectually competent and maintained good relationships with teachers, students and parents. He was promoted to principal. Soon it became clear that he lacked the finesse to deal with newspaper reporters, school-board members and the district superintendent. He fell out of favor with the officials, and his school lost community support. Realizing consciously or subconsciously—it doesn't matter which—that he was incompetent for the proper duties of a principal, Tredwell *Substituted*. He developed an obsessive concern with the movement of students and staff about the school.

"He drew complex plans of traffic-flow,

had white lines painted on floors and arrows on walls, spent hours prowling the building looking for violations of his rules, and bombarded professional journals with articles about his scheme.

"Tredwell's Substitution is a great success. He is active and contented now, and shows no sign of the Final Placement Syndrome."

Peter's alternate escape route is for the employee who is capably and happily doing his work and who wants to avoid ever reaching his level of incompetence.

Merely to *refuse* promotion seldom leads to happiness. It annoys one's superiors, rouses suspicion among one's peers, and shames one's wife and children. Few people can endure all that. So one must contrive never to be *offered* promotion.

The first step is to avoid asking, or seeming to ask, for it. The oft-heard complaint, "My job lacks challenge," is usually understood as showing desire for promotion. So don't give voice to such complaints!

The second step is described by Peter in his lecture, Creative Incompetence: "I have found some employees who are contented in their work, and who seem to be using effective means of maintaining their position.

"Adam Greenaway, a gardener, happily tends the landscaped grounds of the Ideal Trivet Company. He is competent in all aspects of his work but one: He keeps losing delivery slips for goods received. He gives vague explanations such as 'I must have planted the papers with the shrubs.' Most important, he concealed the fact that he wanted to avoid promotion.

"Lack of delivery slips so upsets the accounting department that, when a new maintenance foreman was needed, Greenaway was not considered for the post.

"Thus he could stay indefinitely at a level of incompetence and enjoy the keen personal satisfaction of regularly accomplishing useful work. Surely this offers as great a challenge as the traditional drive for higher rank!"

By his Darwinian Extension Theorem, Peter applies his Principle to the whole human race. Man may go the way of the dinosaur and the sabre-tooth tiger. Those beasts were destroyed by excessive development of the qualities—bulk and fangs—that had originally favored their survival. Man's cleverness was originally a survival characteristic, but now he has become clever enough to destroy himself. If he takes that step, he will achieve his ultimate level of incompetence, in proving himself unfit to live.

"Man's one hope," says Peter, "lies in hierarchiology. I feel that it will soon be recognized as the supreme science. Earlier sociological studies have insufficiently recognized man's hierarchal nature.

"A knowledge of the Peter Principle becomes more and more important as hierarchal systems become stronger. Government and education are prime examples. Both already swollen, both expanding their demands for money and manpower, both extending their influence as more people stay longer in school, and as government controls more functions of life. Even industry, once a stronghold of individualism, is largely an aggregation of hierarchies. My point is that man ought to be using the hierarchal system for his benefit. But he can't possibly use it unless he understands it, and to do that he must understand the Peter Principle. Failing such understanding, the system will destroy the individuals who comprise it."

Many people accept the Peter Principle on first hearing. It sounds so obvious, so like common sense; it explains so aptly a group of hitherto mystifying phenomena.

In academic circles, however, the Principle has made little impression. A few of Peter's subordinates when he was at the University of British Columbia grasped it, but none of his superiors. Some of them saw it as a humorous trifle, others as sociological heresy. Said Peter at the time: "I'm neither primarily funny nor unfunny. I study society scientifically because I must live in it. I present my findings to you because they describe the world you live in.

"Anyway, I'm too busy to worry much about what others think of me. I teach future schoolteachers how to work with handicapped and disturbed children. I'm pursuing two fascinating lines of research: into autism, a profound emotional disorder in which children have no sense of self, and no ability to learn by experience; and into developmental dyslexia, an inability to recognize printed words that often, tragically, pins a 'mentally retarded' label on a genuinely intelligent child. It's all deeply satisfying: I'm about as happy in my work as anyone I know."

The thought then occurred that Peter's hierarchiology might, just might, be *his* form of Creative Incompetence—a means of making himself slightly suspect, and so avoiding an unwanted academic promotion.

"No, no! Of course not!" said the doctor. "But even if it were, of course I wouldn't admit it!"

NOTE

[1] It is Dr. Peter's usual practice to employ fictitious names in his case histories.

12

THE WYNN PRINCIPLE

Richard Wynn

Like most men, I yearn to immortalize my name through famous work. This can be done by recognizing a common phenomenon and expressing it as a scientific principle. Archimedes, Pythagoras, Boyle, and Charles, among others, have accomplished this in the physical sciences. In the social sciences, Gresham's Law, Parkinson's Law, and the Peter Principle have immortalized their discoverers. After nearly a decade of research, I have finally discovered the principle that will immortalize the name Wynn.

Reprinted from *Phi Delta Kappan* © February 1973, by permission of the publisher and the author.

The fateful clue came to me when I learned that the New York City Board of Education renamed its chief school administrator "chancellor." Why this change to a more esoteric job title? A few days later, quite by accident, the answer came to me in a piece of junk mail from a local cemetery. I was immediately struck by the euphemistic language of the letter. One was not asked to buy a cemetery lot but rather to "invest in a memorial estate." It was never suggested that the client's remains would simply be buried there but rather that he would "repose in eternal slumber in the Garden of Peace." The letter made it clear that the deal could be consummated not by an ordinary cemetery lot salesman but by a "pre-need counselor." New York City is right. The superintendent of school, like the cemetery lot salesman, suffers from the banality of his title. We come now to the Wynn Principle: *The esotericism of job titles must be escalated with the rising affluence of a society.*

This trend from banal to more esoteric job titles has been all about us, even in schools. School librarians have become "instructional materials center coordinators." Truant officers have been transformed into "home and school visitors." Dancing teachers have become "instructors in studios of the cultural arts." Secretaries are sometimes spoken of as "executive assistants." Janitors have become "custodians." College deans of men and women have become "vice presidents for student affairs." Book salesmen, later "publishing company representatives," have now become "travelers," evidently because they enjoy traveling more than selling books.

As any scholar of the telephone book yellow pages knows, the trend is well under way in other occupations. Barbers are giving way to "hair stylists." Cosmetic salesladies have been replaced by "beauty consultants" even when their own appearance reveals their ineptitude. Radio and TV announcers have been transformed into "news analysts," which has not gone unnoticed by that diligent observer of the American scene, Spiro Agnew. Stock brokers are almost always "financial securities advisers" nowadays, a change that has cost many of their clients a small fortune. No self-respecting person would patronize a fortune teller, but "consultants in the occult" are doing a thriving business. Termite eradicators are being replaced by "hygienic sanitation services," but don't ask these people to clean out your septic tank. That job calls for "sewage sanitation service." And so it goes.

Why is this move toward more pretentious job titles so pervasive? For one thing, the more esoteric nomenclature creates a certain aura that reduces harassment from clients. You and I would have no compunction about telling a garbage man to keep his grubby hands off the delphinium. But if he were a "sanitation system engineer" you would intervene in his professional practice only at the risk of drowning in your own garbage.

Or take the chancellor of education. No one hesitates these day to storm the office of the superintendent of schools, accuse him of being a fascist pig, drive him out, and rifle his desk. Indeed this has become almost a national pastime. But invading the office of a "chancellor," with its almost divine aura, is a considerably more sobering adventure, to be undertaken only by the most intrepid infidel. The "chancellor" is surely a more formidable figure at the bargaining table than the superintendent. Wouldn't it take a lot more guts to fire a chancellor than a superintendent?

We can now state Corollary Alpha of the Wynn Principle: The degree of harassment from clients is in inverse proportion to the esoterica of one's job title.

Then too, the more exotic titles justify higher wages. Five bucks is plenty for a doctor to examine your hemorrhoids, but $50 is not a bit too much for a proctologist to detect varicose dilations in your rectum. School business managers never made much money, but "vice chancellors for fiscal affairs" drive Cadillacs.

Taking our earlier example, one might reasonably ask the cemetery lot salesman whether $2,000 isn't a lot for a lot. But if you are dealing with a "pre-need counselor," you can't be sure that he doesn't hold advanced degrees in theology, realty, embalming, and psychology. He seems capable of transforming metaphysically your whole concept of death and interment, able to rescue you after death from the status of rotting corpse to some kind of earthly immortality while "slumbering in eternal repose in the Garden of Peace." Doesn't that beat being dead? Two thousand dollars would be a modest sum when viewed as an investment in the perpetuity of self and loved ones. Only a slob could balk at the price now.

These observations permit expression of Corollary Beta of the Wynn Principle: The fee which one can command for his services is in direct proportion to the pretentiousness of his job title.

Think of the greater sense of personal worth and dignity one derives from the nobler job titles. Colleges discovered years ago that promotion from assistant to associate professor could be accepted by faculty in lieu of salary increases with no loss in morale. Who wouldn't prefer "metals reclamation" work to being a junk dealer? No cocktail waitress ever was asked to join the Junior League, but a Playboy Club bunny might have a chance.

Take the most beleaguered occupation of all these days, the policeman. He is in desperate need of status rehabilitation by upgrading his title. The public image of this once respected public servant has sunk to dangerous lows, largely because of the banality of his job title. Nobody likes to be policed. If we could transform his title to "protector of public safety," the endearing acronym "pops" could then replace "pig." Consider the salubrious effect this would have on his image. Think of how much more kindly you could feel toward the man who is crashing his night stick on your head if you knew that your safety was being protected.

Many occupations, like the superintendency and the policman, are overdue for title reform. Prostitutes gave way years ago to call girls, but this ancient profession should now be further enhanced by the more pretentious title "copulation consultant." Pimps could become "intimate interpersonal relations brokers" or "present-need counselors." Undoubtedly the reader will think of other examples.

We can now state Corollary Gamma of the Wynn Principle: One's social status is directly proportional to the esotericism of his job title.

Does the escalation of job titles result in change of function? The evidence suggests that it does not. The "vice chancellor for fiscal affairs" still redlines your requisitions in much the same way that the old business manager did. "Custodians" still rearrange furniture to suit themselves just as janitors did. "Home and school visitors" still run down truants. "Exotic artists" or ecdysiasts still dispense the same old bumps and grinds that strip-tease dancers have these many years. Although salesmen have been displaced almost entirely by "consultants," "analysts," "travelers," and "pre-need counselors," among others, the closing of the sale is no less important. It is only that the sales pitch is now more adroit and erudite.

We come now to Corollary Delta of the Wynn Principle: Job functions are largely unrelated to the escalation of job titles.

Obviously, the process of upgrading job titles is never-ending. Inflation invariably sets in. As titles such as "counselor" or "superintendent" become more common, they must be replaced if esotericism is to be maintained. When cities are teeming with superintendents of sewage, housing, parks, and highways, it is evident that the "superintendent of schools" has been cheapened. But in time the same thing will happen with "chancellors." When we have chancellors of sewage and whatnot, that once noble title will have to be replaced.

This phenomenon leads us to Corollary Epsilon of the Wynn Principle: The esotericism of job titles tends toward endless cycles of inflation in a highly industrialized society.

Undoubtedly other corollaries of this important principle will be derived now that the generalization has been discovered and enunciated. This is the manner in which man's knowledge is extended. The general principle is again stated: *The esotericism of job titles must be escalated with the rising affluence of a society.* It is not imperative that the reader remember the phrasing of the principle, but it is important that the name of its discoverer be remembered: Wynn.

V

STRATIFICATION
Some Are More Equal Than Others!

The Declaration of Independence states that "all men are created equal"—a statement that is more hopeful than factual. In the United States there exists a stratified class structure, and we are all aware that some Americans are more equal than others. As we noted earlier, class ranking significantly affects almost all facets of our lives. Unequal distribution of wealth and occupational opportunity creates inequality in one's chances for life expectancy, health, and education; it affects the kind of legal protection and justice we receive. Class status influences our values, our beliefs, our personalities, and hundreds of other aspects of living in society. Finally, ranking can determine our control over the life chances of others.

This last point—the power of some groups over others—is the hidden agenda of the three articles in this chapter. Cavanaugh, in the first article, notes that people's chances of gaining and holding on to middle-class status are declining since their life chances at gaining middle-class attributes—a college education, a professional job, a home—are also declining, and they are, apparently, powerless to change these conditions. However, most Americans would still rank themselves as middle-class and think that their life chances are improving due to the acquisition of other status symbols. In the second article, Fallers refers to this illusion as the "trickle effect." He notes that although people may not actually be improving their class position, they feel that they are moving upward (*social mobility*) because cheaper copies of cherished consumer goods are trickling down to their level, thus reinforcing their perception that they have a higher class position than they do, and that "equal opportunity" is a reality.

Gans's article on the Dirty Work Movement reveals more directly, while humorously, the power struggle to attain and maintain a class position. For Gans, power rather than occupation is the most important factor in determining class position.

As you read the articles in this chapter, ask yourself why "democratic" Americans accept a class structure whose result is inequality.

13

THE SHRINKING MIDDLE CLASS

Gerald Cavanaugh

Clearly one need not be a Marxist to see a connection between political power and the possession of property. Nor do only Marxists perceive in all settled societies the reality or possibility of class struggle. If the blessed poor are always with us, so too are the damned rich and, in fortunate societies, the vital, moderate middle. The tensions, envy, contempt, and conflict that characterize relations between these classes have exercised social theorists at least since the time of Aristotle. Of all modern societies, only the United States claims to have escaped the condition of—or at least to have blunted the imperatives of—class conflict. The United States has been and is, allegedly, an overwhelmingly single-class—that is, middle-class—society.

This popular self-image of a middle-class country has some basis in statistics and in historical, economic, and social circumstances. The statistics, however, have never warranted so broad a definition of a middle-class society; that conception is, in fact, an "ideology," in the sense of a "false consciousness." And the circumstances that fostered the ideology are rapidly and irreversibly dissolving. That middle class to which most Americans still aspire and in whose reflected glory we all bask— that middle class, never as large as our pro-

pagandists and our self-delusions portrayed it—is rapidly shrinking.

To speak of "shrinking" requires an understanding of the original size of the entity, and here we run into difficulty. The usual definition of "middle class" is a confused mixture of subjective and objective criteria. The image is further blurred by mass media portrayals in which *everybody* is middle class.

Income, life style, social status, family relations, marriage patterns, education, social expectations, and race all enter into the general conception of the American middle class. However, family income is usually the basic determining factor. One may be poor and yet be an aristocrat, but to be middle-class requires a certain minimum family income.

In 1976, Robert Heilbroner defined the "economic middle class" as consisting of those families whose income "ranges from $15,000, where the working class stops, to $32,000, where the upper class begins," and calculated that this included 35 per cent of all families in the nation. Last July, *The New York Times* published a story headed "Tax Cuts to Favor Middle Class," and defined this as "taxpayers in the $15,000-to-$40,000-a-year range." However, an income of $15,000 did not suffice to support a middle-class life style even in 1976; it is certainly inadequate today, when the Bureau of Labor Statistics (BLS) claims $17,106 is required for a "moderate" or "middle-class" standard of living.

The 1978 BLS analysis of urban family budgets concluded that a family income of $25,202 suffices for a minimum "higher-level" standard of living. The "lower-level" minimum is $10,481, while the "poverty line" is $6,200. These figures, as Andrew Levison has emphasized, "automatically define the three distinct socioeconomic cultures in the United States, the culture of poverty, working-class culture, and the life-style of middle-class affluence."

Thus defined, the middle class shrinks from the popular, even "official" 30 to 35 percent of all families to less than 20 percent: Only 18 percent of American families enjoy incomes of $25,000 or more. And even this figure is misleading, since 80 percent of those families have at least two members working and 30 percent include three or more workers.

Having clarified the present size of our "middle class," we may now consider the shrinkage it is experiencing. That shrinkage is the result of fundamental, long-term, structural economic and social changes we have experienced over the past decade—changes that derive from the new form of our "post-industrial" productive system, from demographic pressures, and from the combination of inflation and slow economic growth.

Inflation, for example, has drastically limited access to housing, one of the salient characteristics of middle-class life. In the three decades from 1938 to 1968, Federal programs and economic conditions enabled many middle-*income* families to obtain mortgages on homes, and about half of the country's families did. Today, because of inflation, only the top 20 percent of families can afford new homes. And the situation is even worse than that—almost half the new homebuyers are married, childless, working couples.

This new system of childless families with dual incomes represents, in the words of a spokesman for the U. S. League of Savings and Loan Associations, "an extraordinarily significant social trend. There is no question that savings and loan firms are including sec-ondary incomes and that a lot of homebuyers could not buy homes without them." *The Wall Street Journal* reported last summer that in one area of renovated buildings in New Orleans, the average household had only 2.2 members, and three-fourths of the households had no children. Household income, often based on two paychecks, was in the $15,000 to $20,000 range, compared with average income in the New Orleans area of $9,000. As columnist Sylvia Porter puts it, "The entire prosperity of our economy . . . is based upon the working couple."

Under these conditions, the house becomes not a middle-class haven for raising a family but a setting for a life style which precludes the very thought of children. The middle class thus shrinks even while the demand for housing remains strong.

The same shrinkage applies to another middle-class essential, the college and professional degree. The G. I. Bill and post-Sputnik government expenditures made college and professional schools accessible to millions of youths who ordinarily would have been shut out. Buy by 1970, the gates were again closing because of tuition barriers, a reduction in financial aid, and limitations on admissions, especially at the graduate professional level.

Today, college tuition costs are a burden even for the real middle class, and they show every sign of increasing. The effects of costs and competition are already manifest in the area of advanced professional training. The Bakke case told us much more about the struggle among *whites* to enter professional schools than about affirmative action. Some worthy students are being denied access to advanced training, and some others attempt—sometimes, apparently, with success—to corrupt admissions procedures. In any case, this struggle for advantage is confined, on the whole, to the middle and upper classes. In a no-growth economy with sharply reduced job opportunities, such a struggle can only result in further shrinking the middle class.

Admissions pressures on the best colleges and on professional schools are largely, but not entirely, a demographic effect. But the drive toward higher and professional education is also pushed by the realization that (1) competition is tough and increasing (if only because increasing numbers are applying for limited places), and (2) the nature of our economy has so changed that only the "technocracy," the "knowledge sector," will be in a position to command a "good" job.

Ironically, given the demographic factors and current structural transformations, the middle class will still suffer shrinkage even if it plays the game as conscientiously as it can. By 1990, the number of workers in the prime age group of twenty-five to forty-four will have grown enormously—from 58 million this year to 78 million. This means, says one commentator, "fierce competition for promotions, coupled with substantial career disappointment for many. . . . Persons in the twenty-five-to-forty-four cohort of 1990 will receive especially low relative income for their entire lives. The 'excessive' number of twenty-five-to-forty-four year-olds and the shortfall of younger workers will create major personnel and labor problems on whose effective resolution industrial peace in the 1980s may depend."

This "glut of prime-age workers" will have social consequences, observes another analyst: "Exhortations for social justice will have less appeal where there is sharp competition for limited positions in the upper reaches of the occupational structure. . . . [There will be] an increasingly strident backlash against programs for affirmative action." Not, it should be stressed, that such a reaction will do much to alleviate the situation: The middle class will still shrink.

The problem is not just demographic. While our "post-industrial" productive system demands skilled and highly trained managers—the "knowledge elite"—it needs fewer and fewer of them each decade. What the United States and all Western industrial countries appear to be facing in the 1980s is the prospect of "jobless growth." Even an upturn in business spending, Paul Lewis writes in *The New York Times*, "will merely accelerate the present trend toward replacing human workers with sophisticated new machinery instead of creating additional jobs." According to the Organization for Economic Cooperation and Development, "The evidence that we have is suggesting increasingly that the employment displacing effects of automation, anticipated for the 1980s, are now beginning to arrive on a serious scale in the 1970s."

The baleful effects of automation are hardly new to the world's working classes. What is new about current computerized automation is that it will radically, and negatively, affect middle-class managerial and technical personnel. That is to say, the middle class will shrink still further as both competition and automation tumble members of the technocracy into the ranks of the poorly-paid, overqualified, underemployed. They will enter the "service sector" of the labor force. As the middle class ranks thin and the numbers of the frustrated and relatively deprived grow, we need no Aristotle to remind us that trouble will ensue.

The evidence indicates, then, that our traditional middle class is shrinking. Access to the status and its attributes is increasingly narrowed. Those already within it face enormous and growing competition and inexorable technological forces of displacement. Without structural changes in our economic system, without changes in our social values and in our conception and definition of work, that middle class will continue to shrink.

14

A NOTE ON THE "TRICKLE EFFECT"

Lloyd A. Fallers

Much has been written—and much more spoken in informal social scientific shop talk—about the so-called "trickle effect"—the tendency in U. S. society (and perhaps to a lesser extent in Western societies generally) for new styles or fashions in consumption goods to be introduced via the socio-economic elite and then to pass down through the status hierarchy, often in the form of inexpensive, mass-produced copies.

In a recent paper, Barber and Lobel have analyzed this phenomenon in the field of women's clothes.[1] They point out that women's dress fashions are not simply irrational shifts in taste, but that they have definite functions in the U. S. status system. Most Americans, they say, are oriented toward status mobility. Goods and services consumed are symbolic of social status. In the family division of labor, the husband and father "achieves" in the occupational system and thus provides the family with monetary income. Women, as wives and daughters, have the task of allocating this income so as to maximize its status-symbolic value. Since women's clothing permits much subtlety of expression in selection and display, it becomes of great significance

as a status-mobility symbol.[2] The ideology of the "open class" system, however, stresses broad "equality" as well as differential status. The tendency of women's dress fashions to "trickle down" fairly rapidly via inexpensive reproductions of originals created at fashion centers helps to resolve this seeming inconsistency by preventing the development of rigid status distinctions.[3]

In the widest sense, of course, the "trickle effect" applies not only to women's dress but also to consumption goods of many other kinds. Most similar to women's dress fashions are styles in household furnishings. A colleague has pointed out to me that venetian blinds have had a similar status career—being introduced at relatively high levels in the status hierarchy and within a few years passing down to relatively low levels. Like women's dress styles, styles in household furnishings are to a substantial degree matters of "learning" by lower-status persons that they are status relevant. The trickling down of other types of consumption goods is to a greater degree influenced by long-term increases in purchasing power at lower socio-economic levels. Such consumers' durables as refrigerators and automobiles, being products of heavy industry and hence highly standardized over relatively long periods and throughout the industries which produce them, are much less subject to considerations of taste. They do,

"A Note on the 'Trickle Effect,' " by Lloyd A. Fallers, pp. 314–322, Fall, 1954 *Public Opinion Quarterly*. Reprinted by permission.

however, trickle down over the long term and their possession is clearly status-relevant.

The dominant tendency among social scientists has been to regard the trickle effect mainly as a "battle of wits" between upper-status persons who attempt to guard their symbolic treasure and lower-status persons (in league with mass-production industries) who attempt to devalue the status-symbolic currency. There is much truth in this view. Latterly we have observed a drama of this sort being played out in the automotive field. Sheer ownership of an automobile is no longer symbolic of high status and neither is frequent trading-in. Not even the "big car" manufacturers can keep their products out of the hands of middle- and lower-status persons "on the make." High-status persons have therefore turned to ancient or foreign sportscars.

It seems possible, however, that the trickle effect has other and perhaps more far-reaching functions for the society as a whole. Western (and particularly U. S.) society, with its stress upon the value of success through individual achievement, poses a major motivational problem: The occupational system is primarily organized about the norm of technical efficiency. Technical efficiency is promoted by recruiting and rewarding persons on the basis of their objective competence and performance in occupational roles. The field of opportunity for advancement, however, is pyramidal in shape; the number of available positions decreases as differential rewards increase. But for the few most competent to be chosen, the many must be "called," that is, motivated to strive for competence and hence success. This, of course, involves relative failure by the many, hence the problem: How is the widespread motivation to strive maintained in the face of the patent likelihood of failure for all but the few? In a widely quoted paper, Merton has recognized that this situation is a serious focus of strain in the social system and has pointed to some structured types of deviant reaction to it.[4] I should like to suggest the hypothesis that *the trickle effect is a mechanism for maintaining the motivation to strive for success, and hence for maintaining efficiency of performance in occupational roles, in a system in which differential success is possible for only a few.* Status-symbolic consumption goods trickle down, thus giving the "illusion" of success to those who fail to achieve *differential* success in the opportunity and status pyramid. From this point of view, the trickle effect becomes a "treadmill."

There are, of course, other hypotheses to account for the maintenance of motivation to strive against very unfavorable odds. Perhaps the most common is the notion that the "myth of success," perhaps maintained by the mass-communications media under the control of the "vested interests," deceives people into believing that their chances for success are greater than is in fact the case. Merton seems to accept this explanation in part while denying that the ruse is entirely effective.[5] Somewhat similar is another common explanation, put forward, for example, by Schumpeter, that though the chances for success are not great, the rewards are so glittering as to make the struggle attractive.[6] Undoubtedly both the "success myth" theory and the "gambling" theory contain elements of truth. Individual achievement certainly *is* a major value in the society and dominates much of its ideology, while risk-taking is clearly institutionalized, at any rate in the business segment of the occupational system. Taken by themselves, however, these explanations do not seem sufficient to account for the situation. At any rate, if it is possible to show that the system *does* "pay off" for the many in the form of "trickle-down" status-symbolic consumption goods, one need not lean so heavily upon such arguments.

It seems a sound principle of sociological analysis to assume "irrationality" as a motivation for human action only where exhaustive analysis fails to reveal a "realistic" pay-off for the observed behavior. To be sure, the explanation put forward here also assumes "irrationality," but in a different sense. The individual who is rewarded for his striving by the trickling-down of status-symbolic consumption goods has the *illusion*, and not the *fact*, of status mobility among his fellows. But in terms of his life history, he nevertheless *has* been rewarded with things which are valued and to this degree his striving is quite "realistic."[7] Though his status position *vis-a-vis* his fellows has not changed, he can look back upon his own life history and say to himself (perhaps not explicitly since the whole status-mobility motivational complex is probably quite often wholly or in part unconscious): "I (or my family) have succeeded. I now have things which five (or ten or twenty) years ago I could not have had, things which were then possessed only by persons of higher status."

To the degree that status is *defined* in terms of consumption of goods and services one should perhaps say, not that such an individual has only the *illusion* of mobility, but rather that the entire population has been upwardly mobile. From this point of view, status-symbolic goods and services do not "trickle-down" but rather remain in fixed positions; the population moves up through the hierarchy of status-symbolic consumption patterns.

The accompanying diagram illustrates the various possibilities in terms of the life-histories of individuals. The two half-pyramids represent the status hierarchy at two points in time (X and Y). A, B, C and D are individuals occupying different levels in the status hierarchy. Roman numerals I through V represent the hierarchy of status-symbolic

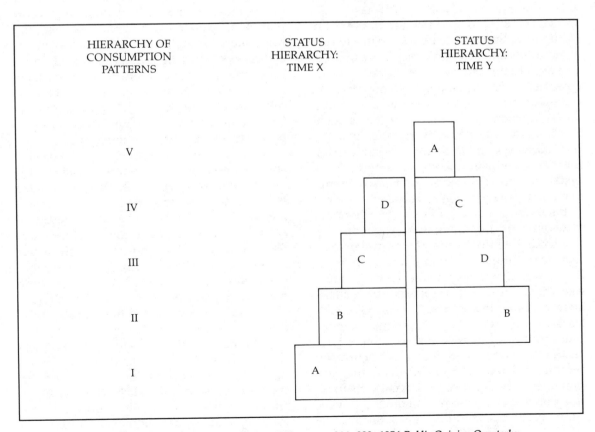

Source: "A Note on the 'Trickle Effect,'" by Lloyd A. Fallers, pp. 314–322, 1954 *Public Opinion Quarterly.*

consumption patterns. Between time periods X and Y, a new high-status consumption pattern has developed and has been taken over by the elite. All status levels have "moved up" to "higher" consumption patterns. During the elapsed time, individual C has "succeeded" in the sense of having become able to consume goods and services which were unavailable to him before, though he has remained in the same relative status level. Individual B has been downwardly mobile in the status hierarchy, but this blow has been softened for him because the level into which he has dropped has in the meantime taken over consumption patterns previously available only to persons in the higher level in which B began. Individual D has been sufficiently downwardly mobile so that he has also lost ground in the hierarchy of consumption patterns. Finally, individual A, who has been a spectacular success, has risen to the very top of the status hierarchy where he is able to consume goods and services which were unavailable even to the elite at an earlier time period. Needless to say, this diagram is not meant to represent the actual status levels, the proportions of persons in each level, or the frequencies of upward and downward mobility in the U. S. social system. It is simply meant to illustrate diagrammatically the tendency of the system, in terms of status-symbolic consumption goods, to reward even those who are not status mobile and to provide a "cushion" for those who are slightly downward mobile.

Undoubtedly this view of the system misrepresents "the facts" in one way as much as the notion of status-symbolic goods and services "trickling down" through a stable status hierarchy does in another. Consumption patterns do not retain the same status-symbolic value as they become available to more people. Certainly to some degree the "currency becomes inflated." A more adequate diagram would show both consumption patterns trickling down and the status hierarchy moving up. Nonetheless, I would suggest that to *some*

degree particular consumption goods have "absolute" value in terms of the individual's life history and his motivation to succeed. To the degree that this is so, the system pays off even for the person who is not status-mobile.

This pay-off, of course, is entirely dependent upon constant innovation and expansion in the industrial system. New goods and services must be developed and existing ones must become more widely available through mass-production. Average "real income" must constantly rise. If status-symbolic consumption patterns remained stationary both in kind and in degree of availability, the system would pay off only for the status-mobile and the achievement motive would indeed be unrealistic for most individuals. Were the productive system to shrink, the pay-off would become negative for most and the unrealism of the motivation to achieve would be compounded. Under such circumstances, the motivational complex of striving-achievement occupational efficiency would be placed under great strain. Indeed, Merton seems to have had such circumstances in mind when he described "innovation," "ritualism," "rebellion," and "passive withdrawal" as common patterned deviations from the norm.[8]

This suggests a "vicious circle" relationship between achievement motivation and industrial productivity. It seems reasonable to suppose that a high level of achievement motivation is both a cause and a result of efficiency in occupation role performance. Such an assumption underlies much of our thinking about the modern Western occupational system and indeed is perhaps little more than common sense. One British sociologist, commenting upon the reports of the British "Productivity Teams" which have recently been visiting American factories, is impressed by American workers' desire for status-symbolic consumption, partly the result of pressure upon husbands by their wives, as a factor in the greater "per man hour" productivity of American industry.[9] Greater productivity, of course, means more and cheaper consumption goods and hence a greater pay-off for the worker. Conversely, low achievement motivation and inefficiency in occupational role performance would seem to stimulate one another. The worker has less to work for, works less efficiently and in turn receives still less reward. Presumably these relationships would tend to hold, though in some cases less directly, throughout the occupational system and not only in the sphere of the industrial worker.

To the degree that the relationships suggested here between motivation to status-symbolic consumption, occupational role performance, and expanding productivity actually exist, they should be matters of some importance to the theory of business cycles. Although they say nothing about the genesis of up-turns and down-turns in business activity, they do suggest some social structural reasons why upward or downward movements, once started, might tend to continue. It is not suggested, of course, that these are the only, or even the most important, reasons. More generally, they exemplify the striking degree to which the stability of modern industrial society often depends upon the maintenance of delicate equilibria.

The hypotheses suggested here are, it seems to me, amenable to research by a number of techniques. It would be most useful to discover more precisely just which types of status-symbolic consumption goods follow the classical trickle-down pattern and which do not. Television sets, introduced in a period of relative prosperity, seem to have followed a different pattern, spreading laterally across the middle-income groups rather than trickling down from above. This example suggests another. Some upper-income groups appear to have shunned television on the grounds of its "vulgarity"—a valuation shared by many academics. To what degree are preferences for other goods and services introduced, not at the upper-income levels, but by the "intelli-gentsia," who appear at times to have greater pattern-setting potential than their relatively low economic position might lead one to believe? Finally, which consumption items spread rapidly and which more slowly? Such questions might be answered by the standard techniques of polling and market analysis.

More difficult to research are hypotheses concerning the motivational significance of consumption goods. I have suggested that the significance for the individual of the trickling down of consumption patterns must be seen in terms of his life-history and not merely in terms of short-term situations. It seems likely that two general patterns may be distinguished. On the one hand, individuals for whom success means primarily rising above their fellows may be more sensitive to those types of goods and services which must be chosen and consumed according to relatively subtle and rapidly changing standards of taste current at any one time at higher levels. Such persons must deal successfully with the more rapid devaluations of status-symbolic currency which go on among those actively battling for dominance. Such persons it may be who are responsible for the more short-term fluctuations in consumption patterns. On the other hand, if my hypothesis is correct, the great mass of the labor force may be oriented more to long-term success in terms of their own life-histories—success in the sense of achieving a "better standard of living" without particular regard to *differential* status. Interviews centered upon the role of consumption patterns in individuals' life aspirations should reveal such differences if they exist, while differences in perception of symbols of taste might be tested by psychological techniques.

Most difficult of all would be the testing of the circular relationship between motivation and productivity. Major fluctuations in the economy are relatively long term and could be studied only through research planned on an equally long-term basis. Relatively short-term and localized fluctuations, however, do occur at more frequent intervals and would provide possibilities for research. One would require an index of occupational performance which could be related to real income and the relationship between these elements should ideally be traced through periods of both rising and falling real income.

NOTES

[1] Barber, Bernard and Lyle S. Lobel, " 'Fashion' in Women's Clothes and the American Social System," *Social Forces*, Vol. 31, pp. 124–131. Reprinted in Bendix, Reinhard and S. M. Lipset, *Class, Status and Power: A Reader in Social Stratification*, Free Press, 1953, pp. 323–332.

[2] It is not suggested that women are *solely* in charge of status-symbolic expenditure, merely that they play perhaps the major role in this respect. See also: Parsons, Talcott, *Essays in Sociological Theory*, Free Press, 1949, p. 225.

[3] Our thinking concerning the status-symbolic role of consumption patterns owes a great debt, of course, to Veblen's notion of "conspicuous consumption" and more recently to the work of W. L. Warner and his colleagues.

[4] Merton, R. K. "Social Structure and Anomie," reprinted as Chapter IV, *Social Theory and Social Structure*, Free Press, 1949.

[5] *Ibid.*

[6] Schumpeter, J. A., *Capitalism, Socialism and Democracy*, Harpers, 1947, pp. 73–74.

[7] By "irrationality" is meant here irrationality *within the framework of a given value system*. Values themselves, of course, are neither "rational" nor "irrational" but "nonrational." The value of individual achievement is nonrational. Action directed toward achievement may be termed rational to the degree that, in terms of the information available to the actor, it is likely to result in achievement; it is irrational to the degree that this is not so.

[8] Merton, R. K., *op. cit.*

[9] Balfour, W. C., "Productivity and the Worker," *British Journal of Sociology*, Vol. IV, No. 3, 1953, pp. 257–265.

15

THE DIRTY WORK MOVEMENT

Herbert J. Gans

It was a small banquet as White House banquets go, but what mattered was that the President chose to memorialize the occasion and to honor the handful of old men able to attend. The men were the surviving members of the DWW, the Dirty Workers of the World; the occasion, the 20th anniversary of the now almost forgotten Dirty Work Movement. The evening was highlighted by the issuance of a new commemorative stamp showing the late Joe Green, the founder of the DWW, as he looked those days, lavatory mop held firmly in the revolutionary posture.

THE DWW'S REVOLUTION

Mr. Green, older readers may remember, was a lavatory attendant at the University of California in Berkeley in the early 1970s; and one day, while cleaning the professional facilities, he chanced on a newspaper headline about the Dirty Word Movement, which had flourished briefly in Berkeley in the mid-1960s. Not the best of spellers, he thought the headline referred to work and mentioned it to his colleagues later that evening. A few days later, the entire Berkeley toilet staff walked off the

From *Social Policy*, March/April 1971, pp. 34–35, published by Social Policy Corporation, New York, N.Y. 10036. Copyright 1971 by Social Policy Corporation.

job, saying they were fed up with doing dirty work.

The men came back when the University raised their wages and renamed them personal service engineers; but in a couple of weeks, they realized that they were still just cleaning johns, and walked off the job again. Soon, lavatory attendants all over the country went on strike; and, finally, the President declared a National Pollution Emergency. He also called for volunteers to solve the problem, as was his fashion, and appeared on television mopping the floor of a White House staff toilet.

By then, however, other workers had begun to leave their jobs. The first to go were hospital orderlies and stockyard slaughterers, but the crisis really deepened when the domestics struck. Washington and Manhattan party-givers had to cancel their parties, after which politics, show business, publishing, and the arts ground to a complete halt. In succeeding weeks there were walkouts by dishwashers and garbage collectors, and when assembly-line workers also quit, the economy just stopped altogether.

In the meantime, Joe Green had organized the Dirty Workers of the World, and after some bitter jurisdictional hassles with existing unions, most of the striking workers were amalgamated into the DWW. And not much later, Joe Green came to the White House to negotiate.

Actually, there was nothing to negotiate; for with the economy at a standstill, the DWW held the trump card. Joe Green made only one demand: the dirtier the work, the more it ought to be paid. The President gave in, his staff quickly prepared the appropriate legislation, and Congress set aside all other business. Since their own salaries would be affected, most Congressmen opposed the bill, and were supported by other salaried groups, including corporation executives, teachers unions, and Washington lobbyists; but pressure from stockholders and property-owners who wanted the economy to start producing again forced them to pass the bill anyway.

A NEW SOCIAL HIERARCHY

During the next year, life in America underwent drastic change. Toilet cleaners became a new economic elite, earning $20 per hour, with three months of paid vacation and a sabbatical every third year. Conversely, movie stars were working for $5 an hour and professors for $3, and Congressional salaries were reduced to $7,500 a year. This, in turn, produced many side effects. Dirty workers now mingled with coupon-clippers in cafe society, while celebrities and politicians had to stay home watching TV. Society pages were filled with accounts of the lavish weekend parties given in the Bahamas by longshoremen, and Joe Green's son married a Philadelphia blue blood.

Naturally, everyone now wanted to go into dirty work; and equally naturally, the DWW closed its membership rolls and renamed itself the Dirty Professionals of the World. The DPW then wrote itself a code of ethics, set up a licensing system, founded a journal to record advances in the dirty professions, and established educational prerequisites for these professions. Universities were quick to develop the appropriate new teaching specialties and research institutes, and the government was quick to provide the grants. The National Institutes of Health awarded Harvard $500,000 to study cross-cultural differences in bedpan cleaning, and MIT received $1 million for advanced work in slaughtering technology.

In the meantime, employers, their costs spiraling, set out to automate dirty work; but, one after another, they learned that it could not always be replaced by technology. A machine was invented to eliminate the coal miner, but none could replace the man who pushed garment trucks on crowded streets and pavements; and the mayor of New York had to resign when his completely automatic garbage-removal system dropped too many empty cans on the parked cars of too many voters.

TOWARD A MORE EQUAL DISTRIBUTION OF DIRT

By now, clean workers were becoming a new underclass, and hippies changed into white shirts to express their sympathies for them. Newspaper editorials celebrated the courageous individualism of the few young people who still sought to prepare themselves for clean jobs; Hollywood made movies about how unhappy the newly rich dirty workers really were; and the best-selling novel of the year was *The Doll Laundry*, the story of three wealthy washerwomen who became drug addicts and finally committed suicide.

These stories helped the clean workers retain their pride in being clean; but as their savings disappeared and their standard of living declined, so did their pride; and before long they began to demand change. The initial onslaught came from those in various occupations who argued that their work was actually dirty and required higher pay. The Army claimed successfully that its blood-letting activities were extremely dirty, and thereafter the surgeons put in a bid for higher salaries. Newspapermen funded studies of the incidence of graphite stains on their hands, and executive secretaries pointed out that they often spilled coffee or whisky on themselves while ministering to the needs of their bosses. Finally, the executives themselves sued for a salary increase, arguing that their work was tension-producing and thus psychologically dirty. Although their case was bitterly contested in Washington, the Supreme Court ruled, in a landmark decision, that emotional factors also had to be taken into account in defining dirtiness. Soon thereafter, the surgeons filed suit for another salary increase on the same grounds, so that, in the end, theirs was again the highest paid occupation in the country. And when the clerk-typists went out on strike, claiming that their work, though clean, was boring, the economy was once more at a standstill.

History repeated itself as the head of the newly organized Clean Workers of America went to the White House to meet with the President. After she pointed out that her union, though barely three weeks old, already had five times as many members as the DWW, the President agreed to her demands, pro-

posing a $10 per hour minimum wage for clean work, and $20 for boring work. Congress passed his bill by acclamation, and thereafter the position of the dirty workers began to decline. The DWW fought hard to salvage at least some benefits, but the Republicans won the next election with a Keep America Clean campaign, and soon after Joe Green died of a broken heart.

THE PRESIDENT WAS DIRTY TOO

Consequently, Washington analysts could not understand why the President had now decided to honor a politically discredited group. True, at the banquet he revealed that he had belonged to the DWW as a young Congressman, supplementing his lowly income by working in the mines on weekends. The President was not given to idle sentimentality, however; and White House correspondents, noting his frequent complaint that the Presidency was a dirty job, were speculating that he might be reviving interest in the DWW to justify a pay increase for himself.

Part Three

MAJOR PATTERNS OF SOCIETY

The major institutions of any society are the family, education, religion, economics, and politics. Although their forms may differ greatly, each of these can be found in every society. An institution is a formal relationship organized around common values to meet basic needs within the society. When a behavior pattern becomes fixed and expected, it can be said to have become part of an institution. Although long-standing normative patterns are difficult to change, new behavior patterns are occurring constantly due to innovations in the material culture (for example, the invention of the auto) or challenges to expected behavior. As the new behavior is adopted, it becomes part of the institutionalized, normative expectation. Then, through the socialization function of that institution, the new behavior is passed on to the rest of society.

All societies have certain functional prerequisites that are necessary for survival. Before we begin our discussion of major social institutions, we should review the prerequisites that social institutions fulfill. According to Talcott Parsons, they are two: first, the social system must be relatively compatible with both the individual members of the society and the cultural system as a whole;

second, the social system requires the support of the other systems around it.

It is the second of Parsons' prerequisites that lead us to expect social institutions to be interdependent and interrelated. What happens in one institution will affect all others. Suppose, for example, there is a recession in the economy. Family members may lose jobs, churches may receive fewer and smaller donations, and politicians may have a hard time getting re-elected.

Each of us is involved with the major institutions at all times. The effects of family, education, religion, economics, and politics on our lives are constant. Illustrations of such effects are seen in the ways family morals or beliefs and our school experiences affect our thinking—and even the nonbeliever will be affected by religious beliefs embodied in laws or reform efforts. Similarly, the economy, with its inflation and unemployment, has an effect on prices and taxes, and politics affects our lives through the passage of laws and expenditure of taxes.

As you read this section, think about the changes that our major social institutions are undergoing and need to undergo—for that is the major theme of each chapter.

MS. Magazine, August 1978. Photo by Carl Fischer. Courtesy the MS. Foundation for Education and Communication.

VI

THE FAMILY
Diversity and Change

Our introduction to the world comes through a primary group: the family. It is the institution with which we have the most contact and the one from which we traditionally receive the most emotional support. We depend on the family for our early nurturance and socialization, and could not survive without it. Society depends on the family to carry out certain vital functions such as reproduction, socialization of the young, and regulation of sexual activity.

The family institution is being strained by the pressure of many ongoing changes in other institutions. In light of this pressure, can the family still fulfill the needs of individuals and society? Will the family maintain its traditional structure? What are future projections for the family? The articles in this chapter address these questions.

In the first article, Bernard notes the increasing strain on the family and on role relations within it, and its effect on marital happiness. Because of such strains, some families are reaching the point at which the rewards of family life are not greater than the benefits derived from divorce. Stresses on the nuclear family that cause divorce can result from the dependence on one person to meet many needs; should this dependency be threatened, the marriage is jeopardized. Premarital concepts of a romantic love that surmounts any crisis turn into the hard reality of day-to-day, postmarital life. Changes in women's roles are introducing changes in family relations and structure, as are changes in the sexual norms and practices of society. These changes, as Bernard notes, directly affect one's view of the happiness of one's marriage. The roles of husband and wife are changing and this may result in a changing perception of marital benefits and happiness. To put it in another manner, our world view of marital and other relationships is colored by the roles we play.

Due to the baby boom of the fifties and sixties, a rising divorce rate, and later marriages, the number of single persons has also increased. Attitudes toward this large population aggregate have also changed along with the growing numbers. Melko and Cargan discuss these attitudinal changes toward singles in their article, "Perceptions of Singlehood." By utilizing the sociological method of context analysis, they trace the attitudes of society toward singles over time.

The family of the future will reflect changes taking place in all institutions of society. The last two articles indicate that families of the future will have a pluralism of forms: Melko and Cargan indicate that there is more tolerance toward a variety of marriage styles and toward those who remain single. The last article also suggests greater future tolerance since there will be different types of families and parenthood, and greater equality in the family.

As you read this section, consider the significance of the family for all of us, and what happens when it does not fulfill its functions for us and for society. Also consider the possible alternatives to the traditional family and whether any of them can help solve our problems as we move into the future.

16

MARRIAGE HIS AND HERS

Jessie Bernard

For centuries men have been told—by other men—that marriage is no bed of roses, a necessary evil, a noose, a desperate thing, a field of battle, a curse, a school of sincere pretense. Supposedly, Oscar Wilde proclaimed marriage a wonderful institution: every woman should be married, but no man. H. L. Mencken is credited with the observation that since it was to man's interest to avoid marriage as long as possible and to woman's to marry as favorably as possible, the sexes were pursuing diametrically antagonistic ends.

These male clichés could hardly have been more wrong. For, contrary to all the charges leveled against it, the husband's marriage, whether he likes it or not (and he does) is awfully good for him. The findings are consistent, unequivocal, and convincing. The superiority of married men over never-married men is impressive on almost every index—demographic, psychological, or social.

After middle age the physical health of married men is better than that of never-married men. But regardless of age, married men

enjoy better mental health and fewer serious symptoms of psychological distress. To take an extreme example, in the United States, the suicide rate for single men is almost twice as high as for married men.

And the actions of men with respect to marriage speak far louder than words—or statistics. Once men have known marriage, they can hardly live without it. Most divorced and widowed men remarry. At every age, the marriage rate for both divorced and widowed men is higher than the rate for single men. Half of all divorced white men who remarry do so within three years after divorce.

Could it be that the gentlemen protest too much? Are their verbal assaults on marriage a kind of compensatory reaction to their dependence on it?

Some men do not marry because they do not want to, for whatever reason, and some because no one wants to marry them. In either case, we are faced with the inevitable and insoluble chicken-and-egg, cause-and-effect question. This selectivity factor is undoubtedly part of the explanation of the superiority married men show over the unmarried, and cannot therefore be ignored in evaluating the impact of marriage. But the weight of the evidence explaining differences by marital status seems to me to be overwhelmingly on the side

"Marriage: His and Hers" as it appeared in *Ms.* Magazine from *The Future of Marriage* by Jessie Bernard (World Publishing Company). Copyright © 1972 by Jessie Bernard. Reprinted by permission of Harper & Row, Publishers, Inc.

of the beneficent effects which marriage has on men rather than on the initial superiority of the married men. Are married men so much better off than the never-married because marriage is good for them or because the less good prospects were selected out of the married population in the first place?

By comparing the married with the widowed, we minimize the selective factor, for the widowed did once choose marriage or were chosen by someone. Such comparisons give us an indication of the value of marriage by showing what happens to men who are deprived of it by death. They are miserable. Widowers show more than expected frequencies of psychological distress, and their death rate is very high.

One would expect the unmarried to be the "easy riders," the men who cannot tolerate the restrictions of conventionality, but seek to satisfy a wide gamut of desires. One study did, indeed, find that the unmarried more than the married felt marriage to be restrictive. It was, however, a more negative kind of reaction—a passive avoidance of the difficulties of marriage—rather than a positive commitment to unlimited wants, desires, or aspirations. Other studies have shown that more single than married men suffer from inertia, passivity, antisocial tendencies, greater moral conflict, and a history of stressful childhoods.

I have emphasized only the documentable, research-based evidence of the benefits of marriage. But every happily married man will be able to add a dozen more: marriage is more comfortable than bachelorhood; sex is always available; responsibility is a rewarding experience. It is reassuring to have a confidante. And then there is love, friendship, and personal service. . . .

The benefits of marriage for men do not come without costs. Some freedom must be surrendered. To be sure, the bachelor party that used to be popular the night before the marriage was a recognition that hereafter there would indeed be sacrifices—no more carousing, no more irresponsible fun.

Economic responsibilities and sexual restrictiveness are the two major costs men feel they pay to maintain a haven. Many husbands therefore name two areas of potential improvement of the state of matrimony. One would be to relieve them from the responsibility for the entire support of wives and children, and the other to make sexual varietism more feasible. Both seem to be in the process of realization.

What will happen to "the husband's marriage" as the wife's economic contribution increases and the couple's fidelity expectations decrease is a matter of sociology in the making.

But at the present time, there is no better guarantor of long life, health, and happiness for men than a wife well socialized to perform the "duties of a wife," willing to devote her life to taking care of him, providing, even enforcing, the regularity and security of a well-ordered home.

The story of the husband's marriage can be short and simple; not so, however, the story of the wife's.

In summarizing the research of a generation, the indicators add up to a sorry betrayal of the bride's ideal. It appears conclusive that more wives than husbands report marital frustration and dissatisfaction. More wives than husbands consider their marriages unhappy, have considered separation or divorce, and have regretted their marriages. Fewer married women than married men report positive companionship. Understandably, therefore, it is mostly the wives who seek marriage counseling and initiate divorce proceedings.

Even among happily married couples, issues such as finances, religion, sex, friends, and life goals show the wives reporting problems in more than twice as many areas as husbands.

Although the physical health of married women is as good as, or even better than that of married men, the women suffer far greater mental-health hazards.

One disheartening study found that more married women than married men have felt they were about to have a nervous breakdown; more have feelings of inadequacy in their marriages and blame themselves for this own lack of general adjustment. Other studies report that more wives than husbands show phobic reactions, depression, and passivity; greater than expected frequency of psychological distress; and mental-health impairment.

If the mental and emotional health of wives—anxious, depressed, psychologically distressed—is so dismal, perhaps we are dealing with a sex difference quite unrelated to marriage. Perhaps the mental and emotional health of wives shows up so poorly simply because they are females—who are "naturally" weak, vulnerable, emotional, moody, and unable to cope.

This interpretation is one version of the perennial charge against women: it's their own fault. When a woman takes her problems to a psychiatrist, the response of the therapist has all too often suggested that her misery was self-generated and could be relieved only by learning to come to terms with her position. (The buck stops with the wife, even though, as several clinicians have reported, both husbands and wives believe that the husband is usually the source of problems in the marriage.)

However, this "it's-merely-a-sex-difference" interpretation cannot account for an intrasex discrepancy: the mental-health picture of wives shows up just as unfavorably when compared with unmarried women. Thus, we are impressed by a study reported in 1938 when marriage was the only alternative lifestyle, and single women were less often glamorized and more often pitied than today. This study nonetheless found that more *married* than single women had their feelings easily hurt, were happy and sad by turns without apparent reason, cried easily, felt hurt by criticism, sometimes felt miserable, found it hard to make up their minds,

were burdened by a sense of remorse, worried over possible misfortune, would cross the street to avoid meeting people, and were self-conscious about their appearance. Recent studies tend to confirm such differences, adding such testimony about wives' feelings as: unhappy most of the time, disliking their present jobs, sometimes feeling they are about to go to pieces, afraid of death, worried about contracting diseases, and bothered by pains and ailments. Many other symptoms of psychological distress, such as nervousness, inertia, insomnia, trembling hands, nightmares, fainting, headaches, dizziness, and heart palpitations, show up *less* frequently than expected among unmarried women and *more* frequently than expected among wives.

All the statistics lead to the inescapable conclusion that single women have it over everyone. The bachelor women report less discomfort and greater happiness. They are more active about working through their problems. They're less often neurotic, antisocial, depressed, or passive. And these differences hold true regardless of age, education, occupation, and income.

Why do married women reveal so many more distress symptoms than both married men and single women? Is it because only distress-prone women prefer to marry? Or because men prefer to marry that type of woman? Or could it be that women start out with an initial advantage which marriage reverses?

Until the resurgence of feminism, very few women remained single because they *did not want* to marry, as in the case of some men. Because of powerful role-conditioning, practically all young women want to marry for lack of other inviting options or available alternatives. And so the root of a woman's single state (in a society in which men traditionally do the proposing) is likely to lie in the behavior of men. The women that men select in marriage reflect what men want in wives.

By and large, research has shown that both men and women tend to marry mates with the same general class and cultural background. But within that common background, men tend to marry women slightly below them in such measurable items as age, education, and occupation.

What men do *not* want in wives may be deduced from evidence gathered in a study of never-married women; the profile reads like an impressive résumé rather than a portrait of a reject. Single women tend to be upwardly mobile; they, more than married women, had started life in lower socioeconomic levels and pulled themselves up educationally and professionally. The implication is that they were "aggressive" and had stronger "achievement motivation" than most women. The talents it takes (for women or men) to achieve the best-paying jobs—competitiveness, aggressiveness, drive, and will to suceed—seem to be precisely those qualities most men fear, suspect, or reject as inconsistent with wifehood.

The second type of woman men do not choose is the too-conventional one. The cliché claims that while men may play around with the freewheeling swinger, they marry the "good girl." Not so, reports a key study. It's the married women who have more often engaged in unconventional heterosexual activities; and it's their single sisters who are more frequently morally strict, conscientious, and scrupulous about family obligations.

An analysis of those women whom men select *out* of the marriage market does little to explain the grim mental-health picture of wives. Sooner or later, practically everyone marries. What, then, is it about marriage itself that can explain the situation?

Years ago, I propounded "a shock theory" of marriage. It was my idea that marriage introduced such profound discontinuities into the lives of women as to constitute a genuine emotional health hazard.

There are some standardized "shocks" that are almost taken for granted. For example, one analyst cites the conflict the bride experiences between her attachment to her parental family and her attachment to her new husband. Another shock marks the end of the romantic idealization when the honeymoon is over and disenchantment sets in. The transition from the best-behavior presentation of the self during courtship to the daily lack of privacy in marriage (hair curlers, the unshaven face) presents its own kind of shock. So does the change that occurs when the wife ceases to be the catered to and becomes the caterer. Discontinuities such as these demand a redefinition of the self, with the assumption of new role obligations.

When another type of shock registers on every woman's scale of myths and misconceptions, there is a sense of betrayal: girls are reared to see themselves as naturally dependent creatures entitled to lean on the greater strength of men. They enter marriage fully confident that these expectations will be fulfilled. They are therefore shaken and dismayed when their husbands turn out to be human. The "strong, protective, superior man" cannot solve his own problems, let alone his helpless wife's. Like everyone else, she was fooled by the stereotypes and by the structural imperatives.

Some of the shocks that marriage may produce have to do with the lowering of status that it brings to women. For, despite the possibilities of a woman's "marrying up," becoming a wife is a step down in the eyes of society. In many states the legal status of wives is lower not only than that of husbands but also than that of unmarried women. But that is relatively minor compared to other forms of status loss, as William Congreve's Mrs. Millamant in *The Way of the World* so well knew when she spoke of "dwindling" into a wife. Even after she had bargained with her husband Mirabell to preserve at least some of her prerogatives in marriage, she said, "These articles subscribed, if I continue to endure you a little longer, I may by degrees dwindle into a wife." And Mirabell recognized that his status would be enhanced: "Well, have I liberty to offer conditions, that when you are dwindled into a wife I may not be beyond measure enlarged into a husband?"

This dwindling takes time—time for a woman to redefine herself and reshape her personality to conform to the wishes or needs or demands of her husband. Roland G. Tharp, a psychologist, concludes from a summary of the research literature that wives "conform more to husbands' expectations than husbands do to wives'." Women who are quite able to take care of themselves before marriage may become helpless after 15 or 20 years of marriage. No wonder sociologist Alice Rossi warns us that "the possibility must be faced . . . that women lose ground in personal development and self-esteem during the early and middle years of adulthood, whereas men gain ground in these respects during the same years." For it is the husband's *role*—not necessarily his own wishes, desires, or demands—that proves to be the key to the marriage and requires the wife to be accommodating.

This in turn tallies with the common finding that wives make more of the adjustments called for in marriage than do husbands. The psychological and emotional costs of these adjustments show up in the increasing unhappiness of wives with the passage of time and in their increasingly negative and passive outlook on life.

One of the basic differences in the wife's and the husband's marriages results from lifestyle—namely, the almost complete change in occupation that marriage brings in her life but not in his. For most women today there are certain years in a marriage when a wife becomes a *housewife*. Even those women who work outside the home are still, in traditional marriages, housewives too. After a nine-to-five day on the job these women tackle the cleaning, cooking, and laundry with the blind obedience of an ordained domestic. Few deny the economic and sociological importance of housework and homemaking. But housewives are not in the labor force. They are not paid for the services they perform.

The low status of the wife's work has ramifications all through her marriage. Since the husband's work is higher than hers in status, earnings, and degree of competition, his needs have to be catered to first.

Eventually the difference in the work of wives and husbands has alienating effects on the relationship. They may not share the same kinds of problems. The couple who began their marriage at the same early stage of their development may find that they and their interests have grown apart in later years. Most often the husband's horizons expand and the wife's contract. "The idea of imprisoning each woman alone in a small, self-contained, and architecturally isolating dwelling is a modern invention," Philip Slater reminds us. "In our society the housewife may move about freely, but since she has nowhere in particular to go and is not party of anything, her prison needs no walls."

Isolation has negative psychological effects on people. It encourages brooding; it leads to erratic judgments, untempered by the leavening effect of contact with others. It renders one more susceptible to psychoses, and heightens one's sense of powerlessness.

We have a ready-made life experiment to demonstrate that it is the role of housewife rather than the fact of being married which contributes heavily to the poor mental and emotional health of wives. By comparing married housewives with married working women, we find that wives who are rescued from the isolation of the household by outside employment show up very well. They may be neurotic, but they are less likely than full-time housewives to be psychotic. In nearly all symptoms of psychological distress—from headaches to heart palpitations—the working women are overwhelmingly better off. In terms of the number of people involved, the housewife syndrome might well be viewed as Public Health Problem Number One. Ironically, the woman suffering from it is not likely to elicit much sympathy. Her symptoms of psychological distress are not worth anyone's attention. Only advertisers take the housewife seriously, and to them she seems only a laughable idiot with a full wallet and an insatiable need for approval. But it's even simpler than that. In truth, being a housewife makes a woman sick.

If we were, in fact, epidemiologists and we saw bright, promising young people enter a certain occupation and little by little begin to droop and finally succumb, we would be alerted at once and bend all our reserach efforts to locate the hazards and remove them. But we are complacent when we see what happens to women in marriage. We put an enormous premium on their getting married, but make them pay an unconscionable price for falling in with our expectations.

If the wife's marriage is really so pathogenic, why do women marry at all? There is a wide variety of reasons: emancipation from the parental home; babies; pressure of social expectations; the absence of any better alternatives.

The real question is not why do young women marry, but why, in the face of all the evidence, do more married than unmarried women report themselves as happy? As, in fact, they do.

The anomaly may be explained by the fact that happiness is interpreted in terms of conformity. Those who do not marry are made to feel failures. Escape from being "an old maid" is one definition of happiness.

Such conformity to the norm of marriage is not merely imposed from the outside. Women have internalized the norms prescribing marriage. And since marriage is set up as the *summum bonum* of life for women, they interpret their achievement of marriage as happiness, no matter how unhappy the marriage itself may be. "I am married, am I not? Therefore I must be happy."

Another way to explain the anomaly of depressed, phobic, and psychologically distressed women reporting themselves as happy may be that they are interpreting happiness in terms of adjustment. The married woman has supposedly adjusted to the demands of marriage; she is reconciled to them. She interprets her reconciliation as happiness, no matter how much she is paying for it in terms of psychological distress.

Another way to solve the paradox of depressed wives reporting their marriages as happy is to view the socialization process as one which "deforms" women in order to fit them for marriage. We cut the motivational wings of young women or bind their intellectual feet, all the time reassuring them that it is their natural destiny and for their own good.

Women accustomed to expressing themselves freely could not be happy in such a relationship; it would be too confining and too punitive. We therefore "deform" the minds of girls in order to shape them for happiness in marriage. It may therefore be that married women say they are happy because they have been made sick.

"But what about love? Isn't that what marriage is all about?" the young bride cries. "None of what you say has even included the word!" True, love has been what marriage has been partially if not all about at least since the 17th century. Love is, in fact, so important to women that they are willing to pay an exorbitant price for it.

But the basic question is, does the satisfaction of these needs for love and companionship have to extort such excessive costs? Can marriage—for women—ever become more often for better than for worse? Perhaps if the ceremonial vows were supplemented with guarantees of human fulfillment, then marriage could become an arena for "enlargement" rather than for "dwindling" into wifely despair.

17

PERCEPTIONS OF SINGLEHOOD: 1900–1975

Matthew Melko
Leonard Cargan

You hear a good deal about singles these days: singles bars, singles comic strips, singles housing. Is there a change taking place? Are there more singles than there used to be? Or have there been closet singles who are coming out?

Whether there are more or not is easily answered from the census data. The answer seems to be yes and no. The percentage of singles (all those not married over the age of 14) was lower in 1975 than in 1900: 37% as compared to 46%. But after a long drop from the 46% of 1900 to 32% in 1960 the percentage of singles began to rise.

Since there has been a distinct increase in the percentage and number of singles, what would be the expected impact on society? With more singles about, the first expectation might be for an increase in the perception of problems, needs and markets involving the young adult.

Obviously, there is a great deal of attention being paid to singles these days. There are singles organizations, articles about discrimination against singles through large economy sizes and family season tickets, much discussion about the transition to widowhood and the problems of the divorced—

particularly of divorced parents. But how much of this attention and concern is new? Is it really greater than it was in the past? And has the discussion matured, or is it merely another generation debating the same old questions?

One simple way to address these questions is to review the titles of *The Readers Guide to Periodical Literature*. Those dealing with singlehood can be counted to get a quantitative picture of the changes that have occurred, and qualitatively evaluated to assess the nature of the change.

The advantages of this method are that the period covered is the same as that covered by the Census statistics, and that the *Reader's Guide* emphasizes popular publications, thus giving a better measure of popular, rather than academic, awareness. The disadvantage is that this approach does not take into consideration the shift in public attention from magazines to television—and, of course, it does not provide quantitative statistics as reassuringly accurate as those provided by census data.

A problem soon encountered in reviewing titles was that the perceptions of the *Reader's Guide* editors about what constituted singles changed over time. The most striking change was the appearance of the concept of Singles, replacing the earlier classification of

---

Bachelors and Spinsters. The present categories for the never-married are Single Men, Single Women, and Single People. The last listing for Bachelors appeared as recently as 1975, however. Spinsters last appeared as a cross-reference in the 1971–72 edition. The listings for Widowhood remained basically the same, usually involving widows, with occasional reference to widowhood and widowers.

Divorce was a principal category in the *Reader's Guide* throughout the 75-year period. An interesting addition, beginning in the 1971–75 period, is the category Children of the Divorced. There were 18 articles in this category dating from 1950 (16 from 1970), and none from before 1950. It seems likely that the increase in divorce is the important factor here, since this increase implies more children of divorced families.

INCREASING INTEREST IN SINGLES

Interest in both the never-married and the divorced quickened in the decade 1966–1975 compared to the previous decade. Articles on the never-married were up 178%; articles on divorce increased by 122%. Since this occurred in a period in which popular weeklies such as *Look* and *Life* were being undermined by television, there seems to be plenty of confirmation that the general awareness of singles was increasing. The percentage of widowed persons remained fairly constant in this period, while the percentage of increase in articles about widowhood was up by only 20%.

A survey of five-year periods in each decade reveals that the category of the never-married received much more attention in the 1970s than it had in any earlier period, including those between 1900 and 1940, when the actual percentage of never-married was considerably higher. The average for the five-year periods examined between 1900 and 1950 was 9 articles as compared with an average of 23 for the 1950–1970 period, and 79 for the 1970s. Interest had more than doubled in the post-

World War II decades and more than tripled again in the 1970s.

There was an average of 4 articles on widowhood in each of the pre-World War II decade periods examined, but an average of 15 in the postwar years, indicating a tripling of interest even though there was no corresponding increase in the percentage of widows and widowers.

The figures on divorce are somewhat surprising for the immediate postwar years. The number of articles devoted to divorce did not reflect the higher percentage of divorce; the number of articles in the 1970s was less than double the number of those appearing in any of the decades in the 1910–1940 period. It may be that as divorce became more acceptable, there was less interest in defending or attacking it.

Despite an increasing interest in singles and the decline in marriage rates, more attention than ever was paid to getting married: articles on how to become more attractive and meet potential mates proliferated. There were 34 articles of this kind from 1950–1975, as opposed to only 9 in the preceding 50 years.

By contrast, in the same period there is no such dramatic increase in concern for the life of the single person: there were 63 articles about it from 1900–1950, but only 55 from 1950–1975. There has been, however, a discernible change in emphasis.

Generally, it appears, the stereotypes of "old maids" and "swinging bachelors" have been replaced with a variety of articles on singles' life. Perceptions of the difficulties of being single also seem to have declined, with more emphasis on everyday coping. But there is still much interest in whether or not singles are happy (leaning both before and after 1950 to the conclusion that they are not), and the need to defend single status still persists. It is still not taken for granted that it is okay to be single. The sexual problems of singles have become an acceptable subject for popular journalism only since 1950.

The lack of two topics is worth noting.

The large increase in the number and percentage of singles from 1960–1975 seems not to be a major topic in itself. There were only two demographic articles, both in the seventies. And there was only one article (in the 1950s) on cause: Why do people marry or remain single? These two topics are related: since there is little awareness of demographic change, there would hardly be much inquiry into why a greater percentage of individuals are remaining single.

MATE FINDING IN AMERICA

Titles about mate finding suggest that the subject and emphasis have not changed much in recent decades. The great majority of these articles were and are written for women. While the singles population was still declining (1950–1960), there was already an increase in suggested aggressive approaches to marriage, particularly among women: "My Mother Said I Should Give It A Try . . ."; "Men That Get Away and Where They Go." Before 1950 there had been no such articles except for sporadic advice on how to be approachable: "How to be Marriageable: Results of a Marriage Readiness Course." And there were hardly any articles about how to meet women, a problem that many men regard as the most important of all. (Such articles can be found, but they were not perceived as problems of singles, only as problems of the young: How do "men" meet "girls"?)

Before 1940, there were few articles openly concerned with actively taking steps toward finding a husband, and only occasional titles such as "Why They Won't Marry the Modern Girl" that suggest one might, by altering conduct or attitude, increase one's chances of being approached. More recent titles suggest a trend toward encouraging feminine initiative (". . . Where to Find Men") that is more a measure of women's growing interest in independence and equality than a change in perception of singles *per se*.

MAKING THE BEST OF BEING SINGLE

Let us consider next the titles that have to do with accepting and finding happiness as a single person. These might be combined under some heading such as "Making the Best of It," again emphasizing that singleness is not a very desirable state.

There are certainly some repeated notes sounded in this series, but also some changes in recent years. The defenses and pleas and plaints of the unmarried ("In Defense of Spinsters"; "Why I Am an Old Maid") disappear after 1960. Instead, the emphasis shifts to the degree of happiness to be found through single status. In recent years it appears that singleness is less to be defended or lamented than to be analyzed. Earlier articles on singles' happiness featured "compensations" or were phrased negatively: "Does It Hurt to Be an Old Maid?" But in the 1960s, the titles become somewhat less defensive: "Pleasures and Pain of the Single Life"; "When Being Single Stops Being Fun." There are more titles emphasizing the positive side of single life ("The Blessings of Bachelorhood"; "A Spinster's Lot Can Be a Happy One"; "Celebrating Singleness: Marriage May Be Second Best"), though bitterness and sadness appear, as in every period: "The Necessary Melancholy of Bachelor" (1900s); "The Sorrowful Mayden . . . and the Social Bachelor" (1920s); "How to be Human Though Single"; "Movin' On—Alone" (1970s). The twin themes of loneliness and unhappiness persist throughout the century.

DAILY LIFE AMONG AMERICAN SINGLES

Finally, there is a set of titles for the concerns of daily living. These include housing, work, money, love, friendship, sex, and a little side advice to marrieds. They treat problems such as the greater difficulty in getting a loan as a fact of life, not as a project for social reform.

In fact, before 1966 there doesn't seem to be a single article on a specific subject relating to single people that is neutral in tone. "How to Travel Alone," for instance, would be a neutral title, but "How to Travel Alone and Like It" assumes that traveling alone would be normally unpleasant unless one took special measures.

Only after the middle 1960s are there pragmatic discussions of birth control ("Should Doctors Prescribe Contraceptives for Unmarried Ladies?"), housing ("Boys and Girls Together: Apartments for Singles Only"), financial problems ("Life Insurance for Single Women"), or institutions ("Church and the Single Person"). There is a particular increase of interest in the sexual problems of singles as distinct from finding a spouse ("Sex as Athletics in the Singles Complex"), and there are the beginnings of articles *for* marrieds *by* singles ("Serving Singles—Don't Play Mix and Match").

But even in the 1970s this acceptance of single life seemed fragile. There were still more articles with defensive overtones, strenuously urging singles to acknowledge how well off they were, or suggesting yet newer ways of finding a potential mate. The acceptance of singlehood or marriage as a choice— no different from the choice of whether to live in the city or the suburbs, or whether to seek a career in business or government—is an ideal that we may in time achieve. But that time has not yet arrived.

18

NORTH AMERICAN MARRIAGE: 1990

Leo Davids

As a preamble for this attempt to predict the options and regulations defining marriage and family life in North America a generation from now, let us consider some of the powerful long-term trends in this area which can be discerned either at work already, or coming very soon. These provide the causal principles that will be extrapolated here to provide a scientific indication of what the mating and parenthood situation is going to look like in another two decades. The remainder of the paper is essentially a working-out of this prediction exercise so that an account of the new situation is built up, which is the best way we have to predict the nature of marriage in 1990.

"PARENTHOOD IS FUN" MYTH WILL DIE

The foundation of almost everything else that is occurring in the sphere of marriage and family life today is a process which will go right ahead in the next decade or two, and will continue to have a vast effect on people's thinking and their behavior. This process is what Max Weber called the *entzäuberung*, the

From *The Futurist*, October 1971, pp. 190–194, published by the World Future Society, 4916 St. Elmo Avenue, Washington, D.C. 20014. Reprinted by permission.

"demystification" or "disenchantment" of human life, which is a hallmark of the modern orientation. Young people, especially, are continually becoming more sophisticated—due to television, modern education, peergroup frankness about all spheres of life, etc.—and they are no longer accepting the myths, the conventional folklore, upon which ordinary social interaction has been based during the past few decades. Thus, for instance, young people are gradually rejecting the myth of "parenthood is fun," realizing that parenthood is a very serious business and one which ought to be undertaken only when people are ready to plunge in and do a good job.

Another grand complex of myths that is gradually being rejected is that of romantic love, under which it is perfectly acceptable to meet a person, form a sudden emotional attachment to that person without any logic or contemplation, and to marry that person on no other basis than the existence of this cathexis. Similarly, the whole institution of "shot-gun weddings," in which an unwanted, unintended pregnancy (usually occurring with a lower class girl) leads to what is called "necessary" marriage, is going to become a quaint piece of history which will be considered with the same glee that modern readers feel when they read about "bundling" in Colonial America. With young men and women who are all fully-informed about reproduction and what can be done to prevent it, such things will occur very rarely; romantic mate-selection, likewise, is going to continue only among the impoverished and marginally-educated segment of society.

Insofar as family life remains almost the only area of modern behavior that has not yet become rational and calculated but is approached with unexamined, time-honored myths, we can expect that this area is "ripe" for fundamental change. When serious, critical examination of all this really gets moving, very great changes will come about in quite a short time.

PROCREATION CAN BE SUBJECT TO COMMUNAL CONTROL

The second independent variable leading to the developments that we are discussing is the total control of human fertility which advances in medical technique have made possible. There is no need here to discuss the pill, the intra-uterine device (IUD), and the many other ways that are in use already to separate sex from reproduction, and therefore to free relations between men and women from the fear or risk of begetting children who would be a byproduct, an unintended side-effect of fulfilling quite other needs. This control of human fertility means that what procreation does occur in the future is going to be by choice, not by accident. Both illegitimacy and venereal disease will be almost extinct, too, in 20 years. It also means that reproduction and child rearing can henceforth be subjected to communal control, will be potentially regulable by society at large. Without contraception, all the rest of these trends and changes would not be occurring at all.

HUSBAND-WIFE EQUALIZATION IS "INEVITABLE"

Women's Liberation, I believe, is not a fad or a current mass hysteria but is here to stay. Once the schools instituted coeducation, male dominance was doomed. Let us rephrase that term for present purposes, calling it Husband-Wife Equalization, as a general name for certain tendencies that have been evident for many years and are continuing today. We all know that marriage has shifted, to borrow a phrase, from institution to companionship. Indeed, through the demystification-sophistication of young women, their employment in full-status work, and because of the control over reproduction that has now become a reality, the equalization (in regard to decision-making) of wives with their husbands has become inevitable. The implications of this are already being voiced, to some extent, in the platforms and proposals of women's rights organizations, and some points will be touched upon herein.

It must be remembered that there will remain in the foreseeable future, a traditionalist minority even in the most advanced and change-prone societies. This segment will expend much effort to maintain patterns of marriage and family living that they feel are right, and which are consistent with the patterns they experienced, when they were children. This traditionalist minority will certainly not be gone, or vanished to insignificant numbers, in the short span of one generation; therefore, any predictions we make must take into account not only what the "new wave" pattern is going to be, but also the fact that there will be a considerable number of people who elect to maintain the familiar value system that they were socialized with, and to which they are deeply committed.

LAW WILL ACCEPT ABORTION AND NEW FORMS OF MARRIAGE

Another trend which is already at work and which, we may assume, is going to accelerate in the future is that legislatures no longer attempt to shape or create family behavior by statute, but are, and increasingly will be, prepared to adapt the law to actual practice, so that it accepts the general viewpoint that public opinion has consensus on. I think that ever since Prohibition, legislators have been forced to agree that sooner or later legal reform must narrow the gap between law on the books and what is really happening in society. It is likely that this reforming and correlation is going to be speeded up in the next few decades, so that the extent to which there is an uncomfortable and problematic contradiction between the law in force and what people are really doing will be virtually eliminated. Thus, all of the ongoing changes with regard to contraception, abortion, new types of marriage con-

tract, etc., will—it is here assumed—be accepted and in a sense ratified by the Law, as the old-style moralists who can still be found in our agencies of social control cease to fight a rear-guard action against the new norms that are, whether they like them or not, emerging. All modes of birth control will become medical problems, free of any statutory limitation.

An important consequence of widespread social-science knowledge among young people today, which is coupled with a greater use of principles drawn from sociology and anthropology in the process of law reform, will be the recognition that continuity or consistency for each person or married couple is necessary, in regard to the larger questions at least, for a particular marriage system to work well in the long run. If the agreements entered into, whatever their content, involve major inconsistency, if people seem to be changing the fundamental norms between them in midstream or giving much more than they receive, then obviously the community has unwisely allowed these people to enter a situation which must lead to disorganization and conflict sooner or later. This realization from our functionalist understanding of how marriage—or any continuing relationship—operates, will lead to acceptance of the clear necessity for such predictability and fairness in every particular case.

So much for the preamble. What are the consequences? **Two major principles underlying our model of marriage in 1990 emerge from the forces and trends listed above. They are: a) the freedom to personally and explicitly contract the type of marriage one wishes; and b) formal public or communal control over parenthood.**

What is meant by the word "marriage," here? To include the newer forms, we require a looser, broader definition than would suffice in the 1950s. Marriage should therefore be understood to refer to a publicly-registered, lasting commitment to a particular person, which generally includes certain sexual or other rights and obligations between these people (that would not be recognized by their community without such married status).

Free choice of the sort of marriage one wishes does not mean that a man and woman (or two men or women?) will write their own original contract incorporating any combination of rules and arrangements that they like. The reason that such freedom would be beyond that envisioned in our thinking, as argued above, is that they would be able to invent a contract that has severe internal inconsistencies or flights of self-delusion, and which therefore sets up strains for their relationship from the outset. The sophistication which anthropological functionalism has brought to us will lead society to channel the choice of marriage into a selection from among a number of recognized types, each of which has been carefully thought through so that it is tenable in the long run. Thus, people will select from among various ways of being married, each of which makes sense by itself and will enable them to function on a long-run basis once they have made this choice. Neither monogamy nor indefinite permanence are important in this respect, so they will not be required. However, the agreed-upon choice will be explicit and recorded so there's no question of deception or misunderstanding, as well as to provide statistical information, and official registration of this choice is an element of marriage which will remain a matter of public concern.

PEOPLE UNFIT TO BE PARENTS WILL BE SCREENED OUT

The right of society to control parenthood is something that can be predicted from a number of things we already know. For one thing, the rising incidence of battered and neglected children, and our almost total inability to really cope with the battered child's problem except after the fact, will certainly lead legis-

lators to planning how those people who can be discovered, in advance, to be unfit for parenthood may be screened out and prevented from begetting offspring who will be the wretched target of their parents' emotional inadequacies. **Furthermore, increasing awareness of the early-childhood roots of serious crime and delinquency will also lead to an attempt to prevent major deviance by seeing to it that early socialization occurs under favorable circumstances. It does not appear that there will be many other really effective ways in which rising crime rates could eventually be reversed.** This, however, will again mean that those who raise children will have to be evaluated for this purpose in some way, so that only those parents who are likely to do a respectable job of early socialization will be licensed to release new members of society into the open community. If such testing and selection is not done, we have no way to protect ourselves from large numbers of young people who have been raised in a way that almost inevitably will have them providing the murderers, rapists and robbers of the next generation. **Since we now begin to have the technology and the knowledge to prevent this, we may confidently expect that parent-licensing is going to come into force soon.**

One other trend, perhaps phrased from the negative side, must also be mentioned here as we try to describe the norms that will probably circumscribe marriage in another generation. This trend is the decline of informal, personal social control over married couples which was formerly exercised by kinsmen and neighbors. It would not make sense to anticipate massive changes in the law and explicit contractual entry into marriage as the normal way to shape married life, if mate selection and the interactions between husband and wife were still under the regulation of custom, vigilantly enforced by aunts, grandfathers or brothers-in-law. It is precisely because the vast mobility of modern living has led, along with other factors, to the isolation of the nuclear family—which is the source of so many problems in the family sphere today—that this new kind of regulation will be called into force and accepted as necessary and proper. The recognition that marriage has left the sphere of *Gemeinschaft* will help to bring about a consensus that the regulation of this area of life will have to be handled like any other kind of socially-important interpersonal behavior in today's *Gesellschaft* civilization.

COURTSHIP MAY BE "DUTCH TREAT"

What will courtship be like in about twenty years? We can assume that courtship will, as it does currently, serve as a testing ground for the kind of marriage that people have in their minds, perhaps even dimly or unconsciously. Thus, insofar as particular young men or women may have begun to feel that the type of marriage they would like is Type A rather than Type B, their courtship would be of the sort that normally leads to Type A, and in a sense tests their readiness to build their relationship along those lines. Only the traditionalist couples will keep up such classic patriarchal customs as the male holding doors, assisting with a coat, or paying for both meals when a couple dines out together. The egalitarians would go "Dutch treat," in other words, each paying for himself, during this spouse research period. Thus, courtship will be of several kinds corresponding to the kinds of marriage that we are about to describe, with the conventional acts and phases in the courtship signaling the present intention of the parties involved to head toward that kind of marriage. Thus, pre-marriage and marriage will exhibit a psycho-social continuity, the early marriage centering on the basic interpersonal stance that is already represented in courtship.

Of course, courtship will serve this testing and assessing function after people have been approximately matched through computer mate-finding methods. Random dating and hopeless courtships will have been largely prevented through the provision of basic cate-goric information which people can use to screen possible spouses, such as total years of schooling completed, aptitude and I Q scores, major subjects (which are related to intellectual interests in a very direct way), religiosity, leisure and recreation preferences, and similar things.

For remarriage suitors, data on wealth or credit and occupation would also be used, along with some indication of attitudes concerning home life and procreation. Since homogamy (similarity between spouses) is recognized as an important indicator of marital success, such information will be systematically gathered and made available to cut down on the wasteful chance element in mate selection. It is only when people are continuing their search for a spouse within the appropriate "pool," defined in terms of those who are at the right point with regard to these variables, that courtship as a series of informal but direct experiments in relationship-building will come into play.

CELIBACY WILL BE LEGITIMIZED

Explicit choice of the kind of marriage one enters into is, of course, an effect not only of the emancipation of women, but of men as well. What will some of the major options be? With the insurance functions that were formerly secured by having children (who would provide during one's old age) being completely taken over by the government (assisted by unions, pension funds and the like), there will be little reason to warn those who choose childlessness against this course. With celibacy no bar to sexual satisfaction, society will accept the idea that some segments of the population can obtain whatever intimate satisfactions they require in a series of casual, short-term "affairs" (as we call them today), and will never enter any publicly-registered marriage. With celibacy or spinsterhood fully legitimized, and with no fear of destitution when one has retired from the labor force, there will undoubtedly be a sizeable number of people who decide not to enter into a marriage of any sort on any terms.

TRIAL MARRIAGE FOR THREE OR FIVE YEARS

Another not-unfamiliar option in this regard will be the renewable trial marriage, in which people explicitly contract for a childless union which is to be comprehensively evaluated after three years or five years, at which point either a completely new decision can be reached or the same arrangement can be renewed for another term of three or five years. This would not be, then, a question of divorce; it is simply a matter of a definite arrangement having expired. The contract having been for a limited term, both parties are perfectly free to decide not to renew it when that term is over. This would be a normal, perhaps minor, part of one's "marital career."

A third option, which introduces very few complications, is the permanent childless marriage; the arrangement between the two adults is of indefinite duration, but they have agreed in advance that there will be no offspring, and of course, there is no question but that medical technology will make it possible for them to live up to that part of the arrangement. Some will choose sterilization, others will use contraceptive methods which can be abandoned if one changes his mind and is authorized to procreate.

Compound marriages will also be allowed, whether they be polygamous, polyandrous or group marriages. However, these communes will not be free of the same obligations that any marriage entails, such as formally registering the terms of the agreement among the members; any significant change in the arrangements among members of such a familial commune will have to be recorded in the appropriate public place in the same way as marriages and divorces which involve only one husband and one wife. There will be great freedom with regard to the number of people in the commune, but internal consistency concerning the give-and-take among the members, their privileges and obligations, will be required. The functional, pragmatic ethics emerging in today's youth culture will be strictly adhered to, some years hence, not as moral absolutes, not because people have come to the belief that these represent the true right and wrong, but in order to prevent serious conflict.

LESS THAN A THIRD OF MARRIAGES WILL PRODUCE CHILDREN

With the majority of young people in society choosing one of the foregoing patterns, the number of marriages in which children are expected will be relatively small; perhaps 25% to 30% of the population will be so serious about having children that they will be prepared to undergo the rigorous training and careful evaluation that will be necessary for them to obtain the requisite licenses. The marriages intended to produce children will usually be classic familistic marriages, in which the general pattern of interaction between husband and wife, as well as the relationship between parent and child, may be fairly similar to the contemporary upper middle-class marriage that we know in 1970. However, three-generation households will probably increase. I see no reason to believe that all of child rearing will be done in a collective way, as in an Israeli kibbutz or in the communes which have been set up in some Communist countries; infant care may gravitate in the direction of day nurseries, however, while school children will live at home, as now.

WOULD-BE PARENTS WILL HAVE TO PROVE THEIR SUITABILITY

The familial pattern, then, explicitly chosen by some men and women to perpetuate the classic familistic marriage, will be intended to provide a home atmosphere approximately similar to that which can be found in those middle class families of today's society that have the best socio-emotional climate. The community will be assured that this home atmosphere is, in fact, most probable, since it has been prepared for, rather than left to an accident of kind fate and to happenstance talents that people bring to parenthood nowadays. All those who desire to become parents, and therefore to exercise a public responsibility in an extremely important and sensitive area of personal functioning, will have to prove that they are indeed the right people to serve as society's agents of socialization. Just as those who wish to adopt a child, nowadays, are subjected to intensive interviewing which aims at discovering the healthiness of the relationship between husband and wife and of the motivation for parenthood, the suitability that the man or woman displays for coping with the stresses of parenthood, as well as the physical and material conditions that the adopted child will be enjoying, the evaluation of mother and father applicants in future will be done by a team of professionals who have to reach the judgment that this particular individual or couple have the background to become professionals themselves: that is, recognized and certified parents.

PARENT-TRAINING WILL BE INTENSE

The course of study for parenthood will include such subjects as: human reproduction and gestation; infant care; developmental physiology and psychology; theories of socialization; and educational psychology. Starting with a foundation of systematic but abstract scientific knowledge, the practical and applied courses in hygienic, nutritional, emotional and perceptual-aesthetic care of children will follow, in the same way as training for medicine and other professions. In addition to the subject matter referred to above, prospective parents will be required to achieve some clarity concerning values and philosophy of life, in which they will be guided by humanistic scholars, and will also

be required to attain a clear understanding of the mass media, their impact on children, and how to manage mass media consumption as an important part of socialization in the modern urban environment. **One side effect of such parent training may be a sharp drop in the power of the peer group, as parents do more and with greater self-confidence.**

Suitable examinations will be devised, and only those who achieve adequate grades in these areas will be given a parenthood license. Some young men and women are likely to take the parenthood curriculum "just in case"; that is, although they have not yet thought through the type of marriage that they desire or the kind of spouse they are looking for, they may continue their education by entering parenthood studies and obtaining the diploma, should it turn out that they elect a classic, child-rearing marriage later on. **Possibly, fathers will be prohibited from full-time employment outside the home while they have pre-school children, or if their children have extra needs shown by poor conduct or other symptoms of psychic distress.**

One of the more striking areas of change, which can serve as an indicator of how different things will be then from what they are now, is age. Age of marriage now is in the early 20's, and child bearing typically occurs when women are in their middle twenties. Also, husbands today are usually about three to four years older than their wives. In another generation, the age of child bearing will probably be considerably advanced, as people who have decided upon parenthood will either be enjoying themselves during an extended childless period before they undertake the burdens and responsibilities of child rearing, or completing the course of study for certification to undertake parenthood. It is probable that women will bear children when they are in their middle and late thirties, so that they will have enjoyed a decade or a decade and a half of companionate marriage in which there was full opportunity to travel, to read, or just relax before they have to spend 24 hours a day caring for a small child. As to the age difference between husbands and wives, which is essentially based on the patriarchal tradition that the man is the "senior" in the home, it will probably disappear in the case of all forms of marriage other than the classic familistic one; there, where people have explicitly decided that the kind of marriage they want is the same as their parents had back in the medievaloid 1970s, or the ancient 1960s, the husband will continue to be a few years older than his wife.

This picture of the marriage situation in 1990 leaves open various questions and problems, which should be touched upon briefly in conclusion. One of the difficulties in this scenario is the question of what authority will make the necessary decisions: What sorts of committees will be in charge of devising the various internally-consistent kinds of marriage, working out the parent education courses, and certifying people for parenthood? There are, after all, political implicatons to controlling marriage and parenthood in this way, and the general public will have to be satisfied that those who exercise authority in this area are, in fact, competent as well as impartial.

Another problem is that of securing complete and valid information: (a) for those who are preparing to locate suitable mates through computer matching, or who are preparing to make a commitment in some specific form of marriage; and (b) concerning those who apply for the parenthood course and later for the license to practice parenthood. Unless we can be sure that the inputs used for making such judgments contain information which is adequate in quantity and true as well, these new systems will not be able to function without a great deal of deviance, and might easily engender problems which are worse than those which we confront today.

WILL CHILDLESSNESS LEAD TO LESS LONG-RANGE INVESTMENT?

A third issue is that of parenthood having tied people to the community, and given them a commitment to the environment: What will childlessness do to one's motivation for planning/preserving; will it de-motivate all long-range investment? Research on this could start now, comparing parents with the childless.

Finally, we have assumed that marriage is going to continue, in some way. That is based on the belief that people will continue to desire a secure partnership with another person or small group, and that youth will feel it is better to institutionally buttress their sharing of life, in general, by setting up a marriage of some kind. This depends, in fact, on the interpersonal climate in communities, and the extent to which people feel isolation and unmet needs that marriage will solve. When marriage is not desired, then we will have discovered new forms of warm, dependable primary association replacing the old institution which has supplied psychological support to people through the millennia.

VII

EDUCATION
Institution in a Cross-Fire

Much of our time up to the age of eighteen—and often beyond—is spent in formal education. All societies are concerned with socializing their young, and schools have become a key mechanism for the formal transmission of knowledge and culture. The functions that schools perform include perpetuating societal values, training young people for their roles in society, and allocating them to societal positions.

Sociologists interested in the institution of education focus on the structure of the system, including the functions performed, the roles played by the various groups involved, the processes that operate within the system, and the pressures from other parts of society that influence the system.

In the first article, Brodinsky discusses some pressures on schools and the resultant changes in the 1970s. A key goal that many of these changes reflect was the attempt by many groups to gain equality—a goal that gained momentum in all institutions in the 1960s and that is being carried on in the programs of the 1970s and 1980s.

Focusing specifically on this issue of equality, Rist discusses what is probably the most troublesome and divisive education issue of our times—desegregation. He succinctly analyzes the desegregation issue, distinguishes between emotions and evidence, and suggests social policies for the future.

In the 1970s schools came under increasing attack from many parents and legislators, who demanded that schools be held accountable for what they were producing. Questions were asked about the value of standardized test scores, students' competence in basic skills, and students graduating without adequate skills. This conservative backlash to the reforms of the 1960s—open education, alternative schools, and others—has led to a demand for change in the schools—not a new phenomenon, we might add. A *Time* magazine article lists a number of concerns with education today: finances, school violence, curriculum reforms, student apathy, and poorly prepared teachers. The article's suggestions may seem radical and might not win favor with many; however, its assessment that change is needed would be endorsed by most of us. The blame for school problems cannot be placed on one group: any change must take students, teachers, administrators, and the family into account. The *Time* magazine article, while not written by sociologists, does endorse the macro-society view of educational problems.

As you read this chapter, consider the following questions: What are some trends that have continued from the 1960s into the 1980s? How do problems faced by schools mirror those in the larger society? What seem to be the current education issues and trends in the 1980s?

19

SOMETHING HAPPENED: EDUCATION IN THE SEVENTIES

Ben Brodinsky

The decade in education began with a volley of gunfire, killing four students at a Kent, Ohio, university campus. It ended with shouts of glee from lobbyists for the National Education Association (NEA) as the House of Representatives gave final approval to a Department of Education.

But neither event has a place among the major developments in education during the 1970s. I mention them because the first was a symbol of the violence and unrest that was sweeping colleges and high schools as the decade opened; the second speaks of the unrelenting reach of the federal government toward public education. Both were dramatic.

As I reviewed educational developments of the past decade, I looked for events that affected schools and colleges in a lasting way, for good or for ill; that stimulated an inordinate volume of public and educational debate; and that lay at the center of national trends and movements.

More than 100 entries met these criteria. But if there was one dominant theme underlying education events of the seventies, it was the yearning for equality. This was the decade in which Americans battled to bring equal

Reprinted by permission of the author.

school dollars to all school districts, whether poor or rich. It also brought new hope for equality to the handicapped, to women, to foreign-language-speaking groups.

It was a decade troubled by controversies over busing, prayer in the schools, the rights of students, and the integrity of textbooks. Educators saw their school budgets eroded by inflation and hit by rising fuel costs. Big cities were pinched by one severe financial crisis after another. Classrooms, hallways, and playgrounds were wracked by student violence and crime.

Biggest newsmakers in education were not educators; they were the U. S. Supreme Court, Congress, executive departments. Operating more than 100 federal aid programs, officials in Washington guided, influenced, or sought to control education to an extent that could hardly be measured or comprehended either by educators or the public.

The climate of the 1970s was not healthy for learning, excellence in education, or intellectual daring. There was little time for improvement of the curriculum, which in many instances retrogressed to the traditionalism of an earlier generation. Little was done for the ailing high schools, and reform efforts left secondary education just about where it was in the 1950s. The concepts of early childhood education failed to make much impression upon the nation's schools.

But it was a decade that gave off heat, steam, or smoke about vouchers, performance contracting, "Sesame Street," the role of private schools, Proposition 13, teacher centers, and the fact that the President's daughter enrolled in an inner-city Washington public school for one year.

Out of the welter of such events I select 10 for elaboration.

SERRANO AND SONS

When the California Supreme Court decreed that school districts relying primarily on the local property tax may be depriving children of equal protection under law (*Serrano* v. *Priest*, 1971), the ruling "shook the foundations of American school finance." Or so it seemed at the decade's beginning. It did not seem so as the decade ended.

But the *Serrano* decision influenced an equally famous case, *Rodriguez*, in which a U.S. district court in Texas agreed that total reliance on property taxes creates sharp differences in the quality of education for children: Rich school districts provide schooling of high quality, poor districts short-change school children.

With what seemed like bated breath, the nation's educators waited for decisive word from the U. S. Supreme Court. When it came, the word (*Rodriguez*, 1973) was by no means resolute. The Court left the use of property taxes for schools pretty much undisturbed, but urged that states correct any constitutional deficiencies by devising new school taxing and spending plans.

Throughout the seventies some 25 states labored to equalize educational opportunities between poor and rich school districts. In these efforts only one thing was certain: The task of reforming school finance has been lifted from the talk stage at educational conferences to the action arenas of state legislatures, courts, and state education agencies.

That may be the decade's most significant achievement in school finance.

What about results? A 1979 Rand Corporation study found that school finance reforms have somewhat loosened school revenue ties to local property and that state treasuries have assumed larger shares of school expenses. But poor schools remain poor, rich schools remain rich, and equalization is still a long way off.

ON BEHALF OF THE HANDICAPPED

When, in 1971, a U. S. district court ruled that Pennsylvania schools must provide education for all retarded children, ages 4 to 21, regardless of cost, the decision proved momentous. It touched off battles for the handicapped in half the states and provided a *cause célèbre* for many professional organizations.

It was a cause calling for humanity, compassion, and dollars. Knock on 10 doors on any street, ran the argument, and behind at least one of them you will find a handicapped child or youth. His chances of getting an adequate education have been slim—clearly a case of deprivation of equal opportunity.

By the middle of the decade about a score of legislatures had enacted laws requiring "appropriate" programs for the handicapped. Educators groaned—and struggled to meet the new challenges. They complained of a lack of special teachers, instructional materials, and funds to do what the laws (or the courts) required. And they kept calling for help from Washington.

Help seemingly came in 1975. Congress passed the Education for All Handicapped Children Act, which has since become famous as P. L. 94–142. Never before has any people in any land accepted so daring a challenge. It requires a massive effort, the provision of individualized schooling for 5 to 7 million physically, mentally, and emotionally handicapped students. It also calls for expensive changes in school plants and facilities to make them accessible to all.

Federal grants to states were the inducements, and a gradual phasing-in was one of the palliatives. But the pain, struggles, and red tape of meeting federal mandates on behalf of the handicapped promoted a rising volume of complaints and doubts among educators: Can "the boldest, most humane of educational ventures" be carried out effectively?

FOR WOMEN AND THE BILINGUAL

From the decade's beginning to its end, American education was embroiled in struggles to achieve equality for women in schools and colleges—and for students to whom English was a second language.

Title IX was the big legal stick Congress handed to those who wanted to end discrimination against women. It was part of the Educational Amendments of 1972. The big year for Title IX was 1975, when federal regulations took effect—and they touched on scores of aspects of hiring, firing, promotion, benefits; on curriculum and extracurriculum; on sports and physical education; on participation of girls and women in school life and educational administration.

Textbook publishers began reexamining their products to root out sexist attitudes and biased reporting. Writers were urged to purge their prose of sexism.

Discrimination against non-English-speaking children had been troubling the conscience of educators for generations. It was not until the 1970s, however, that something practical was done. A Bilingual Education Act, on the statute books since 1965, began to take effect in the mid-seventies with a trickle of federal dollars.

The U. S. Supreme Court decision in *Lau* v. *Nichols* (1974) gave new impetus to the movement. In a case originating on the West Coast, the Court required public schools to "rectify language deficiencies" in order to open up the instructional programs to children who do not speak or understand English.

The initiatives and programs in Washington, state capitals, and local districts on behalf of bilingual students mounted into the hundreds by 1979. Still, advocates charged it was not enough, that funds, teachers, and instructional materials were inadequate to serve the millions of Latinos, Orientals, and American Indians who are entitled to instruction in their native tongues. These advocates had a sound political base; nevertheless, they were challenged by others, educators and laymen, who saw philosophical defects, and even mischief, in bilingual education. The worth and value, the how and why of the movement, will be debated in the next decade, possibly in the next century.

DUE PROCESS FOR STUDENTS

The 1970s gave toughness to the dictum, established in the 1969 *Tinker* case, that "students do not shed their constitutional rights at the schoolhouse gate." Within 60 days in 1975 the U. S. Supreme Court ruled in two cases that students are protected by the due process clause of the Fourteenth Amendment. The decisions created shock waves among educators, or so said the National School Boards Association at the time.

In *Goss* v. *Lopez*, a case involving student suspensions, the High Court said that a student facing suspension must be given oral or written notice of the charges against him and an opportunity to present his side of the story. The majority opinion stated: "We do not believe we have imposed procedures on school disciplinarians which are inappropriate in a classroom setting. Instead, we have imposed requirements which are less than a fairminded school principal would impose upon himself in order to avoid unfair suspensions. . . ."

In *Wood* v. *Strickland*, another suspension case, the Court went further, ruling that a student whose rights have been violated may sue school authorities for damages. Said the Court: "While school officials are entitled to a qualified good-faith immunity from liability of damages, they are not immune from such liability if they knew or reasonably should have known that the actions they took violated constitutional rights of students."

Pained cries from administrators that the rulings meant erosion of local school control, a threat to discipline, and a menace to teachers and principals lasted only a short time. State departments of education soon began publishing impressive brochures detailing student rights (usually coupled with responsibilities), and boards of education wrote or rewrote policies and regulations dealing with due process.

Arbitrary and unilateral procedures against students—where and if they existed—were dealt a blow during the years that historians may call the decade of human rights.

BASICS AND COMPETENCY

"Back to the basics" was the decade's best advertising slogan, a theme for mass media editorials and political oration, and an emotional topic for boards of education and PTA meetings.

The popular outcry was for more and better reading, writing, and arithmetic instruction. But at the movement's height, about mid-decade, demands arose for drill, recitation, more homework, stricter discipline, the teaching of patriotism and an end to social promotions.

A small number of school districts responded by instituting what they called back-to-basics programs, or they set up alternative schools devoted to the three Rs, with history taught by chronology and science by memorization. Other school districts publicized their dedication to fundamental subjects and declaimed: "We've been teaching the basics all along. We've never stopped teaching basics." Still others reexamined their curricular programs and allotted a bit more in time, money, and staff to whatever list of "basics" local communities demanded.

It was not a shining hour for curriculum improvement. Back-to-basics advocates (and they included some educators) gave little, changed little.

More significant were the actions of minimum competency proponents throughout the 1970s. Their arguments ran as follows: Students indeed require a set of basic skills to get along in the world after graduation. These included, over and above the three Rs, skills for citizenship, employment, family life, consumerism, enjoyment of the arts. It's possible to identify these minimum skills, teach them to all (or nearly all) students, and not let anyone move up the educational ladder to graduation until the students pass required tests.

The public liked the idea. States enacted minimum competency laws at a rapid pace throughout the late seventies. Not a state dared neglect demands for such programs. This bright hope for education began to dim, however, by 1979, as educators confronted the problems and the court actions generated by minimum competency laws. Disturbing also was a finding reported by the Education Commission of the States: "No research evidence is available to show that mandated student competency programs are working."

BAKKE AND AFFIRMATIVE ACTION

"The most anxiously awaited court decision of the century." "The most significant civil rights case of the generation." "The most far-reaching educational dispute since the battles for school desegregation."

So ran the hyperbole on the *Allan Bakke* case for more than a year before the U. S. Supreme Court announced its decision on 28 June 1978. National interest was intense, fanned more by words in the mass media than in the literature of education.

The center of attention was a thirty-fivish Marine Corps veteran of Vietnam who was passionately interested in studying medicine. His applications to the University of California Medical School at Davis were denied.

Bakke thought he was rejected because he is white. He saw special places reserved for minority students under a two-track system for applicants. He saw black students admitted who were less well qualified than he when he was rejected.

"Reverse discrimination" was the cry. The lines of legal battle formed, often along racial lines. More beliefs, on both sides of the issue, were filed with the Supreme Court than on any other case within the last 20 years. Hanging in the balance, many thought, was the national policy of affirmative action, under which minority groups were given preference in education and employment. Would the Supreme Court nullify this hard-won right?

When the decision finally came it read: "Affirmed in part and reversed in part." It meant that the Court affirmed Bakke's right to enter the university but rejected the argument that affirmative actions based on race should be outlawed. Admissions programs favoring minorities, the Court said further, must be kept under "strict judicial scrutiny."

Neither whites nor blacks were completely happy with the decision. Few thought that the basic issues of affirmative action or admissions policy were resolved. Most predicted that another generation of court cases would follow the *Bakke* ruling.

CAREER EDUCATION

The average life of an educational reform in the U. S. is about three years. Career education, introduced in 1971 with much fanfare, has outlived most efforts to reform some aspect of schooling. At the end of the decade career education was still alive and doing well, or doing something, in probably a fourth of the nation's school districts.

Credit for the concept goes to Sidney P. Marland, Jr. When he took office as U. S. commissioner of education, he startled the country, and jarred the education community, with a proposal that career education should begin in the first grade and remain a central concept through graduate school.

Was he talking about vocational education? No, but partly yes. Was he talking about occupational information? No, but partly yes. He declined to offer a definition. Career education, he said, should be a bridge between school years and work years; it should stress reality in all classrooms, no matter what subject is taught.

Despite its vagueness, Marland's idea generated enormous public interest, caught the fancy of Congress, and gave rise to a stream of speeches, articles, research studies, and books. Its proponents offered career education as a corrective for problems of dropouts, poor discipline, youth unemployment, apathy in learning. It is a true basic, they said.

In 1975 a research group counted 9,300 school districts where "career education was under way." Even more important, said the research, a fifth of all districts had started inservice programs to help teachers incorporate career concepts into their lessons.

Always a concept in search of a definition, career education was the decade's moderate success story. Countless teachers, for the first time, helped students discover their interests and aptitudes, provided them with the facts about the world of work, and called it career education. When the Dallas school system built and operated a 21-million-dollar facility for the instruction of everything from aeronautics to television, that too went to the credit side of career education.

DECLINING ENROLLMENTS

Few Americans took note when enrollments in the nation's schools dropped by half a million during 1971 and 1972. But when, in 1974, some 700,000 fewer boys and girls entered the elementary grades, both laymen and educators discovered what statisticians had been predicting. The nation's schools had entered a decade-long decline in enrollment. Instead of problems of growth, educators had to meet problems of shrinkage.

What to do with emptying schools and

how to reduce the teaching force, with justice, became major challenges for educators during the seventies.

In some districts school plants went up for sale or rent. In others school boards used freed-up space to expand art, music, science, and library resources and activities. Still others used the new space for adult education or pre-school programs.

But efforts to dispose of surplus teaching stations were usually met with community protests and even court actions. The art of closing a public school was new to most administrators and had to be learned slowly. Advice from experts was to plan ahead four to five years. "In closing schools, figure what it takes to get a bond issue passed," said the Educational Facilities Laboratories of New York, "then double or triple the time."

Long-range planning was also required for solution of staff problems created by enrollment declines. The options included reducing class size and teacher/pupil ratios—if budget and school board policy allowed. In most instances, however, districts resorted to reassignments, voluntary early retirement, freezes on hiring, and reduction in force.

No matter what action was proposed or taken, it created staff anxiety or community discord. And invariably administrators became entangled in the laws, regulations, and nego-tiated contract clauses governing personnel, with lawsuits to follow.

ASSESSMENT, ACHIEVEMENT, SCORES

A daring educational venture of the 1970s was the continual probing into almost impenetra-ble questions: What are American students learning? What do they know and what can they do? And the puzzle of the decade was, Why aren't they doing better?

First facts about the quality of schooling came from the National Assessment of Edu-cational Progress (NAEP) in 1970. This agency, controversial at first, gained credibility as it got down to work measuring student achieve-ment in art, careers, citizenship, literature, mathematics, music, reading, science, social studies, and writing.

Its 1970 findings dealt with science and citizenship, and the report card for elemen-tary and secondary schools was a mix of Cs and Ds, with a few As or Bs. As year after year NAEP poured out thousands of facts about student progress, valuable clues came here and there for curriculum workers, textbook writers, and teacher educators. America accepted periodic assessment of its students as an instrument of education. Funds from the federal government and other sources kept the tests going.

In the middle of the decade NAEP began to send out ominous clues about declines in achievement in science, math, and language arts skills among the groups tested. But NAEP did not prepare Americans for the 1975 shock. The College Entrance Examination Board reported that scores on its Scholastic Aptitude Tests had dropped 10 points on the verbal section and eight points on the math-ematics section from the year before. More-over, the nation learned that the declines, which had begun in the 1960s, would proba-bly continue.

A panel of educators took two years to search for the reasons. Its findings included a long list of factors—from the debilitating role of television to the increase in numbers of minority students taking the tests.

But critics of the schools were convinced that the responsibility lay with "permissive education," "lack of discipline," and "the retreat from the basics."

STRIKES, BARGAINING, POWER

Organized teachers took power during the 1970s.[1] They did it through collective bargain-ing, political action, and use of the strike when necessary.

Opposition to unionism within the profession virtually disappeared during the 1970s. Educators looked at labor tactics, and saw they were good, especially for classroom teachers.

Labor taught American educators that they must organize, must show militance, must have the right to collective bargaining with their employers, and must work only under contracts negotiated in good faith by both sides. The lessons appealed especially to teacher activists; within the decade labor unionism dominated the NEA as well as the AFT and swept into supervisory and administrative groups.

The collective bargaining contract became the main tool for teacher power. Only 15 years ago fewer than 100,000 public school teachers were serving under written contracts. As the 1970s drew to a close, "most" American teachers were covered by contracts negotiated under state laws. Intense lobbying by teachers in all state capitals brought these laws into being.

American education produced few leaders during the 1970s who could be recognized by the public at large. Teacher unionization produced such a leader. He is Albert Shanker, head of the 520,000-member American Federation of Teachers, who taught the ways of the labor union to schoolpeople. Admired, hated, respected, Shanker emerged as a personality who could charm teachers as well as their bosses. "Power is better than powerlessness," said Shanker.

NOTE

[1]Although the National Association of Professional Educators, headquartered in Washington, D.C., claims 46,000 members, its impact was not great enough to gain it listing in the U.S. Office of Education's 1977–1978 *Directory of English Associations*.

20

HELP! TEACHER CAN'T TEACH!

Like some vast jury gradually and reluctantly arriving at a verdict, politicians, educators and especially millions of parents have come to believe that the U. S. public schools are in parlous trouble. Violence keeps making headlines. Test scores keep dropping. Debate rages over whether or not one-fifth or more adult Americans are functionally illiterate. High school graduates go so far as to sue their school systems because they got respectable grades and a diploma but cannot fill in job application forms correctly. Experts confirm that students today get at least 25% more As and Bs than they did 15 years ago, but know less. A Government-funded nationwide survey group, the National Assessment of Educational Progress, reports that in science, writing, social studies and mathematics the achievement of U.S. 17-year-olds has dropped regularly over the past decade.

Rounding up the usual suspects in the

Reprinted by permission from *Time*, The Weekly Newsmagazine. Copyright Time, Inc. 1980.

learning crisis is easy enough. The decline of the family that once instilled respect for authority and learning. The influence of television on student attention span. The disruption of schools created by busing and the national policy of keeping more students in school longer, regardless of attitude or aptitude. The conflicting demands upon the public school system, which is now expected not only to teach but to make up for past and present racial and economic injustice.

But increasingly too, parents have begun to blame the shortcomings of the schools on the lone and very visible figure at the front of the classroom. Teachers for decades have been admired for selfless devotion. More recently, as things went wrong, they were pitied as overworked martyrs to an overburdened school system. Now bewildered and beleaguered, teachers are being blamed— rightly or wrongly—for much of the trouble in the classroom.

One reason is simply that it is easier for society to find someone to blame than to hold up a mirror and see that U. S. culture itself is largely responsible. But the new complaints about teachering also arise from a dismaying discovery: quite a few teachers (estimates range up 20%) simply have not mastered the basic skills in reading, writing and arithmetic that they are supposed to teach.

Of course, among the 2.2 million teachers in the nation's public schools are hundreds of thousands of skilled and dedicated people who, despite immense problems, manage to produce the miraculous blend of care and discipline, energy, learning and imagination that good teaching requires. Many newcomers to the field are still attracted by the dream of helping children rather than for reasons of security or salary. The estimated average salary of elementary school teachers is $15,661, and of high school teachers $16,387, for nine months' work. The average yearly pay of a plumber is about $19,700; for a government clerk it's approximately $15,500. The best-educated and most selfless teachers are highly critical and deeply concerned about the decline in teaching standards and educational procedures. Their frustration is perhaps the strongest warning signal of all.

Horror stories about teaching abound. In Oregon a kindergarten teacher who had been given As and Bs at Portland State University was recently found to be functionally illiterate. How could this be? Says Acting Dean of the School of Education Harold Jorgensen: "It was a whole series of people not looking closely at her."

In Chicago a third-grade teacher wrote on the blackboard: "Put the following words in alfabetical order." During the weeklong teacher strike last winter, many Chicago parents were appalled by what they saw on television news of schools and teachers. Recalls one mother: "I froze when I heard a teacher tell a TV reporter, "I teaches English."

In the Milwaukee suburb of Wales, Wis., school board members were outraged when teachers sent them written curriculum proposals riddled with bad grammar and spelling. Teachers had written *dabate* for *debate*, *documant* for *document*. *Would* was *woud*, and *separate* was *seperate*. Angry parents waved samples of their children's work that contained uncorrected whoppers, marked with such teacher comments as "outstanding" and "excellent."

A Gallup poll has found that teacher laziness and lack of interest are the most frequent accusations of half the nation's parents, who complain that students get "less schoolwork" now than 20 years ago. Whether the parent perceptions are fair or not, there is no doubt that circumstances have certainly changed some teacher attitudes. At a Miami senior high school this spring, one social studies teacher asked his pupils whether their homework was completed. Half the students said no. The teacher recorded their answers in his gradebook but never bothered to collect the papers. Says the teacher, who has been in the profession for 15 years and has now become dispirited: "I'm not willing any more to take home 150 notebooks and grade them. I work from 7:30 a.m. to 2 p.m., and that's what I get paid for." A longtime teacher in a large suburban school outside Boston told *Time* it is common knowledge that some of her colleagues, anxious to preserve their jobs as enrollments dwindle, fail children simply to ensure hefty class size the next year.

The new doubts about teachers have led to a state-by-state demand from legislators and citizen groups that teachers take special examinations to prove they are competent, much like the student competency exams that have become a requirement in 38 states. Asks Indiana State Senator Joan Gubbins: "Shouldn't we first see if the teachers are competent before we expect the kids to be competent?"

With 41 million pupils, public school education is one of the nation's largest single government activities. Current expenditures (federal, state and local) run to $95 billion. So vast and costly an educational system does not cheerfully react to criticism or adapt to change.

The push toward testing teacher competency, however, depends less on Washington than on state and local governments. One of the most instructive battles fought over the issue occurred in Mobile, Ala., and was led by conservative attorney Dan Alexander, president of the board of education. In 1978, after the board required competency testing of Mobile high school seniors, Alexander was besieged by angry parents, at least partly because 53% of the students who took the city's first competency exam flunked it. Recalls Alexander: "Parents came out of the woodwork saying, 'If you're going to crack down on my child, let me tell you about some of my children's teachers.'" One parent brought him a note sent home by a fifth-grade teacher with a master's degree, which read in part: ''Scott is dropping in his studies he acts as if he don't Care. Scott want pass in his assignment at all, he had a poem to learn and he fell to do it." Says Alexander: "I was shocked. I could not believe we had teachers who could not write a grammatically correct sentence. I took the complaints down to the superintendent, and what shocked me worse was that he wasn't shocked."

Alexander made the note public as the kickoff of a campaign for teacher testing. Says he: "Competency testing is probably a misnomer. You cannot test a teacher on whether he's competent, but you certainly can prove he's incompetent." The proposed exams for veteran teachers were blocked by Alexander's colleagues on the board. But they agreed that all new teachers should score at least 500 on the Educational Testing Service's 3¼-hour National Teacher Examination (N.T.E.) which measures general knowledge, reading, writing and arithmetic. Only about half of the Mobile job applicants who took the N.T.E. in 1979 passed.

The American Federation of Teachers, which has 550,000 members, is opposed to testing experienced teachers, though it approves competency exams for new candidates. The much larger National Education Association is against any kind of competency testing for teachers, claiming teacher competency cannot be measured by written tests. Even so, some form of teacher testing has been approved in twelve states.[1] Proposals for teacher testing have been introduced in Colorado, Illinois, Iowa, Kansas, Missouri, New York, Vermont and Wisconsin, and a bill in Oklahoma is scheduled to be signed into law this week. Polls say the teacher-testing movement is supported by 85% of U. S. adults.

Thus far actual test scores of teacher applicants seem depressing. In Louisiana, for instance, only 53% passed in 1978, 63% last year. What about the ones who fail? Says Louisiana Certification Director Jacqueline Lewis: "Obviously they're moving out of state to teach in states where the tests are not required." The results of basic achievement tests taken by job applicants at Florida's Pinellas County school board (St. Petersburg, Clearwater) are not encouraging. Since 1976, the board has required teacher candidates to read at an advanced tenth-grade level and solve math problems at an eighth-grade level. Though all had their B. A. in hand, about one-third of the applicants (25% of the whites, 79% of the blacks) flunked Pinellas' test the first time they took it in 1979.

In 1900, when only 6% of U. S. children graduated from high school, secondary school teachers were looked up to as scholars of considerable learning. Public school teachers were essential to what was regarded as the proud advance of U. S. education. By 1930, 30% of American 17-year-olds were graduating from high school, and by the mid-1960s, graduates totaled 70%. The American public school was hailed for teaching citizenship and common sense to rich and poor, immigrant and native-born children, and for giving them a common democratic experience. "The public school was the true melting pot," William O. Douglas once wrote, "and the public school teacher was the leading architect of the new America that was being fashioned."

The academic effectiveness of the system was challenged in 1957, when the Soviet Union launched its Sputnik satellite. Almost overnight, it was perceived that American training was not competitive with that of the U.S.S.R. Public criticism and government funds began to converge on U. S. schools. By 1964, achievement scores in math and reading had risen to an alltime high. But in the '60s the number of students (and teachers too) was expanding tremendously as a result of the maturing crop of post-World War II babies. In the decade before 1969, the number of high school teachers almost doubled, from 575,000 to nearly 1 million. Writes reading expert Paul Copperman in *The Literacy Hoax:* "The stage was set for an academic tragedy of historic proportions as the nation's high school faculty, about half of whom were young and immature, prepared to meet the largest generation of high school students in American history." To compound the problem, many teachers had been radicalized by the 1960s. They suspected that competition was immo-

ral, grades undemocratic, and promotion based on merit and measurable accomplishment a likely way to discriminate against minorities and the poor. Ever since the mid-1960s, the average achievement of high school graduates has gone steadily downhill.

Ironically, the slide occurred at a time when teachers were getting far more training than ever before. In the early 1900s, few elementary school teachers went to college; most were trained at two-year normal schools. Now a bachelor's degree from college is a general requirement for teaching. Today's teaching incompetence reflects the lax standards in many of the education programs at the 1,150 colleges around the country that train teachers. It also reflects on colleges generally, since teachers take more than half their courses in traditional departments like English, history and mathematics.

Research by W. Timothy Weaver, an associate professor of education at Boston University, seems to confirm a long-standing charge that one of the easiest U. S. college majors is education. Weaver found the high school seniors who planned to major in education well below the average for all college-bound seniors—34 points below average in verbal scores on the 1976 Scholastic Aptitude Test, 43 points below average in math. Teaching majors score lower in English than majors in almost every other field.

Evidence that many graduates of teacher-training programs cannot read, write or do sums adequately has led educators like Robert L. Egbert, president of the American Association of Colleges for Teacher Education, to urge higher standards on his colleagues. The National Council for Accreditation of Teacher Education has become warier about issuing its seal of approval, which is largely honorific, since state boards of education issue their own, often easygoing approval for teacher-training programs. Nevertheless, with an awakened interest in "consumer protection" for parents and pupils, the council denied accreditation to teacher-training programs at

31% of colleges reviewed in 1979, compared with 10% in 1973. Says Salem, Ore., School Superintendent William Kendrick: "For too long, we've believed that if you hold a teaching certificate you can do the job."

Many teachers favor rigorous teaching standards, including the use of compulsory minimum-competency tests—at least for candidates starting out in their careers. They are dismayed by the public's disapproval. Says Linda Kovaric, 32, a teacher at Olympic Continuation High School in Santa Monica, Calif.: "The administration tells you you're doing a crummy job, parents tell you you're doing a crummy job, kids even tell you you're doing a crummy job. A lot of teachers these days feel and look like soldiers who returned from Viet Nam. You see the same glazed look in their eyes."

Many teachers have come to see themselves as casualties in a losing battle for learning and order in an indulgent age. Society does not support them, though it expects them to compensate in the classroom for racial prejudice, economic inequality and parental indifference. Says *American School Board Journal* Managing Editor Jerome Cramer: "Schools are now asked to do what people used to ask God to do." The steady increase in the number of working mothers (35% work full time now) has sharply reduced family supervision of children and thrown many personal problems into the teacher's lap, while weakening support for the teacher's efforts. Says Thomas Anderson, 31, who plans to quit this month after teaching social studies for seven years in Clearwater, Fla.: "I know more about some of my kids than their mothers or fathers do."

A teacher's view, in short, of why teachers cannot teach is that teachers are not allowed to teach. "The teacher today is expected to be mother, father, priest or rabbi, peacekeeper, police officer, playground monitor and lunchroom patrol," says David Imig, executive director of the American Association of Colleges for Teacher Education. "Over and above that, he's supposed to teach Johnny and Mary how to read." Adds Edith Shain, a veteran kindergarten teacher at the Hancock Park School in Los Angeles: "The teacher doesn't know who she has to please. She's not as autonomous as she once was."

In the past 15 years the number of teachers with 20 years or more experience has dropped by nearly half. Four out of ten claim they plan to quit before retirement. In 1965 more than half of America's teachers told polltakers they were happy in their work. Now barely a third say they would become teachers if they had to make the choice again.

For many teachers, whether to leave their profession is not seen as a question of choice, or economics, but as a matter of emotional necessity. The latest pedagogic phenomenon is something called "teacher burnout." It is a psychological condition, produced by stress, that can result in anything from acute loss of will to suicidal tendencies, ulcers, migraine, colitis, dizziness, even the inability to throw off chronic, and perhaps psychosomatic, colds.

This spring the first national conference on teacher burnout was held in New York City. Surprisingly, the syndrome seems nearly as common in small towns and well-off suburbs as in big cities. The National Education Association has already held more than 100 local workshops round the country to help teachers cope with the problem, which University of California social psychologist Ayala Pines defines as "physical, emotional and attitudinal exhaustion." Last March, stress consultant Marian Leibowitz held a burnout seminar in Edwardsville, Ill. (pop. 11,982). It drew a paying audience of 250 to a hall big enough for only 100.

According to Dr. Herbert Pardes, director of the National Institute of Mental Health, what emerges from the familiar litany of teacher complaints is that administrative headaches and even physical assaults on teachers can be psychologically less wounding than the frustrating fact that teachers feel unable to do enough that is constructive and rewarding in their classrooms. Whether it is blackboard jungle, red-tape jumble, a place of learning or a collective holding pen for the hapless young, the modern classroom, teachers claim, is out of teachers' control. Some reasons:

Discipline and Violence. Last year 110,000 teachers, 5% of the U. S. total, reported they were attacked by students, an increase of 57% over 1977–78. Teachers believe administrators tend to duck the subject of violence in the schools to avoid adverse publicity. More than half the teachers assaulted feel that afterward authorities did not take adequate action. Today one in eight high school teachers says he "hesitates to confront students out of fear." One in every four reports that he has had personal property stolen at school.

Since the *Wood* v. *Strickland* Supreme Court decision of 1975, which upheld the right to due process of students accused of troublemaking, the number of students expelled from school has dropped by about 30%. As always in a democracy, the problem of expulsion turns in part on the question of concern for the rights of the disruptive individual versus the rights of classmates and of society. School officials argue that it is wiser and more humane to keep a violent or disruptive student in school than to turn him loose on the streets. But, says John Kotsakis of the Chicago Teachers Union, "schools are now being asked to be more tolerant of disruptive or criminal behavior than society." In a Washington, D. C., high school, a jealous boy tried to shoot his girlfriend in class. The boy was briefly suspended from school. No other action was taken. Says a teacher from that school: "These days if you order a student to the principal's office, he won't go. Hall monitors have to be called to drag him away."

Student Attitudes Toward Learning. In a current hit song called *Another Brick in the Wall,* the rock group Pink Floyd brays: "We don't need no education." There is near unanimity among teachers that many students are defiantly uninterested in schoolwork. Says one West Coast teacher: "Tell me kids haven't changed since we were in high school, and I'll tell you you're living in a fantasy world." A New York panel investigated declining test scores and found that homework assignments had been cut nearly in half during the years from 1968 to 1977. Why? Often simply because students refuse to do them. Blame for the shift in student attitude has been assigned to such things as Watergate, the Viet Nam War, the Me culture. Also to television, which reduced attention span. Now there are 76 million TV homes in the U. S., versus only 10 million in 1950. By age 18, the average American has spent an estimated 15,000 hours in front of the set, far more time than in school. Whatever the figures, teachers agree, television is a hard act to follow.

Shifting Tides of Theory. Because it is American, American education dreams of panaceas—universal modern cures for the ancient pain of learning, easy ways to raise test scores and at the same time prepare the "whole child" for his role in society. Education has become a tormented field where armies of theorists clash, frequently using language that is unintelligible to the layman. Faddish theories sweep through the profession, changing standards, techniques, procedures. Often these changes dislocate students and teachers to little purpose. The New Math is an instructive example. Introduced in the early '60s without adequate tryout, and poorly understood by teachers and parents, the New Math eventually was used in more than half the nation's schools. The result: lowered basic skills and test scores in elementary math. Exotic features, like binary arithmetic, have since been dropped. Another trend is the "open classroom," with its many competing "learning centers," which can turn a class into a bullpen of babble. There was the look-say approach to reading (learning to read by recognizing a whole word), which for years displaced the more effective "phonics" (learning to read by sounding out syllables).

Pedagogues seeking a "science of education" are sometimes mere comic pinpricks in a teacher's side. For example, Ph.D. theses have been written on such topics as *Service in the High School Cafeteria, Student Posture* and *Public School Plumbing*. But many studies are hard on teacher morale. Sociologist James S. Coleman's celebrated 1966 survey of pupil achievement seemed glum news for teachers. That study argued that family background made almost all the difference, and that qualities of schools and teachers, good and bad, accounted "for only a small fraction of differences in pupil achievement." Later researchers, examining Coleman's work, found that pupils do seem to learn more when they receive more hours of instruction.

The sensible thing for any effective teacher would be to fend off such theories as best he can and go on teaching. As teachers are fond of saying, "Teaching occurs behind closed doors." But theory, some of it foolish and damaging, inexorably seeps under the doors and into the classrooms. For example, the sound idea that teachers should concentrate on whetting the interests of students and stirring creativity has been unsoundly used as an excuse to duck detailed schoolwork. Says Columbia's Teachers College Professor Diane Ravitch: "It is really putting things backward to say that if children feel good about themselves, then they will achieve. Instead, if children are learning and achieving, *then* they feel good about themselves." Ravitch believes U. S. education has suffered much from such pedagogic theories, and especially from the notion, which emerged from the social climate of the 1960s, that the pursuit of competency is "elitist and undemocratic."

Textbooks and Paperwork. Teachers are consulted about textbooks but rarely decide what books are finally bought. The textbook business is a $1.3 billion a year industry. Books are ordered by editorial committees and updated at the pleasure of the publisher to sell in as many school systems as possible. Since the late 1960s, according to reading expert Copperman, publishers have found that if a textbook is to sell really well, it must be written

at a level "two years below the grade for which it is intended."

Paperwork done by teachers and administrators for district, state and national agencies proliferates geometrically. Though it all may be necessary to some distant bureaucrat—a most unlikely circumstance—when teachers comply they tend to feel like spindling, folding and mutilating all the forms. Paperwork wastes an enormous amount of teaching time. In Atlanta, for example, fourth- and fifth-grade teachers must evaluate their students on 60 separate skills. The children must be rated on everything from whether they can express "written ideas clearly" to whether they can apply "scarcity, opportunity cost and resource allocation to local, national and global situations."

Administrative Hassles. School procedures, the size and quality of classes, the textbooks and time allotted to study are all affected by government demands, including desegregation of classes, integration of faculty, even federal food programs. One way or another, teachers are bureaucratically hammered at by public health officials (about vaccinations, ringworm, cavities, malnutrition), by social workers and insurance companies (about driver education and broken windows), by juvenile police, civil liberties lawyers, Justice Department lawyers, even divorce lawyers (about child custody).

Mainstreaming as Nightmare. Since the passage of Public Law 94–142 in 1975, it has been federal policy that all handicapped children, insofar as possible, be "mainstreamed," in other words, educated in the same class with everyone else. The law is theoretically useful and just, as a means of avoiding unwarranted discrimination. But in practice it often puts an overwhelming strain on the teacher. "Mainstreaming is ludicrous," says Detroit counselor Jeanne Latcham. "We have children whose needs are complicated: a child in the third grade who has already been in 16 schools, children who need love and attention and disrupt the classroom to get it. Ten percent of the students in Detroit's classrooms can't conform and can't learn. These children need a disproportionate amount of the teacher's time. It's a teacher's nightmare—she can't help them, but she never forgets them."

The tangle of teaching troubles is too complex to be easily unraveled. But one problem whose solution seems fairly straightforward is the matter of illiterate and uninformed teachers. Competency tests can—and should—be administered to screen out teachers, old as well as novice, who lack basic skills. Such screening would benefit pupils, but it would also put pressure on marginal colleges to flunk substandard students bound for a career in teaching. Indiana University Education Professor David Clark asks rhetorically: "Is it more important to make it easy for kids to reach professional level, or to have good teachers?" Pressure is also needed to ensure adequate funding for teacher training. As a typical example, at the University of Alabama last year total instructional cost for a student in a teacher-ed program was $648, in contrast to $2,304 for an engineering student.

In a classic 1960s study titled *The Miseducation of American Teachers*, James D. Koerner, now program officer at the Alfred P. Sloan Foundation, called for the opening of new paths to careers in teaching. At present a state certificate is required for public school teachers, who earn it by completing practice teaching and specialized education courses (such as philosophy of education and educational psychology). According to Koerner there is little evidence that this program of study improves teacher performance. Koerner calls for more intellectually demanding but more flexible requirements to make the field more attractive to talented people who lack specialized teaching credentials. A small step in this direction is a three-year-old pilot program run by the school board in Hanover, N. H. There, college graduates who want to teach are carefully screened for such qualities as imagination and love of children, as well as academic competency. After a year of probationary

teaching, chosen candidates become certified teachers.

It has been argued that teaching needs to be more professional. But in some ways it is too professional now—too encrusted with useless requirements and too tangled in its own obscure professional jargon. The impenetrable language of educators has evolved into what Koerner calls "an artificial drive to create a profession." But it is more damaging to the country than the jargon of law, say, or even government, because it sabotages the use of clear writing and clear thinking by tens of thousands of teachers, and through them, hundreds of thousands of students.

Violence in schools has got to be dealt with effectively. A muscular and unprecedented step in the right direction may have just been taken in California. Over a six-year period, Los Angeles County schools lost an estimated $100 million as a result of school muggings, lawsuits, theft and vandalism while city and school officials ineffectually wrung their hands over jurisdictional problems. Last month the attorney general for the state of California sued, among others, the mayor of Los Angeles, the entire city council, the chief of police and the board of trustees of the Los Angeles Unified School District, demanding that authorities put together some coordinated program to punish the criminals and cut down on violence and theft.

A promising proposal was made by legislators in Pennsylvania last year. They introduced bills requiring that schools report all attacks on teachers to state authorities and that criminal penalties be stiffened for school offenses. Under one of the measures, carrying a gun or knife in school would be treated as a serious crime, and a student who assaulted a teacher would face up to seven years in jail.

Principals need to be more willing to manage their schools. When necessary, the resignation of bad teachers must be sought, even though union grievance procedures can be costly and time consuming. "Too many principals are afraid of grievances," says William Grimshaw, professor of political science at the Illinois Institute of Technology. More important, it should be easier to reward good teachers—if only with public recognition, which is rare at present. As Sylvia Schneirov, a third-grade teacher in Chicago, puts it: "The only praise you get is if your class is quiet and if your bulletin boards are ready when the superintendent comes—you better not have snowflakes on the board when you should have flowers."

Public praise for a job well done matters a great deal. Last year Raj Chopra, the Indian-born superintendent of schools in Council Bluffs, Iowa, raised Council Bluffs' S.A.T. scores, which had slumped below national norms, by starting a systematic campaign to encourage "positive thinking" by—and about—Council Bluffs teachers. Says he: "We make them feel proud of their profession by emphasizing that what they do will have an impact on the country for years to come." On May 6, the city celebrated Teachers Day. Retailers, who had earlier been visited by a "teacher recognition task force," gave discounts to teachers that day.

Teaching children to read and write and do sums correctly is not so complicated a business as it is often made to seem. As Koerner puts it: "Almost any school can significantly improve its performance by the simple act of deciding to do so." Indeed, much of the trouble boils down to a failure of will, of old-fashioned teacherly "gumption" in the schools and outside them. As Marcia Fensin, a former teacher and mother of two daughters enrolled in Chicago's Joyce Kilmer Elementary School, says: "The teachers just don't care. They give busy work straight from the textbooks, and meanwhile our kids are not being motivated."

Ironically though, lack of care about education is also a favorite complaint of educators today. Echoing the view of many in the schools, President Lawrence Cremin of Columbia's Teachers College observes: "By and large, society gets what it deserves out of its school system. It gets what it expects. If

you don't value things, you don't get them."

The evidence suggests that something so simple as caring can improve the schools. One of James Coleman's undisputed findings: all other things being equal, students achieve better in schools that have active Parent-Teacher Associations. PTAs can provide pressure to improve a teaching staff or school programs and facilities. More important, a widely supported PTA is the tangible sign of parental responsibility for education. Caring shows in other ways as well. Observes Cremin: "A number of studies indicate that certain kinds of schools are unusually effective. Whether the students are rich kids, poor kids, blacks, Hispanics or whites, these schools look very much alike on some criteria. The principal leads his teachers. The teachers become committed to teaching the basic skills. Expectations become high. Time is spent on classroom tasks, and a happy order pervades the school. Rules are widely known and quickly enforced. Parents are brought into the act and are supportive. In such schools, black kids learn, white kids learn, green kids learn."

Yet such is the dilemma of education today that even so clear-cut a matter as agreeing to establish very low minimum competency tests for teachers becomes a hot political issue, arousing fear that the tests will only serve as racial discrimination. Significantly, one of the most eloquent advocates of tough standards, and the man who speaks most probingly and practically about American education, its problems and possible salvation, is not an educator but a black leader, the Rev. Jesse Jackson. "Nobody can save us for us but us" is a Jackson slogan. He insists that parents sign a contract stating that they will get personally involved with school and require their children to do two hours of work a night, without benefit of television. "Many of us allow our children to eat junk," Jackson accuses, "watch junk, listen to junk, talk junk, play with junk, and then we're surprised when they come out to be social junkies." And again, "Tears will get you sympathy, but sweat will get you change." Ostensibly, he is exhorting black ghetto kids and their parents. But he could just as well be setting up a program for everyone, blacks and whites, middle-class parents and burnt-out teachers.

The salvation of the public schools lies, most of all, in just such individual dedication to learning, spread society-wide. The schools are simply too big, too close to families and neighborhoods, and too diverse for the improvement of teaching to be ordered by a legislature, Governor, university or school superintendent. They do not need a social program as complex as, say, the Apollo space program, as the continued existence of good public schools throughout the nation shows. They need agreement by the many groups that shape them—parents, teachers, taxpayers, government—that teaching and good teachers are in trouble and need society's support. As to the historic issue, Thomas Jefferson put it well: "If a nation expects to be ignorant and free, in a state of civilization, it expects what never was and never will be."

NOTE

[1] Alabama, Arizona, Arkansas, Florida, Georgia, Louisiana, Mississippi, North Carolina, South Carolina, Tennessee, Virginia, West Virginia.

21

SORTING OUT THE ISSUES AND TRENDS OF SCHOOL DESEGREGATION

Ray C. Rist

Few debates related to domestic social policy have more intensely challenged the viability of the U. S. as a democratic, diverse, and responsive society than has that surrounding the desegregation of our educational systems. The emotions generated by such terms as "forced busing," "the destruction of the neighborhood school," "whites have rights," and "community control" have tended to blur our focus, but the central pivot must remain the interrelations of education, race, and equality. It is only in such a context that a discussion of school desegregation becomes meaningful. Otherwise, one is left to first reify and then parcel out fragments of what is, in fact, a complex mix of law, politics, pedagogics, and cultural values.

In one form or another, the matter of school desegregation has been on the national agenda for more than two decades. The *Brown v. Board of Education of Topeka, Kansas* decision of 1954 has been the touchstone from which

Reprinted from *USA Today,* November 1978. Copyright 1978 by Society for the Advancement of Education.

our society has been grappling with this matter in the courtrooms, the classrooms, the political arenas, and the streets. To mention only Federal troops at Little Rock in the 1950s or the events in Boston and Louisville in the 1970s is to gloss over a generation of conflict. Even so, the direction in which we are headed appears irreversible. The question now is how quickly and in what manner shall we achieve the objectives of constitutional protections and quality educational environments?

It is merely a restating of the obvious to note that there are many misconceptions and misunderstandings regarding school desegregation efforts in the U. S. Further, the infusion of these misconceptions into our national dialogue and policy-making efforts inhibits informed discussion and thwarts successful implementation.

WHAT THE ISSUE IS NOT

The issue is not that of busing *per se*. Of the nearly 42,000,000 children in public elementary and secondary schools, more than 50% (21,800,000) ride buses to school. Of these, an estimated 7% (1,500,000) are bused for reasons of desegregation. Stated differently, participation in a desegregation program through the riding of a bus impacts on three or four of each 100 children in the public schools. Furthermore, when one surveys busing programs across the country, noting the disproportional numbers and years of black children who are bused, the number of white children being bused for any reason related to desegregation may be no more than one in 100.

The issue is not that of *de facto* segregation in either the North or the South. Every standing court order related to school desegregation has been issued on the grounds of *de jure* segregation. In each case where court orders have been issued, the courts have found that the local school districts—and occasionally, the state educational agencies as well—have

systematically carried out policies that led to segregation between black and white students. The stance of the courts, embodied in a massive amount of litigation since the *Brown* decision, has consistently been that *there is no essential difference* in the reasons for ordering system-wide desegregation in either Northern or Southern cities.

The issue is not one of school achievement. Numerous data-collection endeavors provide no uniformity of opinion that desegregation efforts are harmful to student achievement. Rather, it is more realistic to assume that there are specific instances where achievement is hindered, but these are offset by other specific instances where there is no change or academic performance rises.

The issue is not a rejection of the principle of desegregation. Indeed, most Americans say they believe in school desegregation. The percentages have held relatively stable now for more than a decade, in spite of the media sharing few success stories and each and every difficulty. The acceptance among white Americans of multiracial schools as a place for their own children has also been growing. Recent national public opinion data indicates that a majority of white American parents would now be willing to have their children attend a majority black school.

This issue is not that school desegregation can not go smoothly. In the period from 1968 to 1971, a large portion of the South underwent massive desegregation and little was heard about it. Likewise, in the North, Wichita, Las Vegas, Stockton, Providence, Waukegan, Berkeley, Riverside, Portland (Ore.), Racine, Minneapolis, Ann Arbor, and many others have desegregated, mostly on a voluntary basis, and little has been heard. Even in places such as Little Rock and Pontiac, where there was initial violence and controversy, education is now occurring in a calm and non-hostile setting. Recent estimates are that some form of school desegregation has been effected in approximately 3,000 of the nearly 17,000 school districts in the country. Boston and Louisville comprise .0006% of that total. We are enmeshed in selective perception on a national scale.

WHAT THE ISSUE IS

The issue is the apparent randomness of desegregation efforts, leading some to believe that they have been unfairly singled out by the courts or Federal government. The matter of "fairness," of comparing one city's treatment versus another, raises the question of distributive justice. If the resolution of school segregation in Atlanta is vastly different from that in Boston, or Indianapolis from Denver, doubts can justifiably begin to arise. If Atlanta is allowed to retain several all-black schools, why must Boston eliminate each and every one of theirs? The moral force of the law exists only so long as those to whom it applies believe that they have been justly treated. When they believe they have not, the willingness to comply diminishes.

The issue is that the continued exodus of whites from the cities into suburban areas has created a situation where many of the large cities are increasingly, if not predominantly, black. So long as the suburbs are excluded from desegregation plans in these circumstances, substantial desegregation can not occur. If the only required integration is within district, present demographic trends will produce a thorough resegregation of black students in many of the nation's largest cities. The suburbs appear content to have it so. In addition, what such population shifts have created are not only divisions of race, but also of social class. As in Boston, the poor whites and poor blacks are left to be integrated among each other.

The issue is the resistance to Federal intervention and control. Court orders and HEW regulations take options away from local communities to effect their own educational policies. While there has been clear justifica-

tion for such intervention on the part of the Federal government when the dimensions of school segregation were stark and readily visible, the matter at present is more obscure. Not the least of the reasons for this is the lack of an unambiguous position on the part of the Federal government. The failure of the Executive and Legislative branches to take responsible and articulated stands has left the matter entirely in the laps of the courts—and the courts are not the most appropriate places from which to educate people as to their legal and civic responsibilities. The consequence—apparent to state and local officials as well as to laypersons—is that the Executive branch holds one position, the Legislative another, and the courts yet a third. While the first two are seemingly content to make political gain from opposing the rulings of the third, local folks feel they are being pushed about.

The issue is that, even though the courts and educational officials alike have sought to implement integration plans that would provide creative and imaginative additions to the educational system, they have not been able to persuade the communities that desegregation will enhance the quality of their schools. In fact, the opposite is generally believed to be more nearly the truth. While the evidence continues to accumulate that desegregation provides a more equal distribution of educational resources and creates learning opportunities not otherwise available, the white community in particular continues to define school desegregation as little more than the creation of educational disaster zones.

The issue is that the signals from the black community as to the desirability of further school desegregation are increasingly mixed. What in the past gave clear moral legitimation to the desegregation effort was the black community's near unanimity that segregated schools be abolished post haste. (So far as I know, not a single court case pressing for school desegregation has ever been instigated by the white community anywhere in the country.) At present, however, there are an increasing number of persons in the black community willing to trade off desegregation for "community control" of all- or predominantly black schools. This growing diversity of opinion on school desegregation has had the effect of neutralizing large portions of the white liberal community, thus weakening the alliance which was so potent in the 1960s and early 1970s.

SORTING OUT THE TRENDS

For the past decade, primary governmental responsibility for issues of race and schooling has been lodged in the Federal courts. The identification of school desegregation as a judicial matter has by now become so automatic that one has to strain to remember that, during the mid-1960s, it was Congress and the Executive branches of government—not the courts—that exercised leadership in this area. As the policy problem changed its character, becoming national in scope and more politically menacing in form, the coordinate branches of government initially withdrew, then sought to undermine what had become an almost exclusively judicial effort.

The recent public record concerning school desegregation is not a particularly felicitous one, from almost anyone's point of view. The vigor of court action has outstripped the judiciary's willingness—or capacity—to inform the rest of us concerning its justifications for those actions. As a consequence, the great constitutional principles that underlie *Brown* seem destined to be forgotten amidst the tangle of legalisms that have emerged as ostensible elaborations of the Equal Protection Clause. At the Federal level, Congress and the Executive seem capable of expounding only what they oppose—the busing of school children. What they support, what political meanings they would attribute to the phrases "racial justice" and "equal educational opportunity," has to be reckoned a great unknown.

The present flight from responsibility is an altogether unfortunate state of affairs. Questions of race, schooling, and equality have political and moral, as well as constitutional, dimensions. To structure a viable approach for taking on these interrelations, much less assume one can "solve" them, requires different levels to assume responsibility. If the country is to do better in the near future than it has done in the near past, the critical question may be simply stated: Can the non-judicial branches of government at both the state and Federal levels make useful policy and programatic contributions? The possibility for such a response does exist.

Recent judicial decisions also point to another important trend—the inclusion of state educational agencies as parties to the litigation. This is something of a dramatic shift, for, heretofore, the litigation was local citizens or the Justice Department versus the local school board and perhaps the superintendent of schools. Now, the state educational authorities are increasingly being brought into the suits, most often in the role of co-defendant with local educational authorities. Key cases to cite in this regard would include, among others, *Milliken* v. *Bradley* in Detroit, *Arthur* v. *Nyquist* in Buffalo, *Evans* v. *Buchanan* in Wilmington, *U.S.* v. *State of Missouri* in St. Louis County, and *Crawford* v. *Board of Education* in Los Angeles.

As these and other suits have proceeded through the courts, their final adjudications would suggest the following trends with respect to state level involvement in school desegregation. What underlies all these cases, although each was unique, was that the state educational agencies were held responsible for segregatory action and were ordered to be a party to the remedies. To summarize the trends, consider the following:

Where states can be shown to be a party, by acts of either omission or commission, to intentional discrimination in the schools, the courts will order them to participate in the remedies.

Where states accept a responsibility, through either enactment of a state law or passage of a resolution by a state agency, to end discrimination in the schools, the courts will require them to fulfill that responsibility.

Federal courts will not order interdistrict remedies unless each district involved can be found to have *intentionally* taken segregatory actions with interdistrict effects. However, states with enabling legislation may, on their own initiative, merge districts, change school boundaries, order interdistrict transfers, or take other steps to end segregation in their schools without court order.[1]

FURTHER DECLINES
IN SCHOOL SEGREGATION

Progress is being made in the desegregation of public schools in the South, but the picture is not as positive in the North and West. In fact, in some parts of these latter two regions, schools are becoming more intensely segregated. Recently published HEW data indicate, for example, that, in 1970, 74% of all black children in the public schools in Chicago were in schools with 99–100% minority enrollment. In 1974, the comparable figure was 80%. In Los Angeles, the figures for the same years are 55 and 62%, respectively; for Detroit, 36 and 50%, respectively. It should be remembered that these data are for the extreme— 99–100% minority enrollments. The same picture is emerging for Hispanic children. Nearly two-thirds of all Spanish-surnamed students in the New York City schools were in schools with 99–100% minority student enrollments. In fact, on a national average, Hispanic children are now as concentrated in schools with more than 70% minority enrollment as are black students.

In spite of these increased concentrations in various sectors of the country, the national average shows a decline in the levels of school segregation. Whether such a decline will continue depends upon several critical factors. First among these is the matter of how the courts and Federal agencies define *de jure* segregation in areas where schools have never been segregated by law. While there have been individual instances where desegregation efforts have been set back because of judicial rulings that schools are not required to alleviate racial imbalances they did not cause, the more general stance of the courts has been oriented differently. Desegregation has been ordered where school officials were able to maintain segregation by arbitrarily drawing attendance zones, by selectively erecting new schools, and by the assignment of black teachers to black schools. If the courts continue to see such action as having the *intent* to segregate, these actions will be remedied under current statutes governing *de jure* segregation.

A second factor concerns what remedies for segregation will be invoked by governmental agencies and courts. While such efforts as magnet schools, the pairing of schools, and the altering of attendance zones may mitigate segregation, the evidence is overwhelming that the greatest decreases in segregation have come in those districts where students were bused to achieve desegregation. There is little doubt that, if busing as a tool of desegreation is limited or banned, urban areas would revert to having largely segregated schools due to neighborhood patterns.

A third factor, and one related to the second, concerns the future for interdistrict desegregation. If the only required integration in many of our urban areas is that of within-district, present demographic trends will produce a thorough *resegregation* for hundreds of thousands of black students. The reality is that within-district desegregation is simply not possible in many of our large cities. While desegregation can continue to proceed apace in many of our medium and smaller cities and towns, it is increasingly possible in the larger areas only when initiated on a metropolitan basis.

FUTURE IMPLEMENTATION

The matter of school desegregation is likely to be with us for years to come. Despite substantial desegregation in Southern and Border states in recent years, more than half of the black children in these areas are in majority black schools. In the North and West, the figures are even higher. In these regions, more than 80% of all black students are in majority black schools. Similarly, in states where there is a sizable Hispano-American school population, less than half of these students attend majority white schools—and the proportion who do so is generally declining. That so much of the task of desegregation still lies before us, coupled with the realization that desegregation has not fulfilled the expectations many have had, suggests it is time for a reconsideration of the basic and underlying assumptions influencing the present approaches.

Such a period of reevaluation is necessary if the desegregation process is to proceed in such a manner as to maximize the probabilities that the ultimate goals of this major effort at social change will be achieved. While most people sympathetic to these goals will have little quarrel with this admonition in principle, the implications may be less widely accepted.

In order to respond to the conditions listed at the beginning of this article that make school desegregation an "issue," remedies and new initiatives would have to move in ways different than at present. Further, strategies that are at present rejected out of hand—for example, partial desegregation, the preservation of one-race schools, different strategies in different parts of the school district, etc.—may have to be reconsidered. Strategies of school desegregation—be they at the local, state, or Federal levels—can not proceed as if the schools existed in a political and cultural vacuum.

If there is indeed to be future school desegregation in the U. S., the present pattern of sporadic efforts by the courts does not appear to be an effective instrument for achieving it. The more the task of desegregation has fallen to the courts alone, the less systematic, comprehensive, and acceptable the process has become. This is not the fault of the courts, but possibly, just possibly, those who have defaulted will be sufficiently disenchanted with the current state of affairs to reenter the fray and seek new and sensible initiatives. What is lacking at present is not the expertise, not the accumulated wisdom of the past two decades, and not those with leadership skills to see the process through. Rather, what we face is the absence of political will.

NOTE

[1] Bert Mogin, *The State Role in School Desegregation* (Menlo Park, Calif.: Stanford Research Institute, 1977).

VIII

RELIGION
The Supernatural and Society

Religion has been defined by Emile Durkheim, a leading early sociologist, as a more or less coherent system of beliefs and practices that concerns a supernatural order of beings, places, and forces. This rather simplistic definition explains *what* religion is but does not explain *why* it is a universal phenomenon. Religion has been and continues to be a major mode of expression even in today's highly technical world. Why? What functions does religion perform for people and society?

Religion allows for the transcendence of human existence and this gives people a means of dealing with conditions of uncertainty. It helps people to overcome their powerlessness to control the conditions that affect their lives, and it gives them the means to cope with the scarcity of things that satisfy psychological and economic needs. For society, religion provides a means for social control; that is, it helps support some of the primary societal rules.

In the first article, Margolis and Elifson consider these functions in the light of the personal religious experience. In the second article, Mariani notes that such attempts can also be quite lucrative.

All social institutions are interrelated; the societal needs that one institution ministers to are affected by every other institution. In the final article of this chapter, Zwier and Smith delineate the relationship between religion and politics. As you read, think of other institutional relationships and what the implications are of such relationships.

22

A TYPOLOGY OF RELIGIOUS EXPERIENCE

Robert D. Margolis
Kirk W. Elifson

In spite of the extensive research on the phenomena of mystical or religious experiences during the past decade, an important question remains unanswered. Is there a discrete set of characteristics of the religious experience or is there more than one type of religious experience with each type possessing unique characteristics? Stace (1960) argues that there is a unique religious experience with a clearly defined set of characteristics. He presents numerous examples of religious experiences and extracts what he believes to be the defining characteristics. On the other hand, Streng (1970) suggests that it is a mistake to look for a set of core elements of religious experience.

A content analysis of various accounts of religious experiences and subsequent factor analysis of the categories provides some clarification of this issue. If there is indeed only one set of attributes which characterize a religious experience, then only one factor should emerge. Conversely, the emergence of several should provide a typology which specifies (a) different types, if any, of personal religious experiences, and (b) the attributes or characteristics of these experiences.

Previous Typologies: A Discussion and Critique

Many of the attempts to specify the attributes of religious experiences were based on reviews of personal accounts. The first such attempt was by James (1902), who, after presenting numerous examples of religious experiences, arrived at four characteristics common to the experience: ineffability, noetic quality, transiency, and passivity.

Stace (1960) also sought to isolate the attributes of religious experience, and Hood's studies (1973, 1975) have been based on his contribution. Stace limited his inquiry to "a central nucleus of typical cases" (p. 46) and excluded two categories of experiences as not genuine. These two excluded classes were experiences involving visions and voices, and those involving raptures, trances, and hyperemotionalism (p. 54). Such judgments narrow the focus of his inquiry and appear unnecessarily to bias his work from the beginning.

In addition to narrowing his focus by excluding certain experiences as not valid,

From *Journal for the Scientific Study of Religion*, March 1979, Vol. 18, No. 1. Reprinted by permission. This study is based upon an unpublished doctoral dissertation (Margolis: 1977). The authors wish to thank Robert Baker, Richard Gorsuch, Bernard Kempler and an anonymous reviewer for their helpful comments.

much of Stace's inquiry appears to have a moralistic tone not conducive to an objective study by using such phrases as "higher" or "more important experiences" as opposed to "lower" or "inferior experiences" without explanation or apparent justification.

Greeley (1975), in a national survey of 600 respondents who claimed to have had a mystical experience, asked subjects to respond to structured items which he had derived from the writings of Laski (1968) and others, which appropriately characterized their experience. This study is noteworthy in that it employs a large nationwide sample, and it goes directly to people who claim to have had a mystical experience. The list of items is questionable, however, since Laski's sample included primarily her friends and acquaintances. Thomas and Cooper (1977) raised serious doubts concerning the value of any structured question to measure a mystical experience and concluded that since each respondent's interpretation of the meaning of a structured question is vastly different, the use of structured questions to measure mystical experience is not appropriate.

Hood (1973, 1975) has gone beyond the typology stage in developing a scale of mystical experience so that experiences can be placed on a mysticism/non-mysticism continuum. In his 1973 study, Hood operationally defined religious experience by classifying the experiences of his subjects as either mystical or non-mystical based upon criteria developed by Stace (1960). Hood (1975) extended this approach with the development of a mysticism scale containing 32 items. Hood (1973, 1975) does not adopt Stace's categories directly but in some cases deletes categories, combines categories, or substitutes his own terminology. For example, he eliminated Stace's category of paradoxicality. In addition, Stace's category of "unitary consciousness" is renamed "positive affect," and he blurred Stace's basic distinction between introvertive and extrovertive mysticism.

Thomas and Cooper (1977), in reviewing

Hood's Mysticism Scale, concluded that it suffers from the same basic flaw as Greeley's (1975) study—the use of structured questions. In addition, they point out that

the items of the Hood Mysticism Scale are even less specific than the Greeley survey questions. . . . The researcher has no way of knowing from the response to such structured questions whether a respondent has had a mystical experience, one of several types of psychic encounters, or a totally irrelevant experience that was, nonetheless, impressive for the respondent (pp. 14–15).

METHODS

Subjects

A group of religious experiences was collected from 45 subjects. The primary criterion for selecting subjects was willingness to state that they had had a religious experience. In addition, the experience must, in the experimenter's opinion, qualify under Yinger's definition (1970) which states that a religious experience is one which is primarily concerned with people's relationship to some ultimate reality; that is, an experience which has at its core a metaphysical or transcendent quality.[1]

Subjects were solicited in several ways. First, advertisements were placed in several local newspapers. The text of these advertisements read: "Wanted: people who have had a religious or mystical experience to participate in a research study." Subjects were also solicited from local church and religious groups. An attempt was made to contact a wide range of denominations and sects including traditional Protestant prayer meetings as well as Meher Baba and other Eastern religious sects. In all, experiences were collected from approximately eight different religious groups in two states in the Southeastern section of the United States. All subjects who volunteered for this study were screened initially by the experimenter to determine that their experience did conform to the broadly based definition of religious experience given above.[2] This screening was done during the initial telephone or personal contact with the subject. Each subject was asked to describe the experience briefly. The actual number not included was quite small and constituted less than 10% of the total number who volunteered.

The interviews were conducted in an office setting and were tape-recorded and later transcribed. For each experience a standard set of five questions was asked, dealing with antecedent events, the experience itself, and ways in which the experience has affected the subject's life. Although an attempt was made to confine the interview to these five questions, the experimenter frequently probed. Subjects were allowed to volunteer more than one experience. The 45 subjects reported 69 experiences with no subject volunteering more than three experiences.[3] When more than one experience was volunteered, the experimenter repeated the same set of questions for each experience.[4]

Procedures

A content analysis of the reported experiences was performed to determine the primary characteristics of a religious experience. Categories were established by reading the experiences and listing the dominant themes of the experience (Holsti, 1969: 646). Following this, each experience was rated for the presence or absence of each theme and the number of times each theme occurred. After the tabulation was completed, it was decided that any theme which occurred five or more times would be included in the typology.[5] The content analysis was structured so that the themes could be divided into three broad categories: "Before," "During," and "After" the experience. The content analysis yielded a total of 36 themes.

Once the content analysis was completed, the themes of the religious experience were factor-analyzed using principal compo-nent analysis with a oblimin rotation procedure (Harman, 1967).[6] A separate factor analysis was performed on each of the three broad categories: "Before," "During," and "After" the experience. Those factors whose eigenvalues were greater than one were retained and variables with high (+.30 to +1.00) loadings were included in the factors. A typology of religious experience was developed from the factor analysis and included only the part of the analysis which pertained to "During the Experience" factors.

RESULTS

The content analysis of 69 religious experiences yielded the following 20 themes which are presented along with the number of times they occurred: Change in perception of reality (29), Security (28), Nonspecific change in internal state-cognitively oriented (24), Ecstasy (23), Initial negative reaction (22), Visions or voices (22), Experience of divine presence (18), Nonspecific change in internal state-feeling oriented (17), Peace (14), Church service or religious retreat (13), Talking to a friend (12), Out-of-body experience (9), Loss of control (9), Experience of unity or oneness (6), Experience of love (6), Drugs (6), Dream (5), Physical distress (5), and Music (5).

A factor analysis of these themes yielded four factors which are presented in Table 1. Although these factors appear to be quite different, they all seem to be intense emotional experiences, and, with the exception of Factor 2 (Vertigo Experience), they seem to have a positive emotional tone.

Factor 1 (Transcendental Experience) is very similar to the classical mystical experience described by Stace and others. This factor is named "Transcendental Experience" because it involves coming into contact with a higher or metaphysical plane of reality; and this contact dramatically changes the way the subject perceives himself and the world. This factor, of course, was present by definition, given the procedures for recruiting subjects.

Factor 2 (Vertigo Experience) involves at least a temporary disorientation for the subject. It is often triggered by "Drugs" or "Music." "Out-of-the-body experiences" are common, and the individual feels as if he is losing control and often feels frightened initially by his experience. Thus, like the "Transcendental Experience," the "Vertigo Experience" involves a significant alteration in the way the individual perceives himself and his world. Yet his reaction is often one of fear of loss of control rather than feelings of positive affect such as peace, ecstasy, and security.

Factor 3 (Life Change Experience) in many cases involves descriptions of thoughts or feelings that tended to be vague or difficult to specify. Thus, there were many "Nonspecific changes in internal states," both "feeling" and "cognitively" oriented. In many ways, however, this experience seemed to mark the beginning of a life change for the individual in that his thinking or his feelings about himself or his relationship to God were profoundly affected.

Factor 4 (Visionary Experience) often occurred during a "Dream." The subjects frequently reported an "Experience of a divine presence," "Visions or voices," and they often experienced feelings of "Love" or "Ecstasy." It is important to note that this experience, although it is often associated with a dream, is perceived as being a genuine contact with a divine presence.

DISCUSSION

These factors tend to share the characteristics of (a) unity, (b), ineffability, (c) noetic quality, (d) positive affect, and (e) time/space distortions. Unity was one of the attributes mentioned under the "Transcendental Experience" and the "Life Change Experience." The noetic quality seems to correspond to the "new reality" variable in the "Transcendental Experience." In addition, the quality of positive affect seems to be similar to the variables "ecstasy or joy," "peace," and "security" found under the "Transcendental Experience" as well as the variable "quality of love" found under the "Visionary Experience." Although subjects in this study did not mention ineffability as an attribute of the religious experience in the "Life Change Experience" there are many vague references to nonspecific changes in internal states, both feeling and cognitively oriented, which suggest that the experience may have been difficult to describe. The similarities to previous typologies provide a source of external validation for this typology as an accurate representation of the characteristics of a religious experience.[7]

The fact that more than one factor emerged seems to support Streng's (1970) contention of the multi-dimensionality of religious experiences. Although these experiences may share some elements, the continuity of religious life is more like links in a chain which overlap, not a unique set of elements common to all religious experiences.

TABLE 1.
A TYPOLOGY OF RELIGIOUS EXPERIENCE[1]

I. TRANSCENDENTAL EXPERIENCE: (FACTOR I)
1. *Security (.77)*
    a. "There was such a warmth, a feeling of security and love."
    b. "I just felt at peace, as if someone was telling me that everything was going to be all right."
    c. "It felt like coming home . . . that everything was very secure."
2. *Increased feeling of relatedness to God, or the universe (.75)*
    a. "It was like I had been away from God for millions of years and now I was finally going back."
    b. "It was a feeling of being personally known and understood and having a place where you belonged in the whole scheme of things . . . like being in touch with a personal God."
    c. "I felt a total peace with the universe . . . I was in total touch with the life force that's in the Universie."
3. *Feeling of peace (.68)*
4. *A new reality (noetic quality) (.67)*
    a. "I was like mentally in another world."
    b. "I saw that there are different planes—that there are different forms."
    c. "It was a real transformation of how I was in contact with myself and with reality."
5. *Feelings of ectasy or joy (.60)*
6. *Feelings of unity or oneness (.44)*
    a. "I was inside somehow—inside where everything was one and it was God."
    b. "It seemed like a common thing in all of us, one thing we were all part of."
    c. "I saw things without a subject/object duality."
7. *Out-of-the-body experience (.40)*

II. VERTIGO EXPERIENCE: (FACTOR II)
1. *Listening to music (.74)*
2. *Drugs (.66)*
3. *Out-of-the-body (.51)*
4. *Loss of control (.45)*
    a. "I was just shaking all over and crying . . . I couldn't control my emotions."
    b. "I was paralyzed—I couldn't move . . . (I had) feelings of being whipped around by a 90 mile-an-hour wind."
    c. "I was shocked, helpless—either I ignored it or what, I just let loose."
5. *Initial negative reaction (.41)*
    a. "I screamed, I was scared and I hid my head under the pillow."
    b. "It was just a terrible fear. I felt like I would die."
6. *Vision or voices (.40)*
    a. "I heard my name being called . . . over and over again."
    b. "I had a vision of Meher Baba."
    c. "I saw this figure that sort of resembled God."

III. LIFE CHANGE EXPERIENCE: (FACTOR III)
1. *Nonspecific change in internal state (feeling oriented) (.75)*
    a. "It felt like something on rollers came into my body."
    b. "Something came over me like a wave. It was so much of an incredible rush."
    c. "I really felt the presence of the spirit of the Lord . . . It was just kind of a warmth or something. It is kind of hard to describe."
2. *Unity or oneness (.56)*
3. *Talking to a friend (.50)*
    a. "I met a man at work . . . and he witnessed to me about what happened in his own life."

TABLE 1.
(continued)

b. "I met a person who was a friend of mine. He sort of helped me—he didn't advise me but sort of helped me at different times."

c. "A friend of mine had been trying to commit suicide. We had a long talk."

4. *Nonspecific change in internal state (cognitively oriented)* (.43)

a. "And I laid down in my bunk and began to think over my life . . . And it was kind of amazing because I began to see the Bible in a new light."

b. "I started becoming aware of the possibility of mental powers outside and all around . . . I knew something was going to happen."

5. *Attending a church service or religious retreat* (.33)

IV. VISIONARY EXPERIENCE: (FACTOR IV)

1. *Experience of a divine presence* (.70)

a. "And there was a glowing light to my right . . . I knew that was God."

b. "All of a sudden I became aware of God."

c. "I felt like I had died and I said 'I've finally gone to God.'"

2. *Visions or voices* (.68)

3. *A dream* (.57)

4. *Experience of love* (.47)

5. *Experience of ecstasy or joy* (.36)

---

[1]Following each variable is its rotated factor loading.

NOTES

[1]In the absence of any specific acceptable guidelines for including different experiences as "valid" religious experiences, it was decided to adopt the broadest possible definition of religious experience rather than excluding specific experiences based on narrower criteria without adequate empirical justification.

[2]Thomas and Cooper's (1977) criticism of Hood's Mysticism Scale can also be made here; however, an interview allows for eliciting in-depth responses from the subject that are not possible with a self-administered instrument.

[3]While a non-probability sample of 45 respondents may not seem impressive, one contribution of this study is the quality of information on each subject. The possibility of generalizing is limited, but we certainly do not view the typology as final, only a step forward.

[4]The senior author, a clinical psychologist, conducted the interviews and sought to standardize all portions of the interview procedure and thus minimize the procedural variation. None of the subjects exhibited any gross signs of being emotionally disturbed.

[5]Although a theme which occurs five times accounts for less than 8% of the total number of experiences, there were two reasons for choosing a low number as a cutoff point. First, a factor analysis was subsequently to be performed on the themes in the content analysis, and, in a factor analysis, even themes which occur relatively infrequently can have a significant factor loading if they occur often enough in conjunction with other themes. Secondly, five seemed a natural cutoff point since the next lowest theme below five occurred only twice.

[6]A general factor was a theoretical possibility and direct oblimin rotation was employed (Gorsuch, 1974: 192). Higher order factors were not extracted since an examination of the factor correlation matrix revealed no zero-order coefficients greater than .08. Obviously, the analysis was exploratory in nature and did not contain a statistically adequate number of variables (experiences). However, because the original factors comprised the typology, which was then externally validated using independent data, we felt that a factor analysis was warranted. Each of the 36 themes were coded as (1) present of (2) absent for each subject, and then factor analyzed (Gorsuch, 1974: 262).

[7]While only one rater conducted the content analysis, this validation procedure suggests that the scoring procedure was reliable.

REFERENCES

Gorsuch, R. L.
  1974 *Factor Analysis.* Philadelphia: W. B. Saunders.

Greeley, A.
  1975 *Sociology of the Paranormal: A Reconnaissance.* London: Sage.

Harman, H. H.
  1967 *Modern Factor Analysis.* Chicago: University of Chicago Press.

Holsti, O. R.
  1969 "Content analysis," In G. Lindzey and E. Aronson (eds.), *The Handbook of Social Psychology.* Reading, Mass. Addison-Wesley, Vol. 2: 596–693.

Hood, R. W., Jr.
  1973 "Religious orientation and the experience of transcendence." *Journal for the Scientific Study of Religion* 12: 441–448.

  1975 "The construction and preliminary validation of a measure of reported mystical experience." *Journal for the Scientific Study of Religion* 14: 29–41.

James, W.
  1961 *The Varieties of Religious Experience.* New York: Collier.

Laski, M.
  1968 *Ecstasy.* New York: Greenwood.

Margolis, R. D.
  1977 "An empirical typology of religious experience: Its validation and relationship to psychotic experience." Unpublished doctoral dissertation, Georgia State University.

Stace, W. T.
  1960 *Mysticism and Philosophy.* Philadelphia: Lippincott.

Streng, F. J.
  1970 "The objective study of religion and the unique quality of religiousness." *Religious Studies* 6: 209–219.

Thomas, L. E. and P. E. Cooper
  1977 "The mystical experience: Can it be measured by structural questions?" Paper presented at the annual meeting of the American Sociological Association, Chicago, September.

Yinger, M.
  1970 *The Scientific Study of Religion.* London: Macmillan.

23

TELEVISION EVANGELISM MILKING THE FLOCK

John Mariani

Last night I dreamed I died and went to heaven, and God looked just like Fred Silverman. He was surrounded by several blonde female angels in diaphanous robes. Sitting at His left hand was an evocation of Billy Graham, whom He loved well. And at His right hand sat a silver-haired man in ministerial raiment. And God said to this man, "Into thy hands, Robert Schuller, I commend My spirit. Go ye and preach the Gospel to all stations. And don't come back to heaven until you're pulling a 22 Nielsen with a 32 share." And so, brandishing a Bible in one hand and a blow-dryer in the other, Dr. Robert H. Schuller was

From *Saturday Review*, February 3, 1979. Reprinted by permission.

beamed down to a California television tower, from which he emerged incarnate in double-knit robes.

I awoke with a start, and, my slumbers disturbed, proceeded to turn on the television. A celestial chorus singing "In Christ there is no East or West" boomed forth from the tube's warmed-up darkness, followed by the smiling image of a preacher declaiming to a flock of cars at a drive-in church. "This is the day the Lord has made!" he shouted. "Let us rejoice and be glad in it! Turn your hurt into a halo and the scar into a star!" The preacher was Dr. Robert H. Schuller, and I, feeling like Alice peeking through the looking glass, cried out, "This is no dream!"

No, it was simply another telecast of *The Hour of Power,* starring one of the medium's most flamboyant personalities, Reverend Robert Schuller, whose message to America is updated Norman Vincent Peale—positive thinking, Christian fulfillment, religious self-help. Schuller is a stunning speaker, a grand raconteur, and seems wholly sincere. Borrowing a line from "The Birth of the Blues," he tells people to root out their emotional aches and pains: "Don't *nurse* them and re*hearse* them, but dis*perse* them! Or else you will finally develop what psychologists call a neurosis, an abnormal attention to a compulsive emotion, and that will make you sick!"

Schuller is by far the most palatable of TV preachers, as well as the best showman. His brand of Christian optimism works especially well in middle-class markets like southern California, and his advisers have sometimes kept his *Hour of Power* off stations in the more conservative, fundamentalist enclaves of the South. His broadcasts pull in $10.9 million annually in donations, but he has never been accused of fiscal misconduct, as have evangelists like Billy Graham and others who labor in the vineyards of what has often been called "prime-time religion" and "the electric church."

TV evangelism is a booming business. Organized established churches are feeling the pinch, contending that the super-slick show-biz techniques of preachers on the tube take money out of church coffers and bodies out of church pews. Throughout the South and Midwest there are still a number of fundamentalist evangelists on television whose programs serve up equal portions of fire-and-brimstone, choruses of "Will the Circle Be Unbroken," and commercials for plastic, glow-in-the-dark Jesuses.

But the guilt-ridden super-sell and the Elmer Gantryism are now being replaced by mannered, smiling evangelists in vested suits whose telecasts are marked by lavish variety-show production numbers. They broadcast testimonies from Las Vegas entertainers like Robert Goulet and Jerry Lewis, sports figures like Sugar Ray Robinson, born-again government officials (Chuck Colson is a frequent guest). The message is one of pure fervor—good works are unnecessary, social action uncalled for—a video-induced adrenalin for the religious nervous system. A recent Gallup poll financed by 29 religious groups indicates that 34 percent of those questioned considered themselves born-again Christians. Analyzing the survey results, George Gallup, Jr. suggested that the traditional clergy may be unprepared to "deal with religious experience," and recommended providing "a special ministry" to those "people who are all charged up about their faith."

"Charged up" is the key phrase. The devotion of Americans to the television tube and its preachments is so strong that it now acts as teacher, lawgiver, social arbiter, and entertainer all at once, in the same way church liturgy once did. We respond like acolytes to the guiding light of the tube; it mesmerizes us at our most receptive moments, it nourishes our spirit, it refreshes us and puts us to sleep. Thus, the televised confessions of frailty, guilt, misdemeanor, or felony by Chuck Colson and lesser sinners become inspirational events, the modern equivalents of revivalist baptisms. One cannot help but be *charged* by the release and expiation of such images, as if Moses had descended the mountain with horns of light issuing from his head, a gimmick that would immediately take the Israelites' attention away from the static golden calf.

Indeed, the history of evangelism is the history of communication miracles. Even the Old Testament prophets and New Testament saints occasionally spoke in tongues, and the burning bush was a wonder in its day. The Roman Catholics' use of music, theatrics, light, shadow, incense, and extravagant costumes has been criticized by Protestants since the Reformation, and the live telecast of Pope Paul VI's funeral on all three networks had the best color coverage of a spectacle since the '76 Olympics. The churches have always stood ready to embrace new technology: The first books set into movable type were, after all, Bibles. Radio, the voice in the box, was an immediate success with evangelists, but the demands of television—color, light, visual excitement—are only now being realized by preachers and religious groups.

There are at least 25 stations almost wholly devoted to religious programming today. Dr. Schuller's sermons go out to 170 stations nationwide; the Christian Broadcasting Network, currently reaching 130 commercial (the same number as ABC) and 4,000 cable stations in North America, is now beaming the Word to 60 satellite stations in 20 U. S. cities; and Oral Roberts's broadcasts are watched by as many as 62 million people worldwide. What hath God wrought?

Most of these evangelical appeals are low-keyed and designed, like politicians' speeches, to be inoffensive to the largest number of viewers. Sometimes the displays of pecuniary zeal have led to abuses and tasteless exercises in pure greed. The San Francisco-based station KVOF (the "Voice of Faith"), Channel 38, is overseen by Pastor Gene Scott, who tells his audience, "If you are against channel 38, you are not only against me, you are against God," which means that tax collectors are in league with the devil to undermine Scott's ministry. (Studio facilities and transmitters are taxable, and since there may be a profit to Scott, he is also liable for personal income taxes.) San Francisco tax revenuers want Scott to pay $21,300 personal property tax; Los Angeles County wants $150,000; and Hartford, Connecticut, is seeking $80,000. The FCC has made no ruling on the right of tax-exempt church organizations to make direct appeals for donations via television, allowing the evangelists to milk their flock and avoid rendering to Caesar the things that are Caesar's.

Scott's appeals are to the wealthy, and he even asks corporations to contribute 10 percent of their profits. When his station employees sought to form a union, he fired them all. When the *Hartford Courant* blasphemed Scott, the evangelist slapped the newspaper's name on a watermelon, which he then interviewed on the air.

Another California evangelist, Garner Ted Armstrong, was recently excommunicated by his father, Herbert Armstrong (founder of the worldwide Church of God), after several former students at the church's Ambassador College published an 88-page report criticizing the institution's fiscal management and accusing Garner Ted of sexual dalliance with female church members.

One of Armstrong's most celebrated converts, chess master Bobby Fischer, has charged the church with squandering $90,000 of his donations and with using Madison Avenue techniques to win souls. The elder Armstrong, who had in fact once been an advertising man, began preaching the gospel 40 years ago on radio, and his son Garner did his proselytizing on more than 300 television stations until recently. The Church of God brings in $65 million each year.

Possibly the slickest and most sophisticated evangelical network is the PTL (Praise the Lord) Club, which buys $7.4 million of air time annually and reaches 198 affiliates and 3,000 cable stations worldwide. Like the Christian Broadcasting Network, the PTL Club uses a talk-show format modeled on the *Tonight Show*, right down to the plastic ferns and living room furniture one has come to expect on such shows.

The PTL Club is hosted by a jolly, rotund preacher named Jim Bakker, who decided years ago that television is the only medium people respond to these days, and mixing testimony with musical acts (all introduced with appropriate band music just like the Mike Douglas, Merv Griffin, and Dinah Shore shows) brings the Christian message home. Bakker has a sidekick, who is the spitting image of Ed McMahon, whose job it is to laugh at Bakker's jokes and to bolster every sentiment with a soulful, "Praise God!"

A typical PTL Club episode will involve celebrities and preachers as well as simple folk such as the couple who recently told how they forgave the man who raped and murdered their daughter. They had visited him in prison and were now showing the audience snapshots of themselves with their arms around the murderer's shoulders.

On another PTL telecast a guest evangelist brought the metaphysical conceit to a new low when he said, "You know, when you eat onions, you're gonna burp a foul onion smell. But when you eat God, you'll burp a sweet odor to the world." This was followed by a young man with a microphone color-coordinated to his suit, who sang, "Jesus, Jesus, there's something about that name," as if he were auditioning for a gay production of *West Side Story*.

Oral Roberts has changed his role from that of screeching faith healer to become the Ed Sullivan of the evangelical networks. Roberts began his ministry during the Depression, broadcast his first radio shows in 1942, and went on television in 1968. His Mabee Center for TV transmission at Oral Roberts University in Oklahoma beams out a weekly half-hour series and occasional specials with the sophistication of Hollywood's best production units.

Robert's stage is awash in colored lights. The audience is cued, there is a drum roll, spotlights blast the proscenium, and on come a dozen or more smiling faces in a chorus line, singing "God is greater than anyone can tell." The women, ethnically balanced in number, look like variation on Charlie's Angels in discreet ball gowns; the men are all Bruce Jenner look-alikes in J. C. Penney vested suits.

Into the spotlight steps Oral Roberts's son, a midwestern version of Johnny Desmond, who croons songs that might have been written by Barry Manilow. Oral Roberts's wife also makes regular appearances on the show, and her husband has made much of her supportiveness through the years. Roberts himself is perfectly coiffed and has the demeanor of an Oklahoma State football coach giving a pep talk. In direct contrast to his former ministry of faith-healing, he now stresses medical science, soliciting funds to built his City of Faith Hospital. Still, Roberts's request for donations is subtle and incidental to his evangelical message, which is simply, let Christ into your heart and be made whole. We are then treated to a reprise of "God is greater than anyone can tell," and in the fade-out a pleasant announcer makes a last appeal for money.

Recently Oral Roberts was a guest on Robert Schuller's show. Schuller stood there in his gray and black vestments, his arms folded, his smile giving off a sense of dominance as Roberts, in his vested suit, seemed to preach right to Schuller's face. Then the two men grasped hands, gave a benediction, and Schuller gave a speech entitled "Bounce-back-ability," ending with the words, "May God bless you as you worship Him with your offerings."

I do not mean to put Schuller in the same alms-box with the rest of the TV evangelists. He is, I think, a special case, and I do not doubt his utter belief in Christian optimism. Look what God has done for him:

Born an Iowa farm boy, Schuller became a voice crying in the California desert, one freeway exit from Disneyland. Twenty years ago he arrived in the area with $500 in his pocket, and rented space atop the snack bar of the Orange Drive-In Theater. His ads in local newspapers read, "Come as your are/In the family car," for Schuller had a revelation that the automobile was as fine and private a prayer cubicle as a Los Angeleno could want. His present church, a remarkable modern structure with sliding panels that open onto the parking-lot laity, stands in what Schuller calls "a 22-acre shopping center for Jesus Christ." Ah, City of Angels! Souls in sedans! Theology to the Thunderbirds!

Architect Philip Johnson has even designed an all-glass star-shaped cathedral, now being built, of which he says: "A church has no purpose except to back up the ritual of the liturgy. Take the doors. They're 80 feet high and 12 feet wide. And the opening of those doors will look great on TV. Dr. Schuller knows exactly what he's doing."

He must. Schuller's Garden Grove Church (a chapter of the Dutch Reformed) has 9,000 local members. In July of 1970 Schuller began buying cheap local television time—the so-called Sunday morning "ghetto hours"—and *The Hour of Power* was an immediate hit. A year later, against all reasonable conjecture, ratings for the show in New York were boffo. Today Schuller buys about $70,000 worth of air time weekly, although many stations take *The Hour of Power* free of charge and punch it into their FCC-mandated "public interest" slots. Broadcasts, which bring in 40,000 letters each week, and book sales account for $10.9 million each year. All, says producer Mike Mason, is plowed back into the Church. Schuller receives a $39,000 salary and drives a Cadillac Seville given to him by a wealthy parishioner. No one has ever accused Schuller of robbing the coffers of the Garden Grove Church, but he has taken criticism for using show-biz techniques on his broadcasts, although there is much less razzle-dazzle on

The Hour of Power than on most of the evangelical broadcasts.

"But I am *not* an evangelist," insists Schuller. "I have never appeared in a tent and I do not perform faith healing. We went on television because there were no televised church services in the Los Angeles area. People say I don't preach enough about social problems. But if we are to use the media, we must respect the individual's dignity. I can't insult my audience. With my local parishioners I can exhort them to social action, but I must *broad*cast, not *narrow*cast, on television. As for using the medium itself, I think that ceremony fills a need. I am terribly self-critical and never worry about being a media superstar."

But Schuller, along with Billy Graham and Oral Roberts, is indeed a superstar. It was Schuller who was asked to speak at Hubert Humphrey's funeral, and Jesse Jackson has admitted Schuller's influence on his own ministry. Given the bland oratory of most preachers, the pop-baroque exultations of Schuller, together with the visual kick of the medium itself, have turned him into a personality.

Americans need to make the teleological leap, and, like all icons, media personalities become our direct line to hope and easeful grace. I shall never forget the experience of reading the graffiti scrawled on the stone wall that surrounds Elvis Presley's mansion (called, righteously enough, Gracelands). People came from all over the world to display their emotion at this wailing wall, and amidst the "Elvis we love you" inscriptions were Gospel poems and eulogies of folkloric lyricism. One wrote, "Elvis is king, and there is no greater." Another, "Elvis is not dead—he's just on tour with God."

Now do you understand?

24

CHRISTIAN POLITICS AND THE NEW RIGHT

Robert Zwier
Richard Smith

In presidential election years we can expect the quadrennial awakening of political groups seeking to shape the nation's future course. But this year some of those groups are combining politics and religion; they are working to mobilize actual and potential constituencies of born-again Christians in order that the candidates they favor will be selected in November. For many decades the vast majority of conservative Christians have been in a political slumber; now these new groups are sounding the alarm. Concerned that the United States has fallen from a position of world power into decadence and that our society is collapsing under the weight of its own immorality, they call for a return to America's God-inspired foundation of morality, free enterprise, and patriotism. At the ideological heart of many of these organizations are traditional conservative beliefs in individual freedom, limited government and personal diligence.

It is important that Christians become aware of the existence and potential of such movements. Several questions must be addressed. First, what are they and who are their leaders? Second, what are their motivating beliefs about religion and politics? Third, how are they seeking to mobilize Christians? Fourth, can we agree with their views?

A RIGHT-WING VOTING BLOC

Among these new conservative Christian organizations, five are especially prominent: Christian Voice (Robert Grant, co-founder; Richard Zone, executive director; Gary Jarmin, lobbyist); Moral Majority (Jerry Falwell, founder); Christian Voters Victory Fund (Dale Silvers, chairman); Religious Roundtable (Ed McAteer, founder; Richard Viguerie, political operative); National Christian Action Coalition (Robert Billings, president).

These five groups have similar philosophies, tactics and goals. Each represents politically conservative evangelicals seeking to organize the power of a right-wing voting block through the distribution of literature and the broadcast of radio and television programs. Despite their similarities, however, the groups do not always work together. For instance, Moral Majority refused to support the "Washington for Jesus" rally last spring, and Robert Billings of the National Christian Action Coalition has resigned from Christian Voice's policy board, complaining that he was not kept informed.

Reprinted by permission from the October 8, 1980 issue of *The Christian Century.* Copyright 1980 Christian Century Foundation.

Philosophically, there are few disagreements among the groups. Their beliefs reflect a strong element of Bible-quoting fundamentalism and flag-waving patriotism. They share a number of core propositions. The first is that sin and its symptoms are dangerously real in this country. America is suffering from moral decay which, if not stopped, will result in the fall of the country and the rise of atheistic dictatorships. The signs of decay are everywhere: abortion on demand, equal rights for homosexuals, pornography, feminism and drugs, to name but a few. These symptoms, they contend, stem from the philosophy of secular humanism, which holds that God is dead, that people must establish their own moral order, and that individual pleasure is the highest goal.

Furthermore, say these fundamentalist Christians, internal decline is causing the U.S. to lose its position in the world. This nation is a chosen instrument of God, and it carries the major responsibility of implementing God's will in the world. A Christian Voice publicity letter states: "America, as a nation and a people, has stood in her brief history as the mightiest (and perhaps the last) great home of the Faith." Jerry Falwell's television programs are replete with references to the biblical convictions of the founding fathers. Indeed, Falwell has hosted "I Love America" rallies in more than 30 state capitals.

There is a strong conviction that America's prosperity has resulted from its Christian character: faithfulness to God brings material rewards, and "righteousness exalts a nation." Billings's interpretation of our history is illustrative: "You find that anytime America was on its knees, both our economy and our security and our spiritual temperature rose at the same time, and whenever we got off our knees all three have deteriorated."

Next, these interests see the world divided into two main camps. One is the U. S. and its allies—including Israel as God's biblically chosen people—and the other is the godless force of communism, which satanically seeks the total overthrow of the United States. The constant struggle against communism requires the U. S. to maintain its military strength at all times.

TIES TO THE 'NEW RIGHT'

Distinct ideas about the role of government in society are also put forward. Reflecting their conservative views, leaders of these right-wing coalitions believe that God ordained government to protect a nation through strong defense and to enforce fundamental laws, but they do not think that the government should regulate the economy, intervene in the parental responsibility for educating children, or help people who can help themselves. They decry the tremendous growth of federal agencies and the incredible increase in the scope of government control that began during the New Deal administration of Franklin Roosevelt. Christian Voice lobbyist Gary Jarmin argues that

we have to get involved and find a solution that is based on our spiritual beliefs and not on a statist mentality that has so infected even Christian members of Congress. The real gap between us and our liberal brethren is this fundamental point: we believe that free people centered on God can solve these problems . . . but what they have really done is transferred that imperative from themselves to the government.

Finally, these groups believe that Christians have a God-given responsibility to be politically active. In fact, Jerry Falwell has said that the job of a pastor is to save souls, baptize, and get people registered to vote. Failure to register is a sin. If Christians do not act to throw out of office those officials who perpetuate an unchristian, liberal program, the U. S. will crumble and the cause of God's Kingdom will be frustrated.

These views illustrate the close ties these religious groups have with secular New Right organizers. "New Right" is a term referring to a new generation of political activists promising to be far more effective in achieving their policy goals than were such older conservative figures as Republican Senator Barry Goldwater and fundamentalist clergyman Carl McIntire. Despite the reluctance of some to admit their ties with the New Right and their insistence on independence, the linkages are clear. The chief organizers of the New Right are Richard Viguerie and Paul Weyrich. Viguerie has worked with considerable success to implement his 1976 prediction that the "next major growth area for the conservative ideology" would be among evangelical Christians. He heads a coalition of New Right political organizations called the Kingston Group, which Billings and Christian Voice's Jarmin both attend. Other organizations involved in the Kingston Group are Weyrich's Committee for the Survival of a Free Congress (CSFC), Citizens for the Republic (founded by Ronald Reagan), the American Conservative Union, and the National Association of Manufacturers. Richard Zone, Christian Voice operations director, says that the Kingston Group provides a "lot of political perspective. They draw attention to issues we might otherwise have missed."

There are other ties as well. Robert Billings is vice-chairman of Weyrich's Committee for the Survival of a Free Congress—Billings claims Weyrich as his "political mentor"—and Gary Jarmin served as a lobbyist for the American Conservative Union before switching to Christian Voice. His assistant, David Troxler, was formerly an associate director for CSFC.

FAMILY ISSUES

The core propositions shared by these leaders translate into specific positions on issues, and the groups have made their program abundantly clear. Concerning family issues, they fervently oppose abortion, seek a constitutional amendment to prohibit it and laud the recent Supreme Court decision that government has no obligation to pay for the abortions of women on welfare. They oppose homosexuality and contend that homosexuals should not have the same vocational and housing opportunities that others have. They strongly oppose movements for women's and children's rights. For example, they oppose the Equal Rights Amendment, insisting that it would take mothers out of their homes; they oppose government child-care programs for similar reasons. Concerning education, they are adamant in the belief that parents rather than the government should be in control. They oppose government regulation of private schools, and they would prefer to have the federal government get out of education entirely. They also believe that prayer and Bible reading should be restored in all schools, be law if necessary. They opposed the creation of the new Department of Education on the grounds that it was an attempt to increase government control.

In the area of foreign policy, the groups call for increased military spending to ensure that the U. S. will be militarily superior. They believe that the use of force may be necessary to stop the inevitable communist aggression and that the U. S. must remain loyal to those countries that have sided with it against communism (for example, Taiwan).

These groups employ a number of tactics to fulfill their goals; probably their most important activity is the presentation of information about electoral and public-policy choices. Most of the organizations send out newsletters identifying and explaining crucial political issues. So far, mailings have been sent mainly to pastors and Christian educators. Second, the groups have close ties with such Christian broadcasters as Pat Robertson ("700 Club") and Jim Bakker ("PTL Club"). Falwell has his own TV show and has produced additional programs for prime-time viewing.

At least two movements—Christian Voice and the Christian Voters Victory Fund—have compiled ratings of the voting records of members of Congress. The two lists are remarkably similar; their small differences resulted from the fact that the groups used different votes in their calculations. These ratings on the "morality" of legislators have, however, created problems. Besides being denounced by liberal legislators who received low scores, the lists were also attacked by Senator Gordon Humphrey and Representative Robert Dornan, both of whom resigned from the Christian Voice advisory board in protest. The ratings will be used during the fall campaign in an effort to defeat those candidates who received low scores.

Although 1980 is really a trial run as these fundamentalist religionists develop their organizations and perfect their information networks, the ultimate goal is to have an organization in every county and precinct in the country within this decade. At that point the groups will broaden their activities beyond election contests and use their network of Christians to contact legislators before important votes are cast in Congress.

POSITIVE CONTRIBUTIONS

There is little doubt that greater numbers of evangelicals are awakening politically and that these conservative groups are both creating this new activity and benefiting from it. The potential impact is immense, for a solid bloc of several million voters would be able to determine the outcome of many elections. How should we deal with this phenomenon? How should we evaluate the goals, beliefs and tactics of these new groups?

They have made several positive contributions. Most important, they have created an awareness of the interrelationships between political issues and biblical beliefs, accurately pointing to the reality that basic moral questions are involved in choices about defense budgets, tax reform, civil rights and education. For too long evangelicals have been concerned solely with personal morality while ignoring the impact of public-policy choices on the moral and spiritual health of our society. For too long evangelicals have maintained a cautious distance from the political arena. It is time for Christians to realize that Jesus

Christ is Lord of all—and that includes secular politics as well as church matters.

These groups are also correct in their perception that sin is a ubiquitous force. Their call for national and personal repentance may seem strange to many who think of sin as an individual rather than a collective problem, but the very political, economic and social structures of our country are rife with injustice. To be sure, there is considerable disagreement between conservatives and liberals as to what sins must be confessed, but the call for repentance is surely appropriate.

In addition, we must commend these groups for their attempts to remain nonpartisan. None of them makes the claim that the Democrats or the Republicans are more Christian. We should note, however, that because of their core beliefs, more Republicans than Democrats will get their support. Looking at the ratings of the Christian Voters Victory Fund, we see that Republicans consistently score higher. In the Senate, for example, the average rating for Republicans is 56.5, while the average for Democrats is 21.7. In the House, the averages are 79.2 for Republicans and 39.0 for Democrats.

DANGER SIGNALS

Despite the validity of their recognition of a Christian political responsibility, their call for repentance, and their generally nonpartisan appeals, we have several serious disagreements with these groups. The first has to do with their explicit link with ideological conservatism and the implicit suggestion that this ideology is more attuned than is liberalism to the principles found in the Bible. The idea that the principles of God's revelation can be neatly subsumed under the rubric of a humanly devised ideology is pretentious. Any full examination of biblical standards will disclose a subtle blend of "conservatism" and "liberalism." The Bible is full of passages mandating a concern for the poor—a focus too often lacking in laissez-faire conservative circles. The

Bible does not see government as the satanic evil which the conservatives decry; rather, the government is a divinely ordained instrument.

The point here is not that liberalism is closer to the Bible than conservatism but that we are using the wrong level of analysis when we seek to portray either ideology as more Christian. God's will is not subordinate to ideological predispositions; it supersedes them.

Furthermore, there is evidence that these new groups take an inconsistent view of the role of government. For the most part, they desire to limit its power. Yet on certain issues they call for more government involvement. For example, they seek a broad role for government in eliminating abortion, in restricting the rights of homosexuals, in taxing for new weapons systems whose need is unclear, and in mandating prayer and Bible reading in public schools. In short, they do not want government intervention when their own freedoms are at stake, but they are willing to use the power of the government to force life-style changes on others. One does not have to be a proponent of abortion or homosexuality to see the inconsistency. If it is not right to use the government to force one group to tolerate the life style of others, then it is equally wrong to use the government to compel the second group to tolerate the life style of the first.

Likewise, the legislative ratings presented by these groups are flawed. They presume, on the basis of from ten to fifteen votes, to issue final judgments about the morality of individual legislators. In so doing, they again claim that the will of God is bound up with one particular position on very complex issues of national policy. Something is clearly amiss when Christian Voice gives the lowest possible rating to a Baptist minister (William Gray) and to a Catholic priest (Robert Drinan) while giving the highest score to a congressman who has been indicted in the Abscam scandal (Richard Kelly).

The handful of votes selected for examination is not a sufficient basis for judging individual morality. One of the saddest things about these scales is their neglect of votes on environmental and world hunger issues—for the Bible is quite clear on issues of stewardship and compassion. The selectivity of these reports can easily distort their results. Compare, for example, the ratings compiled by the Christian Voters Victory Fund with those of Bread for the World, a group concerned more narrowly with hunger issues. The contrasts are revealing:

Senator	Christian Voters Victory Fund	Bread for the World
Armstrong	100	14
Cranston	0	100
Culver	0	100
Glenn	0	86
Hatfield	25	86
Helms	100	0
Humphrey	100	0
McClure	90	0
McGovern	0	100
Nelson	0	86
Riegle	10	100
Thurmond	90	14

On the basis of these two ratings, can we confidently declare, for example, that Senator Jesse Helms votes more morally than Senator John Culver?

In addition to their selectivity, these ratings can also be criticized by Christians for the specific positions they take. Among Christians there is legitimate disagreement, for instance, about defense policy. The new right-wing groups call for the deployment of several new strategic weapons systems. Yet other Christians interpret the biblical call to be peacemakers as a mandate to reject these new weapons as provocative, more likely to cause a nuclear holocaust than to prevent one, and a costly misuse of precious resources that could be better used to feed hungry people and provide improved health care for the sick and dying.

WHAT IMPACT WILL THEY HAVE?

The issue is not simply the contrasting perspectives of Christians but the claim by these groups that they have the correct, biblical answer and that those who disagree with them are not fit to hold public office because of their immorality. Although Christians of all ideological stripes should be striving constantly to learn the will of God as we face crucial policy choices, we need also to maintain a spirit of humility. We must admit that we do not always clearly understand God's Word, and that we do not fathom the complexities of these policy issues. Every group of Christians, not only the conservative ones discussed here, must refrain from the arrogance of presumed omniscience and must adopt an attitude of humility befitting our sinful nature.

Next, the claim that the United States is *the* instrument to accomplish the will of God is suspect. There is no doubt that God could use, and probably is using, this nation for his purposes, but the claim of these groups carries with it a historical and cultural relativism that seeks to interpret God's plan within a framework of flag-waving nationalism. Their claim further excludes God's use of other countries with strong Judeo-Christian foundations or other religious tenets and ignores the possibility that even "godless" nations are instruments which God can use.

Finally, there is a danger in efforts to use ministers in their pulpits to proclaim the politically conservative gospel. Preaching of the Word, not political mobilization or indoctrination, is the central responsibility of pastors. This statement is not meant to deny pastors a political role or to suggest that their sermons must avoid any consideration of political issues or responsibilities, but it must be stressed that political persuasion is not the first obligation of ministers. There is an additional danger: preaching a political gospel may cause or aggravate splits within churches or denominations and thus hinder the effective proclamation of the gospel of salvation in Christ.

It is too early to tell whether the new conservative Christian groups will have a significant impact on the behavior of the millions of evangelicals in the United States. If these groups do contribute to an increased political awareness and involvement, we can only hope that the newly awakened citizens do not blindly follow the leading of groups that are selective in their interpretations. As this nation faces the threat of nuclear war, the despair of the hungry, and the worldwide depletion of raw materials, Christians must reflect upon their political choices in prayerful humility, blessed with the considerable assurance that God is really in control.

IX

ECONOMICS
The Distribution of the Necessities for Survival

Each society must have a system for the production and distribution of goods and services, and it is the economic institution that fulfills these functions.

The economic institution is supported by and interrelated with all the other social institutions—in particular, the political institution. Consider three influential economic systems: feudalism, colonialism, and capitalism. Strong central government came to an end with the fall of imperial Rome. The result was an end of the central government's function as protector of monetary surety and safety and the beginning of a period in which people were forced to return to the land for survival and to submit to marauding ex-soldiers for protection. With the confiscation of the land and the election of one of their leaders as head-king, a feudal system of government became dominant. Under the colonial system, industry needed workers for the large plantations and mines. However, the natives saw no reason to work for industry since they had their own land for food and shelter. It was the political institution that met the need of this economic system by putting the best native lands into reserve, by requiring taxes to be paid in cash, and by assigning natives, arrested for various reasons, to work on plantations and in mines. Under capitalism, economic organizations—such as the corporation and the union—have developed so powerfully that government has had to become more and more involved in the economic sphere by aiding the purchasing power of the poor and the unemployed, by subsidizing and regulating the corporation, and by regulating the union.

The articles in this chapter reflect this idea of institutional interrelatedness. In fact, in the first article Naisbitt automatically includes political factors in discussing the future of the economy. Salomon and Bernstein, in the second article, continue to note this interrelation, of a capitalist-corporate economy, but from a different perspective—a negative one.

In the last article, the author comments on both ends of the capitalist spectrum: poverty and wealth. In his article, Gans defines poverty and the poor in terms of the functions they perform for the rest of society. Unless viable substitutions to fulfill these functions can be found, Gans states, society will never abolish poverty.

As you read this chapter, think about some current economic problems and how reforms in the areas addressed here might help solve them. Also consider how important economic arrangements are for most aspects of social life.

25

THE NEW ECONOMIC AND POLITICAL ORDER OF THE 1980s

John Naisbitt

To be back in Sweden is always special for me, and I am pleased to be with such a broad representation of Swedish businesses. This morning I will be talking with you about five powerful trends that are restructuring the United States, and to varying degrees, Sweden and the other developed countries of the world. Let me list them first, and then return to each of them for a more detailed discussion.

1. The United States is rapidly shifting from a mass industrial society to an information society, and the final impact will be more profound than the 19th century shift from an agricultural to an industrial society.
2. There is more decentralization than centralization taking place in America—for the first time in the nation's history, the power is shifting not only from the President to the Congress, but—less noticed—from the Congress to the states and localities.
3. We are now a truly global economy because of instantaneously-shared information, and the world is deeply in the process of a redistribution of labor and production. As part of this process all of the developed countries are deindustrializing.
4. The American society is moving in dual directions of high tech/high touch. The introduction of every new technology is accompanied by a compensatory human response—or the new technology is rejected.
5. There are the beginnings of a job revolution in America, a basic restructuring of the work environment from top-down to bottom-up.

Before dealing with each of these structural changes, I will briefly outline our methodology. In developing the Trend Report for our clients we rely almost exclusively on a system of monitoring *local* events and behavior. We are overwhelmingly impressed with the extent to which America is a bottom-up society, and so we monitor what's going on locally rather than what's going on in Washington, or in New York. Things start in Los Angeles, in Tampa, in Hartford, in Wichita, Portland, San Diego, and Denver. It's very much a from-the-bottom-up society.

The tracking concept employed in determining these trends has its roots in World War II. During the war, intelligence experts sought

Used with permission of the author.

to find a method for obtaining the kinds of information on enemy nations that public opinion polls would have normally provided. Under the leadership of Paul Lazersfeld and Harold Lasswell, a method was developed for monitoring what was going on in these societies that involved doing a content analysis of their daily newspapers.

Although this method of monitoring public thinking continues to be the choice of the intelligence community—the United States annually spends millions of dollars doing newspaper content analysis in various parts of the world—it has rarely been applied commercially. In fact, we are the first, and presently the only group, to utilize this concept for analyzing our society. We have been doing content studies every day since 1970 of the 150 major newspapers in the United States.

The reason this system of monitoring the changes in society works so well is that the "news hole" in a newspaper is a closed system. For economic reasons, the amount of space devoted to news in a newspaper does not change over time. So, when something new is introduced into that news hole, as it is called, something or a combination of things has to go out or be omitted. The principle involved here can be classified as forced choice within a closed system.

In this forced choice situation societies add new preoccupations and forget old ones. We keep track of the ones that are added and the ones that are given up. Evidently, societies are like human beings: I do not know what the number is, but a person can only keep so many problems and concerns in his or her head at any one time. If new problems or concerns are introduced, some existing ones must be given up. We keep track of what preoccupations Americans have given up and have taken up. We are keeping track of the changing "share of the market" that competing societal concerns command.

The information collected on various issues or topics is not extrapolated, but is used to look for patterns. For example, there are five states in the United States where most social invention occurs. The other 45 states are, in general, followers. California is the key indicator state; Florida is second, although not too far behind; with the other three trend setter states being Washington, Colorado, and Connecticut.

An example of this phenomenon is provided by a look at who the governors are in these five states. Connecticut and Washington are the only two states where women have been elected governor in their own right. The other states have elected the "new" politician: Graham, Lamm and Brown. The new politics has little to do with the old liberal-conservative dichotomies. Rather, it has to do with appropriate scale decentralization, fiscal conservatism, and a lot of experimentation.

Now let's look at the five trends.

1. The United States is rapidly shifting from a mass industrial society to an information society, and the final impact will be more profound than the 19th century shift from an agricultural to an industrial society.

In 1950—I want to talk about the percentage of labor force in the various sectors—in 1950, 65 percent of the people working in this country were in the industrial sector. That figure today is around 30 percent. It has gone from 65 to 30 percent since 1950. That is a dramatic change. (In 1900, at the turn of the century, it stood at 35 percent.) In 1950, the number of people in the information sector of the society—information occupations—was 17 percent—and now exceeds 55 percent. Information occupations are those involved in the creating, processing, and distribution of information, including banks, stock markets, insurance companies, education, and government.

For years we have been hearing that we are moving into a service society. Yet the service sector (absent information occupations) has remained relatively flat—about 11 or 12 percent for decades. (The character of these service sector jobs has changed—we have few domestics today and a lot of people in fast food jobs—but their ratio to the work force has remained fairly constant.)

It is clear that the post-industrial society is an information society.

One of the important things to notice about this shift is that the strategic resource in the industrial society was capital; the strategic resource in the post-industrial information society is knowledge and data (and that's not only renewable; it's self generating). That explains the explosion of entrepreneurial activity in the United States. Because the strategic resource is now what is in our heads, access to the system is much easier. Not only will we see an impressive increase in the creation of new small firms, but if large institutions are to survive, they will restructure to encourage entrepreneurial activity within their institutions.

Now, the mass instrumentalities that were created, that were consonant with the industrial society are now out of tune with the times. Just as in 1800 the fact that 90 percent of us in the labor force were farmers dictated the societal arrangements of the day, the fact that most of us were in industrial occupations until recently dictated the arrangements of a mass industrial society—which are now out of tune with the new information society. Let me give you three examples. Labor unions. In 1950, with 65 percent of the work force in this country in the industrial sector, more than 30 percent of the workers in the country were members of unions. That's now 19 percent. There's no way that's going to do anything but continue to go down, as we move more and more into the information society. A late entry in mass industrial society, network televison. Network—notice I'm saying network, not television—network television started down last year and it is on a long, slow, irreversible slide downward. I'll talk more about that later. National political parties, which had their heyday in the industrial society, exist today in theory only. Things like department stores and national chain stores which are in tune with the mass, industrial society have been yielding over the last decade and a half to things like boutiques. This phenomenon, the breaking up of mass instrumentalities, you'll see everywhere.

Starting a year ago, the number one occupation in the United States became a clerk, replacing the laborer, and the farmer before that. Farmer, laborer, clerk: a brief history of the United States. (What comes after clerk? I can't decide whether it is soldier or poet.)

In connection with this shift to an information society it is important to notice a powerful anomaly developing: as we move into a more and more literacy-intensive society, our schools are giving us an increasingly inferior product: this is a powerful mismatch. SAT scores (the test to qualify for college) have been going down each year for more than a decade. We all experience that our young people are not outstanding when it comes to writing and arithmetic. Consider this: for the first time in the history of the United States, the generation that is graduating from high school today is less skilled than its parents. Lastly, with the basic restructuring of the society from an industrial to an information society, the traditional groupings of goods and services won't work any more. That is why the economists are almost always wrong. And they will continue to be as long as they rely on the old indices. We need new concepts and new data if we are to understand where we are and where we are going.

2. There is more decentralization than centralization taking place in America—for the first time in the nation's history, the power is shifting not only from the President to the Congress, but—less noticed—from the Congress to the states and localities.

Trends move in different directions, at different speeds. They have different weights. They have different life cycles. About three or four years ago, the heft and feel of the movement toward decentralization became greater than the heft and feel of those forces toward continued centralization.

The two great centralizing events in America's history were the Great Depression and World War II, plus the centralizing impact of industrialization. We are now receding from these centralizing influences.

You remember, in the fifties and into the sixties (and beyond) we began to celebrate ethnic diversity. Polish is beautiful, as well as black is beautiful. We started to celebrate our ethnic restaurants, which of course had been there all the time. An extraordinary thing happened, by the way, in the late sixties. We gave up the myth of the melting pot. For years we had taught our children in fourth grade civics (or thereabouts) that America was a great melting pot, as if we were all put in a giant blender and homogenized into Americans. Now we have given up that myth and recognize that it is our ethnic diversity that has made us such a vital, creative country. Then a phenomenon of the seventies was jurisdictional diversity, geographical diversity. We have no national urban policy today because a (top-down, master plan) national urban policy is out of tune with the times. The only national urban policy that would be in tune with the times is the national urban policy that would respond to local initiatives. It is an inappropriate question to ask, "Are we going to save our cities?" That's an either/or formulation. It doesn't work in the new multiple option society. The point is, we'll save some of our cities; we'll not save others. We'll save some of our cities a little bit; we'll save others a great deal. And it will all turn—again—on local initiative. That's also why we're not getting a national health policy, because you can't do a top-down monolithic kind of policy anymore because of the growing diversity in the United States.

Now, where we feel *centralization* continuing most painfully is in government regulations, as we well know. And that's changing. That's really bending back. It was a Republican Nixon who opened China. A Democrat never could have done that. And I think just so, the Democrats are the only ones who're going to be able to at least get the deregulation started, because Republicans would come

under too much pressure. You know about the airlines, and you know about the trucking industry, which I thought would be the last to go, the railroads, radio. The watershed in this, I think, was in February of 1978, when the U.S. House of Representatives voted against a consumer protection agency. What was not, I think, sufficiently underlined at that time was that the first and second term Democrats voted 43 to 37 against establishing that agency. More and more, we are going to see the political left and right meeting on this issue of being against big government and against government regulations. And that's part of a larger power shift, too, that's going from the President to the Congress and from the Congress to the states, which means more state regulations.

Proposition 13, I think, has to be understood as having a lot more to do with the initiative trend, or the referendum trend, than it has to do with taxes. We are submitting to the political process questions we never submitted to the political process before. The watershed on that was Proposition 15 in California three years ago, when the citizens in California voted on whether or not to build a plant (a nuclear plant, but nevertheless, a plant). We have never submitted that kind of question to the political process before. Business got very involved in that because they had so much at stake. And in the process they helped to legitimize this notion of submitting this kind of question to the political process. There is no end to it. Last November, more than 400 questions were voted on around the country. There have been many votes on where we can and cannot smoke. Five jurisdictions last year voted on using or not using public funds for abortion. Two cities voted on South Africa. Long Beach, California, voted on whether or not to have an oil tanker terminal, and, later, on the color of street lights. We never voted on those kinds of things before, but we're going to see more and more of this. It's a part of this larger, "direct democracy." We'll be voting on a great range of new things, at times "leapfrogging" the traditional political process.

In America, the large, general purpose instrumentalities are folding everywhere. An early sign and instructive analogue of this was the demise of *Life, Look* and *Post,* the huge circulation, general purpose magazines nine years ago. That same year, 300 special purpose magazines were created, most of which are still being published. Four hundred or so were added the following year, and so on. There are now more than 4,000 special interest magazines being published in the United States, and no general purpose magazines. This phenomenon is an analogue for what is going on in the U.S. Two years ago the National Association of Manufacturers and the United States Chamber of Commerce announced they were going to merge for all kinds of wonderful reasons, none of which was true. They were going to merge in order to survive. About a year ago they announced that they couldn't negotiate the merger, so now presumably, they're going to die separately (except that the Chamber has lately become much more responsive to the grass roots, and that may save it). The American Medical Association, another umbrella organization, is getting weaker as the groups within it—the pediatricians, surgeons and so on, and the country and local medical groups are getting stronger.

A year ago two big labor unions, the meat cutters and the retail clerks, merged to form a huge union—for survival. That's the dinosaur effect; they get larger just before they go under. (We haven't noticed it, but there have been 50 mergers of labor unions in the last eight years.)

These kinds of umbrella organizations are out of tune with the times, just as network television now is becoming. ABC, CBS, and NBC will be the *Life, Look,* and *Post* of the eighties and nineties. Back to the magazine analogue, network television will lose ground to new options: the incredible array of cable, video disks, and new special-interest net-

works—a Spanish language network, the all-sports network, the all-news network, the BBC in America network, and so on. My guess is that by the end of the eighties, the three big networks may have fewer than half the viewers they have today.

The cross-over in politics came in 1976—a Presidential year—when the number of people contributing to special interest groups, like "Save the Dolphins" exceeded the number of people who contributed to the umbrella Democratic and Republican parties combined. That trend is continuing. The two great American political parties now exist in name only. We have a Congress filled with independents. We may get some new political parties, but in tune with the decentralization of the country, they will be local, new political parties, not national. We already have the Right-to-Life party on the ballot in New York State. I am aware of your environment party and your health food party here in Sweden. We will have local special-interest parties developing in the U. S.

The magazine analogue is also instructive in connection with leadership. In the United States, we have all noticed a dearth of leadership. We have no great captains of industry any more, no great university presidents, no great leaders in the arts, or in civil rights, or in labor, or in politics. It is not because there is any absence of ambition or talent on the part of those who would be leaders. We don't have any great leaders any more because we followers are not creating them. Followers create leaders—not the reverse—and we followers are not conferring leadership as we did in the past. We are now creating leaders with much more limited mandates: closer to us and on much narrower bands. In the old Taoist model of leadership, "find a parade and get in front of it," we who would be leaders in America are finding much smaller parades—and many more of them.

3. We are now a truly global economy because of instantaneously-shared information, and the world is deeply in the process of a redistribution of labor and produc-

tion. As part of this process all of the developed countries are de-industrializing.

The other side of relying on less centralized political authority is the growing world economic interdependency. Sir Arthur Clarke said that the two inventions that accounted for America's swift economic growth were the telegraph (later the telephone) and the railroads. Similarly, the two great inventions that are making us a global village are the jet airplane and communication satellite. In another way Marshall McLuhan captured the sense of interdependence when he recently said, "There are no passengers on spaceship earth. We are all crew."

We are now a truly world economy because of instantaneously shared information. We have wiped out the "information float." And we are now deeply in a process of re-sorting out who is going to make what in this world. As part of this process all of the non-communist, developed countries are de-industrializing. Even Japan (the most flexible country in the world) is getting out of the steel business and the shipbuilding business. She knows that in these markets (which are at saturation worldwide), South Korea will outdo her in steel, and ships will be more economically built by the new shipbuilders: Brazil, Poland and Spain.

The U. S. and the rest of the developed countries are on the way to losing the following industries: steel, automobile, railroad equipment, machinery, apparel, shoe, textile, and appliance. By the end of the century, the Third World will make 25 percent of the world's manufactured goods. The end of the century is only 19 years away. Remember when President Kennedy was inaugurated? That is how far it is to the year 2000.

We developed nations are probably going to kill ourselves competing over steel and cars, when we should be moving in other new areas as the Third World takes over the old tasks. That is why the Chrysler bailout was so important. That bailout is a big step down, the path of turning the U. S. automobile industry

into an *employment program*, just as Britain turned its automobile (and steel) manufacturing into an employment program. We have to see Chrysler and the other automobile companies in a world context. Consider: In the world automobile market we are reaching saturation; it will soon be a replacement market. There are now 86 countries that have automobile assembly plants. Japan takes 13 man-hours to build a car; the U. S. takes 30 man-hours. Imports passed Ford and became number two to General Motors in 1979 with 20 percent of car sales in the U. S. But in the bellwether state of California imports were 50 percent of car sales last year. It has been part of the conceit of the U. S. automobile companies that they never diversified. They thought they would go on forever. Now even Henry Ford is getting out while the getting's good.

Yesterday is over. We have to look to the new technological adventures: electronics, bio-industry, alternative sources of energy, mining the seabeds. We have to work out policies (or at least let the marketplace do it) to make the transition from the old to the new. By the way: How reliable is the Dow-Jones as a barometer to the economic health of the society or stock market with all those companies from the dying industries on its list? Like the economists, they need a new index.

4. The American society is moving in dual directions of high tech/high touch. The introduction of every new technology is accompanied by a compensatory human response—or the new technology is rejected.

With the introduction of television, for example, came the group therapy movement which, in turn, has led to the personal growth movement and the human potential movement. (Watching TV in bed with someone is, of course, very high tech/high touch.)

Similarly, the high technology of the medical field (brain scanners and heart transplants) has led to a new interest in the family doctor and neighborhood clinics. A novel high tech/high touch example is citizen band

(CB) radio: people using this technology to get in touch with another human being—anybody! And, moving closer to our offices, the high technology of word processing has initiated a revival of handwritten notes and letters. The high technology of chemistry and pharmacology produced the pill which led to a revolution in life styles (away from either/or to multiple-option). Jet airplanes have led only to more meetings. A poignant example of high tech/high touch is how the high technology of life-sustaining equipment in hospitals led to a new concern for the quality of death (and to the hospice movement).

Whenever institutions introduce new technology to customers or employees, they should build in a high touch component; if they don't, people will try to create their own or reject the new technology. That may account, for example, for the public's resistance to automation and electronic accounting. Electronic Funds Transfer (EFT) is failing everywhere.

The high technology of the computer has been somewhat intimidating to many of us, but now I see its high-touch potential as "computer as liberator." Let me explain. A company with 40,000 employees has always treated those 40,000 the same; it had to because that was the only way it could keep track of them. And that has been unfair, because people are different. Now the the computer to keep track, that company can have a different arrangement with each of its employees as to relation of salary to retirement benefits, work hours, job objective and so forth. And that is the trend: each of us having an individually-tailored contract with our employer. Also, the computer will outmode the hierarchical system of organization (and that is liberating!). We had to have a hierarchy in order to keep track of everybody and what they were up to. Now with the computer to keep track we can restructure to horizontal organization of many small entrepreneurial groups. The pyramid has been outdated by the new technology.

5. There are the beginnings of a job revolution in America, a basic restructuring of the work environment from top-down to bottom-up.

Whenever pressing economic trends converge with changing personal values, you get change in a society. That's why we can start to look for some revolutionary changes in the workplace. A whole new attitude toward American workers is on the way. And it could result in a revitalization of the spirit of work and America's sagging productivity.

Here's the situation: The productivity growth rate is on a dismal downswing. Last year was the worst for productivity improvement in the nation's history.

At the same time, over the last two decades, personal values have been changing radically; there's a growing demand for more satisfaction from life. Workers feel it, too. Their psychic pain is reflected in their low productivity. They are sick of being treated like machines in the service of increased productivity. Workers refuse to produce and even deliberately sabotage the products they make.

They are no longer content with the traditional remedies offered up by labor unions, such as more pay, four-day weeks, better health benefits. What they really want, like everybody else, is deep human satisfaction from their work.

But industry had no compelling need to give it to them—until now. These dropping productivity figures will finally force industry, in economic desperation, to give more than token attention to the mental health of workers. The workplace is in for a good shaking up. And the American worker is about to be saved by one of the most unlikely forces in society—call it humanization, personal growth, "the human potential movement," participatory management, the values of the sixties. Call it whatever, it is about to converge with the economic necessity of the seventies and eighties to rescue the America worker from a dead-end existence. For one thing, American industry is beginning to eye the way Japanese companies are run. Japan's productivity runs circles around ours. As I mentioned earlier, it takes Japanese workers 13 man-hours to build a car, compared with 30 man-hours for American workers.

It's often mistakenly thought that Japanese workers are so productive because they perform like robots, ever subservient to authority. The opposite is true. Unlike American workers, the Japanese are given enormous freedom to both plan and execute their work and solve problems alone without the help or interference of managers. The plants are run not from the "top down" like ours where managers deliver orders, but from the "bottom up" where workers make many crucial decisions. Fully 90 percent of Japan's industrial work force is organized in work groups of 8 to 11 people. The whole theory is: the workers know their job better than anyone else, and given a chance, workers will be creative and self-motivated. Interestingly, the Japanese developed some of their management techniques from the theories of our own humanistic psychologists, such as the late Abraham Maslow.

When the Japanese use their techniques on American workers, the changes are astounding. The Japanese Matsushita Company several years ago took over a Motorola plant near Chicago and began to produce Quasar TV sets. The company retained 1000 on-line workers but dismissed half of the 600 supervisors and managers. Within two years, production *doubled* and the reject rate of sets dropped from 60 percent to 4 percent. Moreover, through good quality control, the company reduced its annual warranty costs from $14 million to $2 million. Just think, too, of the countless consumers who were spared the frayed nerves of dealing with defective products. That alone is an important contribution to the nation's sanity.

Our workers are not stupid or lazy. They, like everybody else, want a chance for more personal satisfaction. And they are about to get it—even if the trigger is such an eye-glazing event as lower productivity figures. U. S. industry leaders may not understand such a trend as changing personal values, but they do understand dropping productivity.

Because of how economically interlaced the U. S. is with the rest of the world, the only weapon it has against inflation that is in its full control is productivity improvement. As Peter Drucker says in his new book, "Managing in Turbulent Times," productivity improvement will be management's most important task for the eighties. And in this regard, for the eighties, creative management will be more important than creative technology.

In closing, I want to say that I think the decade of the eighties will be very exciting and uncertain. We must make uncertainty our friend. It is, among other things, the only certainty we have. In the decade of the eighties, we will be restructuring our society from an industrial to an information society; we are decentralizing at home while at the same time we move into a truly world economy where the redistribution of production spells opportunity for all of us; we are becoming an increasingly high touch world as we continue to push high tech; we are becoming a multiple-option, highly market-segmented society; and we will be a more participatory society with greater opportunities for each of us to realize our potential.

In short, we will be a much more complicated society, and the period of working through the structural changes will be painful, but we will be a more interesting, creative, and nourishing society.

26

THE CORPORATE THRUST IN AMERICAN POLITICS

David Salomon
Jules Bernstein

Since the late '60s American business has con-
solidated its organizational structure so as to
vastly increase its political and economic
power. A recent *Fortune* magazine article,
entitled "Business is Learning How to Win in
Washington," detailing many such changes,
opens with a conversation between two lobbyists for the Business Roundtable on how to
defeat the Consumer Protection bill:

Just a few blocks from the White House, in Room 811 of
one of Washington's least memorable office buildings,
this conversation is going on between two men, one of
whom is holding a list of congressmen in his hand:

"Henry Gonzalez of San Antonio . . . should we use
Sears? We have problems with Jake Pickle on this, I'm not
sure we can get him. . . . OK, let's ask Sears about Gonzalez. . . . Delaney of Long Island . . . well, Delaney's a
character, still he was helpful as chairman of the Rules
Committee. . . . Bristol-Myers is close to Delaney, let Bill
Greif handle that. . . .

"Gaydos of Pennsylvania . . . ask Alcoa if they'll do
it, John Harper was very enthusiastic about this one. . . .
Hatfield of Continental could do it but I hate to ask
him. . . . Marks of Sharon, Pennsylvania . . . ask Fer-
guson of General Foods to call Kirby of Westinghouse
about Marks. . . .

"Gore of Tennessee . . . Carrier Corp. and TRW
. . . do we really have a chance with Gore? We really think
we do? Ask Lloyd Hand of TRW. . . . Let's be careful
. . . but if we haven't done our job by now . . . but we
have, we've got the votes and we know it."

From *Dissent*, July 1980. Reprinted by permission.

The secret weapon of this new corporate
campaign is the corporate Political Action
Committee (PAC). The 1975 election laws permitted enterprises to solicit management for
funds and then to donate up to $5,000 to a
political candidate. After the resolution of the
Sun Oil case, which clarified how executives
may be solicited, the use of PACs by corporations has skyrocketed. Today there are more
than 1,000 PACs compared to 139 in 1974. The
total net worth of corporate, trade association
and right-wing PACs is $54 million, in contrast
to $13 million for labor.

The ultraright has entered the PAC arena
in a major way and now controls more than
$6.5 million in PAC funds. These include the
nation's three largest PACs: Ronald Reagan's
Citizens for the Republic ($2.1 million),
National Conservative PAC ($2 million), and
the Committee for Survival of a Free Congress
($1.5 million). Experts anticipate huge increases
in probusiness PACs.

Fortune also reported a growing trend
toward political cooperation among business
groups to defeat proconsumer and prolabor
legislation. Such coalitions offer two major
attractions. First, they permit the business
community to share expenses for lobbying
efforts. Over 100 organizations lobbied against
situs picketing, 400 against consumer protec-

tion, and 600 against labor law reform. In the last case, *Business Week* (11/22/78) reported that $5 million was spent by such groups (not to mention the $2 million spent by the National Right to Work Committee). Second, such coalitions establish huge umbrella organizations, which can draw on extensive grassroots networks, skilled lobbyists, and the clout of prominent corporate Chief Executive Officers (CEO).

Perhaps central to the new business strategy is direct lobbying by businessmen and especially CEOs, who have become the new political power brokers. Unlike older breeds of corporate lobbyists, congressmen know that these individuals often control corporate policy.

In order to exploit this idea, trade associations have established "direct-contact" networks in every state and congressional district. At the push of a Telex button, hundreds of executives are on the phone to their congressmen. The Associated General Contractors organization has 113 "legislative network chapters" around the country, while the Chamber has 2,200 "Congressional Action Committees." Its Washington office distributes 100,000 Action bulletins during the key legislative battles that, *The Nation* recently reported, reach an estimated 7 million people.

Yet, the *sine qua non* of the direct lobbying approach is the Business Roundtable, which *Business Week* has called "the most powerful lobby in Washington." Indeed, the Roundtable is composed largely of CEOs drawn from and limited to the 500 largest companies. Doors open quickly when such powerful figures come "a-calling" on the hill.

The Roundtable's influence stems from the concentrated economic power of its *Fortune* Five Hundred members. Such corporate giants as AT&T, Exxon, IBM, and General Motors each could muster huge organizational resources on their own. In concert, they are the overriding force in the American economy. In 1977 the *Fortune* Five Hundred accounted for 55 percent of the American

GNP with $1.1 trillion in sales. AT&T alone controlled nearly $100 billion in assets, with Exxon and GM second and third at $38.5 billion and $26.7 billion respectively. Furthermore, the Policy Committee of the Roundtable is drawn largely from *Fortune* One Hundred companies; each with assets well in excess of $1 billion and sales of more than $2.5 billion.

This power position makes Roundtable opinion indispensable to government officials and politicians. The Roundtable, for example, has been pivotal in shaping anti-inflation policy. Roundtable members dominated Nixon's Wage and Price Board, while Carter sought and secured initial compliance with his guidelines from Roundtable Executive Committee members AT&T and GM (the Executive Committee is the inner sanctum of the Policy Committee).

The Roundtable's concern with inflation has also taken the form of direct "economic organizing." Since its founding in 1972 it has actively sought to destroy the American building trades unions, sounding its battle cry against "the inflationary impact" of wages in the construction industry. It has organized 55 local "construction user groups" to "encourage" contractor trade associations to go nonunion. As the principal purchasers of industrial construction, Roundtable members have the economic muscle to make this goal seem realizable. In fact, the Construction Users' Anti-Inflation Roundtable, one of three groups from which the Roundtable was formed, has been organizing these chapters since 1969.

As the Roundtable stated in its summary of *Purpose and Challenge*:

Fiscal and monetary policies of the federal government have been blamed for demand inflation and, undoubtedly, must accept their share of the blame as well as require constructive action. *But the part of the total problem here considered is the cost of labor which is again threatening to rise precipitously. Runaway unit labor costs will make economic stability impossible.* [Emphasis added.]

The organization of the Roundtable and its success demonstrate the reason for our new political climate. Economic power is now so concentrated that it can be converted into unprecedented political power and increased economic control.

II

The expansion of corporate power presents issues of immediate concern in, at least, two other areas. They are (1) runaway shops, and (2) increased concentration through conglomeration.

Runaway Shops. Regional redistribution of capital has not only depleted the industrial base of the Northeast but now is a potent political threat in the hands of big business. Recently, Lykes Corporation closed down a 4,200-worker steel plant in Campbell, Ohio, giving only a few days' notice. Thus 80 percent of the town's tax base was eroded overnight and hundreds of families were left without income. There now are no legal restrictions on such practices.

Recently, runaway shops have emerged as a union-busting tactic—for example, the Northeast textile industry. The announcement of GM's Southern strategy has dramatized that no industry, no matter how heavily unionized, is immune from such threats. Only after strong UAW protest did GM discontinue its policy. Other corporate giants, such as GE and Westinghouse, continue to move their operations South and Southwest.

Thus, as an aftermath of this capital relocation, many cities are at the mercy of the large financial institutions. Now the erosion of urban tax bases has led to near-bankruptcy in Newark, Cleveland, and New York. The result, modeled on New York's "Big Mac" (Municipal Assistance Corporation), creates what amounts to a city board of trustees. This board virtually dictates city policy in the name of "fiscal conservation."

Conglomeration. The tendency of companies with large cash reserves to absorb other firms is particularly damaging for two reasons. First, the use of cash reserves to buy existing capital removes investment funds from circulation. The result is a net decrease in employment on the one hand and increased concentrations of economic power on the other. Second, increased economic concentration has led to takeovers of tremendous social importance.

Senator Kennedy, chairman of the Senate Committee on Anti-Trust and Monopoly, has been an outspoken critic of this trend. In a recent interview he stated:

It's very important to look at conglomerate mergers. They've increased steadily since 1972. By 1976, these may include assets valued at more than $5.5 billion, a 300% increase since 1972. . . . The staggering potential for conglomeration is suggested by the fact that Exxon could use just its cash and liquid assets to acquire, for instance, J. C. Penney, DuPont, Goodyear, and Anheuser Busch.

While corporate power has had serious external political effects, it has also undermined internal corporate politics. In a recent book, *Freedom Inside the Organization: Bringing Civil Liberties to the Workplace,* David Ewing comments: "Once a U.S. citizen steps through the plant or office door at 9:00 A.M. he or she is nearly rightless until 5:00 P.M., Monday through Friday." Ewing's work dramatizes the total lack of protection for workers who refuse to pollute and spy or who "blow the whistle" on illegal practices.

While the rights of lower-level employees are being denied, this same rationale is used to shelter top executives from personal responsibility for corporate misconduct. The bottom line of this ethic has been an epidemic of misconduct and crime by corporate executives. The SEC's chief enforcement officer, Stanley Sporkin, recently declared:

Whatever else these [illegal] payments may indicate about corporations and their managements, one thing is certainly clear: many corporate leaders have failed in their duties as stewards of public corporations. I am tired of hearing that all of this corporate bribery, foreign and domestic, has been done in recognition of the reality of the business value and in the name of furthering corporate business.

III

At the core of any effort to shape public opinion is the effort to shape social ideology. Corporate America understands that the prominent scholars of any period shape the ideas of intellectuals, media people, and policy-makers. And while business has always heavily funded the academic world, one recent development demonstrates a new aspect of this trend.

The American Enterprise Institute, founded in the early '70s, has become a predominant focus in American policy study. The AEI has more than 500 centers for Public Policy Research around the country. It maintains a resident faculty of more than 20 scholars, and scores of associated scholars throughout the nation. They produce studies on government regulations, economic, retirement, labor, health, legal, energy, foreign, and defense policy, and they make legislative analyses. With a massive fund-raising drive to gain $60 million, the AEI is planning to endow "Chairs of Free Enterprise" in prestigious universities across the country.

Despite claims that it "does not itself take positions on policy issues," its faculty is top-heavy with conservative analysts—including Paul McCracken, Hubert Stein, Laurence Silberman, Robert Griffin and Milton Friedman. Moreover, an analysis of its board of trustees reveals a 75 percent overlap with Business Roundtable membership.

Corporate Reform. The growth of corporate power has been accompanied by a massive occupation of the political system, and this is undermining the democratic process as we have known it. Yet the truth is that the corporations have no legitimate constituency. They have survived by playing group against group—consumers versus workers, minority-group members versus whites, and women versus men. Inflation has become the new, sophisticated cleaver for promoting such divisions. Labor, government, and consumers have been singled out as the root causes of inflation, and wages, regulation, and social services have been the most visible targets. The poor and the oppressed have been depicted as the cause of society's ills, rather than the victims.

Recently, management theorists have recognized the Achilles heel of corporate America. As the right-wing journalist Irving Kristol has written: "Corporations are highly vulnerable to criticism of their governing structure since there is no political theory to legitimize it." Indeed, the growth of the "corporate-image" business testifies to a growing corporate insecurity, sensing that legitimation cannot keep pace with expansion of power.

We need a broadly based Corporate Reform Movement. Its central focus should be the enactment of a Corporate Reform Act, which subjects corporations to federal regulations similar to those imposed on unions 20 years ago under the Landrum-Griffin Act. Whether such a movement emerges may significantly influence the course of American politics.

27

THE USES OF POVERTY
THE POOR PAY ALL

Herbert J. Gans

Some twenty years ago Robert K. Merton applied the notion of functional analysis[1] to explain the continuing though maligned existence of the urban political machine: if it continued to exist, perhaps it fulfilled latent—unintended or unrecognized—positive functions. Clearly it did. Merton pointed out how the political machine provided central authority to get things done when a decentralized local government could not act, humanized the services of the impersonal bureaucracy for fearful citizens, offered concrete help (rather than abstract law or justice) to the poor, and otherwise performed services needed or demanded by many people but considered unconventional or even illegal by formal public agencies.

Today, poverty is more maligned than the political machine ever was; yet it, too, is a persistent social phenomenon. Consequently, there may be some merit in applying functional analysis to poverty, in asking whether it also has positive functions that explain its persistence.

Merton defined functions as "those

observed consequences [of a phenomenon] which make for the adaptation or adjustment of a given [social] system." I shall use a slightly different definition; instead of identifying functions for an entire social system, I shall identify them for the interest groups, socio-economic classes, and other population aggregates with shared values that "inhabit" a social system. I suspect that in a modern heterogeneous society, few phenomena are functional or dysfunctional for the society as a whole, and that most result in benefits to some groups and costs to others. Nor are any phenomena indispensable; in most instances, one can suggest what Merton calls "functional alternatives" or equivalents for them, in other words, other social patterns or policies that achieve the same positive functions but avoid the dysfunctions.[2]

Associating poverty with positive functions seems at first glance to be unimaginable. One course, the slumlord and the loan shark are commonly known to profit from the existence of poverty, but they are viewed as evil men, so their activities are classified among the dysfunctions of poverty. However, what is less often recognized, at least by the conventional wisdom, is that poverty also makes possible the existence or expansion of respect-

Reprinted from *Social Policy*, July-August 1971, pp. 20–24, published by Social Policy Corporation, New York, NY 10036. Copyright 1971 by Social Policy Corporation.

able professions and occupations, for example, penology, criminology, social work, and public health. More recently, the poor have provided jobs for professional and paraprofessional "poverty warriors," and for journalists and social scientists, this author included, who have supplied the information demanded by the revival of public interest in poverty.

Clearly, then, poverty and the poor may well satisfy a number of positive functions for many nonpoor groups in American society. I shall describe thirteen such functions—economic, social, and political—that seem to me most significant.

THE FUNCTIONS OF POVERTY

First, the existence of poverty ensures that society's "dirty work" will be done. Every society has such work: physically dirty or dangerous, temporary, dead-end and underpaid, undignified and menial jobs. Society can fill these jobs by paying higher wages than for "clean" work, or it can force people who have no other choice to do the dirty work—and at low wages. In America, poverty functions to provide a low-wage labor pool that is willing—or, rather, unable to be *unwilling*—to perform dirty work at low cost. Indeed, this function of the poor is so important that in some Southern states, welfare payments have been cut off during the summer months when the poor are needed to work in the fields. Moreover, much of the debate about the Negative Income Tax and the Family Assistance Plan has concerned their impact on the work incentive, by which is actually meant the incentive of the poor to do the needed dirty work if the wages therefrom are no larger than the income grant. Many economic activities that involve dirty work depend on the poor for their existence: restaurants, hospitals, parts of the garment industry, and "truck farming," among others, could not persist in their present form without the poor.

Second, because the poor are required to work at low wages, they subsidize a variety of economic activities that benefit the affluent. For example, domestics subsidize the upper middle and upper classes, making life easier for their employers and freeing affluent women for a variety of professional, cultural, civic, and partying activities. Similarly, because the poor pay a higher proportion of their income in property and sales taxes, among others, they subsidize many state and local governmental services that benefit more affluent groups. In addition, the poor support innovation in medical practice as patients in teaching and research hospitals and as guinea pigs in medical experiments.

Third, poverty creates jobs for a number of occupations and professions that serve or "service" the poor, or protect the rest of society from them. As already noted, penology would be minuscule without the poor, as would the police. Other activities and groups that flourish because of the existence of poverty are the numbers game, the sale of heroin and cheap wines and liquors, pentecostal ministers, faith healers, prostitutes, pawn shops, and the peacetime army, which recruits its enlisted men mainly from among the poor.

Fourth, the poor buy goods others do not want and thus prolong the economic usefulness of such goods—day-old bread, fruit and vegetables that would otherwise have to be thrown out, second-hand clothes, and deteriorating automobiles and buildings. They also provide incomes for doctors, lawyers, teachers, and others who are too old, poorly trained, or incompetent to attract more affluent clients.

In addition to economic functions, the poor perform a number of social functions.

Fifth, the poor can be identified and punished as alleged or real deviants in order to uphold the legitimacy of conventional norms. To justify the desirability of hard work, thrift, honesty, and monogamy, for example, the defenders of these norms must be able to find people who can be accused of being lazy, spendthrift, dishonest, and promiscuous.

Although there is some evidence that the poor are about as moral and law-abiding as anyone else, they are more likely than middle-class transgressors to be caught and punished when they participate in deviant acts. Moreover, they lack the political and cultural power to correct the stereotypes that other people hold of them and thus continue to be thought of as lazy, spendthrift, and so on, by those who need living proof that moral deviance does not pay.

Sixth, and conversely, the poor offer vicarious participation to the rest of the population in the uninhibited sexual, alcoholic, and narcotic behavior in which they are alleged to participate and which, being freed from the constraints of affluence, they are often thought to enjoy more than the middle classes. Thus many people, some social scientists included, believe that the poor not only are more given to uninhibited behavior (which may be true, although it is often motivated by despair more than by lack of inhibition) but derive more pleasure from it than affluent people (which research by Lee Rainwater, Walter Miller, and others shows to be patently untrue). However, whether the poor actually have more sex and enjoy it more is irrelevant; so long as middle-class people believe this to be true, they can participate in it vicariously when instances are reported in factual or fictional form.

Seventh, the poor also serve a direct cultural function when culture created by or for them is adopted by the more affluent. The rich often collect artifacts from extinct folk cultures of poor people; and almost all Americans listen to the blues, Negro spirituals, and country music, which originated among the Southern poor. Recently they have enjoyed the rock styles that were born, like the Beatles, in the slums; and in the last year, poetry written by ghetto children has become popular in literary circles. The poor also serve as culture heroes, particularly, of course, to the left, but the hobo, the cowboy, the hipster, and the mythical prostitute with a heart of gold have performed this function for a variety of groups.

Eighth, poverty helps to guarantee the status of those who are not poor. In every hierarchical society someone has to be at the bottom; but in American society, in which social mobility is an important goal for many and people need to know where they stand, the poor function as a reliable and relatively permanent measuring rod for status comparisons. This is particularly true for the working class, whose politics is influenced by the need to maintain status distinctions between themselves and the poor, much as the aristocracy must find ways of distinguishing itself from the *nouveaux riches*.

Ninth, the poor also aid the upward mobility of groups just above them in the class hierarchy. Thus a goodly number of Americans have entered the middle class through the profits earned from the provision of goods and services in the slums, including illegal or nonrespectable ones that upper-class and upper-middle-class businessmen shun because of their low prestige. As a result, members of almost every immigrant group have financed their upward mobility by providing slum housing, entertainment, gambling, narcotics, etc., to later arrivals—most recently to Blacks and Puerto Ricans.

Tenth, the poor help to keep the aristocracy busy, thus justifying its continued existence. "Society" uses the poor as clients of settlement houses and beneficiaries of charity affairs; indeed, the aristocracy must have the poor to demonstrate its superiority over other elites who devote themselves to earning money.

Eleventh, the poor, being powerless, can be made to absorb the costs of change and growth in American society. During the nineteenth century, they did the backbreaking work that built the cities; today, they are pushed out of their neighborhoods to make room for "progress." Urban renewal projects to hold middle-class taxpayers in the city and expressways to enable suburbanites to commute downtown have typically been located in poor neighborhoods, since no other group will allow itself to be displaced. For the same reason, universities, hospitals, and civic centers also expand into land occupied by the poor. The major costs of the industrialization of agriculture have been borne by the poor, who are pushed off the land without recompense; and they have paid a large share of the human cost of the growth of American power overseas, for they have provided many of the foot soldiers for Vietnam and other wars.

Twelfth, the poor facilitate and stabilize the American political process. Because they vote and participate in politics less than other groups, the political system is often free to ignore them. Moreover, since they can rarely support Republicans, they often provide the Democrats with a captive constituency that has no other place to go. As a result, the Democrats can count on their votes, and be more responsive to voters—for example, the white working class—who might otherwise switch to the Republicans.

Thirteen, the role of the poor in upholding conventional norms (see the fifth point, above) also has a significant political function. An economy based on the ideology of laissez faire requires a deprived population that is allegedly unwilling to work or that can be considered inferior because it must accept charity or welfare in order to survive. Not only does the alleged moral deviancy of the poor reduce the moral pressure on the present political economy to eliminate poverty but socialist alternatives can be made to look quite unattractive if those who will benefit most from them can be described as lazy, spendthrift, dishonest, and promiscuous.

THE ALTERNATIVES

I have described thirteen of the more important functions poverty and the poor satisfy in American society, enough to support the functionalist thesis that poverty, like any other social phenomenon, survives in part because it is useful to society or some of its parts. This analysis is not intended to suggest that because it is often functional, poverty *should* exist, or that it *must* exist. For one thing, poverty has

many more dysfunctions than functions; for another, it is possible to suggest functional alternatives.

For example, society's dirty work could be done without poverty, either by automation or by paying "dirty workers" decent wages. Nor is it necessary for the poor to subsidize the many activities they support through their low-wage jobs. Thus would, however, drive up the costs of these activities, which would result in higher prices to their customers and clients. Similarly, many of the professionals who flourish because of the poor could be given other roles. Social workers could provide counseling to the affluent, as they prefer to do anyway; and the police could devote themselves to traffic and organized crime. Other roles would have to be found for badly trained or incompetent professionals now relegated to serving the poor, and someone else would have to pay their salaries. Fewer penologists would be employable, however. And pentecostal religion could probably not survive without the poor—nor would parts of the second- and third-hand-goods market. And in many cities, "used" housing that no one else wants would then have to be torn down at public expense.

Alternatives for the cultural functions of the poor could be found more easily and cheaply. Indeed, entertainers, hippies, and adolescents are already serving as the deviants needed to uphold traditional morality and as devotees of orgies to "staff" the fantasies of vicarious participation.

The status functions of the poor are another matter. In a hierarchical society, some people must be defined as inferior to everyone else with respect to a variety of attributes, but they need not be poor in the absolute sense. One could conceive of a society in which the "lower class," though last in the pecking order, received 75 percent of the median income, rather than 15–40 percent, as is now the case. Needless to say, this would require considerable income redistribution.

The contribution the poor make to the upward mobility of the groups that provide them with goods and services could also be maintained without the poor's having such low incomes. However, it is true that if the poor were more affluent, they would have access to enough capital to take over the provider role, thus competing with, and perhaps rejecting, the "outsiders." (Indeed, owing in part to antipoverty programs, this is already happening in a number of ghettos, where white storeowners are being replaced by Blacks.) Similarly, if the poor were more affluent, they would make less willing clients for upper-class philanthropy, although some would still use settlement houses to achieve upward mobility, as they do now. Thus "Society" could continue to run its philanthropic activities.

The political functions of the poor would be more difficult to replace. With increased affluence the poor would probably obtain more political power and be more active politically. With higher incomes and more political power, the poor would be likely to resist paying the costs of growth and change. Of course, it is possible to imagine urban renewal and highway projects that properly reimbursed the displaced people, but such projects would then become considerably more expensive, and many might never be built. This, in turn, would reduce the comfort and convenience of those who now benefit from urban renewal and expressways. Finally, hippies could serve also as more deviants to justify the existing political economy—as they already do. Presumably, however, if poverty were eliminated, there would be fewer attacks on that economy.

In sum, then, many of the functions served by the poor could be replaced if poverty were eliminated, but almost always at higher costs to others, particularly more affluent others. Consequently, a functional analysis must conclude that poverty persists not only because it fulfills a number of positive functions but also because many of the functional alternatives to poverty would be quite dysfunctional for the affluent members of society. A functional analysis thus ultimately arrives at much the same conclusion as radical sociology, except that radical thinkers treat as manifest what I describe as latent; that social phenomena that are functional for affluent or powerful groups and dysfunctional for poor or powerless ones persist; that when the elimination of such phenomena through functional alternatives would generate dysfunctions for the affluent or powerful, they will continue to persist; and that phenomena like poverty can be eliminated only when they become dysfunctional for the affluent or powerful, or when the powerless can obtain enough power to change society.

NOTES

[1] "Manifest and Latent Functions," in *Social Theory and Social Structure* (Glencoe, Ill.: The Free Press, 1949), p. 71.

[2] I shall henceforth abbreviate positive functions as functions and negative functions as dysfunctions. I shall also describe functions and dysfunctions, in the planner's terminology, as benefits and costs.

X

POLITICS
Power and Its Implications

In studying the institution of politics, sociologists concern themselves with the groups involved in the political process and the conditions that tend to generate political involvement or apathy. These interests in turn lead to several related lines of inquiry: (1) the conditions that lead to or prevent political change; (2) the factors in voter participation and ideology; (3) economic power and its effect on the political structure; and (4) the problems of democracy in the bureaucratic organization.

As diverse as these topics may seem, a common sociological question connects them: How is power gained and used? The power of the opposing forces determines what, if any, kinds of political change will occur. A desire to maintain the status quo may create artificial restrictions on voting behavior as well as limit the field to safe candidates; the increasing concentration of economic power may maintain the status quo via election contributions and other types of political involvement; and the effect of control by one group of large organizations (*oligarchy*) may produce the same result.

The theme of this chapter, and of the others in this section, is that of change. This may come as a surprise, since the political structure of this country has seemed to be the steadiest of our social institutions. However, in the first article, Toffler notes that changing social conditions have led to the inability of current political structures to deal with America's needs.

The next two articles indicate that voters apparently agree with this assessment, since they reveal in a Gallup poll the changes they would like to see in the political institution and, in the Nelson article, how they are actually undertaking this change via the direct initiative—a means of gaining power outside of that designated officially by government.

In reading this chapter, keep in mind the social policy changes suggested for American politics and whether they will result in constructive changes. Also keep in mind the effect of these changes on the other social institutions, as well as on society itself.

28

"THE POLITICAL SYSTEM CANNOT COPE" WITH TODAY'S DIVERSITY

Alvin Toffler

"The Structure of Government is Outmoded"

America is engaging in an obsolete ritual as it struggles to select a President. It doesn't matter whether we elect a saint or a genius to the White House. Whoever wins is not going to be able to do very much, because the structure of government is outmoded; it is no longer appropriate to the problems the nation faces as it moves out of the industrial era into a new, "third wave" stage of civilization.

The agricultural revolution of 10,000 years ago launched the first great wave of change. The Industrial Revolution, beginning 300 years ago, touched off the second wave of change; it created a society characterized by mass education, mass consumption, mass entertainment. But today a third wave of change has begun; it is creating a new society characterized by "demassification," with institutions and groups breaking up into smaller entities.

We see it in the breakup of the mass media: The increase in specialized publications and the growth of cable television and satellite networks. We see it in religion, with the rise of specialized groups and cults. We

see it in business, with the new emphasis on market segmentation. We see it in politics, with the breakup of consensus and the rise of single-issue groups. The third wave of change will transform all parts of society.

But this shift from a mass society to a demassified society brings conflict. Those with a vested interest in the mass society resist diversity. Thus the great TV networks fight cable and satellite entrepreneurs. Mass marketers compete with market segmenters. The established religions battle against diverse new theologies. In politics, Washington resists demands for the devolution of power to the regions, states or cities. Across the board, we witness a growing conflict between demassifiers and what might be called "remassifiers": Those who favor the new diversity, and die-hard defenders of the old mass society.

The existing political system is swamped by the new diversity because it was designed for a far more uniform society. It cannot cope with the demassified millions. To function in the real world of the late 20th century, it will have to be restructured.

"Mass Services for a Demassified Public"

Seven years after the OPEC embargo, we have no energy policy. We also have no technology policy, no family policy, no discernible foreign policy. That's not because we have stupid people in power; the reason is that we elect highly intelligent people and then trap them in obsolete organizational structures that make it impossible to arrive at intelligent policies.

Government bureaucracies, for example, are huge factories designed to pump out uniform, standardized services. When consumers become diverse, businesses begin to offer a wider variety of products to serve their needs, but government is less responsive to diversity—so many government programs are turning out mass services for a demassified public. The result is a fantastically wasteful and dangerous mismatch. Even the recipients of government aid are often hurt by it, and the public grows increasingly sullen and alienated.

Because citizens have so little control over the government bureaucracy, they strike back in anger. It is not that the public is without compassion and social decency, but people are trying to assert control over programs—force different policies. When they find they can't, they say, "Kill the whole thing!" Hence, Howard Jarvis and his imitators.

Government programs must be demassified.

Election By "Fake Majority"

Because of the growing diversity in society, it's difficult to put together a majority behind any issue or candidate. We use the election system to compel a vote between two candidates—which forces what appears to be a majority, but it is a mythical or fake majority. Even if 51 percent of the population votes for one candidate, the next morning that 51 percent has broken into 10,000 different, transient interest groups, and there is no longer majority support.

Toward "A Constitutional Crisis"

We're trying to run the United States with a 200-year-old government structure that was created to serve a population of only 4 million relatively homogeneous people.

While the Constitution and the Bill of Rights are stunning achievements, we're putting them under far greater pressure than most people suspect, and we're heading toward a constitutional crisis sometime in the next 10 or 20 years. You can't revolutionize technology, communications, family life economics and world relationships—and expect the old structures of government to stay the same. They will have to be redesigned.

Sorting Out "The Rights We Want to Protect"

Though I cherish it, the Bill of Rights needs to be expanded. It says nothing about dangers to the individual arising out of genetic engineering. It says nothing about the dangers of computer invasions of privacy. It says nothing about many of the problems just beginning to loom on the horizon. Unless we do some anticipatory thinking about the rights that we want to protect, we're going to find ourselves losing many of them. We need a Bill of Rights for the 21st century.

We also need to decentralize a great deal of decision making. It is not possible for the White House and the Congress and the federal bureaucracies to make intelligent decisions about one tenth of the many problems with which they now try to cope. Politicians are overwhelmed by the need to make instant decisions about things they know very little about.

Washington is not going to surrender power to the regions or to the states or even to nongeographical groupings in the society without a struggle. And that struggle is going to take many forms: It may be a battle over revenue sharing; it may be a battle over special grants to cities and states; it may be a battle for minority rights. Congress is grappling with those very problems right now without any framework for understanding the long-range picture.

Greater Power at "The Transnational Level"

Even as we move some power downward to cities, states and regions, we also need to move other types of power upward to international agencies. I have in mind such things as control of the seas and control of outer space. These problems are so large they can no longer be handled at the national level. While the idea of moving power downward has a great deal of political support, moving power up to the transnational level has very little political backing—and yet may be equally important.

Our "Country of Emerging Regional Nations"

Economically, the fast-emerging reality is that we have several nations within the United States. We no longer have a national economy. We now have regional economies, each as large and complex as the national economy was 30 or 40 years ago.

But we are still trying to manage the economy as though it were still a single, uniform structure. So we see liberals and conservatives playing an absurd ping-pong match over increasing or decreasing the money supply and raising or lowering taxes. Such central manipulation produces uneven, irregular and contradictory effects: The same action by the Federal Reserve Board that helps Sunnyvale, Calif., where jobs are too abundant, is going to hurt Youngstown, Ohio, where the steel mills are closing and people are unemployed.

It's like a doctor prescribing the exact same medicine for everyone in the hospital whether they have ulcers, gallbladder trouble or hyperthyroidism.

We're going to have to come to terms with the fact that the United States is a country of emerging regional nations based on well-defined, divergent regional economies. Unitary national policies won't do. And political power will eventually have to reflect that new economic reality.

Action to Avert Violent Dissension

All the other industrial countries are feeling the same pressures. Their political systems are just as obsolete. The British, French, Japanese and Soviet political systems were all designed to operate either in an agrarian or in an industrialized society. They were not designed to function in societies moving beyond industrialism into an age of demassification.

If this country is intelligent and anticipates the emergence of real regional economies and cultures—and begins to move that way—we may be able to avoid the kind of secessionist movements verging on the violent that we now see in France, Brittany, Corsica, Quebec, Western Canada, Scotland, Wales and so on. We need to anticipate the problems and head them off by voluntarily and intelligently devolving power before demands by diverse groups take a violent form.

29

SIX POLITICAL REFORMS
MOST AMERICANS WANT

George Gallup

In conducting thousands of surveys on almost every conceivable issue for nearly half a century, I have learned three significant things about our fellow citizens. One is that the judgment of the American people is extraordinarily sound. Another is that the public is almost always ahead of its leaders. The third is that the electorate has become better educated and more sophisticated politically than ever before.

This is why I am so disturbed by the disillusionment Americans have expressed, through our surveys, with the workings of the political system. Too many Americans regard politics as a "dirty business." In a poll last year evaluating honesty and ethics in 20 occupations, U. S. Senators and Congressmen stood 10th and 13th, respectively, on the list. In an earlier poll, two out of three persons interviewed believed that some legislators had won election by employing "unethical and illegal methods" in their campaigns; even today, only one third of those polled approved of the way Congressmen were doing their jobs. Two out of three American parents would not like to see their children enter politics as their life's work.

Disgust with politics has not, however, diminished Americans' faith in their country. In the latest Gallup surveys, three citizens out of four give the United States a "highly favorable" rating, with only about 2 percent rating it unfavorably; and 68 percent expressed, in an earlier poll, confidence in the nation's future. But what the surveys also make abundantly clear is that the public wants the political health of the nation improved. Here is what the polls show on six major proposed political reforms:

Reform 1. By 60 percent, with 30 percent opposed and 10 percent undecided, Americans favor a resolution offered by freshman Senators John Danforth (R., Mo.) and Dennis DeConcini (D., Ariz.) that would *limit the tenure of representatives in Congress to a maximum of 12 years.* That means no more than two six-year terms for Senators and six two-year terms for members of the House.

U. S. Presidents have been limited to two terms since 1951, and a 12-year restriction for U. S. legislators was advocated by Harry S. Truman and Dwight D. Eisenhower. Stated Eisenhower: "Each man so serving would tend to think of his Congressional career as

Reprinted with permission from the August 1978 *Reader's Digest*. Copyright © 1978 by the Reader's Digest Association, Inc.

an important and exciting interlude in his life, a period dedicated to the entire public rather than as a way of making a living. The members would probably give more attention to national good and less to their personal political fortunes."

One major advantage of the plan is that it would tend to make ability, rather than length of service, the criterion in filling committee chairmanships. Another is that it would bring in younger men and women, perhaps more in tune with the will of the people than those who have been following the same mental routines for decades. There are those who argue that it might deprive the nation of the services of individuals of extraordinary talent, and government is so complex that years are required for a legislator to familiarize himself with it. But room would also be made for individuals of equal, or greater, talent, who might otherwise never get to Congress.

Reform 2. Sums spent on election campaigns average at least $100,000 for those seeking seats in Congress. A candidate must either be wealthy or look for contributions, which may come from those seeking legislative favors. In a poll last year, 57 percent (32 percent opposed and 11 percent undecided) of Americans advocated that *the government provide a fixed amount of money for Congressional election campaigns, and contributions from all other sources be prohibited* (the ban to include use of the candidate's personal funds). The additional cost to taxpayers would be an estimated $2 per adult citizen. It could be the bargain of the century.

Would government funding of campaigns encourage a horde of minor, frivolous candidates? Perhaps, but the problem has been dealt with successfully in Great Britain. There, candidates must put up a substantial money deposit, which must be forfeited if they do not draw at least 12.5 percent of the vote.

Reform 3. [This] would end the chaotic system of nominating Presidential candidates in state-by-state primaries or by state and national conventions. Sixty-eight percent of the voters favor (with 21 percent opposed and 11 percent undecided) *a nationwide primary, to be held on the same day in all 50 states, in which voters would choose the Presidential candidates for their parties by popular vote.*

This proposal has had overwhelming support for nearly a quarter-century. Under the present system, many citizens are denied the opportunity to vote for the candidate of their choice because not all candidates enter all state primaries. And at political conventions the party "pros" often pay little attention to the popular will.

Reform 4. The seemingly interminable Presidential campaigns, which stretch over the better part of a year (from the first primaries in January to the November elections), exhaust the candidates, thoroughly bore the electorate—and end up changing few votes. By a majority of 68 percent to 21 percent (with 11 percent undecided), Americans would like to *shorten the campaign period.* They favor advancing election day to September, and holding the inauguration in November of the election year to allow an incoming President more time to prepare his recommendations for the opening of Congress in January.

Reform 5. Probably the least popular political institution in America is the Electoral College, with its "unit rule" whereby a candidate who wins a plurality in a state gets *all* of that state's votes. The public has favored doing away with the Electoral College since the first survey was taken on this issue in 1948. In a 1977 poll, 75 percent approved amending the Constitution to provide *direct popular election of the President* (14 percent were opposed and 11 percent undecided).

Such a bill actually passed the House of Representatives by a lopsided margin in 1969—only to be filibustered to death by Senators who felt that it would diminish their states' power. But the Electoral College system makes possible the election of a President who receives fewer popular votes than his opponent. This has occurred three times (John Quincy Adams, Rutherford B. Hayes and Benjamin Harrison), and almost happened again in 1968 and in 1976.

Reform 6. Perhaps the most controversial innovation Americans advocate is the right to be consulted on important legislation. By a majority of 57 to 21 percent (with 22 percent undecided), in a recent Gallup poll, they supported a proposal introduced by Senators James Abourezk (D., S.D.) and Mark Hatfield (R., Ore.) that would allow *Americans to initiate federal legislation when a group of voters equal to three percent of the number who voted in the last Presidential election sign a petition requesting such a vote.* Although the procedure would be new to the federal government, it is a familiar practice in almost half the states.

The initiative—or the threat of invoking one—should expedite passage of legislation bottled up in Congress for years. Were the measure in effect now, our Gallup surveys indicate that:

Mandatory busing to achieve racial balance in schools would be abolished by 65 percent of the voters.

The Equal Rights Amendment for women (ERA) would be approved by a majority of 57 percent, including more men than women.

Tough gun-control laws requiring the licensing of all firearms carried outside the home would be enacted by 77 percent, including a large majority of gun owners.

Achieving the reforms referred to in this article would necessitate amending the Constitution in some cases. The customary procedure requires passage of each amendment by two thirds of each House of Congress, then three fourths of the states must approve. It is unlikely, however, that many Congressmen or Senators would approve legislation diminishing their powers and curtailing their continuance in office.

A surer way to get the proposals considered by the nation, as President Eisenhower pointed out, is through the alternate method of amendment prescribed by the Constitution—a constitutional convention, which can be assembled at the request of two thirds of the states. (The amendments would also have to be ratified by the legislatures of three fourths of the states. However, they require only a simply majority vote to be passed at the constitutional convention itself.)

Amending the Constitution that has served the nation so well is not a step to be undertaken lightly, and some suggest that a constitutional convention might itself carry risks. But the measures described here, in my opinion, would help restore the kind of government that the framers of that document actually had in mind—a government that owes nothing to political bosses, pressure groups or campaign contributors, guided only by the will of the people.

30

POWER TO THE PEOPLE
THE CRUSADE FOR DIRECT DEMOCRACY

Michael Nelson

Starting sometime next month, we can expect to suffer the usual plague of end-of-the-decade assessments. Judging from the early returns, the verdict on the Seventies seems fairly predictable. The instant historians will tell us that this has been a placid decade, notable mostly for being different from the last one. The Sixties, they will say, were above all a time of direct-action politics—demonstrations, mass participation, plebiscitary rather than representative democracy. By contrast— a contrast that then-and-now pictures of Jerry Rubin, Rennie Davis, and Berkeley's Sproul Plaza will underscore—the Seventies have been apolitical.

Some will mourn the passing of Sixties-style politics, others will rejoice. Both will miss the point. For Americans in the Seventies did not turn away from the politics of direct action, they merely domesticated it, institutionalized it, and embraced it in the bosom of the middle class.

Nothing illustrates this better than the rising use of the initiative, a device by which— in the 23 states and more than 100 cities that allow it—citizens can draft a piece of legislation, place it on the ballot by petition, and

have their fellow voters directly decide on election day whether it should become law or not. (Initiatives are different from referendums, which allow voters to accept or reject laws already passed by the legislature.) By the end of 1979, some 175 initiatives will have been voted on at the state level since 1970, almost twice as many as in the 1960s. The rate of initiative use accelerated through the decade, from 10 in 1970 to more than 40 each in 1976 and 1978. Two states and the District of Columbia have added the initiative process to their constitutions, and at least 10 others now are considering doing so. In one of them, New York, the initiative idea is being pushed by an unlikely coalition of the League of Women Voters, the Conservative Party, the local branch of Ralph Nader's Public Interest Research Group, and an ad hoc organization called V.O.T.E., which is headed by a conservative investment banker who says he hopes to become New York's Howard Jarvis.

Coalitions like this one (which, to confuse matters further, bears the editorial imprimatur of the *New York Times* and *Newsday*, as well as a host of conservative upstate newspapers) make it hard to characterize the rising initiative tide in standard liberal-conservative terms. So does the sponsorship in Congress of the proposed constitutional amendment to

From *Saturday Review*, November 24, 1979. Reprinted by permission.

allow national initiatives, which ranges from senators like Mark Hatfield on the left to Dennis DeConcini in the middle and Larry Pressler on the right. Among conservative columnists, George F. Will has condemned the initiative, Patrick Buchanan has praised it, and James J. Kilpatrick has been all over the lot. Liberals such as Tom Wicker (pro) and the *New Republic's* Henry Fairlie (con) can be found on either side.

Most distressing of all to those who like their politics tidy has been the extraordinary range of purposes to which the initiative has been put. Last year, for example, Oregon voters passed an initiative that restored capital punishment, but defeated one to restrict state funding of abortions. (They also decided to break the dentists' monopoly on the sale of false teeth.) Michigan voted to raise the drinking age from 19 to 21, but spurned a conservative educational "voucher" plan that would have subsidized parents' decisions to send their children to private schools. (Californians may be voting on a similar plan next June.) An Alaska initiative to set aside some 30 million acres of land for small homesteaders was approved; another to ban no-deposit bottles failed. Californians turned down an anti-smoking proposal; they also refused to require school boards to fire homosexual teachers. A Montana initiative to place restrictions on nuclear power-plant licensing and operations won. A North Dakota plan to regulate health-care costs lost. Collective-bargaining rights did well in Michigan and Missouri, while casino gambling did poorly in Florida.

The most celebrated initiative of 1978 was, of course, California's Proposition 13, the astonishingly popular proposal by Howard Jarvis and Paul Gann to reduce property taxes in the state by 57 percent. Its success in June quickly triggered a middle-class "tax revolt" that terrified liberals in other states. James Farmer, the erstwhile civil rights leader who now heads a group called the Coalition of American Public Employees, complained that "the tax revolt represents nothing more

than the overthrow of equity among taxpayers." Worried commentators predicted that right-wing Jarvis fever would sweep the initiative states in November.

It did not quite turn out that way, however. Although Proposition 13 clones passed in two small states, Idaho and Nevada, they failed in Michigan and Oregon. Four state initiatives to limit increases in government spending passed, but two were turned down. Still others failed to garner enough signatures to get on the ballot. This year Nevada voters repealed the state's 3.5 percent sales tax on food, a reform dear to liberal hearts. And next year a whole host of tax initiatives—liberal, conservative, or both—will come up at the polls. Ohio and Massachusetts proposals . . . would cut property taxes but make up the lost revenues with increased levies on business. Interestingly enough, political scientist Austin Ranney found that in the 33 years prior to 1978, the initiative served as a tool for liberals on tax issues. Their side triumphed 77 percent of the time.

The lack of a clear ideological tilt in the initiative process also is evidenced by the new style of initiative politicians who have led the direct-action efforts of the 1970s. Thus far, arch-conservative Howard Jarvis is the one national celebrity to come out of the initiative movement—he even made *People* magazine's list of "The 25 Most Intriguing People of 1978." But Pat Quinn of Chicago is a more typical wielder of the initiative tool. Quinn is a full-time law student at Northwestern University who, as "a 40-hour-a-week hobby," heads an 8,000 member organization called the Illinois Coalition for Political Honesty. (Members are defined simply as those who pass petitions to get initiatives on the ballot.) Although he got into state politics seven years ago in the traditional way, as an aide to victorious gubernatorial candidate Dan Walker, Quinn's experience in the campaign and in the Walker administration was discouraging. "I became disillusioned in the potential of candidate politics," he says. "You get candidates who either can't deliver on their promises after the election, or don't want to. With initiatives you can address the issues directly."

Illinois has allowed an initiative process since 1970, but neither Quinn nor anybody else had much sense of its potential until his brother Tom came home in 1975 from college in California, where he had gotten involved in a successful campaign to pass a candidate-and-lobbyist-disclosure initiative. "Illinois at that time had around 20 state legislators convicted or under indictment, and the legislature wasn't doing anything about ethics," Pat recalls. "It also had a rule that allowed legislators to draw their whole year's pay on the first day of the session, so even if they were sent to jail in the middle of the year, they still kept the rest of their year's salary. Five of us—me, my brother, and three friends—started a petition drive to get that changed, so at least they'd be paid the same way everybody else is. The issue took off and we got enough signatures to put it on the ballot. Within a month the legislature gave us what we wanted on their own, but we decided to keep the Coalition for Political Honesty going and see what else could be done by initiative."

The coalition's current plan is for a 1980 initiative that, if passed, would overhaul the legislature completely. Presently, Illinois is divided into 59 districts, each of which elects three legislators-at-large. In Quinn's view, the combination of a large number of legislators (177, third highest in the nation) and a small number of districts gives Illinois the worst of both worlds—"too many politicians, but too little representation." His initiative would double the number of districts to 118 and assign one representative to each, thus reducing the membership of the legislature by one third. "A change like this is the kind of thing a legislature will never make by itself," says Quinn, "because it would threaten the jobs of the legislators who would have to make it. They get paid $28,000 a year and for many it's a second job. The initiative is the only tool a citizen has."

Quinn, a young liberal, and Jarvis, an aging conservative, have a good bit more in common than first meets the eye. So do the conservative tax "revolters" in Idaho and the liberal tax "reformers" in Ohio, the conservative pro-voucher people in California and the liberal anti-dentists in Oregon, and other seemingly dissimilar groups of activists. For whatever their political coloration, the greater part of initiative users seem motivated by a basic shared concern: They regard the government itself as just another self-serving interest, one that is all the more threatening because it cannot be reformed except from outside, through direct-action politics.

Looking back over the history of political reform in this century, it is remarkable how many fundamental political changes were hastened by initiative after state legislators balked, reluctant to alter the rules of the game by which they had been elected. Long before Congress and the state legislatures saw the handwriting on the wall, initiatives in several states already had been passed to repeal the poll tax, establish woman suffrage, provide for direct election of United States senators, and institute primary elections. Similarly, the Seventies have been marked by a whole host of ethics, disclosure, and "sunshine-in-government" initiatives, passed by voters after legislatures had turned them down. Austin Ranney finds that historically, the initiative has been used more to alter government and political processes than for any other purpose.

In this light, it also seems apparent that the Proposition 13-inspired "tax revolt" has been aimed less at taxes per se than at the ever larger and more prosperous government bureaucracies that are collecting and spending them. In California, for example, powerful government-employee unions, along with their colleagues in the legislature, beat back fairly modest efforts to reduce ever more burdensome property taxes for years, even after the state treasury accumulated a multi-billion-dollar surplus. Finally, things reached the point where the lamentations of public officials simply were not believed. One poll taken on the eve of Proposition 13 found 88 percent of Californians insisting that "if government services were made more efficient, the current level of services could be provided even though budgets were reduced."

This perception of selfish behavior *by* government officials *for* government officials seems to exist among voters everywhere. A nationwide survey commissioned by the *Washington Post* found that three out of four citizens said they too would vote for a Proposition 13-style tax cut if they had the chance. But an even higher percentage also said that it wasn't so much the taxes that bothered them as the way the money was being wasted. Given a choice of low taxes or high taxes that are spent efficiently, two-thirds picked the latter. "Their real concern," the *Post* concluded, "is that it is the bureaucracy, not the public, that benefits from taxes."

Are people correct in attributing many of the ills of government to the self-serving behavior of the governing class of legislators and bureaucrats? It would be surprising if they were not. It is almost an axiom of sociological theory that when organizations grow larger and more powerful—as all levels of governments have in order to meet our demand for a militarily powerful welfare state—they develop interests of their own, different from those they were created to represent. This clearly has happened at the state and local level, where the number of government employees has tripled from four million in 1950 to 12 million today, with their unions vigorously advocating both higher benefits and higher taxes to finance them. But nowhere is the rise of a governing class more evident than in Washington, D. C. "Right now there are two popular clichés about Washington," writes *Washington Post* reporter Nicholas Lemann, "and both of them, like most clichés, have a lot of truth in them. The first is that Washington is a company town, where everything revolves around the federal government and

there's always just one topic of conversation. The second is that Washington has become the national capital of affluence as well as of government."

It was inevitable, then, that someone would take the initiative to Washington.

As it turned out, there were two people. John Forster and Roger Telschow, fresh out of college, had spent 1976 working in state initiative campaigns all over the country. "We were really struck at the time by the contrast between the enthusiasm people had about initiatives and the indifference they felt toward the presidential and congressional elections," says Telschow. After the election, the figures bore them out: Though voter turnout had dropped for the fourth straight time since 1960, initiative use reached a postwar high. Deciding that national initiatives on citizen-proposed federal laws were an idea whose time had come, they set off for Washington to try to get Congress to pass a constitutional amendment permitting such an innovation. Here is how the national initiative would work:

Citizens initiating a new law would have 18 months to collect petitions with valid signatures equal in number to 3 percent of the votes cast in the preceding presidential election—at present that would be 2.5 million. The Justice Department would then check the signatures for validity. If it certified them within 120 days of the next national election, the proposed initiative would go on the ballot right away; otherwise it would have to wait two years until the next election.

The initiative, if passed by a simple majority of voters, would become law 30 days after the election. As with any other legislation, it would be subject to judicial review and congressional override, though the latter would require the two-thirds vote of Congress and presidential concurrence. Finally, the initiative could not be used to declare war, call up troops, or propose constitutional amendments.

Initiative America (which is what the two

young men named their organization) can be described generously as a shoestring operation; in Washington's constellation of elaborate and well-financed interest groups, it is the equivalent of a lemonade stand in midtown Manhattan. But through sheer energy, will, and talent, Forster and Telschow managed to do everything a shoestring operation can do in politics. In 1977, they persuaded Senator James Abourezk to sponsor their amendment. They then roused interest among press and pollsters—Cambridge Survey Research found three-to-one public support for the idea, for example, and George Gallup included it in a *Reader's Digest* article on the "Six Political Reforms Americans Want Most." Because of this attention, and because Abourezk was a member of the constitutional amendments subcommittee, Senate hearings soon were held on it.

The power of a good idea, of course, can take it only so far through an amendment process that requires the support of two-thirds of each house of Congress and three-fourths of the states—especially an idea whose premise is that Congress has not been representing the people adequately. But Forster and Telschow felt that once Senate hearings rendered the idea respectable, they would be able to rally a coalition of open-government groups like Common Cause behind it.

What followed was a bitterly disappointing experience, one that illustrates yet another sociological axiom: Adversarial organizations end up more alike than different. "We found out that these Washington-based 'people's groups' have become little bureaucracies of their own," recalls Forster. "They see the initiative as a threat to their interests. They thrive on the fact that they can claim to represent people to the government on various issues. If people had an initiative to turn to, two things would happen: One, they could represent themselves, and two, the scene of the action would shift from Washington to the country. That would diminish the public-interest groups' importance. They prefer not to change the rules, even if there doesn't seem to be any chance of winning under the status quo."

Stalled in the Washington community, Initiative America's great hope for the future is that its proposal will be picked up in next year's presidential campaign. This would not be altogether surprising. The governing class's popular standing has been steadily declining. Support for the initiative amendment may prove a constructive way of tapping the public's dissatisfaction. So far, only Jimmy Carter and Howard Baker have brushed off Initiative America, and Jerry Brown, Ronald Reagan, Edward Kennedy, and John Connally are among those who at least have expressed interest. Kennedy, for example, has told Initiative America that he would "like to be with you on this," and Brown's *éminence grise*, Jacques Barzaghi, recently informed board member David Schmidt that Brown might campaign hard on the proposal, which he already has endorsed.

Although it is far from certain that the 1980s will see the adoption of the national initiative amendment, there are a couple of predictions about the coming decade we can safely make.

The first is that, with the bicentennial of the Constitution looming in 1987, we are going to be hearing more than ever about the "intentions of the framers." In the case of the national initiative amendment, those intentions should be fairly easy to ascertain. Democracy was a dirty word at the Philadelphia convention—speakers used it only to raise the specter of mob rule and demagoguery—and any proposal to allow citizens to initiate and decide laws on their own surely would have been hooted off the floor.

Should we be bound by this? No, and I don't think the Founding Fathers (Warren Harding's phrase, not theirs) would want us to be so bound, any more than they would have when we abolished the poll tax, required direct election of senators, and gave the vote to blacks and women—other proposals that were or would have been dismissed at the Constitutional Convention. The authors of the Constitution were aware that they had no monopoly on truth for the ages. Indeed, their most important intention was that the plan of government they drafted be able to adapt to changing times and new kinds of experience. That is why they defined the nature and powers of its institutions in flexible language and why they included an amendment process.

Changing conditions have already altered the nature of our political system, in ways that make the initiative now seem constitutionally appropriate. "Admittedly," argues Professor Henry Abraham of the University of Virginia, "the Founding Fathers envisaged lawmaking to be the province of the people's representatives in assembled Congress, but as our history has demonstrated, laws—or, if one prefers, policies *cum* laws—are increasingly made and applied not only by Congress but by the Chief Executive; by the host of all-but-uncontrollable civil servants in the executive agencies and bureaus; and by the judiciary. Why not permit another element of our societal structure to enter the legislative realm, namely, the people in their sovereign capacity as the ultimate repositor of power under our system, as envisaged by the letter and the spirit of the Preamble to the Constitution?"

As Abraham suggests, the theories of the framers about how their plan of government really would work out in practice were just that—theories. Seventy-five years of experience with state initiatives (Oregon held the first one in 1904) can be safely said to have demonstrated the groundlessness of their fears. Historically, only about one-fifth of the initiatives filed have gotten enough petition signatures even to reach the ballot. And only about one-third of those that have reached the ballot have been passed by voters. This is hardly the "mobocracy" the framers feared democracy would breed.

The other sure prediction that we can make about the 1980s is that the politics of direct action will become even more widespread. For not only has initiative use been increasing, but also the use of other pressure tactics that lie outside the normal processes of representative democracy—with no sign that the basic dissatisfactions with the governing class that have caused all this are abating. Demonstrations, for example, now seem as American as apple pie. In Washington alone, the National Park Service currently issues a record 750 to 1,000 demonstration permits every year, many of them to groups opposing abortion, Equal Rights Amendment proponents, tractor-driving farmers, and other activists from the middle class. Surveying a wide range of poll data, political scientists Robert Gilmour and Robert Lamb recently concluded that "Mass protest, civil disobedience, and illegal disruption are now a part of the accepted political scene."

The Seventies also saw the rise of forms of direct-action politics that Sixties activists overlooked. The most spectacular recent example is the movement for a constitutional convention to consider a balanced-budget amendment. Presently, 30 states have demanded that Congress issue such a call, only four short of the required two-thirds. So plausible has the idea become that White House adviser Patrick Caddell felt comfortable suggesting to Jimmy Carter that he call for a constitutional convention that would reconsider the whole document. (Caddell made his recommendation in the famous "crisis-of-confidence" memorandum that persuaded Carter to cancel a planned energy speech and retreat to Camp David for two weeks in July.) Carter declined the suggestion, but Jerry Brown has endorsed the effort to bring about a balanced-budget convention.

There is no telling what innovations the Eighties will bring in the way of direct-action politics—in Columbus, Ohio, people are already "participating" in televised local government meetings through their two-way cable television system. But whatever these innovations may be, they probably will make the initiative look good to its current opponents by comparison. The initiative is, after all, a technique of the ballot, not the streets or the living room. This not only makes it close kin to the standard system of representative democracy, but it also seems to strengthen that system in the long run. Thus political scientist Charles Bell recently reported that "half the high [election] turnout states use the initiative while only 14 percent of the low-turnout states use it." A Caddell poll found that 74 percent of the voters said they would be more inclined to vote in candidate elections if they also could vote on issues. And far from weakening state legislatures, initiatives seem to prod them on to better things. Eight of the 10 legislatures ranked highest by the Citizen's Conference on State Legislatures are in initiative states.

The assault on the governing class of officials will continue. Whether it will come through the ballot box or some less pleasant route is up to them.

Part Four
SOME PROCESSES OF SOCIAL LIFE

An early pioneer in sociology, Auguste Comte, divided sociology into two major parts: statics and dynamics. Statics is the study of order whereas dynamics is the study of social progress. Although the terms utilized by Comte have changed, this basic division of sociology remains in use as the study of social structure, functions, and social change. This section deals with some of the factors of dynamics.

In the preceding sections, we noted that individuals are transformed into social beings through group interactions in a specific cultural context. We saw that socialization not only transforms people into social beings but also makes them viable members of society by imbuing them with the culture of the society. The major institutions are an essential part of the process. But society is not just structure and institutions; it is also the process of intermingling and the results of that interaction. Results that bring about change can either aid or hinder individuals or society in meeting their needs.

The intermingling of the world's peoples has produced group relations that sometimes lead to stereotyping, prejudice, and discrimination. The articles in the chapter on minority relations discuss what is happening to some specific minorities who are attempting to change their experience.

To function smoothly, society requires normative behavior of its members. The socialization process generally results in individuals who follow the norms of society. However, different socialization processes will result in different interpretations of the norms and produce what we call *deviance*. Deviants may be any people whom society has labeled as different. In the second chapter, we will read not only about the myths concerning deviants, but also about the effects of labeling.

The next two chapters deal with population and the urban scene, and are related in many ways. Population growth has led to the development of urban areas that fulfill necessary functions for the population. But there is another side to population growth. Unchecked growth can mean enormous consumption of energy, thereby creating numerous problems.

The theme of the last two chapters is change. All societies undergo change, but change can be so rapid that a society may find itself with few norms to guide behavior. This can result in such collective behaviors as fads, panic, and even revolution. Another effect of rapid change may be a society's inability to keep its beliefs and value systems in line with changes in its material system. Despite these factors, change is not all bad, or all dysfunctional. In fact, the possibilities open to us through societal change can be both exciting and fulfilling.

As you read these chapters, keep in mind the constant pressures on institutions to change, caused by the conditions and processes discussed in this section.

XI

MINORITY RELATIONS
"We" and "They"

"We" and "they," in-groups and out-groups—these are the categories people use to order their complex world. How easy it is to judge by generalization rather than fact; to maintain our ethnocentric attitude favoring the "we," the in-group, our group. If categorization served only as a means of ordering our lives, would it be bad? But this consciousness of difference has created policies from slavery and subjugation to separation and pluralism; and some of these policies, in turn, have led to reactions by minority groups ranging from social protest to insurrection.

Prejudicial attitudes can be seen in many forms and against many different people. Prejudice usually surfaces in various discriminatory acts such as restricted housing or jobs. Usually, those who utilize prejudice and discrimination need no evidence to support their biased acts, but they will utilize it if evidence is available. The problem is not mitigated when the basis for such "evidence" is false. So argues Daniels in the first article, concerning the Jensen IQ study.

The Josephy article is an illustration of institutional racism and shows that discrimination is no less harmful when practiced by the government. He indicates social policies necessary to effectively address discrimination against the American Indian at the structural level.

Conflict theorists note that not all people have equal rights to obtain their share when it comes to scarce resources. The result is often conflict, utilizing prejudice and discrimination, among the have-nots for such resources that are available. The final article in this chapter addresses this issue with two aggregates not often thought of as objects of discrimination: the elderly and the young.

If racism, prejudice, discrimination, and stereotyping are to be reduced, then individuals and groups must recognize the effects of structural level prejudice and discrimination on their own beliefs and actions. Only in this manner can they overcome their own ethnocentrism and view others from a cultural relativist's perspective. As you read these articles, think of ways that this can be done in our society.

31

THE SMART WHITE MAN'S BURDEN

Norman Daniels

The ancient controversy about nature versus nurture may seem like a dusty academic parlor game. It is nothing of the sort. When an obscure professor of education at Berkeley named Arthur Jensen published a study in 1969[1] that seemed to prove that up to 80 percent of our intelligence is determined by the genes we inherit and then related his findings to black children's poor performance in school, various influential magazines and newspapers were quick to sense a revolution in the way Americans should think about race, education, poverty, and crime.

For forty years, said *Fortune* magazine, "the established dogma in the social sciences has been that all people are born alike and it is environment that makes them behave differently." This environmentalist dogma underlay most of the reform programs of the Sixties. But, said *Fortune*, the elimination of environmental disadvantages through compensatory education and the war on poverty has clearly not done away with differences between blacks and whites in school success, employment rates, or income. Thus, environmentalism failed because it called for the impossible: the elimination of human differences that are rooted in genetic inheritance.

There is, said *Fortune* somewhat triumphantly, a "basic intractability in human nature, a resistance to being guided and molded for improving society." *Fortune*'s sister, *Time*, argued similarly in a series called "Second Thoughts About Man," then wondered whether these second thoughts wouldn't lead to a "new quietism, a readiness to accept things as they are rather than to work for things as they might be."

The Atlantic, a magazine that usually takes its intellectual responsibilities seriously, set out to bring this revolutionary perspective to its readers by publishing Harvard Prof. Richard Herrnstein's skillful popularization of Jensen's argument.[2] Herrnstein argued that our "meritocratic" society selects people for "success in life"—school performance, income, job status—on the basis of largely inherited differences in intelligence that Jensen had apparently demonstrated.

The Jensen-Herrnstein "vanguard" position[3] rests squarely on the concept of IQ. It draws its evidence from certain "life experiments," notably studies of twins and adopted children, which supposedly measure the precise contribution of genes or environment to our IQ and in turn our "success in life." Their "IQ Argument," sometimes labelled "jensenism," can be stated in four steps:

1. IQ measures a general trait, intelligence.
2. IQ is highly heritable; about 80 percent of

observed IQ differences between individuals are genetic in origin.

3. Genetic factors (up to 80 percent of the whole) are implicated in average black-white and social class intelligence differences.

4. Differences in success in life strongly correlate with and are caused by differences in intelligence.

The implications of this argument for social policy strike many people as obvious and far-reaching. Jensen and Herrnstein, for example, both seem to favor more rigorous educational tracking systems adapted to inherited differences. "The false belief in human equality," writes Herrnstein, "leads to rigid, inflexible expectations, often doomed to frustration, thence to anger . . . we should be trying to mold our institutions around the inescapable limitations and varieties of human ability." He complains of "withholding educational advantages from gifted people." Jensen has appeared before various Congressional committees to deliver his message that money spent on compensatory education programs is "lavish" and "extravagant" and one Congressman has inserted the whole of his 1969 study into the Congressional Record. In 1970 *Life* quoted Daniel Moynihan, then a White House adviser, as saying that "the winds of Jensen were gusting through the capital at gale force." The 1973–74 Nixon budget proposes to demolish what is left of compensatory education programs and other programs aimed at creating educational equality. More chilling is the call by some jensenites for the exercise of "eugenic foresight" or that of the physicist William Shockley for voluntary sterilization programs for people with lower than normal IQs. Only this past May, Jensen himself carried the logic of his theories to a point just shy of a call for eugenic foresight. Comparing the low birthrate of affluent (therefore successful, therefore intelligent) whites with the high rate of poor (therefore unsuccessful, therefore unintelligent) blacks,

Jensen concluded that "dysgenics [an undesirable change in the gene pool] with respect to the intelligence of our population is not just a possibility. It is *highly probable*" (his emphasis). Herrnstein, in a recent *Science* article, demurs only that "voluntary sterilization is not a politically feasible solution."

Perhaps the most damaging effects of the IQ argument, however, will be on the expectations of teachers, college administrators, employers, and social workers who come to think of blacks and working class people as genetically less intelligent. Nobel Laureate Shockley, who has Jensen's scholarly blessings, seems to encourage this attitude: "Nature has color-coded groups of individuals so that statistically reliable predictions of their adaptability to intellectually rewarding and effective lives can easily be made and profitably be used by the pragmatic man in the street."

It is absolutely crucial to Jensen's and Herrnstein's arguments that a person's score on an IQ test does in fact indicate his intelligence. But what is intelligence? Unfortunately, there is no generally accepted theory on the matter, an embarrassing point that our authors try to get around by asserting simply that intelligence *is* what IQ tests measure.

There are two things to be said about this stance. First, it's no way out. Scientists usually know what they are measuring and what their measuring instruments do. Second, having IQ tests doesn't obviate the need for a theory of intelligence. It assumes one. IQ tests give us, says Herrnstein, a "single number measuring a person's intellectual power." In this view, intelligence is a single, measurable, super-capacity underlying other skills; it is stable, "conferred" in the first fifteen years of life, and it sets a limit on what a person can learn or do. Are these assumptions warranted? I think not.

The fact that "intelligence" is a noun shouldn't delude us into believing that it names some single attribute we can attach a number to, like "height." In life, we face a variety of tasks and environments. Intelligence takes many forms: a machinist suggests a new production technique, a housewife manages in spite of inflation, a hustler helps build a huge conglomerate. Similarly, how intelligent a person's behavior is will vary with time. Why should we suppose that these changes are fluctuations from some fixed, basic level? Most important, what a person of almost any IQ can learn or do depends on what he wants to do and on what kind of education and training he is given. Jensen says high IQ is needed for high "educability," which he defines as "the ability to learn the traditional scholastic subjects under conditions of ordinary classroom instruction" . . . and thereby innocently opens a can of worms. *What* conditions of "ordinary classroom instruction"? Are social class or race biases in our schools included in these "conditions"?

Moreover, what reasons do we have to suppose that IQ tests measure "intellectual power," an underlying capacity, rather than just achievement? The test items themselves seem to tap specific bits of knowledge—as in the vocabulary test—or the acquisition of specific skills and values. On the Stanford-Binet picture test, for example, a child is marked "right" if he picks out as "pretty" a white, prim-looking woman, and he is marked "wrong" if he picks a woman with Negroid features and slightly unkempt hair.

Jensen and Herrnstein give two reasons. First, they claim that the more intelligent the child, the quicker he assimilates what's in his environment regardless of the values that might be in the test items. In other words, they take precocity as a measure of capacity. But this makes sense only if the children come out of virtually identical environments; otherwise, "precocity" will reflect only different training and exposure. And even if environments were identical—which we know they are not—we would still have the untested assumption that precocity in performance is a measure of capacity and not, say, motivation.

Jensen and Herrnstein's second reason for thinking IQ tests measure capacity is that IQ correlates moderately well with success in school and later job status, and these are assumed to be well correlated with intelligence. Unhappily, this argument doesn't help much either. There is little reason to assume that success in school or on the job is much related to intelligence. Other things, like class background, correlate even better with such achievement than IQ does. Anyway, even if IQ and intelligence were each fairly well correlated with school success, this doesn't by itself mean they are correlated well or at all with each other. Finally, of course, "correlation" does not mean "causation," as Herrnstein occasionally suggests.

Given the questionable assumptions behind IQ tests, it would be an incredible coincidence if IQ tests did indeed measure some common quality of intelligence. But I don't think it is any accident that IQ tests have been constructed with assumptions that are so politically useful. From the start, the developers and promoters of this test technique were all convinced of hereditary, race, and class differences in intelligence. Tests that failed to confirm those assumptions were treated as failing to measure intelligence. Thus, when Sir Francis Galton devised tests that failed to show intelligence was correlated with "preeminence" in society, he threw out his tests, not his thesis that "the average intellectual standard of the Negro is some two grades below our own."

It is no wonder that various American psychologists (Terman, Thorndike, Otis, Goddard, Yerkes) who believed in race and class intelligence differences were so happy when Binet, a Frenchman, developed a handy instrument. Terman, who in 1916 developed the American version of Binet's test, already believed that low intelligence "is very, very common among Spanish, Indian and Mexican families of the Southwest, and also many Negroes. Their dullness seems to be racial, or

SOME PROCESSES OF SOCIAL LIFE

at least inherent in the family stocks from which they come." He suggested, "Children of this group should be segregated in special classes . . . there is no possibility at present of convincing society that they should not be allowed to reproduce." He argued for a major testing program: "When this is done there will be discovered enormously significant racial differences which cannot be wiped out by any scheme of mental culture." Terman's elitism was echoed by Goddard. Based on early IQ tests used on Ellis Island, Goddard reported that over 80 percent of all immigrants were "feeble-minded." IQ tests were used to justify deportations and eventually immigration quotas.

If IQ does not measure intelligence, then Step 2 of the IQ argument, the claim that about 80 percent of IQ differences between individuals are genetically based, loses much of its significance. But let's look anyway at the experimental evidence for the high "heritability" estimate since it appears to be the strongest step in the IQ argument.[4]

If scientists could raise genetically unrelated people in identical, laboratory controlled environments, like rats, then they could estimate "heritability" directly: all variations in IQ would be due to genes. But people are not rats, and we cannot really determine when two environments are identical. To settle the "nature versus nurture" controversy, therefore, scientists are forced to turn to "life experiments" in place of lab experiments; in particular, to cases of genetically identical people (one-egg twins) raised separately. For, logically, any difference in the IQs of identical twins must be due to environment. If the difference is small, then the contribution of environment is small and that of genes high.

There have been four major studies of separated twins, and their results appear to give Jensen and Herrnstein considerable support. The IQs of the twins show far less variation than IQs in the population as a whole, indicating a small environmental contribu-

tion. In Sir Cyril Burt's study of fifty-three twin pairs, for example, IQs of twins raised separately showed rather high (.771) correlations, supporting Jensen's calculation of about 80 percent heritability. Jensen combines the data from all four studies since they agree in their basic results, and claim to use standard tests and procedures; furthermore, they have been reviewed by others with no serious challenge. Finally, Jensen supplements the evidence for high heritability from the twin studies with evidence from other "life experiments." For example, adopted children's IQs seem to correlate better with their natural mothers' IQs than with their adopting mothers'. And kinship studies comparing closeness of genetic relation to similarity in IQ are compatible with a high estimate of heritability. The data, as scientists would say, look pretty "hard."

That's what Professor Leon Kamin, chairman of the Princeton Experimental Psychology Department, may have thought before he began to scratch a little at this evidence. His study gives strong reason to think the data may not be so hard after all.

First, Kamin argues, it is important to see how well designed the existing "life experiments" are. If the life experiments on twins are to give an accurate estimate of the environmental contribution to IQ, it is essential that the separated twins be randomly placed in the full range of environments that a society offers. Otherwise, there will be less IQ variation than there should be and it will look as though genes contribute more than they do. Did the four studies Jensen and Herrnstein rely on really provide the full range of environments needed? It appears not.[5]

For one thing, the twins in all four studies either went to adoptive homes or else one member of a pair was raised at home. Adoptive families, however, are generally well above average for their communities in economic security, cultural and educational status; they are smaller than average, and have older than average parents. Besides, adoption agencies match children's characteristics (or those of the natural parents) to characteristics of the adopting family, for religion, sex, age, color and complexion, physique, medical history and family background.

But there are even more specific problems with the studies. In over half of Burt's cases, one of the twins stayed in the natural parent's home. In general, these twins shared similar geographical regions, similar social and religious customs; they often played together and shared the same school system. Shields, the author of another study, claims his twins had different environments, but his report documents extensive similarities. For example, Benjamin and Ronald were "brought up in the same fruit-growing village, Ben by the parents, Ron by the grandmother . . . [and were] . . . in school together." Jessie and Winifred were "brought up within a hundred yards of each other . . . wanted to sit at the same desk." Bertram and Christopher were raised by paternal aunts "amicably living next door to one another."

Burt's is the only one of the four studies that even attempts to show that the twins went into homes of differing socio-economic status. But, according to Kamin, the data in the paper where he makes this claim do not exactly match data on the same twins published by his assistant and, in several places, fail to match data that Burt sent to Jensen. Nevertheless, in spite of these devastating problems, and in spite of the coincidental fact that Burt's original data sheets have been conveniently destroyed, Jensen sticks to his guns.

Kamin has probed another key feature of experimental design in the twin studies. To carry out an estimate fairly, it is necessary that the IQ tests be standardized with regard to sex and age. After all, one-egg twins are the same age and sex as well as being look-alikes, and it wouldn't be very scientific if the twins' IQs were made to look more similar simply because they had the same age and sex. Yet the IQ tests used for Jensen's estimate were not standardized for age and sex. Kamin has

shown that the high correlations of twins' IQs in one of the studies can be accounted for almost entirely by the failure to standardize the tests for age alone.

Anyone who has taken a psychology course knows that one must always try to compensate for or weed out the bias of the person doing an experiment. One needs uniform tests and testing procedures. One should make sure, for example, that each member of a twin pair was tested by a different person. Knowing the results of one twin's IQ test might lead to biasing, even unconscious biasing, of the result on the other twin. Unfortunately for Jensen, experimenter bias is evident in the twin studies. In all but five of thirty-eight cases, Shields tested both members of a twin pair himself and found an average difference of 4.9 points, a small difference pointing to a large genetic contribution. In the five other cases, he tested one twin and his assistant the other. Here they found a 13.2-point average difference, about normal for the population as a whole and compatible with a nearly zero estimate of heritability. Shields ignores this discrepancy. Burt also apparently tested almost all the twins in his study himself so we have no way of knowing how much he may have "unconsciously" biased the results. This factor alone should lead us to throw out more than two-thirds of the data for the four combined studies.

In addition, there is some evidence that selective exclusion of data in the Shields study, as well as in Burt's procedure of "adjusted assessments" if scores seemed too far off, operated to increase similarities in twins' IQs. In fact, Burt didn't even administer standard tests in all cases. He admits in a footnote to giving "personal interviews" and "camouflaged IQ tests" and then later refers to them as "tests of the usual type."

Finally, there is an even more serious problem with the data. Burt, who may not even have used standard test procedures, nevertheless managed to find correlations that remain identical to the third decimal place in spite of sample size changes of over 100 percent—just about a mathematical impossibility. For instance, Burt's papers report the same .771 correlation for twins reared separately in three studies, one involving twenty-one twin pairs (1955), one involving "over thirty" pairs (1958), and finally fifty-three pairs (1966). Even a college chemistry student knows better than to report data like that in his lab reports—they'd be thrown out as "fudged." It might be noted that Burt, in 1909, before any IQ data were available, remarked that his smarter subjects tended to be "blond."

The "hard data" for Jensen's estimates has turned to mush. With regard to every crucial feature of experimental design, to say nothing of experimenter integrity, the famous twin studies fall apart. Yet these "life experiments" are the cornerstone of Jensen's estimate of heritability.

The third step in the IQ argument asserts that the high 80-percent heritability of IQ for individuals can be used to explain the 15-point difference in the mean IQ of blacks and whites or the 30-point difference between the mean IQ of lower and upper classes. To go from individual to group differences is a big, in fact fatal, leap, since "heritability" is *defined* only for individual differences, and in *Genetics* Jensen himself warns against it. But later he leaped with abandon, as when he commented in the *New York Times*, "The number of intelligence genes seems lower overall in the black population than in the white."

In *Educability* (pages 155–156), Jensen again attempts the leap from individuals to groups, this time by bamboozling the reader with a mathematical argument. Basically, using mathematical equations, he says that if heritability is high (80 percent) and if IQ is well-correlated (.5) with success, then mathematics tells us genes must play some role in determining success. However, he neglects to tell the reader that the "some role" genes "must" play could be completely insignificant; it has to be only slightly more than zero. And he fails to warn the reader that his argument

depends crucially on heritability being as high as he says it is. This argument hardly fools the reader familiar with mathematics and is completely unfair to the non-mathematical reader.

While making the same jensenian jump from individuals to groups (social classes), Herrnstein tries to back away from the delicate issue of black-white differences. "We do not know why blacks bunch toward the lower end of the social scale," he writes on page 14. Again on page 186, "The only proper conclusion is that we do not know whether . . . [racial differences in IQ are] . . . more genetic, less genetic, or precisely as genetic as might seem to be implied by a heritability of .8." But if "bunching" blacks into the poorest section of the working class is a mechanism that can "environmentally" lower black IQs, then why doesn't "bunching" most working-class people into working-class living conditions "environmentally" lower *their* IQs? Herrnstein cannot admit that working-class living conditions can significantly lower IQs; that would undermine his entire thesis that class differences in IQ are highly heritable. His only way out of the dilemma is to say that working-class environments depress black IQs but not white IQs, a difficult argument to defend.[6]

The last step of the IQ argument, the "meritocracy" thesis, claims that success in life is in large part determined by high IQ. Jensen uses this step to explain why blacks, with their lower average IQs, have low "educability" and therefore are found disproportionately in the lower end of the working class. Does "low IQ," however, explain racist wage differentials or "last hired, first fired" policies exercised by many companies? In 1967, thousands of jobs were given to blacks in the auto industry following the Detroit riots. Was this higher level of "success" a result of boosted IQ? Jensen, it seems, would have us forget all we know about economic, political, and social forces and believe instead that all along some Invisible Hand has been selecting people for subtle, inherited differences in IQ, differences that in time impose education, unemployment, and welfare burdens on society (page 16).[7]

But if Jensen, who thinks the white population averages out genetically superior to the black population, is still in the grip of the White Man's Burden, then Herrnstein, whose social concern for the implications of IQ in the meritocracy is seemingly cleansed of racial overtones, is in the grip of The Smart Man's Burden. Herrnstein reveals the onus of the Smart Man's Burden in his famous "syllogism":

1. If differences in mental abilities are inherited, and
2. If success requires those abilities, and
3. If earnings and prestige depend on success,
4. Then social standing (which reflects earnings and prestige) will be based to some extent on inherited differences among people.

Herrnstein reveals the agonies of the Burden in his *Atlantic* lament: "As the wealth and complexity of human society grow, there will be precipitated out of the mass of humanity a low-capacity (intellectual and otherwise) residue that may be unable to master the common occupations, cannot compete for success and achievement, and are most likely to be born to parents who have similarly failed." A residue which, one gathers, will make huge demands on the good will and tax moneys of its betters. It is a little perplexing that Herrnstein's anguish is not geared toward concrete suggestions about how to ameliorate the "inevitable" situation through "effective compensatory education." Rather, it seems geared toward preparing the "residue" to accept its fate, for he goes no further than to suggest increased use of the IQ and other tests to make possible a "more humane and tolerant grasp of human differences," which is to say, a more rapid and rigid determination of just who the "residue" is.

Is there any reason to believe that high IQ is a prerequisite for success, or that there is a causal relation between IQ and "success in life"? Herrnstein's evidence is that IQ is a moderately good predictor of "success" and, further, that since people with high-status jobs tend to have higher average IQs, there is some reason to think high IQ is a prerequisite for performing the jobs. But other things statistically predict "success" even better than IQ, notably class background and number of school years completed. Independent of these other factors, IQ is no good at all as a predictor of "success in life."[8]

But isn't high IQ needed for performing high-status jobs? Probably not. People with high-status jobs may have high average IQs not because they have to be "smarter," but because these jobs require educational credentials and high IQ is correlated with getting these credentials even if it is not needed for them. Herrnstein here relies on equating high IQ with high "educability" or "trainability," but there is plenty of evidence that this equation is totally without basis. In fact, within job categories or types, performance on jobs or "success" at the job is notoriously *unrelated* to IQ.

Far more plausible than the thesis that getting ahead in America requires "intelligence," as measured by IQ, is the thesis that getting ahead requires other motivational and attitudinal traits. Competitiveness, servility (in appropriate situations), and hopefulness are possible candidates, as is a considerable tolerance of boredom. Whether highly "heritable" or learned, such traits are a debatable measure of "merit," nor do they necessarily represent the survival of the "fittest."

But even if one granted Herrnstein his "meritocracy" thesis, his conclusion doesn't follow. In his syllogism, he subtly equates "high heritability" with "fixedness" or "resistance to change in all circumstances." Even if IQ is highly heritable in our society, it does not follow that better education directed at the disadvantaged would not significantly boost mean IQs for society and make many more people "eligible" for high IQ jobs. Similarly, "high heritability" does not mean that new educational techniques won't be found that tend to benefit lower IQs more than higher ones, with the result that IQ differences are substantially reduced. In such a new environment, IQ might even lose its (supposed) high heritability. In other words, the question of "meritocracy" aside, Herrnstein makes his syllogism seem to work by giving a misleading picture of the implications of high heritability.

There seems to be no reason, then, for accepting anything about Herrnstein's famous syllogism, either its premises or its conclusion. Nor will we inevitably have to groan under the Smart Man's Burden.

Is anything left of the IQ argument, that vanguard position of the new "revolution" in the social sciences? IQ does not measure intelligence. High heritability estimates of IQ are based on useless studies and maybe even fudged data. Anyway, these estimates cannot be used to explain group differences. Finally, IQ seems to have nothing important to do with "success." This is all that's left of the IQ argument that *Fortune*, *Time*, *Atlantic*, the *New York Times*, and other prominent newspapers and magazines have made so famous. Will the scholarly refutations of jensenism be made as famous? Will the press now give as much attention to showing what's wrong with jensenism as they have given to making it nearly a household word in Washington and a guide for the "pragmatic man in the street"? That may be up to the reader.

NOTES

[1]Jensen's paper in the *Harvard Educational Review* is reprinted with supplementary papers in *Genetics and Education* (Harper & Row, 1972). He develops his thesis on race differences in *Educability and Group Differences* (Harper & Row, 1973).

[2]Herrnstein's *Atlantic* article, "IQ" (September 1971), is the basis for his recent book, *IQ in the Meritocracy* (Atlantic-Little, Brown, 1973).

[3]As self-styled "revolutionaries" challenging an "egalitarian orthodoxy," the two professors signed an advertisement in *American Psychologist* comparing their unfriendly reception by academics and students to the attempts to suppress Galileo, Darwin, Einstein, and Mendel.

[4]The high heritability estimate appears likely only if we ignore opposing evidence based on IQ boosting studies. Programs that "improve" the child's environment by subjecting the children to intensive tutoring, or by coaching mothers on how to play with and read to their children, produced dramatic 15- to 30-point IQ gains which seem to be longlasting. It is hard to see how coaching a mother an hour or so a week even scratches the surface of the differences between lower- and upper-class living and child-rearing conditions. In my own view, since low IQ is no sign of "stunted intelligence," I think programs

geared to boosting IQ, rather than teaching children something useful, are a waste of time. But by claiming that "environmentalism" is in a crisis, in spite of all this pro-environmentalist evidence, Jensen and Herrnstein seem to be attempting an unwarranted shift in the burden of proof.

[5]Kamin delivered a paper analyzing the existing data at a recent meeting of the Eastern Psychology Association, making most of the points I cite above. It is rather sad that Herrnstein, who has constantly complained of alleged infringements on his "academic freedom" and who charges his critics with failing to consider his arguments, has resorted in a recent issue of *Science* to charging Kamin with being "blinded" by Marxism (for which there seems to be no evidence). Presumably, Herrnstein had better be prepared to charge the whole membership of the Eastern Psychology Association since they voted by a two-to-one margin "to censure the use of inconclusive evidence concerning the heritability of IQ."

[6]Herrnstein could still say that things like "racist insults" are what depress black IQs. But does he think poor whites suffer no insults or discrimination?

[7]Jensen, showing an astonishing ignorance of history, says: "It is more likely—though speculative of course—

that Negroes brought here as slaves were selected for docility and strength rather than mental ability, and that through selective mating [with slave owners?] the mental qualities never had a chance to flourish."

[8]For evidence of this, see Samuel Bowles' and Herbert Gintis's recent study in *Social Policy*. One might try to save Herrnstein's claim by arguing that IQ is a factor needed

for success in school and thus indirectly for success in life. But if class background is held constant, IQ still plays only a minimal role in predicting school success. And it is further arguable that it plays that role only because it measures values and attitudes and not because it measures intelligence.

32

FREEDOM FOR THE AMERICAN INDIAN

Alvin M. Josephy, Jr.

During the last few years there has been an outpouring of information on American Indians. Books and magazine articles; radio and television documentaries, discussions and commentaries; movies; and newspaper reports and editorials have focused attention with new and more accurate perspectives on Indian cultural backgrounds, Indian-white history, and present-day Indian needs and aspirations.

One result is that non-Indian Americans today are more understanding than they have ever been of the Indian side of what happened in the *past*. The Native Americans who resisted the intruding whites from the time of Jamestown and Plymouth to the last battle on the plains are now seen as patriotic peoples who struggled righteously for their lives, lands, freedom, religious beliefs, and means of livelihood. Although Indian scholars, still to come, will add breadth and depth to the record from their own cultural and tribal insights,

the long history of past shame is clear for all who will read or listen.

Despite all that has been written and said, however, what is more important to the contemporary Indian—his own problems, wants, and goals of *today*, not of the past— seems still confusing to most non-Indian Americans, not alone among the nation's opinion makers and the general public, but in the areas of the federal government that deal with Indian affairs. As a result, sound and harmonious relations between Indians and non-Indians appear to many people to be as elusive today as they were to the whites and Native Americans of the past.

The fault is often ascribed to two principal gaps in thinking, one historic and the other cultural. On the historical level, the non-Indian has become aware of what happened in the past, but he feels that that is all over and cannot be undone, and that the Indian of 1973—a full century after Custer—should "shape up" and be like everyone else. The continuation of reservations puzzles him. Are they concentration camps, or what? He is

From *The Critic*, Sept./Oct. 1973, pp. 18–27. Reprinted by permission of the author.

SOME PROCESSES OF SOCIAL LIFE

mystified by the special relationship between the federal government and the Indians that seems to perpetuate, at one and the same time, an incompetent, sometimes corrupt, bureaucratic rule by Washington over the Indians, and a helpless, but apparently willing, dependence by the Indians on the federal treasury. Why does it go on? Who is at fault?

The Indians, at the same time, view history differently. Once, they knew, they were free people, thoroughly capable of governing themselves, and all of the present-day United States was theirs. The white man subjugated and dispossessed them. The small portions of land that were left to them (land that had never belonged to anyone else)—or that were given to them by the government, because all of their own territory had been stolen from them—were set aside as reservations for their sole possession and use, with guarantees made to them in solemn treaties that the federal government would protect these reservations for as long as the Indians wished. As payment for the land that was taken, the government promised services—education, health facilities, vocational training, roads, and so forth.

There are about 1,000,000 Indians in the United States today (the estimates of their pre-Columbian population in the same area range from 850,000 up to 9,800,000). About half of them live on reservations and half in urban and rural areas. But almost all of them consider themselves the descendants and inheritors of the peoples who made the treaties with the federal government. To them, not only is the history of the past very much alive, but they are the continuers of that history. Small as their numbers may be, they are the Indian past that is still running like an unbroken thread through our body politic and through many present-day concerns. The land of the reservations is all they have left, but it is still theirs and no one else's. Although it is only a token of what they once had, it is sacred to them for what it means as the repository of their tribal culture, history, and tra-

ditions; the burial grounds of their fathers; the homes of their families; the last tie they possess with their mother, the Earth, and with all of nature; the firm root of their existence as Indians and tribal peoples; and the basis of whatever prospects they have for a future as Indians. Their history, up to the present day, has been one of struggle to force the government to live up to its treaty promises and protect the reservations against the erosions and exploitation of non-Indians. Far from being concentration camps, in short, the reservations are beloved and guarded as homelands by the tribes, and the people can come and go from them as they please.

This sense of an unbroken connection with the historic past reflects the first gap of information between Indians and non-Indians. The Indian is very much aware of the details of the treaties and promises made to his ancestors; the white man, in or out of government, is not. The Indian is also aware of the details of federal-Indian relations from the time when the treaties were made. They include broken promises; zigzagging policies of different administrations in Washington; frauds, lies, and injustices by the score; stern rule by tyrannical agents, missionaries, and army officers; punishments; denial of rations; the stamping out of native languages, religion, and culture; the shanghaiing of children for enforced attendance at distant white men's schools; the smashing of tribal institutions, values, and standards, and the substitution of alien forms; the bringing of poverty with no solutions; and, finally, prejudice, persecutions, neglect, aimlessness, and death. The Indians knew this history, year by year, on one reservation after another. The whites know it only vaguely—in stereotypes and fuzzy generalizations, no more graphic than was the list just recited. The Indian therefore knows exactly what he would like to end; the white man would agree that it should be ended, but he is not exactly sure of what— other than poverty—there is to end.

The cultural gap between Indians and

non-Indians is even wider than the historical. Since 1924, Indians have been citizens of the United States. They have the vote and in almost all ways except the most important—the possession of freedom (to be discussed later)—they are considered like all other Americans. They need, use, and enjoy the material traits of modern-day civilization. Some of them are thoroughly acculturated, and even assimilated, into the white man's society. Many are truly bicultural, at home on reservations but equally able to get on in white men's cities. But almost all of them are knowingly and feelingly still Indians, possessors of cultural values, standards, and beliefs that they inherited from their peoples and that differ profoundly from those of the non-Indians.

A whole literature exists on Indian life and beliefs. They differed in some ways from tribe to tribe, but there were many samenesses. The Indians' concepts of their relations to their fellowmen, to the supernatural, and to nature and the Earth were basically somewhat similar among tribes in all areas of the Western Hemisphere. To non-Indians, with a background of Judeo-Christian religion and philosophy and Western European socioeconomic and political development, Indian ways were different and, therefore, inferior. Cooperation rather than competition; group orientation rather than personal ambition; stewardship of nature rather than its conquest; brotherhood with all creation rather than dominion over it—these were just a few among many of the Indians' ways which were brushed aside and ignored by the white conqueror.

But they did not die. The cultural values, too, are part of the Indian thread that still runs through the United States, believed in and observed by peoples of Indian blood and background, whether they live on reservations or in cities. The proof of their ability to endure exists strikingly in the Atlantic coastal states where Indian tribes were smashed into small and powerless fragments, then overrun,

absorbed, and forgotten by non-Indians long before the American Revolution. Today their descendants have emerged as cohesive groups—Penobscots, Micmacs, Malecites, Passamaquoddies in Maine; Wampanoags in Massachusetts; Narragansets in Rhode Island; Niantics, Pequots, Mohegans, and others in Connecticut; Patchogues, Shinnecocks, and Montauks, among others, in New York; Chickahominys, Powhatans, and Rappahannocks in Virginia; Croatans (descendants, perhaps, of those who absorbed Raleigh's "Lost Colony" in 1587) in North Carolina; and many others—still Indians, still proud of their tribal heritages, still clinging to their ancestral cultural values—which continue to be markedly different from those of the rest of American society.

If those values have persisted in the East among people who have been overrun and submerged by the white man for more than two centuries, then how strong they must still be among the more recently conquered peoples, like the Sioux, Cheyenne, Navajos, and many dozens of others in the West, who continue to observe such spiritual ceremonies as the Sun Dance, use their own curers and purify themselves with the sweat bath, go on vision quests, and honor their holy men. And how impossible, it seems to imply, it has been—and will be—for the white man to eradicate them and turn the Indian fully into a white man, living in complete accordance with the white man's cultural values.

Almost all Indians (and, in fairness, some white men) have viewed such an effort as immoral and, indeed, incredibly shortsighted and self-defeating. But the drive and power of the dominant culture have shown neither interest in, nor patience with, the Indians' ways. The white man has not cared to understand Indian culture, much less consider that it could co-exist with his own, and he is totally at sea when the Indian clothes his words and actions in terms of his own culture, as he did recently in stating his purposes during the occupations of Alcatraz Island, the Bureau of

Indian Affairs Building in Washington, D. C., and the region of Wounded Knee in South Dakota. There was, of course, nothing novel about the white man's reactions to each of these confrontations. He viewed them as lawless outbursts by radical minorities among the Indians and missed the point entirely that though they were desperate attempts (the only methods left to the Indians) to call the nation's attention to their terrible oppression and suffering (something many whites did understand), they were even more important as efforts to break the bonds of their yearnings to save themselves as Indians by saving their Indian cultural traditions and heritage. Not all Indians approved of the militant and violent tactics and damage at the Bureau of Indian Affairs and at Wounded Knee. But most Indians knew what it was all about, agreed with the aims of the occupiers, and prayed for their safety and success.

In a sense, those recent Indian-white confrontations, accompanied by patronization, brutal insensitivity, and lack of understanding on the part of too many whites who were involved, illuminated the depth of the historical and cultural gaps that still separate Indians and non-Indians. In a way, also, they climaxed the long centuries of a misguided white policy toward Indians that began in the first English colonies on the Atlantic. Until 1890, it was one of assimilate or die. Since then, and until today, it has been assimilate or stagnate in poverty. Both ideas, one a continuation of the other, have been at the heart of the nation's Indian policy since the first Administration of George Washington. The most benign concept of white men toward Indians has been that of saving them by turning them, as quickly as possible, into white men—Christianizing them, settling them down as farmers or mechanics, cutting their hair, clothing them as whites, educating them without reference to their own history, culture, language, or background, and getting them to disappear as white men in the white man's world. Programs changed from one

administration to the next, but each was designed to speed up the assimilation process—and each, in turn, failed. As part of the process, the Indian was stripped and robbed of whatever might impede assimilation—among them, his freedom of religion, his tribal institutions, his mythology and artistic inheritance, and his land and resources. In 1934 he regained his religious freedom. But assimilation is still the aim of national Indian policy. Hobbled by the historic and cultural gaps which perpetuate his ignorance and confusion about the Indians' real needs and goal, the non-Indian American continues to view assimilation as the best—indeed, the only—destiny for the Indians. He gives this as a mandate to the federal government, which through appropriate committees in Congress and the Bureau of Indian Affairs (the executive branch's agency in the Department of the Interior charged with handling relations with the Indians), persists in trying to carry it out. In the process, Indian lands and resources, the basis for continued Indian life, are not protected (the whittling away of Indian assets increasing, of course, Indian poverty), and Indian self-determination, even though proclaimed as an Administration goal by President Nixon in July, 1970, is frustrated.

Serious as they have been as impediments blocking the non-Indians' understanding and support of Indian aims, the historic and cultural gaps obfuscated the actual mainspring of the nation's traditional Indian policy and the true motive behind the drive to force Indian assimilation. Stated bluntly, it has been—and continues to be—the acquisitive greed for Indian lands and resources. Many non-Indians undoubtedly believe that the era when the Indians were defrauded and cheated of their lands is over. But the facts are the opposite. Indians have never been permitted rest in their fight to save what they have. Today the assault against the reservations is more massive and threatening to them than at any time in the recent past. Dams are flooding the best parts of their lands. Rights-of-way for railroad lines, transmission lines, highways, and other facilities are slicing through the reservations. Leases for huge real estate developments, white men's resorts, coal strip mines, and power, gasification, and petrochemical plants are being approved for the reservations by the Department of the Interior.

All these developments, plumped down on top of the Indians, industrializing their lands, and making less of the reservation available for them, may be viewed as hastening assimilation. But that is putting the cart before the horse. The real effect is that the reservations are being taken away from the Indians and turned into white men's domains. The methods used, moreover, are the same as those of the past. The Navajos, Hopis, Crows, Northern Cheyennes, and many others have all been victimized by fraud, cheating, lies, and deceit in the leasing of their lands and resources during the last few years.

Scores of Indians are articulate today in expressing their people's needs and demands. Individuals, tribes, and regional and national Indian organizations have grown expert in using the white man's own media to try to communicate what they want. In time, they will undoubtedly bridge the historic and cultural gaps, bringing non-Indians to see their destiny as they see it. But achieving that destiny will be impossible until the mainspring of national Indian policy is, so to speak, smashed, and the taking of Indian lands and resources is checked. The only instrument with which this can be accomplished is what all Americans, save Indians, possess: freedom. Without it, as they now are, their lands, lives, decisions, and fate are at the mercy of a government primarily responsive to outside aggrandizers. Without it, their boundaries of existence narrow and their future as Indians shrivels. To the Indians, there is method in the determination of the government, up to now, to talk self-determination and freedom for them, but in practice to deny it.

What is the relation of the government to the Indians that denies them freedom? In 1934, the Indian Reorganization Act imposed on almost every tribe in the country a uniform type of government, modeled after the white man's ways, with constitutionally-elected tribal officers, a tribal council, or legislature, and tribal courts. For most tribes, it was a tragic mistake. The Indians were used to their own traditional forms of government—whether by clan leaders, traditional chiefs, councils of elders, or some other group or individual—and, in large numbers, they resented and boycotted the alien system that was foisted on them. Constitutions were accepted by small voting minorities in many tribes, and to this day the tribal governments are divisive institutions on numerous reservations, ignored by majorities of the people. Worse still, the powers of the Indian governments were limited. Over all important matters, the Bureau of Indian Affairs maintained absolute control, with the right to approve or veto. Much like the native legislatures in British colonial governments, the tribal councils became little more than ceremonial rubber stamps for the real authority that lay with the white man.

As a consequence, the tribal governments became responsive, and responsible, to the Bureau of Indian Affairs, rather than to their own people. The Bureau, in turn, being responsible to Congress for "no trouble on the reservations," ran the tribes in collusion with pliant and venal tribal officers who basked in the prestige and petty rewards of their positions. This situation, in which reservation peoples often refer to their office holders as "Uncle Tomahawks," and "Apples" (red outside, white inside), has perpetuated dependence, dulled initiative, and made a sham of real self-determination. Though the present administration regards the tribal councils as the organs of Indian freedom, the real boss is still the Bureau of Indian Affairs.

The question of the authority of the Bureau has been muddied by its position as trustee of Indian lands and resources, a function which almost every tribe wishes it to continue to fulfill. How, asks the Bureau, can we give up ultimate authority and still act responsibly as trustee? The answer lies in an analogy. A bank can be a trustee for a white man's money or property, carry out that function with or without consultation with its client, and have no authority over any other part of that person's life. But, beginning with its trust responsibility over tribal property, the federal government, through the Bureau of Indian Affairs, has insidiously extended its governance over every other portion of an Indian's life. To be convinced, one has only to sit for a day in the outer office of a Bureau agency on any reservation and see the stream of Indians coming in, hat in hand, for advice, approval, and permission in a hundred personal and varied matters. Relatively few Indians turn to their own tribal institutions. They go to the government for approval of wills, for advice on travel, and for a weekly or monthly allowance doled out to them arbitrarily from part of the rental receipts from land leased to whites.

With great truth, Warren H. Cohen and Philip J. Mause wrote in the *Harvard Law Review* in June, 1968: "Although normal expectation in American society is that a private individual or group may do anything unless it is specifically prohibited by the government, it might be said that the normal expectation on the reservation is that the Indians may not do anything unless it is specifically permitted by the government."

This is not freedom.

As a result of the confrontations at the Bureau of Indian Affairs Building and at Wounded Knee, federal-Indian relations are today in a state of crisis. The Indians have made known their needs and demands, but Administration officials and Congress—either through lack of understanding, or because of a determination not to lose control of the Indians and their resources, have responded

so far with proposals that are superficial and relatively meaningless—little more than a moving around of chairs, so to speak. None of their reactions go to the heart of relations between the Indians and the federal government, and nothing they propose can therefore succeed in satisfying the Indians or the challenges that the Indians have raised.

Yet the time for a revolutionary change in federal-Indian relations is here and now. The Indians have expressed it, and the form of that change can be stated in the following terms:

1. Within every town, city, county, and state, free Americans have local governments of their own choosing, free of interference by the federal government. Their systems of mayors, town managers, city councils, or whatever, are their own business. Federal officials or agents may be in those areas to carry out the delivery of federal programs to local citizen groups, who may be considered the clients or beneficiaries of the programs. But the local affairs of the people are not the concern of the federal personnel. If there is a local political problem, the people have the means through their own systems of government to handle it themselves. Their governments normally are responsive and accountable to the people. In times of local conflict, the federal officials sit in a corner and read a newspaper. The problem is not theirs.

   The Indian tribes must attain the same level of freedom. The dominant society must stand back and enable the people of each tribe to create governments of their own choosing with the full freedom to manage and control their own affairs. If such governments are established, they will of necessity be responsive and responsible to their individual peoples and will provide the basis for what is now missing: the enforcement of the government's trusteeship obligations over lands and resources; protection of treaty rights; the design and execution of development programs that the people really want and will make succeed; educational and other institutions that have meaning for their people; contracting with nongovernmental, as well as governmental, agencies for technical assistance, credit, and services; and the effective safeguarding of their people against discrimination, abuse, and injustices.

2. Simultaneously, the Bureau of Indian Affairs must be stripped of its authority over the tribes and become, in fact as well as in theory, a service organization, limited in its functions to the delivery of expertise, services, and credit to Indian clients at their request. The present status of the Bureau, on reflection, is ludicrous. In effect, it is charged with being an entire supergovernment over the tribes, with departments and individuals supposedly expert in every phase of modern-day community activity and individual life. It must be expert on the reclamation of stripmined land, on the buying of school books, on marital problems, on water rights law, on the harvesting of timber, on corporate relations, on the hiring of a lawyer, and on tens of thousands of other matters, many of them vital to Indian concerns. All these spheres of expertise are often centered in one all-powerful bureaucrat or in a small group of his assistants, whose judgments are often autocratically imposed on the Indians, whether they are right or wrong, wanted or unwanted. It is an impossibility to be so infallible, not only in so small an agency, but in one in which mediocrity and incompetence have been hallmarks.

When a tribe needs technical assistance for its people, it should have the freedom to seek the best and, by contract underwritten by the federal government, make its own arrangements with the private, as well as the public sector. But the most important principle must be one, again, of freedom: the B.I.A. personnel, as well as all federal officials, must relate to the Indians and their governments on nontrustee affairs in the same manner in which federal agents relate to non-Indian citizens and their local governments. In Indian matters, they should no longer be permitted to take sides, and they should not have the right to interfere. Their sole duties should be to deliver services adequately funded by the federal government as guaranteed by treaties.

In such a state of affairs, with totally free governments of their own choosing, and with the right to manage and control their own lives as they see fit, Indian initiative will inevitably be unfettered. Compared with the past and present record of the white man thinking for the Indian and doing everything for him—a record replete with maladministration, petty tyranny, and failure—the future will seem like an age of miracles. Even if there are mistakes, internal conflicts, and inefficiency, it can be no worse than what has been and what is. Moreover, it will be the Indians' own business; they have the right, like everyone else, to make mistakes and, by making them, learn and gain experience. If they have truly accountable governments, with such safeguards as methods for referendums, the handling of corruption, and the protection of individual and tribal rights, all must ultimately be far superior to what now exists.

3. To carry out the trustee function, a special management-and-legal apparatus should be created within the federal government, separate from the B.I.A. service delivery organization, responsible to the Indians alone, and charged with a commitment to the trust obligation. Its functions must be the management of trustee affairs and the determined protection of tribal lands, water rights, and mineral and other

resources. Its relationship to the Indians should approximate that of a bank and lawyer to their client, and it should have nothing to do with any other phase of the Indians' life.

This relationship between the federal government and the Indians would provide the underpinnings for the settling and solving of all other matters. There are numerous demands of a bewildering variety that must be negotiated between free Indians and the federal government. The Indians participating in "The Trail of Broken Treaties," which occupied the Bureau of Indian Affairs Building in October, 1972, presented the government with a set of twenty demands which should provide guidelines for such negotiations.

They include, among other points, a review and rectification of broken treaties; the enforcement of treaty rights; the re-establishment of a treaty-making relationship between the tribes and the government; and the inclusion of off-reservation Indians and members of tribes not now federally recognized as recipients of programs for Indians.

What has been proposed here is not in conflict with any Indian demand. It is addressed to the non-Indian, in and out of government, who is confused about the present status of the Indian and the substance of what he wants. It calls only for Indian freedom—the prerequisite for meaningful negotiations for everything else.

33

OLD VS. YOUNG IN FLORIDA PREVIEW OF AN AGING AMERICA

Rasa Gustaitis

A 14-year-old who lives in one of the beach-front condominiums in Ft. Lauderdale knows that elderly women clutch their purses as he passes on his bike. So he likes to ride up behind them close and slow, just to tease.

He is a clean-cut, polite youngster, a nice boy by any mother's definition, and he means no harm. Nevertheless, he relishes this private little joke on the aged. It is his way of

From *Saturday Review*, February 16, 1980. Reprinted by permission.

getting a bit of revenge for the many times he has been made to feel suspect and unwelcome simply because of his youth.

His story is not an unusual one in Broward County, where the old and the young are engaged in what almost amounts to a war of generations. Only newcomers are likely to be surprised by the hostility between the two combatants. A recently arrived New Yorker, for instance, was shocked that the other customers in a restaurant refused to sit next to her and three children. A co-worker at her office explained: "Kids make noise, they throw things—who needs it?" The young can be equally scathing toward the elderly. "The problem with the o.p.s (common term for "old people" here) is not how to take care of them; it's how to keep them from killing the rest of us," remarked a young policeman's wife.

For the moment the U. S. remains largely free of the generational hostility so evident in Broward County. But there is good reason to believe that within decades the attitudes prevalent there will have spread throughout America. For demographically, Florida, and especially Broward, mirrors the future of the nation.

The number of old people in the U. S. has been growing faster than the general population. Between 1970 and 1978, the total population increased by 7 percent, while the elderly population grew 20 percent. In Florida, the growth of the elderly population has been even more dramatic: Their numbers have jumped 50 percent between 1970 and 1978, according to Jacob Siegel, senior demographic statistician at the population division of the Census Bureau. And while it is estimated that 11 percent of the current U. S. population is over 65, in Florida nearly 18 percent is elderly. Within the next 50 years, close to one out of every five Americans will be over 65. In Florida, the traditional population pyramid will be turned upside down. Those over 65 will outnumber those under 14.

The vast social and political consequences of this concentration of the elderly can already be seen in Broward County, located northeast of Miami. Broward has long been a mecca for the retired. Today over one-third of the county's population is over 60, and the number is on the rise. The conflict between the young and the old is possibly the most ominous fallout from this immense migration.

There are many reasons why the two groups have been cast as adversaries—differences of values and life styles, for instance. But ultimately the struggle comes down to one major issue: money, particularly government money. Both old and young rely heavily on the government for needed social services. However, the ability of the government to provide these services in an inflationary economy has shrunk, while the elderly continue to expand in number and power. The net result is almost inevitably more for the old, less for the young. There is no way to prove categorically that a direct trade-off favoring the old at the expense of the young is taking place. Yet signs of the trend are unmistakable. The fate of certain public spending programs, the widespread discrimination against children and young people in housing, the increasingly punitive attitude toward youthful offenders in the schools and in the criminal justice system, and the political clout of the old all testify to the pervasiveness of the climate created by the growing elderly population.

The aged in Florida have bought the American promise of work followed by earned leisure. So now they shy away from social concerns with the catchphrase, "We've paid our dues." Thus, when Dade County proposed a drastic budget cut last summer, hoping thereby to avert a tax-cut initiative of disastrous proportions, the biggest slice came out of Headstart, a preschool program. As it turned out, the ballot initiative included a printing error that would have almost completely abolished taxes. It failed, and children's advocates soon succeeded in restoring the Headstart budget to the amount of the previous year. Nevertheless, with inflation taken into account, the net effect was still a cut.

Spending for schools has also shrunk in Florida, although dollar levels have remained relatively stable. In 1978 Florida, one of the richest states, spent the smallest percentage of its wealth on education, according to an indepth report by the *Miami Herald*. In per pupil expenditures it ranked 32nd of the 50 states. Although Governor Robert Graham has announced that the state will increase spending by 10 percent in 1980, he has simultaneously proposed that the percentage of property taxes going to schools, which has already dropped in the last 10 years, should be still further reduced. According to Scott Rose, school finance expert in Pinellas County, the proposed levels will not permit schools to keep pace with inflation. As the proportion of the elderly in Florida grows, and as inflation keeps shriveling incomes, public support for education can be expected to erode even more—especially since in some areas a growing proportion of the public-school children will come from minority groups. In the words of Hillsborough County School Superintendent Raymond O. Shelton, "It's going to be difficult to keep education in the limelight as a high priority social issue."

Cutbacks have hit other youth-related programs as well. Six years ago, Dr. Georgia Reynolds, a physician who has specialized in community health practices, started a mobile health unit for preschoolers. Not long ago, Broward County failed to find the funds needed to keep the program alive. The failure has had a price. Visiting child-care centers, Dr. Reynolds found "children who had not seen a doctor since they dropped out of the baby clinic before age one. They had problems that could easily have been remedied earlier. But by the time the kids are five or six, not much can be done." She saw cases of amblyopia (lazy eye), children who were neglected and malnourished. "One three-year-old girl was totally deaf and nobody knew it. We had her in a special program within a week." When asked why the mobile health unit had been discontinued, Dr. Reynolds replied, "I think it's the old people, mostly. They say they've already paid their dues." Having struggled to raise their own children and to make sure that they are not a burden to them, many elderly want simply to be left alone to enjoy their "golden years."

A direct consequence of this attitude has been widespread discrimination in housing against young couples and children. (Florida has no law forbidding housing discrimination against children. When a St. Petersburg city councilman proposed that a local antidiscrimination ordinance be extended to cover exclusion of children, other councilmen quickly rebuffed him.) The old and the young probably live more separate existences in Florida than anywhere else in the world. Promised a life of carefree safety in the sun, the elderly settled in droves in developer-built communities that had been designed to keep apart, rather than join, people of different ages, races, and classes. As a result, Broward today is a sprawling county with no focus. Each of its municipalities has a separate government and a separate—sometimes almost nonexistent—system of taxation. The smallest is Lazy Lakes, with 550 people; the largest, Ft. Lauderdale, with 160,000. Across the patchwork of these communities, running roughly along the railroad tracks that parallel the water, live most of the county's blacks, squeezed more tightly together as real estate prices keep rising. The wealthy elderly tend to live along the beach; the poorer, farther inland; and families with children cluster in whatever developments accept them.

Just how difficult it can be to cross the borders is evidenced by the story of the eight-year-old boy who came for an overnight stay with his great-grandparents at one of the many expensive adults-only condominiums. When the child arrived, the doorman handed him a sheet of rules: "Children require the constant supervision of those responsible for them. They must be kept from interfering in any way with the quiet and comfort of residents." The grandparents, nearly 80, were a lively couple fond of dancing and ocean cruises, but they regarded the rules as reasonable. After all, hadn't they chosen to live there precisely to be free from disturbances?

A young woman recounted that when she looked for an apartment with her husband she was asked several times by a rental agent whether she was planning to have children. She assured him that she was not, yet was nevertheless turned away with a suspicious look. For a single woman with more than one child, the options are far slimmer. Carol Fleck, a divorced mother of three, frantically searched for months after her apartment building was turned into a condominium. She had decided she could not afford to buy in, but soon discovered that no place would rent to anyone with three children. "I make more than most of the women in my office—$220 a week before taxes. And my oldest, who is 20, has a job, so we can pay a bit more," she said. "But I've looked everywhere. Occasionally apartments will take a 16-year-old, but my youngest is nine."

What underlies the discrimination against the young in housing is, of course, fear—a fear that also accounts for the harsh penalties meted out to the young lawbreakers in Florida. In the popular view, brutal and drug-crazed young hoods are particularly partial to old people as victims. This image is wrong—the elderly are victimized less than other age groups, and when the perpetrator is a youth, the victim is most often another youth—but it is constantly reinforced by the press. Last year, the media devoted much attention to 85-year-old Ralph Germano, who was attacked in his Miami home by five juveniles. He was taunted, beaten, and left bleeding on the floor, not to be found until 12 hours later. He died 37 days after the assault. One of his attackers, Eve Postell, is now the youngest female serving a life sentence in Florida's adult prison system. She is 13 years old.

The entire Florida prison population has been getting younger, as more and more juveniles like Eve are funneled into it. The view expressed by David Waksman, the assistant state attorney who prosecuted Postell, is all too typical: "These kids have shown they can't be rehabilitated," he told the *St. Petersburg Times*. "There is only one thing left. Warehouse them so they won't mug or kill anybody." He added: "Eve will be out one day and I would hate to see her then. She'll probably be 10 times worse, but that's a lot better

than having her on the street. What else can we do?"

Such attitudes have led some to predict that Florida, which has more people on death row than any other state and was the first state to put a prisoner to death against his will in 10 years, may also become the first to execute a juvenile. "I don't see why all the time and money should be spent on people who have no consideration for their victims," commented an elderly woman, secretary in a church in Pinellas County. "We're much better off without them."

This severity toward the young is especially ironic in light of the fact, pointed to by Gary Feinberg, a sociologist at Nova University, that the elderly have much in common with the young. "Both have only one aim: fun. . . . "What we do as recreation—drinking, smoking, driving," says Feinberg, "they do as a way of life. Both old and young are on the outside of society." Both are aliens.

Perhaps because of this, there is a similarity in the pattern of crimes committed by the old and by juveniles. Elderly shoplifters have become a serious problem in Broward County, and vandalism and assaults by the elderly have also risen. Feinberg talks of "elderly delinquency," which he says has been spawned by the "short-run hedonism" of people who live for today because they do not have a strong grasp on tomorrow and who have no meaningful social role.

In spite of all the elderly population's struggles to mold Florida into their private world, life there is a bitter disappointment to many who worked so hard to afford it. They believed the ads: Harry is lounging by his pool, a cold drink in his hand, and he's phoning the boys back at the plant in drizzle city. Wish you were here. Smiles all around. The ad does not show that the call may be the high point of Harry's week (and how many times can he make such a phone call?). A few days spent next to the pool, and Harry may be feeling the sort of depression children experience at Christmas or on birthdays when the presents have all been opened and there's nothing more to do. "We used to go down to the beach when we first came," said a 55-year-old resident of a condo along the water. He had retired early from a small business he owned and operated in California. "But now we don't go much. Maybe because it's so close. Maybe if we had to drive there we'd go more."

Some people don't have cars or can't drive. For them, Florida is particularly desolate. The streets were designed for cars, not pedestrians, and public transportation is sparse. "We had a guest from Germany," a retired Ft. Lauderdale woman reported, "who kept asking, 'Where are all the people?'"

Where many of them are is at home, sitting in front of the TV, in an air-conditioned room. Others, to be sure, have made a successful adjustment. They enroll in classes, they engage in volunteer work. Some even find romance. One businessman was reunited with his World War I sweetheart at a writing workshop. Both had raised families and were widowed. They rediscovered each other and now spend part of their year at his home in Ft. Lauderdale, part in hers on Long Island.

But they are the rare exceptions. Too often the elderly merely "hang out," perhaps in the shopping center, one of the few places they can easily get to by public transit. They wander, they watch different kinds of people mingling, they browse in the shops—and sometimes they take something.

"They rarely do it out of economic need," said Peter Vallone, counselor at the county criminal justice division's pretrial intervention program. "Seems that a lot are acting out against the establishment. They're lonely. They've lost a mate. So they strike out against society," he said, echoing a similar wisdom about juveniles. Some shoplift to get attention or to keep from being bored. "A lot are on drugs and they're spacey," said Jacob Messina, a planner in the criminal justice division. "Nothing illegal about the drugs, of course. They are medication." Law enforcement officers are sympathetic to the elderly—far more

so than they are to juvenile offenders. A few officers are even embarrassed. Yet stores insist on pressing charges because they "lose millions a year on this problem," according to Vallone. Jail sentences are rare, however. "Our facilities are so bad they would die," said Sandra Hunter, supervisor of the county probation department.

Arrest is often a blessing in disguise for the elderly because it leads to sessions with a counselor who can become a lifeline. "For the first time in a long while someone is paying attention to them," said Hunter. "One man was stealing five wallets a day. He had a quota. He didn't need the wallets, but he did have a need. One of our volunteers got him involved in building doll houses. He doesn't steal anymore." Sometimes arrest means a call to a distant son or daughter who has failed to heed many plaintive invitations to come down to visit. The arrest becomes a reproach: See what you let happen to your father? And to get an extra bit of attention, one of the counselors has noticed, many are arrested on their birthdays.

In the meantime, the juvenile justice system, which was meant to provide just that sort of support for youngsters, is being abandoned as a failure—largely because of pressure from the elderly.

The political arena is the main battleground in the conflict between the generations. Because the elderly can vote—nationally, 15 percent of those who cast ballots are over 65—they have legislative power, and they use it to further their interests. The House Select Committee on Aging, set up only four years ago, is now one of the largest committees and one of the most sought-after assignments in Congress. It was expanded last year from 32 to 45 members after almost a fourth of the House requested a seat.

The committee is chaired by 79-year-old Claude Pepper, a Democrat from Dade County who has proved to be one of the most successful legislators on the Hill. . . . Pepper was responsible for the bill that abolished mandatory retirement from federal employment at 70 and raised the age limit from 65 to 70 in private employment. "We've had good luck with other legislation too," he said in an interview, referring to housing and home health-care bills for the elderly.

By contrast, Pepper said, youth-oriented legislation has had a hard time finding support. Recently he fought against a bill that would have made certain expenditures—child care, shelter, and medical costs—nondeductible from income when determining eligibility for food stamps. If passed as written, the bill would have disqualified many families and elderly people. Pepper was able to protect the elderly from the proposed cuts, but not young families.

Further proof that the tide is shifting in favor of the old is the fate of a proposal for a federally funded national child care program. Advocates have all but given up on the bill. Its sponsor, Senator Alan Cranston (D-Calif.), has not scheduled hearings because the political climate is too adverse.

The political power of the elderly is, as one would expect, particularly evident in Florida, where almost a third of the ballots are cast by seniors. In Broward County the figures are even more startling. An aide of Representative Edward Stack, who at 69 is the oldest freshman in the House, estimated that half of the voters who turned out in his district in the fall of 1977 were 65 or over. The state, moreover, has some very determined lobbyists for the elderly. "There are numerous, excellent elderly advocacy groups. They do their homework, and when they address an issue they are well prepared," said Betty Lou Barbieri of the Community Action Agency in Dade County. "Would that I could say that of the advocacy groups for children."

The two most effective lobbying groups are the American Association of Retired Persons, to which nearly half of Florida's retired people belong, and its parent organization, the American Retired Teachers Association,

which has put forward proposals that have sometimes sparked the ire of the rest of the population. In one community, residents of a project for the elderly demanded that a traffic light be installed, even though one existed a block away, and the new light would have meant terrible traffic snarls. In Dade County, after a group of senior citizens demanded reduced cab fare for elders, the *Miami Herald* objected in an editorial that such a subsidy "would discriminate against all persons under 65. They could not use the service, regardless of need, yet would have to subsidize the elderly, all of whom would be eligible, also regardless of need."

To be fair, elderly advocacy groups have also been instrumental in passing legislation that benefits society as a whole. Thanks to the elderly lobby, Florida is the first state to require pharmacists to inform customers about less expensive generic alternatives to brand-name prescription drugs. Largely because of the elderly lobbyists, too, the state has revoked a ban on advertising by optometrists, thereby encouraging price competition. It has also outlawed the 99-year recreational lease that forced many condominium buyers to pay gigantic fees for use of pools and gyms.

The best hopes for a happy resolution to the old versus young conflict lie precisely at the intersection of self-interest and public interest. Advocates of state-subsidized day care, for instance, scored a victory in Florida, although such programs are being cut back in many states. Advocates in the state persuaded legislators that "day care is not a youth issue; it is an economic and labor-related issue," according to Phoebe Carpenter, coordinator of community child care in central Florida. Her group had produced a study which showed that when adequate day care is available, welfare case loads drop by 50 percent and family income rises, thus easing the tax burden for other citizens. By couching the argument in those terms, Carpenter said, "We lost some supporters and won others. We lost do-gooders and won bankers and chambers of commerce. We lost the liberals and won conservatives."

Similar arguments are likely to be made by other advocates for children and youth in the coming years. Instead of talking in terms of children's needs and appealing for sympathy, they will talk of taxpayer benefits.

Appeals to a sense of fairness and social justice worked politically in the expansive civil-rights Sixties and ceased to be effective in the "era of limits" decade just ended. But the Eighties could turn out to be a time of synthesis, when self-interest demands the well-being of the entire body social—including both the old and the young.

XII

DEVIANCE
What Does It Mean?

Deviance is one of the most myth-laden of social issues. The trouble with myths is that they often contain a grain of truth, which can make their distortions difficult to demonstrate. Most often, myths are simplistic explanations based on a person's particular set of biases.

One common myth is based on the idea that crime is genetic; that is, that there is a relationship between the committing of crime and one's race, or that criminals reflect a distinctive physical type. In fact crime, like all human behavior, is learned—there is no monopoly on crime by any race, ethnic group, or physical type; we all commit crimes.

Another myth concerns the kind and amount of crimes being committed. The mass media concentrate on crimes that elicit reader/listener interest—crime against persons. In fact, F.B.I. reports show that most crime is against property.

Equally misleading is the myth that crime rates are increasing. It's true that crime statistics appear to show an increase, but they do not tell the whole story. Some of the increase simply reflects improved methods of data collection.

A final myth expounds the idea that punishment and incarceration reduce crime. When we consider the high incidence of repeated criminal behavior despite severe punishment, we can conclude that apparently there is little or no relationship between incarceration and the reduction of crime.

As we noted, however, all of these popular myths do contain a grain of truth. For example, blacks do have a higher crime rate in some of the more publicized crimes, and incarcerating criminals does reduce crimes against the public—as least while they are in prison. When we take this type of information out of context, however, we create myths that can be very difficult to disprove.

In the first article, Rosenhan deals with another aspect of these myths—the official definitions of deviance. He notes how labeling a person as deviant causes him to be seen as deviant even if he is not. More importantly, once labeled as such, he will never again be considered "normal," despite normal behavior. It would seem then that the label defines the action rather than the action speaking for itself. When reading this article, think about other "deviancies" that may be artifacts of a label.

McCarthy, in the second article of this chapter, also deals with the myth of how deviance is created. However, the source this time is a direct result of our culture—a culture that emphasizes a male behavior pattern more stereotypical than real but that nonetheless is real in its consequences: the depersonalization of women. This article is an example of the outcome of a seemingly harmless belief. Can you think of other "harmless" beliefs? How would you deal with them?

The final article turns from the sources of deviance to the myth regarding the treatment of the deviant—treatment that sometimes seems to create further deviance. In this case, the issue may be even more significant, since the deviant is a juvenile and we are dealing with the possibility of a lifelong career of crime. In reading this article you may want to ask yourself whether such a system is good or bad, and whether it is also a good way to treat adult criminals.

34

ON BEING SANE IN INSANE PLACES

D. L. Rosenhan

If sanity and insanity exist, how shall we know them?

The question is neither capricious nor itself insane. However much we may be personally convinced that we can tell the normal from the abnormal, the evidence is simply not compelling. It is commonplace, for example, to read about murder trials wherein eminent psychiatrists for the defense are contradicted by equally eminent psychiatrists for the prosecution on the matter of the defendant's sanity. More generally, there are a great deal of conflicting data on the reliability, utility, and meaning of such terms as "sanity," "insanity," "mental illness," and "schizophrenia."[1] Finally, as early as 1934, Benedict suggested that normality and abnormality are not universal.[2] What is viewed as normal in one culture may be seen as quite aberrant in another. Thus, notions of normality and abnormality may not be quite as accurate as people believe they are.

To raise questions regarding normality and abnormality is in no way to question the fact that some behaviors are deviant or odd. Murder is deviant. So, too, are hallucinations. Nor does raising such questions deny the existence of the personal anguish that is often associated with "mental illness." Anxiety and depression exist. Psychological suffering exists. But normality and abnormality, sanity and insanity, and the diagnoses that flow from them may be less substantive than many believe them to be.

At its heart, the question of whether the sane can be distinguished from the insane (and whether degrees of insanity can be distinguished from each other) is a simple matter: do the salient characteristics that lead to diagnoses reside in the patients themselves or in the environments and contexts in which observers find them? From Bleuler, through Kretchmer, through the formulators of the recently revised *Diagnostic and Statistical Manual* of the American Psychiatric Association, the belief has been strong that patients present symptoms, that those symptoms can be categorized, and, implicitly, that the sane are distinguishable from the insane. More recently, however, this belief has been questioned. Based in part on theoretical and anthropological considerations, but also on philosophical, legal, and therapeutic ones, the view has grown that psychological categorization of mental illness is useless at best and downright harmful, misleading, and pejorative at worst. Psychiatric diagnoses, in this view, are in the minds of the observers and are not valid summaries of characteristics displayed by the observed.[3,4,5]

Reprinted by permission from *Science*, Vol. 179, January 19, 1973, pp. 250–258. Copyright © 1973 by the American Association for the Advancement of Science.

Gains can be made in deciding which of these is more nearly accurate by getting normal people (that is, people who do not have, and have never suffered, symptoms of serious psychiatric disorders) admitted to psychiatric hospitals and then determining whether they were discovered to be sane and, if so, how. If the sanity of such pseudopatients were always detected, there would be prima facie evidence that a sane individual can be distinguished from the insane context in which he is found. Normality (and presumably abnormality) is distinct enough that it can be recognized wherever it occurs, for it is carried within the person. If on the other hand, the sanity of the pseudopatients were never discovered, serious difficulties would arise for those who support traditional modes of psychiatric diagnosis. Given that the hospital staff was not incompetent, that the pseudopatient had been behaving as sanely as he had been outside of the hospital, and that it had never been previously suggested that he belonged in a psychiatric hospital, such an unlikely outcome would support the view that psychiatric diagnosis betrays little about the patient but much about the environment in which an observer finds him.

This article describes such an experiment. Eight sane people gained secret admission to 12 different hospitals.[6] Their diagnostic experiences constitute the data of the first part of this article; the remainder is devoted to a description of their experiences in psychiatric institutions. Too few psychiatrists and psychologists, even those who have worked in such hospitals, know what the experience is like. They rarely talk about it with former patients, perhaps because they distrust information coming from the previously insane. Those who have worked in psychiatric hospitals are likely to have adapted so thoroughly to the settings that they are insensitive to the impact of that experience. And while there have been occasional reports of researchers who submitted themselves to psychiatric hospitalization,[7] these researchers have commonly remained in the hospitals for short periods of time, often with the knowledge of the hospital staff. It is difficult to know the extent to which they were treated like patients or like research colleagues. Nevertheless, their reports about the inside of the psychiatric hospital have been valuable. This article extends those efforts.

PSEUDOPATIENTS AND THEIR SETTINGS

The eight pseudopatients were a varied group. One was a psychology graduate student in his 20's. The remaining seven were older and "established." Among them were three psychologists, a pediatrician, a psychiatrist, a painter, and a housewife. Three pseudopatients were women, five were men. All of them employed pseudonyms, lest their alleged diagnoses embarrass them later. Those who were in mental health professions alleged another occupation in order to avoid the special attentions that might be accorded by staff, as a matter of courtesy or caution, to ailing colleagues.[8] With the exception of myself (I was the first pseudopatient and my presence was known to the hospital administrator and chief psychologist and, so far as I can tell, to them alone), the presence of pseudopatients and the nature of the research program was not known to the hospital staff.[9]

The settings were similarly varied. In order to generalize the findings, admission into a variety of hospitals was sought. The 12 hospitals in the sample were located in five different states on the East and West coasts. Some were old and shabby, some were quite new. Some were research-oriented, others not. Some had good staff-patient ratios, others were quite understaffed. Only one was a strictly private hospital. All of the others were supported by state or federal funds or, in one instance, by university funds.

After calling the hospital for an appointment, the pseudopatient arrived at the admissions office complaining that he had been hearing voices. Asked what the voices said, he replied that they were often unclear, but as far as he could tell they said "empty," "hollow," and "thud." The voices were unfamiliar and were of the same sex as the pseudopatient. The choice of these symptoms was occasioned by their apparent similarity to existential symptoms. Such symptoms are alleged to arise from painful concerns about the perceived meaninglessness of one's life. It is as if the hallucinating person were saying, "My life is empty and hollow." The choice of these symptoms was also determined by the *absence* of a single report of existential psychoses in the literature.

Beyond alleging the symptoms and falsifying name, vocation, and employment, no further alterations of person, history, or circumstances were made. The significant events of the pseudopatient's life history were presented as they had actually occurred. Relationships with parents and siblings, with spouse and children, with people at work and in school, consistent with the aforementioned exceptions, were described as they were or had been. Frustrations and upsets were described along with joys and satisfactions. These facts are important to remember. If anything, they strongly biased the subsequent results in favor of detecting sanity, since none of their histories or current behaviors were seriously pathological in any way.

Immediately upon admission to the psychiatric ward, the pseudopatient ceased simulating *any* symptoms of abnormality. In some cases, there was a brief period of mild nervousness and anxiety, since none of the pseudopatients really believed that they would be admitted so easily. Indeed, their shared fear was that they would be immediately exposed as frauds and greatly embarrassed. Moreover, many of them had never visited a psychiatric ward; even those who had, nevertheless had some genuine fears about what might happen to them. Their nervousness, then, was quite appropriate to the novelty of the hospital setting, and it abated rapidly.

Apart from that short-lived nervousness, the pseudopatient behaved on the ward as he "normally" behaved. The pseudopatient spoke to patients and staff as he might ordinarily. Because there is uncommonly little to do on a psychiatric ward, he attempted to engage others in conversation. When asked by staff how he was feeling, he indicated that he was fine, that he no longer experienced symptoms. He responded to instructions from attendants, to calls for medication (which was not swallowed), and to dining-hall instructions. Beyond such activities as were available to him on the admissions ward, he spent his time writing down his observations about the ward, its patients, and the staff. Initially these notes were written "secretly," but as it soon became clear that no one much cared, they were subsequently written on standard tablets of paper in such public places as the dayroom. No secret was made of these activities.

The pseudopatient, very much as a true psychiatric patient, entered a hospital with no foreknowledge of when he would be discharged. Each was told that he would have to get out by his own devices, essentially by convincing the staff that he was sane. The psychological stresses associated with hospitalization were considerable, and all but one of the pseudopatients desired to be discharged immediately after being admitted. They were, therefore, motivated not only to behave sanely, but to be paragons of cooperation. That their behavior was in no way disruptive is confirmed by nursing reports, which have been obtained on most of the patients. These reports uniformly indicate that the patients were "friendly," "cooperative," and "exhibited no abnormal indications."

THE NORMAL ARE NOT DETECTABLY SANE

Despite their public "show" of sanity, the pseudopatients were never detected. Admitted, except in one case, with a diagnosis of schizophrenia,[10] each was discharged with a diagnosis of schizophrenia "in remission." The label "in remission" should in no way be dismissed as a formality, for at no time during any hospitalization had any question been raised about any pseudopatient's simulation. Nor are there any indications in the hospital records that the pseudopatient's status was suspect. Rather, the evidence is strong that, once labeled schizophrenic, the pseudopatient was stuck with that label. If the pseudopatient was to be discharged, he must naturally be "in remission"; but he was not sane, nor, in the institution's view, had he ever been sane.

The uniform failure to recognize sanity cannot be attributed to the quality of the hospitals, for, although there were considerable variations among them, several are considered excellent. Nor can it be alleged that there was simply not enough time to observe the pseudopatients. Length of hospitalization ranged from 7 to 52 days, with an average of 19 days. The pseudopatients were not, in fact, carefully observed, but this failure clearly speaks more to traditions within psychiatric hospitals than to lack of opportunity.

Finally, it cannot be said that the failure to recognize the pseudopatients' sanity was due to the fact that they were not behaving sanely. While there was clearly some tension present in all of them, their daily visitors could detect no serious behavioral consequences—nor, indeed, could other patients. It was quite common for the patients to "detect" the pseudopatients' sanity. During the first three hospitalizations, when accurate counts were kept, 35 of a total of 118 patients on the admissions ward voiced their suspicions, some vigorously. "You're not crazy. You're a journalist, or a professor [referring to the continual note-taking]. You're checking up on the hospital." While most of the patients were reassured by the pseudopatient's insistence that he had been sick before he came in but was fine now, some continued to believe that the pseudopatient was sane throughout his hospitalization.[11] The fact that the patients often recognized normality when staff did not raises important questions.

Failure to detect sanity during the course of hospitalization may be due to the fact that physicians operate with a strong bias toward what statisticians call the type 2 error.[5] This is to say that physicians are more inclined to call a healthy person sick (a false positive, type 2) than a sick person healthy (a false negative, type 1). The reasons for this are not hard to find: it is clearly more dangerous to misdiagnose illness than health. Better to err on the side of caution, to suspect illness even among the healthy.

But what holds for medicine does not hold equally well for psychiatry. Medical illnesses, while unfortunate, are not commonly pejorative. Psychiatric diagnoses, on the contrary, carry with them personal, legal, and social stigmas.[12] It was therefore important to see whether the tendency toward diagnosing the sane insane could be reversed. The following experiment was arranged at a research and teaching hospital whose staff had heard these findings but doubted that such an error could occur in their hospital. The staff was informed that at some time during the following 3 months, one or more pseudopatients would attempt to be admitted into the psychiatric hospital. Each staff member was asked to rate each patient who presented himself at admission or on the ward according to the likelihood that the patient was a pseudopatient. A 10-point scale was used, with a 1 and 2 reflecting high confidence that the patient was a pseudopatient.

Judgments were obtained on 193 patients who were admitted for psychiatric treatment. All staff who had had sustained contact with or primary responsibility for the patient—attendants, nurses, psychiatrists, physicians, and psychologists—were asked to make judgments. Forty-one patients were alleged, with high confidence, to be pseudopatients by at least one member of the staff. Twenty-three were considered suspect by at least one psychiatrist. Nineteen were suspected by one psychiatrist *and* one other staff member. Actually, no genuine pseudopatient (at least from my group) presented himself during this period.

The experiment is instructive. It indicates that the tendency to designate sane people as insane can be reversed when the stakes (in this case, prestige and diagnostic acumen) are high. But what can be said of the 19 people who were suspected of being "sane" by one psychiatrist and another staff member? Were these people truly "sane," or was it rather the case that in the course of avoiding the type 2 error the staff tended to make more errors of the first sort—calling the crazy "sane"? There is no way of knowing. But one thing is certain: any diagnostic process that lends itself so readily to massive errors of this sort cannot be a very reliable one.

THE STICKINESS OF PSYCHODIAGNOSTIC LABELS

Beyond the tendency to call the healthy sick—a tendency that accounts better for diagnostic behavior on admission than it does for such behavior after a lengthy period of exposure—the data speak to the massive role of labeling in psychiatric assessment. Having once been labeled schizophrenic, there is nothing the pseudopatient can do to overcome the tag. The tag profoundly colors others' perceptions of him and his behavior.

From one viewpoint, these data are hardly surprising, for it has long been known that elements are given meaning by the context in which they occur. Gestalt psychology made this point vigorously, and Asch[13] demonstrated that there are "central" personality traits (such as "warm" versus "cold") which are so powerful that they markedly color the meaning of other information in forming an impression of a given personality.[14] "Insane," "schizophrenic," "manic-depressive," and "crazy" are probably among the most powerful of such central traits. Once a person is designated abnormal, all of his other behav-

iors and characteristics are colored by that label. Indeed, that label is so powerful that many of the pseudopatients' normal behaviors were overlooked entirely or profoundly misinterpreted. Some examples may clarify this issue.

Earlier I indicated that there were no changes in the pseudopatient's personal history and current status beyond those of name, employment, and, where necessary, vocation. Otherwise, a veridical description of personal history and circumstances was offered. Those circumstances were not psychotic. How were they made consonant with the diagnosis of psychosis? Or were those diagnoses modified in such a way as to bring them into accord with the circumstances of the pseudopatient's life, as described by him?

As far as I can determine, diagnoses were in no way affected by the relative health of the circumstances of a pseudopatient's life. Rather, the reverse occurred: the perception of his circumstances was shaped entirely by the diagnosis. A clear example of such translation is found in the case of a pseudopatient who had had a close relationship with his mother but was rather remote from his father during his early childhood. During adolescence and beyond, however, his father became a close friend, while his relationship with his mother cooled. His present relationship with his wife was characteristically close and warm. Apart from occasional angry exchanges, friction was minimal. The children had rarely been spanked. Surely there is nothing especially pathological about such a history. Indeed, many readers may see a similar pattern in their own experiences, with no markedly deleterious consequences. Observe, however, how such a history was translated in the psychopathological context, this from the case summary prepared after the patient was discharged.

This white 39-year-old male . . . manifests a long history of considerable ambivalence in close relationships, which begins in early childhood. A warm relationship with his mother cools during his adolescence. A distant relationship to his father is described as becoming very intense. Affective stability is absent. His attempts to control emotionality with his wife and children are punctuated by angry outbursts and, in the case of the children, spankings. And while he says that he has several good friends, one senses considerable ambivalence embedded in those relationships also. . . .

The facts of the case were unintentionally distorted by the staff to achieve consistency with a popular theory of the dynamics of a schizophrenic reaction.[15] Nothing of an ambivalent nature had been described in relations with parents, spouse, or friends. To the extent that ambivalence could be inferred, it was probably not greater than is found in all human relationships. It is true the pseudo-patient's relationships with his parents changed over time, but in the ordinary context that would hardly be remarkable—indeed, it might very well be expected. Clearly, the meaning ascribed to his verbalizations (that is, ambivalence, affective instability) was determined by the diagnosis: schizophrenia. An entirely different meaning would have been ascribed if it were known that the man was "normal."

All pseudopatients took extensive notes publicly. Under ordinary circumstances, such behavior would have raised questions in the minds of observers, as, in fact, it did among patients. Indeed, it seemed so certain that the notes would elicit suspicion that elaborate precautions were taken to remove them from the ward each day. But the precautions proved needless. The closest any staff member came to questioning these notes occurred when one pseudopatient asked his physician what kind of medication he was receiving and began to write down the response. "You needn't write it," he was told gently. "If you have trouble remembering, just ask me again."

If no questions were asked of the pseudopatients, how was their writing interpreted? Nursing records for three patients indicate that the writing was seen as an aspect of their pathological behavior. "Patient engages in writing behavior" was the daily nursing comment on one of the pseudopatients who was never questioned about his writing. Given that the patient is in the hospital, he must be psychologically disturbed. And given that he is disturbed, continuous writing must be a behavioral manifestation of that disturbance, perhaps a subset of the compulsive behaviors that are sometimes correlated with schizophrenia.

One tacit characteristic of psychiatric diagnosis is that it locates the sources of aberration within the individual and only rarely within the complex of stimuli that surrounds him. Consequently, behaviors that are stimulated by the environment are commonly misattributed to the patient's disorder. For example, one kindly nurse found a pseudopatient pacing the long hospital corridors. "Nervous, Mr. X?" she asked. "No, bored," he said.

The notes kept by pseudopatients are full of patient behaviors that were misinterpreted by well-intentioned staff. Often enough, a patient would go "berserk" because he had, wittingly or unwittingly, been mistreated by, say, an attendant. A nurse coming upon the scene would rarely inquire even cursorily into the environmental stimuli of the patient's behavior. Rather, she assumed that his upset derived from his pathology, not from his present interactions with other staff members. Occasionally, the staff might assume that the patient's family (especially when they had recently visited) or other patients had stimulated the outburst. But never were the staff found to assume that one of themselves or the structure of the hospital had anything to do with a patient's behavior. One psychiatrist pointed to a group of patients who were sitting outside the cafeteria entrance half an hour before lunchtime. To a group of young residents he indicated that such behavior was characteristic of the oral-acquisitive nature of the syndrome. It seemed not to occur to him that there were very few things to anticipate in a psychiatric hospital besides eating.

A psychiatric label has a life and an influence of its own. Once the impression has been formed that the patient is schizophrenic, the expectation is that he will continue to be schizophrenic. When a sufficient amount of time has passed, during which the patient has done nothing bizarre, he is considered to be in remission and available for discharge. But the label endures beyond discharge, with the unconfirmed expectation that he will behave as a schizophrenic again. Such labels, conferred by mental health professionals, are as influential on the patient as they are on his relatives and friends, and it should not surprise anyone that the diagnosis acts on all of them as a self-fulfilling prophecy. Eventually, the patient himself accepts the diagnosis, with all of its surplus meanings and expectations, and behaves accordingly.[5]

The inferences to be made from these matters are quite simple. Much as Zigler and Phillips have demonstrated that there is enormous overlap in the symptoms presented by patients who have been variously diagnosed,[16] so there is enormous overlap in the behaviors of the sane and the insane. The sane are not "sane" all of the time. We lose our tempers "for no good reason." We are occasionally depressed or anxious, again for no good reason. And we may find it difficult to get along with one or another person—again for no reason that we can specify. Similarly, the insane are not always insane. Indeed, it was the impression of the pseudopatients while living with them that they were sane for long periods of time—that the bizarre behaviors upon which their diagnoses were allegedly predicated constituted only a small fraction of their total behavior. If it makes no sense to label ourselves permanently depressed on the basis of an occasional depression, then it takes better evidence than is presently available to label all patients insane or schizophrenic on the basis of bizarre behaviors or cognitions. It seems more useful, as Mischel[17] has pointed out, to limit our discussion to *behaviors*, the stimuli that provoke them, and their correlates.

It is not known why powerful impressions of personality traits, such as "crazy" or "insane," arise. Conceivably, when the origins of and stimuli that give rise to a behavior are remote or unknown, or when the behavior strikes us as immutable, trait labels regarding the *behaver* arise. When, on the other hand, the origins and stimuli are known and available, discourse is limited to the behavior itself. Thus, I may hallucinate because I am sleeping, or I may hallucinate because I have ingested a peculiar drug. These are termed sleep-induced hallucinations, or dreams, and drug-induced hallucinations, respectively. But when the stimuli to my hallucinations are unknown, that is called craziness, or schizophrenia—as if that inference were somehow as illuminating as the others.

THE EXPERIENCE OF PSYCHIATRIC HOSPITALIZATION

The term "mental illness" is of recent origin. It was coined by people who were humane in their inclinations and who wanted very much to raise the station of (and the public's sympathies toward) the psychologically disturbed from that of witches and "crazies" to one that was akin to the physically ill. And they were at least partially successful, for the treatment of the mentally ill *has* improved considerably over the years. But while treatment has improved, it is doubtful that people really regard the mentally ill in the same way that they view the physically ill. A broken leg is something one recovers from, but mental illness allegedly endures forever.[18] A broken leg does not threaten the observer, but a crazy schizophrenic? There is by now a host of evidence that attitudes toward the mentally ill are characterized by fear, hostility, aloofness, suspicion, and dread.[19] The mentally ill are society's lepers.

That such attitudes infect the general population is perhaps not surprising, only upsetting. But that they affect the professionals—attendants, nurses, physicians, psychologists, and social workers—who treat and deal with the mentally ill is more disconcerting, both because such attitudes are self-evidently pernicious and because they are unwitting. Most mental health professionals would insist that they are sympathetic toward the mentally ill, that they are neither avoidant nor hostile. But it is more likely that an exquisite ambivalence characterizes their relations with psychiatric patients, such that their avowed impulses are only part of their entire attitude. Negative attitudes are there too and can easily be detected. Such attitudes should not surprise us. They are the natural offspring of the labels patients wear and the places in which they are found.

Consider the structure of the typical psychiatric hospital. Staff and patients are strictly segregated. Staff have their own living space, including their dining facilities, bathrooms, and assembly places. The glassed quarters that contain the professional staff, which the pseudopatients came to call "the cage," sit out on every dayroom. The staff emerge primarily for caretaking purposes—to give medication, to conduct a therapy or group meeting, to instruct or reprimand a patient. Otherwise, staff keep to themselves, almost as if the disorder that afflicts their charges is somehow catching.

So much is patient-staff segregation the rule that, for four public hospitals in which an attempt was made to measure the degree to which staff and patients mingle, it was necessary to use "time out of the staff cage" as the operational measure. While it was not the case that all time spent out of the cage was spent mingling with patients (attendants, for example, would occasionally emerge to watch television in the dayroom), it was the only way in which one could gather reliable data on time for measuring.

The average amount of time spent by attendants outside of the cage was 11.3 percent (range, 3 to 52 percent). This figure does not represent only time spent mingling with patients, but also includes time spent on such chores as folding laundry, supervising patients while they shave, directing ward cleanup, and sending patients to off-ward activities. It was the relatively rare attendant who spent time talking with patients or playing games with them. It proved impossible to obtain a "percent mingling time" for nurses, since the amount of time they spent out of the cage was too brief. Rather, we counted instances of emergence from the cage. On the average, daytime nurses emerged from the cage 11.5 times per shift, including instances when they left the ward entirely (range, 4 to 39 times). Late afternoon and night nurses were even less available, emerging on the average 9.4 times per shift (range, 4 to 41 times). Data on early morning nurses, who arrived usually after midnight and departed at 8 a.m., are not available because patients were asleep during most of this period.

Physicians, especially psychiatrists, were even less available. They were rarely seen on the wards. Quite commonly, they would be seen only when they arrived and departed, with the remaining time being spent in their offices or in the cage. On the average, physicians emerged on the ward 6.7 times per day (range, 1 to 17 times). It proved difficult to make an accurate estimate in this regard, since physicians often maintained hours that allowed them to come and go at different times.

The hierarchical organization of the psychiatric hospital has been commented on before,[20] but the latent meaning of that kind of organization is worth noting again. Those with the most power have least to do with patients, and those with the least power are most involved with them. Recall, however, that the acquisition of role-appropriate behaviors occurs mainly through the observation of others, with the most powerful having the most influence. Consequently, it is understandable that attendants not only spend more time with patients than do any other members of the staff—that is required by their station in the hierarchy—but also, insofar as they learn from their superiors' behavior, spend as little time with patients as they can. Attendants are seen mainly in the cage, which is where the models, the action, and the power are.

I turn now to a different set of studies, these dealing with staff response to patient-initiated contact. It has long been known that the amount of time a person spends with you can be an index of your significance to him. If he initiates and maintains eye contact, there is reason to believe that he is considering your requests and needs. If he pauses to chat or actually stops and talks, there is added reason to infer that he is individuating you. In four hospitals, the pseudopatient approached the staff member with a request which took the following form: "Pardon me, Mr. [or Dr. or Mrs.] X, could you tell me when I will be eligible for grounds privileges?" (or ". . . when I will be presented at the staff meeting?" or ". . . when I am likely to be discharged?"). While the content of the question varied according to the appropriateness of the target and the pseudopatient's (apparent) current needs the form was always a courteous and relevant request for information. Care was taken never to approach a particular member of the staff more than once a day, lest the staff member become suspicious or irritated. In examining these data, remember that the behavior of the pseudopatients was neither bizarre nor disruptive. One could indeed engage in good conversation with them.

The data for these experiments are shown in Table 1, separately for physicians (column 1) and for nurses and attendants (column 2). Minor differences between these four institutions were overwhelmed by the degree to which staff avoided continuing contacts that patients had initiated. By far, their most common response consisted of either a brief response to the question, offered while they were "on the move" and with head averted, or no response at all.

The encounter frequently took the following bizarre form: (pseudopatient) "Pardon

TABLE 1.
SELF-INITIATED CONTACT BY PSEUDOPATIENTS WITH PSYCHIATRISTS AND
NURSES AND ATTENDANTS COMPARED TO CONTACT WITH OTHER GROUPS

Contact	(1) Psychiatrists	(2) Nurses And Attendants	University Campus (nonmedical) (3) Faculty	University Medical Center Physicians (4) "Looking For A Psychiatrist"	(5) "Looking For An Internist"	(6) No Additional Comment
Responses						
Moves on, head averted (%)	71	88	0	0	0	0
Makes eye contact (%)	23	10	0	11	0	0
Pauses and chats (%)	2	2	0	11	0	10
Stops and talks (%)	4	0.5	100	78	100	90
Mean number of questions answered (out of 6)	[1]	[1]	6	3.8	4.8	4.5
Respondents (No.)	13	47	14	18	15	10
Attempts (No.)	185	1283	14	18	15	10

[1]Not applicable.

me, Dr. X. Could you tell me when I am eligible for grounds privileges?" (physician) "Good morning, Dave. How are you today?" (Moves off without waiting for a response.)

It is instructive to compare these data with data recently obtained at Stanford University. It has been alleged that large and eminent universities are characterized by faculty who are so busy that they have no time for students. For this comparison, a young lady approached individual faculty members who seemed to be walking purposefully to some meeting or teaching engagement and asked them the following six questions.

1. "Pardon me, could you direct me to Encina Hall?" (at the medical school: ". . . to the Clinical Research Center?").
2. "Do you know where Fish Annex is?" (there is no Fish Annex at Stanford).
3. "Do you teach here?"
4. "How does one apply for admission to the college?" (at the medical school: ". . . to the medical school?").
5. "Is it difficult to get in?"
6. "Is there financial aid?"

Without exception, as can be seen in Table 1 (column 3), all of the questions were answered. No matter how rushed they were, all respondents not only maintained eye contact, but stopped to talk. Indeed, many of the respondents went out of their way to direct or take the questioner to the office she was seeking, to try to locate "Fish Annex," or to discuss with her the possibilities of being admitted to the university.

Similar data, also shown in Table 1 (columns 4, 5, and 6), were obtained in the hospital. Here too, the young lady came prepared with six questions. After the first question, however, she remarked to 18 of her respondents (column 4), "I'm looking for a psychiatrist," and to 15 others (column 5), "I'm looking for an internist." Ten other respondents received no inserted comment (column 6). The general degree of cooperative responses is considerably higher for these university groups than it was for pseudopatients in psychiatric hospitals. Even so, differences are apparent within the medical school setting. Once having indicated that she was looking for a psychiatrist, the degree of cooperation elicited was less than when she sought an internist.

POWERLESSNESS AND DEPERSONALIZATION

Eye contact and verbal contact reflect concern and individuation; their absence, avoidance and depersonalization. The data I have presented do not do justice to the rich daily encounters that grew up around matters of depersonalization and avoidance. I have records of patients who were beaten by staff for the sin of having initiated verbal contact. During my own experience, for example, one patient was beaten in the presence of other patients for having approached an attendant and told him, "I like you." Occasionally, punishment meted out to patients for misdemeanors seemed so excessive that it could not be justified by the most radical interpretations of psychiatric canon. Nevertheless, they appeared to go unquestioned. Tempers were often short. A patient who had not heard a call for medication would be roundly excoriated, and the morning attendants would often wake patients with, "Come on, you m-----f-----s, out of bed!"

Neither anecdotal nor "hard" data can convey the overwhelming sense of powerlessness which invades the individual as he is continually exposed to the depersonalization of the psychiatric hospital. It hardly matters *which* psychiatric hospital—the excellent public ones and the very plush private hospital were better than the rural and shabby ones in this regard, but, again, the features that psychiatric hospitals had in common overwhelmed by far their apparent differences.

Powerlessness was evident everywhere. The patient is deprived of many of his legal rights by dint of his psychiatric commitment.[21] He is shorn of credibility by virtue of his psychiatric label. His freedom of movement is restricted. He cannot initiate contact with the staff, but may only respond to such overtures as they make. Personal privacy is minimal. Patient quarters and possessions can be entered and examined by any staff member, for whatever reason. His personal history and anguish is available to any staff member (often including the "grey lady" and "candy striper" volunteer) who chooses to read his folder, regardless of their therapeutic relationship to him. His personal hygiene and waste evacuation are often monitored. The water closets may have no doors.

At times, depersonalization reached such proportions that pseudopatients had the sense that they were invisible, or at least unworthy of account. Upon being admitted, I and other pseudopatients took the initial physical examinations in a semipublic room, where staff members went about their own business as if we were not there.

On the ward, attendants delivered verbal and occasionally serious physical abuse to patients in the presence of other observing patients, some of whom (the pseudopatients) were writing it all down. Abusive behavior, on the other hand, terminated quite abruptly when other staff members were known to be coming. Staff are credible witnesses. Patients are not.

A nurse unbuttoned her uniform to adjust her brassiere in the presence of an entire ward of viewing men. One did not have the sense that she was being seductive. Rather, she didn't notice us. A group of staff persons might point to a patient in the dayroom and discuss him animatedly, as if he were not there.

One illuminating instance of depersonalization and invisibility occurred with regard to medications. All told, the pseudopatients were administered nearly 2100 pills, including Elavil, Stelazine, Compazine, and Thorazine, to name but a few. (That such a variety of medications should have been administered to patients presenting identical symptoms is

itself worthy of note.) Only two were swallowed. The rest were either pocketed or deposited in the toilet. The pseudopatients were not alone in this. Although I have no precise records on how many patients rejected their medications, the pseudopatients frequently found the medications of other patients in the toilet before they deposited their own. As long as they were cooperative, their behavior and the pseudopatients' own in this matter, as in other important matters, went unnoticed throughout.

Reactions to such depersonalization among pseudopatients were intense. Although they had come to the hospital as participant observers and were fully aware that they did not "belong," they nevertheless found themselves caught up in and fighting the process of depersonalization. Some examples: a graduate student in psychology asked his wife to bring his textbooks to the hospital so he could "catch up on his homework"—this despite the elaborate precautions taken to conceal his professional association. The same student, who had trained for quite some time to get into the hospital, and who had looked forward to the experience, "remembered" some drag races that he had wanted to see on the weekend and insisted that he be discharged by that time. Another pseudopatient attempted a romance with a nurse. Subsequently he informed the staff that he was applying for admission to graduate school in psychology and was very likely to be admitted, since a graduate professor was one of his regular hospital visitors. The same person began to engage in psychotherapy with other patients—all of this as a way of becoming a person in an impersonal environment.

THE SOURCES OF DEPERSONALIZATION

What are the origins of depersonalization? I have already mentioned two. First are attitudes held by all of us toward the mentally ill—including those who treat them—attitudes characterized by fear, distrust, and horrible expectations on the one hand, and benevolent intentions on the other. Our ambivalence leads, in this instance as in others, to avoidance.

Second, and not entirely separate, the hierarchical structure of the psychiatric hospital facilitates depersonalization. Those who are at the top have least to do with patients, and their behavior inspires the rest of the staff. Average daily contact with psychiatrists, psychologists, residents, and physicians combined ranged from 3.9 to 25.1 minutes, with an overall mean of 6.8 (six pseudopatients over a total of 129 days of hospitalization). Included in this average are time spent in the admissions interview, ward meetings in the presence of a senior staff member, group and individual psychotherapy contacts, case presentation conferences, and discharge meetings. Clearly, patients do not spend much time in interpersonal contact with doctoral staff. And doctoral staff serve as models for nurses and attendants.

There are probably other sources. Psychiatric installations are presently in serious financial straits. Staff shortages are pervasive, staff time at a premium. Something has to give, and that something is patient contact. Yet while financial stresses are realities, too much can be made of them. I have the impression that the psychological forces that result in depersonalization are much stronger than the fiscal ones and that the addition of more staff would not correspondingly improve patient care in this regard. The incidence of staff meetings and the enormous amount of record-keeping on patients, for example, have not been as substantially reduced as has patient contact. Priorities exist, even during hard times. Patient contact is not a significant priority in the traditional psychiatric hospital, and fiscal pressures do not account for this. Avoidance and depersonalization may.

Heavy reliance upon psychotropic medication tacitly contributes to depersonalization by convincing staff that treatment is indeed being conducted and that further patient contact may not be necessary. Even here, however, caution needs to be exercised in understanding the role of psychotropic drugs. If patients were powerful rather than powerless, if they were viewed as interesting individuals rather than diagnostic entities, if they were socially significant rather than social lepers, if their anguish truly and wholly compelled our sympathies and concerns, would we not *seek* contact with them, despite the availability of medications? Perhaps for the pleasure of it all?

THE CONSEQUENCES OF LABELING AND DEPERSONALIZATION

Whenever the ratio of what is known to what needs to be known approaches zero, we tend to invent "knowledge" and assume that we understand more than we actually do. We seem unable to acknowledge that we simply don't know. The needs for diagnosis and remediation of behavioral and emotional problems are enormous. But rather than acknowledge that we are just embarking on understanding, we continue to label patients "schizophrenic," "manic-depressive," and "insane," as if in those words we had captured the essence of understanding. The facts of the matter are that we have known for a long time that diagnoses are often not useful or reliable, but we have nevertheless continued to use them. We now know that we cannot distinguish insanity from sanity. It is depressing to consider how that information will be used.

Not merely depressing, but frightening. How many people, one wonders, are sane but not recognized as such in our psychiatric institutions? How many have been needlessly stripped of their privileges of citizenship, from the right to vote and drive to that of handling their own accounts? How many have feigned insanity in order to avoid the criminal consequences of their behavior, and, conversely, how many would rather stand trial than live interminably in a psychiatric hospital—but are wrongly thought to be mentally ill? How many have been stigmatized by well-intentioned, but nevertheless erroneous, diagnoses? On the last point, recall again that a "type 2 error" in psychiatric diagnosis does not have the same consequences it does in medical diagnosis. A diagnosis of cancer that has been found to be in error is cause for celebration. But psychiatric diagnoses are rarely found to be in error. The label sticks, a mark of inadequacy forever.

Finally, how many patients might be "sane" outside the psychiatric hospital but seem insane in it—not because craziness resides in them, as it were, but because they are responding to a bizarre setting, one that may be unique to institutions which harbor nether people? Goffman[4] calls the process of socialization to such institutions "mortification"—an apt metaphor that includes the processes of depersonalization that have been described here. And while it is impossible to know whether the pseudopatients' responses to these processes are characteristic of all inmates—they were, after all, not real patients—it is difficult to believe that these processes of socialization to a psychiatric hospital provide useful attitudes or habits of response for living in the "real world."

SUMMARY AND CONCLUSIONS

It is clear that we cannot distinguish the sane from the insane in psychiatric hospitals. The hospital itself imposes a special environment in which the meanings of behavior can easily be misunderstood. The consequences to patients hospitalized in such an environment—the powerlessness, depersonalization, segregation, mortification, and self-labeling—seem undoubtedly countertherapeutic.

I do not, even now, understand this problem well enough to perceive solutions. But two matters seem to have some promise. The first concerns the proliferation of community mental health facilities, of crisis intervention centers, of the human potential movement, and of behavior therapies that, for all of their own problems, tend to avoid psychiatric labels, to focus on specific problems and behaviors, and to retain the individual in a relatively nonpejorative environment. Clearly, to the extent that we refrain from sending the distressed to insane places, our impressions of them are less likely to be distorted. (The risk of distorted perceptions, it seems to me, is always present, since we are much more sensitive to an individual's behaviors and verbalizations than we are to the subtle contextual stimuli that often promote them. At issue here is a matter of magnitude. And, as I have shown, the magnitude of distortion is exceedingly high in the extreme context that is a psychiatric hospital.)

The second matter that might prove promising speaks to the need to increase the sensitivity of mental health workers and researchers to the *Catch 22* position of psychiatric patients. Simply reading materials in this area will be of help to some such workers and researchers. For others, directly experiencing the impact of psychiatric hospitalization will be of enormous use. Clearly, further research into the social psychology of such total institutions will both facilitate treatment and deepen understanding.

I and the other pseudopatients in the psychiatric setting had distinctly negative reactions. We do not pretend to describe the subjective experiences of true patients. Theirs may be different from ours, particularly with the passage of time and the necessary process of adaptation to one's environment. But we can and do speak to the relatively more objective indices of treatment within the hospital. It could be a mistake, and a very unfortunate one, to consider that what happened to us derived from malice or stupidity on the part of the staff. Quite the contrary, our overwhelming impression of them was of people who really cared, who were committed, and who were uncommonly intelligent. Where they failed, as they sometimes did painfully, it would be more accurate to attribute those failures to the environment in which they, too, found themselves than to personal callousness. Their perceptions and behavior were controlled by the situation, rather than being motivated by a malicious disposition. In a more benign environment, one that was less attached to global diagnosis, their behaviors and judgments might have been more benign and effective.

NOTES

[1] P. Ash, *J. Abnorm. Soc. Psychol.* 44, 272 (1949); A. T. Beck, *Amer. J. Psychiat.* 119, 210 (1962); A. T. Boisen, *Psychiatry* 2, 233 (1938); N. Kreitman, *J. Ment. Sci.* 107, 876 (1961); N. Kreitman, P. Sainsbury, J. Morrisey, J. Towers, J. Scrivener, *ibid.*, p. 887; H. O. Schmitt and C. P. Fonda, *J. Abnorm. Soc. Psychol.* 52, 262 (1956); W. Seeman, *J. Nerv. Ment. Dis.* 118, 541 (1953). For an analysis of these artifacts and summaries of the disputes, see J. Zubin, *Annu. Rev. Psychol.* 18, 373 (1967); L. Phillips and J. G. Draguns, *ibid.* 22, 447 (1971).

[2] R. Benedict, *J. Gen. Psychol.* 10, 59 (1934).

[3] See in this regard H. Becker, *Outsiders: Studies in the Sociology of Deviance* (Free Press, New York, 1963); B. M. Braginsky, D. D. Braginsky, K. Ring, *Methods of Madness: The Mental Hospital as a Last Resort* (Holt, Rinehart & Winston, New York, 1969); G. M. Crocetti and P. V. Lemkau, *Amer. Social. Rev.* 30, 577 (1965); E. Goffman, *Behavior in Public Places* (Free Press, New York, 1964); R. D. Laing, *The Divided Self: A Study of Sanity and Madness* (Quadrangle, Chicago, 1960); D. L. Phillips, *Amer. Sociol. Rev.* 28, 963 (1963); T. R. Sarbin, *Psychol. Today* 6, 18 (1972); E. Schur, *Amer. J. Sociol.* 75, 309 (1969); T. Szasz, *Law, Liberty and Psychiatry* (Macmillan, New York, 1963); *The Myth of Mental Illness: Foundations of a Theory of Mental Illness* (Hoeber Harper, New York, 1963). For a critique of some of these views, see W. R. Gove, *Amer. Sociol. Rev.* 35, 873 (1970).

[4] E. Goffman, *Asylums* (Doubleday, Garden City, N. Y., 1961).

[5] T. J. Scheff, *Being Mentally Ill: A Sociological Theory* (Aldine, Chicago, 1966).

[6] Data from a ninth pseudopatient are not incorporated in this report because, although his sanity went undetected, he falsified aspects of his personal history, including his marital status and parental relationships. His experimental behaviors therefore were not identical to those of the other pseudopatients.

[7] A. Barry, *Bellevue Is a State of Mind* (Harcourt Brace Jovanovich, New York, 1971); I. Belknap, *Human Problems of a State Mental Hospital* (McGraw-Hill, New York, 1956); W. Caudill, F. C. Redlich, H. R. Gilmore, E. B. Brody, *Amer. J. Orthopsychiat.* 22, 314 (1952); A. R. Goldman, R. H. Bohr, T. A. Steinberg, *Prof. Psychol.* 1, 427 (1970); unauthored, *Roche Report 1* (No. 13), 8 (1971).

[8] Beyond the personal difficulties that the pseudopatient is likely to experience in the hospital, there are legal and social ones that, combined, require considerable attention before entry. For example, once admitted to a psychiatric institution, it is difficult, if not impossible, to be discharged on short notice, state law to the contrary notwithstanding. I was not sensitive to these difficulties at the outset of the project, nor to the personal and situational emergencies that can arise, but later a writ of habeas corpus was prepared for each of the entering pseudopatients and an attorney was kept "on call" during every hospitalization. I am grateful to John Kaplan and Robert Bartels for legal advice and assistance in these matters.

[9] However distasteful such concealment is, it was a necessary first step to examining these questions. Without concealment, there would have been no way to know how valid these experiences were; nor was there any way of knowing whether whatever detections occurred were a tribute to the diagnostic acumen of the staff or to the hospital's rumor network. Obviously, since my concerns are general ones that cut across individual hospitals and staffs, I have respected their anonymity and have eliminated clues that might lead to their identification.

[10] Interestingly, of the 12 admissions, 11 were diagnosed as schizophrenic and one, with the identical symptomatology, as manic-depressive psychosis. This diagnosis has a more favorable prognosis, and it was given by the only private hospital in our sample. On the relations between social class and psychiatric diagnosis, see A. deB. Hollingshead and F. C. Redlich, *Social Class and Mental Illness: A Community Study* (Wiley, New York, 1958).

[11] It is possible, of course, that patients have quite broad latitudes in diagnosis and therefore are inclined to call many people sane, even those whose behavior is patently aberrant. However, although we have no hard data on this matter, it was our distinct impression that this was not the case. In many instances, patients not only singled us out for attention, but came to imitate our behaviors and styles.

[12]J. Cumming and E. Cumming, *Community Ment. Health 1*, 135 (1965); A. Farina and K. Ring, *J. Abnorm. Psychol. 70*, 47 (1965); H. E. Freeman and O. G. Simmons, *The Mental Patient Comes Home* (Wiley, New York, 1963); W. J. Johannsen, *Ment. Hygiene 53*, 218 (1969); A. S. Linsky, *Soc. Psychiat. 5*, 1966 (1970).

[13]S. E. Asch, *J. Abnorm. Soc. Psychol. 41*, 258 (1946); *Social Psychology* (Prentice-Hall, New York, 1952).

[14]See also I. N. Mensh and J. Wishner, *J. Personality 16*, 188 (1947); J. Wishner, *Psychol. Rev. 67*, 96 (1960); J. S. Bruner and R. Tagiuri, in *Handbook of Social Psychology*, G. Lindzey, Ed. (Addison-Wesley, Cambridge, Mass., 1954), vol. 2, pp. 634–654; J. S. Bruner, D. Shapiro, R. Tagiuri, in *Person Perception and Interpersonal Behavior*, R. Tagiuri and L. Petrullo, Eds. (Stanford Univ. Press, Stanford, Calif., 1958), pp. 277–288.

[15]For an example of a similar self-fulfilling prophecy, in this instance dealing with the "central" trait of intelligence, see R. Rosenthal and L. Jacobson, *Pygmalion in the Classroom* (Holt, Rinehart & Winston, New York, 1968).

[16]E. Zigler and L. Phillips, *J. Abnorm. Soc. Psychol. 63*, 69 (1961). See also R. K. Freudenberg and J. P. Robertson, *A.M.A. Arch. Neurol. Psychiatr. 76*, 14 (1956).

[17]W. Mischel, *Personality and Assessment* (Wiley, New York, 1968).

[18]The most recent and unfortunate instance of this tenet is that of Senator Thomas Eagleton.

[19]T. R. Sarbin and J. C. Mancuso, *J. Clin. Consult. Psychol. 35*, 159 (1970); T. R. Sarbin, *ibid. 31*, 447 (1967); J. C. Nunnally, Jr., *Popular Conceptions of Mental Health* (Holt, Rinehart & Winston, New York, 1961).

[20]A. H. Stanton and M. S. Schwartz, *The Mental Hospital: A Study of Institutional Participation in Psychiatric Illness and Treatment* (Basic, New York, 1954).

[21]D. B. Wexler and S. E. Scoville, *Ariz. Law Rev. 13*, 1 (1971).

35

PORNOGRAPHY, RAPE, AND THE CULT OF MACHO

Sarah J. McCarthy

"Never mind these cross burnings by the Ku Klux Klan," he said, "they are only fantasies—charades acted out by hardware salesmen and feedstore clerks hiding under white sheets. We must concern ourselves with real problems—poverty, unemployment, and real lynchings. For too long we have played into whitey's hands acting like darkies with wide eyes as white as moons, hair shot straight in the air like Buckwheat's, afraid of everything—spiders, our own shadows, ghosts. It is possible, too," continued the black man with radical credentials, "that these ghoulish parades will satiate them, drain off their aggression like steam from a boiler. In the end, things could get much worse for us if we take Klan rallies away."

As far as I know, this conversation is purely fictional. Along with all of the other outrages and indignities, blacks at least were not saddled with intricate Freudian catharsis

This article first appeared in *The Humanist*, Sept./Oct. 1980 and is reprinted by permission.

theories that justified the perpetuation of Klan rallies, cross burnings, and little Black Sambo. A lot of people understood when blacks objected to Kingfish and Sapphire and to the plaster of Paris jockeys that held lanterns on suburban lawns. Almost no one argued for the retention of Stepin Fetchit as a kinky sexual turn-on. But for women, who oppose violent pornography, things are different.

According to the California Department of Justice, pornography in this nation is a $4 billion-a-year business, outselling the combined sales of the movie and record industry. No mere whisper in the corner of our culture, the combined circulation of the porn magazines is 16 million monthly copies, and in an era of what Robin Morgan has named "Brutality Chic," the violence in these magazines is increasing. Snuff films, in which there is a simulated, or sometimes actual, murder of a woman, are selling for $1500, and at least one feminist with radical credentials has come close to defending them. Deirdre English writes in the April 1980 Mother Jones: "The fact remains that, no matter how disturbing violent fantasies are, as long as they stay within the world of pornography they are still only fantasies. The man masturbating in a theater showing a snuff film is still only watching a movie, not actually raping and murdering." Referring to feminist groups who are organizing against violent pornography, English continues: "There is something wrong with attacking people not because of their actions but because of their fantasies—or their particular commercial style of having them."

But oppressed groups have never just concentrated their efforts on actions. The attitudes and prejudices that underlie racist acts such as job discrimination, have always been dealt with, and yet, English asks that women dispassionately separate reality from fantasy. Are we to assume, then, that fantasy has no roots in attitudes? She asks us to consider the possibility that sexual violence is not just a result of "sex-role brainwashing" induced by pornography and other cultural conditioning, but that the violence may be the "expression of something profoundly real in the male psychology."

And what about the psychology of this man who is masturbating to a snuff film, how did he get this way, and what should women have to say about him? How and where did he acquire this penchant, or particular commercial style, of masturbating to women's deaths? And what sort of man reads Hustler? Is his psyche a boiling cauldron of male rage of mythic proportions brought on by centuries of mothering? Are his hormones raging out of wack, or has he simply evolved this way like an elephant seal?

Studies such as those done by the President's Commission on Obscenity and Pornography are not really germane to today's questions because they did not study the effects of the violent pornography that has since become commonplace. According to F.B.I. Uniform Crime Statistics, a twelve-year-old girl in the United States has a one in three chance of being raped in her lifetime, and if the research in social psychology and behaviorism in the past twenty years is valid, we can expect not a catharsis effect from the increase in violent porn, but a skyrocketing of rape statistics. For if psychologists have learned anything at all in the past twenty years, it is that societal "brainwashing" is very real and very deep, and that the power of the socialization process in shaping our behavior should not be underestimated.

In 1961, Stanford psychologist Albert Bandura concocted a series of experiments to study how children were affected by the observation of adult aggression. He invited a group of preschool children to observe adults playing with a Bobo doll (a five-foot inflated plastic doll). The adults punched the doll, sat on it, hit it with a mallet, tossed it in the air yelling things such as "Sock him in the mouth." Another group of children were asked to watch an adult who sat quietly playing with some tinker toys, ignoring the presence of the doll. When the children who had not witnessed the adult aggression were left alone in the room with the Bobo doll, they exhibited little or no aggression. Those who had watched the violent display were twelve times as likely to be physically aggressive, and twenty-four times as likely to verbally aggress against the doll. Reporting on this study, authors of the textbook *Social Psychology*, Freedman et al., concluded:

The children in this situation learned to attack a certain type of doll. They might also attack the same type of doll in a different situation, and perhaps a different kind of doll, as well. Just how far this would extend—whether or not they would also punch their brothers and sisters—is not clear; but it is clear that they would be somewhat more likely to attack some things than they were before. Through the process of imitation, these children showed more aggressive behavior.

Another study that illustrates the power of the socialization process and the impact of social role on behavior is the Stanford Prison Experiment. Stanford psychologist Philip G. Zimbardo, interested in the psychological effects of imprisonment, set up a mock prison complete with cells in the basement of Stanford's psychology building. He advertised in the local newspapers for volunteers who would live as guard and prisoner for $15 per day, selecting only those who were judged to be emotionally stable, physically healthy, mature, law-abiding citizens. The sample of white, middle-class, college-aged males was divided by a flip of a coin into guards and prisoners. At the start there were no measurable differences between them. To duplicate a real prison, the prisoners were de-individualized by having to identify themselves by numbers rather than their names, to dress in knee-length smocks, to wear stocking caps that mimicked the shaved heads often found in real jails, and to obtain permission from the guards to engage in routine activities such as letter writing, cigarette smoking, or even going to the toilet.

The guards were likewise cast into their roles with all of the necessary paraphernalia and trimmings such as identical khaki uniforms, silver mirror sunglasses, billy clubs, whistles, handcuffs, and keys. "Although they received no formal training from us in how to be guards," says Zimbardo, "for the most part they moved with apparent ease into their roles. The media had already provided them with ample models of prison guards to emulate."

Since Zimbardo was as interested in the guard's behavior as he was in the prisoner's, "They were given considerable latitude to improvise and to develop strategies and tactics of prisoner management." Within hours the guards and prisoners were involved in a grimly serious power struggle:

Guard K: "During the inspection, I went to cell 2 to mess up a bed that the prisoner had made, and he grabbed me screaming. He grabbed my throat, and although I was really scared, I lashed out with my stick and hit him in the chin."

Guard M: "I was surprised at myself. . . . I made them call each other some names and clean the toilets with their hands. I practically considered the prisoners cattle, and I kept thinking: I have to watch out for them in case they try something."

Guard A: (From his diary) Prior to the experiment: "As I am a pacifist and nonaggressive individual, I cannot foresee a time when I might maltreat other living things."
First day: "Feel sure that the prisoners will make fun of my appearance and I evolve my first basic strategy—mainly not to smile at anything they say or do which would be admitting this is only a game. . . . After we had our lights out Guard D and I held a loud conversation about going home to our girlfriends and *what we were going to do to them.*" (Italics, mine)
Third day: "This was my first chance to exercise the kind of manipulative power that I really like—being a very noticed figure with almost complete control over what is said. When the parents talked to the prisoners, I sat on the edge of the table dangling my feet and contradicting anything I felt like. . . . This was the first part of the experiment I was really enjoying. . . . 817 is being obnoxious and bears watching."
Fourth day: "The psychologist rebuked me for handcuffing and blindfolding a prisoner . . . and I resentfully replied that it is both necessary security and my business anyway."
Fifth day: "I harass Sarge who continues to stubbornly overrespond to commands. I have singled him out for special abuse both because he begs for it and because I simply don't like him. The real trouble is that 416 refuses

to eat his sausage . . . we throw him into the hole (a small dark closet) ordering him to hold sausages in each hand. We have a crisis of authority; this rebellion potentially undermines the complete control we have over the others. I am very angry with this prisoner. I decided to force-feed him, but he wouldn't eat. I let the food slide down his face. I didn't believe it was me doing it. I hated myself for making him eat, but I hated him more for not eating."

Guard A was not the only one to become so swept away with all of this. The other guards, the prisoners, and Zimbardo, too, as he candidly admits, got carried away. Zimbardo was caught up in a very serious role of warden. When rumors of an impending prison break organized by prisoner 819 spread like wildfire through the basement prison, Zimbardo made a frantic call to the real jail in Palo Alto to see if they would house his prisoners. In the midst of this flurry, a fellow psychologist passed through to see how things were going. "What's your independent variable?" he asked. "Who has time to worry about independent variables," Zimbardo lashed out, "Can't you see I've got a prison break on my hands?"

Zimbardo concludes: "We had to end this experiment. We were caught up in the passion of the present, the suffering, the need to control people instead of variables, the escalation of power and all of the unexpected things that were erupting around and within us. So our planned two weeks simulation ended after only six (was it only six?) days and nights."

The frightening lesson of this experiment is the ease with which people who have no particular aggressive or authoritarian characteristics can, in a matter of hours, act in pathological ways when such behavior is viewed as appropriate to one's immediate environment or social role. For those who are suspicious of sex-role theory as it relates to female-male behavior, it is noteworthy that the guard-prisoner roles enacted in this experiment took only hours, rather than centuries, to develop. And these two studies are by no means isolated examples. There is a large body of research which indicates that people are a lot more malleable than previously thought; that we are like chameleons changing our colors from yellow to green to brown in response to our immediate background. Few people or chameleons will risk clashing with their environment. This does not mean, however, that we are blank slates. Behaviorist B. F. Skinner has written that all reinforcers (rewards and punishments) ultimately derive their power from evolutionary selection. We, just like chameleons, have probably inherited this fine-tuned responsiveness, this flexibility to the environment, because it has had survival value. Humans and other animals who were not highly responsive to the rewards and punishments meted out by the physical and social environment are presumably extinct (except, of course, for those intrepid few who are to be found on endangered species or socially ostracized lists).

That is the bad news, but there is a core of good news at the heart of all of this, and it is that people are educable, that consciousness can be raised as well as lowered, and that people are as responsive to a healthy world as they are to a bad one. In a very real sense, humans are the self-creating species, for so much of our behavior depends upon the environment that we create. Or, as Skinner writes in the last line of *Beyond Freedom and Dignity*: "We have not yet seen what man can make of man." With all of this in mind, it seems very reasonable to assume that this violence that lurks deep in the male psyche has been taught, and that if it has been learned, it can be unlearned.

Nazi Germany and the Jonestown suicides powerfully demonstrate the pliability of people to their cultural ideologies. Nazi Germany offered proof that people will kill millions of their fellow citizens in response to the demands of their culture, and Jonestown took things one step further. People are capable of killing themselves and their children in response to such demands.

Contrary to previous theories that the instinct for self-preservation was the most basic and powerful of human drives, the Guyana suicides demonstrate that the socialization process is even more powerful. In a 1972 *Esquire* article, "If Hitler Asked You to Electrocute a Stranger, Would You? . . . Probably," by Philip Meyer, Yale psychologist Stanley Milgram tells of his quest to understand how and why an entire nation could be mobilized to mass-murder under Hitler. At first, Milgram subscribed to the Germans-are-different theory as the most likely explanation for the Holocaust. This theory had been advanced by William Shirer in *The Rise and Fall of the Third Reich*, ". . . the Nazi regime has expressed something very deep in the German nature," a theory much like the men-are-different or violence-deep-in-the-male psyche hypotheses.

Milgram first set out to devise a test that would document his assumption that Germans were more obedient, and then he planned to test for factors in their culture that had caused such behavior. He devised an obedience test, but he never took it to Germany. His first unexpected findings were that Americans were highly obedient. "I found so much obedience," says Milgram softly, a little sadly, "I hardly saw the need for taking the experiment to Germany."

Milgram's test consisted of having subjects "shock" people who made mistakes on a learning task. (Unknown to the subjects, the machine was not really connected.) Two-thirds of those tested among thousands of subjects, shocked to the end of the scale when the experimenter requested that they do so, even though the machine read "lethal voltage" and the victims were screaming in mock pain.

"Many subjects will obey the experimenter no matter how vehement the pleading of the person being shocked," says Milgram in his book *Obedience to Authority*. He continues:

A commonly offered explanation is that those who shocked the victim at the most severe level were monsters, the sadistic fringe of society. But if one considers that almost two-thirds of the participants fall into the category of "obedient" subjects, and that they represented ordinary people from all walks of life, the argument

becomes very shaky. Indeed, it is highly reminiscent of the issue that arose in connection with Hannah Arendt's book, *Eichmann in Jerusalem* (1963). Her conception of the banality of evil comes closer to the truth than one might dare imagine. The ordinary person who shocked the victim did so out of a sense of obligation—a conception of his duties as a subject. . . .

The force exerted by the moral sense of the individual is less effective than social myth would have us believe. Though such prescriptions as "Thou shall not kill" . . . occupy a preeminent place in the moral order, they do not occupy a correspondingly intractable position in the human psychic structure. A few changes in newspaper headlines, a call from the draftboard, orders from a man with epaulets, and men are led to kill with little difficulty. Even the forces mustered in a psychology experiment will go a long way toward removing the individual from moral controls. Moral factors can be shunted aside with relative ease by a calculated restructuring of the informational and social field.

What comprises the informational and social field of the young American male? Increasingly, a primary source of sex education for teenaged boys is pornography. It would be wise to learn what it is that Larry Flynt and others are telling our children.

"There's still something to be said for bashing a woman over the head, dragging her off behind a rock, and having her," said one of the guys in the February 1980 *Penthouse*, which has a monthly circulation hovering around five million, equal to or surpassing *Playboy*. Larry Flynt's *Hustler* ranks third with an approximate circulation of two million monthly copies. "Women Who Flirt with Pain" was the cover hype for a *Penthouse* interview with an assortment of resident Neanderthals (a name that would swell them with pride).

"We're basically rapists, because we're created that way," proclaims Dale. "We're irrational, sexually completely crazy. Our sexuality is more promiscuous, more immediate, and more fleeting, possibly less deep. We're like stud bulls that want to mount everything in sight."

Some of this information is not pleasant reading, but one of the primary purposes of feminists against pornography is to educate

SOME PROCESSES OF SOCIAL LIFE

women and men who do not usually read porn, to show them how far from cheesecake things have come. When women talk about porn, it is important that we show it for what it is, how really raunchy things are, because men and boys are reading it, and we think that it is an incitement to rape. Much of pornography, and indeed our objections to it, hinges on violence and degradation, rather than sexuality.

The letters-to-the-editor in the February *Penthouse* contains an ugly letter from someone who claims to be a sophomore at a large midwestern university, and who is "into throat-fucking." He writes of Kathy and how he was "ramming his huge eleven-inch tool down her throat." Kathy "was nearly unconscious from coming." Gloria Steinem writes in the May 1980 *Ms.*: "Since *Deep Throat*, a whole new genre of pornography has developed. Added to the familiar varieties of rape, there is now an ambition to rape the throat. Porn novels treat this theme endlessly. Real-life victims of suffocation may be on the increase, so some emergency room doctors believe."

Another issue of *Penthouse* contains an article about what they have cleverly called "tossing." A college student from Albuquerque, who drives a 1974 Cadillac and who is "attracted to anything in a skirt," tells how it's done. "How did you get into tossing?" the *Penthouse* interviewer asks. "It just happened," says Daryl. "I was doing it in high school two years ago and didn't know I was. I'd date a chick once, fuck her in my car, and just dump her out. Literally."

Women against porn groups have come under fire for their difficulty in making clear the dividing line between pornography and erotica, but since we are generally opposed to censorship, this blurry grey area need not be our major concern. Feminist analysis and education around pornography has mushroomed far beyond the traditional pro- or anti-censorship dichotomy. Just as an EPA report of air pollution need not imply closing down the factory, or a diagnosis of alcoholism does not imply prohibition, a diagnosis of cultural pollution due to pornography does not imply censorship.

Women have generated a lot of powerful and profound thoughts about pornography; the lack of legalistic precision makes them no less profound. One of the more succinct thoughts was presented by Robin Morgan in *Going Too Far*. "Pornography is the theory," she said, "and rape is the practice." Gloria Steinem, writing in the November 1978 *Ms.*, in the article, "Erotica and Pornography, A Clear and Present Difference," says that "Erotica is about sexuality, but pornography is about power and sex-as-weapon—in the same way we have come to understand that rape is about violence, and not really about sex at all. Erotica is sexual expression between people who have enough power to be there by positive choice."

The slide shows put together by Women Against Violence in Pornography and Media and Women Against Pornography in New York make it clear that these groups are not antisex but antiviolence, particularly sexual violence. The slide show includes a *Hustler* cover picture of a nude woman being pushed head first into a meat grinder, coming out at the bottom as ground meat. I write these graphic descriptions hesitantly because they are so offensive, and then I remind myself that the picture was plastered on newstands from coast to coast in gas stations and drug stores, bought by fifteen-year-olds and their fathers. This issue sold two million copies, maybe more since it was promoted as *Hustler*'s last all-meat issue following Larry Flynt's rebirth at the hands of Ruth Carter Stapleton. Women should know about this. Inside this last all-meat issue is a nude woman lying on a plate looking like a piece of chicken covered with ketchup, and another who is laid out on a hamburger bun, also covered with ketchup. Another issue of *Hustler* displaying the pits of cynicism chic has a drawing of a man's scrotum pushed up against the ear of a retarded girl, his penis presumably filling up her empty head and semen squirting out the other ear. The text reads, "Good Sex with Retarded Girls—you can do anything you want cause who would believe a scrunched face retarded girl?" Will anyone print this, I wonder as I type? I was bleeped once for telling this story on a radio talk show, but Larry Flynt and Hugh Hefner are not censored.

The rest of the slide show is more of the same: women hanging on crosses, their nipples being pulled with pliers, and a kiddie porn section that assures anyone with child abuse on his mind that it's okay, the kids will love it. "I never dreamed it would be this wonderful," said one nude little girl in saddle shoes; and a little girl in a *Playboy* cartoon, getting dressed as she leaves the apartment of a sixty-year-old man, says, "And you call *that* being molested?" *Hustler* used to run a regular kiddie corner called "Chester the Molestor." And, of course, there are men out there who believe this stuff. Such propaganda to rape will cause rape to become as common as smoking in the boys room or "kicking ass" after football games.

There is a long macho tradition in this culture that pronounces certain kinds of violence as perfectly appropriate, even expected, just as Nazis were expected to gas Jews, Klansmen to lynch blacks, and hunters to harvest deer. It did not require rage for an Eichmann to kill a Jew, or for a subject in a psychology experiment to electrocute a stranger, and it probably does not usually require rage for men to rape women. Because it would require a state of raging hatred for women to rape and murder men, women assume that it must be the motive behind male violence toward women, but I think such an assumption is a mistake. To assume this is to ignore or deny male cultural learning, the things they have been taught about women and themselves. Though I'm sure male rage exists, just as female rage exists, it is probably not the primary cause of rape. What we may be dealing with is the banality of rape, the sheer ordinariness of it as the logical end of macho,

the ultimate caricature of our sexual arrangements. Some men may think that rape is just the thing to do. Its source could, in large part, be due to something as mundane as faulty sex education, rather than a wellspring of rage of mythic proportions. In many subcultures within the United States, violence against women has become acceptable, expected, and even trendy. In *Against Our Will*, Susan Brownmiller says it well:

Does one need scientific methodology in order to conclude that the antifemale propaganda that permeates our nation's cultural output promotes a climate where sexual hostility directed against women is not only tolerated, but ideologically encouraged? . . . Yet when it comes to the treatment of women, the liberal consciousness remains fiercely obdurate, refusing to be budged, for the sin of appearing prissy in the age of the so-called sexual revolution has become the worst offense of all.

In a chapter on rape and war, Brownmiller writes of some Americans in Vietnam. John Smail, a squad leader in the Third Platoon, said that rape was an everyday affair. "You can nail just about everybody on that—at least once. The guys are human, man." "Rape was," in the words of another Vietnam veteran, "pretty SOP—standard operating procedure, and it was a rare G. I. who possessed the individual courage or morality to go against his buddies and report, let alone stop, the offense."

Also in *Against Our Will*, Veteran George Phillips tells writer Lucy Komisar:

"They only do it when there are a lot of guys around. You know, it makes them feel good. They show each other what they can do. They won't do it by themselves."
     "Did you rape too?"
     "Nope."
     "Why not?"
     "I don't know, I just got a thing. I don't—of course, it got around the company, you know, well, 'the medic didn't do it.' "
     "Did anybody report these incidents?"
     "No. No one did. You don't dare. Next time you're out in the field you won't come back—you'll come back in a body bag."

Feminist thinkers like Brownmiller and Morgan and many others have generated most of the creative thoughts about pornography, and Brownmiller is right about them not needing scientific methodology to legitimize the plain common sense that is at the heart of the argument. However, occasionally science, too, exhibits a certain amount of common sense, and in this case the methodology of behaviorism and social psychology do buttress feminist arguments about porn in particular, and sex-role development in general.

Most psychologists, biologists, and even sociobiologists today see the heredity-environment arguments as a false dichotomy, preferring instead an interactionist position. For example, the human capacity for language is innate, but the actual use of language, down to the last vowel and consonant, depends upon our immediate environment. Even the precise dialect with which we speak, unless we make a concise effort to the contrary, is determined by whether we live in Boston or Alabama or Brooklyn. The capacity for aggression is also thought to be innate, as best demonstrated by the rage of a newborn infant; but the expression of that anger, in childhood and adulthood, in its intensity and its focus, depends upon one's social environment. Attitude and interpretation are crucial to the expression of anger. A hitchhiker will feel natural anger if he is trying to get a ride on a cold, rainy night if large cars with one occupant keep passing him. If the car passing him is an occupied ambulance, his reaction will be different.

Another avenue of psychological research has been sex hormone research, both in regard to rape and to sex differences in general. As far as I know, sex hormones results have been very ambiguous, with some researchers indicating that they have found links between aggression and the male hormone, testosterone, and others challenging those findings. It seems that nothing definitive can be said at this point about the effects of sex hormones on human behavior. It does not seem illogical, though, given the evolutionary history of our species, that males could conceivably have a somewhat greater tendency toward aggression. A greater tendency, if in fact that is the case, does not translate into an irresistible compulsion to rape.

There is a principle highly thought of in the sciences called the Principle of Parsimony. It states that one should never employ a more complex explanation for an event when a less complex one will suffice, a principle that surely seems to apply to current discussion about the roots of male violence against women. In a culture that promotes the cult of macho, rapes should be expected.

Sociobiologists may argue that there is a link between sex and violence in the male brain, but recent research has unearthed a similar linkage in the female brain and nervous system. The September 16, 1978 issue of *Science News* has an article "Sex and Angry Women":

Numerous studies over the years have shown that certain types of erotic literature, pictures, and films can increase aggression in males. Generally more explicit sexual depictions tend to make men—already angered by experimenters—more angry and aggressive. At the same time, softer-core erotic materials seem to soothe the hostility in angry males.

In one of the first such experiments involving women, Robert A. Baron of Purdue University tested forty-five undergraduate women. The subjects were either angered (by unflattering personal evaluations from another student) or not angered and then exposed by varying degrees of erotic pictures of men and women, as well as to nonerotic pictures. Baron reported at the American Psychological Association meeting that heightened sexual arousal does increase aggression in women, as well as men; and there is indication that it may take less to make women more angry than it does for men.

This is an interesting line of research, especially in view of the fact that, when women are questioned about their "rape fantasies," it is always assumed that they are fantasizing about themselves as the victims of a rape rather than as the aggressor. There are, of course, perfectly understandable reasons for some women to have had fantasies in which they were raped. Women have almost always needed a pretext to have sex, and force is the most guiltless pretext of all. Women's rape fantasies, however, are nothing like real rapes. In a fantasy the woman controls the rapist, even chooses him. A real rape has nothing to do with choice or control, and the result of it is violence and degradation, not sexual pleasure.

Researchers Feshbach of UCLA and Malamuth of Manitoba reported that 51 percent of the men they interviewed after watching violent pornography said there was at least some possibility they would commit rape if assured they would not be caught. "There seems to be within the general population a high proportion of men who are similar to rapists," Malamuth says. "It's only a matter of degree." Professor Ed Donnerstein of the University of Wisconsin found that rapists were aroused by films that showed violence against women, even if they had no sexual content at all. Donnerstein is fast emerging as the primary aggression researcher in the area of social psychology, primarily aggression against women as incited by violent porn. In a paper titled "Pornography Commission Revisited: Aggressive-Erotica and Violence Against Women," Donnerstein reports that:

There is good evidence to suggest that the observation of such aggressive acts could reduce restraints against subsequent aggressive behavior. Furthermore, as noted in the work of Berkowitz, one important determinant of whether an aggressive response is made is the presence of aggressive cues. Not only objects, but individuals can take on aggressive-cue value if they have been associated with observed violence. This increase in aggression should be especially true for previously angered individuals who are already predisposed to aggress. . . . The present results show that exposure to an aggressive-erotic film was able to increase aggression to a higher level than that of the erotic film.

Donnerstein also reports that angered males who had watched the aggressive-erotica displayed aggression selectively to females but not to males. This study further demonstrates the point that interpretation and attitude as well as imitation cause aggression to be selectively exhibited. Once a particular person is seen as a scapegoat, he or she will be the target for aggression. Donnerstein asks, "Why would the aggression against the female be increased after exposure to the aggressive-erotic film? One potential explanation is that the female's association with the victim in the film made her an aggressive stimulus which could elicit aggressive responses."

These research results, of course, directly contradict Freud's theory of catharsis, as does much of the psychological research. In fact, in *Social Psychology* (Freedman et al.) it is said that: "The vast majority of laboratory experiments have shown that observing aggression provokes greater aggressive behavior, not less. The catharsis effect simply does not occur in these experiments, except in rare instances."

There are probably as many reasons for rape as there are for murder. As well as the condoned red-blooded-American-boy rapes, there are those that can be quietly placed on the doorstep of patriarchal religion. Dread of women grows easily in men who have been taught by puritanical religions that sex is sinful, who must be forever on guard against modern-day temptresses, the daughters of Eve and Salome, Bathsheba and Delilah, who are about to rob them of their morality, their strength, their garden. For they are all there in the Bible—Sarah, Anne, and Mary—divided like the sheep and the goats into good and bad women, forever categorized as Madonnas or whores. The lucky whores who were forgiven were permitted to wash their master's feet with their hair.

Mary Daly, in *Beyond God the Father*, writes of the scapegoat syndrome and how society as we know it has a perverse need to create the "other" as an object of condemnation so that those who condemn can judge themselves as good. She quotes St. Augustine:

What can be more sordid, more devoid of modesty, more full of shame than prostitutes, brothels, and every other evil of this kind? Yet remove prostitutes from human affairs and you will pollute all things with lust; set them among honest matrons, and you will dishonor all things with disgrace and turpitude.

SOME PROCESSES OF SOCIAL LIFE

She then quotes St. Thomas Aquinas:

... prostitution in the world is like filth in the sewer. Take away the sewer and you will fill the place with pollution; take away prostitutes from the world and you will fill it with sodomy.

And, of course, there was St. Paul who proclaimed that it was better to marry than to burn. (I have a special fondness for this one because a religious uncle passed it along to my husband in the reception line at our wedding.)

In view of all this, it is not surprising that men like the Hillside Strangler and Jack the Ripper, and the son of Jack the Ripper now operating in Britain, have vented their rage against prostitutes, temptresses whom they would resist even if they had to kill them.

Given the antiwomen and antisex attitudes that flourish in many religious and right-wing groups, it is understandable that many women and liberals are somewhat suspicious of the new feminist antiporn groups. Most women would have to be dragged kicking and screaming before they would again be hoisted upon the pedestal, placed there like "Christmas card virgins with glued hands" as Marge Piercy has written.

The President's Commission on Obscenity and Pornography reported that a "recent survey showed that 41 percent of American males and 46 percent of American females believe that sexual materials lead people to lose respect for women." In the book *Philosophy and Women*, Ann Garry writes:

If a person makes two traditional assumptions—that sex is dirty and that women fall into two classes, good and bad—it is easy to see how that person might think that pornography could lead people to lose respect for women or that pornography itself is disrespectful to women. If one sees these women as symbolic representations of all women, then all women fall from grace with these women. . . . Can we imagine 41 percent of men and 46 percent of women answering "yes" to the question, "Do movies showing men engaging in violent acts lead people to lose respect for men?" Think of the following: women are temptresses, blacks cheat the welfare system, Italians are gangsters, but the white males in the Nixon administration were an exception—white males as a group did not lose respect because of Watergate and related scandals.

And what of women, what of their role in this, for surely we have a role, just at the prisoners in Zimbardo's prison had their part to play? Sally Kempton has written, "It is hard to fight an enemy that has outposts in your head." There can be no doubt that both the father-confessors of patriarchal religion and the sugar daddies like Hugh Hefner, who pass out goodies for women who take off their clothes, have outposts in our heads. There are none of us who has not been caught in their cross-fires, and they are both our enemy.

Society, religion, and biology (for example, unwanted pregnancies) have insisted that women say no to sex when they meant yes. This is the mustard seed of truth that lies at the heart of the rumor that women want to be raped. The female side of rape is the sexual credibility gap: women who said "No" because they had no other choice, when they meant "Yes." The lies of these women were not lost on men who latched onto this wonderfully self-serving nugget, and the message spread like wildfire that women want to be forced. Myths die hard, even after sexual revolutions, especially when one's ego and sexual gratification are at stake.

There is another women's problem. It is one to be seen in women's literature over the centuries—some have called it the Compassion Trap, some have personified it as Lady Bountiful; Robin Morgan has named it the Pity the Poor Rapist mentality—it is the problem of self-abnegation, the denial of one's self. Black feminist poet and author Alice Walker has written of it in *Meridian*. Lynne is a white woman who has gone South in the sixties to work for civil rights, where she marries a black man, Truman. Lynne and Truman have a friend named Tommy Odds who one day has his lower arm shot off in a demonstration. Because he was angry, and because Lynne was white, he wanted to make love to her.

For of course it was Tommy Odds who raped her. As he said, it wasn't really rape. She had not screamed once, or even struggled very much. To her, it was worse than rape because she felt that circumstances had not permitted her to scream. As Tommy Odds said, he was just a lonely one-arm nigger down on his luck that nobody had time for anymore. But she would have time—wouldn't she? Because she was not like those rough black women who refused to be sympathetic and sleep with him—was she? She would be kind and not like those women who turned him down because they were repulsed and prejudiced and the maroon stump of his arm made them sick. She would be a true woman and save him—wouldn't she?

"But Tommy Odds," she pleaded, pushing against his chest, "I'm married to your friend. You can't do this."

Water stung in her eyes as she felt her hair being tugged out at the roots.

"Please don't do this," she whimpered softly.

"You knows I cain't hep myself," he said in loose-lipped mockery.

His hand came out of her hair and was quickly inside her blouse. He pinched her nipples until they stung.

"Please," she begged.

There was a moment when she knew she could force him from her. But it was a flash. She lay instead thinking of his feelings, his hardships, of the way he was black and belonged to people who lived without hope; she thought about the loss of his arm. She felt her own guilt. And he entered her and she did not any longer resist but tried instead to think of Tommy Odds as he was when he was her friend—and near the end her arms stole around his neck, and before he left she told him she forgave him and she kissed his round slick stump that was the color of baked liver, and he smiled at her from far away, and she did not know him. "Be seein' you," he said.

The next day Tommy Odds appeared with Raymond, Altuna, and Hedge.

Women are beginning to fight back, speak out against rape images wherever they are to be found. Women Against Pornography in New York is conducting tours of the Times Square porn district for other women who have been too intimidated to go alone, and organized a "Take Back the Night" march in which ten thousand people marched. Women Against Violence Against Women in Los Angeles and NOW organized a boycott of all Warner Communications products, beginning with the "Some Girls" album by the Rolling Stones, and its corresponding billboard that read "I'm Black and Blue from the Rolling Stones and I Love It." A group of women spray painted the billboard during the night, and the next day it was removed. At a press conference in Los Angeles, the President of Warner Communications recently announced that WCI "opposes the depiction of violence against women or men on album covers or in related promotional materials." Women Against Violence in Pornography and Media in San Francisco put together a slide show of pornographic images of women to raise public consciousness about this issue, to show that we have come a long way from cheesecake to the meat-grinder. Women Against Sexist Violence in Pittsburgh recently held a conference on pornography as an incitement to rape, and held workshops at which they discussed the possibility of legislation that would outlaw only violent pornography.

There are women walking around New York and Los Angeles, Chicago and Pittsburgh with big black and gold buttons that announce: "Women Against Pornography: It's About Time."

36

THE SEARCH FOR JUVENILE JUSTICE

Michael Serrill

"These are the armies of the night!" blares the advertising slogan for the controversial film *The Warriors*. The "armies" are made up of youthful thugs, some as young as 12. In New York City, the film tells us, there are tens of thousands of them wandering the streets and subways in loosely federated packs. Given half a chance each one of them will happily kill.

The Warriors is only the latest in a long series of media presentations, fictional and factual, that seem designed to depict young criminals, and sometimes teen-agers generally, as ogres. As always, it is hard to tell whether the media are molding the public mood or merely reflecting it. But there is little doubt that the public mood as regards juvenile crime is sour, even venomous. The people—at least those who influence state legislatures—want children accused of violent crimes locked up and locked up for a good long time.

Legislatures in at least a dozen states have obliged. They have passed laws making it much easier for serious juvenile offenders to be tried and sentenced in the adult courts, lowered the age of majority for those accused of a variety of crimes, and stipulated that cer-

tain juvenile offenders must be sent to secure state institutions. They have effectively dismissed the traditional belief that children are less responsible for their acts than adults.

While this harsh line has been capturing the headlines, a much quieter but equally powerful countermovement has succeeded in gaining the release from state institutions of thousands of children who are neglected, abused, or minor criminal offenders. The efforts of "child advocacy" groups have ranged from massive class-action lawsuits—one succeeded in having the entire Texas juvenile corrections system declared unconstitutional—to a Colorado suit in which a teen-ager has charged his mother and father with "parental malpractice."

But the get-tough forces and the children's rights' groups will agree on one point: The existing juvenile justice system has no consistent standards for the treatment of any juvenile in trouble, whether he is a murderer or an orphan, whether he has committed assault or been victimized by it. In several states, conservative and liberal groups have joined in an effort to rewrite the juvenile laws so that they define specifically the rights and obligations of juveniles in trouble, and the rights and obligations of the courts and other agencies that attempt to redirect their lives. The most comprehensive new statute took

From *Saturday Review*, June 23, 1979. Reprinted by permission.

effect in Washington State a year ago and is widely regarded as a model for juvenile law reform.

The target of every effort to rewrite the juvenile laws is a single institution: the juvenile court (also known as "family" and "domestic relations" court). Its sustaining beliefs have been that troubled children must be treated differently from their adult counterparts, that they bear little or no responsibility for their acts, and that the state's obligation is to do everything necessary to resolve the social or familial problems that brought them to court. The court's mandate in almost every state has been to look at each individual case and take whatever action is in the "best interest" of the child. The word "punishment" has been anathema. Juvenile court judges have thus come to see themselves as administrators of social-service agencies rather than courts of law.

The broad discretion of the juvenile courts has been under relentless attack for many years now. The anti-institution forces claim that judges have always taken the easy way out by sentencing too many of their charges to training schools. The pro-institution forces charge that the judges, obsessed with fulfilling juveniles' social needs, have lost sight of their obligation to protect the community.

Until just a few years ago, the United States relied almost entirely on large public institutions for the imprisonment and treatment of juvenile offenders of all kinds. The entire legal and philosophical justification for the existence of these institutions—many of which were, and are, operated directly by juvenile courts—has been that they are rehabilitative. It is technically illegal in many states to send a child to an institution if it is not in his "best interest."

But in the late Sixties and early Seventies, a reform movement revealed many juvenile institutions as brutal, dehumanizing places where children had their heads shaven, were marched around in formation, were assaulted and held for years without hearings to deter-

mine if they could be released. There was a tide of revulsion against these conditions in the late Sixties that depopulated both adult and juvenile jails.

The culmination of the movement to get juvenile offenders out of public institutions came in 1971 and 1972, when Massachusetts Department of Youth Services Commissioner Dr. Jerome Miller stunned the juvenile justice community by closing down all of the state's juvenile training schools, which once held more than 1,000 children. The youngsters were sent home or were placed in privately operated "group homes"—small residences for eight to 12 children—or were placed in foster care. By 1974, almost all of the major states had reduced their juvenile institution populations by over half. Experiments were launched with a dozen different kinds of community programming.

But the anti-institution movement has run up against several obstacles in recent years. A controversial seven-year study of the experiment in Massachusetts by the Harvard Law School concluded that the children treated in community programs in 1973 were just as likely to commit new crimes as those released from institutions in 1968. A more recent and even more hotly debated study of community programs for hard-core delinquents in Chicago came to a still more discouraging conclusion: Teen-aged offenders sent to institutions or other highly structured programs were less likely to commit new crimes when released than those held in more therapeutic programs.

Even if the reformers could prove that community programs are effective, they would be fighting an uphill battle against the many politicians who are determined that violent juvenile criminals be locked up, whether it does them any good or not. Between 1960 and 1975 the number of juveniles arrested for FBI Index crimes increased 283 percent. More than half of all arrests for serious crimes are of youths under 18. While 20 years ago juvenile delinquents confined their criminal activity to shoplifting, car theft, and burglary, they now commit robbery, rape, arson, and murder.

There is no scientific evidence that this explosion of juvenile crime has anything to do with juvenile court or corrections procedures; sociologists, in fact, are at a loss to explain why it has happened. But the angry political response was predictable. (It is ironic, however, that it has come now, since crime rates among both adults and juveniles have been declining since 1976.) New York and California, along with a growing number of smaller states, have stiffened penalties for juvenile crimes or lowered the age at which juveniles can be prosecuted as adults. There are several teen-agers among the 500 men and women on death rows around the country.

New York, which has a reputation as the state that is softest on juvenile criminals, passed a law last summer mandating that all 13-year-olds charged with murder and all 14- and 15-year-olds charged with murder and 14 other crimes be initially prosecuted in the adult courts. Maximum terms in institutions were expanded from 18 months to as long as life. (At least with respect to convicted offenders, New York's reputation for leniency is undeserved. It is one of only three states that send all 16- and 17-year-olds, whatever their crime, to adult prisons. On a given day, New York has more than 2,000 offenders aged 16–18 in adult jails, compared with about 40 in California.)

The anti-institution reformers have held their own against this tide of reactions, but not without some abandonment of their own ideals. The new laws which they have proposed effectively sacrifice the serious offenders to the brutalities of institutions while allowing—in Washington, mandating—lesser penalties for minor offenders and "status" offenders—runaways, truants, "ungovernable" children, and all others whose offense would not be punishable in an adult court.

While a number of states, under pressure from various interest groups, have made piecemeal reforms in their juvenile codes and procedures, only Washington has attempted to restructure the entire system. On July 1, 1978, a new juvenile code went into effect in Washington that glistens with modernity. It includes almost all the elements that reform groups have advocated.

The new law diverts all status offenders and many minor offenders out of the criminal justice system altogether. They will be dealt with by community agencies that will mete out both sanctions and social services. Chronic and serious juvenile law violaters must be sent to institutions under the new law. The judges no longer have a choice. Every ounce of their discretion has been taken away from them, at least as far as dispositions are concerned.

The state now operates under a point system, with each juvenile offender receiving a certain number of points based on his age, prior record, and current offense. Those who accumulate more than 110 points are committed to the state for a fixed period of time based on the same three factors. They cannot be paroled; parole release has been abolished. Those with less than 110 points cannot go to institutions, but they are not let off scot-free. They must make restitution to their victims, pay fines of as much as $100, and do as much as 150 hours of "community service"—work in local government or private programs for no pay. If they fail to live up to the terms of their restitution and community-service agreements, they can be locked up in the local juvenile detention center for as long as 30 days.

The new code comes as close as that of any other state to constituting a "bill of rights" for children. Children are no longer the chattels of their parents. If they run away from home and are picked up by police, they can refuse to go back home. When the new structure is fully in place, those who refuse to go home will be taken to non-secure "crisis residential centers," where they can stay up to 72 hours while counselors negotiate between the parents and children to resolve the family problem that caused the child to leave home. If the problem is not resolved within 72 hours, the case will be taken to court. But the judge cannot order the child to go home if the child doesn't want to, as he could before the new law was passed, and as judges in other states still can. If the child refuses to cooperate the judge cannot declare him "ungovernable" and send him to an institution. Parents, judges, probation counselors, and community workers can recommend counseling or therapy for both delinquent and nondelinquent youths, but the youngsters have the right to refuse it. Those who are delinquent enough to be sent to institutions also have the right to refuse counseling and therapy; they cannot be punished for not cooperating and, since their terms are fixed, they cannot be denied release.

The Washington law is being held up as a model by reformers inside and outside the state. But for all its virtues, it has yet to squarely confront the problems raised by serious offenders. The new law provided no additional funds to expand school and counseling programs for the 625 children (down from 1,500 in the late Sixties) in Washington's seven institutions. The main emphasis of the law was to expand services for the minor and status offenders who were diverted out of institutions by the law. The hard core of juvenile offenders are locked up at places like the Green Hill School in Chehalis. Green Hill includes two maximum security units. These are new and clean, but very prisonlike buildings where serious offenders are required under Washington's new juvenile law to spend at least 90 days. Most spend much longer there—some as long as a year. Some of them go to school a few hours a day; for the rest of the day the staff has to scramble to find something for them to do. There are no vocational education programs they can attend, according to "group-life" counselor Allie Thurman, and the counseling they get is minimal. "It makes me sick—the waste," says Thurman angrily, waving his hand toward the 16 boys meandering aimlessly around the narrow day

room at Fir Cottage, one of Green Hill's two maximum-security units.

The inmates are quick to second the point Thurman was making.

"They don't do nothin' for you here," said one boy in Fir Cottage matter-of-factly as a half-dozen of his fellow inmates nodded agreement. Asked what they could do for him, the boy, convicted of armed robbery and assault and serving 40 months, said they could teach him a trade. He could think of nothing else. He said he didn't need "treatment"; he wasn't sick.

Thurman and many other staff members at Green Hill denounce the "determinate" sentencing and absence of parole of the new juvenile code. Green Hill, the state's oldest and most secure facility, currently holds 112 boys, most of them convicted of violent crimes. Before the new law went into effect last July, most delinquents spent less than a year in the institution; now they are being sentenced to terms as long as four years.

Law enforcement officials respond to criticisms of harshness by pointing to the gross deficiencies, as well as the injustice, of the old system. The determinate-sentence aspect of the law, for example, was pushed—in fact, written—by officials of the King County (Seattle and environs) prosecutor's office and the Seattle police department. Like their counterparts in most cities, the police and prosecutors in Seattle had long been angry at the fact that the seriousness of a teen-ager's crime and the length of his criminal record seemed to have nothing to do with the disposition of his case. Seattle Assistant Chief of Police Elmer E. Knechtel, who spent more than 20 years in the department's juvenile bureau, can tell countless "horror stories" about juveniles who committed crime after crime with seeming impunity. "We had a kid who had been arrested 64 times," Knechtel recalls, "35 of them for felonies. And he had never done time in an institution." Knechtel says that 30 years ago juveniles comprised 20 to 25 percent of those arrested for burglary and 33 percent of those arrested for car theft. By 1977, he said, the respective percentages had risen to 63 and 82 percent. At least some of this change, said Knechtel, "has got to be due to the fact that we didn't do anything about it."

But the ire of law-enforcement officials was aroused not merely by leniency but by an almost wild inconsistency in sentencing, apparently unrelated to the severity of the crime involved. Jay Reich, head of the juvenile division of the King County prosecutor's office, describes an example of this "bizarre" process. "We had back-to-back cases before the same judge. The first case was a young gal who had been convicted of prostitution at age 14 and had tremendous dependency problems. She was committed to the state institution. . . . The next case before the judge was a 16- or 17-year-old male who had been convicted of rape in the first degree. He was given four weekends in detention, because he was amenable to the social services available in the community. . . . There was no sense of proportionality or predictability. I don't know what the message given to the kids was about committing crimes."

Though grave injustices of this sort appeared to provide adequate justification for a more rational, and harsher, system of punishment, even enforcement officials expect the new toughness to have little or no effect on juvenile crime rates. Warren Netherland, director of the Division of Juvenile Rehabilitation, which runs the state institutions, admits, "As near as I can tell, there is nothing that any part of the criminal justice system does that affects crime rates. The thing we [in the juvenile system] have going for us more than anything else is maturity. A lot of credit we take for programs would probably happen if we did nothing."

In fact, it is hard to find anyone, in Washington or elsewhere, who thinks he has found a method of rehabilitating criminals, juvenile or adult. The advantages of the new system, says state Representative Mary Kay Becker, one of its principal backers in the legislature,

are not that it will reduce crime or rehabilitate more offenders, but that it is more fair and more honest. The juveniles who are sent off to institutions should be the first to know, she added, that "we are not sending [them there] to do them any good. We're sending them there because their behavior has demonstrated that they are a menace to society."

The trend to deal more seriously with serious offenders and less harshly with others is likely to continue. The Office of Juvenile Justice and Delinquency Prevention, created by Congress in 1974, has adopted regulations forbidding any state or county agency that receives its funds from placing nondelinquents or status offenders in secure institutions. It also forbids the mixing of delinquents and nondelinquents and the mixing of adult and juvenile offenders in any program. At stake is more than $100 million annually in federal juvenile-justice funds. There was great indignation among local officials at this federal attempt to coerce them. But in the end the money was too attractive to ignore, and most of them are making grudging attempts to comply. The number of juveniles in state correctional institutions has been steadily declining since at least 1965, when there were about 43,000, to 26,000 today; this decline has continued in the past few years despite an increase in the number of serious offenders sent to institutions.

Furthermore, the effort to expand the due process rights of juveniles got a powerful push on February 12, when the House of Delegates of the American Bar Association approved no less than 17 volumes of "standards" for the operation of juvenile courts and correctional systems. Portions of the standards have already been incorporated verbatim into the Washington State law and into proposed new laws in several other states. The ABA recommends a "due process model" in which juvenile defendants are entitled to the full panoply of due process rights now provided for adults, including open hearings (all are now closed, to protect the child from the glare of publicity) and jury trials, which no state now permits. Perhaps the most radical ABA recommendation is that the sentences of juvenile offenders be standardized according to the severity of the offense, the age of the child, his criminal record, and that his "social history" play no role in deciding a disposition.

Although the object of these recent reforms is a more fair and just juvenile system, there remains the danger that the agencies of government will see their entire mission as the imposition of *legal* justice and forget about the equally pressing imperative of *social* justice. While it may not be the courts' proper role to address the history of poverty, discrimination, abuse, and deprivation that most defendants carry with them to the courtroom, it is certainly someone's responsibility. If the new juvenile sentencing systems mean that delinquent youngsters' individual problems and needs will be ignored, then this attempt at reform, like those before it, will be a failure.

SOME PROCESSES OF SOCIAL LIFE

XIII

POPULATION AND ECOLOGY
People and Pollution

Population and related ecological problems are with us today and will remain with us for many years to come—if we survive. This is the verdict of many experts, called demographers, who study changes in human populations. Three variables are crucial to population change: fertility (the birthrate), mortality (the death rate), and migration (population movement). In studying populations, demographers focus on how these variables affect three different areas:

1. Population growth and decline: the size of the population
2. Population distribution: where the population is located
3. Population composition and structure: the characteristics of the population, such as age, sex, education and so forth

Each of these three areas must be examined to understand the population picture in the United States and the world today. Our three articles deal with these factors and their effect on world food and energy resources.

We must be concerned with the rapid growth rate many countries are experiencing, both for humanitarian reasons and because of the increasing demand on scarce resources. The Population Reference Bureau estimates that in developing countries population can double every twenty to thirty-five years. This means that natural resources, food production capacity, and other essentials must double in the same period just in order to maintain present life styles. Yet most countries are demanding more food, improved communications, education, scientific advances, and higher standards of living at a time when resources and capacities to produce are already severely strained.

In the first article, Brown et al. support the Bureau's claim by noting that unchecked population growth in the world has a detrimental effect on twenty-two important dimensions of life, ranging from education to environment, from quality of life to availability of food. The authors conclude that the threat to the quality of life should receive more attention, especially from those in positions of power.

In the next article, "Taking Shape: A Bigger, Different Population," population changes in the United States during the 1980s are outlined. These changes are affecting the distribution of the population, its age and racial composition, and the life style of the future, from family life to available consumer goods to the crime rate.

The final article takes a refreshing look at one of the byproduct problems of population—pollution. According to McCloskey, reducing this problem has been good for you and me and for business as well.

Through these articles runs the theme of cooperation among developed and developing societies, among the members of any society to protect scarce natural resources and to gain resources needed for survival. As you read this chapter, consider the implications of population changes on our lives in the United States, the imbalance between rich and poor countries, and the results of world population growth on the imbalance of resources.

37

THE POPULATION PROBLEM IN 22 DIMENSIONS

Lester R. Brown
Patricia L. McGrath
Bruce Stokes

The food dimension of the population threat remains paramount, yet in their Malthusian mindset, population analysts often neglect the threat's numerous other, often newer manifestations.

We have identified 22 dimensions of the population problem, including hunger, that deserve attention. Selection of the problems discussed was based simply upon evidence that population growth contributes in some degree to each of them. Collectively, they portray the stresses and strains associated with continued population growth in a world already inhabited by four billion people.

1.   Literacy

In many countries of Asia, Africa, and Latin America, the number of illiterates is rising as population grows more rapidly than schools can be built and staffed with teachers. Millions of children move toward adulthood without any instruction at all; others enroll in the primary grades but drop out without ever learning to read or write. Those countries

Reprinted by permission from *The Futurist*, October 1976, pp. 238–245, published by the World Future Society, 4916 St. Elmo Avenue, Washington, D. C. 20014.

with the least to spend on education and literacy usually have the highest birthrates.

In 1950, 700 million illiterates comprised about 44% of the world adult population. Today, more than a quarter of a century later, there are 800 million illiterates. While the percentage of illiterates declined from 44% to 34% between 1950 and 1970, the absolute number unable to read or write has continued to grow. Illiteracy is most acute in areas with rapid population growth.

2.   Oceanic Fisheries

The hope that man will be able to turn to the oceans to satisfy his food needs as population pressures on land-based food resources mount is being shattered due to increasing competition and conflict over scarce supplies of fish. From 1950 to 1970 the world fish catch more than tripled, from 21 to 70 million tons. But between 1970 and 1973 the longstanding trend was reversed and the fish catch declined by nearly five million tons.

Many marine biologists now feel that the global catch of table-grade fish is at or near the maximum sustainable level. Of the 30 or so leading species of commercial-grade fish, a number are now overfished; that is, stocks will not sustain even the current catch. Without cooperative global management of oceanic fisheries and control of the swelling flow of pollutants, the catch could decline even further.

3. Natural Recreational Areas

Ski slopes, golf courses, beaches, city parks, wildlife preserves, and campgrounds are all utilized by increasing numbers of people each year. Access to what some view as a public resource has become an increasingly sensitive issue as rising population pressure combines with higher incomes to create a demand for more recreation facilities. City dwellers stream out in ever-increasing numbers to seek the therapy of nature. But what they all too often find is the same congestion they left behind—bumper-to-bumper traffic, noise, air pollution, and crowded, overflowing recreation areas.

International hotels are springing up in isolated places like Machu Picchu, the lost city of the Incas. A real estate firm has begun selling off some of the world's few remaining uninhabited islands through advertisements in London newspapers. So many trekkers have come to the Himalayas that they are exacerbating the firewood shortage as well as littering the lower slopes of the mountains with discarded gear. The growth of luxurious tourist hotels near Mount Everest has required the installation of special landing strips and water systems, both jeopardizing a fragile environment.

4. Pollution

As the human population has increased in numbers and become more concentrated, its potential for disrupting the earth's ecosystem has grown. Each additional person, especially in affluent societies, increases the burden on what is, in many areas, an already overburdened environment. A study of air pollution in Swedish cities has demonstrated the link between population density and air pollution: the concentration of sulfur dioxide in the cities' air, the result of burning fossil fuels in cars, generating plants, and industry, was highest in cities with the largest populations.

The Mediterranean Sea now serves as a sewer for over 400 million people. Although its ecological balance had never been seriously jeopardized until the mid-twentieth century, overpopulation, the tourist boom, industrial development, and maritime irresponsibility now threaten to turn the Mediterranean into a dead sea.

5. Inflation

Inflation results when demand exceeds supply. World demand for goods and services has expanded at about 4% per year from 1950 to 1975, nearly tripling during the 25 year span. About half of all production gains were absorbed by population growth, which averaged close to 2% per year during the period, and about half by increases in per capita consumption. Meanwhile, it has become increasingly difficult, for a combination of economic and political reasons, to expand the supply of many strategic goods commensurately. The result has been scarcity-induced inflation.

6. Environmental Illnesses

As population grows, health problems often intensify. More and more people concentrated in urban areas generate ever greater amounts of pollution, overwhelming human and natural efforts to clean the air and water. Air pollution and the diseases it causes are increasingly prevalent in some cities. Dust, sulfur dioxide, and other by-products of burning of fossil fuels have been directly linked to illness and death. A recent study conducted in Nashville, Tennessee, showed that the incidence of heart disease in polluted areas was nearly double the normal rate. A similar study of non-cigaret smokers in California indicated that men who live in cities die of lung cancer over three times as often as their counterparts in relatively unpolluted rural areas.

7. Hunger

The dominant single factor reshaping world food-trade patterns in recent decades is the difference in continental rates of population growth. A comparison of North America and Latin America, two regions roughly equal in size and resources, illustrates the devastating role of rapid population growth. As recently as 1950, both North America and Latin America had essentially the same population size, 163 and 168 million respectively. But the difference since then explains why North America emerged as the world's breadbasket while Latin America became a net food importer. While North America's population growth has slowed substantially since the late fifties, that of many Latin American countries has expanded at an explosive 3% or more yearly. If North America's 1950 population had expanded at 3% per year, it would now be 341 million rather than the actual 236 million. Those additional 105 million people would absorb virtually all the current exportable surpluses, and North America would be struggling to maintain self-sufficiency.

None of the basic resources required to expand food output—land, water, energy, fertilizer—can be considered abundant today. In some countries, the area under cultivation is actually declining as a result of population-induced phenomena like desert encroachment, soil erosion, or urban sprawl. As a result, food production has lagged behind demand in virtually every geographic region except North America.

8. Housing

Providing decent living quarters for rapidly increasing populations seems dishearteningly difficult today. As a result of the swelling demand for houses, the land, lumber, cement, and fuel required have risen beyond the financial means of many of the world's four billion people. The expectation that a growing share of each nation's people would be able to enjoy a home of their own has now been dimmed considerably by the impact of rapid population growth and associated material scarcities.

9. Climate Change

Humans generate airborne dust in every daily activity from suburban driving to tilling the soil. Around large cities, where millions of individual actions each generate their own small quantity of dust, the particles often act as cloud seeders, increasing rainfall. The impact of the world's four billion people on climate can already be measured locally wherever population density is great. Even more worrisome, local changes may also be triggering shifts in global climatic patterns and trends.

10. Overgrazing

When human population in the poor countries grows, the livestock population is almost always increased commensurately in order to expand draft power, food supplies, or family wealth and security. As herds of cattle multiply, they can denude the countryside of its natural grass cover, particularly if they are not properly controlled. Literally millions of acres of the world's cropland, mostly in food-deficit areas of Asia, the Middle East, Africa, and the Andean countries, are abandoned each year because severe soil erosion has so lowered productivity that the land cannot sustain local inhabitants using existing agricultural technologies.

History provides us with graphic examples of human abuse of the soil. North Africa, once the fertile granary of the Roman Empire, is now largely barren and unproductive. The Fertile Crescent of the Tigris-Euphrates Valley may have supported more people in the pre-

Christian era than it is able to support today. In North America, the Chihuahuan Desert in New Mexico and the Sonoran Desert in Arizona are now believed by some analysts to have been expanded by overgrazing in the few hundred years since the arrival of Europeans.

11. Crowding

Aerial photographs of Java reveal that people are actually moving into the craters of occasionally active volcanoes in their search for land and living space. Periodic evacuations and loss of life result. In Bangladesh, people are driven by population pressure into flood-prone lowlands and onto low coastal islands previously uninhabited because of the danger of tidal waves and typhoons. When such "natural" disasters occur, the loss of life may be attributed largely to overcrowding.

The more people there are on earth, the more people there are per square mile. Nothing can change that fact. Crowding and its side-effects, competition and aggression, can induce stressful situations, and stress seems to be a major factor governing susceptibility to heart disease, high blood pressure, skin disorders, and stroke; behavioral problems like child abuse, alcoholism, and homicide also seem to be stress related.

12. Income

With the perceptible economic slowdown that has occurred in most of the world during the seventies, population growth may offset all economic growth in some countries, actually preventing rather than just reducing any gains in per capita income. The prospect of slower increments in living standards, or even declines in some countries, is not just a remote possibility. In India, real income per person declined from $45 per year in 1972 to $41 in 1973, a decline of nearly 10%. In Bangladesh the downward spiral is further advanced, and is compounded by the new malady of political instability. The number of new mouths to be fed has simply exceeded the capacity of the country's farmers to expand their output.

13. Urbanization

During the nineteenth century industrial revolution in England, the flow of people from countryside to city was mainly a result of job opportunities in the city. Today, the process of urbanization has accelerated in the developing countries, but it is more a measure of rural despair than of urban opportunity. Plots of rural farmland are divided and subdivided by each successive generation until the pieces are too small to provide a livelihood. The inevitable result is a rural exodus. If projected trends materialize, the twentieth century will be the one in which human society is converted from a primarily rural society to one that is primarily urban.

14. Deforestation

As the human population has expanded over the century, the earth's forests have receded. Trees have been cut to make room for agriculture, to provide wood for shelter, firewood for fuel, and, in recent centuries, newsprint for newspapers. The two principal causes of deforestation are directly linked to population growth: land clearing for agriculture and wood gathering for fuel. Tree harvesting for lumber is a third, but globally less significant, source of deforestation. Areas such as the Middle East, which were densely settled long ago, lost their stock of trees in ages past. Today, many poor countries in other regions are passing through the same stages of forest destruction at a historically unprecedented pace.

15. Political Conflict

As expanding populations exert more and more pressure on limited resources, both local and global, their impact on politics—the task of determining who gets what—becomes increasingly evident. Additional people place additional demands upon a political system at the same time that they impede that system's ability to respond satisfactorily. By constantly complicating resource allocation decisions, population growth can affect not only political stability within national borders but also the relations among states.

Population's role in international conflict has consisted of exacerbating existing tensions—and creating new ones. The 1969 war between El Salvador and Honduras was triggered by soccer riots, but the underlying cause was the wholesale migration of Salvadorans from their crowded country into less-populous Honduras, where they began asserting an economic importance offensive to Hondurans. The 1971 Indo-Pakistani War was detonated at least in part by the sudden pressure placed on India's resources by the millions of East Pakistani refugees fleeing Pakistan's civil war.

Where population growth contributes to poverty and unmet demands, it may also encourage terrorism. Terrorism has long been a tool of those seeking power. Now it has become a survival tactic for poor people. In Colombia, police officials estimated that as many as 10,000 kidnappings took place in 1975.

16. Minerals

The future availability of mineral supplies at reasonable cost will depend on slowing growth in demand as well as on expanding reserves. New technologies—especially recycling, the potential of which has barely been tapped—present opportunities for limited stretching of mineral reserves. Yet the reality that mineral resources have limits is irrefutable, regardless of price and technology. If mined long enough, any mineral resource must sooner or later be exhausted.

17. Health Services

Population growth affects health in many ways. Women who have large families often start childbearing early in life. Teenage mothers have higher mortality rates and suffer a greater incidence of disease than mothers who are more mature. Crowding, when accompanied by poor sanitation, fosters the spread of infectious diseases. Large family size strains food budgets and leads to poor nutrition, which in turn weakens the body and makes it vulnerable to disease.

Faced with the overwhelming task of providing housing, education, and employment for twice their present populations by the end of the century, most developing nations will have little time, expertise, or money to expand health services. In many countries, governments will have trouble just maintaining the current level of inadequate health care.

18. Water

Brooklyn, New York, was a sparsely populated village in the nineteenth century, and like most communities, supplied itself with fresh water by sinking wells to tap what then seemed like an inexhaustible supply of underground water. As the area changed from a collection of small farms to a heavily populated borough, expanding demand slowly lowered the level of underground fresh water, and salt water seeped into the city's supply, rendering it useless. With no other source of drinkable water, Brooklyn was forced to obtain its supplies from distant sources in upstate New York, an area with fewer people and fewer demands on its water supply.

Examples of population growth exerting pressure on water supplies are legion. From Manila—where the population may double in 15 years—to the grazing range of the Ethiopian Plateau, the limited availability of fresh water is undermining health, restricting food supplies, and diminishing hopes of economic development. Population pressure on water supplies is most evident in agriculture, with irrigation needs representing one principal source of future world water demand. Producing enough food to keep one person alive requires enormous quantities of water. Up to 120 gallons of water are needed to grow the grain used in a loaf of bread. A pound of meat, which requires direct water consumption plus water to grow the animal feed, can require 200 times that amount. Per capita daily water use in the United States has increased more than 75% in the last 25 years. World water use is expected to triple by the early twenty-first century if projected population and per capita consumption trends materialize.

19.   Unemployment

During the spring of 1973, when a national election campaign was in progress in Colombia, the *New York Times* reported that both major political parties had opened campaign offices in New York City in order to solicit votes from the estimated 80,000 Colombians residing illegally in the city. For New Yorkers, this dramatized the difficulty that developing countries have in providing jobs for their rapidly expanding populations. The U. S. Immigration and Naturalization Service estimated in 1974 that 7 to 12 million illegal immigrants reside in the United States. As many as two-thirds are Mexicans. The willingness of millions to sever ties with their home communities, their cultures, and often their families to submit themselves to the humiliation associated with illegal immigration indicates the extent of their desperation.

Economists estimate that for every 1% growth in the labor force, a 3% rate of economic growth is required to generate jobs. With current technology, countries experiencing a 3% rate of population growth therefore require a 9% rate of economic growth just to maintain employment at the current level. Attaining full employment would require an even faster rate of economic expansion. But economic growth rates have been falling during the seventies rather than rising; fewer jobs are being created even while the number of potential workers is climbing at an unprecedented rate.

In Latin America, the first region to experience rapid population growth, the number of unemployed tripled in the 15 years from 1950 to 1965. India is now beleaguered with 100,000 new entrants into the labor force each week. At least 15% of the labor force is reported jobless in Pakistan, Sri Lanka, Malaysia, and the Philippines. Perhaps 25% of Indonesia's potential labor force may now be out of work.

Reducing birth rates and instituting progressive economic policies can both increase the capital available for creating jobs in the near term and eventually reduce the number of jobs needed.

20.   Endangered Species

The earth's history is one of species evolving, flourishing, and disappearing. But recent studies suggest that extinction is no longer a slow process. The number of plant and animal species threatened with extinction now far exceeds the number of new species appearing.

During the past four decades, the number of Bengal tigers roaming the Indian subcontinent has dropped from about 40,000 to 2,000, as India's growing human population has reduced the tigers' range. (Each tiger needs at least 10 square miles to forage for game.) Over half of southern Florida's plant species now verge on extinction, because of a tripling of the human population during the past quarter century. Throughout the United States, the Smithsonian Institution estimates that a tenth of the 20,000 species, sub-species and varieties of plants native to the United States are now threatened with extinction.

In Kenya, the human population density

in the savanna is now increasing alarmingly. In the struggle to produce more food, farmers there plow grasslands that are the home of most of the country's big game. African naturalists fear that the consequent loss of fresh water supplies and open land will gradually eliminate wildlife.

21. Energy

Every person added to the world's population requires energy to prepare food, to provide clothing and shelter, and to fuel economic life. The amount of energy used every day by the world's four billion consumers, for everything from heating water to running the most sophisticated computers, is rapidly increasing. Each increment in demand is another claim on shrinking energy reserves. The squeeze on energy supplies is being felt all over the world. In the shadow of the Himalayas, the pressure of population growth is depleting firewood resources at an alarming rate. Estimates of proven U. S. petroleum reserves have been scaled down in recent years, while population continues to grow. Countries historically energy self-sufficient, such as the U. S. and Romania with its once-rich Ploesti oil fields, are steadily depleting their reserves of oil, becoming dependent on imported supplies.

22. Individual Freedom

As more and more people require space and resources on this planet, more and more rules and regulations are required to supervise individual use of the earth's resources for the common good. To safeguard the environment, regulations limiting industrial pollution have been established. Local governments in the U. S., representing the interests of their constituencies, now have the authority to shut down plants when air pollution exceeds specified limits, or when plants continue to pollute in violation of the environmental statutes.

Requirements for the common good have also filtered down to the individual level in the form of hunting permits, fishing licenses, health certificates, drivers' licenses, and building permits. Land use provides another obvious example of encroaching regulation. Zoning laws regulate the use of privately owned land. Sewer moratoriums have effectively prevented some landowners from developing their property. The need for more extensive political control is painfully illustrated by the tragedies born of the unregulated use of common resources like air and water. A finite world pressed by the needs of increasing numbers of inhabitants can no longer afford such uncontrolled self-seeking. One possible result of the re-emergence of scarcity may be the resurrection in modern form of the pre-industrial polity—a polity in which the few govern the many and in which government is no longer of or by the people. From the effects of population pressure, Robert Heilbroner, in *An Inquiry into the Human Prospect*, has inferred that military-socialist governments are the only regimes capable of establishing workable economic and social systems. And from the difficulties and dangers of continued growth, he anticipates a drift toward authoritarian measures as the only means by which a suicidal Hobbesian struggle might be avoided.

Conclusion

This inventory of the many consequences of population growth underlines both the complexity of the problem and the urgency of efforts to slow population growth everywhere. Each person added to the world's population puts at least some additional pressures on the earth's resources, on its food, energy, water, and space. If the person is affluent, then the pressure on resources will be far greater than if the person is poor. Population growth threatens rich and poor alike. Pollution affects everyone; there are no ecological islands.

Our analysis suggests strongly that the threat posed by population growth deserves much more attention than it is now getting. Leaders can no longer afford the luxury of insisting that population is someone else's problem or that it can only be solved by future generations.

As the dimensions of the population problem become more apparent, some national political leaders are beginning to respond. Perhaps the most encouraging development over the past year has been the sharp increase in requests from developing countries for assistance in family planning. The principal aid agencies in this field—the United Nations Fund for Population Activities, the International Planned Parenthood Federation, and the U. S. Agency for International Development—are being overwhelmed with requests for assistance. As of 1976, the principal constraint on efforts to make family planning services available to all who want them is not so much apathy in the developing countries as a lack of financial and technical assistance from the rich countries. How we respond to the population threat may do more to shape the world in which our children and grandchildren will live than anything else we do.

38

TAKING SHAPE: A BIGGER, DIFFERENT POPULATION

Of all the factors that will affect people's lives in the '80s, few will have a bigger impact than the shifts ahead in America's population—

Growth in the number of Americans will speed up. Population will expand by about 21 million in the coming decade, or 3 million more than in the 1970s. By 1990, the country will have an estimated 242 million people.

The big increase will be in older, more affluent age brackets. Four fifths of the population growth will be in persons in their 30s and 40s, most of the rest in the age 60-and-older group.

Births will increase from 33 million in the 1970s to 39 million in the '80s. This upswing is to result from a large increase in women in their childbearing years, not from any increase in the birth rate.

The number of Americans under age 20 will fall below 30 percent of the population for the first time in history. The reason: A sharp decline in the number of teen-agers, resulting from the smaller rate of births in the '60s and '70s.

People over 65, most of them retired, will account for 1 out of every 8 Americans by the end of the decade. Increased longevity because of better health care will raise the number of people in this age group by 5 million, to a total of 30 million by 1990.

A dramatic increase is expected in the oldest age bracket, people 75 or over. Growth of this age group during the '80s will total 2.6 million, accounting for 12 percent of the nation's total population growth and bringing

Reprinted from *U.S. News & World Report.* Copyright 1979 U.S. News & World Report. Used with permission.

the number of such senior citizens to more than 12 million.

These changes in the nation's population picture for the decade ahead are computed by the magazine's Economic Unit, based on official projections. For a look at what these shifts will mean—

A CHANGING LABOR FORCE

The American labor force will grow more slowly and increase in experience as fewer young workers seek jobs. Unemployment is expected to lessen.

The biggest decline will be largely in unskilled young men age 16 through 24, as the size of this age group shrinks. One result will be growing difficulty for the armed services in enrolling new recruits.

Women will be joining the labor market in even greater numbers. Some 50 percent of those age 25 to 54 worked at or sought paid jobs in 1970, and about 60 percent do so now. But more than 70 percent will be in the job market by the end of the 1980s, for a total of 38 million.

Somewhat fewer men in the 25-to-54 age group will join the work force. Their total will reach 46 million by the end of the 1980s. As more men opt for early retirement, the portion of working-age males participating in the job market will continue its slow decline, from 80 percent in 1970 to 78 percent in 1980 and to 76 percent in 1990.

Blacks in the labor force will increase at a faster rate than whites will. By 1989, the U. S. job force will have about 15 million blacks, with men and women in nearly equal numbers.

Employment will rise by more than 16 million over the coming decade, compared with an increase of 18 million in the 1970s. At the end of the '80s, about 113 million Americans will have jobs. With fewer hard-to-place teen-agers on the market, one of the most nagging problems of the 1970s will ease as unemployment declines to possibly 5 percent of the labor force.

NEW CONSUMER DEMANDS

Business will see its customers change, requiring many firms to take a fresh look at their retail-sales strategies. For example, the decline in today's big teen-age market will result in less demand for such things as blue jeans, records, tapes, old cars, some athletic gear and "junk food" products consumed by high-school students.

But an increase in the number of births will bring an upturn in the presently lagging demand for baby food, infants' clothes, toys and services.

Demand will increase, too, for a broad spectrum of goods and services needed by larger numbers of people in their 30s and 40s. With growing families and rising incomes, they will require more cars, furniture, clothes, vacation facilities, outdoor equipment and especially housing—both homes and apartments.

Biggest increase in demand will come from the burgeoning number of Americans over 65, many of them healthier and wealthier than today's senior citizens. This points to a new boom in the leisure industry—from hobbies and movies to ocean cruises and recreational vehicles. It also will spur demand for nursing homes, health clinics and retirement developments.

THE IMPACT ON SCHOOLS

Most communities will find their school systems unbalanced during the coming decade. Fewer teen-agers will mean that many high schools will have to close down or cut back. Grade schools that were closed during the '70s may have to be reopened during the '80s, as the number of births increases and the trend to preschool classes extends to more segments of the population.

SOME PROCESSES OF SOCIAL LIFE

Colleges, which expanded rapidly during the past decade, already are finding their supply of students dropping off. Many institutions will be forced to contract sharply or close down altogether as the number of potential collegians age 19–22 descends further and faster during the '80s. The alternative: New, stepped-up emphasis on graduate work and classes for retirees or working students.

LIFESTYLES AND FAMILIES

The day of the big family will recede further, population experts say, as the '80s bring a jump in the number of people living alone or as childless—often unmarried—couples.

While the total number of households—separate living units of one person or more—rises from 80 million in 1980 to a record 97 million in 1990, the average size of the American household thus will continue to decrease. From 3.3 people in 1960, it will drop to 2.7 in 1980 and to a low of 2.5 by 1990.

The number of individuals living alone, often as a result of divorce, is expected to increase more than any other category, up from less than 7 million in 1960 to more than 25 million by the end of the '80s. This compares with an increase in the number of families from 45 million to 68 million during the same period.

COMING RACIAL SHIFTS

Blacks will increase both in numbers and as a proportion of the population during the next decade, giving them increasing political and economic muscle. They now total about 26 million or 11.8 percent of Americans. By the end of the '80s, they will number 30 million, or 12.2 percent.

Asians and other racial minorities are expected to increase even faster, but from a relatively small base—up from 1.3 percent of the population in 1970 to 2.7 percent by 1990.

Whites will increase in number from just over 190 million now to 207 million at the end of the '80s. As a share of the population, whites will decline from 86.2 percent now to 85.1 percent.

CRIME AND PUNISHMENT

The rate of serious crime in America, headed upward again at this time, is almost certain to subside in the 1980s, criminologists say. The reason: A decline in the number of teen-agers and young adults. Those under 25 accounted for 56 percent of all arrests in 1977, the latest figures available.

With any substantial decrease in the rate of crime, planners foresee a lessening need for costly new police equipment, new jails and correctional institutions. There is even hope that these cutbacks may help to hold down the steady increase in city and state taxes.

As population patterns change, the impact will be felt by industry, residential areas, schools, local governments and nearly everyone.

POPULATION SWINGS AHEAD

Within the big metropolitan areas, people will continue to move away from the central cities to the suburbs, leaving just 22.9 percent of Americans living inside the cities, down from 27 percent today. The suburbs will continue to expand as more blacks, low-income whites and blue-collar families move in—but not as fast as in the 1970s.

The big swing to the sun belt will continue, with vast numbers moving from the North and East to the South and West. Biggest gainers from this shift will be California, Florida and Texas, which will each add at least 2.5 million people if present trends continue.

What it all adds up to is that population changes of many kinds, now under way, are set to have widespread effects on life in America during the decade ahead.

39

ENVIRONMENTAL PROTECTION IS GOOD BUSINESS

Michael McCloskey

At a time when inflation is on everyone's mind, many people wonder how heavy a toll the economic troubles ahead will take on the environmental movement. Is there a basic incompatibility between economic functions and environmental goals?

Environmentalists have been accused of being radicals who seek a condition of "no growth" and a return to a primitive style of life. Of course, none of this is true. Environmentalists seek responsible behavior by business people, behavior that does not degrade the environment others must share, or impoverish the future. We seek constructive growth that improves general conditions at reasonable costs. We are against the brand of progress that means that only a few gain and most lose.

As environmentalists, we spend most of our time advocating positive changes in public policy to improve the environment. We are *for* mass transit, *for* solar power, *for* recycling, *for* reclaiming wastewater, *for* water and energy conservation, *for* reforestation and *for* true sustained yield, *for* integrated pest management, *for* irrigation with nutrient-rich wastes, *for* reclamation of derelict lands, *for* renovation of urban housing and infilling, *for* clean air and water, *for* open space and parks, and *for* better public health programs.

Unfortunately, most of these positive projects compete with proposals counter to them, and in dealing with our competition we are often tagged as negative. While it may seem to be no more than a matter of semantics, this negative side of the coin seems to draw more publicity.

But many businesses live well with the programs we advocate, and the record is getting better all the time. Of all businesses and industries that produce pollution, 80% now comply with federal pollution laws. More industries than municipalities met the 1977 water-pollution cleanup standards. Only 600 of some 4000 industrial dischargers are not yet in compliance.

Pollution-control programs, far from being a burden on the economy, have produced one of the fastest-growing industries in America. There are now more than 600 companies manufacturing control equipment. Others make cooling towers, scrubbers, precipitators, catalytic converters, pyrolitic processors and mufflers. Firms producing air- and water-pollution control equipment had sales of $1.8 billion in 1977. Their sales are growing at a rate

From *Sierra*, March/April 1981, pp. 31–33. Reprinted by permission.

twice as fast as the rest of U. S. industry and are expected to triple by 1985, reaching $5 billion.

All together, more than $47 billion is now spent annually in the United States to prevent environmental abuse; about $27 billion of this is spent in response to environmental legislation. The total environmentally related spending amounts to 1.3% of the Gross National Product. By 1986, nearly $710 billion may have been spent on environmental programs, with $477 billion of it triggered by federal programs. Most of this money will be routed through the accounts of businesses that make or maintain pollution-control equipment.

As many as a million workers may soon be employed in this work. Each additional billion dollars spent on pollution control creates 40,000 new jobs; annually, 160,000 new jobs are created in the pollution-control field. The bulk of these jobs will be in industry and local government, with skilled operators constituting the largest category. In addition, 1.5 million new jobs could be created through transportation reforms alone with measures that environmentalists advocate.

And these figures do not tell the whole story. Other environmentalist-supported programs also provide business opportunities: processing recycled materials, manufacturing buses and trains for mass transit, building and selling solar collectors, rehabilitating older homes and installing insulation and energy-conserving equipment. Public incentive programs supported by environmentalists help foster all these businesses.

As firms find that older plants do not justify further investment in controls, they often choose new locations to build plants that are usually more profitable. So far some 118 old plants have been closed, with some 22,000 workers affected. But in most cases, the businesses that closed relocated to better advantage. Of the plants that closed ostensibly for environmental reasons, 60% were shown in one survey to be old or obsolete.

Environmental programs are designed to improve living conditions for everyone, and business shares in these benefits. Property values as a whole are protected by good environmental-control programs. Residential values are protected by good planning and by strong zoning standards. Strong air-quality controls prevent damage to structures from corrosion; paint jobs last longer; sensitive crops and yard plants suffer less. Current damage from uncontrolled air pollution in these categories may approach $3 billion annually. Strong water-pollution controls improve the safety of drinking water and the quality of the water required for some sensitive industrial processes. Such controls, as well as those on toxic substances and pesticides, help assure the health of commercial fisheries. Mass transit improves the mobility of the work force, and energy and water conservation help reduce operating costs.

Most of these programs, moreover, help produce a healthier and happier work force that spends more time on the job. Air pollution, for example, is more than an annoyance. It limits lifespan, curtails vigor and reduces resistance to disease. It raises both morbidity and mortality rates. Achieving national air-quality standards for industry would reduce mortality losses to the economy by $36 billion annually. Toxic substances in air, water, foods and other products can produce cancer; between 60% and 90% of all cancers are induced by the environment, and the incidence of such cancer is growing at a rate of 2% a year. Cancer is twice as prevalent in polluted central cities as it is in suburbs.

But the key question remains: do the investments required for these programs stifle business? Studies in recent years suggest that pollution-control investments now amount to 4.7% of new investments in plants and equipment. This percentage has been falling in recent years, although it may rise a little to meet deadlines coming due in 1983. For a few industries, such as steel and nonferrous metal smelters, pulp processors and electric utilities, the investment rates are much higher. In the next few years, the steel industry may have to invest about 20% of its capital outlays in pollution controls.

Some steel plants and copper smelters have been notorious foot draggers, and have not been making scheduled investments to cure their conspicuous problems within a reasonable time. Now, suddenly, time has run out on them, and the whole bill is coming due. One study found that it costs three times more to install pollution controls all at once than to phase in the installations over a period of time.

But in general, the amounts being invested by industry are only a small share of new capital being invested. Capital costs for control equipment have been overestimated both by the Environmental Protection Agency and by industry, a recent study found; EPA's cost projections were closer to the actual figures than industry's.

Whatever the projections have said, a recent study for the Council on Environmental Quality confirms earlier findings that pollution-control investments displaced little productive new investment. In fact, a survey by the Bureau of Economic Analysis a few years ago showed that only 2% of the firms affected were postponing other investments because of the squeeze for capital. One should also bear in mind that these are largely one-time increases in outlay. Once a plant has been upgraded to meet control standards, the investment does not have to be repeated. Annual growth in the GNP is probably only 1% lower because of these outlays; over a ten- to fifteen-year period, the growth might be only 1% to 2% lower than it would have been with no pollution-control investment.

One reason for the small negative effect on GNP is that pollution-control investments are often made by making industrial processes more efficient. One division of Dow Chemical found that new investments in pollution control cut operating costs by the $2 million that the control equipment cost. Alcoa cut energy consumption in its plants by 30% when it introduced new technology to reduce fluoride and tar emissions. The 3M Company changed its processes to reduce air and water pollution and saved $11 million in costs. The Great Lakes Paper Company found a water-pollution treatment system that reduced annual operating costs by $14 million a year. A National Science Foundation study of five other nations also found the environmental investments stimulated technological innovation generally.

Of course, most businesses will try to pass on any added costs to consumers. Still, these increases are dwarfed by the general rates of inflation. Over the past decade, the Consumer Price Index has probably risen by only 1.5% because of spending on pollution control. The rate of inflation may be increased by 3.6% by 1985 because of these one-time expenditures, but this does not represent an erosion of purchasing power; it is a small part of the runaway rates of inflation that have been compounding from year to year. Besides, with pollution-control investments, the public is getting more for its money—better water and air, better health, more productive crops and longer-lasting buildings and homes. In 1977, estimated economic benefits from air-pollution controls exceeded their costs.

Other objectives of environmental programs are basically anti-inflationary. Environmentalists believe in husbanding natural resources to prevent waste and premature depletion. As resources are depleted, scarcity ensues and prices inflate. Environmentalists want to ration nonrenewable resources, to limit their depletion and extend their availability. Policies of planned obsolescence, conspicuous consumption, throwaway goods, depletion allowances and maximum growth have caused us to exhaust our high-grade resources. We have used up the bulk of our easily extracted oil and gas and must now look for them in remote and difficult places. A lack of sound conservation policies in the past is adding to the inflation we must now bear.

SOME PROCESSES OF SOCIAL LIFE

We should rethink all government policies that encourage depletion, waste and sprawl. Sprawl stands as an instructive example of waste. It has been encouraged by various federal policies: tax deductions, mortgage insurance and freeway aid. Lessening sprawl with policies that encourage multifamily low-rise housing would provide both environmental and economic benefits. A study done for the Council on Environmental Quality showed that such housing costs 44% less per occupant to construct than does single-family housing, and it also produces 45% less pollution, consumes 35% less water, uses 44% less energy and does not preempt as much land. This example shows that environmentally backed programs often help keep costs down.

Environmentalists have also been trying to keep costs down in energy. They advocate relying on the energy sources that cost the least. For example, energy conservation averages about $4 billion, ranging down to as little as $1.5 billion, in capital costs per quadrillion BTUs. In contrast, nuclear power may cost between $70 billion and $90 billion per quad.

If the country chooses high-cost forms of energy, the capital requirements could be prodigious. Over the next decade, investments from these energy industries could range from $800 billion to $1 trillion or more, tying up anywhere from half to two thirds of all capital available to all industry.

Clearly, capital-intensive energy technologies will cause severe competition for capital and inflate its cost. In contrast, energy plans geared primarily to conservation might require only a third as much capital, perhaps less. The $430-billion difference between the two forecasts is nearly as great as the total amount required over the same period for pollution-control programs.

The conclusion we can draw from these numbers and contrasts is that, taken as a whole, environmental programs will do more to help our economy than to burden it. The conserver society we advocate is probably the only pattern for the future of our economy that can work.

America: the third century

XIV

THE URBAN SCENE
From Cities to Suburbs and Return

Cities developed centuries ago as agricultural surplus freed people from farming. Those not needed in the vital task of feeding the population were attracted to urban areas both by the work opportunities and by the excitement of city living. This process of migration to cities continues today in many parts of the world. However, the rapid expansion of cities has caused strains on communications, transportation, distribution of needed goods and services, making cities less desirable places in the eyes of many.

As cities in the United States have become more crowded, a reverse trend has taken place. Many have sought relief from the congestion of cities by moving to suburbs. This movement was at its peak in the 1960s. Initially it was the well-to-do who could afford suburban living, but today persons of many income levels are attracted to suburbs. This movement to and growth of the suburbs has brought big-city problems such as crime, pollution, congestion, racial tensions, housing shortages, and energy shortages to what was believed to be utopian communities. The fact is that many of these problems also existed in the suburbs in addition to problems specific to them.

Recently there has been another change in this pattern of movement. No longer are suburbs expanding as they did in the 1960s; inner cities are attracting more industry and individuals who stay or return due to massive facelifts and lower transportation costs. Investment of money by both the federal government and private companies has enabled cities to revitalize decaying downtowns and become attractive, desirable places again. The first article discusses these changes taking place in many cities and suburbs.

The energy crisis is also affecting the distribution of people and industry in cities and suburbs. With gasoline costly and in short supply, many persons will need to give up private autos for alternative transportation such as mass transit, and will live closer to their jobs. In many countries mass transit is well-developed, rapid and convenient. Why is this not true of most cities in the United States? Kwitny takes us back to the roots of the "great transportation conspiracy," explaining how several corporations conspired to eliminate cheap, efficient mass transit from many cities. Thus, what appeared to be a problem arising naturally from population growth and movement was actually the result of a criminal conspiracy.

The last article presents us with some alternative plans for cities in an energy-short world. Van Til explains the options available to us and the implications of each option.

As you read this chapter, consider the changes taking place in the cities and suburbs with which you are familiar, and what future changes might come about as a result of energy shortages and transportation problems.

40

COMEBACK FOR CITIES, WOES FOR SUBURBS

Lawrence Maloney
Donald L. Battle

The face of urban America—its congested cities and sprawling suburbs—is being transformed in ways that are surprising even the experts.

Little more than a decade ago, U. S. cities were torn by riots that erupted despite a flurry of federal programs aimed at easing urban woes. Now, at the beginning of a new decade in which government handouts may prove much harder to come by, the outlook for many of the nation's big urban centers, ironically, is upbeat.

Meanwhile, the suburbs, which have attracted the bulk of the nation's wealth and jobs since World War II, are beginning to suffer the nagging problems of crime, pollution, troubled schools and even poverty. Fewer residents are leaving cities for the white picket fences of suburbia, and more suburbanites are coming back. More companies, too, are setting up shop in the downtowns, as cities switch from hubs of industry to regional magnets for trade and tourism.

All this doesn't mean that the great advantages enjoyed by many suburbs over cities will disappear overnight. However, more

observers now agree that a slow but sure equalizing process is under way in many metropolitan areas. Says urbanologist Louis Masotti of Northwestern University: "People realize that suburbs aren't Shangri-La any more. At the same time, the cities are becoming more exciting."

SPRUCING UP THE DOWNTOWNS

What is turning the heads of even the pessimists is the massive facelift going on in cities across the land. Once the seedy part of the city, Downtown U.S.A. is being rediscovered by more businesses and by families seeking an alternative to suburbia.

Spurred by federal aid and by lucrative real estate tax breaks, private developers are pouring billions of construction dollars into center-city skyscrapers, shopping plazas, hotels, apartments and condominiums. At the same time, factory lofts, brownstone buildings and waterfront warehouses are being recycled by developers and by families fleeing the rising costs of commuting. Says Charles Leven, an urban specialist at Washington University in St. Louis: "We're getting a miniature version of what happened in the

1950s when people fled to the suburbs. We're now seeing some flight back to the city."

Much of the resurgence is due to the maturing of urban-renewal programs and the emergence of cities as regional service centers. In many communities, the service or white-collar industries located in downtown areas are growing at a faster clip than other employment sectors. The space requirements of businesses ranging from the arts and tourism to banking and insurance are triggering a construction boom. Among the many examples:

New York's Wall Street area will have a 69-million-dollar facility housing the American Stock Exchange. The plans call for construction of three new hotels and a convention center.

Chicago will redevelop a seven-block area—for 500 million dollars—anchored by a 2,100-room Hilton Hotel.

Miami is planning a 50-story World Trade Center catering to international firms.

Denver, scrambling to furnish office space in its role as headquarters for the Rocky Mountain energy industry, is in the midst of a billion-dollar building boom.

Washington, D. C., will break ground in April for a convention center that already has stimulated interest for additional hotel space and 14 new office buildings.

Eight new office buildings went up in San Francisco last year, and two more are set for completion in 1981.

Los Angeles will begin construction in June of a 71-million-dollar wholesale-produce mart.

In St. Louis, 19th-century lofts and warehouses are being recycled into offices along the Mississippi River.

Detroit's 350-million-dollar Renaissance Center, a high-rise office-and-hotel com-

plex located in the downtown area, already has pumped more than 1 billion dollars into the city's economy.

The reasons that service industries are attracted to downtown areas are many. Despite advances in communication, daily face-to-face contact still is needed by many workers such as lawyers, bankers and the media.

Surveys by the Real Estate Research Corporation of Washington, D. C., give another view: "We expect less pioneering with respect to office location in the early '80s than was seen during the 1970s. There will be fewer remote, suburban office parks, due in part to the energy crisis and . . . to limitations on sewer and water-extension capacity."

There also is a growing interest among corporations in keeping the inner city viable. Explains E. Eddie Henson, president, Williams Realty Corporation, Tulsa: "The core of cities is the figurehead or central image. If you let it deteriorate or die, it has a bad effect on the total community."

Many downtowns, too, are luring foreign firms and banks that want to be near their U. S. customers. Foreign institutions, taking advantage of what they perceive to be a relatively stable American economy, are investing millions of dollars in U. S. real estate, especially in cities. For example, Ackerman & Company, an Atlanta real-estate firm, has purchased 350 million dollars in real estate for Dutch pension funds and insurance companies in the last three years. About half of those acquisitions are downtown office buildings.

HIGHER REVENUES, MORE JOBS

The benefits of this revival go far beyond the companies involved. Cities are reaping gains in jobs and tax revenues. In Sacramento, a 15-block Capitol Mall redevelopment produced 1.7 million dollars last year in property taxes, compared with $180,000 prior to the new construction. When completed in four years, the new headquarters building for PPG Industries and Grant Street East—a combination office, hotel and commercial complex—will add at least 1.1 million dollars to Pittsburgh's coffers each year.

Thousands of jobs also are being created. Eleven new commercial and office buildings will bring 40,000 jobs to Chicago's Loop area. Over the last decade, rebuilding efforts in Baltimore have added 30,000 jobs to the center city, bringing the number of downtown workers to 120,000.

Those jobs and the burgeoning force of service workers are, in turn, sparking demand for downtown shops. In Philadelphia, the Gallery, an enclosed mall with 100 shops only a few blocks from City Hall, has become so successful that a second phase containing another 100 outlets is planned. Sales are running well above those of comparable stores in suburban malls.

Retail sales in Miami, a city that has become a Mecca for Latin American tourists, were up 35 percent last year. In Denver, the demand for downtown stores has spawned plans for construction of a 13-block pedestrian shopping mall. Also among the many cities that have built malls to boost the fortunes of downtown merchants and encourage energy conservation are Chicago, Portland and Seattle.

Says Mathias DeVito, president of the Rouse Company, Columbia, Md., a firm that pioneered development of suburban centers: "Downtown retail sales are coming back so demonstrably that over the next 10 years every city will have a shopping mall."

Along with shops and offices, more builders are including apartments and condominiums as part of their multiple-use complexes. Michael J. Moloney, housing and urban-redevelopment director in Phoenix, notes that interest in downtown living is "phenomenal."

At this point, there is no flood of people abandoning suburbs for the city. Increasingly, however, people who might have moved from cities are staying put, fixing up old town-houses or converting commercial buildings into apartments and condominiums.

No one knows exactly just how much urban rehabilitation is going on. A 1976 survey by the Urban Land Institute suggests that nearly half of the 260 cities with populations of 50,000 or more were experiencing renewal, but most observers say that revitalization has stepped up substantially since then, with whole neighborhoods being reborn.

Cities in the forefront of this resurgence, such as Boston, Chicago and Washington, D. C., have the ability to attract large populations of higher-income professionals, points out economist Richard Nathan, the director of Princeton University's Urban and Regional Resource Center. These cities also have become regional centers for trade, banking and other services.

Examples of a residential spurt are everywhere. In Miami, work is under way on Plaza Venetia, a three-phase complex of apartments, shops, hotels, a marina and restaurants. Oakland's Hong Kong U.S.A. project will include condominium towers, as well as stores, a hotel and offices. Other cities, such as Boston, Baltimore, St. Louis and San Francisco, are capitalizing on the ambiance of their waterfronts to spur construction and renovation of homes.

In San Diego, the Marina-Columbia project represents the first urban-residential development there since the early 1900s. Already, about 3,000 people have expressed interest in buying condominiums there, and a lottery may be needed to handle the demand. Similarly, the first privately financed, nonsubsidized homes built in downtown Detroit in 20 years are selling for $67,000, making them competitive in price with suburban homes.

Behind the lure of city living are changes in American lifestyles. A realty-company survey, for example, indicates that 70 percent of Tulsa respondents feel that the downtown is a good place to work. A few short years ago, that figure was only 20 percent. The same survey showed a fourfold increase in the number of people who were interested in living in the central business district.

Observers trace this shift, in part, to a worsening energy crisis and a change in demographics. While most families with children still seek out the suburbs, there is a growing group of people who desire the advantages of city living. Masotti of Northwestern notes that people are marrying later, opting for smaller families and finding less need than in the past for single-family suburban homes that require gasoline-guzzling automobiles and time-consuming commutes. In many of these cases, busy working couples want to be near their places of employment. Still another segment of city dwellers consists of "empty nesters"—former suburban residents who have raised their families and now want to be close to the cultural attractions of cities.

This new-found love affair with the cities—and the building triggered by it—has reached a point where people worry about the displacement of the poor. In Washington, D. C., a recent study found that 25,000 residents have been forced to move from their homes over the last five years because of condominium conversions, renovations and rising housing prices. Some experts predict that cities could become "battlegrounds" in the 1980s if ways aren't found to let the urban poor share in the rebirth of cities.

HELP FROM THE GOVERNMENT

Although companies and individuals have led the way in moving cities toward rebirth, government also has played a role. Local officials not only are offering attractive tax-rebate plans to businesses but also are forming redevelopment agencies to cut red tape, assemble tracts of land for companies and speed loans at lower interest rates.

The federal government has lent a hand through revenue sharing and community-development funds as well as through Urban Development Action Grants (UDAG), a pro-gram which many observers consider to be the most successful urban effort in years.

UDAG takes an approach that could become commonplace in the money-tight 1980s: Using federal dollars to spur private investment in cities. Since April of 1978, the Department of Housing and Urban Development has awarded 1.2 billion dollars in action grants to cities. That money has in turn leveraged more than 6.5 billion dollars in private funds from bankers and companies interested in halting urban decay and encouraging economic development. In fact, HUD won't release money unless a city can prove that the private sector has formally agreed to participate in the projects, which include commercial and residential buildings and land assembly for developers.

Action grants, a 400-million-dollar annual program, form the cornerstone in a Carter urban policy that has been gutted by the budget squeeze. Two years ago, the Carter administration unveiled an ambitious urban program—one that would have cost more than 13.5 billion dollars in the two years ending Sept. 30, 1980. But in the wake of Proposition 13 fever, the administration trimmed some of its requests and was blocked by Congress on others. In the end, the White House received only 2.5 billion dollars.

Still, the Carter administration has been praised by many mayors for several policy shifts that have helped cities on their road to recovery, including efforts to locate more government facilities in cities and to target more federal grants to distressed areas. Also praised: A "community conservation" policy that allows mayors to ask the government to do an analysis before approving federal funds for highways and other projects in suburbs.

Such efforts have angered suburban leaders, who argue that their constituents are being asked to subsidize cities, while getting little in return. Booming sun-belt cities, too, are critical of Carter efforts to funnel more federal aid to troubled frost-belt cities. Sun-belt mayors already have succeeded in forcing a change in the formula for awarding action grants to allow more money to go to "pockets of poverty" in otherwise healthy cities. Infighting among cities could intensify, if the President's new anti-inflation plan forces cuts in urban programs.

Federal assistance is needed, experts contend, because the revival of cities, though more visible every day, is still tenuous. If a recession hits, warns economist Thomas Muller of the Urban Institute in Washington, D. C., several cities would suffer seriously, having to lay off workers and curtail services.

Others worry that cities for too long have neglected repairs on bridges, roads and other facilities and also have skimped on the funding of pension plans for public workers—problems that could haunt them later in the '80s.

Even so, many cities are in better financial shape than earlier in the decade, says George Peterson, director of public finance for the Urban Institute. The experience of New York City, which was on the edge of bankruptcy in 1975 and has slowly fought its way back with massive federal and state support, has scared other cities into tougher money management. That is evident in the squabbles that cities such as Chicago and Philadelphia have had recently with public employees over contracts and personnel cuts.

Still, urbanologists believe that this harder line is a good sign that cities are coming to grips with their problems—problems that have yet to be faced by suburbs.

SUBURBS: STILL BOOMING, BUT . . .

While cities try for a comeback, the suburbs face a different challenge: How to grow without inheriting a host of urban ills.

Areas that were sleepy villages 20 years ago have blossomed into surging centers of commerce and industry. But with that dramatic growth have come many problems formerly associated with urban cores: Crime, congestion, troubled schools, racial tensions, housing shortages. There are predictions, too, that future expansion—and the wealth it brings—will be slowed by energy shortages.

This shift comes after a long period in which suburbs reigned as the center of urban vitality. Explains urban geographer Peter O. Muller of Temple University in Philadelphia: "The big development of the '60s and '70s was that cities turned inside out. More people now identify with suburban realms. The idea of a city and its subservient suburbs is dead and buried."

The movement of population and jobs bears that out. In the 1960s, suburbs grew four times faster than center cities and, by 1970, had more housing units than either cities or rural areas. Suburban jobs increased by 44 percent in the 1960s, while employment in center cities dropped 7 percent. In 1973, for the first time, suburbs provided more jobs than cities did.

Muller and other experts point to the creation of minicities outside of metropolitan areas. In these suburban complexes, thousands of people now live, work, shop and play. In such a setup the center city is no more, no less important than the others.

Before long, experts predict, these new minicities will be bogged down with many of the problems of older cities. For now, though, their story is one of incredible growth.

For example, in Tyson's Corner, Va., only a half-hour drive from the nation's capital, there was virtually no office space as late as 1966, reports David A. Edwards, executive director of the Economic Development Authority of Fairfax County, Va. Now, 50 major companies are locating in the area each year. By 1986, an estimated 12 million square feet of office space will be completed, the equivalent of 12 major city blocks in Washington, D. C.

This is in addition to a major shopping center now being expanded and other shops, hotels and apartments. Notes Edwards:

"Tyson's Corner has become the downtown for many people, especially families with children."

Northwest of Chicago, the village of Schaumburg—another minicity—had less than 1,000 people in 1960. Now it has 54,000, in the wake of a development spree that brought 11.2 million square feet of office and industrial space, most of it since 1970, plus construction of one of the country's biggest and most profitable shopping centers, Woodfield Mall.

The village's cut of the sales taxes from commercial enterprises makes up half its budget and has enabled the community to build some of the finest municipal facilities in the Chicago area, says Mayor Herbert Aigner. Also benefiting: Parks, libraries, schools and other items funded by property taxes from Schaumburg's lucrative business establishments.

Although these and other mushrooming suburbs may still lag behind cities in cultural offerings, urban expert Hugh Wilson of Adelphi University in New York notes that most suburbs still offer far better schools, more living space and less pollution, which is why people are still "voting with their feet" and heading for suburbia.

FAMILIES UNDER STRAIN

Along with the growth and a more pleasant environment have come serious problems. Many suburban communities that opened their arms to large commercial developments with an eye to boosting the tax base have not been as generous in allowing home building. Bans on sewer construction, zoning restrictions, minimum lot sizes, delays in approving projects and slow-growth plans have all led in many areas to a housing squeeze.

The result: Soaring home prices. From 1969 through 1979, inflation pushed the median price of a new home from $25,600 to $62,900, a 146 percent jump. During that same period, median family income grew by about 103 per-

cent. Annual price increases of 25 percent or more have been common in booming suburban communities of California—and developers often have had to resort to lotteries and other methods to handle the crush of would-be buyers.

In many cases, such buyers get in over their heads in order to sample the good life of suburbia. Last year, a study of families in Fairfax County, Va., by the Mount Vernon Center for Community Mental Health found that many families were under tremendous strains.

"People are getting tied into massive mortgage payments that can only be handled with dual incomes," explains psychologist Robert Weigl of the center. "Then a child appears on the scene or some other reason causes someone to drop out of the work force, and the troubles worsen."

Weigl says that many suburban families, even those with incomes of $40,000 to $45,000, simply devote too much of their energy to money matters. The result, according to the study: Marital strains, divorce, alcoholism, problems with child rearing, weak ties with friends and neighbors.

To ease the cost burden, more suburban communities in the months ahead may be forced to allow more moderately priced housing. In California, for example, suburban communities are being pressured by the state to design "inclusionary" programs that provide housing for families that earn between 80 and 120 percent of an area's median income. Such families generally have a maximum annual income of $24,000, too much for government housing subsidies and too little to qualify for most new homes.

To comply, some communities are changing their zoning to let builders put up higher-density projects with less costly homes. However, most builders are opposed to inclusionary zoning—an idea which experts say is sure to spread throughout the country—because it means higher home prices for families not eligible for discounts.

In many places, the drive to open up suburbia to moderate-income families is being waged in the courts. That's the case in some suburbs of New York City: Communities that have lured a steady stream of companies from the city but have been slow in permitting the building of homes workers can afford. Under pressure from the courts, for example, Bedminister, N. J., has been forced to undergo a rezoning that will allow a subsidiary of the Johns-Mansville Corporation to build a 2,200-unit subdivision on a single site, 25 times as many homes as would have been permitted originally.

Federal authorities are involved, too. The Department of Housing and Urban Development has withheld community-development funds from suburbs that have failed to permit construction of more affordable homes. And Department of Justice officials in late January threatened to bring lawsuits against suburbs that use large-lot zoning and other techniques that have the effect of barring minorities. On March 7, the department filed a suit charging the Detroit suburb of Birmingham with adopting land-use policies that prevent racially integrated low-income housing.

Even so, some progress has been made in making suburban living accessible to moderate-income people and minorities. A recent study by the Suburban Action Institute in New York City found many examples of suburbs that have designed good plans for providing lower-cost housing. Paul Davidoff, the institute director, also points to the rising population of middle and upper-income blacks in the suburbs, where the number of blacks increased by 34 percent between 1970 and 1977. However, observers note that blacks still make up less than 6 percent of the suburban population and tend to settle in traditionally black areas.

AS WORRIES PILE UP—

Debates over the economic and social mix of its people aren't the only question clouding suburbia's future. In some communities—including the booming minicities—the love affair with growth is cooling as residents confront traffic snarls, increasing pollution, overloaded services and disappearing green space.

In Newport Beach, Calif., where the Irvine Company and other developers have built a huge office-and-retail complex, the new City Council has voted changes in zoning laws that will reduce home building by 50 percent and commercial building by 60 percent. It's the same story in Schaumburg, where one official admits that the growth controls are not far off because of traffic congestion.

Racial unrest persists, too. Harassment of black families continues in some suburbs, including isolated instances of cross burnings by the Ku Klux Klan in areas of Long Island, N. Y., and suburban Washington, D. C. Fair-housing groups also have found that middle and upper-income blacks still tend to be steered by real-estate agents to specific suburbs.

For the nation's older suburbs—the ones bordering major cities—there are other problems. Declining school enrollments lead to empty buildings ripe for vandalism. Recent FBI statistics show that crime in many suburban areas has been growing faster than in large cities.

In the close-in suburbs, there is little vacant space left for new buildings that would shore up the tax base and allow for improvements on decaying public facilities. Political battles also are brewing between older residents, who hold most of the power in established suburbs, and young families. A report by the Urban Land Institute, a Washington research group, found that the number of elderly households in the suburbs rose by 31 percent between 1970 and 1976, compared with a 10 percent rise in central cities. While many of these people are well off, a substantial number are in real need and are pressing for new services.

Notes historian Richard Wade of the City University of New York: "The crisis of the inner cities will move to the inner suburbs in the 1980s."

What may help older suburbs is the energy crisis. Experts predict that rising fuel costs will curb suburban sprawl and give a new lease on life to close-in areas. Developers already are putting up townhouses on passed-over land, and large, old homes are being split up into apartments for young families.

Muller of Temple University also believes that the rising cost of energy and housing will lend more stability to the suburbs. People will tend to stay put, instead of seeking a bigger home and more space in more remote suburbs.

AN END TO RIVALRY?

Some experts predict that, as suburbs take on more of the problems of cities, there will be increased cooperation in solving areawide problems.

That already is happening in many areas. Councils of government, which began in the 1950s purely as planning vehicles, are taking on more power and sparking areawide solutions in the management of sewer systems, emergency medical services, public transit, pollution control, energy conservation and other essential services.

In Portland, Oreg., for example, a Metropolitan Service District was set up last year, with 12 elected officials representing 24 cities and three counties. Already, that body has succeeded in establishing an urban-growth boundary to limit sprawl and has set up programs to cope with flooding and traffic problems that individual jurisdictions bickered over for years.

Most instances of regional cooperation still fall short of creating ways for cities and older suburbs to share in the property-tax bonanza of growing suburbs. In the entire country, only one tax-sharing system exists— in the Minneapolis-St. Paul region.

In fact, some experts believe that suburban interests may become more competitive— and less sympathetic to city problems—as they gain more political clout after the 1980 census. One clue is the creation of a Suburban Caucus in Congress. Its goal: To see that suburbs get a bigger chunk of federal funds.

Complains Representative Ronald M. Mottl (D-Ohio), the caucus chairman: "Suburbs send $3 to Washington and get $1 back. It's just the opposite for cities."

Suburban leaders are up in arms, too, over White House efforts to curb suburban projects that could hurt the economies of established communities. An example of that policy is the administration's community-conservation program made public last fall. Under that approach, a mayor can ask the federal government to investigate and even halt suburban developments, such as an office park or shopping center, that would damage the health of cities. This tool is limited to projects in which federal funds are involved.

Several city officials have asked for such reviews, and results already are showing up. One example: In Charleston, W. Va., last year, officials successfully blocked federal funds for an access road to a proposed regional shopping center. Now, the project will be built downtown.

What these trends show, according to urban observers, is that suburbs, while winning the economic battle with cities, may have lost the look of utopia that lured so many millions of families since World War II. In effect, they have become more like cities, a development that some observers believe may help to heal the bitter rivalries of the past.

41

THE GREAT TRANSPORTATION CONSPIRACY

Jonathan Kwitny

When Charlie Wilson was toiling in the General Motors executive suite, earning his future Cabinet appointment as secretary of defense, GM, along with some of the oil companies, was steering the country toward its current energy predicament. Few remember it, but before the automobile companies became predominant, the country relied on centrally generated electricity for city transportation. It was relatively clean and energy-efficient. There were streetcars and off-street railways. There were also trackless trolleys—electric buses powered by overhead wires and able to maneuver through traffic.

Without realizing, much less debating the consquences, the country turned its transportation policy over to GM and its automotive allies. What followed was the destruction of mass transit; the country became almost totally reliant on the private automobile, with its necessary consumption of foreign oil. Of course, most people would consider it unfair to blame the demise of mass transit on several big corporations. They just manufactured the car and the bus—to the delight of millions.

But it wasn't that simple. When GM and a few other big companies created a transportation oligopoly for the internal-combustion

engine—so convenient until the cheap gasoline ran out—they did not rely just on the obvious sales pitch. They conspired. They broke the law. This was all proved at a little-remembered trial in a federal court in Chicago, in 1949. After more than a month of sworn testimony, a jury convicted the corporations and several executives of criminal antitrust violations for their part in the demise of mass transit. The convictions were upheld on appeal.

In many places, mass transit didn't just die—it was murdered. No doubt the mass availability of the automobile inevitably would have changed travel habits to a great degree, but it will never be known to what extent electrified transport would have died on its own. The big conspirator companies were unwilling to entrust their fates to the market. Instead, they methodically removed the competition. In knowing violation of the Sherman Antitrust Act, they used their economic power to take over a small bus company and, through it, acquired and dismantled one electrified mass-transit system after another, replacing them with buses. The buses, besides being built and supplied by GM and the oil companies, never had the same appeal for riders that the electrified transit systems did, and merely added to the allure of the private car. Then the big companies that orchestrated the demise of the trolley tried to cover over their own tracks as surely as they covered over the tracks of many a rail line. The GM conspiracy case is a fine example of what can happen when important matters of public policy are abandoned by government to the self-interest of corporations—something that is occurring right now in the realm of energy.

References to the conspiracy over the years have been few and cursory. It was cited briefly in 1974 by Congressional-committee staff member Bradford Snell in "American Ground Transport," his report on monopolistic practices in the automobile industry. The committee published the report along with a reply by General Motors, which mostly repeated the defenses that jury had chosen not to believe at the trial: that the dismantled electrified transit systems weren't profitable, and that the whole thing was an innocent effort to help a customer, the affiliated bus company.

There was no evidence in the committee report, or in an obscure book that mentioned the case last year, or in some occasional references Ralph Nader has made to the case, that the trial transcript itself had been dug up and consulted. GM's reply said that because the indictment dealt with antitrust violations—"a close point of law," in GM's words—the case "lends no support" to the notion that GM induced the destruction of mass transit. The transcript of the trial, however, says otherwise.

The transcript and other evidence from the GM case are in two battered packing cartons in a federal warehouse near Chicago. That material makes this point beyond a reasonable doubt: There was for many years a criminal conspiracy behind our national transportation policy, and it was directed by some of the biggest corporations in the country. As spelled out in the court record, the conspirators did their work in many cities. They schemed from the mid-1930s through the 1940s. Electrified-rail mass-transit systems, which carried millions of riders, were bought and junked. Tracks literally were torn out of

the ground, sometimes overnight. Overhead power lines were dismantled, and valuable off-street rights of way were sold.

After reading the testimony and court filings, I interviewed dozens of transit officials all over the country to find out if the old electrified system could have served us today with both convenience and savings in energy. No more than three of these officials were even aware of the GM conspiracy case, and none knew the details. They were, however, aware that a series of "mistakes" had been made in transportation planning back in the 1930s and 1940s.

What keeps millions of American city dwellers and suburbanites from greatly reducing their use of gasoline by riding transit lines today is the enormous cost of building new trolley systems. But evidence from the trial shows that this cost might have been, to a large degree, avoided. Transit officials who remember the rails, power lines, and generating stations that were once in place say these facilities, if left intact, could have formed the nucleus for a modern American transit system. Electrified trains and trackless trolleys are not only cheaper to run than automobiles, they are substantially cheaper to run than diesel buses. Riders tend to prefer them to buses. The difference in cost can be expected to widen with each oil-price increase and with the introduction of new power-conserving devices on railcars and trolleys. But in most American cities the rails and wires are gone.

Americans didn't need a lot of arm twisting to give up mass transit for the private car. Gasoline was twelve cents a gallon in the 1930s, and the air was clean. Although the internal-combustion engine was no doubt attractive, some big companies promoting the engine evidently considered the attraction insufficient for the product to succeed legitimately. The conspirators in this case included not only General Motors but also Standard Oil of California, Phillips Petroleum, Mack Manufacturing (the big truck maker), and Firestone Tire & Rubber, among others. Though all were convicted of antitrust violations for what they did, the token punishments they received scarcely marred the success of their venture.

Ironically, a congressional antitrust action in 1935 was what made it possible for the conspiracy to succeed as easily as it did. The new law tried to break up electric-utility monopolies and required power companies to divest themselves of ancillary businesses. Most of the nation's transit systems had been started by electric-utility companies before the days of household power. By the 1930s, the retail sale of electricity had become the main business of these power companies, and transit was just a sideline. But the forced sell-off came just when the internal-combustion engine was ready to substitute for electrified transit.

It was at about this point that the GM conspirators got together with a tiny, family-owned bus service and tutored and bank-rolled it as it gobbled up one trolley system after another. The front for GM was National City Lines, Inc. After it had destroyed scores of rail and trolley systems on the pretext that buses would be more profitable, National City Lines showed its commitment by promptly getting out of the bus business and putting its assets into intercity trucking.

Perhaps the most striking example of what happened is in Los Angeles, which has become a frightening mutation of human life produced by the automotive gene. Though hard to believe now, Los Angeles once had a heavily used urban rail system extending from Newport Beach and Long Beach, through downtown, on to Pasadena, and into the San Fernando Valley—perhaps the best system in the country. The conspirators bought and dismantled it in stages during the 1940s. Taxpayers now are faced with building a similar system at a cost of billions. Year after year they have rejected the idea because of this cost.

Because the conspirators continued to deny the charges even after conviction, we are deprived of the kind of thorough narrative that might have been provided if even one guilty executive had crossed over and testified for the government. But the corporate letters and memoranda unearthed by federal prosecutors, and the explanations offered by the executives who tried to justify their actions in their own defense, tell a vivid enough story. It left the jury no reasonable doubt that the big motor, tire, and oil concerns knew they were breaking the law and acted deviously to cover up for it.

The story personalized itself in the unlikely career of E. Roy Fitzgerald, who quit school in the seventh grade to work, as irony would have it, in a railroad camp. In the 1920s he and two brothers saved up enough money to start a bus service over the two miles between Eveleth and Leonidas, Minnesota. By 1933 they had moved up to a somewhat longer intercity route, from Chicago to Paducah, Kentucky. That was when a GM salesman began talking to them about the virtues of local bus service, and persuaded them to buy the transit franchise in Galesburg, Illinois, which was for sale at the time. GM said it would be glad to help Fitzgerald and his brothers meet the purchase terms if they would agree to replace the existing streetcars with GM buses.

Fitzgerald apparently didn't know it, but GM had been trying to create a successful showcase for its buses for many years, according to the testimony of Irving Babcock, president of the GM truck and bus division. "We were having great difficulty in convincing the power companies to motorize and give up their streetcars," Babcock testified. So, he said, "I went to my executive committee and asked for an appropriation to invest $300,000 to help finance a few of these small cities." GM bought the transit systems in Kalamazoo and Saginaw, Michigan, and Springfield, Ohio, and proceeded to convert them from rail to bus.

But the transit industry missed the hint. Cities refused to give up their rail lines voluntarily, despite the presence of these showcases and the best efforts of GM salesmanship. So GM decided that more force-feeding was necessary, and to accomplish this in the best public-relations light, GM chose to stop buying transit systems directly and to act instead through an independent, or purportedly independent, bus operator. It was at this point that GM signed a deal with Roy Fitzgerald.

So Galesburg, too, lost its streetcars. Where there were rails one day, there was asphalt the next. The enthusiastic Fitzgerald caught wind of opportunities in a few more Illinois towns, and soon he was in Detroit, in the office of Babcock himself, to negotiate financing to take over the transit franchise in East St. Louis. Such direct dealing with the GM division president indicates that Fitzgerald was no ordinary customer. He had GM's money behind him, which made it easy to buy transit systems, particularly after Congress, in forcing utilities to divest, forced them onto the market. Undeniably, as GM's defense kept pointing out, urban railway companies suffered a profit drop-off in the 1930s, and some were losing money. But, as Herbert Listman, general sales manager of the bus division at GM, testified, the same was true of other businesses during the Depression—including bus lines.

On the strength of GM's checkbook, Fitzgerald moved from East St. Louis to Joliet, Illinois, where, he testified, "they discontinued operating streetcars in the city one night and we started operating modern buses . . . the next day." Quickly into the fold came Tulsa, Oklahoma; Jackson, Michigan; and Montgomery, Alabama. General Motors even provided engineering surveys showing Fitzgerald's operation just what to do. By 1936, Fitzgerald had moved into Beaumont and Port Arthur, Texas, and Cedar Rapids, Iowa. Again, rail lines were either torn up or paved over. Fitzgerald instructed the transit systems he was dealing with that he could buy in only "if a deal could be made with the city for complete bus operation—that we were not interested in operating streetcars."

The Fitzgerald bus systems were now big business, and clearly some kind of corporate structure was needed. Just as clearly, it was not really Fitzgerald's business, so he could not set up the corporate structure on his own. Early in 1936 he and his chief underling, Foster C. Beamsley, met in Detroit again with GM division president Babcock and sales manager Listman. They decided to form National City Lines, Inc., as a holding company for the various transit ventures. Obviously there would be further expansion—opportunities beckoned all over the map. Apparently hoping not to have to foot the bill for all this, the GM men suggested that National City Lines try to finance its expansion with bank loans and a public stock sale.

The result of these money-raising efforts over the next six months is significant because it contradicts the cover story that GM and the other conspirators later put forward. The companies argued in court that they had gone in with Fitzgerald to create modern, profitable bus lines out of broken-down rail systems. But the financial community disagreed at the time. The banks refused to lend any money. "They did not think it was the proper time," Fitzgerald explained on the witness stand. National City Lines did succeed in raising $1.9 million from a public stock sale, but only after agreeing to the most extreme terms—15 percent off the top as fees to the brokers, which was practically Mafia rates.

Moreover, $1.9 million wasn't nearly as much as was needed. So in October Fitzgerald and Beamsley were back in Babcock's office at GM for more capital. Also present was Glenn Traer, an executive from Greyhound, the bus company. Babcock later testified that GM had gone to Greyhound earlier to help pay for the takeover and destruction of some of the rail lines Fitzgerald had started with in Illinois. (Neither Greyhound nor any of its executives was charged in the conspiracy case.) Now Greyhound agreed to participate with GM in a much wider venture, but only if others were brought in to share the load. A lot of money would be needed. The B. F. Goodrich Company seemed a logical choice to approach because a tire concern would certainly benefit from transforming city railways into paved streets. But B. F. Goodrich declined to join the conspiracy. So Firestone was approached and agreed to come in. By their later actions, the conspirators appear to have been well aware that they were violating the Sherman Antitrust Act, which prohibits companies from joining together to restrain competition or to sabotage competitors.

But they were quite undeterred by the law, which may be a fair comment on its general effectiveness.

Eventually the conspirators invested about 10 million 1930s dollars in the plot. GM and Firestone stationed their own service personnel where Fitzgerald operated his buses. Stuart Moore, a Greyhound maintenance executive, was put on the National City Lines staff and board of directors to help supervise the conversion of the rail systems. At least one government regulator, who acknowledged at the trial that he had helped engineer official approval for what the GM conspirators did, was later made a paid consultant for the fraudulent holding company.

In midsummer of 1937, the conspirators resolved to expand the bus scheme to the Western states. But the financing problem remained, and Traer, the Greyhound executive, was sent out to raise cash. "Well," he reported back to Babcock, "I talked to investment houses, brokers, and private capital. . . . I couldn't get the money." If the city bus was indeed a brilliant new idea that was sweeping the country on its own merit, as the conspirators later contended, the country's capital markets were curiously slow to catch on. The only way the GM group could raise more money was to bring in more conspirators. An oil company seemed a logical bet, so Traer and Babcock went to Standard Oil of California.

"We could see . . . from our standpoint, it was going to create a market for our product—gasoline, lubricating oils, and greases,"

a Standard Oil executive recalled from the witness stand. "If the Fitzgeralds were able to accomplish anything along this line on the Pacific coast, then other people would do it, and that would open up even more markets for us," he said. So Standard Oil came in.

Then the conspirators went to Mack Trucks—GM's supposed direct competitor in the bus-making business. A Mack officer named Roy Hauer showed up on Roy Fitzgerald's farm in the winter of 1937–38 and agreed that the new law forcing electric companies to sell their transit businesses provided a rare opportunity. So officers from Mack Trucks, Standard Oil, and General Motors all met in the office of Greyhound Bus Lines in Chicago and decided who was going to pay Fitzgerald to dismantle the West Coast rail system.

Part of the deal was that Fitzgerald's operations would buy at least 42.5 percent of their buses from General Motors and 42.5 percent from Mack (an obvious Sherman violation), with the other 15 percent to be decided by need. At the trial, Fitzgerald said that the new bus lines promised to make big money for his investors; that was why they invested, he testified. But there were indications from the investing companies themselves that they expected their profits to come not from bus operations at all but from the sale of their products after electrified transit was destroyed. An internal memo at Mack, for example, spoke of a "probable loss" on the bus-line stock, but said it would be "more than justified" by "the business and gross profit flowing out of this move in years to come."

Nor does it appear that GM expected to make its principal profit from the sale of buses, the new form of mass transit. If it did, there is no satisfactory explanation in the trial record for why GM gave half the prospective bus business away to Mack, its supposed competitor. Another explanation, of course, is that the real profits were going to be made from the sale of cars (in Mack's case, trucks) after the destruction of mass transit opened the way for a huge public network of streets and highways. That this is what happened offers some justification for the explanation that it was intended.

The agreements under which the conspirators provided money did not require merely that all buses, tires, and petroleum products be purchased from the particular supplier who was putting up the cash. The contracts also specified that the transit systems could never buy another streetcar or any other piece of equipment that would "use any fuel or method of propulsion other than gasoline." (In the early 1940s, when the diesel bus came into vogue as a replacement for the older, gasoline-engine models, it was discovered that diesel equipment violated this restrictive clause. Accordingly, the clause was changed, specifically to permit the purchase of diesel fuel.)

As operations spread around the country, more capital was needed and the conspirators decided to bring in others who would benefit from what they were doing. A plan was devised to carve up the United States among various oil companies; each one was to be awarded a region in which it would supply the bus companies run by National City Lines. Texaco was approached to handle the Midwest and South; its sales department liked the idea, but the top executives turned it down, saying only, according to Fitzgerald's testimony, that they were "not interested."

Phillips 66 was offered the same deal and showed unrestrained enthusiasm. At the negotiations with Phillips, Fitzgerald was accompanied by R. S. Leonard, a finance officer of Firestone, and Victor Palmer, the treasurer of Standard Oil of California—a competitor of Phillips. The transaction was sealed personally by Frank Phillips, the petroleum company's founder and chairman, and Kenneth S. Adams, the president and heir to Phillips's position as head of the company. According to Fitzgerald, Phillips told him that "anywhere along the line that I might feel that his people were doing anything to us that

might change this deal, he would be glad to have me come back and talk to him."

Meanwhile, the GM transit juggernaut rolled on. Butte, Montana; Fresno, Oakland, Stockton, and San Jose, California; Portsmouth and Canton, Ohio; Terre Haute, Indiana. In St. Louis, the whole electric utility had gone into bankruptcy receivership. Seven banks had taken over, and were glad to have an investor named Fitzgerald buy control of the streetcar system, which became a bus system.

Roy Fitzgerald was being made into the biggest transportation tycoon since Jay Gould. His capacity to manage it all was finally spread so thin that it was decided the West Coast portion should be split off and run separately. Victor Palmer left his job as treasurer of Standard Oil of California to take over the presidency of the West Coast bus systems, which were called Pacific City Lines. John L. Wilson, a Mack executive, was made president of the St. Louis system and was given seed money to buy and convert the Lincoln, Nebraska, transit system in his own name.

In general, the conspirators took great pains to disguise their involvement. They clearly didn't want the public to know who was really behind all the marvelous new transit systems that Roy Fitzgerald and General Motors were designing. Firestone executive Leonard wrote a chummy letter to Phillips stating that Firestone was keeping its transit investments secret by investing in the names of two employees acting as nominees, and hinting that Phillips might do the same thing (apparently Phillips didn't). At one point, even National City Lines, the front group, operated behind a front name of its own, the Andover Finance Company, in order "to make investments in situations beyond the legal limits," in the words of a Fitzgerald aide. Standard Oil of California made its investments in the name of two nominee companies, because, Standard's treasurer, Henry Judd, testified: "We didn't want to be criticized. . . . We didn't want to have the people in the community feel that if the service was not what they wanted . . . the complaints would rest with the Standard Oil Company of California." This seems strange behavior from companies that defended themselves on the grounds that they had performed noble public service by hastening the advent of the bus. At one point, B. F. Stradley, acting treasurer of Phillips, wrote to Harry L. Grossman, vice-president and secretary of GM's bus division:

From our conversation, it appears there may be a difference of opinion between us in respect of the propriety and perhaps the legality of certain requirements which we have in mind in respect of the agreement covering the purchase of stock in American City Lines [a proposed National City Lines affiliate]. We shall be glad to present our views to you at any time . . . although it occurs to me that it might not be well to discuss the problem jointly with the American City Lines group since by so doing it would become obvious that our meeting was prearranged.

The same letter noted that the details of the transaction had already been discussed with Firestone.

Fitzgerald himself obviously knew that there was something wrong with talking to representatives of more than one supplier at a time, because from the witness stand he kept denying that he had ever done so. In the face of all the evidence, he insisted that he had merely gone around independently trying to raise money from the most logical investors he could think of, his suppliers. For example, there was a meeting in April 1939 to discuss the formation of an affiliate that later took over and wrecked the suburban Los Angeles rail transit system. Fitzgerald testified that the only people there were himself and Russell M. Riggins of Phillips. He specifically swore, on questioning, that R. S. Leonard of Firestone hadn't joined the discussions at all.

Yet the prosecution produced a letter from Riggins to Leonard saying, "It was a real pleasure to again have the opportunity to be with you" at what Riggins called "the big meeting last Monday," as a result of which "everything has been mutually agreed upon."

Sacramento, Salt Lake City, Portland, Tampa, Mobile, Baltimore, El Paso, and Spokane were taken over. The takeover of Los Angeles had been carefully plotted for a couple of years. In 1941, the Glendale and Pasadena railway systems were bought and transformed into all-bus operations according to an engineering plan drawn up by General Motors. The Long Beach system was bought and scrapped.

In its reply to the Congressional staff study's account of the Los Angeles takeover, GM argued that the bus-for-rail substitution there was accomplished gradually over four decades, starting before GM even got into the bus business. But the trial testimony of Henry C. Judd, treasurer of Standard Oil, was pretty blunt:

"Mr. Fitzgerald called me on the telephone [in December 1944]. He told me that they had made an offer for the purchase of the [downtown] Los Angeles railway, and that it had been accepted, and that he would like to have us put $1 million into [the deal]."

Besides its own contribution, Standard used its influence to pry loose another $5 million from Bank of America to finance the takeover.

Soon after the war, GM, Standard Oil, Firestone, and Phillips all got out of their stock ownership in the transit systems. Mack and Greyhound already were long gone. Victor Palmer, leaving the presidency of Pacific City Lines, was welcomed back to the executive payroll at Standard. Money had been made, all right, but not on transit company stock. As Herbert Listman, general sales manager for GM buses, testified, "It was the policy of General Motors to get out of all these investments. They were temporary finance plans. . . . They have served their purpose."

Soon, National City Lines was out of the bus business, too. What was left were cars.

Those indicted and convicted of violating the Sherman Antitrust Act were National City Lines, Pacific City Lines, Firestone Tire & Rubber, General Motors, Phillips Petroleum,

Mack Manufacturing, Standard Oil of California, Federal Engineering (a Standard Oil subsidiary), E. Roy Fitzgerald, Foster G. Beamsley, H. C. Grossman (assistant secretary of GM), Henry C. Judd, L. R. Jackson (vice-president of Firestone), B. F. Stradley (secretary and treasurer of Phillips), and A. M. Hughes (vice-president and director of Phillips). These few took the rap for everyone involved.

Recalling the old rail network in Los Angeles, Gerald Haugh, currently general manager of the bus system in the city's Long Beach section, says, "It would be great if we had it all back again. It could have been modernized. You'd have tried to extend the rails out into those areas where people were buying. It would have been a hell of a lot cheaper than to do it today. It was a damn shame they took up the tracks."

As for the people who took up the tracks, they suffered little for it. U. S. District Judge William J. Campbell sentenced the guilty corporations to pay fines of $5,000 each (except for Federal Engineering, a Standard Oil subsidiary, which had to pay only $1,000). The guilty individuals paid fines of exactly $1 each. The defendants also had to pick up the court costs, which totaled a not too princely $4,220.78.

A few years after the trial, Julius and Ethel Rosenberg paid the death penalty for treason in a case that unfolded at about the same time as the GM conspiracy case. The Rosenbergs' crime, as it turned out, had no appreciable effect on the future of the country. On the other hand, what the transit conspirators did was destroy mass-transit systems that today could benefit millions of citizens and, ironically, make for improved national security by reducing reliance on foreign oil. And they did it for no greater cause than their own profit.

42

A NEW TYPE OF CITY FOR AN ENERGY-SHORT WORLD

Jon Van Til

The spectre of a permanent oil shortage has loomed ever larger in the United States in recent years. At the same time, the future of nuclear energy is very much in doubt and solar and other renewable energy sources are still in the early stages of development. Conservation measures, it is said, could allow us to maintain much of our high standard of living in the face of worsening energy shortages—perhaps even achieving as much as 50% savings in energy use—but these savings cannot be accomplished overnight and would require massive changes in life-styles.

Even with substantial conservation, a permanent energy shortfall would have a tremendous impact on the American way of life—not just on the way people live but also on where they live. For this reason, it is imperative that we do some serious thinking—and, hopefully, careful planning—about future energy supplies.

HOW MUCH ENERGY?

To stimulate systematic thinking about the influence of energy on our lives, I have developed five scenarios, the first three of which

From *The Futurist*, June 1980, pp. 64–70, published by World Future Society, 4916 St. Elmo Avenue, Wash., D.C., 20014. Reprinted by permission.

are based on those developed by the Energy Policy Project of the Ford Foundation in 1974. The last two are based on more recent research suggesting that no-growth or even declining-supply scenarios are distinctly possible visions of the future.

It is, of course, impossible to determine which of these scenarios will prove to be the most accurate in the years ahead. However, each is possible, and increasingly it is beginning to appear that the least energy-rich visions are at least as likely to emerge as the more bountiful ones. In any case, it is wise to be prepared to deal with a wide range of alternative energy futures. Thus, for better or worse, I offer the following five scenarios:

1. Pre-1973 trends projected. An orderly transition takes place from oil and coal to eventual exploitation of breeder technology. Energy use continues to grow at a 3.5% annual rate.

2. Modest Growth. Energy use continues to grow, but at a slower rate (1.9% per year). The trend is toward a viable multi-based energy future, including nuclear energy. An orderly transition from oil to coal to nuclear power as the primary energy source takes place—along with increased development of renewable energy sources. The successful implementation of a number of conservation measures permits continued economic expansion with largely unchanged patterns of energy usage.

3. *Steady-state of energy availability after 1990.* The energy supply grows slowly until 1990 and then levels off. As oil is exhausted, it is replaced by coal and renewable energy sources. Increasing demands for energy for industrial and household uses are accompanied by intensified conservation efforts, since the energy supply is no longer growing.

4. *Steady-state of 1973 level of energy usage through the year 2000 and beyond.* The energy supply stabilizes at the 1973 level, with the development of renewable sources begun in the late 1970s continuing to permit an orderly transition as oil becomes increasingly scarce. A heavy emphasis is placed on conservation, and a dramatic decline in per capita citizen and household use of energy takes place.

5. *Decline to 75% of 1973 level of supply by year 2000, with even grimmer future prospects.* Renewable energy sources are not developed, and frequent crises occur as the traditional non-renewable energy sources are exhausted and nuclear power continues to be plagued with difficulties.

These scenarios contain variations not only in the *amount* of energy available, but also in the *forms* that energy will take.

Energy comes in a variety of forms—each having different properties. Some forms of energy are permanently depleted upon use, and others are perpetually renewed. Some forms are relatively easy to transport, while other forms, because they require continuous transmission or are relatively unconcentrated, are not economical for purposes such as fueling motor cars. Energy sources also differ in the amount of pollutants resulting from their use. Finally, we may distinguish between sources that require central generation and refinement and those that permit local generation.

When these characteristics are considered in relation to principal energy sources available, four different patterns of energy form and structure emerge. First, there is a group of energy sources that are non-renewable, difficult to transport, highly-polluting, and centrally generated. This group includes coal and nuclear fission (in its present forms), applied to the generation of electrical power. A second category of energy sources includes those that are non-renewable, transportable, highly-polluting, and centrally-refined. This category includes oil and its derivative, gasoline. Third is a group of sources that are renewable, difficult to transport, potentially highly-polluting, and centrally-generated. This category includes the two nuclear forms yet to be commercially developed—breeder and fusion sources. Finally, there is a group of sources that are renewable, generally non-transportable (but not entirely so), low-polluting, and potentially decentrally-generated. This category includes the various forms of solar energy, including hydroelectric, methane, and wind power—the soft energy paths.

HOW MUCH ENERGY FOR TRANSPORTATION?

Today's spread-out residential patterns—featuring urban sprawl and heavy commuter traffic from remote areas into urban centers—were built on the assumption that cheap and abundant gasoline would always be available for transportation. However, there is wide agreement among experts that, in the event of a severe energy shortfall, the amount of energy available for transportation would be deeply cut. My own most pessimistic scenario envisions a loss in transportation energy of 52% by the year 2000. And such a drastic shortfall in energy for transportation will have a major impact on future residential patterns.

Pursuing further the implications of the 52% decline scenario, it quickly becomes apparent that an even greater decline will ensue in energy available for automobiles. Energy for transportation must be shared among seven major categories of use, according to the Ford Foundation study. The Ford planners see the demand for three of these uses—automobiles, buses, and airplanes—as being highly elastic, while energy use for rail, farm machinery, and ships is viewed as highly inelastic. Truck use is seen as moderately elastic. Transportation energy, after all, is used both for passenger transit and the shipping of freight, and the latter purpose is more inelastic in the event of energy shortfall.

The energy trade-offs required in the most pessimistic scenarios (steady-state and declining-growth) would be among the most difficult decisions made in American history—and would surely require a rationing system for users.

The impact of an energy shortfall on individual mobility is likely to be substantial. If a mix of transit options aimed toward maximum feasible mileage is chosen (see Table 1) the 1973 constant level (scenario four) will produce almost as many miles of transit per capita as the steady-state after 1990 scenario (scenario three), and the 75% level scenario

TABLE 1.
TRAVEL IN MILES PER CAPITA FOR FIVE ENERGY SCENARIOS IN THE YEAR 2000

The following table shows the number of miles that could be traveled per capita in the United States in the year 2000 under five different energy scenarios, assuming in each case a mix of transit options aimed toward maximum feasible mileage is chosen.

	SCENARIO 1 Pre-1973 projected	SCENARIO 2 Modest growth	SCENARIO 3 Steady-state after 1990	SCENARIO 4 1973 ZEG	SCENARIO 5 75% decline	Actual 1970 levels
Auto	9,410	9,410	7,570	3,784	1,992	8,210
Bus	255	255	1,365	3,938	3,448	240
Air	4,190	3,905	1,955	1,238	326	780
Rail	125	410	590	1,106	1,106	60
Totals	13,980	13,980	11,480	10,066	6,872	9,290

The following major assumptions were made in compiling these figures:

Scenario 1—Autos carry an average of 1.4 persons in city driving and 2.4 in rural travel. Buses carry 15 persons per vehicle-mile. Autos get 10.4 miles per gallon in city driving.

Scenario 2—Autos get 25 miles per gallon and carry an average of 1.4 persons per vehicle in cities and 2.4 in rural travel. Planes increase their passenger load by from 54% to 67% and also reduce flight speed to permit a 4.5% reduction in fuel use. For rail travel, the number of passenger-miles per available seat is tripled.

Scenario 3—Autos get 33 miles per gallon and carry 1.4 persons per vehicle in cities and 2.4 in rural travel. Buses carry 19.5 persons per vehicle-mile. Six percent of the population is in new towns, requiring 50% auto usage. Ten percent of urban traffic is carried by bikeways and walkways. Planes increase their passenger load by from 54% to 67% and also reduce flight speed to permit a 4.5% reduction in fuel use. Plane trips of 400 miles or less are replaced by train travel. Rail passenger-miles per available seat are tripled.

Scenario 4—Autos get 33 miles per gallon and carry 1.4 persons per vehicle in cities and 2.4 in rural travel. Buses carry 30 persons per vehicle-mile. Six percent of the population is in new towns, requiring 50% auto usage. Planes increase their passenger load by from 54% to 67% and also reduce flight speed to permit a 4.5% reduction in fuel use. Plane trips of 400 miles or less are replaced by train travel. Rail passenger-miles per available seat are tripled.

Scenario 5—Autos get 33 miles per gallon and carry 1.4 persons per vehicle in cities and 2.4 in rural travel. Buses carry 30 persons per vehicle-mile. Six percent of the population is in new towns, requiring 50% auto usage. Ten percent of urban traffic is carried by bikeways and walkways. Planes increase their passenger load by from 54% to 67% and also reduce flight speed to permit a 4.5% reduction in fuel use. Rail passenger-miles per available seat are tripled.

Source: Van Til, 1979

SOME PROCESSES OF SOCIAL LIFE

(scenario five) will produce just two-thirds the miles of the two preceding scenarios, or five-sixths the level of present travel. On the other hand, continued reliance on the automobile as the primary conveyance will yield far less mileage per capita.

WHAT FORM MIGHT OUR CITIES AND SUBURBS TAKE?

Now, what impact will these energy patterns have on the way in which we will choose, or be compelled, to organize our cities and suburbs in the years ahead? To answer this question, it will help to have in mind the major patterns that human settlements might assume. One highly useful way of viewing these possibilities was suggested by Catherine Bauer Wurster some 15 years ago. Combining two dimensions in her analysis—degree of concentration or dispersion, and degree or region-wide specialization or sub-regional integration—Wurster derived four models of the future of American urbanization: "present trends projected," "general dispersion," "concentrated super-city," and "constellation of relatively diversified and integrated cities."

The first type, "present trends projected," involves a continuing trend toward suburban expansion, with a lesser degree of urban concentration, all within a regional pattern of economic specialization. This type closely resembles the shape of the contemporary Northeastern metropolitan centers. The second type, "general dispersion," is the vision of metropolitan sprawl that characterizes so many of America's newer Sun Belt cities. The third type, the "concentrated super-city," is the one envisaged by visionary architects like Soleri and Small, in which a population density much greater than that of present-day Manhattan is accommodated in an urban megastructure. The fourth type, "constellation of relatively diversified and integrated cities," involves more concentration than the present form, but also provides a high degree of subregional integration,

allowing particularly for people to live near their places of employment. Its closest embodiment is in the commercial cities of the eighteenth century.

HOW WILL ENERGY PATTERNS AFFECT RESIDENTIAL PATTERNS?

Examining Wurster's typology, in combination with the constraints implied by the five energy scenarios, suggests the set of interrelations depicted in Table 2. The table presents my estimation of the viability of each urbanization model in each energy scenario, and suggests that the options will decrease dramatically as energy prospects diminish.

Thus the first model, "present trends projected," is well-suited to energy-rich scenarios, but becomes increasingly unviable as we move toward energy-poor conditions; this model involves more dispersion than concentration, and implies an increasing dependence upon automobile transit. Such dependence is unlikely to be sustained in energy scenarios 3, 4, and 5, which provide fewer auto miles per person in the year 2000 than at present. Nor is such dispersion consistent with a large increase in dependence upon bus and rail transit, which themselves require a greater concentration of population in residential clusters than can be anticipated in the projection of present trends. In sum, it is unlikely that the projection of present trends can accommodate a decline in energy available for transit, or a decline in automobile miles per person. Therefore, the first Wurster model can be sustained only in the two most plentiful energy scenarios.

Obviously, the general dispersion model is even less viable, barring a return to agrarian economic patterns and life styles. It can be sustained under current economic expectations only by an increase in energy available for transit, and by a substantial increase in miles per person available by automobile. Only the most plentiful energy scenario, pre-1973 projected, meets these criteria clearly.

TABLE 2.
VIABILITY OF URBANIZATION MODELS IN THE YEAR 2000

The amount of energy available in the year 2000 will largely determine which types of cities will be viable. Under the most energy-abundant scenario, all four types of cities could be supported, but the choices narrow until, under the most austere senario, only one type of city is viable.

URBANIZATION MODELS	SCENARIO 1 Pre-1973 projected	SCENARIO 2 Modest growth	SCENARIO 3 Steady-state after 1990	SCENARIO 4 1973 ZEG	SCENARIO 5 75% decline from 1973
Present projected	Yes	Yes	Question-able	Probably No	No
General dispersion	Yes	No	No	No	No
Concentrated super-city	Yes	Question-able	No (too expensive to build)	No	No
Diversified-integrated	Yes	Yes	Yes	Yes	Yes

Source: Van Til, 1979

Under the three least bountiful energy scenarios, general dispersion is simply an unworkable form.

The concentrated supercity model (such as the megaliths of Paolo Soleri) is energy-efficient *once built*, but too expensive to construct save under energy-rich conditions—a cruel paradox. It might well have been built earlier, but it is not a present option for salvation from energy shortfall.

Thus we are left with the diversified-integrated model, the form of the old commerical city, as the one most congenial to an energy-short future. Only this form provides clear energy savings, without extensive ruralization, for its social organization could be maintained even in the face of very tight energy supplies:

What fuel there is available for transportation could be allocated on the highest priority to the transport of resources and the delivery of goods.

Workers could be strongly motivated to reside within walking or bicycling distances of their jobs, supplemented by increased bus availability and use of precious auto-mobile mileage (where winter climate or physical limitation require). This approach would require the development of "motel-type" housing permitting the maximum of worker mobility with the minimum of moving costs.

Personal transportation by fuel-powered vehicle could be substantially curtailed; whenever possible, communication could be conducted by telecommunications (including telephone). Pleasure travel would be drastically limited (particularly air travel, which would be largely limited to national defense and the use of top elites' business travel) and would be greatly reduced from present levels.

The distribution of goods and services could be provided within subregional centers, as would, insofar as feasible, the production of goods and services.

As for capital construction in a time of constraint, it is clear that insufficient energy will be available for the sort of crash building program of more energy-efficient dwellings envisaged in recent years by Paolo

Soleri, Glen Small, and other architects. Policy makers will seek to maximize the usage of existing shells, and will approve construction of new ones only on a modest basis. There simply will not be sufficient resources for a policy of reconstruction. In the case of energy shortfall, we shall have to rely on the stock of shells we have in existence for our basic residential, commercial, and industrial needs.

Therefore, in an energy-short future, American settlement patterns might take the following form:

Residential and economic patterns emerge around a number of regional nodes, within which most transportation, except that used for production, is confined.

The most desirable housing within these subregional centers is located within two kilometers of the node, with other housing concentrated within a kilometer radius of the node.

The locations of these nodes emerge on the basis of current land use, and they occupy, in large part, existing shells. Node development occurs where there is a high density of building space (residential, commercial, industrial) and where there is proximity to the circulation system of the energy-poor society (rail lines for goods transport; interstate highways for goods transport; limited transport of persons by buses and automobiles).

Land outside the 10-kilometer radius of subregional nodes is available for settlement only by farmers, self-sufficient nomads, and workers in the long-term vacation business. Included in this category is a large portion of current suburban land, most existing towns with populations under 10,000 and almost all land in mountainous and rural areas.

Such a settlement pattern would obviously differ greatly from that of the present. Least changed from the present pattern would be the middle-sized cities of the Northeast, already concentrated in land-use. They would diversify in production, but would largely rely on existing shells. Larger cities, and smaller more spread-out cities, would see the development of multiple nodes within their present limits, each of which would take on an increasing autonomy. And most different would be the spread-out cities, and most present suburbs and small towns, much area within which would become largely depopulated as it falls outside the radius of the subregional nodes that would develop around present malls, apartment centers, suburban town centers, and other areas of potential concentration.

Almost all new construction would be contained within the nodes; house and land prices would skyrocket within the central ring in particular; and resettlement compensation would be required to assist those suburbanites whose real estate investments would be almost totally lost by the shifting residential patterns. Cultural experience would continue to be most accessible in those nodes that were formerly the central cities of great metropolises: and these would become the most highly valued places of residence in the new immobile urban world.

It is probably unlikely, given the traditional American resistance to long-range planning, that any foresightful effort to reshape settlement patterns to accommodate energy shortfall will be undertaken. Rather, we shall more likely be left to muddle through with the guidance provided by a market economy and reactive political leadership. These market and political forces will surely cushion the impact of energy shortfall, bringing sharply increased prices for land and houses that are centrally located. Such a policy will be justified by many as a prudent course, given the uncertainties of future restrictions on energy.

However, without a strong planned commitment to guide this process of concentration, it is likely that, under conditions of shortfall, inequalities between citizens will be exacerbated, elites will monopolize access to energy for their own personal use, and levels of social tension and disruption will rise as real living standards for most Americans plummet to intolerable levels. In such a future, neither democracy nor social order will be assured.

CONCLUSION: THE ENERGY BASES OF OUR FUTURE SOCIETY

We now face a historic choice of three energy paths—one soft, one hard, and one, quite possibly, only hypothetical:

The Hard Path. We can continue to rely on non-renewable energy sources, but all of these have serious limitations. Oil is simply running out, worldwide, and will be subject to increased price inflation and uncertainty of supply throughout the remainder of this century; in the twenty-first century, oil is likely to be perceived as a precious mineral to be employed only for selected industrial applications. The use of coal for the production of electricity will be limited by the pollution it produces, as well as by the difficulty with which its mining rate can be accelerated. And non-renewable nuclear production will continue to be plagued by the legacy of Three Mile Island (which greatly increased the unattractiveness of nuclear power to potential investors), problems of disposal, and the terrorist threat. It now appears likely that few new non-renewable nuclear installations will ever be built in the United States, and that those on line will simply be shut down permanently as they fail. Most are likely to be out of commission by the last decade of this century. Thus the hard energy path of non-renewable fuel appears to be conducive only to a low-transportation, low-energy future— one that can only be sustained, with some substantial discomfort, by the multi-nucleated, urbanized settlement form referred to earlier as "diversified-integrated." As Amory Lovins has noted, "Centralized energy sources encourage industrial clustering and urbanization."

The Renewable Nuclear Path. We can maintain an increasingly desperate faith in the eventual development of the elusive energy path, renewable nuclear. This path could sustain, if developed, three of the four urbanization models—assuming that sufficient transportable fuel remains available (or can be generated to power electric autos) to provide the physical mobility required by the spread pattern of contemporary cities and metropolitan areas. Renewable nuclear is another centralized energy source and thus would encourage urbanization and industrial clustering. Indeed, the urban form most congenial to an energy-rich renewable nuclear future would likely be the concentrated supercity, with its limited needs for automobile transportation and its huge energy needs for construction. Centralized residential patterns would minimize the transmission costs of nuclear-powered electricity, but would also maximize citizen anxiety and insecurity regarding the safety of living so close to large nuclear installations. This drawback might bring increased support for the diversified-integrated urbanization model, which would provide some insulation from centralized plants, though resulting in increased electricity costs and reduced access to urban amenities for many people.

The Soft Path. Finally, we can convert as rapidly as possible to the soft energy path, thereby permitting the greatest choice of settlement patterns, as only the concentrated super-city is eliminated. Present trends could be sustained by a determined conservation effort, maximum solar retrofitting, and development of alternative liquid fuels to supplement oil for the powering of automobiles, trucks, and airplanes. As Lovins noted in his book *Soft Energy Paths*, "Soft technologies can match any settlement pattern, their diversity reflecting our own pluralism."

Clearly, the solar path contains within it strong decentralizing forces. As architect Sim

Van der Ryn has noted, the typical half-acre suburban plot is ideally suited to the collection and recycling of solar energy, as well as to the growing of a significant proportion of family food needs.

Nonetheless, the centralizing tendencies of solar energy should not be ignored, involving as they do a focus on the conservation of energy for transportation, retrofitting of existing structures, and some central generation of power. These tendencies suggest more directly the viability of the diversified-integrated model. Perhaps with the limits on node size somewhat relaxed, this model would prove congenial in a solar future, but the most attractive aspect of that future may involve its ability to avoid the *forced* choice of the diversified-integrated model.

A great challenge of the solar future will be to permit a level of physical mobility adequate to the needs and wishes of the American population. The dispersed utopia, congenial as it is to the practical visionaries of the "appropriate technology" movement, is nonetheless one in which little consideration has been given to personal mobility—whether by automobile, bus, or air. How in such a future will work be organized? Will commuting actually be substantially replaced by home-based communications? And, how will the tendency to travel—for recreation, escape, family-linkage, and for the sake of travel itself—be curbed by the organization of decentralized living centers, each themselves remote from centers of urban life and culture? These questions are critical in developing an image of a solar society that will begin to appeal to more than just a hip young segment of American society, themselves very much attracted in their own behavior to the travel ethic made possible by energy abundance. As long as the solar path is seen to lead to a sedentary and isolated "utopia," it is not likely to gain wide support. Amory Lovins, for one, is optimistic that a mobile solar future is possible, maintaining that grain and wood alcohol can be used to produce enough fuel to sustain the present high levels of personal transit.

However optimistically or pessimistically we view what lies ahead, though, it is apparent that urban futures are only one set of human futures inextricably linked to the energy futures from which we shall choose in the coming years. Our utopias will either forebode gloom or anticipate joy in large part in relation to the availability of energy to sustain those visions of life.

It is highly likely that the city, renewed and as the node, or center of nodes, in an energy-conserving future, will play an invigorated role in the society of that future. But the very existence of those city-nodes depends upon the development of the right mix of the right energy forms. The choice of that mix, and those forms, is one that all Americans must join in making in the next very few years. For the sake of our children's future, and any futures that lie beyond, it must be the correct decision—one wisely based on the knowledge of the interrelations of spatial, energy, and societal futures.

XV

COLLECTIVE BEHAVIOR
When Norms Get Lost in the Shuffle

There are times when the norms that guide societal behavior break down. At these times, *collective behavior*—behavior that is both spontaneous and unorganized—may become the norm. Fads, crazes, riots, and panics are all examples of collective behavior; natural disasters, social movements, public opinion, and crowds can create collective behavior situations.

Most of us have been involved in several forms of collective behavior; when we watch a demonstration at a fair, we are a *casual crowd*; when we cheer at a football game, we are an *expressive crowd*; when we join a campus confrontation, we are an *acting crowd*. In each of these situations, however, we maintain a degree of anonymity, because the activities are both temporary and impersonal.

Another form of collective behavior in which many of us have been involved is the social movement; this represents a group of people who are attempting to resist or bring about change. There are many recent examples: the Civil Rights Movement, the Women's Movement, various educational reform movements, and fundamentalist Christian movements. A movement may have a short life span, or it may be institutionalized, a stable part of the ongoing society; its ideas may be rejected, moderately accepted, or overwhelmingly adopted by the society at large.

In the first article Motley describes humorously but poignantly her involvement in the Women's Movement. This is the type of movement that evolves due to a belief that reforms are needed in certain aspects of society. Motley describes the phenomenon that causes many to leave movements: burnout.

The Jonestown Peoples Temple settlement became known worldwide through broadcasts about the mass murder/suicide of hundreds of people. How could one charismatic leader with a persecution complex take so many with him to death? Hall analyzes this phenomenon and the events leading up to the suicide/murders. Social scientists vary in their interpretations of the bizarre events at Jonestown—some considering them to reflect hysteria, others, crowd contagion. Whatever the explanation, events leading up to the deaths fit Smelser's six basic conditions for collective behavior: (1) structural conduciveness—a settlement located in an isolated area where Jones had total control; (2) structural strains—the immediate strains of the numbers of people to be fed and housed in the jungle setting; (3) generalized belief—an apocalyptic sect, believing that the world was doomed and the afterlife was wonderful; (4) precipitating factors—Congressman Ryan's visit and the increasing persecution complex of Jones; (5) mobilization for action—an organizational structure that was prepared for this ultimate event; and (6) mechanisms for social control—few obstacles to carrying out the plan and few means of escape from it.

A riot or other crowd activity can also be explained using Smelser's conditions for collective behavior. Try following the same steps as you read the article by Dye. He outlines the findings of the National Advisory Committee on Civil Disorders and presents a sociological theory of the causes of riots: the relative deprivation theory.

As you read these articles, consider some collective behavior situations in which you have been involved, and whether they fit the patterns described.

43

SOMETIMES I GET TIRED OF WOMEN'S LIB

Dana Tueth Motley

In 1963 I worked as a clerk-stenographer at the University of Illinois, in Urbana. My husband was a student there, and I was earning my P.H.T. (Putting Hubby Through). I wanted to go to college myself, eventually, and since university employees were eligible to take courses with the approval of their department heads, I decided to enroll. But when I asked for his approval, my department head said no. My immediate supervisor pointed out to him that the bookkeeper in our office took off many hours a week to attend classes for his Ph.D. degree. That, said the department head, was different. We "girls" groused about the situation on coffee break but we did not really question it. That was the way things were.

By the time the Women's Movement had begun gathering momentum, in the late 1960s, I was already a full-time student. (My husband was now putting *me* through school.) I was an early sympathizer with the Movement, and as time went by, I became more committed and then active. I attended meetings, parties and rallies. I typed, called, wrote, baked, talked, discussed, debated, argued and generally wore myself to a frazzle for the cause. I "burned out."

One reason I wore out, I think, is that by nature I'm not a social activist. In general I don't care two hoots for politics, and I'm on the shy side. If equal rights for women were not so important to me, I never would have become involved. But another reason I wore out is that I had to ask myself more and more often if people even want the ERA. In particular, do women want it? Not enough of them seem to. If they don't want it, why am I beating *my* brains out to get it passed? I think of several of this past year's incidents that continue to bother me.

As my best friend at work leaves an office party one of my bosses, hearing us planning to attend a feminist meeting the following week, tells her: "What do you want to get mixed up in all that for?" She laughs apologetically, waves and is gone. "Now there goes a real nice woman," he tells me. *Not like you*, he means. He thinks feminists are neurotic. I tell my friend about this the following Monday. She listens in silence and does nothing. Well, I tell myself, that's her business.

Another office party. A coworker tells me she has been reading my letters to the editor of a local newspaper. I know better than to ask her what she thinks of them. After a few moments she says, "I'm for equal pay and all that." (I wish I had a dime for every time I've heard that remark.) "We're still a long way from equal pay," I reply. She agrees, and adds:

"But I like to have my cigarettes lighted and doors opened for me." I comment feebly, "Well, good manners are always in order." Only later, in bed, do I think of what I should have said, what I *will* say next time: "What makes you think that if you get equal pay for equal work, you will have to forfeit men's good will?"

I read an article about a woman who has been elected to the U.S. Senate. I go from paragraph to paragraph, looking for the inevitable answer to the inevitable question. There it is. No, the Senator answers, she does not consider herself a feminist. Women truck drivers, blacksmiths, mechanics, farmers—not one of them ever does. Why not?

My husband's 20-year-old cousin has spent the summer as a legislative aide in Springfield. She is telling us at dinner about an ERA demonstration in the state House of Representatives. I am interested until it dawns on me that she thinks the women involved are crazy. I tell her I'm for the ERA. She says women don't need the ERA—she personally has never suffered from discrimination. My heart begins to pound. I say, "Well, I have!" I light a cigarette and choke out something about how things have changed a lot in 15 years, but I'm too upset to make much sense.

At a feminist meeting one of our members proposes that we pass a resolution supporting the anti-nuclear movement. I say we must not allow ourselves to be sidetracked—we must concentrate on women's issues. She responds with a lecture, telling us feminism involves everything, and certainly nuclear energy. I cut in rudely to ask whether Martin Luther King would have involved himself in the antinuclear issue. A young college student whom I have never seen before says King was involved in the Vietnam war. I suggest that this was because Blacks especially were affected adversely by the war. I plead that we make more of an effort to appeal to a broader political spectrum of women, that involvement in "radical" causes will weaken our own cause and alienate women who are moderate

or conservative. But we end up voting to join a coalition of "progressive" groups. We live in a college town. Many of our members are students. Most are leftist or liberal. I feel alienated.

I read the responses of people who answered the question, "Do you support the ERA?" in a free weekly newspaper I picked up at the grocery store. One young woman says she is "kind of neutral." She thinks it's "up to the individual." She is an engineering student. If other people want the ERA, she writes, it is fine with her, "but for me, I don't need it." I see red. I write to her that it is necessary for people to organize in order to overcome discrimination. I add that organized feminists have already made significant changes, that 15 or 20 years ago women did not enter the engineering field; that every woman, whether she knows it or not, owes her greater expectations and opportunities to the feminist movement. I feel like a pompous fool when I have to write letters like this.

I see my state representative on television. He is talking about a bill to raise the drinking age from 19 to 21. He has assured me by letter and telephone that he supports women's rights—but not the ERA. He is a lawyer and he thinks that the ERA has terrible legal ramifications—though he does not specify what they are. He is for the E and the R, not the A. I pretend to accept his assertion that he's with us, but I know better. I also know he will be re-elected—people in my state don't seem to give a damn about the ERA.

I see a coffee mug while browsing at the supermarket. Emblazoned on the mug are the words: "I want the perfect secretary. One who can type fast and run slow." I grab the mug and march up to the service desk, where I politely tell the manager that this mug is insulting to secretaries. He says that he agrees with me but that some people like the mugs. I persist, telling him no secretary should have to look at this while taking dictation, that secretaries work hard and should not have to put up with insults, that sexual harassment is already a problem. He smiles tightly. I hand him the cup and leave. Back at home, I call a friend. She commiserates. I say we should call the media, buy all the cups and then dash them to the sidewalk in front of the store. We discuss whether we would wind up in jail. We discuss the depth of our commitment— whether we would be willing to go to jail for the cause or not. It is a wet Sunday afternoon. We drift to other topics and then hang up. I feel impotent.

It's been a long day. A bus driver is telling us that there are two sides to the ERA. It infinitely dismays me to hear people still debating whether women should have equal rights. The assumption seems to be that even though equal rights for women under the law is quite clearly what the amendment states, it won't work out that way—women will get more than they bargained for. And I get the impression that this would delight a lot of people. I tell the bus driver there were two sides to the civil rights issue for Blacks, too. One side was held by the KKK. He grunts and looks aggravated.

I ask three closet ERA supporters at work to buy tickets to a fund-raising party. Two are going to be out of town. The third has to attend a wedding. I lose my temper and tell them the idea isn't so much to attend the party as to support the ERA. I stalk off, raving to a friend, "I've certainly bought enough Girl Scout cookies around this joint." And that I don't want anyone to come whining to me when the ERA fails again in Springfield. I know I have no right to judge these women, but I was so sure they would buy tickets. One does come back to buy one. The second says she will buy one next payday. I don't want to feel I've coerced them, but I do.

One of my male coworkers, a devoted admirer of Phyllis Schlafly, earnestly tells me that some women *like* to stay at home; that his wife does; that not every woman is cut out for a career. I tell him that that isn't what the ERA is about. I tell him that the ERA will guarantee more security for homemakers. He quotes a passage from the Bible about women submitting to their husbands. He and I have had this conversation before. We will have it again.

I'm talking to my mother, who after many discussions now backs the ERA but who feels that most people have too much trouble just surviving to devote time and energy to a political cause. I explain to her that I'm campaigning for her, for her mother, for myself— for all women. I talk about Susan B. Anthony, the fight to get the vote, Sojourner Truth. I start to tell her about Sojourner's famous speech, but when I get to the "And ain't I a woman too?" I break down in tears. My mother looks worried. She tells me she thinks I ought to get out of "all this" for a while.

As I'm leaving the office my closest coworker tells me men don't treat women well any more because of all this "women's lib stuff." She is what we in the Movement call "male-defined"—she believes a woman's role in life is to find a man and stand by him. I am so shocked by her remark that I say, "That's right," and walk out the door.

At another feminist meeting we discuss the Nestlé boycott, African women, the J. P. Stevens boycott, Karen Silkwood—everything, it seems, but the ERA. We're going to focus our energies on abortion, not the ERA. I've helped the abortion movement when I could, but now I want the ERA desperately. One woman tells me people are tired of working for the ERA. I go home and rip my bumper sticker off the car and my feminist credo by Jill Ruckelshaus off the mirror, and throw away all the buttons I've picked up at various women's fair booths ("ERA Yes," "ERA No Time Limit on Equality," "I'm a Housewife for ERA," "ERA Yes *again*," "Keep Abortion Safe and Legal," and "Failure Is Impossible"). "I am through," I rave. "Those women don't care about equal rights; they're just a bunch of self-aggrandizing eggheads." My husband has been watching a movie on television. He offers me his bowl of popcorn.

I get a new ERA bumper sticker. A male

driver passes me and gives me a dirty look. A lot of women won't put those bumper stickers on their cars. I understand why. One of my friends, returning from a conference, had her car bumped from behind all the way home.

I write the Star to complain about an article that says women invite rape by the way they do their hair, the way they dress, the way they walk, anything at all. It is irresponsible, I point out in my letter, to print an article that blames women for men's violent behavior. I get a thank-you-for-your-interest reply. It is signed by a woman.

I make the mistake of mentioning my letter to my coworker. She tells me she feels sorry for all the falsely accused men who are sent to prison for rape. Their lives are ruined, she says. I begin to argue with her. I don't make a dent.

A man and I are discussing women's rights, and sooner or later he asks me where my husband stands on the issue. I reply that my husband is 100 per cent behind equal rights for women. The man either doesn't believe me or thinks I've got my husband buffaloed.

I'm tired. I need a break. Other women are going to have to carry the burden awhile. It bothers me that I don't begin to measure up to Susan B. Anthony. And then I come across something she is quoted as having said: "I really believe I shall explode if some of you young women don't wake up and raise your voices in protest. . . . I wonder if when I am under the sod—or cremated and floating in the air—I shall have to stir you and others up. How can you not be all on fire?"

That's what I wonder. And I wonder, too, what's so frightening about this simple sentence, the body of the Equal Rights Amendment: "Equality of rights under the law shall not be denied or abridged by the United States or by any state on account of sex."

44

APOCALYPSE AT JONESTOWN

John R. Hall

The events of November 1978 at Jonestown, Guyana have been well documented, indeed probably better documented than most incidents in the realm of the bizarre. Beyond the wealth of "facts" which have been drawn from interviews with survivors of all stripes, there remain piles of as yet unsifted documents and

Published by permission of Transaction, Inc., from *Society*, Vol. 16, No. 6. Copyright © 1979 by Transaction, Inc.

tapes; if they can ever be examined, these will perhaps add something in the way of detail. But it is unlikely they will change very much the broad lines of our understanding of Jonestown. The major dimensions of the events and the outlines of various intrigues are already before us. But so far we have been caught in a flood of instant analysis; some of this has been insightful, but much of the accompanying moral outrage has clouded our ability to comprehend the events themselves. We need a more considered look at what sort of social phenomenon Jonestown was, and why (and how) Reverend Jim Jones and his staff led the 900 people of Jonestown to die in mass murder and sucide. On the face of it, the action is unparalleled and incredible.

"CRAZY LIKE A FOX"

The news media have sought to account for Jonestown largely by looking for parallels "in history"; yet we have not been terribly enlightened by the ones they have found, usually because they have searched for cases which bear the outer trappings of the event, but which have fundamentally different causes. Thus, at Masada, in 73 A.D., the Jews who committed suicide under siege by Roman soldiers knew their fate was death, and chose to die by their own hands rather than at those of the Romans. In World War II, Japanese kamikaze pilots acted with the knowledge that direct, tangible, strategic results would stem from their altruistic suicides, if they were properly executed. And in Hitler's concentration camps, though there was occasional cooperation by Jews in their own executions, the Nazi executioners had no intentions of dying themselves.

Besides pointing to parallels which don't quite fit, the news media have targeted Jim Jones as irrational, a madman who had perverse tendencies from early in his youth. They have labeled the Peoples Temple as a "cult," perhaps in the hope that a label will suffice when an explanation is unavailable. And they have quite correctly plumbed the key issue of how Jones and his staff were able to bring the mass murder/suicide to completion, drawing largely on the explanations of psychiatrists who have prompted the concept of "brainwashing" as the answer.

But Jones was crazy like a fox. Though he may have been "possessed" or "crazed," both the organizational effectiveness of the Peoples Temple for more than 15 years, and the actual carrying out of the mass murder/suicide show that Jones and his immediate staff knew what they were doing.

Moreover, the Peoples Temple only became a "cult" when the media discovered the mass suicide. As an Indiana woman whose teenager died at Jonestown commented, "I can't understand why they call the Peoples Temple a cult. To the people, it was their church. . . ." It is questionable whether the term "cult" has any sociological utility. As Harold Fallding has observed, it is a value-laden term most often used by members of one religion to describe a heretical or competing religion, of which they disapprove. Of course, even if the use of the term "cult" in the press has been sloppy and inappropriate, some comparisons, for example to the Unification Church, the Krishna Society, and the Children of God, have been quite apt. But these comparisons have triggered a sort of guilt by association: in this view, Jonestown is a not so aberrant case among numerous exotic and weird religious "cults." The only thing stopping some people from "cleaning up" the "cult" situation is the constitutional guarantee of freedom of religion.

Finally, "brainwashing" is an important but incomplete basis for understanding the mass murder/suicide. There can be no way to determine how many people at Jonestown freely chose to drink the cyanide-laced Flav-r-ade distributed after Jonestown received word of the murders of U.S. Congressman Leo Ryan and four other visitors at the airstrip. Clearly over 200 children and an undetermined number of adults were murdered. Thought control and blind obedience to authority ("brainwashing") surely account for some additional number of suicides. But the obvious cannot be ignored: a substantial number of people—"brainwashed" or not—committed suicide. Insofar as "brainwashing" occurs in other social organizations besides the Peoples Temple, it can only be a necessary and not a sufficient cause of the mass murder/ suicide. The coercive persuasion involved in a totalistic construction of reality may explain in part *how* large numbers of people came to accept the course proposed by their leader, but it leaves unanswered the question of *why* the true believers among the inhabitants of Jonestown came to consider "revolutionary suicide" a plausible course of action.

In all the instant analysis of Jones' perversity, the threats posed by "cults" and the victimization of people by "brainwashing," there has been little attempt to account for Jonestown sociologically, and as a religious phenomenon. The various facets of Jonestown remain as incongruous pieces of seemingly separate puzzles; we need a close examination of the case itself to try to comprehend it. In the following discussion based on ideal type analysis and *verstehende* sociology, I will suggest that the Peoples Temple Agricultural Project at Jonestown was an apocalyptic sect. Most apocalyptic sects gravitate toward one of three ideal typical possibilities: (1) preapocalyptic Adventism, (2) preapocalyptic war, or (3) postapocalyptic other-worldly grace. Insofar as the Adventist group takes on a communal form, it comes to approximate the postapocalyptic tableau of other-worldly grace. Jonestown was caught on the saddle of the apocalypse: it had its origins in the vaguely apocalyptic revivalist evangelism of the Peoples Temple in the United States, but the Guyanese communal settlement itself was an attempt to transcend the apocalypse by establishing a "heaven-on-earth." For various reasons, this attempt was frustrated. The Peoples Temple at Jonestown was drawn back into a preapocalyptic war with the forces of the established order. "Revolutionary suicide" then came to be seen as a way of surmounting the frustration, of moving beyond the apocalypse, to "heaven," albeit not "on earth."

In order to explore this account, let us first consider the origins of Jonestown and the ways in which it subsequently came to approximate the ideal typical other-worldly sect. Then we can consider certain tensions of the Jonestown group with respect to its other-worldly existence, so as to understand why similar groups did not (and are not likely to) encounter the same fate as Jonestown.

"A PROPHET CALLS THE SHOTS"

An other-worldly sect, as I have described it in *The Ways Out*, is a utopian communal group which subscribes to a set of beliefs based on an apocalyptic interpretation of current history. The world of society-at-large is seen as totally evil, and in its last days; at the end of history as we know it, it is to be replaced by a community of the elect—those who live according to the revelation of God's will. The convert who embraces such a sect must, perforce, abandon any previous understanding of life's meaning and embrace the new worldview, which itself is capable of subsuming and explaining the individual's previous life, the actions of opponents to the sect, and the demands which are placed on the convert by the leadership of the sect. The other-worldly sect typically establishes its existence on the "other" side of the apocalypse by withdrawing from "this" world into a timeless heaven-on-earth. In this millennial kingdom, those closest to God come to rule. Though democratic consensuality or the collegiality of elders may come into play, more typically, a preeminent prophet or messiah, legitimated by charisma or tradition, calls the shots in a theocratic organization of God's chosen people.

The Peoples Temple had its roots in amorphous revivalistic evangelical religion, but in the transition to the Jonestown Agricultural Mission, it came to resemble an other-worldly sect. The Temple grew out of the interracial congregation Jim Jones had founded in Indiana in 1953. By 1964, the Peoples Temple Full Gospel Church was federated with the Disciples of Christ. Later, in 1966, Jones moved with 100 of his most devout followers to Redwood Valley, California. From there they expanded in the 1970s to San Francisco and Los Angeles—more promising places for liberal, interracial evangelism than rural Redwood Valley. In these years before the move to Guyana, Jones engaged himself largely in the manifold craft of revivalism. Jones learned from others he observed—Father Divine in Philadelphia and David Martinus de Miranda in Brazil, and Jones himself became a purveyor of faked miracles and faith healings. By the California years, the Peoples Temple was prospering financially from its somewhat shady "tent meeting" style activities, and from a variety of other petty and grand money-making schemes; it was also gaining political clout through the deployment of its members for the benefit of various politicians and causes.

These early developments give cause to wonder why Jones did not establish a successful but relatively benign sect like Jehovah's Witnesses, or, alternatively, why he did not move from a religious base directly into the realm of politics, as did the Reverend Adam Clayton Powell, from his Harlem congregation to the U. S. House of Representatives. The answer seems twofold. In the first place, Jim Jones seems to have had limitations both as an evangelist and as a politician. He simply did not succeed in fooling key California observers with his faked miracles. And for all the political support he peddled in California politics, Jones was not always able to draw on his good political "credit" when he needed it. A certain mark of political effectiveness concerns the ability to sustain power in the face of scandal. By this standard, Jones was not totally successful in either Indiana or California: there always seemed to be investigators and reporters on the trails of various questionable financial and evangelical dealings.

Quite aside from the limits of Jones' effectiveness, the very nature of his prophecy directed his religious movement along a different path from either "worldly" politics or sectarian Adventism. Keyed to the New Testament Book of Revelations, Adventist groups receive prophecy about the apocalyptic downfall of the present evil order of the world and the second coming of Christ to preside over a millennial period of divine grace on earth. For all such groups, the Advent itself makes social action to reform "this" world's institutions irrelevant. Adventist groups differ from one another in their exact eschatology of the last days, but the groups that have survived, like the Seventh Day Adventists and Jehovah's Witnesses, have juggled their doctrines which fix an exact date for Christ's appearance. Thus they have moved away from any intense chiliastic expectation of an imminent appearance, to engage in more mundane conversionist activities which are intended to pave the way for the Millennium.

"APOCALYPSE NOW"

Reverend Jones himself seems to have shared the pessimism of the Adventist sects about reforming social institutions in this world (for him, the capitalist world of the United States). True, he supported various progressive causes, but he did not put much stake in their success. Jones' prophecy was far more radical than those of contemporary Adventist groups: he focused on imminent apocalyptic disaster rather than on Christ's millennial salvation, and his eschatology therefore had to resolve a choice between preapocalyptic struggle with "the beast" or collective flight to establish a postapocalyptic kingdom of the elect. Up until the end, the Peoples Temple was directed toward the latter possibility. Even in the Indiana years, Jones had embraced an apocalyptic view. The move from Indiana to California was in part justified by Jones' claim that Redwood Valley would survive nuclear holocaust. In the California years, the apocalyptic vision shifted to Central Intelligence Agency persecution and Nazi-like extermination of blacks. In California too, the Peoples Temple gradually became communalistic in certain respects; it established a community of goods, pooled resources of elderly followers to provide communal housing for them, and drew on state funds to act as foster parents by establishing group homes for displaced youth. In its apocalyptic and communal aspects, the Peoples Temple more and more came to exist as an ark of survival. Jonestown, the Agricultural Project in Guyana, was built beginning in 1974 by an advance crew that by early 1977 still amounted to less than 60 people, most of them under 30 years old. The mass exodus of the Peoples Temple to Jonestown really began in 1977, when the Peoples Temple was coming under increasing scrutiny in California.

In the move to Guyana, the Peoples Temple began to concertedly exhibit many dynamics of other-worldly sects, though it differed in ways which were central to its fate. Until the end, Jonestown was similar in striking ways to contemporary sects like the Children of God and the Krishna Society (ISKCON, Inc.). Indeed, the Temple bears a more than casual (and somewhat uncomfortable) resemblance to the various Protestant sects which emigrated to the wilderness of North America beginning in the seventeenth century. The Puritans, Moravians, Rappites, Shakers, Lutherans, and many others like them sought to escape religious persecution in Europe in order to set up theocracies where they could live out their own visions of the earthly millennial community. So it was with Jonestown. In this light, neither disciplinary practices, the daily round of life, nor the community of goods at Jonestown seem so unusual.

"THE JUNGLE IS ONLY A FEW YARDS AWAY"

The disciplinary practices of the Peoples Temple—as bizarre and grotesque as they may sound, are not uncommon aspects of other-worldly sects: these practices have been played up in the press in an attempt to demonstrate the perverse nature of the group, so as to "explain" the terrible climax to their life. But as Erving Goffman has shown in *Asylums*, sexual intimidation and general psychological terror occur in all kinds of total institutions, including mental hospitals, prisons, armies, and even nunneries. Indeed, Congressman Leo Ryan, just prior to his fateful visit to Jonestown, accepted the need for social control: " . . . you can't put 1,200 people in the middle of a jungle without some damn tight discipline." Practices at Jonestown may well seem restrained in comparison to practices of, say, seventeenth-century American Puritans who, among other things, were willing to execute "witches" on the testimony of respected churchgoers or even children. Meg Greenfield observed in *Newsweek* in reflecting on Jonestown, "the jungle is only a few yards away." It seems important to recall that some revered origins of the United States lie in a remarkably similar "jungle."

Communal groups of all types, not just other-worldly sects, face problems of social control and commitment. Rosabeth Kanter has convincingly shown that successful communal groups in the nineteenth-century U. S. often drew on mechanisms of mutual criticism, mortification, modification of conventional dyadic sexual mores, and other devices in order to decrease the individual's ties to the outside or personal relationships within the group, and increase the individual's commitment to the collectivity as a whole.

Such commitment mechanisms are employed most often in religious communal groups, especially those with charismatic leaders. Other-worldly communal groups, where a special attempt is being made to forge a wholly new interpretation of reality, where the demand for commitment is especially pronounced (in a word, where it is sectarian)— these groups have tremendously high stakes in maintaining commitment. These groups are likely to seek out the procedures most often effective at guaranteeing commitment. After all, defection from "the way" inevitably casts doubt on the sanctity of the way, no matter how it is rationalized among the faithful. Thus, it is against such groups that the charges of "brainwashing," chicanery, and mistreatment of members are most often leveled. Whatever their basis in fact, these are the likely charges of families and friends who see their loved ones abandon them in favor of committing material resources and persons to the religious hope of a new life. Much like other-worldly sects, families suffer a loss of legitimacy in the "defection" of one of their own.

The abyss that comes to exist between other-worldly sects and the world of society-at-large left behind simply cannot be bridged. There is no encompassing rational connection between the two realities, and, therefore, the interchange between the other-worldly sect and people beyond its boundaries becomes a struggle either between "infidels" and the "faithful" from the point of view of the sect, or between rationality and fanaticism from the point of view of outsiders. Every sectarian action has its benevolent interpretation and legitimation within the sect and a converse interpretation from the outside. Thus, from inside the sect, various practices of "confession," "mutual criticism," or "catharsis" sessions seem necessary to prevent deviant worldviews from taking hold within the group. In the Peoples Temple, such practices included occasional enforced isolation and drug regimens for "rehabilitation" akin to contemporary psychiatric treatment. From the outside, all this tends to be regarded as "brainwashing," but insiders will turn the accusation outward, claiming that it is those in the society-at-large who are "brainwashed." Though there can really be no resolution to this conflict of interpretations, the widespread incidence of similar "coercive persuasion" outside Jonestown suggests that the fact it was practiced at Jonestown is not so unusual, at least within the context of other-worldly sects, or total institutions in general, for that matter.

What is unusual is the direction which coercive persuasion or "brainwashing" took. Jones worked to instill devotion in unusual ways—ways which fostered the acceptability

of "revolutionary suicide" among his followers. During "white nights" of emergency mobilization, he conducted rituals of proclaimed mass suicide, giving "poison" to all members, saying they would die within the hour. According to one defector, Deborah Blakey, Jones "explained that the poison was not real and we had just been through a loyalty test. He warned us that the time was not far off when it would be necessary for us to die by our own hands." This event initially left Blakey "indifferent" to whether she "lived or died." A true believer in the Peoples Temple was more emphatic: disappointed by the string of false collective suicides, in a note to Jones he hoped for "the real thing" so that they could all pass beyond the suffering of this world. Some people yielded to Jim Jones only because their will to resist was beaten down; others, including many "seniors"—the elderly members of the Peoples Temple—felt they owed everything to Jim Jones, and provided him with a strong core of unequivocal support. Jones allowed open dissension at "town meetings" apparently because, with the support of the "seniors," he knew he could prevail. Thus, no matter what they wanted personally, people learned to leave their fates in the hands of Jim Jones, and accept what he demanded. The specific uses of coercive persuasion at Jonestown help explain how (but not why) the mass murder/suicide was implemented. But it is the special use, not the general nature of "brainwashing" which distinguishes Jonestown from most other-worldly sects.

MEAT EATERS AND BEAN EATERS

Aside from "brainwashing," a second major kind of accusation about Jonestown, put forward most forcefully by Deborah Blakey, concerns the work discipline and diet there. Blakey swore in an affidavit that the work load was excessive and the food served to the average residents of Jonestown, inadequate.

She abhorred the contradiction between the conditions she reported and the privileged diet of Reverend Jones and his inner circle. Moreover, because she had dealt with the group's finances, she knew that money could have been directed to providing a more adequate diet.

Blakey's moral sensibilities notwithstanding, the disparity between the diet of the elite and of the average Jonestowner should come as no surprise: it parallels Erving Goffman's description of widespread hierarchies of privilege in total institutions. Her concern about the average diet is more the point. But here, other accounts differ from Blakey's report. Maria Katsaris, a consort of Reverend Jones, wrote her father a letter extolling the virtues of the Agricultural Project's "cutlass" beans used as a meat substitute. And Paula Adams, who survived the Jonestown holocaust because she resided at the Peoples Temple house in Georgetown, expressed ambivalence about the Jonestown community in an interview after the mass murder/suicide. But she also remarked, "My daughter ate very well. She got eggs and milk everyday. How many black children in the ghetto eat that well?" The accounts of surviving members of Reverend Jones' personal staff and inner circle, like Katsaris and Adams, are suspect, of course, in exactly the opposite way as those of people like the "Concerned Relatives." But the inside accounts are corroborated by at least one outsider, *Washington Post* reporter Charles Krause. On his arrival at Jonestown in the company of U. S. Congressman Leo Ryan, Krause noted, "contrary to what the Concerned Relatives had told us, nobody seemed to be starving. Indeed, everyone seemed quite healthy."

It is difficult to assess these conflicting views. Beginning early in the summer of 1977, Jones set in motion the mass exodus of some 800 Peoples Temple members from California to Jonestown. Though Jonestown could adequately house only about 500 people by then,

the population quickly climbed well beyond that mark, at the same time ballooning way past the argicultural base of the settlement. The exodus also caused Jonestown to become "top heavy" with less productive seniors and children. Anything close to agricultural self-sufficiency then became a more elusive and long-range goal. As time wore on during the group's last year of existence, Jones himself became ever more fixated on the prospect of a mass emigration from Guyana, and in this light, any sort of long-range agricultural development strategy seemed increasingly irrational. According to *The New York Times*, the former Jonestown farm manager, Jim Bogue, suggested that the agricultural program at Jonestown would have succeeded in the long run, if it had been adhered to. But with the emerging plans for emigration, it was not followed, and thus became merely a charade for the benefit of the Guyanese government. This analysis would seem to have implications for *internal* conflicts about goals within Jonestown: for example, Jim Jones' only natural son, Stephan Jones, as well as several other young men in the Peoples Temple, came to believe in Jonestown as a socialist agrarian community, not as an other-worldly sect headed up by Jim Jones. Reflecting about his father after the mass murder/suicide, Stephan Jones commented, "I don't mind discrediting him, but I'm still a socialist, and Jim Jones will be used to discredit socialism. People will use him to discredit what we built. Jonestown was not Jim Jones, although he believed it was."

The "seniors" who provided social security checks, gardened, and produced handicraft articles for sale in Georgetown in lieu of heavy physical labor, as well as the fate of agricultural productivity—these both reinforce the assessment that Jim Jones' vision of the Peoples Temple approximates the "other-worldly sect" as an ideal type. In such sects, as a rule, proponents seek to survive *not* on the basis of productive labor (as in more "worldly utopian" communal groups), but on the basis of patronage, petty financial schemes, and the building of a "community of goods" through proselytism. This was just the case with Jonestown: the community of goods which Jones built up is valued at more than $12 million. As a basis for satisfying collective wants, any agricultural production at Jonestown would have paled in comparison to this amassed wealth.

But even if the agricultural project itself became a charade, it is no easy task to create a plausible charade in the midst of relatively infertile soil reclaimed from dense jungle; this would have required the long hours of work which Peoples Temple defectors described. Such a charade could serve as yet another effective means of social control. In the first place, it gave a purposeful role to those who envisioned Jonestown as an experimental socialist agrarian community. Beyond this, it monopolized the waking hours of most of the populace in exhausting work, and gave them only a minimal (though probably adequate) diet on which to do it. It is easy to imagine that many city people, or those with bourgeois sensibilities in general, would not find this their cup of tea in any case. But the demanding daily regimen, however abhorrent to the uninitiated, is widespread in other-worldly sects. Various programs of fasting and work asceticism have long been regarded as signs of piety and routes to religious enlightenment or ecstacy. In the contemporary American Krishna groups, an alternation of nonsugar and high-sugar phases of the diet seems to create an almost addictive attachment to the food which is communally dispersed. And we need look no later in history than to Saint Benedict's order to find a situation in which the personal time of participants is eliminated for all practical purposes, with procedures of mortification for offenders laid out by Saint Benedict in his *Rule*. The concerns of Blakey and others about diet, work, and discipline may have some basis, but they have probably been exaggerated, and in any

case, they do not distinguish Jonestown from other-worldly sects in general.

COMMUNITY OF GOODS

One final public concern with the Peoples Temple deserves mention because it so closely parallels previous sectarian practice: the Reverend Jim Jones is accused of swindling people out of their livelihoods and life circumstances by tricking them into signing over their money and possessions to the Peoples Temple or its inner circle of members. Of course, Jones considered this a "community of goods" and correctly pointed to a long tradition of such want satisfaction among other-worldly sects; in an interview just prior to the mass murder/sucide, Jones cited Jesus' call to hold all things in common. There are good grounds to think that Reverend Jones carried this philosophy into the realm of a con game. Still, it should be noted that in the suicidal end, Jones did not benefit from all the wealth the way a good number of other self-declared prophets and messiahs have done.

As with its disciplinary practices and its round of daily life, the community of goods in the Peoples Temple at Jonestown emphasizes its similarities to other-worldly sects—both the contemporary ones labeled "cults" by their detractors, and historical examples which are often revered in retrospect by contemporary religious culture. The elaboration of these affinities is in no way intended to suggest that we can or should vindicate the duplicity, the bizarre sexual and psychological intimidation, and the hardships of daily life at Jonestown. But it must be recognized that the Jonestown settlement was a good deal less unusual than some of us might like to think: the things which detractors find abhorrent in the life of the Peoples Temple at Jonestown prior to the final "white night" of murder and suicide are the core nature of other-worldly sects; it should come as no surprise that practices like those in Jonestown are widespread, both in historical and contemporary other-worldly sects. Granted that the character of such sects—the theocratic basis of authority, the devices of mortification and social control, and the demanding regimen of everyday life—predispose people in such groups to respond to the whims of their leaders, whatever fanatic and zealous directions they may take. But given the widespread occurrence of other-worldly sects, the other-worldly features of Jonestown are in themselves insufficient to explain the bizarre fate of its participants. If we are to understand the unique turn of events at Jonestown, we must look to certain distinctive features of the Peoples Temple—things which make it unusual among other-worldly sects, and we must try to comprehend the subjective meanings of these features for various of Jonestown's participants.

RACE AND IDEOLOGY

If the Peoples Temple was distinctive among otherworldly sects, it is for two reasons: first, the group was far and away more thoroughly racially integrated than any other such group today. Second, the Peoples Temple was distinctively proto-communist in ideology. Both of these conditions, together with certain personal fears of Jim Jones (mixed perhaps with organic disorders and assorted drugs), converged in the active mind of the reverend to give a special twist to the apocalyptic quest of his flock. Let us consider these matters in turn.

In the Peoples Temple, Jim Jones had consistently sought to transcend racism in peace rather than in struggle. The origins of this approach, like most of Jones' early life, are by now shrouded in myth. But it is clear that Jones was committed to racial harmony in his Indiana ministry. In the 1950s, this formation of an interracial congregation met with much resistance in Indianapolis, and this persecution was one impetus for the exodus to California. There is room for debate on how far Jones' operation actually went toward racial equality, or to what degree it simply per-

petuated racism, albeit in a racially harmonious microcosm. But the Peoples Temple fostered greater racial equality and harmony than that of the society-at-large, and in this respect, it has few parallels in present-day communal groups, much less mainstream religious congregations. The significance of this cannot easily be assayed, but one view of it is captured in a letter from a 20-year-old Jonestown girl: she wrote to her mother in Evansville, Indiana that she could "walk down the street now without the fear of having little old white ladies call me nigger."

Coupled with the commitment to racial integration, and again in contrast with most other-worldly sects, the Peoples Temple moved strongly toward ideological communism. Most other-worldly sects practice religiously inspired communism—the "clerical" or "Christian" socialism which Marx and Engels railed against. But few, if any, to date have flirted with the likes of Marx, Lenin, and Stalin. By contrast, it has become clear that, whatever the contradictions other socialists point to between Jones' messianism and socialism, the Reverend Jim Jones and his staff considered themselves socialists. In his column "Perspectives from Guyana," Jim Jones maintained, "neither my colleagues nor I are any longer caught up in the opiate of religion. . . ." Though the practice of the group prior to the mass murder/suicide was not based on any doctrinaire Marxism, at least some of the recruits to the group were young radical intellectuals, and one of the group's members, Richard Tropp, gave evening classes on radical political theory. In short, radical socialist currents were unmistakably present in the group.

PREACHING ATHEISM

It is perhaps more questionable whether the Peoples Temple was religious in any conventional sense of the term. Of course, all utopian communal groups are religious in that they draw together true believers who seek to live out a heretical or heterodox interpretation of the meaningfulness of social existence. In this sense, the Peoples Temple was a religious group, just as Frederick Engels once observed that socialist sects of the nineteenth century paralleled the character of primitive Christian and Reformation sects. Clearly, Jim Jones was more self-consciously religious than the socialist sects were. Though he "preached atheism," and did not believe in a God that answers prayer, he did embrace reincarnation, and a surviving resident of Jonestown remembers him saying, "Our religion is this: your highest service to God is service to your fellow man." On the other hand, it seems that the outward manifestations of conventional religious activity—revivals, sermons, faith healings—were, at least in Jim Jones' view, calculated devices to draw people into an organization which was something quite different. It is a telling point in this regard that Jones ceased the practice of faith healings and cut off other religious activities once he moved to Jonestown. Jones' wife Marceline once noted that Jim Jones considered himself a Marxist who "used religion to try to get some people out of the opiate of religion." In a remarkable off-the-cuff interview with Richard and Harriet Tropp—the two Jonestown residents who were writing a book about the Peoples Temple—Jones reflected on the early years of his ministry, claiming, "what a hell of a battle that (integration) was—I thought 'I'll never make a revolution, I can't even get those fuckers to integrate, much less get them to any communist philosophy.' " In the same interview, Jones intimated that he had been a member of the U. S. Communist party in the early 1950s. Of course, with Jones' Nixonesque concern for his place in history, it is possible that his hindsight, even in talking with sympathetic biographers, was not the same as his original motives. In the interview with the Tropps, Jones hinted that the entire development of the Peoples Temple down to the Jonestown Agricultrual Project derived from his communist beliefs. This interview and Marceline Jones' comment give strong evidence of an early communist orientation in Jones. Whenever this orientation originated, the move to Jonestown was in part predicated on it. The socialist government of Guyana was generally committed to supporting socialists seeking refuge from capitalist societies, and they apparently thought Jones' flexible brand of Marxism fit well within the country's political matrix. By 1973, when negotiations with Guyana about an agricultural project were initiated, Jones and his aides were professing identification with the world-historical communist movement.

THE PERSECUTION COMPLEX

The convergence of racial integration and crude communism gave a distinctly political character to what in many other respects was an other-worldly religious sect. The injection of radical politics gave a heightened sense of persecution to the Jonestown Agricultural Project. Jim Jones seems to have both fed this heightened sense of persecution to his followers, and to have been devoured by it himself. Jones manipulated fears among his followers by controlling information and spreading false rumors about news events in the United States. With actual knowledge of certain adversaries, and fed by his own premonitions, Jones spread premonitions among his followers, thereby heightening their dedication. In the process, Jones disenchanted a few, who became Judas Iscariots, in time bringing the forces of legitimated external authority to "persecute" Jones and his true believers in their jungle theocracy.

The persecution complex is a stock-in-trade of other-worldly sects. It is naturally engendered by a radical separation from the world of society-at-large. An apocalyptic mission develops in such a way that "persecution" from the world left behind is taken as a sign of the sanctity of the group's chosen path of salvation. Though racial and political persecution are not usually among the themes of other-worldly persecution, they do not totally break the other-worldly way of interpreting experience. But the heightened sense of persecution at Jonestown did reduce the disconnection from society-at-large which is the signature of other-worldly sects.

Most blacks in the U. S. have already experienced "persecution"; if Jim Jones gave his black followers some relief from a ghetto existence (which many seem to have felt he did), he also made a point of reminding the blacks in his group that persecution still awaited them back in the ghettos and rural areas of the United States. In the California years, for example, the Peoples Temple would stage mock lynchings of blacks by the Ku Klux Klan, as a form of political theater. And according to Deborah Blakey, Jones "convinced black Temple members that if they did not follow him to Guyana, they would be put into concentration camps and killed."

Similarly, white socialist intellectuals could easily develop paranoia about their activities; as any participant in the New Left movement of the 1960s and early 1970s knows, paranoia was a sort of badge of honor to some people. Jones fed this sort of paranoia by telling whites that the CIA listed them as enemies of the state.

Jones probably impressed persecution upon his followers to increase their allegiance to him. But Jones himself was caught up in a web of persecution and betrayal. The falling out between Jones and Grace and Tim Stoen seems central here. In conjunction with the imminent appearance of negative news articles, the fight over custody of John Victor Stoen—Grace's son whom both Jones and Tim Stoen claimed to have fathered—triggered Jones' 1977 decision to remove himself from the San Francisco Temple to Guyana.

We may never know what happened between the Stoens and Jones. According to Terri Buford, a former Jonestown insider, Tim Stoen left the Peoples Temple shortly after it became known that in the 1960s he had gone on a Rotary-sponsored speaking tour denouncing communism. Both sides have accused the other of being the progenitors of violence in the Peoples Temple. To reporters who accompanied Congressman Ryan, Jones charged that the Stoen couple had been government agents and provocateurs who had advocated bombing, burning, and terrorism. This possibility could have been regarded as quite plausible by Jones and his staff, for they possessed documents about alleged similar Federal Bureau of Investigation moves against the Weather Underground and the Church of Scientology. The struggle between Jones and the Stoens thus could easily have personified to Jones the quintessence of a conspiracy against him and his work. It certainly intensified negative media attention on the Temple.

For all his attempts to garner favor from the press, Jones failed in the crucial instance: the San Francisco investigative reporters gave horror stories about the Peoples Temple and Jones' custody battle a good deal of play. Jones may well have been correct in his suspicion that he was not being treated fairly in the press. After the mass murder/suicide, the managing editor of the *San Francisco Examiner* proudly asserted in a January 15, 1979 letter to the *Wall Street Journal* that his paper had not been "morally neutral" in its coverage of the Peoples Temple.

The published horror stories were based on the allegations by defectors, the Stoens and Deborah Blakey foremost among them. How true, widespread, exaggerated, or isolated the incidents reported were, we do not know. Certainly they were generalized in the press to the point of creating an image of Jones as a total ogre. The defectors also initiated legal proceedings against the Temple. And the news articles began to stir the interest of government authorities in the operation. These developments were not lost on Jim Jones. The custody battle with the Stoens seems to have precipitated Jones' mass suicide threat to the Guyanese government. Not coincidentally, according to Jim Jones' only natural son, Stephan Jones, at this point the first "white night" drills for mass suicide were held

(Stephan Jones connects these events with the appearance of several negative news articles).

With these sorts of events in mind, it is not hard to see how it came to be that Jim Jones felt betrayed by the Stoens and the other defectors, and persecuted by those who appeared to side with the defectors—the press and the government foremost among them. In September 1978, Jones went so far as to retain well-known conspiracy theorist and lawyer Mark Lane to investigate the possibility of a plot against the Peoples Temple. In the days immediately after he was retained by Jones, Mark Lane (perhaps self-servingly) reported in a memorandum to Jones that "even a cursory examination" of the available evidence "reveals that there has been a coordinated campaign to destroy the Peoples Temple and to impugn the reputation of its leader." Those involved were said to include the U. S. Customs Bureau, the Federal Communications Commission, the Central Intelligence Agency, the Federal Bureau of Investigation, and the Internal Revenue Service. Lane's assertions probably had little basis in fact: though several of the named agencies independently had looked into certain Temple activities, none of them had taken any direct action against the Temple, even though they may have had some cause for doing so. The actual state of affairs notwithstanding, with Lane's assertions, Jones had substantiation of his sense of persecution from a widely touted theorist of conspiracies.

The sense of persecution which gradually developed in the Peoples Temple from its beginning and increased markedly at Jonestown must have come to a head with the visit there of U. S. Congressman Leo Ryan. The U. S. State Department has revealed that Jones had agreed to a visit by Ryan, but withdrew permission when it became known that a contingent of "Concerned Relatives" as well as certain members of the press would accompany Ryan to Guyana. Among the Concerned Relatives who came with Ryan was the Stoen couple; in fact, Tim Stoen was known as a "leader" of the Concerned Relatives. Reporters with Ryan included two from the *San Francisco Chronicle,* a paper which had already pursued investigative reporting on the Peoples Temple, as well as Gordon Lindsay, an independent newsman who had written a negative story on the Peoples Temple intended to be (but never actually) published in the *National Enquirer.* This entourage could hardly have been regarded as objective or unbiased by Jim Jones and his closer supporters. Instead, it identified Ryan with the forces of persecution, personified by the Stoens and the investigative press, and it set the stage for the mass murder/suicide which had already been threatened in conjunction with the custody fight.

The ways in which the Peoples Temple came to differ from more typical other-worldly sects are more a matter of degree than of kind, but the differences together profoundly altered the character of the scene of Jonestown. Though the avowed radicalism, the interracial living, and the defector-media-government "conspiracy" are structurally distinct from one another, Jim Jones drew them together into a tableau of conspiracy which was intended to increase his followers' attachment to him, but ironically brought his legitimacy as a messiah into question, undermined the other-worldly possibilities of the Peoples Temple Agricultural Project, and placed the group on the stage of history in a distinctive relationship to the apocalypse.

VIRTUOSI OF THE COLLECTIVE LIFE

Other-worldly sects by their very nature are permeated with apocalyptic ideas. The sense of a decaying social order is personally experienced by the religious seeker in a life held to be untenable, meaningless, or both. This interpretation of life is collectively affirmed and transcended in other-worldly sects, which purport to offer "heaven-on-earth," beyond the effects of the apocalypse. Such sects promise the grace of a theocracy in which followers can sometimes really escape the "living hell" of society-at-large. Many of Reverend Jones' followers seem to have joined the Peoples Temple with this in mind. But the predominance of blacks and the radical ideology of the Temple, together with the persistent struggle against the defectors and the "conspiracy" which formed around them in the minds of the faithful each gave the true believers' sense of persecution a more immediate and pressing, rather than "other-worldly" cast. Jones used these elements to heighten his followers' sense of persecution from the outside, but this device itself may have drawn into question the ability of the supposed charismatic leader to provide an other-worldly sanctuary. By the middle of October, a month before Congressman Ryan's trip in November 1978, Jones' position of preeminent leadership was beginning to be questioned not only by disappointed religious followers, but also by previously devoted "seniors" who were growing tired of the ceaseless meetings and the increasingly untenable character of everyday life, and by key virtuosi of collective life who felt Jones was responsible for their growing inability to deal successfully with Jonestown's material operations. Once those who were dissatisfied circumvented Jones' intelligence network of informers and began to establish solidarity with one another, the "conspiracy" can truly be said to have taken hold within Jonestown itself. If the times were apocalyptic, Reverend Jones was like the revolutionary millenarians described by Norman Cohn and Gunther Lewy. Rather than successfully proclaiming the postapocalyptic sanctuary, Jones was reduced to declaiming the web of "evil" powers in which he was ensnared, and searching with chiliastic expectation for the imminent cataclysm which would announce the beginning of the kingdom of righteousness.

Usually, other-worldly sects have a sense of the eternal about them: having escaped "this" world, they adopt the temporal trappings of "heaven," which amounts to a time-less bliss of immortality. But Jim Jones had not really established a postapocalyptic heavenly plateau. Even if he had promised this to his followers, it was only just being built in the form of the Agricultural Project. And it was not even clear that Jonestown itself was the promised land: Jones did not entirely trust the Guyanese government, and he was considering seeking final asylum in Cuba or the Soviet Union. Whereas other-worldly sects typically assert that heaven is at hand, Jones could only hold it out as a future goal, and one which became more and more elusive as the forces of "persecution" tracked him to Guyana. Thus, Jones and his followers were still within the throes of the apocalypse, still, as they conceived it, the forces of good battling against the evil and conspiratorial world which could not tolerate a living example of a racially integrated American socialist utopia.

In the struggle against evil, Jones and his true believers took on the character of what I have termed a "warring sect"—fighting a decisive Manichean struggle with the forces of evil. Such a struggle seems almost inevitable when political rather than religious themes of apocalypse are stressed, and it is clear that Jones and his staff at times acted within this militant frame of reference. For example, they maintained armed guards around the settlement, held "white night" emergency drills, and even staged mock CIA attacks on Jonestown. By doing so, they undermined the plausibility of an other-worldly existence. The struggle of a warring sect takes place in historical time, where one action builds on another, where decisive outcomes of previous events shape future possibilities. The contradiction between this earthly struggle and the heaven-on-earth Jones would have liked to proclaim (for example, in "Perspectives from Guyana") gave Jonestown many of its strange juxtapositions—of heaven and hell, of suffering and bliss, of love and coercion. Perhaps even Jones himself, for all his megalomaniacal ability to transcend the contradictions which others saw in him (and labeled him an "opportunist" for), could not endure the struggle for his own immortality. If he were indeed a messianic incarnation of God, as he sometimes claimed, presumably Jones could have either won the struggle of the warring sect against its evil persecutors or delivered his people to the bliss of another world.

In effect, Jones had brought his flock to the point of straddling the two sides of the apocalypse. Had he established his colony beyond the unsympathetic purview of defectors, Concerned Relatives, investigative reporters, and governmental agencies, the other-worldly tableau perhaps could have been sustained with less-repressive methods of social control. As it was, Jones and the colony experienced the three interconnected limitations of group totalism which Robert Jay Lifton described with respect to the Chinese Communist revolution: (1) diminishing conversions, (2) inner antagonism (that is, of disillusioned participants) to the suffocation of individuality, and (3) increasing penetration of the "idea-tight milieu control" by outside forces. As Lifton noted, revolutionaries are engaged in a quest for immortality. Other-worldly sectarians in a way short-circuit this quest by the fiat of *asserting* their immortality—positing the timeless heavenly plateau which exists *beyond* history as the basis of their everyday life. But under the persistent eyes of external critics, and because Jones himself exploited such "persecution" to increase his social control, he could not sustain the illusion of other-worldly immortality.

On the other hand, the Peoples Temple could not achieve the sort of political victory which would have been the goal of a warring sect. Since revolutionary war involves a struggle with an established political order in unfolding historical time, revolutionaries can only attain immortality in the widescale victory of the revolution over the "forces of reaction." Ironically, as Lifton pointed out, even the initial political and military victory of the revolutionary forces does not end the search for immortality: even in victory, revolution

can only be sustained through diffusion of its principles and goals. But as Max Weber observed, in the long run, it seems impossible to maintain the charismatic enthusiasm of revolution; more pragmatic concerns come to the fore, and as the ultimate ends of revolution are faced off against everyday life and its demands, the quest for immortality fades, and the immortality of the revolutionary moment is replaced by the myth of a grand revolutionary past.

The Peoples Temple could not begin to achieve revolutionary immortality in historical time, for it could not even pretend to achieve any victory against its enemies. If it had come to a pitched battle, the Jonestown defenders—like the Symbionese Liberation Army against the Los Angeles Police Department S.W.A.T. (strategic weapons and tactics) Team—would have been wiped out.

But the Peoples Temple could create a kind of "immortality" which is really not a possibility for political revolutionaries. They could abandon apocalyptic hell by the act of mass suicide. This would shut out the opponents of the Temple: they could not be the undoing of what was already undone, and there could be no recriminations against the dead. It could also achieve the other-worldly salvation Jones had promised his more religious followers. Mass suicide united the divergent public threads of meaningful existence at Jonestown—those of political revolution and religious salvation. It was an awesome vehicle for a powerful statement of collective solidarity by the true believers among the people of Jonestown—that they would rather die together than have the life that was created together subjected to gradual decimation and dishonor at the hands of authorities regarded as illegitimate.

Most warring sects reach a grisly end: occasionally, they achieve martydrom, but if they lack a constituency, their extermination is used by the state as proof of its monopoly on the legitimate use of force. "Revolutionary" suicide is a victory by comparison. The event can be drawn upon for moral didactics, but this cannot erase the stigma that Jonestown implicitly places on the world that its members left behind. Nor can the state punish the dead who are guilty, among other things, of murdering a U. S. congressman, three newsmen, a Concerned Relative, and however many Jonestown residents did not willingly commit suicide. Though they paid the total price of death for their ultimate commitment, and though they achieved little except perhaps sustenance of their own collective sense of honor, still those who won this hollow victory cannot have it taken away from them. In the absence of retribution, the state search for living guilty, as well as the widespread outcry against "cults," take on the character of scapegoating. Those most responsible are beyond the reach of the law: unable to escape the hell of their own lives by creating an other-worldly existence on earth, they instead sought their "immortality" in death, and left it to others to ponder the apocalypse which they have unveiled.

45

VIOLENCE IN AMERICAN CITIES

Thomas R. Dye

The civil rights legislation of the 1960s had relatively little impact on the black masses in urban ghettos. The breakthroughs that the civil rights movement made in open public accommodations, fair employment, fair housing, and voting rights may have opened new opportunities for the educated black middle class, but the undereducated black poor living in the ghetto environment could not really take advantage of these new opportunities. The victories of the civil rights movement were primarily *symbolic* victories; the *actual* conditions of ghetto blacks in income, education, health, employment, housing, and other conditions of life were left unchanged. It was inevitable that the resentment, bitterness, and frustration of the ghetto masses would find expression in some fashion.

Civil disorder and violence are not new on the American scene. On the night of December 16, 1773, a group of "agitators" in Boston, Massachusetts, illegally destroyed 342 chests of tea. And violence as a form of political protest has continued intermittently in America to the present day. The nation itself was founded in armed revolution. Yet even though domestic violence has played a prominent role in America's history, the ghetto riots of the 1960s shocked the nation with the most massive and widespread civil disorders ever to face the nation. All these riots involved black attacks on established authority—policemen, firemen, National Guardsmen, whites in general, and property owned by whites. Three of these riots—Watts, California, in 1965 and Newark and Detroit in 1967—amounted to major civil disorders.

From *Politics in States and Communities*, 2nd ed., by Thomas R. Dye, © 1973. Reprinted by permission of Prentice-Hall, Inc., Englewood Cliffs, N.J.

The Watts riot in August 1965 was described in the McCone Commission's report:

In the ugliest interval . . . perhaps as many as 10,000 Negroes took to the streets in neurotic bands. They looted stores, set fires, beat up white passers-by whom they had hauled from stopped cars, many of which were turned upside-down and burned, exchanged shots with law enforcement officers, and stoned and shot at firemen. The rioters seemed to have been caught up in an insensate rage of destruction. By Friday, disorder spread to adjoining areas, and ultimately, an area covering 46.5 square miles had to be controlled with the aid of military authority before public order was restored. . . .

Of the 34 killed, one was a fireman, one was a deputy sheriff, and one a Long Beach policeman [the remainder were Negroes].

More than 600 buildings were damaged by burning and looting. Out of this number, more than 200 were completely destroyed by fire. The rioters concentrated primarily on food markets, liquor stores, furniture stores, clothing stores, department stores, and pawn shops.

. . . We note with interest that no residences were deliberately burned, that damage to schools, libraries, churches and public buildings was minimal, and that certain types of business establishments, notably service stations and automobile dealers, were for the most part unharmed.[1]

In the summer of 1967, New Jersey's governor proclaimed Newark a city "in open rebellion," declared a state of emergency, and called out the National Guard. For four consecutive days and nights snipers fired at police and firemen, looters made off with the inventories of scores of stores, and arsonists set fire to large portions of commercial property in the black section of that city. More than four thousand city policemen, state troopers, and National Guardsmen were required to restore order. Before the riot was over, twenty-three persons had been killed, and property damage was widespread. Of the dead, only two were white—a policeman and a fireman. Of the black dead, two were children and six were women.

But it was Detroit that became the scene of the bloodiest racial violence of the twentieth century. A week of rioting in Detroit, July 23–28, 1967, left forty-three dead and more than one thousand injured. Whole sections of the city were reduced to charred ruins and smoke. Over thirteen hundred buildings were totally demolished and twenty-seven hundred businesses sacked. Detroit's upheaval began when police raided an after-hours club and arrested the bartender and several customers for selling and consuming alcoholic beverages after authorized closing hours. A force of fifteen thousand city and state police, National Guardsmen, and finally federal troops fought to quell the violence. Most of the looted retail businesses were liquor stores, grocery stores, and furniture stores. Many black merchants scrawled "Soul Brother" on their windows in an attempt to escape the wrath of the black mobs. Eventually, homes and shops covering a total area of fourteen square miles were gutted by fire. Firemen who tried to fight fires were stoned and occasionally shot by ghetto residents. Of the forty-three persons who were killed during the riot, thirty-three were black and ten were white. Among the dead were one National Guardsman, one fireman, one policeman, and one black private guard. Both the violence and the pathos of the ghetto riots were reflected in the following report from Detroit:

. . . a spirit of carefree nihilism was taking hold. To riot and destroy appeared more and more to become ends in themselves. Late Sunday afternoon it appeared to one observer that the young people were "dancing amidst the flames."

A Negro plainclothes officer was standing in an intersection when a man threw a Molotov cocktail into a business establishment on the corner. In the heat of the afternoon, fanned by the 20–25 mile per hour winds of both Sunday and Monday, the fire reached the home next door within minutes. As its residents uselessly sprayed the flames with garden hoses, the fire jumped from roof to roof of adjacent two- and three-story buildings. Within the hour the entire block was in flames. The ninth house in the burning row belonged to the arsonist who had thrown the Molotov cocktail. . . .

. . . employed as a private guard, fifty-five year old Julius L. Dorsey, a Negro, was standing in front of a market, when accosted by two Negro men and a woman. They demanded he permit them to loot the market. He ignored their demands. They began to berate him. He asked a

SOME PROCESSES OF SOCIAL LIFE

neighbor to call the police. As the argument grew more heated, Dorsey fired three shots from his pistol in the air.

The police radio reported: "Looters, they have rifles." A patrolcar driven by a police officer and carrying three National Guardsmen arrived. As the looters fled, the law enforcement personnel opened fire. When the firing ceased, one person lay dead. He was Julius L. Dorsey. . . .[2]

The National Advisory Commission on Civil Disorders concluded:

1. No civil disorder was "typical" in all respects . . .
2. While civil disorders of 1967 were racial in character, they were not *inter*-racial. The 1967 disorders, as well as earlier disorders of the recent period, involved action within Negro neighborhoods against symbols of white American society—authority and property—rather than against white persons.
3. Despite extremist rhetoric there was no attempt to subvert the social order of the United States. Instead, most of those who attacked white authority and property seemed to be demanding fuller participation in the social order and the material benefits enjoyed by the vast majority of American citizens.
4. Disorder did not typically erupt without preexisting causes, as a result of a single "triggering" or "precipitating" incident. Instead, it developed out of an increasingly disturbed social atmosphere, in which typically a series of tension-heightening incidents over a period of weeks or months became linked in the minds of many in the Negro community with a shared network of underlying grievances.
5. There was, typically, a complex relationship between the series of incidents, and the underlying grievances. For example, grievances about allegedly abusive police practices . . . were often aggravated in the minds of many Negroes by incidents involving the police, or the inaction of municipal authorities on Negro complaints about police action.
6. Many grievances in the Negro community resulted from discrimination, prejudice, and powerlessness which Negros often experience. . . .
7. Characteristically the typical rioter was not a hoodlum, habitual criminal, or riff-raff. . . . Instead, he was a teenager or young adult, a lifelong resident of the city in which he rioted, a high school drop-out—but somewhat better educated than his Negro neighbor—and almost invariably underemployed or employed in a menial job. He was proud of his race, extemely hostile to both whites and middle class Negroes and, though informed about politics, highly distrustful of the political system and of political leaders.
8. Numerous Negro counter-rioters walked the streets, urging the rioters to "cool it." . . .
9. Negotiation between Negro and white officials occurred during virtually all of this disorder. . . .
10. . . . Some rioters may have shared neither the conditions nor the grievance of their Negro neighbors; some may have coolly and deliberately exploited the chaos created by others; some may have been drawn into the melee merely because they identified with, or wished to emulate, others.
11. The background of disorder in the riot cities was typically characterized by severely disadvantaged conditions for Negroes, especially as compared with those of whites. . . .
12. In the immediate aftermath of disorder, the status quo of daily life before the disorder generally was quickly restored. Yet despite some notable public and private efforts, little basic change took place in the conditions underlying the disorder. In some cases, the result was increased dislike between blacks and whites, diminished inter-racial communication, and the growth of Negro and white extremist groups.[3]

ASSESSING THE CAUSES OF RIOTS

One explanation of urban violence is that it is a product of the relative deprivation of ghetto residents.[4] *Relative deprivation* is the discrepancy between people's expectations about the goods and conditions of life to which they are justifiably entitled and what they perceive to be their chances for getting and keeping what they feel they deserve. Relative deprivation is not merely a complicated way of saying that people are deprived and therefore angry because they have less than what they want; it is more complex than that. Relative deprivation focuses on (1) what people think they *deserve*, not just what they want in an ideal sense, and (2) what they think they have a *chance* of getting, not just what they have.

Relative deprivation differs considerably from the *absolute deprivation* hypothesis. The absolute deprivation idea suggests that individuals who are the most deprived are those who are most likely to rise up. Of course, it is true that conditions in America's ghettos provide the necessary environment for violence. Racial imbalance, de facto segregation, slum housing, discrimination, unemployment, poor schools, and poverty all provide excellent kindling for the flames of violence. But these underlying conditions for violence existed for decades in America, and the nation never experienced simultaneous violent uprisings in nearly all its major cities before the 1960s. This suggests that the deprivation itself is not a sufficient condition for violence. Some new ingredients were added to the incendiary conditions in American cities which touched off the violence of the 1960s.

Relative deprivation focuses on the distance between current status and expectation level. According to this hypothesis, it is neither the wholly downtrodden—who have no aspirations—nor the very well off—who can satisfy theirs—who represent a threat to civil order. The threat is posed by those whose expectations about what they deserve outdistance the capacity of the political system to satisfy them. Often, rapid increases in expectations are a product of minor symbolic or token improvements in conditions. This leads to the apparent paradox of violence and disorder occurring at the very time that improvements in the conditions of blacks are being made. It is hope, not despair, that generates civil violence and disorder. Masotti and Bowen remark: "The reason why black Americans riot is because there has been just enough improvement in their condition to generate hopes, expectations, or aspirations beyond the capacities of the system to meet them."[5]

The civil rights movement made many blacks acutely aware of discrimination in American society and reduced their tolerance for injustice. The civil rights movement increased the aspiration level of the black masses and inspired impatience and hostility toward the "white establishment." The civil rights movement had to awaken blacks to their plight in American society before progress could be made in eliminating discrimination, but the price of this awakening was a major increase in aspiration levels and the risk of frustration and bitterness when aspirations were unfulfilled. The breakthroughs that the established civil rights movement made in

public accommodations, employment, voting, and office-holding in the 1960s may have opened new opportunities for the educated middle class. But the undereducated black poor, living in the ghetto environment, could not really take advantage of many of these opportunities. The movement increased their expectation level, but it failed to significantly alter their condition in life. Thus, it is no coincidence that the urban disorders followed on the heels of some of the most significant legislative gains in the civil rights struggle.

Once racial violence has broken out anywhere in the nation, the mass media play an important role in disseminating images of violence as well as the symbols and rationalizations of the rioters. Television offers the rioter a mass audience. It was not unknown for rioters to leave the scene temporarily to hurry to their television sets to see themselves. Moreover, television images may reinforce predispositions to participate and even to legitimatize participation. Television enables blacks in one ghetto to see what blacks in another ghetto are doing, and it explains simultaneous rioting in ghettos across the nation.

THE NATIONAL ADVISORY COMMISSION ON CIVIL DISORDERS

In July 1967, in the midst of widespread urban disorder, President Lyndon B. Johnson appointed a National Advisory Commission on Civil Disorders to study the riots and to make necessary recommendations. In its official report the commission enumerated "three of the most bitter fruits of white racial attitudes":

Pervasive discrimination and segregation. The first is surely the continuing exclusion of great numbers of Negroes from the benefits of economic progress through discrimination in employment and education, and their enforced confinement in segregated housing and schools. The corrosive and degrading effects of this condition and the attitudes that underlie it are the source of the deepest bitterness and at the center of the problem of racial disorder.

Black migration and white exodus. The second is the massive and growing concentration of impoverished Negroes in our major cities resulting from Negro migration from the rural South, rapid population growth and the continuing movement of the white middle-class to the suburbs. The consequence is a greatly increased burden on the already depleted resources of cities, creating a growing crisis of deteriorating facilities and services and unmet human needs.

Black ghettos. Third, in the teeming racial ghettos, segregation and poverty have intersected to destroy opportunity and hope and to enforce failure. The ghettos too often mean men and women without jobs, families without men, and schools where children are processed instead of educated, until they return to the street—to crime, to narcotics, to dependency on welfare, and to bitterness and resentment against society in general and white society in particular.[6]

The commission admitted, however, that "these facts alone—fundamental as they are—cannot be said to have caused the disorders." The commission identified three "powerful ingredients" that had "begun to catalyze the mixture":

Frustrated hopes. The expectations aroused by the great judicial and legislative victories of the civil rights movement have led to frustration, hostility and cynicism in the fact of the persistent gap between promise and fulfillment. The dramatic struggle for equal rights in the South has sensitized Northern Negroes to the economic inequalities reflected in the deprivations of ghetto life.

Legitimation of violence. A climate that tends toward the approval and encouragement of violence as a form of protest has been created by white terrorism directed against nonviolent protest, including instances of abuse and even murder of some civil rights workers in the South; by the open defiance of law and federal authority by state and local officials resisting desegregation; and by some protest groups engaging in civil disobedience who turn their backs on nonviolence, go beyond the Constitutionally protected rights of petition and free assembly, and resort to violence to attempt to compel alteration of laws and policies with which they disagree. This condition has been reinforced by a general erosion of respect for authority in American society and reduced effectiveness of social standards and community restraints on violence

and crime. This in turn has largely resulted from rapid urbanization and the dramatic reduction in the average age of the total population.

Powerlessness. Finally, many Negroes have come to believe that they are being exploited politically and economically by the white "power structure." Negroes, like people in poverty everywhere, in fact lack the channels of communication, influence and appeal that traditionally have been available to ethnic minorities within the city and which enabled them—unburdened by color—to scale the walls of the white ghettos in an earlier era. The frustrations of powerlessness have led some to the conviction that there is no effective alternative to violence as a means of expression and redress, as a way of "moving the system." More generally, the result is alienation and hostility toward the institutions of law and government and the white society which controls them. This is reflected in the reach toward racial consciousness and solidarity reflected in the slogan "Black Power."[7]

The commission warned that "our nation is moving toward two societies, one black, one white—separate and unequal." The principal "blame" for the riots was placed upon whites rather than blacks: "What white Americans have never fully understood—but what the Negro can never forget—is that white society is deeply implicated in the ghetto. White institutions created it, white institutions maintain it, and white society condones it."[8] The commission recommended massive federal aid programs in employment, education, welfare, and housing, but it suggested no new departures from traditional programs in these areas. The commission called for the creation of two million new jobs in the ghettos, the elimination of de facto segregation, the construction of six million new units of public housing, and more liberal welfare benefits. In the commission's words: "These programs will require unprecedented levels of funding and performance, but they neither probe deeper nor demand more than the problems which called them forth. There can be no higher priority for national action and no higher claim on the nation's conscience."

NOTES

[1] Governor's Commission on the Los Angeles Riots, John A. McCone, Chairman. *Violence in the City—An End or a Beginning* (Sacramento: Office of the Governor of California, 1965), pp. 3–5.

[2] National Advisory Commission on Civil Disorders, *Report* (Washington, D. C.: Government Printing Office, 1968), p. 4.

[3] *Ibid.*, pp. 110–12.

[4] For a full discussion of the *relative deprivation* explanation as well as alternative explanations, see Dan R. Bowen and Louis H. Masotti, "Civil Violence: A Theoretical Overview," in *Riots and Rebellion*, ed. Masotti and Bowen (Beverly Hills: Sage Publications, 1968). See also James C. Davies, "Toward a Theory of Revolution," *American Sociological Review*, 27 (February 1962), 6; and Ted Gur, *Why Men Rebel* (Princeton: Princeton University Press, 1970).

[5] Masotti and Bowen, *Riots and Rebellion*, pp. 24–25.

[6] National Advisory Commission on Civil Disorders, *Report*, pp. 203–4.

[7] *Ibid.*, pp. 204–5.

[8] *Ibid.*, p. 2.

XVI

SOCIAL CHANGE
Society in Flux

Social change is the alteration, over time, of a basic pattern of social organization. It involves two related types of changes: changes in folkways, mores, and other cultural elements of the society; and changes in the social structure and social relations of the society. An example of a change in the cultural elements would be women entering the labor force, whereas the rise of secondary-group relationships with a corresponding increase in formal organization would be an example of structural change.

Social change happens through the triple impact of *diffusion* (the spread of ideas across culture), *discovery* (unpremeditated findings), and *invention* (purposeful new arrangements)— each of which is expanding at a geometric rate. This means that the period of time over which an initial invention evolves may require centuries, but once it is established, further changes related to that invention are rapid. For example, it took less than fifty years to go from the Wright brothers' twelve-second flight to supersonic travel and trips to the moon. Similarly, the rates of diffusion and discovery are now greater due to advancements in communication and travel. Rapid social change has had mixed results. Sometimes change is generally beneficial and therefore easily accepted; sometimes change is detrimental, and its acceptance can lead to disorganized behavior. Many variables affect the ease of acceptance, including the rate of change, attitudes toward the change, and the parts of society affected by the change.

In the first article, Reinhold notes the effect that a past social event has had on current styles of living and thinking. These effects might be considered surprising since they were thought to arise from fads started by a socially condemned aggregate. As you read this article, you might ask yourself why America so readily accepted the ideas of the Woodstock generation.

The second article, by Goodman, also examines a heritage from the past. He analyzes the predictions made by George Orwell in his famous book, *1984*, and points out that most have come true. Since Orwell's book is about a negative utopia, the fulfillment of his predictions would not appear to be a good omen.

The final article carries the theme of change a bit farther into the future. Cornish's look at the '80s gives us a choice of agendas for the future. Will it resemble Reinhold's future, with freedom of thought and life style, or Orwell's utopian "Big Brother" society?

46

THE LEGACY OF WOODSTOCK

Robert Reinhold

In thousands of small, almost imperceptible ways, in the routine transactions of daily work, play and family life, Woodstock nation is alive in Des Moines.

It is not altogether obvious here in Iowa or on the rest of the American scene. Gone, for the most part, are the more vivid signs of the national cultural and political awakening that was symbolized by that extraordinary youth gathering at the Woodstock Festival in New York State 10 years ago this month.

It was billed as a rock music concert, but, in the minds of many there, it was a victory celebration, the culmination of a decadelong youth crusade for a freer style of life, for peace and tolerance—a crusade rooted in such national forces as the civil rights drive and other movements of the time. For them, Woodstock marked rebellion against what was seen as an old, repressive and corrupt order and the proclamation of a new order.

The jeans with embroidered bell bottoms and the beads have given way to jackets and ties and other more conservative garb. The psychedelic rock of Jimi Hendrix, Sly and the Family Stone, and Jefferson Airplane has faded into the slick disco sounds of Donna Summer and the raucous rock of Kiss and Ted Nugent. And the radical politics spurred by the Vietnam War has mostly reverted to more conventional politics, and even apathy.

But if the political heat has dissipated, the spirit of openness and tolerance that marked that countercultural era have lingered, despite suggestions by some that the nation is returning to the quiescent, more conformist 1950s. Much of what the counterculture produced has spread far from its point of origin on college campuses and filtered through all social classes. It has also left this Middle Western commercial center of 200,000 people—and thousands of other small and large places across the country—different in many subtle but significant respects.

Not everyone applauds the differences. Sociologists and historians who have monitored these changes generally agree that this country is today markedly different from what it was in the 50s. They are not unanimous, however, about whether the changes are for the better.

Some applaud the relaxed attitudes toward sexual freedom, drug use and unconventional behavior. But others with radical political sympathies dismiss the life style changes as superficial ones that have left economic and racial inequalities unremedied. And still others see a weakening of the national moral fabric

Mr. Reinhold is a correspondent of *The New York Times.* From "Changes Wrought by 60s Youth Linger in American Life" by Robert Reinhold, *The New York Times,* Aug. 12, 1979, pages 1 and 38. © 1979 by The New York Times Company. Reprinted by permission.

and a new cultural norm that deters those with traditional values from pursuing them.

Anyone who doubts that things have changed should talk to Billie B. Wallace, the 53-year-old Chief of Police, who said that when the force hires new, young officers these days it accepts them if they assert that they no longer smoke marijuana. It's not that the chief has much sympathy for smoking dope; the police found that they could scarcely find any new recruits otherwise.

Or, stroll through the offices of the once-starchy Equitable Life Insurance Company of Iowa in its ornate tower on Locust Street, where beards, casual clothes and relaxed work habits are now the norm.

A HIGH FOR PROFESSIONALS

Or, visit the Our Place discotheque on Walnut, where young homosexuals with influential positions in television, law enforcement, teaching and other professions openly dance together every weekend, sniffing butyl nitrite, a solvent that produces a rushing, throbbing sensation.

Or, witness the extent to which women here, as elsewhere, have penetrated professions once largely closed to them. Feminist stirrings have even cropped up among farm women who inhabit the vast agricultural lands that stretch to eternity in all directions from Des Moines.

Or, talk to landlords like Lee and Ruth Williams, both 46 years old, who no longer care much whether the couples they rent apartments to are married or not.

Or, visit the Down Home Music Festival where a few thousand young people draped themselves over a cow pasture a couple of weekends ago and anesthetized themselves with beer and marijuana. Among the revelers was a young man in faded jeans and a bandanna around his hair, obviously quite high; on Monday morning he returned to his job as an assistant county prosecutor.

The spirit of Woodstock was quickly eroded by the economic recession that followed it in the 70s, which in some cases undermined the financial freedom that gave so many youths the wherewithal to hitch around the country and attend rock festivals. They soon found themselves competing for scarce jobs and places in professional schools. And some found that middle-class values were not as repugnant as they once thought.

But still the youngsters of the Woodstock generation are filtering into and altering the way of life of Des Moines. They are its young teachers, police officers, newspaper and television reporters, lawyers, business people and parents. While they have mostly shed the beads, long hair and political concerns of the 60s, they are bringing to their careers new attitudes about sex, drugs, marriage and work that undoubtedly were shaped in part by their youthful experiences with the counterculture.

In the process, they are altering the definition of news in the newsrooms, changing the character of police work and law enforcement, expanding the limits of acceptable language, gradually liberalizing business and work practices and bringing new priorities to the classroom.

The changes should not be exaggerated. Chief Wallace may be willing to hire former marijuana smokers as policemen, but not homosexuals. The Williamses may rent to unmarried couples, but they would hesitate to take a racially mixed couple. And few people here would risk walking down the street openly smoking marijuana, as many do in New York and San Francisco.

NARROWED GENERATION GAP

But throughout the country the older generation has made some accommodations. Interviews with young and old indicate that the much-discussed generation gap has narrowed.

"What we've got is an interpenetration of the generations; people find they are no longer so far apart," said John R. Searle, a philosopher at the University of California at Berkeley, who served on the President's Advisory Commission on Campus Unrest in 1970. "I am deeply struck by the fact that we now have a great deal of tolerance for all kinds of life styles. There has been a terrific decline in political activity since the 60s, but an awful lot of the cultural changes are still with us."

But others who had expected, or at least hoped for, an enduring political transformation to result from the new leftist movement that was intertwined with the counterculture are less impressed. Christopher Lasch, the social historian at the University of Rochester who is the author of "The New Narcissism," agrees that young people have brought more social tolerance to American life. But, he adds, "I really do not think they are changing institutions."

"There are powerful economic coercions that cannot be altered simply by changes in life style," he said, adding that even many of the cultural changes are misdirected. "Young teachers may smoke grass and talk wistfully about helping out, but education is deteriorating."

David Riesman, the Harvard sociologist, declares, not altogether approvingly, that "the counterculture has triumphed." He decries what he calls "the tyranny of enlightenment."

"It is marvelous to have relaxation of the older constraints from which Sinclair Lewis fled," he said. "But in many places the newer values have such near-total hegemony that people with older values are persecuted." While Professor Riesman says he applauds the natural-food and environmental movements, he feels that the counterculture has "seriously damaged" American intellectual life, high culture and national productivity.

Others are more sympathetic about the residue of the 60s but uncertain about how durable it is. "I agree that the sensibilities of the 60s are being quasi-institutionalized," said Bennett Berger, a sociologist at the University of California at San Diego who is the author

of the forthcoming book on communes called "Ideological Work."

"But what that means in terms of consequences is problematical," he added. "Exactly how these new sensibilities are making inroads in established institutions is hard to prove. People are struggling with contradictions between what's in their heads and what they've got to face."

The shift in values that Woodstock represented was resisted then and still is among those who saw it as an unraveling of the American moral fiber. Indeed, a backlash of sorts is evident in the evangelical religious movement, in the political strength of the anti-abortion drive, in the back-to-basics trend in education. Chief Wallace here attributes rising crime to the willingness of society to mete out "swift and sure" justice to young people. And Professor Riesman says that the only students properly prepared for college now are products of single-sex parochial schools.

Whatever the case, signs of change are everywhere. In the industrial, working class city of Pittsburgh, where there were only two bars for homosexuals in 1969, there are now a dozen, plus two churches and five activist groups catering to homosexuals.

Natural-food stores have sprouted from coast to coast, even in towns like Oskaloosa, Iowa; population 11,000. The national Safeway supermarket chain carries bean curd and alfalfa sprouts.

And the use of marijuana is now commonplace among virtually all social strata in small towns and large cities. The police seldom make much effort to curtail it.

LIBERALIZED VIEWS ON SEX

Reflecting that, a *New York Times*/CBS News Poll taken last month found that 55 percent of the populace saw nothing wrong with premarital sex, well over double the number in a Gallup poll taken the month of the Woodstock Festival in 1969. And the proportion approving the full legalization of marijuana use has doubled from 12 to 25 percent of Americans in the last decade.

The trends vary, of course, from place to place. The Woodstock period scarcely touched many rural towns or remote Appalachia. And even in sophisticated places such as New York and environs, many young people have never tried marijuana. But the effects, some subtle, some obvious, linger, and Des Moines, certainly not as liberal as New York or Boston but by no means a hick town, provides as typical an example as any.

Consider, for example, Jeff Hunter. The son of a wealthy developer and now 28, he tuned out and turned on 10 years ago. With long hair and beard, he dropped in and out of three colleges, traveled with a rock band, sold pretzels and mescaline on the streets of Boston and bummed around Europe and North Africa.

Now he is back in Des Moines and married. His hair is cut short and is receding, he wears a blazer and striped ties and prefers sipping Johnnie Walker Red to smoking Panama Red. Like his father, he is going into business, starting by learning how to manage the Hotel Fort Des Moines. But he insists that he is different.

'AESTHETICS ARE IMPORTANT'

"In my father's day, the buck was almighty," he said. "I am much more concerned about how it is done. I take a lot of pride in this hotel. The aesthetics are important to me. I think more about what impact this or that economic move will have on the community." He hopes to restore an ornate century-old downtown office building.

But like so many young people, he finds that his liberal social sensibilities often clash with the responsibilities of work. He remembers with anguish the self-contempt he felt the day he shooed away a man going through the hotel's garbage. "What are you doing, Hunter?" he recalled saying to himself.

Not far away Luther T. Hill, executive vice president of the Equitable Insurance Com-

pany, sits in his 18th-floor office, the embodiment of the conservative Middle Western businessman with his short gray hair, gold-watch fob and Harvard law degree on the wall. Yet he, too, was touched by Woodstock.

"There was a day when no man would come to work here without a suit and tie," he said, adding that they are rare now. "There was a time when beards were frowned on; now they are common. Also, young people are less willing to wait patiently for older employees to retire. There is much more movement. There was a time when we would not consider rehiring people who left; now we think they can be the best employees."

The younger generation has compelled even such a strict law-and-order man as Billie Wallace, the Chief of Police, whose four children range in age from 22 to 29, to rethink things. Eight years ago one of his daughters brought home a boy with a full beard.

"I'll never forget the first time she brought him home," he said. "I looked at that beard and turned right off." But the girl married the youth, and Mr. Wallace now considers him "one of the finest young men I know."

"He desensitized Billie Wallace on beards," he said.

His ideas about police work have changed, too. "We started very, very dogmatic in resisting drugs," he said, whispering the word "drugs" in mock horror. "Prior to Vietnam we scratched any police applicant who admitted ever using marijuana. But we found that if we wanted any police recruits we had to modify that stance."

One of the new breed of officers is George Simmer, 31, a tall, blond product of small-town Iowa. Even though he never had much in common with the long-hairs when growing up, he freely admitted in his police lie detector test that he had smoked marijuana sometimes. He says he does not any longer, but he frequently does not bother to make arrests for possession of small amounts, knowing there will usually be no prosecution.

The professions are changing too. Dwight

M. Davis, superintendent of schools, says that young teachers today are more likely to want jobs teaching the poor and handicapped.

"In the past teachers felt the best jobs were with high achievers," he said. "Now many of our top young candidates feel more of a commitment to work with the disadvantaged."

FROM PROTESTS TO GOLF

Over at the newsroom of *The Des Moines Register*, the young reportorial staff has had its impact. "The atmosphere around the newsroom is much more relaxed than when I started in 1970," said Jim Healey, the newspaper's music critic. "Everybody was uptight about drugs then. Now the focus is not on those transgressions because the people writing about it are doing it. To them, that's not news anymore."

Indeed, the counterculture has seeped into corners of Des Moines society that would have shunned it a dozen years ago. Gerald Crawford is a 29-year-old lawyer who marched against the war in college. Now he dresses in dark suits, plays golf, drives a Mercedes and gambles in Las Vegas. He reports that at half the parties attended by professional people here about half the people will smoke marijuana or snort cocaine, and few are shocked.

Much of this has not been easy for institutions like the church to accept, but it, too, is different now. Young Roman Catholic couples in Des Moines can find a sympathetic ear in the Rev. Frank Palmer, the 43-year-old director of family life education for the diocese. He still believes in virtues of marriage and close-knit family life, but he welcomes some of the changes wrought by the 60s:

"We are not quite as sheltered as we were before. The whole 60s was a period of questioning of all the sacred cows, the schools, the churches, the government. That was good. I welcomed that. There is a lot of questioning still. We are coming to realize there are not as many absolutes as we thought there were."

47

COUNTDOWN TO 1984: BIG BROTHER MAY BE RIGHT ON SCHEDULE

David Goodman

George Orwell wrote *1984* to warn the Western world about what he thought the future might hold. But though Orwell succeeded in creating a gripping vision of a thought-controlled, totalitarian world, his novel has failed to halt the forces that he saw leading the way towards totalitarianism. Now, with only a few years to go until 1984, the Western world is potentially much closer to his vision than most people realize. Though *1984* has failed as a warning, it has been succeeding brilliantly as a forecast.

The novel is filled with predictions, from the details of international treaties that would someday avert nuclear war to the future methods used by dictators to guarantee internal security against revolutionaries. Fortunately, some of Orwell's most terrifying forecasts have not yet come true—Big Brother does not stare from every available wall and many personal liberties have remained intact—but a surprising number of Orwell's speculations are now fact, and many others could become so in the near future.

Even as the book was being published, some of Orwell's predictions were beginning

to come true. In the novel *1984*, Orwell pictures a world controlled by three great superpowers—Oceania, Eurasia, and Eastasia—which have achieved social and political stability by locking themselves into a nuclear stalemate. In 1949, the year in which the book first appeared and three years after Orwell began *1984*, 12 Western allies formed the North Atlantic Treaty Organization; the Soviet Union exploded its first atomic bomb; and the Chinese communists proclaimed a People's Republic in China. In the novel *1984*, the three superpowers wage continuous "warfare of limited aims" in a quadrilateral of land that includes much of Africa, the Middle East, and Southeast Asia. Today, the U. S., the U.S.S.R., and China struggle to gain influence throughout the Third World.

Even more accurate than Orwell's predictions of international relations are his forecasts of future developments in science and technology. Although the people of *1984* live close to the poverty level, technological progress is not wholly retarded, and throughout the novel Orwell speculates about dozens of future inventions. He talks about lenses in space, for instance, that would focus the heat of the sun on the enemy. These devices closely resemble the solar collectors that engineers

Reprinted by permission of the author.

are now designing to orbit the earth and beam down microwaves. Orwell mentions the possible use of disease germs immunized against all possible antibodies. Today, work on synthetic RNA and recombinant DNA points toward a major breakthrough in this field within the next five to ten years.

However, some readers object to considering the world of *1984* as even a possible future. Instead of a forecast, they prefer to see *1984* as a grim fantasy—Orwell's extrapolation of only the bleakest of his surroundings into a world where the houses are rotting, the roads are pockmarked by bomb craters, electric power comes on only sporadically, the water is cold, the soap gritty, and the cigarettes crumble to pieces.

But many of the social trends of the last three decades have been towards Orwell's *1984* vision, not away from it, and when the social developments are considered along with the technological similarities between Orwell's vision and the modern day, a future resembling *1984* must certainly be seen as *possible*.

Even more alarming is the realization that certain "triggering incidents" could make Orwell's future a *probable* one. In fact, these triggering incidents might even make the world of *1984* a *preferable* future, because eternal warfare and a loss of liberty would be viewed as the price that must be paid to avoid catastrophic destruction.

FROM POLYGRAPH TO PREDICTIONS

The government of Oceania monitors Party members by means of a remote sensor of human heartbeat. The sensors are located in the two-way telescreens built into every lodging, government office, and public square in Oceania. By tuning in on a certain person, government police can detect when he is lying or engaging in subversive activity.

I am particularly interested in these sensors because I invented such a device, and thus unwittingly helped to make one of

Orwell's predictions come true. My work on the invention began when I was a doctoral candidate at the University of California at Irvine and wanted a way to measure simultaneously several of the physiological variables in salamanders. There must be a better way, I thought, than plunging painful electrodes into a salamander's body.

And I found a better way, thanks to the electric field of extremely minute voltage that surrounds the bodies of all living organisms. A colleague and I developed very delicate voltage sensors that can measure this electric field, and researchers can now detect and record from a distance an animal's heartbeat, respiration, muscle tension, and body movements.

I took great satisfaction in the remote sensor until 1972, when I moderated a program on future studies at the University of California at Irvine. I had just finished recommending that remote sensing be used for painfree research on animals and human burn victims when a student named Marilyn Hart spoke up. She reminded me that in *1984* Big Brother uses such a sensor for a much more sinister purpose—to spy on the thoughts of suspect Party members. After the class was over I looked in my own copy of *1984* and discovered that she was right: Orwell's protagonist, Winston Smith, tries to sit as far away as possible from the remote sensor in the telescreen because "you could not control the beating of your heart, and the telescreen was quite delicate enough to pick it up."

The Orwellian applications of the remote sensor had never occurred to me, and I was shocked to realize that I could be an inadvertent collaborator with Big Brother. I continued reading *1984* and soon resolved to identify the predictions Orwell had made in the book and find out how many had come true.

Several months later, with my colleagues Gary Swift and William Sparks, I counted the predictions that Orwell makes in *1984*. We identified 137 specific predictions, which we divided into two categories—(1) scientific and technological predictions and (2) social and political predictions. We found that about 80 of Orwell's predictions had already (in 1972) been realized.

More than 20 predictions related directly to psychobiology, my own field, but I felt reluctant at first to discuss the psychobiological aspects of *1984* with others in my profession; after all, it is not pleasant to think that we have been preparing a *1984* world. But because of several startling revelations, my reluctance dissolved. First of all, it became known in 1975 that a group of brain researchers, funded by military intelligence, had been working covertly on methods of hypnotic interrogation and behavior control through ultrasonics and electromagnetic radiation. Then, in July 1977, it was revealed that the U. S. Central Intelligence Agency had spent nearly $25 million studying behavior-altering drugs like LSD and pentothal.

In 1978 I returned to the list of 137 Orwellian predictions that we had compiled six years earlier. This time I found that *over 100 of the predictions had come true.* There is now no doubt in my mind that *1984* describes a future that is clearly possible.

THE SCIENTIFIC AND TECHNOLOGICAL PREDICTIONS

The governments of *1984* are able to exercise such strict control over their citizens largely because they have adapted the fruits of science and technology to their own ends. Thus, although the scientists and technicians of Oceania are not free to study subjects of their own choosing, the government sponsors huge research projects in certain areas. Specifically, scientists are either psychologist-inquisitors engaged in perfecting psychoscience mind control, or physicists, chemists, or biologists seeking to create ever greater weapons of destruction.

Orwell therefore presupposes a fairly high level of research and development in the world of *1984*, and either explicitly or implic-

itly he speculates about many future developments in science and technology. I have chosen 30 of these as a sample, and have divided them into three categories—the sciences of the military, the police, and the psychoscientists—to examine Orwell's foresight in each.

Military science. In the years right after World War II, most of the military devices Orwell envisioned were either nascent ideas held by a handful of scientists or wild speculations still limited to science fiction. But since that time, scientists in the service of the military have doggedly kept pace with Orwell's imagination: today, not one of the ideas listed is beyond contemporary capabilities. For instance, Orwell foresaw "vast laboratories" where "teams of experts are . . . planning the logistics of future wars." Such laboratories have their real-life counterparts today in the RAND Corporation and other think tanks serving the military. The Doomsday researchers of *1984* try to figure out "how to kill several hundred million people in a few seconds without giving warning beforehand." Today the solution is at hand as scientists miniaturize atomic weapons (the smallest in the U. S. arsenal is only six inches in diameter), concoct more deadly chemical and biological weapons (the latter made all the more frightening by the possible use of manufactured virulent microbes), and strengthen enhanced ion beams and laser "death rays" (now proven capable of stopping antitank missiles in flight). Moreover, as Orwell imagined over 30 years ago, planes can refuel in flight as they fly toward enemy targets; ballistic missiles can hit a large city block from a launching pad a continent away; and projectiles such as the cruise missiles operate according to guidance signals from self-contained intelligence.

Orwell's scientists are working to develop "poisons capable of being produced in such quantities as to destroy the vegetation of whole continents." The U. S. military's "Agent Orange," a defoliant widely used in Vietnam, meets that requirement. Orwell's soil submarine would "bore its way under the soil like a submarine under water." U. S. government scientists recently suggested building a machine that would melt its way through the ground with the heat from a nuclear reactor in its prow. Orwell imagined floating fortresses—man-made islands that would prowl the sea lanes and then be able to remain stationary for months or years. Such floating fortresses have not yet appeared, but if a prototype of such an island-weapon could be created before the late 1980s, then all of these "Orwellian" military technologies could be operating within the next five to ten years.

Police science. The technology of police surveillance and citizen control has kept abreast of progress in military science. Orwell accurately foresaw the development of large data banks—today's electronic computers—that would contain detailed information about all Party members. Furthermore, the invention of fiber optics and microwave communications allows modern technologists to store and retrieve this information with the same speed as the inquisitors of Oceania.

Orwell also predicted that television would help solve the police problems of *1984*. He writes of large public television screens in every meeting hall that continuously pour forth news, spurious statistics, and political propaganda. All home televisions are two-way flush-mounted telescreens, equipped with scanning lenses, powerful omnidirectional microphones, and remote sensors of heartbeat. With the telescreen, the government keeps its citizens under almost constant surveillance. Externally and internally, Big Brother Is Watching You.

To improve the telescreens, the scientists of Oceania are hard at work devising tone-of-voice analyzers and brainwave sensors. Eventually, they hope to enable the secret police to reach their ultimate goal: "To discover, against his will, what another human being is thinking."

All of these devices are within the state of the art of today's technology. Ours could become the most snooped-on, computer-analyzed society in history. Television scanners equipped with electronic detectors of heartbeat, brainwaves, and voice stress could collect physiological and behavioral data which could then be conveyed by microwaves or fiber optics to a central data bank for instantaneous cross matching with the electronic profiles of known subversives and dissidents. Suspected persons could be traced, arrested, and imprisoned—just as in *1984*.

Psychoscience. All told, Orwell managed to foresee some of the most important devices of the last three decades. But nowhere was his foresight sharper than in the field of psychoscience. In Oceania, no man's thoughts are inviolate. The Thought Police can tell from a person's "friendships, his relaxations, his behavior toward his wife and children, the expression on his face when he is alone, the words he mutters in sleep, even the characteristic movements of his body" whether he is being faithful to the Party. After identifying a dissident, the Thought Police use drugs, electric shock, and intricate forms of mental and physical torture to force a person to conform to Party norms.

In recent years, the science of psychoscience has gone even beyond that of *1984*. Since 1963, the number of brain scientists has increased tenfold to more than 6,000. In the U. S., the Bureau of Narcotics, the Department of Justice, and the CIA have become new sources of research funds. The broadening interface of academic science and government control has already begun spilling into the laboratory from the pages of *1984*.

More than 3,000 therapies to modify behavior are now recognized. Many suggest little more than transmogrified torture: Modern therapists may systematically pound the body or administer electric shocks to improve people's health or cure them of inappropriate habits. Even Orwell's most frightening treatment, a prolonged and intimate contact with a dreaded phobic stimulus (rats in the case of Winston Smith), has been brought into modern therapy under the name of implosion or "flooding."

Truth drugs have recently begun to play a larger role in improving rapport during psychotherapy: nitrous oxide, carbon dioxide, ether, hallucinogens like LSD, sodium pentobarbital, and sodium amytal have all been used to induce an uncensored flow of thoughts; sodium amytal generally is considered the best disinhibitor. For a severe mental case, a psychosurgeon may still be permitted to perform a lobotomy—a severing of some neural tracks of the brain's frontal lobes.

Researchers now routinely insert electrodes into the orgasm center of the brain. Other implant techniques enable scientists to inject chemicals like cocaine directly into the brain, or even to insert supercooled electrodes to freeze certain brain tissues. Some daring psychoscientists have even tried to use the body's own immunological system to destroy certain specified nerve cells, thus altering behavior.

The result of all this scientific progress is a psychocivilized society—a world where people achieve better living through surgery, electric currents, drugs, flooding, structural integration, bioenergetics, hypnosis, and control of body language. Clearly, few, if any, of the possibilities for mind control that Orwell foresaw go beyond the therapy sessions of today's researchers. With respect to the brain and behavior, 1984 science is here now.

THE SOCIAL AND POLITICAL PREDICTIONS

Our studies indicate that all of Orwell's scientific and technological predictions have either already come true or could soon come true. But such a judgment cannot be rendered so easily on Orwell's social and political forecasts.

To some futurists, many of these social and political speculations still seem incredible: In Oceania, no part of a Party member's life is personal, not even his thoughts. The government, through the Thought Police, works to convince everyone that external reality does not exist, that the only measure of the past is people's memories and written records, both of which are altered constantly to suit Party dogma. Oceania is a country of constant fear, where public executions, search without warrant, and imprisonment without cause are commonplace.

Some futurists, in fact, hardly acknowledge Orwell as a prophet at all. Both Richard Farmer in The Real World of 1984 (David McKay Company, New York, 1973) and Jerome Tuccille in Who's Afraid of 1984 (Arlington House, New Rochelle, New York, 1975) foresee a "satisfied plenty" and "exuberant democracy" ahead for the American people. Although they admit that technological change is altering people's lives, they believe that people will come to accept technological advancement as inevitable and learn to use technology to further, rather than destroy, human privacy.

But the social trends of the last 30 years have brought the West closer to 1984 than ever before, and these trends could rapidly accelerate under certain circumstances. Of course, the correspondence between Orwell's world and our own varies widely depending on the specific feature under consideration, but the overall drift is obvious.

Doublethink. In 1984, doublethink is a mental facility required of every good Party member. Orwell defines it as "the power of holding two contradictory beliefs in one's mind simultaneously, and accepting both of them." Furthermore, "the process has to be conscious, or it would not be carried out with sufficient precision, but it also has to be unconscious, or it would bring with it a feeling of falsity and hence of guilt."

Essentially, doublethink is Orwell's projection of the tendency he saw in people to subvert reality to ideological abstractions. Orwell especially detested this trait in the liberal Soviet sympathizers who became apologists for Germany after the Hitler-Stalin pact, and this incident formed much of the base for doublethink in *1984*. But doublethink marks all political propaganda to some extent. A recent example was in the late 1960s when the Nixon administration overtly promoted domestic law and order and decried all forms of "civil disobedience" while covertly ordering telephone taps, sponsoring break-ins, opening the mails, keeping its "enemies" under surveillance, and committing other ostensibly lawless acts.

Denial of objective reality. The Party in *1984* teaches its members that "reality is not external. Reality exists in the human mind, and nowhere else." In this way, the good Party member learns how to sift his sense impressions through an ideological filter, acknowledging acceptable information and ignoring everything else.

Such solipsism is now widespread in our age of growing social confusion and eroding traditional values. The increasing use of alcohol and other drugs may be an attempt to avoid a look at life that would be too painful to bear. Politicians also deny objective reality by backing policies that are unrelated to the actual needs of their constituencies.

Newspeak. The linguists of Oceania are busy replacing traditional English with Newspeak, a language so impoverished that "a heretical thought . . . should be literally unthinkable, at least so far as thought is dependent on words."

Today the steady degradation of the English language is a constantly lamented fact. Verbal test scores have fallen for a decade; bureaucratic gobbledygook grows more dense as the problems of government grow more complex; and politicians continue to mangle the language with their neologisms (as when bombing raids become "protective reaction strikes").

Mutability of the past. In Oceania, history is completely rewritten every day to suit the needs of the Party. Day-to-day falsification of published records helps assure the stability of the regime in power. One of the Party's slogans is "Who controls the past controls the future; who controls the present controls the past."

Revising the records of the past to fit current policies has long been standard procedure in many countries and has recently become increasingly common in the Western world. Histories are rewritten, tape recordings erased, records deliberately "lost," and past statements dismissed as "inoperative."

Big Brother. The gigantic face of Big Brother, the supposed ruler of Oceania, peers down from posters pasted on buildings and billboards. "He is a face on the hoarding, a voice on the telescreen. . . . Big Brother is the guise in which the Party chooses to exhibit itself to the world. His function is to act as a focusing point for love, fear, and reverence, emotions which are more easily felt toward an individual than toward an organization."

With today's paternalistic government and powerful presidency, Big Brother may be somewhat diffused but just as strong. An interesting aspect of Big Brother's presence lies in the composition of his face. He is worshipped solely because of the strength, charisma, and self-assurance that seem to exude from his features. Today, television personalities (and especially newsmen) are often chosen because they have this same kind of face.

Continuous war. The three super-powers of *1984* have adopted continuous war as an expedient to "use up the products of the machine without raising the general standard of living." In this way, "the consequences of being at war, and therefore in danger, makes the handing-over of all power to a small caste seem the natural, unavoidable condition of survival."

Today's arms race is the equivalent of Orwell's continuous war. In addition, the current struggles in Africa, the Middle East, and Southeast Asia show many of the same qualities as the war in *1984*. With regards to the Orwellian purpose of continuous war, the experiences of the 1960s are enough to remind us that some of the worst violations of personal liberties have occurred during time of

war, usually in the name of national security.

Breakup of the family. One of Oceania's greatest methods of personal disorientation is the dissolution of the family. Breaking the emotional ties between man and woman, parents and children, eliminates bonds that would detract from a person's absolute devotion to the State.

In America, the divorce rate more than doubled between 1963 and 1975, with more than one out of every three marriages now ending in divorce. The subsequent withdrawal into self has contributed to a growing aimlessness and a wide search for something to replace personal relationships. Might not the new something be a political adventure?

Unwarranted search and surveillance. In Oceania, as in most totalitarian states, due process of law is merely a toothless legalism. A man's home is the government's castle. Any citizen can have his dwelling ransacked and possessions seized as evidence to be used against him. Telescreens provide almost complete physical surveillance, and even the mind is not exempt from probe.

Personal privacy has steadily eroded in recent years. The surveillance of alleged subversives by U. S. government agencies has been documented by congressional testimony. Both government agencies and private companies employ investigators to make personal credit checks. Some journalists use hidden microphones to collect information for their articles. And satellites orbit the earth maintaining constant surveillance of areas as small as a square yard.

Public hangings. The government of Oceania uses public executions as a warning to critics and malingerers. The criminal displayed after execution by hanging encourages the populace not to break the law or go against Party dogma.

In the U. S., a well-known Texas politician recently recommended public hangings as a deterrent to crime after the Gary Gilmore incident. More generally, the increasing

acquiescence of the American public toward violence in the movies and TV bears a close resemblance to the mood of savagery that marks the people of Oceania. The vicarious pleasure taken in violence is one of the strongest parallels between modern society and the world of *1984*.

The social trends of today clearly indicate a general decay of individual liberties, rational thought, personal privacy, and self-determination; a *1984*-type future is getting closer every year. But the critics of *1984* are quick to point out that "it can't happen here" and that *1984* certainly could not come true only five years from now. They maintain that our democratic beliefs run too deep to be destroyed by a predatory Big Brother.

They are partially right. None of the social trends have yet reached the intensity that Orwell envisioned in *1984*, and at the current rate of "progress" an Orwellian future is definitely more than just five years away. Unfortunately, the trends could speed up. Not one of Orwell's predictions is beyond the range of possibility, and almost any of the social and political trends described above could be brought to a head by just *a single triggering incident*.

THE TRIGGERING INCIDENT

Orwell wrote *1984* partially to deprecate the excesses that the Soviet and German states committed before and during World War II, but the novel is not simply a polemic against collectivist societies or a diatribe against dictatorship. During most of his adult life, Orwell was disturbed by the wave of totalitarianism sweeping the world, and he often pointed out how the mentality leading to its spread was growing in England. In his 1939 novel *Coming Up for Air*, Orwell's English protagonist muses about "all the things you've got in the back of your mind, the things you're terrified of, the things you tell yourself are just a nightmare or only happen in foreign countries. The bombs, the food queues, the rubber trun-

cheons, the barbed wire, the colored shirts, the slogans, the enormous faces, the machine guns squirting out of bedroom windows. It's all going to happen . . . it's just something that's got to happen."

In the course of Orwell's novels, it finally did happen in *1984*. Orwell did not believe that the state he described in the novel would come to the West in just that form, but he did believe that something resembling it could arise. In 1949, right after the book was published, he said: "I believe . . . that totalitarian ideas have taken root in the minds of intellectuals everywhere, and I have tried to draw these ideas out to their logical consequences. The scene of the book is laid in Britain in order to emphasize that the English-speaking races are not innately better than anyone else and that totalitarianism, if not fought against, could triumph everywhere."

Today, the fight against totalitarianism in America has been scaled down from the national obsession of the 1940s and 1950s to become the concern of a limited number of specialists. And yet many of the features of totalitarianism are still growing. If these trends continue, how many years will pass before the tyranny of totalitarianism overtakes the West?

Moreover, what if these trends suddenly quicken? The prospect is so distressing that most people would sooner not think about it. But the facts suggest that a number of different types of events could bring about the abrupt appearance of a *1984*-type government. One such development is the sudden appearance of terrorist groups armed with atomic weapons.

The terrorists would not even have to use atomic weapons to cause a massive reshuffling of social priorities. If they simply issued a clearly credible threat of nuclear attack, governments would have to take drastic steps to stop them or minimize possible damage. Such governmental action would almost inevitably result in some curtailment of individual rights.

Furthermore, most people would willingly agree to give up those rights, as shown by the willingness of airline passengers to waive some of their rights in the face of a real or imagined threat by terrorists. How many more rights would people yield in the face of a threat to thousands of lives or to the structure of their society?

Many people clearly might view a *1984*-type world as a *preferable* future when the alternative is nuclear destruction. If terrorists actually exploded an atomic weapon somewhere in the Western world, the willingness of people to give up their liberties would greatly intensify. A nuclear explosion could easily infuse society with the siege mentality and war hysteria that the Oceania government adapts to its purposes. Some suggestion of what might happen is the state of virtual warfare that prevailed in Italy during the kidnapping of former premier Aldo Moro.

By actually exploding a nuclear weapon, terrorists could destroy almost the entire government of a major country. The result could be a power vacuum that would be filled by either the most powerful insurgent group fighting to gain control or by the group most desiring of power. In neither case would there likely be an overriding concern for individual rights.

Thus a future similar to that of *1984*, where survival is bought only at the price of subservience, could come on schedule if terrorists gain access to atomic weapons in the years before 1984. And, regrettably, the evidence suggests that nuclear technology now is sufficiently diffused that such a contingency is well within the realm of possibility.

For example, a professor at a large American university announced last summer that he had devised a way to immensely simplify the separation of uranium isotopes. By using a carbon dioxide laser, enough weapons-grade U^{235} for a bomb could be produced in about a year; the critical mass for U^{235}, when encased in a beryllium neutron reactor, is only 11 kilograms. The professor pointed out that the cost, approximately $100,000, is within the capabilities of many small organizations.

SOME PROCESSES OF SOCIAL LIFE

Several published reports of past years have documented the laxness of the safeguards applied to uranium and plutonium. And if the material is available, the know-how needed to make an atomic bomb is easily acquired. Last year, two college students announced that they had managed to design a working model of an atomic bomb using only unclassified information.

The proliferation of atomic weapons makes a future like *1984* look almost probable. A well-known rule of thumb states that technology of any kind usually takes 30 years to move from the innovators to the consumers. Since atomic bombs were first exploded in 1945, the time may have come for the general distribution of small, portable, and potentially catastrophic nuclear weapons.

Nuclear terrorism is only one type of development that might usher in *1984*. Almost any major disruption of life in the Western world could lead to some loss of personal liberties. Almost any large economic or ecological catastrophe could clear the way for the rise of totalitarianism. For instance, a massive famine in Mexico could lead to a stampede of refugees into the U. S., forcing the American government into much more vigilant security; a conventional border war could escalate into a major nuclear confrontation; and any nuclear war between superpowers would undoubtedly cause a substantial clampdown on individual liberties. The political situation of Orwell's *1984* arises out of a limited nuclear war that Orwell foresaw happening in the 1950s; luckily, that Orwellian prediction did not come true. But the possibility for such a war increases as nuclear weaponry becomes more refined and available.

MUST WE LIVE THIS FUTURE?

The possibility of Orwell's *1984* becoming reality—perhaps even before the date he specified—is clear. Whether or not it really happens will depend on what we do today. We must prepare to act on two fronts—to *prevent* the triggering incidents from taking place, and to *reverse* the social trends that are leading the Western democracies towards *1984*.

In pondering these problems, we should not expect answers from government bureaucracies. As Willis W. Harman of SRI International has noted: "Society tends to hide knowledge from itself that is superficially threatening to the status quo, even though this knowledge may be badly needed to resolve its most fundamental problem." Being organizations that act to define society's status quo, bureaucracies are far too inertia-bound to discover innovative solutions to the potential threat of totalitarianism. Current administrators, trained to react only after a crisis has occurred, cannot confront the challenges of this second phase of the Atomic Age, when weapons-making information is widely disseminated.

An approach that might form a viable starting point for an initiative to prevent *1984* conditions is the suggestion of biophysicist and futurist John Platt that the countries of the world establish Councils of Urgent Studies. These councils would study what Platt calls the "crisis of crises"—the flood of world problems that are occurring simultaneously in the current age of transformation. In doing this, they would have to give immediate attention to the specific crises that could lead to *1984*.

Forming the councils would be a project similar to mobilizing the country's top minds during wartime. "We need full-time interdisciplinary teams," Platt contends in his book *Perception and Change: Projections for Survival*. These teams must include "natural scientists, social scientists, doctors, engineers, lawyers, and many other trained and inventive minds, who will put together our stores of knowledge and powerful new ideas into action-oriented, policy-directed 'social inventions' that will have a chance of being adopted soon enough and widely enough to be effective."

Platt's councils would have two main tasks: first, to identify and appraise potential

problems before they become uncontrollable and, second, to solve them. The councils would devise possible solutions to future problems and then seek to implement them by communicating with policy-makers and the general public. With respect to nuclear terrorism, for instance, the councils could study the political and social consequences of terrorist attacks and originate plans to enable society and its institutions to survive.

Platt's Councils of Urgent Studies proposal is only one approach towards finding some way to protect individual liberties in the years ahead. Others need to be developed and implemented lest the remainder of George Orwell's prophecies be realized.

48

AN AGENDA FOR THE 1980s

Edward Cornish

As the 1970s came to an end, newspapers and magazines published numerous articles predicting developments during the new decade. Most of the articles were based on the assumption that the trends of the 1970s will continue through the 1980s: Population will continue to grow, the economy will pursue its current lackluster path, and computer technology will proliferate at an ever-increasing rate. But the 1980s may turn out to be a decade when many important trends change direction. If so, forecasts made simply projecting current trends into the future may result in more than the usual number of embarrassing failures to anticipate correctly the shape of things to come.

The world seems to have entered a phase in which some key trends have lost their force and the structure of many institutional arrangements has been seriously under-

From *The Futurist*, February 1980, pp. 5–13, published by World Future Society, 4916 St. Elmo Avenue, Washington, D.C. 20014. Reprinted by permission.

mined. For instance, economic growth, which was so strong during the 1950s and 1960s, has greatly slowed in many countries, and some now find their economies stagnant or even declining. The relative decline in the power of the United States—the nation that once provided protection for non-communist countries around the world—has led to new uncertainties about the stability of the international order. Additional sources of major change may be found in the massive transfer of wealth from the industrialized nations to the oil-producers; the decline of the dollar; the growing chaos in financial markets; the increasing stridency of the developing nations' demands on the developed countries; and the seemingly irresistible spread of nuclear weapons. The resulting tensions could lead to serious confrontations and breakdowns that would greatly alter the world that might be anticipated simply by extending current trends a few years into the future.

Extending current trends into the future is not a bad way to begin thinking about the

future, but it is unwise to stop there. Yet most of the recent articles about the 1980s give little consideration to any forecast except the one they regard as most probable, which, of course, is the one created by simply extending the trends. This practice of excluding alternative possibilities is risky because it suggests that we need give no thought to any possibility except the one chosen as most likely. If something else happens—something deemed to have a lesser chance of realization and therefore not worth considering—we will be totally unprepared. The "single-forecast" practice presumably led the French army in the 1930s to develop the Maginot Line—a series of fortifications admirably suited to the trench warfare of the 1914–18 period but laughably inadequate against the assault of Nazi Germany in 1940.

The articles about the 1980s also seem to assume that the best people to make forecasts are specialists, especially if they are also government officials. For instance, the person best qualified to forecast the future of the automobile might be an automobile specialist in the Department of Transportation. Yet experience has shown over and over again that developments in any given field may be revolutionized by events occurring outside that field, and presumably beyond the purview of the specialist. Artificial fibers such as nylon and dacron drastically altered the clothing business, but the fibers were developed by the chemical industry, not the clothing industry. During the 1970s, the greatest development in the typesetting industry was perhaps the application of computer technology to typesetting; this resulted in a massive displacement of earlier methods of typesetting and the redundancy of thousands of typesetters in newspapers.

Another characteristic of the forecasts that have appeared recently is their generally optimistic tone. Perhaps nowhere is this more evident than in *The Exciting '80s* by Arnold Barach (Kiplinger Washington Editors, Washington, D. C., 1979). Although Barach is care-ful to insert occasional caveats and disclaimers, the general mood of the book is strongly upbeat: Readers can look forward to a generally rosy future, thanks to new technological developments and continued economic growth.

THE EMERGENCE OF FUTURISM

The 1960s saw the emergence of the future as a subject for serious study in its own right. It was a decade highlighted by the pioneering work of Olaf Helmer and his colleagues at the Rand Corporation; Bertrand de Jouvenel's Futuribles project in Paris; and the founding of the Hudson Institute and the World Future Society. What, if anything, can the emerging study of the future contribute to people's understanding of the new decade? Perhaps the most important insight that futurists can offer is that the future cannot be predicted! The future is not a world that lies before us quietly awaiting our arrival but rather a world that we ourselves are creating. The future, then, is not fixed. Many different "futures" may develop out of the present moment in which we live. For that reason, we should explore a number of possible future worlds, not just a single "most likely" possibility. Again and again, experience has shown that something viewed as wildly improbable or even impossible turns out to be what actually occurs. We may lack the time to study carefully all the possibilities, but experience suggests that we ought to at least look at more than one. Even if no one possibility turns out to be precisely on target, the experience of considering several alternatives keeps our minds open and ready for whatever contingencies may actually occur.

The "alternative futures" approach opens the gateway to a future that we choose and shape rather than one that is simply thrust upon us when we have reached the appropriate moment in time. To develop a series of alternative futures, we can start by developing a "standard" or "surprise-free" forecast, based on the assumption that present

trends will continue, but after that we should develop others. One possibility is an "optimistic" scenario postulating that things will be much better than we currently expect; another possibility is a "pessimistic scenario" that assumes many of the bad developments that we think are possible will in fact occur. Many more scenarios could be developed but these three (standard, optimistic, and pessimistic) give us a basis for the all-important psychological leap into the future.

Here are three highly abbreviated scenarios for the 1980s:

Standard scenario. Many things will happen during the 1980s, but essentially the decade will see a continuation of the trends of the 1970s. World population will grow; but living standards will remain about the same. Terrorism may increase, and there may even be a few small wars, but probably no World War III. Many advances will occur in technology, especially electronics and communications, but the economic benefit of these advances will be largely offset by the shrinkage in the amount of prime natural resources—petroleum, metal ores, forests, farm land, etc.

Pessimistic scenario. The world economy will deteriorate badly in the 1980s due to high population growth, the exhausting of natural resources, failure of nations to curb inflation and soaring debt, and other factors. The developed countries will face soaring unemployment; the developing countries experience mass famines. Economic difficulties will lead to political unrest, with revolutions likely not only in the poor countries but also in the rich. As political chaos mounts, many democratic regimes will collapse, and amid the chaos, new dictators will rise. Major wars—both civil and international—will occur, and there is the possibility of World War III.

Optimistic scenario. New communications devices will spearhead a parade of new technological devices that will solve most of the pressing problems of the 1970s. Microprocessors will vastly increase the efficiency with which energy is used, enabling people to keep their homes warm and drive their automobiles with far less expenditure of fuel than is now required. Breakthroughs in energy production will substantially free the world from its enslavement to petroleum and natural gas. New birth control methods will curb population growth in the developing countries, thus preventing starvation and making it possible for them to advance economically. Artificial intelligence will provide an exciting new alternative for decision-making, and increasingly, electronic devices will be entrusted with arbitrating differences among nations. At the same time, human wishes will be expressed on a mass basis through computer-communications devices hooked up to homes everywhere. As the nations move toward an anticipatory democracy mode, with huge electronic "town meetings" involving millions of people, the world will move rapidly toward peace and prosperity.

Each of the foregoing scenarios may be viewed as possible! We cannot say that it simply could *never* possibly happen, although we may view one or more scenarios as highly improbable. Probably none of the scenarios offers an accurate description of the 1980s but they anticipate at least some features of the decade.

By considering three alternative views, we are forced to see the future as a domain of possibilities rather than a realm of fixed realities that we can do nothing to change. The alternative scenarios require us to think a little about many more possibilities than we would have considered if we had viewed the future in terms of a single forecast. We now see the future not as a world that is forced upon us, but as a world that we ourselves create.

CRITICAL CHOICES

Besides developing a number of scenarios for the 1980s, we can explore the new decade by identifying some of the significant issues about which people will have to make choices.

These issues are often called "problems," but they are not problems in the scientific sense. A scientific problem is a matter of factual knowledge, and scientists can gradually work toward an answer that will satisfy most scientists as being correct. But the policy choices that will exercise us during the years ahead do not have "correct" answers; instead, they are challenges to us to make choices about what sort of future we want to create.

The 1980s—more than any previous decade—will be a period in which human choice will operate more decisively than ever before. The rapid development of technology has freed man from slavery to environmental and biological circumstances. No longer is he a prisoner of a particular geographic locality, because he can travel easily to the other side of the world. He can converse with people around the globe via new electronic devices. New biomedical advances are making it possible for him to have a longer life and better health. Improved economic systems have removed—at least in many nations—the once ever-present danger of starvation.

Each of the following "critical choices" can serve as the topic for a mind-stretching debate about the future. They have no right answer that a teacher can look up in the back of a book. Instead, they represent challenges that will probably remain with the world throughout the 1980s.

Complexity and democracy. The increasing complexity of modern life makes it more and more difficult for voters to understand policy issues and make wise choices among candidates. Many voters give up and stop voting at all.

What can be done to enable people to be effective participants in elections and the formation of public policies?

The enormous scale of industrial society. The modern world has developed an economic system that depends heavily on the mass production of goods by means of a heavily specialized, centralized system. In recent years, critics have suggested that many problems—pollution, family breakdown, and so on—might be alleviated through smaller-scale production ("Appropriate Technology") and the decentralization of activities.

Should efforts be made to reduce the size of factories so that each community could produce more of the goods that it uses rather than being dependent on distant suppliers for most of its needs?

Industries endangered by foreign imports. Many workers find their jobs are threatened by goods imported from other nations and demand "protection"—tariffs, quotas, regulations, and other measures designed to reduce the influx of foreign goods. But such "protectionism" deprives consumers of the chance to buy better or cheaper goods from abroad and is generally deplored as hurting the overall economy. However, if domestic industries are not protected, they may go bankrupt, throwing whole regions into an economic depression. Government officials may talk about "retraining" displaced workers, but retraining may not work well because older workers cannot always acquire new skills that might command the premium wages they were receiving earlier. Nor do they wish to leave their home communities for a distant location.

What should government do when domestic industries are threatened by imports?

Minority cultures. Most nations contain groups of people with a cultural tradition different from that of the dominant culture. Canada, for example, has a large group of French speakers; France has Basques and Bretons; Britain has Welsh-speakers, and so on. These groups generally want to enjoy the economic benefits obtainable through the national society but also want to preserve their own cultural heritage. But they cannot do the one without sacrificing, at least to some degree, the other. For instance, an American Indian must learn English if he wants a high-paying job, but as he learns English he tends to lose his native culture.

Should minorities be assimilated as rapidly as possible into a nation's dominant culture? Should

the world aim for a single culture in the interest of economic efficiency or should it seek to preserve a wide variety of cultures in the interest of greater long-term creativity and security?

Nuclear power. Electricity and other forms of energy are essential to a modern civilization, but traditional sources like petroleum and natural gas have become increasingly expensive. Nuclear power offers a partial solution to the problem but presents certain dangers: Nuclear materials or equipment might be used by terrorists or militarists and there is also the danger of accidental explosions or leaks of radioactivity.

Can we live with nuclear power? Can we live without it? If we must live with nuclear power, what can be done to minimize the risks?

Crime. Many social thinkers once believed that crime would disappear as more people were given jobs and education. Unfortunately, in many instances crime has risen—not fallen—as society provided more schools and better economic conditions.

What can be done to reduce crime in the future? Should penalties be heavier?

Electronic voting. New communications technology makes it feasible for citizens to vote or express their views regularly and often on a wide range of issues without leaving their homes.

Should governments move to create "electronic town-meetings" on a nationwide basis to decide public issues? Should political leaders be subject to instant recall by an electronic ballot?

Family breakdown. The family has traditionally been the social institution charged with producing and rearing children to become members of the future society. But the traditional family consisting of father, mother, and children appears to be disintegrating. The divorce rate has risen dramatically in recent years and more women who have children outside of wedlock have elected to keep their children rather than turning them over to adoptive parents.

What, if anything, should be done to halt the disintegration of families?

Growing armaments. The world's nations constantly strive to acquire new weapons for "security" purposes. Yet the growing arsenal of weaponry seems to decrease rather than increase international security. Many developing countries devote more of their precious foreign exchange to acquiring weapons than to alleviating the suffering of their poverty-stricken people.

What can be done to slow or halt the arms race? What can be cone to prevent a Third World War?

Migration. People want the freedom to travel and live wherever they choose, but when they settle in other nations they often create cultural and political problems within their adopted countries. As transportation systems improve, it becomes physically easier for people to move from one country to another and increasing numbers may elect to do so, but violence and turmoil may result if millions of people from low-wage countries elect to move into nations where wages are higher.

What limits should be placed on international migration?

Poverty in wealthy nations. During the past few decades, living standards have risen dramatically in the developed countries, but there remain wide discrepancies in individual income. Many countries have sought to insure that all citizens have a certain minimum standard of living by means of welfare payments and free goods and services. Meanwhile, governments require well-to-do people to pay increasingly heavy taxes as their incomes rise. Some Swedish scholars have recently proposed that limits be placed on consumption— for instance, a legal limit on the amount of housing or the number of automobiles a person can have. In Sweden and elsewhere, however, experience suggests that policies aimed at equalizing the standard of living tend to undermine the incentive to work. And when people work less they produce less for everyone.

Should there be a minimum standard of living to which all citizens are entitled even if they refuse to work? Should there be limits placed on people's

consumption of goods? Should a government try to give all its citizens the same standard of living?

Credentialing. Many employers now insist that prospective employees have certain educational credentials, such as a university degree. But such a requirement often excludes from consideration people who would be excellent employees.

Should it be made illegal to discriminate on the grounds of alleged educational deficiencies?

Rich versus poor nations. The citizens of some nations enjoy a very high average standard of living while people in other countries are desperately poor. Some people feel that the rich countries should provide free assistance to the poor nations—much like the welfare payments made within the rich countries to their poorer residents. Other people feel that the rich nations have no such obligation and the poor countries are poor because they have not curbed their population growth.

How should the rich countries help the poor countries? Is it fair to tax the poor in the rich countries in order to help the rich in the poor countries?

Ownership of the oceans. Nations have steadily extended their claims to the areas of the ocean off their shores. Thus the oceans, which once were regarded as the common property of mankind, are now passing into national or even private ownership. National or private ownership is not necessarily bad: If the resources of the ocean are to be developed, property rights must be respected, that is, ocean farmers who cultivate sea plants and fish need to have their investment protected or they will cease their efforts. At present, many resources of the ocean are being ruthlessly exploited because no nation owns them and therefore has the incentive and authority to safeguard them.

Who should own the oceans? How should conflicting claims to ocean resources be mediated?

Automobiles. Most people like to use automobiles for many of their transportation needs, because the automobile offers door-to-door convenience, privacy, etc. But the automobile uses large amounts of increasingly scarce and expensive gasoline and exacts huge human costs (about 50,000 dead and 100,000 maimed each year in the United States alone).

Should the use of the automobile be discouraged? If so, what alternative forms of transportation should be promoted?

Extended human life. Biomedical research may soon discover how to extend the human life-span by many years. Conceivably, some people alive today may live to be two or three centuries old. If so, some people might retire at 65 and collect retirement benefits for centuries, eventually bankrupting pension funds and imposing a huge burden on younger workers.

How is society to adjust to an extended human life-span?

The value of human life. Many people are kept alive in hospitals even though they are in acute pain or may never be able to resume normal living. Keeping them alive is enormously expensive both to their relatives and to society at large. The dilemma is becoming increasingly important as medical technology makes it possible to keep many people alive indefinitely provided special equipment is used.

Is life an absolute value that society can deprive none of its members of under no circumstances? Who should bear the cost of keeping people alive when they have no reasonable expectation of being able to resume their normal lives again?

The cost of government regulations. Governments have instituted numerous regulations to protect consumers against dangerous products, workers against accidents and discrimination, and citizens against pollution. But the cost of meeting government regulations now is widely viewed as a problem in its own right. Large companies pass the costs along to customers in the form of higher prices; small firms often find themselves unable to cope with complex government regulations and survive; new innovative technology—which could improve productivity (thereby reducing inflation)—is held back by regulations.

What should be done to make government reg-

ulations less burdensome? Should there be "sun-set" provisions so that legislation automatically becomes inoperative after a certain number of years?

New technology. Progress depends on the development of new technology, but new technology often turns out to be dangerous or to have undesirable long-term consequences (thalidomide and DDT, for example).

How can technology best be assessed in advance of its wide-scale use? How can we have technology assessment without technology "arrestment"—a serious slowdown in the arrival of useful new technology that can help us to accomplish our purposes?

Destruction of the environment. In many areas, people are destroying their natural environment in a wide variety of ways. Nepalese peasants searching for firewood denude the neighboring mountains, exposing the soil to rains that wash it away, leaving bare rock. Elsewhere, cattle farmers allow herds to become too numerous for grasslands and the land turns to desert.

What should be done to halt environmental destruction?

Extinction of many animals and plants. The growing human population is threatening the survival of thousands of plant and animal species. By the end of the twentieth century, some researchers believe that over half a million species now alive may be extinct.

What can be done to preserve these species, which might be extremely valuable to humanity at some later date?

Artificial conception and birthing. Biologists have succeeded in fertilizing human ova outside a woman's uterus. Soon it may be possible to rear embryos in a solution until they are ready to be "born." It may be possible for a laboratory to produce thousands or even millions of living babies that could be sold to whoever wants them.

Who are the parents of babies born in this manner—that is, who is responsible for bringing them up? Should such experiments be allowed to continue?

Smoking. Medical experts now are gener-

ally agreed that cigarette smoking can seriously harm people's health—perhaps even when they themselves do not smoke but are in the presence of smokers.

Should smoking be banned in public places? Do people have the right to smoke even though they are harming their health in doing so?

Drugs. The use of marijuana and narcotics has increased greatly since World War II. Illegal trafficking in drugs is now immense: Narcotics are said to be America's largest import except for petroleum.

Should marijuana be legalized but regulated like alcohol? What about the "hard" drugs like heroin and cocaine?

Responsibility for health. Society has long acted as if physicians and hospitals were responsible for people's health. Research has revealed, however, that an individual can do more to keep himself healthy than the best doctor—simply by following such rules as not smoking, not overeating, and so on.

If individuals refuse to follow health rules, should they be punished for doing so, since the cost of their illness may have to be borne by others?

Terrorism. Many groups have discovered that they can get attention for their cause by committing acts of violence—bombings, assassinations, kidnappings, and so on.

How can the international community put down terrorism without unduly restricting people's freedoms?

Disorder in the financial world. Rampant inflation and the declining dollar have led to widespread uncertainty in international finance. Billions of dollars now race back and forth across national frontiers beyond the control of central banks. A sudden movement somewhat could trigger an international economic crisis.

What can be done to restore order in the world's financial markets?

Choosing the sex of one's children. Physicians are currently developing various means whereby parents can decide whether to have a boy or a girl.

Should parents choose the sex of their children? What can be done to prevent the sex-ratio

SOME PROCESSES OF SOCIAL LIFE

from becoming unbalanced so that there are far more men than women—or vice versa?

Overpopulation. Some countries are doing little to reduce the birthrate of their people with the result that the nations are increasingly overpopulated. With more and more mouths to feed, the food supply inevitably runs short.

If a nation refuses to curb its population growth, is the international community required to alleviate the resulting starvation? If so, will that not make the problem just that much worse?

Licenses for parents. Many children today are born to parents who do not want them or cannot provide adequately for them. Society now requires people to have a license if they want to drive but makes no such requirement for becoming a parent, which is a much more complex task.

Should people who want to have children be required to meet at least some minimum standards?

The policy choices listed above constitute only a sampling of the stupendous agenda that faces the world today. Since these choices are genuine, we cannot know in advance what will eventually be chosen. We can, of course, state our views about what *should* be chosen, but that is a very different thing from predicting successfully the choices that will be made.

RETURN OF HALLEY'S COMET

There are, of course, a few predictions for the 1980s that can be made with considerable confidence. For instance, Halley's comet will make one of its rare appearances to earthly viewers. It will be most visible in the sky from November 1985 to January 1986. Halley's comet travels in a very long orbit around the sun; most of the time it is too far away from earth to be visible to the naked eye, but every 76 years the comet comes into the neighborhood of the earth. Sir Edmund Halley, for whom the comet is named, was a close friend of Sir Isaac Newton, and he used Newton's gravitation principle to calculate the orbits of a number of comets. In doing so, Halley

noticed that a comet was reported in the same position of the sky in 1531, 1607, and 1682, moving along an identical path. Halley theorized that all the sightings were of a single comet and predicted that the comet would reappear in another 76 years. Halley's predictions were confirmed in 1759 and again in 1835 and 1910.

Such precise predictions by astronomers fill ordinary mortals with awe. They seem to challenge futurists thinking about human life on earth to produce predictions of similar accuracy and precision. Some futurists may feel ashamed that they fail so miserably in their efforts to make accurate precise predictions, but they should not feel any chagrin. Halley's comet is an inanimate object that has no choice about its actions and operates far beyond the power of human beings to alter its behavior. By contrast, futurists deal with the actions of human beings, who constantly make choices about what they shall do. Unlike astronomers, whose predictions are hardly more than statements about the periodic behavior of inanimate objects, futurists are engaged in the far more complex task of helping human beings to create a better future world. It is not the task of futurists to predict exactly what people will do in the future, but rather to help people to understand the possibilities of the future so that a better world can be created.

The 1980s promise to be a fascinating and exciting decade. We human beings will be making many crucial choices that will affect human life profoundly in an infinite number of ways. The 1980s will probably not be a tranquil period—too many powerful forces have been set loose for that—but it may be a period during which great progress will be made despite much turbulence. One thing we can feel pretty confident about: We will make a great many choices that will dramatically shape the world in which we will live in the years to come. The fact of choice is what makes the future of the world so unpredictable—but far more interesting than Halley's comet.

GLOSSARY

CHAPTER I. SCIENCE AND SOCIOLOGY

1. "THE PROMISE" *Mills*
   Sociological Imagination: The capacity to understand the most impersonal and remote changes in terms of their effect on the human self and to see the relationship between the two.
   Personal Trouble: A private matter that occurs within the character of an individual and within the range of that individual's immediate relations with others.
   Public Issue: A matter that transcends the local environment of an individual and the range of that individual's inner life.

2. "STRIPTEASERS" *Skipper*
   Sensationalism Principle: If a study is novel and concerns sex, its scholarly aspects will be ignored while its sensational aspects are stressed.
   Erotic Principle: If a study is novel and concerns sex, it will be a subject of curiosity and humor for some, and ridicule and scorn for others.
   Evergreen Principle: If a study is novel and concerns sex, its newsworthiness is endless.
   Instant Expert and Expert-by-Association Principle: If a study explores a new area of investigation, its authors will be considered instant experts in that area.
   Conversation Piece Principle: If a study is novel and concerns sex, it will have wide variety of appeal and be used in a variety of conversations.

3. "THE AMERICAN SOLDIER—AN EXPOSITORY REVIEW" *Lazarsfeld*
   Criterion of Significance: A means of judging importance.

CHAPTER II. SOCIALIZATION

4. "FINAL NOTE ON A CASE OF EXTREME ISOLATION" *Davis*
   Socialization: The process of learning cooperative group living.
   Learning Stage: The expected knowledge and ability at a particular age.

5. "HOMOGENIZING THE AMERICAN WOMAN: THE POWER OF AN UNCONSCIOUS IDEOLOGY" *Bem and Bem*
   Sex-Role Socialization: Learned patterns of behavior expected of each sex; these patterns differ by society.

6. "THE SOUNDS OF SILENCE" *Hall and Hall*
   Silent Language: Communication which takes place through gestures, facial expressions, and other body movements.

CHAPTER III. CULTURE

7. "BODY RITUAL AMONG THE NACIREMA" *Miner*
   Culture Hero: A person recognized as heroic within a given society.
   Ethos: The distinguishing attitudes, habits, and beliefs of a group.
   Masochistic Tendency: The tendency to receive pleasure from being hurt or dominated.
   Sadistic Specialist: A person who receives pleasure from dominating others or from giving pain.

8. "ONE HUNDRED PERCENT AMERICAN" *Linton*
   Americanism: A belief originating in the United

States or sympathetic toward the United States and its values.

Insidious Foreign Ideas: "Treacherous" thoughts from other countries.

9. "THE CHANGING DOOR CEREMONY" *Walum*
Social Ceremony: A conventional social act.
Door Ceremony: A conventional social act concerning the opening and closing of doors.
Ideology of Patriarchy: Characteristic beliefs associated with the father or eldest son as head of the family.
Anomie: A state of being without norms or rules to guide behavior.

CHAPTER IV. INTERACTION AND GROUP BEHAVIOR

10. "SOME SOCIAL STRUCTURE DETERMINANTS OF INCONSISTENCY BETWEEN ATTITUDES AND BEHAVIOR: THE CASE OF FAMILY VIOLENCE" *Dibble and Straus*
Role Expectations: Behavior expected from one occupying a particular position.
Division of Labor: Economic and other activity specialization.

11. "THE PETER PRINCIPLE" *Hull*
Level of Incompetence: The point at which no more rank promotions will be obtained.
The Peter Principle: In a hierarchy each employee tends to rise to his or her level of incompetence; eventually every post tends to be occupied by an employee incompetent to execute its duties.
Final Placement Syndrome: The miseries that accompany the level-of-incompetence position.
Process of Substitution: Substituting irrelevant, but within competence, duties for those that actually are required of the level-of-incompetence position.
Creative Incompetence: An imaginative way to avoid promotion to a position of incompetence.
Darwinian Extension Theory: The belief that cleverness may destroy humanity.

12. "THE WYNN PRINCIPLE" *Wynn*
The Wynn Principle: "The esotericism of job titles must be escalated with the rising affluence of a society."
Corollary Alpha: The greater the esoterica of a job title, the less the degree of harassment from clients.
Corollary Beta: The greater the pretentiousness of a job title, the greater the fee commanded for services.

Corollary Gamma: The greater the esoterica of a job title, the greater one's social status.
Corollary Delta: Job titles are largely unrelated to job functions.
Corollary Epsilon: Cycles of inflation are related to the esoterica of job titles.

CHAPTER V. STRATIFICATION

13. "THE SHRINKING MIDDLE CLASS" *Cavanaugh*
False Consciousness: Incorrect belief regarding status position.
Ideology: A group's explanation of life's relevant aspects.

14. "A NOTE ON THE 'TRICKLE EFFECT' " *Fallers*
Trickle Effect: The tendency for new styles of fashion to pass down through the status hierarchy.
Trickle Hypothesis: The trickle effect is a means for maintaining motivation, and thus efficiency, in occupational performance.
Myth of Success: A means of deceiving people into believing that chances of success are greater than they really are.
Gambling Theory: The belief that struggle is worthwhile since rewards are so great.

15. "THE DIRTY WORK MOVEMENT" *Gans*
Psychologically Dirty: Tension producing work.

CHAPTER VI. THE FAMILY

16. "MARRIAGE: HIS AND HERS" *Bernard.*
Shock Theory of Marriage: Marriage produces discontinuities (in beliefs, values, and behavior) that can cause emotional problems.
Romantic Idealization: Fanciful beliefs held about marriage.

17. "PERCEPTIONS OF SINGLEHOOD: 1900–1975" *Melko and Cargan*
Singles: Actually all unmarried persons but sometimes used to refer to the never married only.

18. "NORTH AMERICAN MARRIAGE: 1990" *Davids*
Romantic Love: Love based on physical and mental attraction.
Battered Child: A physically abused child.
Celibacy: Abstention from sexual relations.
Trial Marriage: A contract for a marriage for a specific period of time which can be renewed.

CHAPTER VII. EDUCATION

19. "SOMETHING HAPPENED: EDUCATION IN THE SEVENTIES" *Brodinsky*
Equal Opportunity: Regardless of status, same chances for employment, promotion, and so on, are provided.
Due Process: Fair judicial hearing when accused of misbehavior.

20. "HELP! TEACHER CAN'T TEACH!" *Time*
Basic Skills: Teaching of reading, writing, and arithmetic.
Mainstreaming: Incorporating physically or mentally handicapped students into regular classrooms and schools.

21. "SORTING OUT THE ISSUES AND TRENDS OF SCHOOL DESEGREGATION" *Rist*
De Facto Segregation: Segregation entrenched in social customs and institutions.
De Jure Segregation: Segregation entrenched in law.
White Flight: Exodus of white population from center cities presumably due to minority concentrations or school desegregation.

CHAPTER VIII. RELIGION

22. "A TYPOLOGY OF RELIGIOUS EXPERIENCE" *Margolis and Elifson*
Typology: A classification of theological types.
Noetic Quality: An intellectual experience.

23. "TELEVISION EVANGELISM: MILKING THE FLOCK" *Mariani*
Evangelism: The revival of commitment to Christ.
Mesmerizes: Hypnotize or fascinate.

24. "CHRISTIAN POLITICS AND THE NEW RIGHT" *Zwier and Smith*
Free Enterprise: Privately-owned businesses are free to organize and operate.
Laissez-Faire: A doctrine asserting the belief of nongovernment interference in business.

CHAPTER IX. ECONOMICS

25. "THE NEW ECONOMIC AND POLITICAL ORDER OF THE 1980s" *Naisbitt*
Decentralization: The dispersal of functions and powers from a central authority.
Deindustrialization: The dispersal of industry or its reduction.

Entrepreneurial: Organizing, managing, and assuming risks of a business.

26. "THE CORPORATE THRUST IN AMERICAN POLITICS" *Salomon and Bernstein*
Situs Picketing: Posting demonstrators at a specific location.
Sine Qua Non: An essential item.
Runaway Shops: Moving industries to nonunionized areas.

27. "THE USES OF POVERTY: THE POOR PAY ALL" *Gans*
Functional analysis: A means of analysis that examines the objective consequences of an action, a law, or the like.
Latent Function: A consequence that is not readily apparent.
Dysfunction: An objective consequence that hinders the fulfillment of a goal.

CHAPTER X. POLITICS

28. "THE POLITICAL SYSTEM CANNOT COPE WITH TODAY'S DIVERSITY" *Toffler*
Demassifiers: Breaking up of larger groups into smaller ones.
Remassifiers: Creating different large groups.
Genetic Engineering: Chemical or physical manipulation of inherited biological properties.

29. "SIX POLITICAL REFORMS MOST AMERICANS WANT" *Gallup*
The Initiative: Drafting of a piece of legislation by the citizens and putting it on the ballot by petition.

30. "POWER TO THE PEOPLE: THE CRUSADE FOR DIRECT DEMOCRACY" *Nelson*
Plebiscitary: A vote by the people.
Sunshine-In-Government: Committee meetings open to public attendance.

CHAPTER XI. MINORITY RELATIONS

31. "THE SMART WHITE MAN'S BURDEN" *Daniels*
White Man's Burden: Belief that whites must bring "civilization" to natives of other countries.
Hereditarian: Believes intelligence is primarily genetically determined.
Environmental Disadvantages: One's environment disallows optimal development of one's abilities.
Meritocracy: Rule by those of greatest merit; for example, intelligence or abilities in warfare.

32. "FREEDOM FOR THE AMERICAN INDIAN" *Josephy*
Bureaucratic Rule: Organization or society run by formal organizational procedures.
Acculturate: Adaptation of aspects of a culture which is not their own.
Assimilate: Adoption of the dominant set of cultural traits by the culturally different group.

33. "OLD VS. YOUNG IN FLORIDA: PREVIEW OF AN AGING AMERICA" *Gustaitis*
War of Generations: Conflict between youth and older citizens.
Population Pyramid: Age structure of a population.

CHAPTER XII. DEVIANCE

34. "ON BEING SANE IN INSANE PLACES" *Rosenhan*
Pseudopatient: A pretend patient.
Type 1 Error: A false-negative error; for example, diagnosing a sick person as healthy.
Type 2 Error: A false-positive error; for example, diagnosing a healthy person as sick.
Depersonalization: Removing a sense of the individual from treatment.

35. "PORNOGRAPY, RAPE, AND THE CULT OF MACHO" *McCarthy*
De-Individualized: Referring to people by numbers rather than names.
Authoritarian Characteristics: Resignation to authority.

36. "THE SEARCH FOR JUVENILE JUSTICE" *Serrill*
Class-Action Lawsuits: Legal action on behalf of all persons with identical interests in the wrong doing.
Anathema: A person intensely disliked or cursed by religious authority.

CHAPTER XIII. POPULATION AND ECOLOGY

37. "THE POPULATION PROBLEM IN 22 DIMENSIONS" *Brown, McGrath, and Stokes*
Scarcity-Induced Inflation: Higher prices brought on by a shortage of goods.
Urbanization: The proportion of people living in urban areas grows faster than does that of people living in rural areas.

38. "TAKING SHAPE: A BIGGER, DIFFERENT POPULATION" *U.S. News and World Report*
Birth Rate: Number of births per year per 1,000 members of a society.

Labor Force: Employed or members of the working-age population seeking employment.

39. "ENVIRONMENTAL PROTECTION IS GOOD BUSINESS" *McCloskey*
Toxic Substances: Poisonous items.
Planned Obsolescense: Limited lifespan of a product by design.
Conspicuous Consumption: Display of wealth via flamboyant or wasteful use of consumer goods.

CHAPTER XIV. THE URBAN SCENE

40. "COMEBACK FOR CITIES, WOES FOR SUBURBS" *Maloney and Battle*
Balance of Power: Status quo relationship between groups holding power.

41. "THE GREAT TRANSPORTATION CONSPIRACY" *Kwitny*
Mass Transit: Transportation facilities aimed at serving large numbers of the public.

42. "A NEW TYPE OF CITY FOR AN ENERGY-SHORT WORLD" *Van Til*
Non-Renewable Energy: Fuels which cannot be replaced once used.
Multi-Based Energy: Fuels and energy resources from a variety of sources.

CHAPTER XV. COLLECTIVE BEHAVIOR

43. "SOMETIMES I GET TIRED OF WOMEN'S LIB" *Motley*
ERA: Equal rights amendment; proposes no discrimination on the basis of sex.
Movement: A large number of people united to bring about or prevent some social change.
Burnout: Intense involvement in a movement or activity leads to fatigue with the effort.

44. "APOCALYPSE AT JONESTOWN" *Hall*
Cult: Loosely structured association of people who share unique religious values.
Verstehen: Subjective interpretation of an individual's behavior and intentions.
Total Institution: All aspects of behavior controlled while confined; for example, mental institutions, prisons.
Ideal Type: Abstract description constructed from observations of real cases.

45. "VIOLENCE IN AMERICAN CITIES" *Dye*
Ghetto: Area of city in which a particular group is concentrated.

Relative Deprivation: Deprived feeling of status or goods due to comparison.

White Exodus: Movement of white residents from an area usually due to concentration of minority members.

CHAPTER XVI. SOCIAL CHANGE

46. "THE LEGACY OF WOODSTOCK" *Reinhold*

    Tolerate: To allow.

    "Theory of Enlightenment": Such total belief in newer values that older persons suffer from persecution.

47. "COUNTDOWN TO 1984: BIG BROTHER MAY BE RIGHT ON SCHEDULE" *Goodman*

    Doublethink: Holding two contradictory thoughts at the same time and believing both of them.

    Psychoscientists: Scientists who work with the brain.

    Psychocivilized Society: Surgery allows people to achieve better living.

48. "AN AGENDA FOR THE 1980s" *Cornish*

    Alternative Futures: Multiple predictions.

    Biomedical: Study of ability of humans to survive and operate in abnormal environments.